The Short Oxford History of the Modern World

General Editor: J. M. Roberts

The Short Oxford History of the Modern World
General Editor: J. M. Roberts

The Crisis of Parliaments: English History 1509–1660
Conrad Russell

The Old European Order 1600–1800
Second Edition
William Doyle

The Limits of Liberty: American History 1607–1992
Maldwyn A. Jones

The British Empire 1558–1995
Second Edition
T. O. Lloyd

Modern India: The Origins of an Asian Democracy
Judith M. Brown

Barricades and Borders: Europe 1800–1914
Third Edition
Robert Gildea

Rebellions and Revolutions: China from the 1800s to 2000
Second Edition
Jack Gray

British History 1815–1914
Second Edition
Norman McCord and Bill Purdue

The European Dynastic States 1494–1660
Richard Bonney

Empire, Welfare State, Europe: History of the United Kingdom 1906–2001
Fifth Edition
T. O. Lloyd

Endurance and Endeavour: Russian History 1812–2001
Fifth Edition
J. N. Westwood

British History

1815–1914

Second edition

Norman McCord

and

Bill Purdue

OXFORD
UNIVERSITY PRESS

OXFORD
UNIVERSITY PRESS

Great Clarendon Street, Oxford OX2 6DP

Oxford University Press is a department of the University of Oxford.
It furthers the University's objective of excellence in research, scholarship,
and education by publishing worldwide in

Oxford New York

Auckland Cape Town Dar es Salaam Hong Kong Karachi
Kuala Lumpur Madrid Melbourne Mexico City Nairobi
New Delhi Shanghai Taipei Toronto

With offices in

Argentina Austria Brazil Chile Czech Republic France Greece
Guatemala Hungary Italy Japan Poland Portugal Singapore
South Korea Switzerland Thailand Turkey Ukraine Vietnam

Oxford is a registered trade mark of Oxford University Press
in the UK and in certain other countries

Published in the United States
by Oxford University Press Inc., New York

British Library Cataloguing in Publication Data
Data available

Library of Congress Cataloging in Publication Data
Data available

Typeset by Newgen Imaging Systems (P) Ltd., Chennai, India
Printed in Great Britain
on acid-free paper by
Biddles Ltd., King's Lynn, Norfolk

ISBN 978–0–19–923319–9   978–0–19–926164–2 (Pbk)

10 9 8 7 6 5 4 3 2 1

Preface

The period covered by this book has probably attracted more attention from historians than any other. This is scarcely surprising, for in a variety of historical aspects those decades were of cardinal importance. They brought the development of one of the world's greatest empires and the evolution of the world's first great industrial society, and they still offer to the student the engrossing spectacle of a decentralized rural society facing enormous and unprecedented pressures of economic and social change coupled with accelerating population growth—and facing those difficulties with notably little internal conflict and bloodshed. In the development of government and administration too, those decades were of crucial importance in the transformation of Britain from a little-governed nation to a modern State equipped with large and expanding agencies of official activity.

This period also remains a focus of argument and disagreement among historians, partly because of its imagined close relevance to our own society. The assumption of close connection has led to the frequent use of nineteenth- and early-twentieth-century history as a convenient source of ammunition with which to fight our own political and ideological controversies.

The synthesis offered here cannot be complete, for the volume of writing on the economic, social, and political history of this period is too great for any one volume to cover it in its entirety. Inevitably, much of the account relies on the published work of many writers. In some cases, as for example, to Professor Norman Gash, Dr Boyd Hilton, Dr E. H. Hunt, and Dr David Philips, the debt is a considerable one. We hope that our borrowings have been adequately acknowledged in the notes and apologize if in any instances we have inadvertently omitted to ensure so.

The terminal date for the first edition of this book, published in 1991, was set at 1906 and we are grateful to Oxford University Press for extending the coverage of the volume to 1914. We consider this a more appropriate termination which enables us to take British history up to the brink of the First World War. We have also endeavoured in this revised edition to take account of at least some of the many works on different aspects of the period published in the last fifteen years. The new end date has necessarily involved changes to the organization of the later sections of the book which is now divided into four main chronological parts, roughly 1815–30, 1830–50, 1850–80, and 1880–1914. Within each the first chapter offers a succinct political narrative, the second a discussion of developments in government and administration, and a third surveys economic and social developments. An argument could readily be advanced for reversing this sequence, but it seems likely that many potential readers would find the initial provision of a political narrative useful. The significance of the expansion of both central and local government during these years seemed to warrant a separate consideration. A short Biographical Appendix gives brief notes on some of the principal individuals mentioned.

Norman McCord reaffirms his gratitude to the then staff of Newcastle Central Library, especially Mr Frank Manders, for the provision of facilities while he was writing the first edition, and for the help and encouragement he then received from the General Editor of the series, Professor J. M. Roberts. Bill Purdue gives his thanks to the Open University for the periods of study leave which facilitated his work on the present volume. We are both grateful to the staff of Oxford University Press for the scrupulous care with which the text has been handled by them.

N. Mc
University of Newcastle upon Tyne
A. W. P
Open University
October 2006

Contents

List of tables

Introduction

The choice of a *period* is among the most basic, contestable, and revealing of all the techniques of the historian. It is basic because any attempt to make sense of the past must involve breaks, developments, beginnings, and endings, all of which are challenged by continuities. It is contestable because other historians will discern different patterns and revealing because it exposes the historian's preoccupations and sympathies.

Our period is 1815–1914 and thus takes its enclosing dates from the ending of one great European war and the beginning of another. Few would argue with the end date. The first edition of this book by Norman McCord ended with the great Liberal electoral victory of 1906 and the political and economic consequences of that victory were profound enough to justify this, but the idea of the First World War as the great watershed rightly endures. The year 1815 is also a convenient historical demarcation and the reason is obvious. Contemporaries had no doubt that the defeat of Napoleon and the subsequent peace settlement marked the end of an era. Britain emerged victorious from more than twenty years of almost continuous warfare, and with the prestige of the nation, the government, and the existing order greatly enhanced. The period 1815–1914 has also a unity when it comes to foreign policy and international affairs in that during it there was no war on the European continent to match in scale or duration either the Napoleonic wars or the First World War, nor any extensive British military action in Europe.

From the viewpoint of political, social, and economic developments in British history, the starting point of 1815 is more contestable. One recent magisterial survey of the period 1783–1846 has referred to 1815 as 'a date which was of no more than military significance'.[1] In the last decade or so, historians have begun to write about the 'long eighteenth century' lasting from 1688–*c*.1832[2] and it has been suggested that the essential characteristics of British society that prevailed during this period persisted until the late 1820s and early 1830s. One interpretation emphasizes the religious dimension and sees the repeal of the English Test and Corporations Act and the Catholic Emancipation Act as marking the

1. Boyd Hilton, *A Mad, Bad & Dangerous People? England 1783–1846* (2006), 670.
2. See Frank O'Gorman, *The Long Eighteenth Century 1688–1832* (1997).

effective demolition of the confessional state in England (together with Wales) and Scotland. A 'confessional state' is one which gives full rights of citizenship only to members of established churches, in these instances members of the Anglican Church in England and Wales and the Presbyterian Church in Scotland.[3] Were one to seek a starting point that reflected economic history, one might go further back to the 1780s, traditionally the decade in which that now controversial concept, the 'Industrial Revolution', began to 'take off',[4] or further forward to the 1830s, when railways and steam power came into more general use. There is, however, much to be said for starting with Britain at the end of more than twenty years of warfare, at a time when the political and religious arrangements arrived at in 1688 were substantially intact but when economic and social change was altering rapidly the Britain over which Church and State presided. Our period encompasses the reigns of six monarchs including the last five years of the reign of George III, though he inhabited a confused twilight world at Windsor and it was his eldest son who, as Regent, held centre stage, and the first four years of the reign of George V. For the greater part of our near 100 years Queen Victoria was on the throne and the association between her reign and indeed the nineteenth century and cultural, religious, and social attitudes remains strong to the degree that one could contest the long eighteenth century with the long Victorian period, its making, its high summer, and its legacy. Paralleling, punctuating, and dividing the concepts of Regency, Victorian, and Edwardian are readings of the past which discern unities based upon inherent characteristics, ages of improvement, of progress, of aristocracy, of atonement, of industrialization, of equipoise, and of imperialism, even an age of uncertainty.[5] The interpretations which such 'ages' represent and the contrasts between them are what makes history a live and dynamic discipline in which the most apparently definitive interpretation only lasts until the next one.

Trends and preoccupations in historical writing have quickly succeeded each other in recent decades and this second edition takes note of such developments. Class-based interpretations of British history are much less influential than they were in the 1960s and 1970s and even when *British History 1815–1906* was published in 1992. Few would now talk confidently about a British working class, while the implausibility of the term the 'middle class' has long been recognized. We continue the approach of the previous volume, which is to emphasize that the majority of the population can usefully be described, at least from the 1830s

---

3. J. C. D. Clark, *English Society 1688–1832* (1985).

4. W. W. Rostow, *The Stages of Economic Growth* (1960).

5. Examples are: Asa Briggs, *The Age of Improvement* (1959), Norman Gash, *Aristocracy and People: Britain 1815–65*, Boyd Hilton, *The Age of Atonement: The Influence of Evangelicalism on Social and Economic Thought 1785–1865* (1988), W. L. Burn, *The Age of Equipoise* (1964), and Richard Shannon, *The Crisis of Imperialism 1865–1914* (1974). An illuminating essay by David Eastwood, 'The Age of Uncertainty', *Royal Historical Society Transactions*, 6th series, VIII (1998), surveys interpretations of the early nineteenth century.

when class terminology began to be widely used, as the 'working classes' but that the horizontal divisions of society were complex, multi-layered and overlapping, while other divides such as those between urban and rural, the 'respectable' and the 'not respectable', and the serious and the pleasure-loving, cut across the social strata.

That other division, between the sexes, has become ever more prominent in historical writing during the latter decades of the twentieth century. There can be little doubt that women were insufficiently in the foreground of histories of modern Britain written before then. Ironically, given that feminist histories tended to emerge from radical and socialist schools of historical writing, it was precisely by these schools that women had been most neglected. No doubt, the long-term aim of historians should be to integrate the history of women with the history of society and necessarily most social, cultural, economic, and religious, if not political, developments affected both sexes, while women identified themselves as much by their social position or even religious leanings as by their sex. Nevertheless in a period when society was patriarchal, as with differing emphases it had always been, and when gender differences and roles were taken for granted it is essential to attempt to understand women's position in terms of the context of the society in which they lived. This has, of course, been characteristic of the best of recent 'women's history'.[6]

The history of the 'working class' or the 'common people' school of historical writing with its emphasis upon the separate nature of the politics and the institutions of the people has now given way to an interest in the 'popular', its culture, imagery, and language. At the heart of much of this work has been the question whether there was a great division between the cultures of the pre-industrial or pre-modern worlds and that of the industrial and urban society which emerged in the course of the nineteenth century. The significance of the leisure habits of society, the subject matter and imagery of popular literature, and the influence of the public house or the social world of the street had their place in the first edition of this book but recent work demands their more extended treatment in the present volume.

Our title is *British* history but a further historiographical development makes the question of national identity a central historical preoccupation. How British was Britain in 1815 or indeed in 1914? To what extent was Scottish, English, or Welsh identity submerged in or merged with a sense of being British? It has been suggested that a British identity was created in the eighteenth century on the basis of economic prosperity, the empire, and Protestantism, and that the eventual success of British arms against Napoleon further consolidated it.[7] Whether a

6. See for instance Amanda Vickery, *The Gentleman's Daughter: Women's Lives in Georgian England* (1998) and 'Golden Age to Separate Spheres? A Review of the Categories and Chronology of English Women's History', *Historical Journal*, 36 (1993), 383–414; K. D. Reynolds, *Aristocratic Women and Political Society in Victorian Britain* (1998).

7. Linda Colley, *Britons. Forging the Nation 1707–1837* (1992).

sense of British identity was superimposed over other national identities, or whether British identity was largely an expanded Englishness is debateable.[8]

A common acceptance of British identity, usually cohabiting with Welsh, Scottish, and English identity as well as with strong affiliations to cities and counties was largely unquestioned in our period. These multiple identities are important because, even as Britain became more centralized, other national and regional influences remained potent and were on the whole a source of strength, as, for example, with the regional basis of army regiments, to Britain.

To the English it was all too easy to see Britain and England as virtually synonymous and indeed most Europeans seem to have shared this view. From outside Europe, things looked different and few, if any, referred to an English Empire. To Americans in 1812 it was the British who were a coming and it was to Britain that colonies and later dominions gave allegiance. The role of the Empire in consolidating British identity was considerable.

An important question, which reverberated throughout our period, was the degree to which largely Catholic Ireland, bound to the United Kingdom by the Act of Union of 1800, could associate with the other kingdoms. Hindsight may suggest that this union was bound to fail and that what Bernard Shaw termed 'John Bull's Other Island' was too different in culture, religion, and national aspiration to remain under a common government with Britain. We should be wary of seeing such an outcome as inevitable. The Irish Question was both constant and multi-faceted but the Irish role in the British army and in the administration of the Empire bound many Catholic Irish to the Union while economic ties were close. Certainly the virtually complete political independence of southern Ireland in the form of the Irish Free State gained in 1921 was not foreseeable even in 1914. The impact of the Union upon British politics was considerable; without the Irish connection it is unlikely that the Catholic Emancipation Act would have been passed in 1829, that the Liberal Party would have split in the 1880s, or even that the reduction of powers of the House of Lords in 1911 would have been implemented.

What sort of people the British were and whether and/or how they changed over our period has intrigued historians. Were they a 'polite and commercial' or a riotous and violent people at the beginning of the nineteenth century?[9] Were they serious-minded and religious during the early and mid-Victorian 'Age of Improvement'? Were they forever nostalgic countrymen even though they created the first industrialized and urbanized society? Was Edwardian Britain buoyant, pleasure-loving, and confident or apprehensive and much divided?

8. O'Gorman, *The Long Eighteenth Century*, 99; Jeremy Black and Donald Macraild, *Nineteenth Century Britain* (2003), 6.

9. A recent Oxford University Press volume in the New Oxford History of England series proffers a very different title to its predecessor volume: Boyd Hilton, *A Mad, Bad and Dangerous People? England 1783–1846* (2006) as opposed to, Paul Langford, *A Polite and Commercial People: England 1727–1783* (1992).

Had the British public and their popular culture been tamed, trained, subdued or become more responsible during the course of ninety-nine years?

The British were a much more governed people at the end of our period than at the beginning and the process of the growth of government and administration is one of our main themes. This process went against the grain of tradition of economical and limited government and there were losses in terms of liberties as well as gains in terms of order, social welfare, and hygiene in an increasingly complex, urbanized, and interdependent society.

Throughout most of our period, government was the responsibility of an elite, though arguably one open to successful men of talent, prodded by new circumstances and problems and by pressure from below. Pragmatism rather than an inexorable march towards democracy and social reform best describes the failures and considerable success of this elite in presiding over rapidly changing circumstances at home and abroad.

Part I

1

Political developments

1815–1830

The victory of Britain and its allies and the inauguration of peace did not provide the government and its ministers with easy years to enjoy this triumph. The years of war had not frozen Britain in the context of the early 1790s but had rather seen social and economic pressures and problems subordinated to the war effort even as they became more serious, while the urgent necessity for national unity had divided and made unpatriotic reformist movements amongst the elite and the broader populace. The government was faced with pressing problems: a rising population, a depression in agriculture, which set in soon after the war's end, major social problems consequent upon economic change and the difficulty of finding work for the soldiers and sailors who were no longer required. Economic and social problems fanned radical discontent.

The role of both government and Parliament was smaller than it was to become in later generations. Nevertheless, the ministry's reaction to the problems of the early years of peace exerted a significant influence on the development of British society. Ministers were aware that the population was rising and that increased numbers could only be supported by economic growth. That required internal peace and an adequate level of social cohesion. Although the functions and powers of government in the first years of peace were limited, misjudgements here could imperil both internal order and economic expansion.

The Liverpool government

The major effect of the wars with France on British politics had been a strengthening of the forces concerned to promote internal stability and prosecute the war effectively. There was a complementary weakening of the opposition Whig Party which fell apart as its members divided over their reactions to the French Revolution and to the war. The adhesion of the more conservative Whigs under the Duke of Portland to the government of William Pitt in 1793 marked a decisive parting of the ways between them and the supporters of Charles James Fox who remained dedicated to support for the principles of the French Revolution, to reform at home, and opposition to the measures that the government took against radical and revolutionary activities. With the exception of a so-called 'Ministry of all the talents' which was formed after Pitt's death in 1806, and included Fox and other more radical Whigs, but lasted only a year, government continued to lie in the hands of the political heirs of the Younger Pitt, those who had supported his pre-war administration in the years after 1784, and the Portland Whigs.

The government which held office in 1815 had been formed three years earlier, when Lord Liverpool found himself elevated unexpectedly on the death of Spencer Perceval at the hands of a deranged assassin. There is no easy or all-embracing word with which to describe the government. Historians have for long debated when party politics emerged in Britain. Much depends on what we mean by party, and a tight modern definition involving national organizations, party programmes, and disciplined voting in Lords and Commons will not find parties existing in early nineteenth-century Britain. On the other hand, the terms 'Tory' and 'Whig' had long been used, did represent attitudes and principles, and meant something to contemporaries. Political allegiance, nevertheless, often remained vague and fluid. The description 'Tory' is the most questionable, for the Opposition (a term which itself was just coming into general usage) were happy enough to be Whigs. Liverpool's government is often referred to as Tory though many of its members would not have described themselves as such. To some extent the political context had been established by the Whig Opposition during the French Revolutionary and Napoleonic Wars, for what was seen as their extreme and disloyal opinions and tactics had created a broad and diverse body of support for a government party, which included self-conscious Tories, ex-Whigs and competent men of government. Pitt saw himself as a Whig but, ironically, is often seen as the founding father of a new Tory Party; it was his dramatic clashes with Fox and the foundation of Pitt and Fox clubs after the deaths of both politicians that did much to harden allegiances and give new meaning to the labels of Tory and Whig. What resulted under Liverpool was a government which was essentially a coalition; despite all the disadvantages of having to hold balances between conflicting views and conflicting individuals, it had the advantages of a broad and responsible grouping which contained many able men. If we must be cautious as to the use of the word 'Tory' to describe this government, there can be no doubt that during the 1820s it came to be used by many contemporaries and was accepted by some ministers as a description of themselves. Most historians have used the term to describe the governments of that decade albeit with caveats.[1] As Frank O'Gorman has argued, it was a very different kind of Toryism from that of the eighteenth century. The Divine Right of Kings and passive obedience had been dropped 'in favour of the loyalism of the 1790s, the

1. B. W. Hill, *British Parliamentary Parties 1742–1832* (1984), argues that 'The government headed by Perceval, later by Liverpool, came under the latter to be generally accepted as Tory', p. 195. Boyd Hilton, *A Mad, Bad and Dangerous People*, 709 fn., favours 'conservative' as the best description of governments between 1815 and 1830.

ideology of Burke, the wartime sacrifice of the revolutionary and Napoleonic period, the defence of Protestantism and, not least, nostalgia for the towering figure of William Pitt'.[2] There was one fundamental common basis to both supporters of the administrations and those of the Opposition in that both sides were firmly dedicated to the 1688 constitutional settlement and 'saw themselves as the heirs of early-eighteenth century Whigs'.[3]

Almost all the senior ministers were drawn from the aristocracy, though, unusually, a high proportion of them represented recent promotions to that category. Liverpool himself was a second-generation peer; his father had been born into a junior branch of an Oxfordshire gentry family, and had risen first as a civil servant and then as a prominent political figure. The Foreign Secretary, Lord Castlereagh, was also only second-generation nobility, from an Irish family with a recent infusion of Indian wealth. The Home Secretary, Lord Sidmouth, was the son of a doctor and had entered politics as a friend of Pitt; his peerage only dated from 1805. Lord Eldon, the Lord Chancellor, son of a Newcastle coal merchant,[4] had in his youth eloped with the daughter of a wealthy tradesman, and subsequently made his way to high rank as a lawyer and politician. Wellington was a younger son of a minor Irish noble family (recent arrivals in the peerage of Ireland); his rise to personal pre-eminence and dukedom was largely his own work. George Canning, who became President of the Board of Control for India in 1816 and Foreign Secretary in 1822, owed his career to his own talents and timely help from an uncle who was a successful banker. His father had been an unsuccessful lawyer, disinherited by his own father, who had died in 1771, leaving his widow to pursue a career as an actress of no great distinction. The Liverpool Cabinet was not an assembly of Britain's bluest blood, but predominantly a group of men whose eminence was either their own work or of recent making. Unmerited pretension in the aristocracy was not something which aroused their instinctive loyalties.

Much depended on the character and behaviour of the Prime Minister himself. For long after his death the reputation of Lord Liverpool was to be that of an amiable figurehead presiding over a Cabinet which included men of greater talents. The young Disraeli satirized him as 'the Arch Mediocrity'. That malicious portrait has now been discredited, as research has disclosed both the merits and the services of the man who held the premiership for fifteen difficult years.

In grasp of principles, mastery of detail, discernment of means, and judgement of individuals he was almost faultless. Cautious and unhurried in weighing a situation, he was

2. O'Gorman, *The Long Eighteenth Century*, 285. Pitt's 'towering stature' was to some extent part of a hagiography that developed after his death. He had held the country together but his wartime strategies and alliances had not met with great success. The reputation of Fox was, similarly, burnished after his death.

3. J. C. D. Clark, *English Society 1688–1832* (1985), 357.

4. Lord Eldon's father was a comparatively well-off man. Newcastle coal-fitters controlled and organized the conveyance of cargoes of coal out of the Tyne and William Scott owned several keelboats (coal barges) and a public house, while he was involved in maritime insurance. His social position was, however, modest.

prompt and decisive when the time came for action. In debate he was not only informed, lucid and objective, but conspicuously honest . . . Though his colleagues might occasionally disagree with him, he never lost their respect or their trust. He repaid them in full. He never dismissed a minister; he was never ungrateful or disloyal . . . He was a man whom it was almost impossible to dislike; and he himself could find something to like in almost everyone.[5]

This assessment surely contains many of the qualities of a great Prime Minister. In the kind of political world in which he worked, and with the prickly personalities of some of his colleagues, Liverpool's talents proved indispensable in holding together the ministerial team during his long years of ascendancy. His cool and balanced approach to human foibles enabled him to handle skilfully someone like Canning, at once one of the most able and the most wayward of the 'Tory' politicians of these years. This quality is also well illustrated by his comment on Lord Wellesley, Wellington's elder brother and someone who combined considerable influence and accomplishments with vanity and unreliability, 'The truth is, he is a great *compound*, and if one is to have the use of him it must be by making as little as possible of some of his absurdities . . . a man may be wise in some things and most foolish in others.'[6]

Ministerial changes

The ministry's long tenure of office naturally saw changes in personnel. Some of these were relatively isolated events, such as Canning's return to office in 1816; his previous exclusion had been largely due to his own responsibility for earlier disputes within the government. Liverpool was anxious to strengthen the front bench in the Commons, and Canning had come to appreciate that reconciliation with his old colleagues offered his only hope of a successful career. The death of the President of the Board of Control for India offered the opportunity for Canning's appointment, though Liverpool's choice was unwelcome to some of the other ministers, and Canning had already set his sights higher. The entry into the Cabinet of the Duke of Wellington in 1819 was another useful individual acquisition. In the early 1820s other ministerial changes arose from retirements of older ministers, and the consequent promotion of younger men who had made their mark in junior posts. Men like Peel, Huskisson, and Robinson had

---

5. A notable biography of Liverpool has done much to set the record straight: N. Gash, *Lord Liverpool* (1984). This book has been drawn on heavily for the account of Liverpool's administrations given in this chapter. The summary quotation here is taken from the brief essay by the same author in H. Van Thal (ed.), *The Prime Ministers* (1974), i. 287. Another perceptive account is given by J. E. Cookson, *Lord Liverpool's Administration, 1815–22* (1975). Boyd Hilton, 'The Political Arts of Lord Liverpool', *Royal Historical Society Transactions*, 5th series, No. 38 (1988), 147–70, demurs somewhat from Gash's view, acknowledging Liverpool's political acumen but pointing to his 'hypersensitivity about his own feelings' and arguing that 'whatever his secret as a prime minister, it was not that of the cool and calculating unruffler of other men's feathers'.

6. Gash, *Lord Liverpool*, 204.

first joined the ranks of ministerial supporters as young men attracted by the stance of the patriotic wartime government. Peel, for example, entered Parliament in 1810 at a time of grave national crisis. The factious tactics of the Whig Opposition made their party appear disloyal and unattractive to most young entrants to the political scene. Coming from a Church-and-King family background, it was natural for Peel to rally to the Pittites. A group of able young men had been recruited to the government in this way; they had now risen in status and experience to the point at which they were ready to take on greater responsibilities. When Lord Sidmouth retired from the Home Office in 1822 at the age of 65, Peel had earned the succession by reliability in support of the government, a successful term in the onerous office of Chief Secretary for Ireland in 1812–18, recent services in connection with the return to the gold standard, and distinction in parliamentary debate.[7] (It was typical of Liverpool's sympathetic handling of colleagues that Sidmouth was allowed to remain in the Cabinet without a ministerial appointment after he left the Home Office.) A similar transition took place at the Exchequer; the elderly Vansittart went to the Lords as Chancellor of the Duchy of Lancaster, to be succeeded at the Exchequer by Frederick Robinson, who had earned his promotion by loyal service in lesser posts since 1809. These changes did not involve any shifts in the government's policies. The newer members of the Cabinet were newcomers neither to administration nor to support for the ministry's policies.

Ministerial promotions do not always involve easy decisions; Liverpool's appointment of William Huskisson as President of the Board of Trade in 1823 resulted in the aggrieved resignation of the Vice President, Wallace, who felt with some reason that this promotion over his head represented a slight on his own contribution to the government's work in recent years. That Wallace was a long-standing personal friend of the Prime Minister did not make this decision easier, but Liverpool made what he thought to be a necessary appointment in the public interest.

The major change at the Foreign Office had more complex and tragic causes. From the formation of the Liverpool government in 1812, it had depended heavily on the services of Lord Castlereagh in the joint roles of Foreign Secretary and Leader of the House of Commons. Though not a great orator, Castlereagh was a competent minister who was generally respected in Parliament. He had carried much of the burden of defending the government's policies in both foreign and domestic affairs. In the summer of 1822, his mental health began to deteriorate, with delusions of conspiracies against him. Castlereagh's suicide in August may have been precipitated by attempts to blackmail him on grounds of alleged homosexuality.[8] Although his manner had worried both the King and some of his colleagues in previous weeks, this was an unexpected catastrophe for the

---

7. For Peel's early career, N. Gash, *Mr. Secretary Peel: The Life of Robert Peel to 1830* (1961).
8. J. W. Derry, *Castlereagh* (1976), 227–8. See also Wendy Hinde, *Castlereagh* (1981).

government, but provided an occasion to resolve another problem. Canning had resigned again in 1820 in disagreement with his colleagues' handling of the Queen Caroline affair (see pp. 29–31 below). His departure was viewed with equanimity by many of the other ministers, who neither liked nor trusted him, but Liverpool himself was aware of the loss to the government of Canning's abilities both as a minister and as a leading debater in the Commons. It had been mainly owing to Liverpool's own efforts in bridge-building that another reconciliation with Canning had been effected. At the time of Castlereagh's death, Canning was about to sail to India to become Governor General. The sudden death of Castlereagh opened to Canning the inheritance he had coveted for many years—the combined mantle of Foreign Secretary and Leader of the House of Commons. Liverpool insisted on this strengthening of the ministerial team, against hostility both from the King and from most of his Cabinet colleagues, an illuminating instance of his personal ascendancy. The return of Canning strengthened the Cabinet and improved its debating strength in the House of Commons, but at the cost of some friction within the inner circles of the administration. Canning's obvious personal ambition, and the distrust many of his colleagues felt for him, led to bickering which was to trouble the ministry in ensuing years.

Historians have debated the significance of the Cabinet changes between 1821 and 1823. It has been described as, a 'changed course in a way rarely hitherto achieved by long-serving administrations'.[9] Much depends on whether differences between members of the Cabinet are seen as largely personal or as to do with distinctions between 'high Tories' and 'liberal Tories', the former more sympathetic to the interests of agriculture and unconvinced of the need for political, administrative, and economic reforms while the latter favoured the interests of commerce and felt that practical reforms in response to popular feeling were necessary.[10] Few governments or cabinets have been without divisions and there were certainly differences over policy between the members of Liverpool's administration. There was, however, considerable continuity in policies before and after the extended reshuffle and if, subsequent to it, there was a new emphasis upon reforms, this may well have been due to a pragmatic approach to problems and pressures as they arose. Governments cannot enjoy the convenient separations of problems and policy areas available to historians who describe and analyse them. They face complex mixtures of problems requiring decisions at the same time.

Government and Opposition

In tackling its problems, the Liverpool government could reasonably reckon on one strong point in its favour: there were no good reasons to believe that any

9. B. W. Hill, *British Parliamentary Parties*, 211.
10. Boyd Hilton, 'The Political Arts of Lord Liverpool', 169.

other group was in a better position to take on the responsibilities of office. Within an often divided and incoherent opposition, two main elements may be singled out. The first, the only alternative administration in terms of the political realities of the day, was the aristocratic Whig grouping, of which Earl Grey was the most obvious leader. The opposition to Pitt's government in the years after 1784 had been weakened by the secession to the government of the Portland Whigs in 1794. In the immediately post-war years the Whig Opposition suffered further losses when a group led by Lord Grenville effectively moved into support of the Liverpool ministry between 1817 and 1821. Of the Opposition leaders, few if any seemed more attractive claimants for public responsibilities than Liverpool and his colleagues.

In the relatively fluid parliamentary politics of the early nineteenth century, the Whigs could sometimes inflict defeats on the government; they could never persuade either the electorate or the independent MPs to withdraw from Liverpool's government that general confidence which entitled an administration to remain in office. There were a number of occasions when the Cabinet had to make it clear that if independent MPs continued to support the regular Opposition in harassing the government the result would be its resignation. This threat, with the implication that a Whig government might follow, always proved enough to produce a more tractable disposition on the back benches of the House of Commons. If the Liverpool government was not always popular, the Opposition could never muster enough support to oust it, either in Parliament or in the country at large.

The second source of opposition consisted of various radical groups which were vociferous but not powerful. The proposals favoured by radicals included extensions of the parliamentary franchise and redistribution of parliamentary seats, together with drastic cuts in taxation and government spending. There were no particular reasons why Liverpool and his colleagues should have been much impressed either by these proposals or by the personalities of most prominent radicals. In its handling of national finances the Cabinet could well believe that its policies were more attuned to the needs of British society than the uncritical demands for reduction in expenditure voiced by the Opposition. Nor was it easy to believe that the ills of that society would be cured by a dose of instant democracy, given contemporary levels of education, literacy, information, and communications.

The attitudes of the aristocratic Whigs to the tumults inspired by radicals in the post-war years were neither consistent nor particularly admirable. When it came to the crunch, between deciding to support the existing order or to join in radical demands for its drastic reshaping, most Whigs would rally to the party of order, even if in quieter times they might speak loudly of the need for change. Nor did the aristocratic leaders of the Whig Party view the radical leaders who emerged in these years with any liking or respect. As Grey, increasingly seen as the principal

Opposition leader, commented of the best-known radical leaders in 1819:

Is there one among them with whom you would trust yourself in the dark? Look at them, at their characters, at their conduct. What is there more base, and more detestable, more at variance with all tact and decency, as well as all morality, truth and honour? A cause so supported cannot be a good cause.[11]

The spectacle of a popular demagogue like Henry 'Orator' Hunt deliberately trying to work up popular feeling, but rapidly changing his tune when agitation seemed dangerous, was no more attractive to aristocratic Whigs than to government ministers. Liverpool and his colleagues could well believe that, whatever imperfections their regime might include, none of the obvious alternatives offered any likely improvements. Nor had ministers any reason to be ashamed of the beliefs which inspired their policies. They saw themselves as the heirs of Pitt, and frequently declared that their principles were his. They shared with almost all of their contemporaries the belief that the State had only a limited role. Liverpool once told the House of Lords that 'by far the greater part of the miseries of which human nature complained were in all times and in all countries beyond the control of human legislation.'[12] On another occasion he noted that 'it is the duty of government and of Parliament to hold the balance between all the great interests of the country, *as even as possible*.'[13]

Government and monarchy

While members of the government were unfailingly loyal to the Crown, and saw themselves as the King's ministers, this loyalty had proper limits. It did not compel them to remain in office if the sovereign rejected their advice on matters which they considered of vital importance. Despite Liverpool's continual anxiety that the King was about to replace him,[14] ministers were capable of facing George IV with a choice between sacrificing his own preferences and accepting the resignation of his ministers in the knowledge that he could not find more acceptable ones. This was a sanction only to be used reluctantly, but when it was employed it proved effective in disciplining their nominal master. Equally they were not prepared to cling to office in circumstances which might bring discredit not only on themselves but on the King's government generally. In 1819, after a number of defeats and narrow majorities in the House of Commons, Liverpool determined that the time had come when the government must either see its major policies endorsed in Parliament or make way for other ministers:

I am quite satisfied, after long and anxious consideration, that if we cannot carry what has been proposed, it is far, far better for the country that we should cease to be the

11. Quoted by W. R. Brock, *Lord Liverpool and Liberal Toryism, 1820–1827* (2nd edn., 1967), 117–18.
12. Gash, *Lord Liverpool*, 147.   13. Ibid. 184.
14. Williams and Ramsden, *Ruling Britannia*, 180.

Government. After the defeats we have already experienced during this Session, our remaining in office is a *positive* evil. It confounds all idea of government in the minds of men. It disgraces us *personally* and renders us less capable every day of being of any real service to the country, either now or hereafter.[15]

This firmness, which in 1819 as on other occasions brought a recovery in the ministry's fortunes, was not based on any rigidity of policy. Although ministers had strong views in all policy fields, there was always room for flexibility and pragmatism in the day-to-day conduct of affairs; Liverpool argued that, 'sometimes, to avert a present and very pressing evil, we are obliged to depart from what is sound, both in principle and in practice'.[16]

Although ministers were divided on one major issue of the day, the question of extending political rights to Roman Catholics, they were otherwise agreed on the undesirability of any drastic change in the political system they had inherited. Averse to major changes in the electoral system, they were willing to show a modest pragmatism here as elsewhere. The Cornish borough of Grampound had an unsavoury reputation for electoral corruption, and in 1821 the House of Commons resolved to deprive the borough of its two MPs. Liverpool was prepared to accept this, but refused to accept the proposal that the confiscated seats should be given to Leeds; instead he used his influence in the House of Lords to see to it that the seats went instead to increase the number of county seats for Yorkshire. A cautious programme of change in representation as occasional opportunity and expediency dictated was acceptable, but not any sudden thoroughgoing remodelling of the system. Even the ministers and Tory MPs who advocated Catholic Emancipation were opposed to any general changes in the franchise or distribution of parliamentary seats.

Government and party

Much the same attitude was evident in ministers' attitudes towards party. Liverpool and his colleagues saw nothing wrong in a situation in which not much more than a quarter of the MPs were closely allied in support of the government. Within this grouping, some sixty office-holders formed a core around which others assembled out of conviction or hope of future favours, or both. The Opposition could never muster any larger number of dedicated supporters, and the parliamentary struggles depended essentially on enlisting the support of uncommitted Members. The government did not even regard it as essential for them to retain the undeviating support of their recognized partisans, and Liverpool went so far as to declare that he would 'never attempt to interfere with the individual member's right to vote as he may think consistent with his duty upon any particular question'.[17]

15. Gash, *Lord Liverpool*, 142.   16. Ibid. 146.
17. Brock, *Lord Liverpool*, 101.

Such attitudes, no doubt prompted by admirable motives, could add to the government's problems in contriving parliamentary majorities for important legislation. These were compounded by the weakening of the government's patronage. For most of the previous century, administrations had been able to buy support by an unscrupulous deployment of a considerable range of offices, sinecures, pensions, and honours. This was a declining asset. The campaign for 'economical reform' from the 1780s and the continuing rage for cutting public expenditure went far to deprive the government of patronage resources by abolishing offices which were either pure sinecures or were not 'efficient' posts.

Public opinion not only demanded the elimination of such posts but also watched with increasing care the ways in which the remaining patronage of government was employed. It was still possible to restrict such patronage for the most part to government supporters, but those appointed had to be capable of carrying out the duties of the post concerned, by the (not unduly exigent) standards of the day. Liverpool and his colleagues were still able to some extent to find billets for relatives or friends, but demand far exceeded supply. Moreover, ministers themselves were unwilling to exploit their patronage as unscrupulously as some of their predecessors had done. Most Civil Service posts were given to men who were capable of discharging the relevant duties with reasonable success; this often involved the rejection of unsuitable but importunate candidates from the ranks of the ministry's supporters.

In the past Church patronage had been a source of political manipulation, but here too the Liverpool administration moved with the times, the Prime Minister himself, whose evangelical Christianity was sincere if undemonstrative, in the forefront. Although one of his cousins was promoted to a minor bishopric in 1825, it is not clear that the promotion was undeserved. In other cases of ecclesiastical preferment in the government's gift, Liverpool showed a tenacious determination to insist on meritorious appointments, even at the cost of clashes with senior colleagues.[18] A similar high-mindedness was evident in other areas of patronage. Liverpool himself was not a supporter of Catholic Emancipation, but in sharing out electoral patronage made available to him by borough patrons he was scrupulously even-handed as between 'Protestants' and 'Catholics' (as opponents or supporters of emancipation were nicknamed) among the government's supporters. Such limitations on the government's exercise of patronage, whether enforced or voluntary, made it harder to cement together a sufficient corps of reliable supporters in Parliament.

Law and order

Within the limited role marked out for governments, some items had an undoubted place. It was certainly a duty of government to maintain law and order.

18. Gash, *Lord Liverpool*, 203–4, 240.

That this might not be an easy task was obvious enough, for recurrent disorder, especially at times of economic depression, had been common for centuries.[19] Riot was a prescriptive mode of bringing grievances to the notice of established authority. Most of the popular demonstrations of discontent stemmed from economic and social problems rather than any widespread revolutionary intent. The regularity with which the incidence of tumult varied with economic conditions suggests that political disaffection was neither very widespread nor very deep-rooted, for surely genuinely convinced radicals would be ready to demonstrate in good years as well as bad. Although history has, especially in the recent past, made much of the demonstrations of discontent in the 1815–30 period, there is no convincing evidence that they were any worse than in earlier periods.

Ministers were well aware of the importance of their decisions in the sphere of public order. The cohesion of society could be imperilled either by excessive repression or by a failure to preserve public order. The economic growth which was necessary to support a growing population could only be achieved if internal stability could be maintained. The Liverpool government, however, found its role as conservator of civil peace difficult enough, especially in the first years after 1815. Civil police resources were weak. The reduced peacetime army and navy could be relied on, but the armed forces were a last resort, traditionally to be called on to act in support of the civil power only when that power was unable to control a dangerous situation. In addition to the paucity of peacekeeping resources, there were other complications involved in the maintenance of law and order. This was a society in which there was a considerable respect for the principle of law, however much lawbreaking there might be in practice. It was not always easy to know just what the law was in relation to questions of public order. For example, when and how a public meeting might become an illegal assembly provided questions which neither government nor magistrates found it easy to answer. On one occasion the Lord Chancellor, Lord Eldon, noted that 'An unlawful assembly, *as such merely*, I apprehend can't be dispersed; and what constitutes *riot* enough to justify dispersion is no easy matter to determine, where there is not actual violence begun on the part of those assembled.[20] Magistrates seeking Home Office advice on this issue could receive an unhelpful response, such as the statement that a public meeting became an illegal assembly when it proceeded to act illegally. Magistrates, and members of the armed forces, were well aware that juries could not always be trusted to give unflinching support to guardians of public order who had acted energetically in circumstances of uncertain legality. Much of the 'repressive' legislation of the 1815–20 period consisted of attempts to clarify the law of public order and provide for the speedier trial of offenders against it.

19. J. Stevenson, *Popular Disturbances in England, 1700–1870* (1979); E. P. Thompson, 'The moral economy of the English crowd in the eighteenth century', *Past and Present*, 50 (1971); A. Booth, 'Food riots in north-west England, 1790–1801', *Past and Present*, 77 (1977).
20. Stevenson, 346 n. 19.

In fulfilling its role as the chief guardian of civil peace, the Liverpool government was not indifferent to suffering or unsympathetic to those protesting against justified grievances. Provided that protests were kept within reasonable bounds, it was possible for both central and local authorities to show restraint in handling even spirited demonstrations of discontent. At the end of a prolonged strike by merchant seamen in 1815, the government's attitude was expressed in letters from the Home Secretary, Lord Sidmouth: 'it is now my earnest wish ... that, as the law is no longer violated, that Consideration and Liberality may be manifested by the Shipowners, which is due to British Seamen'; 'it is His Lordship's most anxious Desire, that only cases of very prominent Delinquency should be made the Subject of Prosecution'. The Duke of Northumberland, Lord Lieutenant of the county principally affected, in his letters to the Home Office, laid the principal responsibility for the episode on the employers concerned, and praised the restraint of the striking seamen. The commander of the army in the northern district, Lt Gen. Wynyard, told Sidmouth that 'The conduct of the Shipowners, in shifting this distressing business from their own, to the shoulders of the Government, seems to me as disgraceful as it is cowardly.'[21]

The Home Office papers contain many instances in which ministers, officers of the armed forces, and local magistrates expressed sympathy for poorer people labouring under genuine suffering or justified grievances. Employers were often criticized either for treating their dependants unfairly or for trying to shift on to those in authority responsibility for awkward situations which the employers themselves had created. At the same time the government could be scathing in its attitude towards magistrates who seemed to be failing in the discharge of their responsibilities. For most of the time, those in authority perceived a distinction between the more or less traditional demonstrations of discontent which sought to bring about beneficial intervention by those in authority, and subversive activities aimed at undermining the existing order of society.

The Liverpool government was soon left in no doubt that the transition to peace in 1815 was not to see the beginning of a period of domestic tranquillity. Even during the last months of the war, the enactment of the Corn Law of 1815 was accompanied by attacks on the houses of ministers and MPs; as a precaution, army reinforcements were moved to the capital. At the same time, the episode illustrated some of the ways in which the administration's enemies were divided. 'Respectable' opponents of the Corn Law, such as the eleven peers, including two royal dukes, who entered a formal protest against the Act on the journals of the House of Lords, would have nothing to do with the violence of the London crowds, and were quick to disavow any sympathy with them. Sir Francis Burdett, although one of the most prominent radical politicians of the day, repudiated any connection with the violence and intimidation seen on the streets of London.[22]

---

21. PRO, HO 42/196 contains the series of letters relating to the end of the strikes referred to here.
22. Stevenson, *Popular Disturbances in England* frequently mentions such divisions. The Lords' protest against the 1815 Corn Laws is reproduced in N. McCord, *Free Trade* (1970), 46–9.

During the difficult years to come, the Liverpool government could rely on the fact that what was seen as mob violence alienated moderate opinion and swung support towards the ministry. With the final enactment of the Corn Law towards the end of March 1815 that particular tumult subsided, but the focus of disorder now shifted to the provinces.

A rapid reduction in the Royal Navy, and the paying off of the large fleet of hired merchant shipping which the war effort had required, was made necessary by the clamour for economy. This produced sudden and large-scale redundancies among seamen and sparked off the great strikes of 1815, already referred to. Peace also brought a sharp reduction in government expenditure on such items as munitions and uniforms. Radical and Whig politicians were happy to take the lead in the pressure for drastic cuts in public spending and lower taxation, in ways which might embarrass the government; the social consequences of this pressure were ignored.

Apart from substantial reductions in the armed forces, the first post-war years saw dislocation in export markets, together with poor harvests and high food prices. The combined pressures brought on a rash of disturbances in many parts of the country. The response of the authorities varied with the nature of the outbreaks. Two examples will illustrate these reactions. In July 1816 groups of unemployed miners began to march towards London, dragging with them wagons of coal, with the intention of petitioning the Prince Regent to intervene to obtain work for them. The government responded by ordering the London stipendiary magistrates to intercept the marchers, who were supporting themselves by begging en route.[23] These agents met the marchers and in accordance with instructions from the Home Secretary persuaded them to abandon their plan, on the grounds that their behaviour was illegal. The demonstrators were promised that their petition would be laid before the Prince Regent by the Home Secretary, and the magistrates provided money to meet the costs of the march home.

Events in the spring and early summer of 1816 in rural eastern England presented a more sombre picture. Here the disorder had many precedents. In reaction to high food prices and a variety of local grievances, crowds gathered in many different places, with corn mills, food shops, and the homes of their owners the principal targets of violence. There was some intimidation, extortion, and destruction of property; many people were put in fear by the outbreaks. The government responded by dispatching a special judicial commission to the affected areas, which condemned to death twenty-four men convicted of participation in the riots; five of the capital sentences were carried out, and most of the remainder were commuted to long sentences of transportation instead. These rural outbreaks provided the most serious episodes in a summer which saw scattered demonstrations of discontent in many parts of the country.

23. PRO, HO 41/1, 3 July 1816. This document provides a fine example of early 19th-cent. bureaucratic prose. The incident is summarized in N. Gash, *Aristocracy and People* (1979), 78.

Disturbances included sporadic attacks on machinery credited with causing unemployment in Leicestershire and Nottinghamshire, although these 'Luddite' outbreaks were not on as large a scale as those of 1811–12.

Spa Fields

In the following winter the centre of trouble briefly moved to London again, with major demonstrations at Spa Fields on 15 November and 2 December.[24] The moving spirits in organizing these meetings were a group of extreme radicals who found inspiration in the writings of Thomas Spence, an advocate of the communal ownership of land. The ringleaders were James Watson, a radical London apothecary, and his son of the same name, who hoped to inspire a massive popular response to their initiative. They invited William Cobbett, Major John Cartwright, Sir Francis Burdett, and Henry Hunt, all of them leading radicals with established national reputations. The first three prudently stayed away and Hunt, although he did turn up, disappointed the meeting's organizers by carefully larding his speech with explicit denunciations of violence and illegality, and by urging the crowd to disperse peacefully at the end of the meeting.

This was not what some militants had wanted, and at the second meeting on 2 December, before Hunt had arrived, a breakaway group of about 200 men split from the main gathering and began a march towards the Tower, perhaps with memories of the Bastille in mind. Most of this little corps scattered when confronted by the Lord Mayor and a handful of constables. A few of the most determined, having ransacked a gun shop and wounded a bystander, made their way to the Tower, where they milled about ineffectively for some time before being dispersed by troops. The younger Watson had been primarily responsible for the episode, and now fled abroad; a seaman, Cashman, was later executed for his part in the rising.

Again radical disunity was obvious; Hunt himself described the outbreak as 'a disgraceful and contemptible riot'. At the same time, the performance of the forces of law and order, though successful in the event, had not been efficient (the troops in the Tower, for example, were without ammunition). The Home Secretary had already been arguing the need for legislation to strengthen the law on public order. Early in 1817 these arguments were strengthened by incidents during the state opening of Parliament. The Prince Regent on his way to Westminster was given a hostile reception and windows on the royal coach were shattered by either shots or, more likely, stones.

It was difficult for ministers to know just how dangerous the discontent was. A considerable volume of information was received, especially at the Home Office, but its quality varied. Some letters came from alarmists, including the minority of magistrates who were prone to panic. To their exaggerated fears were

---

24. Stevenson, *Popular Disturbances in England*, 193–6.

added the reports of informers who infiltrated subversive political movements; since they hoped to be paid by results, there was no inducement for them to minimize the dangers present. It might be profitable for them to act as agents provocateurs, as some of them, including the notorious 'Oliver the Spy', certainly did.[25] On the other hand there was much correspondence of a more balanced and sensible nature, pointing out that most of the current troubles had little to do with political subversion but rather with attempts to induce the authorities to act to remedy pressing grievances. There could be no doubt that radical extremists were contemplating violent revolution, but it was possible to believe that their influence was very limited.

Faced then with conflicting evidence, ministers compromised by producing emergency legislation in 1817, but made it more moderate than Sidmouth would have preferred. In securing its passage ministers moved carefully, arranging first for both Houses of Parliament to appoint Committees of Secrecy to consider the situation. With evidence of disorder and subversion duly submitted, these committees reported in favour of legislative action which ministers could then proffer as meeting the wishes of the legislature. The most important new weapon given to government was the temporary power to imprison without trial persons suspected of treasonable activities; the government's own attitude here was indicated by Liverpool's admission in the Lords that this power was 'most odious', only to be justified by clear necessity. Other Acts strengthened the law against attacks on the Prince Regent, provided stiff penalties for attempts to subvert members of the armed forces, and extended the powers of magistrates to prohibit meetings thought to be seditious.

Little use was made of these new powers. The suspension of habeas corpus in 1816, which allowed arrest without trial, was renewed from June 1817 until January 1818, but only forty-four arrests were made under this. Of those arrested, the majority were released before the end of 1817 and the rest by the following January. Those arrested included some dangerous characters. The Spencean Arthur Thistlewood, for instance, was locked up without trial after he had issued a theatrical challenge to a duel to the Home Secretary, but in the summer of 1819 he was free again, and engaged in revolutionary plotting. Meanwhile the government's action in strengthening the law of public order seemed justified by disturbances later in 1817, though in the event the only significant eruption came in the tragic Derbyshire rising. A few hundred men from industrial villages like Pentrich assembled under the leadership of Jeremiah Brandreth, believing that they formed one small component in a widespread insurrection. In fact they were pathetically isolated, and easily dispersed by a small force of troops at Nottingham. During their outbreak there had been attacks on some houses, in the course of which a servant had been killed. This in itself would have led to capital sentences, even if no treasonable purpose had been involved. Brandreth

25. Ibid. 209–10.

and two of his associates were hanged and thirty transported for their part in this misconceived if genuine attempt at revolutionary insurrection. During these trials the government spy 'Oliver' was shown to have acted as an agent provocateur. This did not help the reputation of the government, whose enemies accused it of trapping weak and misguided men into disastrous courses. In the absence of adequate police resources, given the undoubted presence of real revolutionaries, it was difficult to see how government could refrain from trying to plant agents within subversive groups, but such agents were rarely trustworthy.

Repressive legislation and special judicial commissions were not the only responses of ministers to the domestic troubles of these years. The new Acts of Parliament reaching the statute book in 1817 included a measure seeking to curtail truck, that is, the practice of paying wages in goods, which might include drink, instead of money. Another Act of 1817 made available loans for public works to increase employment, while another was designed to encourage emigration for those who could not find adequate employment at home.[26] The latter months of 1817 and most of 1818 were relatively tranquil, but in the matter of law and order as in other spheres 1819 was to prove a crisis year.

Peterloo

At the end of 1818 there was a resurgence in radical activity. New organizations, sometimes calling themselves Political Protestants, appeared in various parts of the country, and preparations began for a series of political rallies to take place in 1819. One device much canvassed with a view to exploiting weaknesses in the electoral system was to call public meetings in the large towns which as yet had no MPs of their own; these meetings would proceed to choose a popular representative as a kind of challenge to the legal system of representation in Parliament. It was this campaign which led indirectly to the tragedy of Peterloo.

In the early summer of 1819 there were mass meetings in London and in various provincial centres. Although the majority of the crowds which assembled were made up of relatively poor people, the radical movement enjoyed the support of some men of higher social standing. One of the most active leaders in 1819 was Sir Charles Wolseley, seventh Baronet, of Wolseley Hall, Staffordshire, who had been present at the fall of the Bastille in 1789, and indeed claimed to have participated in that assault. He presided at a reform meeting at Stockport in June, and a month later on the strength of such services a mass meeting at Birmingham selected him as 'legislatorial attorney' or democratic representative of that town. From the government's point of view this provided an opportunity to retaliate, for such an election was plainly illegal. Wolseley was arrested, and a royal proclamation stressed that such pseudo-elections could not be allowed to continue.

26. M. W. Flinn, 'The Poor Employment Act of 1817', *Economic History Review*, 2nd ser., 14 (1961), 82–92.

The Manchester Radical Union, which had come into existence as part of the political upsurge of these months, had planned to follow the Birmingham example with a mass meeting and a popular election on 9 August. After a warning from magistrates that this would not be allowed, the plans were altered; the date was postponed to 16 August, and the idea of holding an election was dropped in favour of resolutions advocating a peaceful and legal campaign for parliamentary reform.[27]

On 16 August the great meeting assembled on St Peter's Fields, on the outskirts of Manchester. Parties marched in from outlying communities, while a group of magistrates watched the proceedings with mounting anxiety from a house nearby. There were doubts about the legality of the meeting and fears concerning what it might lead to. After most of the crowd had assembled, the magistrates decided that they would arrest the principal speaker, Henry Hunt, before he began his speech. The local constables declared that they could not implement the order without military protection. The most accessible military force was the Manchester and Salford Yeomanry, volunteer cavalry drawn from the dominant social groups of the district and imperfectly trained. A yeomanry force escorted the constables to the hustings erected for the speakers and Hunt was duly arrested. Then in trying to withdraw the yeomanry became trapped inside the huge crowd. Their predicament could be seen by the magistrates, who dispatched to their rescue a body of regular Hussars which had arrived on the scene. As these disciplined professional troopers forced their way into the crowd there was a panic, and at the end of the day eleven people had been killed and hundreds injured. There was evidence that the yeomanry themselves had panicked and struck out wildly with their weapons, also suggestions that some of them had been drinking before the meeting. Robert Southey, then, along with his fellow 'Lakeland Poets' Wordsworth and Coleridge, completing his journey from youthful radicalism to literary supporter of the Tories, felt that the fault lay 'in employing the yeomanry instead of the [better disciplined] regular troops'.[28]

Hunt and nine other radicals were tried at York in March 1820 on charges of sedition arising from the meeting and after a trial lasting two weeks Hunt and four others were found guilty. It is significant, however, that they were charged on seven counts and only found guilty on one, that of 'intending disaffection and hatred of the king and constitution'.[29]

The tragedy at St Peter's Fields was promptly christened Peterloo, in ironical reference to the British Army's victory at Waterloo a few years earlier, and it is as the Peterloo Massacre that it is enshrined in history. It was not in any literal sense a massacre—if the troops available in the Manchester area had been massed against the meeting, or if the army's firearms had been used, the death toll could

27. For Peterloo, Stevenson, *Popular Disturbances in England*, 213–17, and the associated footnote references, provide a modern summary account.
28. W. A. Speck, *Robert Southey: Entire Man of Letters* (2006), 179.
29. R. Poole, ' "By the Law or the Sword": Peterloo Revisited', *History*, vol. 91, no. 302, April 2006.

have been more than eleven. The reality, however, was tragic enough, and the Manchester magistrates had managed things badly. It is possible to see some reasons why this had happened.

The tenor of the advice which the Home Office gave to local magistrates was that they were responsible for the maintenance of law and order in their districts, but that they should not overstep their legal powers. As recently as 4 August, Sidmouth had warned the Manchester magistrates against precipitate action when faced with a large meeting which was not clearly illegal. On the other hand immediate decisions on how to respond had to be left to the men on the spot. The royal proclamation of 30 July had enjoined magistrates to 'bring to justice . . . all persons who have been or may be guilty of uttering seditious speeches and harangues'.[30] On 16 August it had been reported to the magistrates that the mass meeting was causing alarm in the district, and their principal spokesman later noted that he had come to the conclusion that Manchester was endangered by the possible consequences of the great radical gathering.[31] At least the decision to arrest Hunt before he could begin to stir up the crowd was an intelligible one. It is possible to argue, however, that the magistrates' intervention was not in accordance with the general tenor of the advice coming from the Home Office, although that advice was not precise in nature.

The news from Manchester was unwelcome to the government. Liverpool's own reaction was that the action of the magistrates had been 'justifiable' but not 'prudent'.[32] At the same time, ministers felt that they had no choice but to back up the local representatives of law and order. To have joined in the chorus of condemnation which was gathering about Peterloo would be to undermine the confidence of the unpaid local magistracy on which so much depended, and encourage the faint-hearted among them to avoid unpleasant responsibilities. Whatever their private doubts, ministers authorized a message from the Prince Regent congratulating the Manchester magistrates on their 'prompt, decisive and efficient measures'. Most of the Cabinet was dispersed during the parliamentary recess, but it is unlikely that the absentees would have dissented from the judgement that, since the government could not remain silent or condemn the magistrates, an endorsement of their conduct was the only possible course to adopt. Sidmouth, in response to the growing radical activities of 1819, had already been pressing for further legislation; Liverpool had been less convinced of the need for this, but the political aftermath of Peterloo made it necessary to give a clear indication of the government's determination to stand firm.

It was natural that radicals should point to the bloodshed at Peterloo, and the government's support of the magistracy there, to show the need for a drastic change in the country's system of government, however exceptional that event had been. Left to themselves, the radicals were unlikely to mobilize the kind of

30. R. Walmsley, *Peterloo: The Case Reopened* (1969), 137 n.
31. Ibid. 166.   32. Gash, *Lord Liverpool*, 144.

power which could be effective in that society. It was one thing to attract thousands of people to great meetings of protest in hard times, and to tell them that their privations were the direct result of mismanagement and oppression by a corrupt and extravagant government. It was quite another matter to make such numbers support more drastic courses of action, or even to remain interested in reform when better times came. The immediate aftermath of Peterloo, nevertheless, saw an unusual coming together of the ministry's foes as, after some hesitation, aristocratic Whigs moved to associate themselves with the wave of radical protest. This conjunction was marked by the holding of a series of mass meetings, given countenance by the attendance of many of the government's political rivals among the leading Whigs. The resolutions at these post-Peterloo meetings were usually drawn up with a studious moderation which could keep this kind of uneasy alliance together; commonly they denounced the action of the Manchester magistrates and the government's backing of them, enunciated a claim for a right to meet freely to discuss matters of public interest, but steered clear of such controversial matters as the need for, or the desirable extent of, parliamentary reform. In Yorkshire, where the local Whig aristocrats were strong, the Lord Lieutenant, Earl Fitzwilliam, summoned a formal County Meeting and drafted the protest resolutions himself. The government's reaction was swift; Fitzwilliam was dismissed as Lord Lieutenant, for the government had determined to fight back.

The Six Acts

Parliament was called together in November 1819, and by then the Home Office had assembled a dossier of evidence gathered from local correspondents, suggesting that the radical agitation remained formidable, and that it presented a definite threat to public order. Attempts by the Whig parliamentary Opposition to secure a public inquiry into Peterloo were easily defeated, and the government had little difficulty in securing reassuring majorities for the six Acts with which it aimed to strengthen the forces of order. These Acts are worth careful consideration, for they undoubtedly represented the peak of legislative repression enacted by the Liverpool administration; their reputation in this light has given the Six Acts of 1819 a notoriety which may well surprise anyone who takes the trouble to read them.[33] Considering the nature of contemporary society, the policies in matters of public order of regimes elsewhere in Europe, and the parallel provided by the penal code for non-political offences in the Britain of these years, the Six Acts must appear distinctly mild rather than draconian. Unofficial military drilling was banned (a prohibition still in force under later legislation),

33. The Six Acts were 60 Geo. III, c. 1 (the Training Prevention Act), 60 Geo. III, c. 2 (the Seizure of Arms Act), 60 Geo. III, c. 4 (Misdemeanours Act), 60 Geo. III, c. 6 (Seditious Meetings Prevention Act), 60 Geo. III, c. 8 (Blasphemous and Seditious Libels Act), 60 Geo. III, c. 9 (Newspapers and Stamp Duties Act).

magistrates in areas of apprehended subversion could search houses and other buildings for arms, political meetings could only be held with a magistrate's permission; the latter two statutes were temporary, and no attempt was made to extend them when they expired. There were provisions to limit a defendant's power to postpone trial by taking advantage of legal technicalities, to tighten up the law relating to the stamp duty on newspapers, and for the suppression of publications deemed to be blasphemous or seditious. The penalties provided for breaches of the legislation were not severe. Moreover, there was no sustained effort to implement the new legislation.

The Cato Street conspiracy

Events in the next few months seemed to vindicate the government's initiative. In February, with the aid of an informer involved in the plotting, ministers became aware of a scheme hatched by Thistlewood and a group of similar militant radicals to murder the entire Cabinet. Forewarned, the authorities were able to trap the conspirators in a house in Cato Street, although one of the official party was killed in the fracas which ensued. Thistlewood and four of his fellow conspirators were executed on 1 May. The spring of 1820 also saw minor outbreaks of disaffection in places like Barnsley, Sheffield, and Huddersfield, though none of these presented serious problems to the authorities.

As far as the problem of internal security was concerned the Liverpool government had by now weathered the storm, and in comparison the remainder of its tenure posed no comparable dangers. The cumulative evidence of popular dissatisfaction which had been presented by the years 1815–20 was, however, sufficient to make acute and thoughtful men reflect that the pressure for change was increasing. In May 1820, soon after the crushing of Thistlewood's Cato Street conspiracy, Peel asked one of his colleagues,

Do you not think that the tone of England—of that great compound of folly, weakness, prejudice, wrong feeling, right feeling, obstinacy, and newspaper paragraphs, which is called public opinion—is more liberal—to use an odious but intelligible phrase—than the policy of the Government? Do not you think that there is a feeling, becoming daily more general and more confirmed—that is, independent of the pressure of taxation or any immediate cause—in favour of some undefined change in the mode of governing the country?[34]

Dissatisfaction with the government was about to find another focus, not in anything arising from the social ills of a changing economy, but in a reverberating scandal produced by the royal family.[35]

34. L. J. Jennings (ed.), *The Croker Papers* (1884), i. 170.
35. Gash, *Lord Liverpool*, gives a clear account of the Queen Caroline affair, and of the Liverpool government's role in it.

The Queen Caroline affair

For years there had been a problem caused by the breakdown of relations between the Prince Regent and his wife Caroline. The Prince had been secretly married to Mrs Fitzherbert, a Roman Catholic, but the marriage had no legal validity as it was contrary to the Royal Marriages Act. His marriage to Princess Caroline of Brunswick Wolfenbuttel had been undertaken in the interests of pro-creating an heir and getting his debts paid off by Parliament. It was not a success. The couple had quarrelled in the early days of the marriage, and their only child, Princess Charlotte, died in 1817. The Princess of Wales lived abroad, and her behaviour had already provoked investigations which uncovered misconduct which went beyond mere indiscretion. After a confidential inquiry in 1818, nei-ther the government nor the Prince Regent had any doubt that Caroline had committed adultery during her sojourn abroad. The death of Princess Charlotte strengthened the determination of the Prince Regent to rid himself of a wife he loathed, and the whole unsavoury mess—complicated by the fact that the Prince Regent's own private life was notoriously lax—blew up with the death of the old invalid King George III early in 1820.

The new King now demanded that his ministers take action to rid him of his adulterous Queen. Conscious of the dreadful opportunity for a damaging scan-dal which was now unfolding, the Cabinet first reluctantly accepted George IV's demand that Caroline be excluded from the usual prayers for the royal family included in the Anglican liturgy. At the same time they pinned their hopes to the possibility of inducing the new and unwelcome Queen to see reason and accept a substantial income in return for staying abroad out of the way. Tortuous nego-tiations ensued, in which the radical lawyer Henry Brougham acted as a slippery and untrustworthy contact with Caroline, but eventually the attempts to reach a satisfactory settlement broke down. Caroline decided that she would come to England and claim the proper rights of a queen consort, despite the reputation she had acquired among those who knew something of her escapades abroad. Brushing aside warnings from the government, in June 1820 she came to London and placed herself under the protection of radical leaders in the capital. The Cabinet had warned the Queen that if she flouted their advice and came to Britain to make trouble, they would have no choice but to yield to the importun-ities of her royal husband, and take action to obtain a divorce.

In July Liverpool introduced into the House of Lords a Bill of Pains and Penalties which would have dissolved the royal marriage and deprived Caroline of the rights and privileges of a queen consort. The parliamentary proceedings which ensued involved the public rehearsing of evidence against the Queen, including extensive examination of foreign domestic servants about her conduct abroad and her relations with male friends. It was a remarkable instance of the washing of dirty linen in public. Faced with the opportunist hostility of Whig peers, and George IV's own reputation as a libertine, the proceedings were an ordeal for ministers. There was an outburst of popular sympathy for the Queen, seen as an injured innocent persecuted by a depraved royal husband. The popular outcry was by no means confined to London. In Scotland, where the liturgy prohibition did not apply, many clergy, both secessionist and established, prayed for the Queen and, at 'the first anti-governmental demonstration in the Scottish capital in the post-war period', 17,000 signatures were collected in Edinburgh, calling on the King to dismiss his ministers.[36] The chances of passing the bill through all of its parliamentary stages, against formidable opposition in both Houses and hostile popular clamour, became increasingly remote.

The Cabinet began to retreat when it decided that it could not carry the whole bill; after a fierce struggle with the King, it was decided to drop the formal divorce, on which some of the bishops had expressed doubts, in order to save the rest of the bill. This scheme was frustrated by an adroit parliamentary manoeuvre by Earl Grey, who persuaded most of the Whig peers to vote for the retention of the divorce stipulation, which ministers knew they had no real chance of fighting through the Commons. After the bill passed its second reading in the Lords by a majority of only nine, the government bowed to the inevitable and announced that it would not proceed further with the measure.

With the Caroline affair, popular culture, the monarchy, tensions between the sexes, and politics came together.[37] It is impossible to characterize popular culture neatly in political terms. It is at once traditionalist and radical, prepared to challenge the establishment but usually in defence of some 'age old' right or sentiment and to assault change or modernization on the same terms. There were many paradoxes in the agitation: the demonstrators gave expression to dissatisfaction with King and government but they did so by supporting a member of the royal family; Whigs and radicals may have taken up Caroline's cause for diverse ends and to discredit the monarchy but the crowds in supporting the Queen expressed a somewhat unorthodox monarchism. There was a long popular cultural tradition by which women saw themselves as the guardians of morality taking the lead in hounding sexual deviancy or marital betrayal. This could result in 'rough music' for errant wives or harsh husbands and in this instance popular and especially female popular culture decided that Caroline was the 'woman wronged'.

The whole affair had poisoned relations between the sovereign and his ministers, and brought discredit on just about every person and institution which the scandal touched. Nevertheless, although the business continued to rumble on after the end of the parliamentary proceedings, Lord Eldon's prediction that the agitation would 'die away like all other nine days' wonders' proved largely correct.[38] Caroline's past behaviour had been less than circumspect; the poet Robert

36. N. Gash, *Aristocracy and People: Britain 1815–1865* (1979), 109.
37. See Flora Fraser, *The Unruly Queen: The Life of Queen Caroline* (1996), 450–1; Tamara L. Hunt, 'Morality and Monarchy in the Queen Caroline Affair', *Albion*, 23 (1991).
38. H. Twiss, *The Public and Private Life of Lord Chancellor Eldon*, vol. 2 (1846), 19.

Southey mocked her as 'Carolina purissima'.[39] There was a reaction as details of Caroline's past became well-known and loyalist addresses swung opinion against her.[40] At her husband's orders, the Queen was turned away from the doors of Westminster Abbey during the coronation ceremony, but the London crowd proved more interested in the coronation procession and she was supported only by what the contemporary commentator, Croker, called a 'thin and shabby mob'.[41] Ultimately Caroline was brought to accept a substantial pension, which did much to discredit her in the eyes of erstwhile supporters. One of the most unsavoury episodes in the history of the monarchy was brought to an end by the Queen's death early in August 1821, although her death temporarily revived her cause. She had expressed a wish to be buried in her old home of Brunswick; the government tried to organize a quiet departure for her cortege, but the London crowd forced the authorities to take the procession through the city, after a clash with the escorting troops in which two Londoners were killed. At the end of 1820 Canning, whose relations with Caroline many years previously had at the least been indiscreet, had insisted on resigning from the government.[42] This weakened the government front bench, but the rift proved short-lived, so that Canning was again available to enter the Cabinet after Castlereagh's suicide in 1822.

The behaviour of the London crowd at the Queen's funeral was one reason why the new Home Secretary, Peel, made a strenuous effort in 1822 to obtain the formation of a new police force for the capital. Appreciating that there would be strong feeling against arming the executive with such a weapon, he tried to procure from a parliamentary select committee a willing assent for the project of 'obtaining for the Metropolis as perfect a system of police as was consistent with the character of a free country'. On this occasion, however, the device misfired, and the committee decided that

It is difficult to reconcile an effective system of police, with that perfect freedom of action and exemption from interference which was one of the great privileges and blessings of society in this country; and Your Committee think that the forfeiture or curtailment of such advantages would be too great a sacrifice for improvements in police, or facilities in detection of crime, however desirable in themselves if abstractedly considered.[43]

The would-be reformer was obliged to withdraw his proposal, though a few years later more careful preparation of the ground was to produce a different result (see pp. 50–1 below).

Acutely distressing to ministers though the Queen Caroline affair had been, once it was over a more tranquil period ensued. Although there was a continuing crop of minor demonstrations of discontent and industrial disputes, improving

39. W. A. Speck, *Robert Southey: Entire Man of Letters* (2006), 184.
40. Jonathan Fulcher, 'The Loyalist Response to the Queen Caroline Agitations', *Journal of British Studies*, 34 (1995), 499–501.
41. L. J. Jennings (ed), *The Croker Papers*, i, 196.
42. David Saul, *Prince of Pleasure* (1998), 237.
43. Gash, *Mr. Secretary Peel*, 313.

economic conditions gave the Liverpool ministry an easier time. The 1815–21 period had seen the administration buffeted by the strains of the immediate post-war years, and facing problems in the maintenance of law and order. During the same period, other aspects of the ministry's responsibilities had also posed problems.

Economic policy

The management of the State's finances was an important part of the government's work, and in this area Liverpool and his colleagues had clear ideas as to which policies were in the public interest. They were well aware that the population was growing fast and that only economic growth could provide the resources needed to support the increased numbers. While they were prepared to sympathize and cooperate in the desire of the tax-paying electorate to see government carried on as economically as was practicable, the ministers' perception of the sensible limits of this attitude was not generally shared. It was not simply that ministers were anxious to retain a revenue adequate to meet the State's essential services in the new peacetime situation, for they had ideas which went beyond this static conception. They believed that it ought to be possible to manipulate even the reduced peacetime revenue to encourage prosperity in the interests of the whole national community. At the same time, unlike many taxpayers, the ministers could see that it was impossible to reduce taxes to the low pre-war levels, if only because of the huge sums which must now be allotted to service the swollen National Debt.

At the end of the war, although the bulk of the State's revenue came from indirect taxation in various forms, there remained the direct property or income tax which had been imposed on the wealthier sectors of society as a wartime expedient. Liverpool and his colleagues planned to maintain the income tax into the peacetime years, at a reduced rate, in order that the complex tariff system might be simplified and reduced to encourage the growth of commerce. The two elements were interdependent, for indirect taxation could only be cut if the administration could retain the income tax to meet necessary expenditure. The income tax was unpopular, and it was widely believed that its original imposition had been accompanied by an undertaking to discontinue it when peace came. Apart from the actual cost to the small but influential minority which paid it, the inquisitorial nature of income tax, with officials prying into details of personal finances, was widely disliked.

The government did its best to sweeten parliamentary and public opinion in 1816, by agreeing to levy the tax at a much reduced rate, which should still have given the Treasury a useful £6 million a year. Anxious consultations and estimates of probable support led the Cabinet to believe that it could carry the measure by something like 40 votes in the Commons. It is an illuminating indication of the independence of most MPs that in the event the crucial resolution was defeated by almost the same margin, 238 votes to 201, with many of the government's usual supporters in the hostile lobby. Whig and radical MPs, however, provided the bulk of the votes which frustrated the government's plan.

In more modern times such a defeat on a major element in the Budget would imperil a government's existence, but in 1816 the Liverpool Cabinet could survive this kind of rebuff, provided it retained the general confidence of Parliament. The vote meant, however, that for some years to come the administration found itself in a difficult financial position. It could not implement its desire to liberalize the tariff system, which was increasingly seen as an impediment to increased trade and prosperity, because it needed the revenue from tariffs to pay its way. The loss of direct taxation on the rich involved an increased reliance on duties levied on articles of general consumption. Moreover, without the income tax the ordinary revenue was not even sufficient to meet necessary expenditure. This meant repeated recourse to further borrowing to make ends meet, which increased instead of diminishing the burden of the National Debt.

The 1815 Corn Law

In one respect the government had already felt obliged to add to the country's tariff restrictions, though this time primarily for protective rather than revenue purposes. The Corn Law of 1815 was an attempt to cushion the country's most important economic interest, agriculture, against post-war difficulties. High wartime food prices had begun to fall as early as 1813, and the drop in cereal prices continued into 1815; the average price of wheat, which had stood at 118s. 9d. per quarter at the beginning of 1813, was down to 60s. 8d. by January 1815.[44] It was recognized that something would have to be done to offset this trend, and the obvious course was to enact tariff protection for home produce. In 1814 a parliamentary committee had recommended that an acceptably remunerative price for wheat would be 80s. per quarter, and in 1815 the dominant landed interest was unlikely to accept any lower level of protection.

Liverpool himself, and William Huskisson, then a junior minister whom the Prime Minister often consulted on economic matters, already believed that a sliding scale of duties, varying with home prices, would work more smoothly than the prohibition of imports until a certain price level was reached. In the end, though, they found it politic to accept the simpler solution which the 1814 committee had advocated. The 1815 Corn Law imposed a new range of duties on agricultural imports, with the 80s. figure selected as the cut-off point for wheat. No foreign wheat was to be imported until the average home price reached that figure, though produce from British colonies was allowed to enter at a lower

---

44. Gash, *Lord Liverpool*, 117. For the background to the 1815 Corn Law, D. G. Barnes, *A History of the Corn Laws from 1660 to 1846* (1930). A perusal of the successive early 19th-cent. Corn Laws, especially those of 1815, 1828, and 1842, provides a good illustration of the growing sophistication of government activity.

level. The prosperity of home agriculture was not the only objective here. Wartime experience had recently indicated that as a matter of national security it was desirable to limit dependence on foreign food supplies. The government also hoped that if the landed interest could be conciliated by this major concession then perhaps its representatives might be induced to look favourably on the remainder of the ministry's financial proposals. The illusory nature of this hope was made clear in 1816, not only by the defeat on the income tax, but also by the way in which the House of Commons took the bit between its teeth in a campaign to cut government spending to the bone.

Cheap government

It could fairly be said that this campaign was pursued to an unreasonable extreme. On the one hand, it was carried to a point which imperilled the proper functions of government, including the needs of national security. On the other hand, the 'economists' were blind to the constructive elements within the ministry's own conception of national finances, including the view that the retention of a modest element of direct taxation could provide an opportunity to encourage healthy economic growth by cutting customs duties. The scale of the cuts in the sums allotted for the maintenance of the armed forces meant that both army and navy were reduced below what the government felt to be safe figures. The destruction on grounds of economy of some of the ancillary services which had been built up during the war left the army dangerously weak in such areas as transport and medical care, in ways which pointed forward to the sufferings of the troops in the Crimea forty years later.

The campaign for economy was eagerly embraced by the Opposition in Parliament, and on this issue the administration could not count upon their usual supporters to provide a defensive majority. Under pressure from a tax-paying electorate, many MPs could not easily stand by the government in matters of taxation. The parliamentary crusade against remaining sinecures and pensions was pressed on such a scale that the ministry was increasingly deprived of traditional means of rewarding merit and long service as well as less elevated uses of patronage. True, there were some beneficial side-effects of the campaign. The disappearance of sinecures and other discretionary awards in the gift of government meant that Parliament had to act to introduce a system of superannuation for civil servants, if as yet on a limited scale. But government was left living from hand to mouth for the revenue with which to meet essential expenditure. In this area, the Liverpool government had to face not only Whig opposition in Parliament, but also radical rhetoric out of doors. The radical politicians of the years after 1815 rarely if ever showed any appreciation that increased State action financed by higher taxation might prove a beneficial agency of social improvement. Instead, in chorus with the Whigs, the growing volume of radical propaganda placed a continuing emphasis upon allegations of excessive taxation and government extravagance.

A turning-point came in 1819. After four years of battering and defeats on issues of public finance, Liverpool and his colleagues decided that they had endured enough; if the House of Commons was not willing to trust them with adequate resources then they would resign. The occasion for this determination was not simply of the government's making. The decision on whether or not Britain ought to return to a currency tied to a gold standard had been postponed for some time after the war, but by 1819 such a decision was becoming impera-tive. The Bank of England formally asked the government for an inquiry which would lead to a conclusion. The ministry responded by arranging for the appointment of a strong select committee to study the matter; Peel was the chairman, and ministers were well represented in the committee's membership. After a full exploration of the question, and a careful study of rival theories of currency, the committee reported that the ready exchange of banknotes for gold should be implemented by 1823; in fact, improving economic conditions enabled the major changes to be implemented as early as 1821.

The government had, however, taken a wider view of the problems of public finance, by obtaining at the same time a parallel select committee to consider the broad field of government finance. Carefully managed by front-bench members, this committee was induced to make a powerfully argued report, broadly back-ing the administration's views in revenue matters. It was not possible to bring back an income tax, but the committee declared that budgeting should aim at providing an annual surplus of at least £5 million, which might be used either for debt redemption or beneficial cuts in the taxes which impeded commerce. The report provoked a parliamentary battle, with the Whig Opposition trying to reject the committee's conclusions in order to maintain a constant pressure on government spending and revenue. In the event the skilful handling of the committee's proceedings by ministers paid off, and the Commons endorsed the recommendations of their select committee by a healthy majority of more than 200.[45]

This success, together with economic revival in the years after 1821, which made indirect taxation more productive, enabled the Liverpool government to embark upon a policy of cautious fiscal reform during the early 1820s. In May 1820 Liverpool himself, in one of his best parliamentary performances, made it clear that he was intellectually convinced that movements in the direction of free trade were in the best interests of the whole national community. This was no doctrinaire position, but rather a general belief which might be implemented pragmatically, with exceptions recognized where particular circumstances justi-fied them. Nor was this any sudden conversion to the merits of freeing trade from tariff barriers, or the consequence of recent ministerial changes. The reduc-tions in tariffs, the partial relaxation of the Navigation Acts which protected British shipping, and the development of reciprocal trading concessions with

45. Gash, *Lord Liverpool*, 142–3.

other countries represented the kind of policies which the Liverpool government would have liked to implement earlier.[46] They now became practicable, partly because of the more favourable economic climate, the successful conversion of parliamentary opinion, and perhaps also because the ministry had earlier swallowed so much in the way of sweeping away vulnerable elements in public finance.

By 1825 much had been done to free British commerce from obsolete restrictions and vexatious duties; the heirs of Mr Pitt could feel that in these respects they had been pursuing policies which he would have approved. It was not the imposition of complete free trade, but rather a programme of tidying up and streamlining the old cumbrous array of restrictions on commerce. Liverpool and his colleagues were aware that to proceed much further in these matters the reimposition of a significant element of direct taxation would be necessary, but they knew that it was politically impossible to reimpose an income tax in the immediate future.

Foreign policy

Apart from the maintenance of law and order and the health of the national finances, another accepted responsibility of early nineteenth-century governments was the conduct of relations with other states.[47] As Foreign Secretary, Castlereagh played a prominent role in the last years of the war and in the making of the peace settlement of 1815. Thereafter he pursued a policy of cooperation with continental powers, including a France restored to the community of nations. This policy of collaboration, marked by periodic congresses for the amicable settlement of problems, came under strain as differences emerged between Britain and her continental associates. From the beginning British participation in the 'Concert of Europe' had been seen by the Liverpool government primarily as the best mode of safeguarding British interests, rather than the result of any wider ideological commitment to the congress system. When, in the years after 1818, issues arose which divided British interests from those of her continental allies, a definite cooling and separation developed. The existence of disagreement had surfaced as early as September 1815, when Britain refused to subscribe to the declaration of a Holy Alliance between Russia, Austria, and Prussia, aimed at the maintenance of monarchical power in Europe. Although Castlereagh privately described this agreement as 'a piece of sublime mysticism and nonsense', in public the amenities were preserved, with Britain's abstention ascribed to the nature of her established parliamentary regime and the incapacity of George III.

46. J. H. Clapham, *An Economic History of Modern Britain: The Early Railway Age* (1930), discusses the economic reforms of these years.

47. C. K. Webster, *The Foreign Policy of Castlereagh, 1815–1822: Britain and the European Alliance* (1925); H. W. V. Temperley, *The Foreign Policy of Canning, 1822–27* (1925); Wendy Hinde, *George Canning* (1973) and *Castlereagh* (1981).

While the associated continental autocracies were determined to maintain their own form of government, this was no vital interest of Britain. The alignment of restoration Bourbon France with the policy of monarchical supervision of European States was unwelcome, but tolerable as long as the autocratic powers did not act in a manner which appeared prejudicial to Britain's own interests. In the 1820s the international situation developed in ways which showed Britain to be openly at variance with the views of her old allies. The stance of the British government was summarized in a State paper on foreign policy drawn up by Castlereagh in May 1820. This made it plain that Britain would refuse to acknowledge that the continental Great Powers had a right to interfere in the affairs of other States in order to enforce the maintenance of political systems of which they approved. The grand alliance which Britain had joined for the purpose of defeating Napoleon was not, in the British view, 'an Union for the Government of the World or for the Superintendence of the Internal Affairs of other States'. During the 1820s the widening differences of opinion were made clear in the affairs of Spain and Portugal and their colonies, and then in relation to the Greek revolt against Turkish rule. There was little that Britain could do to prevent France acting as the agent of the continental powers in upholding absolute monarchical rule in Spain. Despite British protests, French armies were in Spain from 1823 to 1827. Britain no longer had an army capable of waging a second Peninsular War, nor was Parliament likely to approve of expensive foreign adventures.

There was, however, one mode of retaliation open to Britain. Her naval primacy was still widely accepted, even if the material basis of it had been substantially eroded since 1815. Spain was faced with revolutions in her South American colonies, an area which had become an important market for British commerce. Canning, when he took over the Foreign Office after Castlereagh's death, continued and emphasized his predecessor's policies by making it clear that Britain would not allow the French occupation of Spain to extend to the dispatch of military expeditions to buttress Spanish authority across the South Atlantic. Castlereagh had already conceded belligerent status to the South American rebels, a kind of halfway house on the way to full recognition. After considerable hesitation, at the end of 1824 the Liverpool Cabinet decided to give formal diplomatic recognition to the rebel regimes in Mexico, Buenos Aires, and Colombia, coupling with this recognition the negotiation of commercial treaties. This decision was crucial in allowing the South American republics to establish their independence behind the shield of British naval supremacy.

If forcible intervention in Spain itself was not practicable for Britain, the situation was different as far as Portugal was concerned. A continuing alliance with Portugal was one of the cornerstones of British foreign policy, and the Liverpool government had no intention of allowing Portugal to follow Spain into the ambit of the continental powers. The monarchy in Portugal was at least ostensibly associated with a liberal political system, but during the minority of a young Queen there were repeated attempts, covertly backed by Spain, to replace her by a reactionary uncle. After a series of appeals from a Portuguese government threatened by insurgent attacks from Spanish bases, Britain responded by sending a military force to Portugal late in 1826. The presence of these troops, with their clear message of a British commitment, proved effective in containing the situation in Portugal. At the same time, Britain intervened in relations between Portugal herself and her biggest colony, Brazil. It was under British persuasion that the government of Portugal was brought to accept that Brazil should be an independent State ruled by a member of the Portuguese royal family. In the later 1820s an end to foreign military intervention in the affairs of the Iberian peninsula was brought about by a concerted withdrawal of British forces from Portugal and French forces from Spain.

There was no essential difference in the foreign policies pursued by Castlereagh and Canning, but the latter was more flamboyant in his public justification of these measures. In the course of one of his most famous speeches, he told the House of Commons that 'I resolved that if France had Spain, it should not be Spain with the Indies. I called the New World into existence to redress the balance of the Old.' Given that the major decisions on British foreign policy were agreed in Cabinet, and that the Prime Minister himself kept an effective watching brief in such matters, the egotism of the language was understandably irritating to many of Canning's colleagues. Some of them were in any event unhappy about policies which seemed to encourage revolution and the overthrow of legitimate authority in the Spanish colonies, and the theatrical and personalized nature of some of Canning's foreign policy pronouncements played a part in impairing relations within the Cabinet.

The Greek Revolution began in 1821, after a record of unsuccessful risings against Turkish rule in earlier generations. The official British policy was one of non-intervention, with the intention also of preventing interference by any other powers. In particular, Britain was suspicious that Russia might try to fish in these troubled waters with the intention of extending her influence towards the Mediterranean. The Greek rebels obtained considerable, though not universal, public sympathy in Britain. This was associated with illusions derived from the prominence of classical Greece in the education of the dominant groups. Although it was evidently possible to see the Greek rebels as fellow countrymen of Pericles and Socrates, the Liverpool Cabinet was less romantic in its reactions, remaining unmoved both by the exploits of British volunteers in Greece (where Byron died in 1824) and by the intervention on the Turkish side of the powerful Viceroy of Egypt from 1825. This Egyptian intervention came close to stamping out the Greek revolt, but its harshness provoked an international reaction which in the end was to procure the independence of a small Greek kingdom. When in the summer of 1827, by the Treaty of London, Britain agreed to join France and Russia in imposing a ceasefire in Greece, the motive of the British government was less sympathy for the Greeks than a determination to restrain Russia from independent intervention. The three powers sent naval squadrons to the scene to enforce their will, a move which resulted in a collision with the naval forces of Turkey and Egypt at the battle of Navarino, in October 1827. The annihilation of the Turkish and Egyptian fleet effectively destroyed Turkey's ability to maintain her armies in southern Greece. By the end of the decade the independence of the small Greek kingdom had been assured.

The foreign policy issues of the 1820s had not improved personal relations within the Cabinet. Although Canning's return to senior office in 1822 had been accepted, and he had succeeded to the whole of Castlereagh's official role as Foreign Secretary and Leader of the House of Commons, he could not succeed to the respect with which Castlereagh had been regarded by his colleagues. His flamboyant displays in the course of foreign policy in the years after 1822, and his habit of appealing for support to public opinion outside government and Parliament, did nothing to reduce the suspicion with which he was viewed by many long-serving members of the governing party. More conservative ministers, who could remember what the results of revolution had been nearer home, were less than happy at Canning's willing encouragement of revolutionary regimes in South America. Liverpool was by no means blind either to Canning's faults or to the effect of them on some of his colleagues, but he was also well aware of the Foreign Secretary's talents both as a minister and as a considerable public figure. In practice, he gave Canning steady support. The way in which the premier exerted his own authority on behalf of Canning did nothing to endear that minister to colleagues who saw him either as Liverpool's favourite or as someone who exercised an undue influence over their leader. After 1825 Canning's position was strengthened by a reconciliation with George IV, something made possible by judicious flattery and circumspect behaviour by the Foreign Secretary. Yet such controversial decisions as the recognition of the South American republics were only reached after lengthy arguments in Cabinet, during which Canning found himself opposed by right-wingers, of whom Wellington was perhaps the most strenuous in opposing Canning's policies and methods.

Catholic emancipation

The other problem which deepened divisions within the ministry was the question of Catholic emancipation. The issue was whether the grant of full political rights to Roman Catholics, including entry to both Houses of Parliament, represented an unnecessary and damaging breach in the hallowed Constitution, or a concession which could now safely be made to loyal but Catholic fellow citizens. The division of opinion within the government was not a simple one in terms of age or experience. Both Castlereagh and Canning supported emancipation; Wellington and Liverpool were opponents. After the ministerial changes of the early 1820s most of the leading opponents of emancipation within the government were in the House of Lords, while the majority of the government front bench in the Commons was in favour of the measure. The only Tory politician[48] of the first rank in the Commons who opposed emancipation was Peel; in differing from his front-bench colleagues here, he earned powerful support and goodwill from the largely inarticulate Tory backbenchers, most of whom shared the widespread public hostility to Catholicism.[49] Despite this, there was more support for emancipation within the more sophisticated and tolerant governing groups than in British society in general.

The difference of opinion on this key political issue of the day was one breach between ministers which could not be healed, though it was possible to postpone any drastic consequences. When the Liverpool government had been formed in 1812, it had been agreed that there would be no settled government policy on the Catholic issue, and that individual ministers were free to hold and express their own opinions in the matter. This agreement survived the Cabinet changes of the early 1820s, although their overall effect was to strengthen the position of the pro-Catholic elements within the Cabinet, with the retirement of more conservative older members. An increasing strain was put upon the situation, however, by the fact that the question was repeatedly raised in Parliament, making the rifts between ministers on the issue increasingly obvious.

Although there was never a secure Commons majority for emancipation during Liverpool's premiership, and the Lords could be relied upon to reject any emancipation measure which might on occasion secure a narrow majority in the Lower House, resistance to the proposal seemed to be weakening as the decade wore on. In 1825, when there was a transient majority for an emancipation measure in the Commons, the issue already threatened to break up the government. First Peel and then Canning threatened to resign on the issue and Liverpool himself seriously considered retirement. The intervention of other ministers succeeded in patching things up for the time being, and the tide of parliamentary support for emancipation receded somewhat, but discord between ministers had been made clear during these exchanges. The general election of 1826, which was overall a victory for the government, saw some gains by Tory opponents of emancipation, reflecting the views of much of the electorate.

The 1820s were not then years of continuous tranquillity within the administration, although to outside gaze the ministry seemed to be in a stronger position than in the immediate post-war years. In addition to carrying out the ordinary administrative functions which provided the main work of an early nineteenth-century government, on a number of fronts the Liverpool ministry had useful

---

48. By 1827 the term Tory was becoming accepted by government supporters. Peel, leaving office after Liverpool's stroke, declared, 'I may be a Tory—I may be an illiberal—but the fact is undeniable ... that there is not a single law connected with my name, which has not had for its object some mitigation of the severity of the criminal law; some prevention of abuse in the exercise of it; or some security for its impartial administration.' Quoted by Boyd Hilton, *A Mad, Bad and Dangerous People*, 196.

49. Gash, *Mr. Secretary Peel*, gives a good account of the problem of Catholic emancipation in these years. Gash, *Lord Liverpool*, deals with the matter for the period of Lord Liverpool's administration.

innovations to its credit, a programme made easier by the improved economic conditions of these years.

Law reform

As Home Secretary, Peel took up the issue of reform of the country's penal laws and prisons. This was already in hand when he went to the Home Office, but he pushed the campaign ahead with considerable energy and dexterity.[50] The Gaols Act of 1823 cut through a mass of inchoate legislation about prisons, stretching back to medieval times, and created a system of local prisons, financed by the rates, and controlled by local magistrates. The Act also prescribed a system of regular inspection and reports, including an annual report to the Home Secretary from all of the prison authorities.

The parallel reforms in the penal code were not designed simply to relax the harshness of the law by, for instance, reducing the incidence of death sentences. More compelling was the desire to transform a previously chaotic situation into something clear and effective. Codification and simplification were important components in the changes effected, as well as mitigation of penalties. Peel's legislation covered wide ranges of the law, including various crimes and the law of evidence. A good example was the new statute governing offences against the person; its drafting involved the repeal of 57 earlier statutes and their replacement in this single consolidated Act. Altogether Peel's legal reforms saw an untidy mass of 278 old Acts of Parliament replaced by 8 major statutes expressed in reasonably clear terms. As with most of Peel's policies, the ground for the reforms was meticulously prepared by consultations both with experts in the field and with possible opponents to be conciliated. Because of this, the actual enactment of the legislation caused little difficulty.

Reforms of the public finances, the criminal code, and the prisons were not the government's only positive achievements. We have seen how the repressive legislation of 1817 was accompanied to the statute book by reforms like the Poor Employment Act. The Six Acts of 1819 were also accompanied by ameliorative legislation, including a Factory Act and a measure to protect the wages of merchant seamen, though the former measure proved ineffective in practice.[51] In addition, after a number of previous inquiries and reports by select committees, in 1819 the government introduced an Act which created a Charity Commission, the ancestor of the Charity Commissioners of the present day and a serious attempt to embark upon a course of revising and modernizing the complex charitable institutions of the country.[52] A further Act of 1819 extended the official encouragement given to the growing network of friendly societies, an increasingly

50. Gash, *Mr. Secretary Peel*, chs. 9 and 14.
51. Clapham, *Economic History of Modern Britain*, 376.
52. R. Tompson, *The Charity Commission and the Age of Reform* (1979).

popular form of insuring against illness and bereavement and providing for old age (see pp. 122–4 below).

Repeal of the Combination Laws

In 1824, after an initiative by the radical MP Joseph Hume, the government offered no serious objections to the repeal of the Combination Acts of 1799–1800; the Acts had been largely ineffective, and there had been no sustained official pressure to implement them. Repeal not only allowed organizations which had in effect been clandestine trade unions to emerge openly, but encouraged a considerable increase in strikes in the following months. This induced the government to modify the 1824 settlement by an Act of 1825 which limited the scope of trade union activity and tried to strengthen the law against intimidation of workers by unions. There was also a further Factory Act in 1825; like its predecessors, it imposed only limited restrictions, which depended for their effectiveness on the attitudes of the local and central government agencies involved. The Home Office papers show that some magistrates at least took their responsibilities under the early Factory Acts seriously, and that Peel as Home Secretary backed them.[53] He was prepared to listen to complaints from trade-unionists about inaction on the part of recalcitrant magistrates, and to take steps to ensure that the Acts, however limited, were implemented.

Some Liverpool initiatives

Liverpool himself, as well as supporting his ministers' reforms, took a personal interest in some other measures. His pragmatism was well illustrated by his willingness to contemplate new forms of public spending, even within that general climate of rigid economy. In 1818 he was instrumental in persuading Parliament to make a grant of £1 million for the building of new Anglican churches, especially in urban areas where population increase had outstripped the old parochial system; six years later he secured an additional half million for the same purpose. In 1824 he was responsible for the foundation of the National Gallery; the nucleus of this national art collection came from the estate of a wealthy London merchant, J. J. Angerstein. Liverpool was instrumental in securing the parliamentary vote of £57,000 which secured for the nation an impressive collection which included masterpieces by Titian, Rubens, Van Dyck, Velasquez, Rembrandt, Raphael, and Reynolds, and in persuading Parliament to make available the money which provided a new home for the collection and paid the first staff to look after it. In 1826 Liverpool induced Parliament to authorize the spending of an additional £9, 000 on acquisitions.[54]

53. D. George, 'The Combination Laws', *Economic History Review*, 1st ser., 6 (1935–6), 172–8.
54. Gash, *Lord Liverpool*, 210. For Angerstein see DNB.

Banking reforms

A financial panic occurred in 1825.[55] The previous two years had seen a rapid expansion in the creation of new commercial enterprises, some of them distinctly precarious in character. This led to a banking crash beginning at the end of 1825. Despite attempts by the Bank of England to limit the damage, a number of banks failed, both in London and in the provinces. About eighty country banks failed, and, although some of these contrived to recover, there was widespread dislocation in the financial working of the economy. The government was willing to intervene pragmatically, passing an Act limiting the future circulation of small notes and obliging the Bank of England to publish weekly statements of the amount of its notes in circulation. This produced a revolt by the well-developed Scottish banking sector which valued the £1 note and the resultant outcry led to the exemption of the Scottish note issuing system. Sir Walter Scott was amongst the Scottish defenders of the £1 note and the note still issued by the Bank of Scotland is adorned with his portrait. The Scottish banking system was in many respects more sophisticated than its English counterpart, though this was not to spare it its share of crises and disasters.

Another Act gave the Bank of England the right to create provincial branches, something which Liverpool and his colleagues rightly saw as a useful element of stability in the banking sector. This Act also allowed the creation of joint-stock banks outside a 65-mile radius from London, but it denied partners in these banks limited liability, so that anyone embarking on such an enterprise risked his whole fortune in case of failure; no doubt this was intended to encourage safe banking practices. Within a few years the banking system was significantly altered by the opening of branches of the Bank of England in Gloucester, Swansea, Manchester, Birmingham, Bristol, Exeter, Hull, Leeds, Liverpool, Leicester, Newcastle, and Norwich. In the early days, these formidable competitors for banking business were often unpopular with the country banks, but it gradually became clear that cooperation was the better policy. The presence of the national bank, with its great resources to draw on, became a source of strength in times of economic pressure; in early-Victorian financial crises, the Bank of England branches helped to restrict the damage caused in the provinces by the failure of other banks.

Although the reforms for which the Tory governments of the 1820s were responsible were limited, they represented an increase in State intervention in difficult circumstances and with limited resources of both men and money. Sir John Clapham's general verdict on the government's record may therefore surely stand:

Judged as governments are perhaps entitled to be judged, not by what proved practicable in a later and more experienced day, nor by what reformers and poets dreamed and were not called upon to accomplish, but by the achievements of other governments in their own day, that of Britain in the late twenties of the nineteenth century makes a creditable showing.[56]

55. Clapham, *Economic History of Modern Britain*, 272–6.   56. Ibid. 316.

Years of Tory decline

Once the crucial presiding role of Lord Liverpool came to an end, frictions within the Cabinet on matters of both policies and personalities erupted.[57] The Prime Minister, whose health had been declining for some time, suffered a stroke in February 1827. The immediate reaction of both King and Cabinet was to hold on in the hope that there might be at least a partial recovery, sufficient for Liverpool to remain at the head of the government. This was not to be, however, and at the end of March the King received the premier's formal resignation.

The succession problem was not easy to solve. Canning seemed the obvious choice, by virtue of his long and varied ministerial experience, and the key role in Cabinet, Parliament, and public opinion which he had come to play in the years since 1822. It soon became clear that Canning would not be able to hold together the team which had accepted Liverpool's leadership. Canning could scarcely be expected to agree to serve under any of the other possible candidates, but an important group of Liverpool's colleagues, of whom Wellington and Peel were the most important, made it plain that they would not join a government under Canning. George IV believed that his ministers should rally around the premier he selected, and found this intransigence irritating. On 10 April he formally commissioned Canning to form an administration. Seven members of the Cabinet promptly resigned, including both Wellington and Peel. The ostensible cause was the unwillingness of more conservative ministers to serve under a Prime Minister who was a committed supporter of Catholic emancipation. Canning had made it clear that he would continue the convention of regarding this issue as an open question for ministers, and the explanation of the split in the Tory ranks was less simple. It owed much to the distrust and dislike which Canning had inspired in some of his colleagues over a long period of time. In Peel's case there may also have been a wish to preserve his independence as a possible future contender for the leadership.

Faced with the loss of the right wing of the old Liverpool grouping and the departure of a number of experienced ministers, Canning cobbled together a government by turning to some of the more moderate Whigs. Lord Lansdowne became Home Secretary, Lord Dudley Foreign Secretary, and Tierney also joined the Cabinet as Master of the Mint. Some important ministers remained from the previous administration, including Lord Goderich (formerly F. J. Robinson, Liverpool's Chancellor of the Exchequer), Huskisson, Wynn, and Palmerston. The government was not a strong one, but had it been given time might have established itself as a viable governing coalition. During its brief life its existence deepened the divisions within the old Tory ranks.[58] Wellington and Peel both

---

57. Gash, *Mr. Secretary Peel*, chs. 12–17, provides a good account of the last years of Tory rule as does B. W. Hill, *British Parliamentary Parties*, 217–25.

58. An account of the right-wing opposition to Canning's government is given in R. A. Gaunt, 'The Fourth Duke of Newcastle, the Ultra Tories and the opposition to Canning's Administration', *History*, vol. 88, no. 292 (October 2003), 568–86.

went into parliamentary opposition, with serious consequences. Previously the Liverpool Cabinet had agreed on a proposal to modify the Corn Laws, but when Canning now brought forward this measure Wellington succeeded in wrecking the new government's plan. The Canning government also faced the opposition of many Whigs; Lord Grey, for example, remained on the hostile benches.

Any chance which the new political grouping might have had of attaining stability was in any case soon frustrated by Canning's death. Because of the loss of so many former colleagues, and the weakness of the new government's ministerial team, Canning had been forced to take a great deal upon himself. He was seriously overworked and continued to struggle on when he fell ill. At the beginning of August 1827 the seriousness of his illness became clear and he died only a week later.

The King, still affronted by the refusal of the right-wing Tories to work with the Prime Minister of his choice, tried to keep the Canning team together by commissioning Goderich to form the next government. This experiment proved unhappy. Goderich could not control his colleagues, who found a number of different issues on which to quarrel. By the end of the year it was clear that matters could not continue in this form. Goderich retired, and George IV then sought to recreate the Liverpool front by commissioning Wellington to form a government.

At first sight this seemed successful; the new Cabinet included both Tories who had served with Canning and those who had refused to do so. However, the events of 1827 had emphasized divisions which were not healed by the apparent reunion under Wellington. Huskisson regarded himself as the principal heir to Canning's mantle, and proved a difficult colleague. He thought of himself, not simply as one of Wellington's Cabinet colleagues, but rather as the spokesman for an important 'Canningite' wing of the party. He was also sensitive, and ever-ready to see or suspect a slight where none was intended. Wellington had only limited patience with such personal foibles; he complained at the amount of time he was obliged to spend in coping with 'what gentlemen are pleased to call their feelings'. The new Cabinet did not work together easily, and policy differences were added to personal difficulties.

The Liverpool Cabinet had agreed in its last months that the 1815 Corn Law, with its strict cut-off points for imports, ought to be replaced by a more flexible sliding scale of duties. After the failure to pass such a measure in 1827, the new administration would have to act, but it was not easy to obtain agreement on the level of protection to be afforded. Huskisson wanted a lower level, while Wellington, expressing the wishes of the government's agricultural followers, would have liked a higher scale of duties. Eventually a not very satisfactory compromise was patched together, after considerable argument, and this reached the statute book in the course of 1828.

Another area of disagreement was a belated legacy from the general election of 1826. Following on the example of Grampound a few years earlier, two boroughs,

East Retford and Penryn, stood condemned for electoral corruption, and it was necessary to decide what should be done with the seats involved. The conservatives in the Cabinet preferred a solution of extending the boundaries of the two constituencies, enlarging and hopefully purifying the electorates by bringing in the surrounding rural areas. If this proved unacceptable, then a possible alternative would be to transfer the seats to increase the representation of two large counties, as Grampound's two seats had been given to Yorkshire. A more radical proposal, to which Huskisson and the other Canningites inclined, was to transfer the confiscated seats to large industrial towns as yet without their own MPs. Again a compromise was arrived at with some difficulty—the East Retford constituency was to be enlarged and the Penryn seats were to be given to Manchester. In the event, however, the House of Lords rejected the Manchester allocation, with the result that Huskisson and some of his colleagues opposed the East Retford decision in the Commons.

The matter at issue was scarcely a vital one, but Huskisson chose to submit a precipitate letter of resignation. It was not the first time that he had tried to get his own way by threatening to leave the government; by now Wellington had had enough, and simply accepted the resignation. The other Canningite ministers felt bound to stand by their sectional leader, and effectively the left wing of the old Tory front had broken away.

Religion and reform

The divisions over East Retford and Penryn may not have been seen as of great importance at the time but they can be seen retrospectively as harbingers of the great debate over parliamentary reform which, together with the abolition of the Test and Corporations Act and the Catholic Emancipation Act, was to bring, not only the post-war period of Tory government, but, arguably, the Hanoverian religious and political order, to an end.

Historians have perceived a 'Reform Crisis' of 1828–32 in which religious and political issues were linked. There were paradoxes in the relationship between the cause for greater equality between those of different religious denominations and those who demanded a more representative Parliament and a widened franchise. Not the least of these was the greater prevalence of liberal attitudes towards religious equality amongst wealthier sections of society, who for the most part were already enfranchised, than amongst the lower orders. It is very unlikely that a Parliament elected upon a greatly widened franchise would have passed Catholic emancipation.

There can be little doubt that there was a crisis but there is considerable disagreement over its nature and significance, why it occurred when it did, and whether its outcome was the end of an *ancien regime* or a necessary and wise reform and consolidation of the existing order. A Whiggish view sees the crisis and its outcome as almost inevitable because of social and economic change and because the prevailing political and religious arrangements were no longer apposite in the new context. The old order was still intact in the late 1820s but the influence of those excluded by it had grown stronger while 'the convictions of the governing classes that those exclusions were justifiable grew correspondingly weaker.'[59] J. C. D. Clark, while accepting the gradual weakening of support for the old order, argues for a sudden betrayal from within the ranks of the establishment: 'The years 1800–32 witnessed, then, not so much the progressive advance of a liberal mood shared by all as the gradual numerical erosion of a social, religious and political hegemony from without, and a final and sudden betrayal from within.'[60] Clark sees 'Repeal, Emancipation and Reform' (Repeal of the Test Acts; Catholic Emancipation; and Parliamentary Reform) as intimately linked, with reform as the least important issue, largely quiescent during the 1820s: 'Reform was a consequence of the shattering of the old order by Emancipation.'

An important factor in the events which led to Catholic emancipation was the intrusion of what would later be called the 'Irish Question' into British politics. The Act of Union of 1800 had resulted in the addition of 100 Irish MPs to the House of Commons. Although they could not sit in Parliament, Catholics could vote and in many Irish constituencies they formed a majority of voters.

Though it was possible to argue that both Catholics and Protestant dissenters were in an inferior position under the constitution in England, as were Episcopalians as well as Catholics in Scotland, in practice the position of Protestants who were not members of the established churches involved little practical disadvantage. Anglicans, Presbyterians, and dissenters were united by a common hostility to Catholicism, which had for long made dissenters cautious about making too much of their disabilities under the constitution for the obvious reason that it could help make the case for the removal of Catholic disabilities. This was precisely what happened when, early in 1828, Lord John Russell, a Whig MP, introduced into the Commons a measure for the repeal of the Test and Corporation Acts, the old penal legislation which had been enacted in the seventeenth century to exclude Protestant Nonconformists from public office. Though still on the statute book, these Acts had been ineffective for many years, as Parliament suspended their operation by annual Toleration Acts. This had become a routine parliamentary proceeding, but Russell's proposal to repeal the penal laws, which had the support of two nonconformist pressure groups, a united committee of Baptists, Congregationalists, and Unitarians and the Protestant Society, involved an open abandonment of the principle that membership of the State Church was a prerequisite for full citizenship under the British constitution. In the circumstances it was not possible to mount any effective opposition to Russell's proposal to regularize a long-standing convention and it

59. J. A. Cannon, 'New Lamps for Old: The End of Hanoverian England' in J. A. Cannon (ed.), *The Whig Ascendancy: Colloquies on Hanoverian England* (1981), 103.

60. J. C. D. Clark, *English Society 1688–1832* (1985), 409.

could be seen as an exclusively Protestant measure. This enactment had, nevertheless, unmistakable implications for the position of Roman Catholics. Moreover, opinion in influential circles had been hardening in favour of emancipation, and even Wellington had in his recent pronouncements dropped any doctrinaire opposition to it. On the other hand, he and his principal lieutenant, Peel, had been strenuous opponents of emancipation in the past, and this made things difficult for them in 1828–9.

The repeal of the Test Acts might not, however, have led so swiftly to the removal of Catholic disabilities had it not been for the County Clare Election. Wellington found some difficulty in filling the vacant places in his Cabinet caused by the Canningite resignations. The one appointment which seemed to bring a new accession of strength to the Cabinet proved ironically the occasion of a greater crisis.[61] Vesey Fitzgerald was chosen to fill the place of the Canningite Grant at the Board of Trade. Acceptance of this post involved Fitzgerald in a by-election for his Irish constituency of County Clare. There seemed no initial reason to anticipate difficulty here, for Fitzgerald, though himself of course a Protestant, was a good landlord in Ireland and an advocate of Catholic emancipation. However, there followed an unexpected challenge, when Daniel O'Connell came forward to oppose Fitzgerald in the Clare election. Since 1823 O'Connell had been building up a formidable nationalist agitation in Ireland, aiming in the first instance at Catholic emancipation. Despite sporadic attempts by the authorities to impede its progress, by 1828 his Catholic Association had greatly extended its influence. This challenge to the government was made possible by the legal expedient resorted to in the past to exclude Catholics from Parliament. The law did not forbid them to stand as candidates, but instead obliged elected MPs, before taking their seats, to take a statutory oath drafted in a form which no Catholic could accept. There was nothing to prevent a Catholic appearing as a candidate, though in practice of course it had not happened. It soon became clear that Fitzgerald's seat was in jeopardy; in this Irish county constituency the combined influences of the Catholic Association and the Roman Catholic Church proved stronger than government influence and Fitzgerald's personal standing. O'Connell's election duly came in July 1828, after his opponent had withdrawn from the hopeless contest. O'Connell's clever move placed the Wellington government in a predicament. If ministers took no action it was obvious that the example of County Clare would be imitated in many Irish constituencies at the next general election, which was likely to occur soon. That situation would make a mockery of the legislative Union, with Irish Catholic MPs elected in substantial numbers but denied entry to the Parliament of the United Kingdom. There were other recent developments which weakened the case for resistance.

61. J. A. Reynolds, *The Catholic Emancipation Crisis in Ireland, 1823–9* (1954); for a consideration of the question of Catholic emancipation as a whole see Wendy Hinde, *Catholic Emancipation: A Shake to Men's Minds* (1992).

The ministry saw that prolonged resistance to Catholic emancipation was not likely to be possible in the light of current opinions, while the Irish situation made some accommodation necessary. Warned by the military commander in Ireland that reinforcements would be needed to contain the situation there unless the crisis could be resolved, the government eventually decided that the lesser of the choice of evils before it was to concede Catholic emancipation.

This was particularly difficult for Peel, who had risen to eminence in previous years not so much as an able reformer but rather as the principal champion of the 'Protestant' cause in the House of Commons. He could accept the arguments which now made the concession of emancipation unavoidable, but his previous commitment on the issue seemed so tight that he told Wellington that he could not take personal responsibility for the enactment of a measure so opposed to his earlier stance. However, the Prime Minister, well aware that his front bench in the Commons had been weakened by the loss of the Canningites, believed that Peel's parliamentary talents would be needed to pilot through the controversial measure. Faced with an appeal to his sense of duty, Peel agreed to remain at his post. As some vindication to his troubled conscience, he determined to face his constituents in an attempt to justify his change of front. This was to give a hostage to fortune, since the electorate of Oxford University was fiercely Protestant. Peel was beaten at the by-election he provoked. To keep him in Parliament an unsavoury bargain was made with the owner of the pocket borough of Westbury.

What horrified many contemporaries and still seems surprising was the attitude of the Church of England, for no bishop voted against the measure and the Church was 'complicit in the dismantling of the confessional state'.[62] The affairs of Ireland had intruded into British politics and there can be no doubt that Catholic emancipation was deeply unpopular in Britain. Petitions against it poured in from all over Britain and there was particular outrage in Scotland, Wales, and northern English towns. 'Glasgow sent in over twenty-one hostile petitions, bearing over 24,000 signatures in all.'[63] The bill was duly enacted in 1829, though an attempt was made to limit its effects in the Irish countryside by an arbitrary raising of the level of the Irish county franchise from the traditional 40s. to £10.

The immediate result of the ministry's change of policy on this key issue was to outrage more conservative Tories, who made no secret of their alienation from the administration and their refusal to use their influence further in its support, as well as a broad swathe of public opinion. If Wellington had lost the left wing of his original support in 1828, he had now lost his right wing too, and the government entered its last months in office in an unmistakably weakened state. The measure weakened part of the case against parliamentary reform, which had

62. O'Gorman, *The Long Eighteenth Century*, 356.
63. Linda Colley, *Britons*, 329.

been that any tinkering with the system of representation could lead to great dangers for the propertied classes and might undermine the constitution, and made the bulwarks against radical change, Lords, Church, and King, look weak. It made some ultra Tories favour a wider franchise on the grounds that it was the elite rather than the common people which had favoured emancipation. It thus can be seen as an important factor in reviving pressure for parliamentary reform.

Yet even in these difficult years, the ministry found it possible to notch up some positive successes. The struggle to improve national finances had continued; in 1830 a successful debt-conversion exercise was carried out, which had the effect of reducing the interest paid on £135 million from 4 to 3.5 per cent.[64] Moreover, Peel now found the right time to resurrect his scheme for a London police.

The Metropolitan Police

Taking great care to avoid a repetition of the rebuff of 1822, Peel had been meticulously preparing the ground and gathering evidence since 1826, and early in 1828 he felt ready to propose a new select committee. That inquiry was carefully managed, and fed with masses of detailed evidence from both British experience and foreign police examples. This dexterity was rewarded by the presentation in July 1828 of a report from the select committee, reversing the position of its 1822 predecessor. While admitting that there were problems relating to traditional freedoms, 'these difficulties must be encountered if it be intended to institute an efficient system of Police in this great Metropolis, for the effective protection of property, and for the prevention and detection of crime'.[65] A bill to give effect to the committee's recommendations was prepared in readiness for the 1829 session. By June 1829 the Metropolitan Police Act had reached the statute book.[66]

One major concession had made this legislation easier: the small central City of London was excluded from the scope of the new force, and left to its own authorities. The remainder of London was now to be guarded by the new Metropolitan Police under the direction of the Home Office. Within a few weeks of the enactment of the 1829 Act, the basic lines of the new organization had been worked out. An administrative staff of 5 accompanied an operational force of 8 superintendents, 20 inspectors, 88 sergeants, and 895 constables.

The origins of these grades indicate the novelty of the new institution. Superintendent and inspector were already established titles in other branches of public service, sergeant came straight from army usage, while constable marked an ostensible continuity with an ancient police office. One of the first two Commissioners, Charles Rowan, was an army officer from a minor Irish

64. Clapham, *Economic History of Modern Britain*, 388.

65. Gash, *Mr. Secretary Peel*, 494–5.

66. A study of the creation and early history of the Metropolitan Police is D. Ascoli, *The Queen's Peace: The Origins and Development of the Metropolitan Police Force* (1979), 84–92.

landowning family; army experience and training were also drawn on for such matters as the operational structure of the force and the creation of a system of patrols for individual constables. The other Commissioner, Richard Mayne, was the lawyer son of an Irish judge, and was to serve for 39 years until the age of 72. The senior officers were largely drawn from non-commissioned officers of the Guards or cavalry regiments, and about one-seventh of the constables were also ex-soldiers. Quite deliberately, Peel refused to allow the appointment as superintendents of 'gentlemen—commissioned officers, for instance', because he wanted a group who would satisfactorily do work which was not then regarded as prestigious. Superintendents received £200 p.a., inspectors £100 p.a., while sergeants were given a weekly wage of 22s. 6d., and constables 21s. (less deductions for uniform). Even the two Commissioners were only paid £800 p.a., appreciably less, for instance, than factory inspectors were to receive in 1833.

Despite the speed with which the preliminary work of creating the Metropolitan Police was carried out, the task of establishing the new force on a satisfactory footing took years to complete. This was mainly because of the difficulty of finding and keeping satisfactory recruits, and because of the public suspicion with which the force was viewed at first. In the early years a high proportion of new recruits was rapidly discarded for such offences as drunkenness, insubordination, slackness, or dishonesty. The weeding out process was generally successful, and a renewed parliamentary inquiry into the Metropolitan Police five years after the creation of the force gave full backing to its continuance, noting a significant drop in metropolitan crime since 1829. It was to take more than a quarter of a century before the London police model was imitated everywhere.

The fall of the Tories

With Catholic emancipation out of the way, attempts were made to try to strengthen the ministry again by conciliating some of the recent dissidents. Emancipation had removed one source of discord between government Tories and Canningites, and perhaps Huskisson and his colleagues might be induced to return to the fold. Negotiations to this end had made some progress when Huskisson was accidentally killed at the opening of the Manchester and Liverpool Railway in September 1830. Another principal actor had been removed from the scene a little earlier, in June, with the death of George IV, which necessarily involved a general election. In the existing confusion of parties, this produced no clear result, and it remained uncertain how some of the new MPs would view such questions as the survival of the existing ministry and the desirability of parliamentary reform. The course of political events would have to wait upon the assembly and early debates of the new Parliament before any definite indications would be available.

Meanwhile, the question of parliamentary reform had come forward again in public discussion, although in the last months of the old Parliament a comfortable

213 to 117 vote had defeated Russell's latest move on that issue. In July 1830 news of a revolution in France may have played a part in strengthening a desire for change in Britain, while the outbreak of serious disturbances in the rural south of England in the first of what were called the 'Swing' riots did nothing to help the government. Nor did signs of faltering in important sections of the economy. The new Parliament met for business for the first time early in November, and it soon became clear that the ministry was in serious trouble in the House of Commons. In the debate on the Address in the House of Lords, Wellington responded with more clarity than wisdom to a question from Grey concerning the ministry's attitude towards a reform of Parliament; the Prime Minister declared that 'the legislature and the system of representation possessed the full confidence of the country... He was not only not prepared to bring forward any [such] measure, but... as long as he held any station in the government of the country he should always feel it his duty to resist such measures when proposed by others.' The validity of this trenchant claim, especially the 'full confidence of the country' element, was somewhat impaired when a few days later the ministry felt obliged to abandon a proposed visit by the new King to the Mansion House because they feared a riotous reception en route.

Wellington's intransigence over reform helped to alienate moderate opinion and was widely believed to have sealed the fate of his government. It was uncertain whether ministers would be able to beat off any substantial resolution in the new House of Commons in favour of parliamentary reform, but in the event this issue was not put to the test. On 15 November the House of Commons effectively rejected the ministry's proposals on the new King's Civil List. An amendment calling for an inquiry into the matter by a select committee was carried by 233 votes to 204. Wellington and Peel were now sure that the fall of the government could not be delayed; a government which could not implement its will in such a sensitive matter as the monarch's parliamentary income was obviously vulnerable. On 16 November the two leading ministers announced in the two Houses of Parliament that the administration was at an end; on the same day William IV, who did not share George IV's hostility to the Whigs, sent for their leader, Earl Grey, and commissioned him to form a government. The long period of dominance by the party of government, whether we term it Pittite or Tory or Pittite and then Tory, which had been almost uninterrupted since the younger Pitt's triumph nearly half a century earlier, was now over.

2

Government and administration

c.1815–1830

Britain has often been seen as a unitary state with the 'King in Parliament' being able to legislate for anything that was 'not impossible' by Acts of Parliament.[1] In practice and in law things were not so simple. Scotland retained its own laws and its own religious settlement, even if its political life was increasingly one with the United Kingdom as a whole, while the constitutional settlements of 1688 for both England and Scotland could not be easily overturned. In addition a code and a host of unwritten assumptions helped maintain the relative autonomy of counties and cities within a national framework. There was a feeling that central government should not disregard local interests and the views of local gentry and urban dignitaries, but this was also the consequence of the reliance of government on these very people and the relative paucity of the resources of the centre.

British governments in the early nineteenth century possessed only rudimentary resources in a variety of fields. Arrangements for the drafting of legislation were haphazard, even within major departments of state. Information was inadequate in many crucial areas of public policy. For example, there were as yet no maps covering the country's terrain in any systematic fashion, although the work of the Ordnance Survey was to remedy this during the Victorian period.

The traditional expectation of what was required of government was far less than what would be needed even in the near future but the exigencies of war had already seen an expansion of government's role. Economic and social problems were increasingly requiring the attention of government. Central amongst such problems was population growth.

The existence of accelerating population growth, and the problems which it involved, had only become clear a few years before 1815. In the later eighteenth century there had been uncertainty as to whether or not the population was increasing and about the scale of change involved. The first national census, in 1801, had done much to resolve these doubts, despite important limitations. The motives cited by Charles Abbot, the proposer of the Act which authorized it, are

---

1. Sir W. Blackstone, *Commentaries on the Laws of England* (1765–1769).

worth noting. He considered that

it had long been a matter of surprise and astonishment, that a great, powerful and enlightened nation like this should have remained hitherto unacquainted with the state of its population ... when the subsistence of the people is in question, this knowledge becomes of the highest importance. It is surely important to know the extent of the demand for which we are to provide a supply.[2]

The census of 1801 tried to measure the population of Great Britain in that year, but also involved a rough-and-ready estimate of recent demographic changes. The parish clergy were directed to submit the numbers of baptisms and burials for every tenth year from 1700 to 1780, and then for every year until 1800. The resulting returns were incomplete and imperfect, but provided some indication of the increase in population during the eighteenth century. From 1801 to 1831 the decennial enumeration of the existing population was entrusted to the only body of officials generally available, the Poor Law overseers, most of them unpaid, amateur, annual appointees. Although these duties were to be based on a door-to-door visitation resulting in lists of houses, families, and individuals, there was no effective definition of what constituted a house or a family. Overseers counted as seemed best to them, and there was a good deal of confusion, as well as varying standards of energy and literacy. Few overseers left any record of the basis on which they had formed their calculations. There were more serious gaps, too; for example, the first full census operation in Ireland was not attempted until 1821.

Although these operations were of fundamental importance in providing the first understanding of population change, their relatively crude character provides a good example of the limitations of the official machinery and the statistical information available to the governments of these years. In considering the role and working of government, such limitations are important.

The monarchy

Europe in the years after 1815 was dominated by monarchies, and the United Kingdom of Great Britain and Ireland formally adhered to that pattern of government. All important public appointments were made in the king's name, all Acts of Parliament and government decisions were ostensibly the reflection of the sovereign's will. In practice, of course, the British conventions of government already in 1815 diverged markedly from the workings of continental autocracies, in that the reduction in the monarch's power was well advanced.

This reduction of the monarch's power had not come about because of any great change to the constitution, which remained much as it had been

2. D. V. Glass, *Numbering the People* (1973), 91, 97. A general guide to the census is *Census of Great Britain, 1801–1931*, published as *Guide to Official Sources No. 2* by the Interdepartmental Committee on Social and Economic Research (1951). For a recent study of much demographic material, N. L. Tranter, *Population and Society, 1750–1940* (1985). For Ireland, K. H. Connell, *The Population of Ireland, 1750–1845* (1950).

established after the 'Glorious Revolution' of 1688. The gradual diminution of the powers of the Crown came about neither because monarchs willed it, nor politicians demanded it, but largely because of the accidents of royal lives and the idiosyncrasies of particular monarchs. George III had exercised an effective influence, which was underpinned by the respect which he commanded and his capacity for hard work. He had, before succumbing to an incapacitating illness, been ready to devote endless hours to his work, without even a private secretary to help him, until his eyesight began to fail in 1805; before then he wrote and even copied many of his official letters himself. Even before his illness required that his authority pass to his son as Regent, many decisions had fallen to his ministers. George IV, whether as Prince Regent or as King, had neither his father's reputation for probity and moral conduct, nor his willingness to work hard at the business of governing, though he was not devoid of acuteness and was effective in some other aspects of his role (see pp. 90, 101–3 below). From the time that he first assumed the regency, he exploited his own private secretary as a useful buffer between himself and the routine grind of government.[3] The vagaries which dictate royal successions played a part in his performance as king: a handsome, though prematurely portly, young prince had given way to a stout middle-aged figure by the time he became Regent in 1811, and an obese, breathless, and gouty figure became King in 1820. George IV's reign saw, therefore, a decline in royal political influence and the limited talents of his brother and successor, William IV, precluded any significant recovery of royal authority during his reign. Such personal failings mattered and as has been argued with reference to Catholic emancipation and parliamentary reform, 'There was nothing predictable about the events of 1827–32, and a different attitude on the part of the last two Hanoverian monarchs might well have proved crucial.'[4]

A further factor was the decline in the amount of patronage available to the monarch, for the ability to dispense positions and sinecures had always been an important weapon when it was necessary to find support in the House of Commons. Economical reform was largely responsible for this decline: 'In response to a critical motion by Brougham, Castlereagh claimed that...1800 [offices] had gone since 1810 and of the 80 or so placemen who could be identified in the Commons, two-thirds were so only in the sense that they held ministerial or "efficient" office.'[5]

In addition, the long continuation in office, first of Pitt's ministry after 1783 and then of Lord Liverpool's ministry after 1812, encouraged the evolution of a kind of collective ministerial experience and authority. The young politicians whom Pitt had encouraged were by the 1820s mature political figures, well used

---

3. Sir Robert Mackworth Young, 'The royal archives and Prince Albert', in A. M. Birke (ed.), *Prince Albert Society Papers* (1985).

4. Jeremy Black, 'The House of Hanover', in W. M. Ormrod (ed.), *The Kings and Queens of England* (2001), 235.

5. Williams and Ramsden, *Ruling Britannia*, 180.

to working together, and capable of mounting a collective defence of the government's position against the whims of any wayward monarch.

Ministers of the Crown

While there was wide acceptance of the principle that it was the king's prerogative to choose his ministers, this power was curtailed in practice by the need to select ministers who could command the general confidence of Parliament, and especially the House of Commons, which controlled the purse-strings of the State. Even if the monarch could still block the appointment of an individual, or the appointment of an individual to a specific post, these were prerogatives which were increasingly difficult to enforce. There were powerful conventions which prescribed the proper categories from which ministries might be selected. Some ministerial posts necessarily involved a great deal of administrative work by the ministers themselves, so that it was desirable that a Cabinet should include at least some men of administrative ability and experience. In that inherently unequal society, ministers also had to be drawn from groups which possessed wealth, security, and an assured personal status within the community. In 1812, ten of the fourteen members of Liverpool's Cabinet possessed hereditary titles; most of the others received peerages within the next few years.

Most peers did not seek an active political career in ministerial office. The minority who were both sufficiently interested and sufficiently able to do so normally served an apprenticeship in junior ministerial posts before being considered for Cabinet office. Those in high office in 1815 had been in great measure moulded by considerable administrative experience in previous years, often years of great difficulty for ministers. A few typical lifespans will illustrate the scale of the changes and problems faced by this relatively small group of politically influential aristocrats—Liverpool 1770–1828, Eldon 1751–1838, Wellington 1769–1852, Grey 1764–1845. During these years Britain experienced large-scale demographic, economic, social, and political changes in ways which were unforeseeable and often posed difficult problems for the country's governors.

It is sometimes supposed that those who governed Britain in these years were ill acquainted with the society they ruled. Such an impression is at best a half-truth. While members of Lord Liverpool's Cabinet might not have fully understood conditions in cotton factories or coal mines—at that time not very typical situations in society—collectively they could bring to bear an impressive range of experience and knowledge of different parts of the country. Ministers normally possessed substantial estates, and spent considerable periods of time there. Liverpool's main estates were in Oxfordshire, Eldon possessed property in both Dorset and Northumberland, Sidmouth in Berkshire, Castlereagh and Palmerston in Ireland, Mulgrave in Yorkshire, Peel in Staffordshire and Lancashire, Wynn in Wales, Wellington and Palmerston in Hampshire, Robinson in Yorkshire, Surrey, and Lincolnshire, Camden in Sussex, Bathurst in

Gloucestershire. Given that landowners were unlikely to be ignorant of conditions in their own home areas, the cumulative range of regional knowledge was extensive. Few would have denied that Viscount Melville had extensive knowledge of the Scottish economy and society. Nor was it the case that early nineteenth-century ministries were drawn entirely from the long-established landed aristocracy. Many of Liverpool's long-serving Cabinet, including the Prime Minister himself, came from families which had only recently made their way into the highest ranks of society (p. 11 above).

The Cabinet

The collective authority of the Cabinet was by 1815 well understood, but there was still much that was nebulous about the conventions which governed its workings. Arrangements for Cabinet meetings and agendas were wholly unsystematic. During the Regency period, Lord Holland noted that 'There are no precise laws or rules, nor even any well established or understood usages which mark which measures in each Department are or are not to be communicated to the Cabinet.'[6] Any member of the Cabinet might initiate a meeting, and at times even the Prime Minister might not be aware of the purpose for which a Cabinet meeting had been called.[7] Despite this continued informality, the superior authority of the Cabinet in government was well established.[8]

The Prime Minister

Within this collective authority, the pre-eminent position of the Prime Minister was also by 1815 reasonably clear. The Prime Minister, once commissioned to form an administration, proceeded to select his own colleagues, and a condition of their continued tenure of office was his willingness to continue working with them. Liverpool's long premiership, from 1812 to 1827, following on that of the Younger Pitt, 1783–1801 and 1804–6, did much to consolidate the position of the Prime Minister. No one in the Liverpool administration doubted that the ministry had a chief who was much more than a figurehead. This is not to say that the first minister was an autocrat. His own room for manoeuvre was often restricted by the realities of contemporary politics; in practice successful Prime Ministers preferred to get their own way by argument, cajolery, sweet reasonableness, and the influence of their personal prestige, rather than by any peremptory dealings with their colleagues.

6. Holland, *Memoirs of the Whig Party* (1852–4), ii. 85.
7. A. Aspinall, 'The Cabinet Council, 1783–1835', *Proceedings of the British Academy*, 38 (1952), 145–252.
8. It has been argued that Liverpool sought to keep politics and policy separate and thus preferred to keep policy-makers out of the Cabinet but that after 1822 policy was increasingly discussed and made in the Cabinet. Boyd Hilton, 'Lord Liverpool: the art of politics and the practice of government', *Transactions of the Royal Historical Society*, 38 (1988), 147–70.

Central administration

Some ministerial posts involved the headship of a major administrative department. This was the case with the three Secretaries of State, Foreign, Home, and
War and Colonies—or the Treasury, the Post Office, and the Board of Trade. In a
few cases, departments employed a staff distinctly numerous by contemporary
standards. The revenue offices, including Customs, Excise, and the administration of other indirect taxation such as the stamp duties, employed nearly 20,000
officials. This included local officers all over the country as well as a headquarters
staff. In 1815 the Post Office employed about 1,500 officials, again with a national
coverage. The supporting services for the armed forces, including the naval
dockyards, together possessed a work force of about 4,000.[9] These numbers, sufficient to arouse the suspicion and resentment of many of the taxpayers who had
to pay for them, were hardly out of proportion with the work which those
departments had to perform.

Although Scotland retained its own recognized church and legal system, the
office of Secretary of State for Scotland and the institution of the Scottish Privy
Council had become moribund. In practice, Henry Dundas, the 'uncrowned
King of Scotland' had controlled Scottish affairs as well as patronage during Pitt's
ministries and his son, the second Viscount Melville, continued to do the same
until 1827.

At the centre of government, the resources available were often tiny in relation
to the responsibilities involved. In most major departments, the senior minister
presided over one or two junior ministers and a small staff of those who were
coming to be called civil servants, a term which still appeared newfangled in
these years.[10] In the early decades of the century, ministers themselves still
did much of the routine departmental work; the long-serving members of
Liverpool's government had accumulated a body of experience and precedents
which made them especially useful in this role. As Foreign Secretary, for instance,
Castlereagh made little personal use of his staff, and Canning drafted his own
dispatches.[11] The civil servants in a major department of state—commonly
described as clerks—spent much of their time in routine labours such as copying
and recording correspondence. Often even trivial decisions would be taken by
either an undersecretary or by the senior minister himself. Although this
involved a great deal of relatively low-level work by ministers, the total amount
of government activity was in normal circumstances so small that such a personalized system could still work in the years after 1815. Moreover, there was a
long period in the summer, while Parliament was in recess, in which the tempo
in government offices usually sank to a slow pace, and long holidays were taken

9. N. Gash, *Aristocracy and People: Britain 1815–1865* (1979), 51.
10. D. M. Young, *The Colonial Office in the Early Nineteenth Century* (1961), 8.
11. C. Webster, *The Foreign Policy of Palmerston* (1951), 58; C. Webster, *The Art and Practice of Diplomacy* (1961), 181–96.

by both ministers and their staff. When the Peterloo crisis blew up in August 1819, more than half of the Cabinet were abroad, and only four Cabinet ministers could be readily assembled for important meetings in the following month.[12]

The Civil Service

The ministerial heads of the various departments made the appointments to vacant clerical posts in their offices. For the most part such ministerial patronage was secure, and ministers could choose officials from among their own personal friends, relatives, dependants, or acquaintances. Matters were not always so simple, though. The existence of a vacancy in a salaried government appointment was the signal for intense pressure on the minister, either from hungry applicants themselves, or from men of influence who knew that to secure appointments for their clients was a demonstration of their own importance. Conscientious ministers, such as Peel, found the distribution of patronage in these conditions one of the most distasteful responsibilities of government.

These appointments had obvious attractions. A government clerk's normal conditions of employment were less than arduous. A clerk in the Home Office or the Colonial Office would not be expected to begin work before about 11 a.m. and might well be finished for the day by 4 p.m. Salaries, at least for the more respectable grades of government work, were sufficient to sustain an agreeable standard of living. In 1816, Colonial Office clerks received a salary of £80 during their first five years, rising to £160 for the next five years, £200 after ten years, £300 after fifteen years, and £400 after twenty years' service.[13] In addition there were various perquisites, such as the London agencies for individual colonies, from which Colonial Office clerks might obtain substantial extra earnings. Annual holiday entitlements for clerks in central government offices were usually about ten or twelve weeks.

As yet there were no systematic provisions for superannuation or retirement. Sir John Barrow occupied the key civil service position of Secretary to the Admiralty from 1804 to 1845 (with one brief interval out of office) before retiring in his early eighties. Pensions were normally granted to civil servants on retirement, but these were very much individual arrangements rather than the working of an understood scheme. At the Colonial Office Richard Penn was on the strength from 1801 to 1825 (during which time he made a reputation as a humorous author); when he retired at the age of 40 he was given an annual pension of £750. His colleague, John Forbes, retired in 1824 at the age of 38 after a similar stint in office; his pension was only £200.

Such undemanding but rewarding employments were much sought after, and it was rare for nominations to be secured simply on grounds of ability.

12. N. Gash, *Lord Liverpool* (1984), 144.
13. Young, *The Colonial Office in the Early Nineteenth Century* gives a full discussion of the Colonial Office and its staff in this period.

On 25 October 1825, George IV wrote to his Colonial Secretary to ask a favour: 'I wish in the course of a year you could give one, the lowest clerkship in your office, for a lad of eighteen. A year hence will do.' This royal request was accepted and acted upon.[14] As Home Secretary, Lord Sidmouth appointed two members of his own family to clerkships; his successor, Peel, gave clerkships to three members of a family with whom he was on friendly terms. In addition he gave two similar posts to the two Redgrave brothers, also personal acquaintances. These two appointments were made when the brothers reached the age of 13. Like many of their contemporaries as civil servants, these youthful officials proved equal to the modest levels of administrative skill demanded of them, while the less than onerous nature of their work gave them ample opportunity to develop interests and acquire national reputations in the world of art.[15] Appointment to lucrative administrative posts by patronage was not a peculiarity of government in these years, for similar practices pervaded the whole of society, as it had done in earlier periods. In industry, commerce, banking, estate management, the allocation of apprenticeships in skilled trades, and a wide variety of other spheres, the existence of influential friends or relatives was vital in securing individual advancement. The practices of the State merely reflected the normal and traditional habits of an inherently unequal society.[16]

Even in the early years of peace after 1815 there was a tendency for the volume of work in government offices to increase. Between 1822 and 1830, the number of out-letters copied annually at the Home Office rose from 400 to 1,400; at the Colonial Office, the number of letters received increased from 4,487 in 1816 to 7,491 in 1824.[17] Although there were small increases in establishments, some key ministries continued to operate with what now appear tiny staffs. When Canning became Foreign Secretary, he found an office staff of twenty-four, and the Home Office managed with about the same number.[18] The Board of Trade, which was acquiring new responsibilities in the post-war years, increased its headquarters staff from twenty to twenty-six during the 1820s. In comparison, the principal London banks would employ between thirty-two and fifty-six clerks in their head offices at this time.[19]

The administrative procedures used by government departments rarely showed any sophisticated techniques; even such basic functions as filing and accounting were often defective. At the Home Office, the administrative chores were allocated to officials in a time-honoured but antiquated fashion; a few clerks were seriously overworked, while others had little to do and felt no obligation to help less fortunate colleagues. The quality of office procedures in the

---

14. Young, *The Colonial office in the Early Nineteenth Century*, 268.   15. Ibid. 97.

16. Ibid. 262–72 for Colonial Office patronage. For Home Office examples, A. P. Donajgrodzki, 'New Roles for old: the Northcote–Trevelyan Report and the Clerks of the Home Office, 1822–48', in G. Sutherland (ed.), *Studies in the Growth of Nineteenth-Century Government* (1972), 82–109.

17. Donajgrodzki, 'New roles for old', 93 n. Young, *The Colonial Office in the early Nineteenth Century*, 283.

18. Young, *The Colonial Office in the Early Nineteenth Century*, 81.   19. Ibid. 284.

years after 1815 is exemplified in the regular preparation of an emergency summary of the shipping situation, a practice inaugurated during a critical stage in
the Napoleonic War; this procedure continued unnoticed for sixteen years after
the end of the war.[20] The preservation of any kind of order or continuity in
central administration owed more to the existence of a kind of collective
memory in the offices than to any skilful filing and indexing of documents. One
of Peel's principal contributions to the skills of government was his work as
Chief Secretary for Ireland and later as Home Secretary in trying to implement a
more orderly and businesslike range of office procedures; by 1830 much still
remained to be done.[21]

The armed forces

The central civil departments of state were small and in consequence inexpensive. Far and away the biggest public-spending departments were the army and
navy, which also had more recent wartime experience of administrative expansion than any of the civil ministries. The coming of peace brought a rapid reduction in the size of the military and naval establishments. The five years after 1815
saw the numbers in the army drop from 300,000 to 88,100 men. Even in 1827,
however, the army and navy between them cost £16 million, well over a quarter
of total central government spending, at a time when more than half of the
national revenue went to service the National Debt. The whole of the State's civil
expenditure amounted to much less than the cost of the armed forces.[22]

In a period of unrelenting parliamentary and public pressures for economies
in public spending, governments found it difficult to preserve armed forces capable of fulfilling the responsibilities which faced them at home and overseas. In
November 1816, the Home Secretary, Lord Sidmouth, noted that 'We must expect
a trying winter, and it will be fortunate if the Military establishment which was
pronounced to be too large for the constitution of the country shall be sufficient
to preserve its internal tranquillity.'[23]

Although the post-war years saw governments facing internal pressures which
sometimes seemed threatening, the armed forces remained loyal to the existing
order, and offered an important source of stability. One reason for this was that
the officers of the cavalry and infantry establishments did not form a detached
professional corps, but were closely linked to the dominant groups in society.
Officers' salaries were so low that it was difficult for an officer to live comfortably
on his army pay, especially in fashionable units. This financial pressure was

20. Ibid. 184.

21. N. Gash, *Mr. Secretary Peel: The Life of Sir Robert Peel to 1830* (1961), ch. 4.

22. J. H. Clapham, *An Economic History of Modern Britain: The Early Railway Age, 1820–1850*
(1930), 319. The standard account of the naval administration in these years is C. J. Bartlett, *Great
Britain and Sea Power, 1815–1853* (1963); this gives an admirable discussion of government problems
in this sphere.

23. J. Stevenson, *Popular Disturbances in England, 1700–1870* (1979), 207.

compounded by the traditional system of purchase of commissions, which treated them as a form of private property which could, under certain conditions, be bought and sold. Entry into the commissioned ranks in cavalry and infantry regiments was normally a matter of patronage combined with purchase of a commission. A high proportion of these officers was drawn from the aristocracy and gentry, and the great majority of them came from social groups with some supplementary private income.[24]

Such a system may seem almost grotesquely inefficient by later standards, but in contemporary terms it could be easily justified. If national stability depended upon the continued loyalty of the armed forces in troubled times, then it was important that the army should be led by men closely attached to the existing order. In a celebrated State paper, Wellington summed up these arguments:

it is promotion by purchase which brings into the service men of fortune and education; men who have some connection with the interests and fortunes of the country, besides the commission which they hold from His Majesty. It is this circumstance which exempts the British army from the character of being a 'mercenary army' and has rendered its employment, for nearly a century and a half, not only not inconsistent with the constitutional privileges of the country, but safe and beneficial.[25]

This close connection between the army and the civil power helps to explain the success with which the small home army was used in a police role in the years after 1815. It was rare to find military officers employed on police duties eager to promote conflict and bloodshed, common instead to find army officers trying to bring about conciliation and pacification. Those who commanded the army were not a military caste separated from the rest of society; they were, rather, a part of a coherent governing group well aware of the dangers which unjustified repression might create. If the industrial areas of Britain saw a disproportionate amount of disturbances in these years, it was unlikely that aristocratic officers would be content to act simply as the police agents of mill owners or mine owners, probable instead that they would view such parties with condescension and superiority.

Law and order

Apart from the armed forces, in the years before the development of civil police forces the maintenance of law and order depended upon the local magistracy and their usually weak and often unpaid police resources. Each parish possessed a constable, an unpaid amateur elected by the parish vestry (the council or governing body of the parish) to hold an office going back to Norman or Anglo-Saxon times. It was not a popular duty, and by the early nineteenth century the victims of the vestry election often paid a substitute to do the actual work.

---

24. The standard work here is A. Bruce, *The Purchase System in the British Army, 1660–1871* (1980).
25. Ibid. 65–6.

As with many other minor local government posts, the job of parish constable might now be a paid perquisite held by a local inhabitant, perhaps for many years, in addition to some other form of employment. Towns often used local Improvement Acts to obtain authority to raise some kind of watch. In the Black Country, Walsall had a small force for watching, at night only, from 1811, and Wolverhampton followed suit three years later.[26] Although these tiny and cheap police resources appear unimpressive, they were not always absurdly inadequate in relatively close-knit local communities where communal social disciplines remained effective. They could in some circumstances even appear adequate, as in another growing Black Country community, Darlaston, which

although a big and important town, had neither magistrate nor courthouse. An infirm old man acted as the constable, watchman and beadle. If he wanted to take anyone up, he had merely to go to the culprit and say 'Come'. Strangely enough, the men thus apprehended nearly always did as bidden, and were then walked off to Bilston, one mile distant, where there was a magistrate.[27]

For most criminal acts of a relatively minor nature, justice remained a local matter. Where any kind of formal prosecution was launched, only a small minority of cases went anywhere beyond the Courts of Petty or Quarter Sessions, staffed by the unpaid local magistrates.

The high courts

It is an indication of the decentralized nature of authority in Britain that there were no intermediate tribunals between these local courts and the high courts centred in London. A team of twelve common-law judges staffed the main central courts and also travelled on the assize circuits twice in each year.[28] The Lord Chancellor was the most important influence in determining judicial appointments, although the Prime Minister was often involved in selection for the highest judicial positions. A distinguished legal career was a normal prerequisite, but other considerations could also play a part. Here is Lord Eldon explaining to the Prince Regent in 1818 the rationale behind a recent appointment: 'Mr. Richardson was educated at Harrow, and afterwards at Oxford, where he greatly distinguished himself. For his principles as to State & Church I believe him to be perfectly sound: as a lawyer . . . he is represented to me as exceedingly learned. He is, as the times require, firm.'[29]

Judges, like army officers, were usually drawn from the propertied groups, though rarely from the upper ranks of the aristocracy, for whom the long grind of a legal training might be unattractive. As with other branches of the upper

26. D. Philips, *Crime and Authority in Victorian England: The Black Country, 1835–1860* (1977), 54–5.
27. Ibid. 53.
28. D. Duman, *The Judicial Bench in England, 1727–1875* (1982) provides a detailed examination of the judges of this period.
29. Ibid. 80.

reaches of civil authority, they were reasonably well paid, relatively much more so than their modern successors; a long judicial tenure would suffice to endow a family with a very comfortable standard of living. As with other civil establishments, the official patronage attached to the courts provided a useful supplement to judicial salaries. In 1825 three-quarters of the substantial incomes received by officials of the Court of King's Bench went to sons of previous Chief Justices of that court.[30]

The existence of such practices was for many years deemed compatible with the prestige and authority of the courts, but already in 1815 the traditional system of payment by a variety of salaries, fees, and perquisites was becoming less acceptable. In 1825, in parallel with similar changes in a wider range of public employment, a simple salary structure replaced the older pattern of paying judges partly by salary and partly by diverse fees.[31] In general, the calibre of the judges in these years was reasonably high, and their tenure was largely protected from political interference by Acts of 1702 and 1761. Like the army, the working of the upper courts provided an example of a major function of the State entrusted to men who were themselves drawn from and associated with the propertied groups which dominated a society that was, as it always had been, profoundly unequal.

The Empire

Britain's limited administrative resources were not concerned only with the United Kingdom. Despite the setback of the War of American Independence, in 1815 Britain was mistress of a great overseas empire.[32] The end of the Napoleonic War saw it increased by the acquisition of seventeen colonies conquered during the war. Imperial dependencies had been acquired in a haphazard sequence and from a variety of motives, but most of the new annexations were retained for some kind of strategic purpose. Ceylon's main attraction was the magnificent harbour and potential eastern naval base offered by Trincomalee; Malta was held for its strategical position in the Mediterranean; and Cape Colony because it commanded the route to India. There was no symmetry in character or function in the British overseas possessions after 1815. Some were remnants of the old colonial system, such as the old West Indian colonies, which retained their local legislative assemblies. Most of the newer acquisitions had no tradition of self-government, and came to be ruled as direct dependencies. They were primarily controlled by the Colonial Office, in ways which were later to be rationalized to represent 'Crown Colony' status. Even in the West Indies, direct rule was applied to new possessions like St Lucia. Because of the particular nature of Canada's recent history, and the conjunction there of both British and French colonial

---

30. D. Duman, *The Judicial Bench in England, 1727–1875*, 119 and n.   31. Ibid. 122–4.
32. For a general account, D. K. Fieldhouse, *The Colonial Empires* (1966), 242–302.

traditions, that part of the empire possessed a peculiar version of the traditional pattern of colonial government. Under the legislation of 1791, there were representative assemblies in both Upper and Lower Canada. In the early post-war years, colonial administration was very untidy. Patronage could be important in this sphere too, as the arrangements for governing St Lucia demonstrated; fourteen of the official appointments there were made by the Secretary of State for the Colonies, nine by the island's army commander, six by the Ordnance Department, one by the Paymaster General, and four by the Treasury.[33]

The most peculiar overseas anomaly was the British position in India.[34] The rise of Britain to a dominant position in this subcontinent was one of the most remarkable political developments in the history of the modern world. The administration of Britain's Indian possessions and dependencies in the years after 1815 reflected the role of the chartered East India Company in building up the British position there. Although from time to time there were proposals for placing Indian affairs directly under the Colonial Office, such administrative rationalization was not effected. Instead Indian administration was left to the directors of the company, under the general supervision of a government-appointed Board of Control. Though the East India Company remained an important commercial enterprise, it retained most of the patronage for posts in India. The government, through the Board of Control, influenced the key political appointments in India and in the last resort the board could enforce its will by sending direct orders to the Governor General, but this power was rarely used. In effect, though not in theory, the Board of Control became an imperfect ministry for India, while the political and administrative staff appointed by the company became a kind of embryonic Indian civil service.

The success of the British in eighteenth-century India had been facilitated by the chronic instability and disunity of the native powers there. It was by exploiting this disunity, in the first place for reasons of self-defence, and later for expansion, that the small resources of the British in India had been able to exert so effective a leverage. Under the expansionist regime of Lord Hastings between 1813 and 1823, Britain's paramount position in India became established. By 1818, after the militant Governor General's campaigns against the unstable Maratha states, Britain controlled, either directly or indirectly, by far the greater part of the subcontinent; only the Punjab and Sind retained any real independence.

British rule in India took two main forms. Large areas—primarily the three great 'presidencies' of Bengal, Bombay, and Madras—were annexed as British territory, ruled by the East India Company as the agent of the British State. In order that this system might operate with reasonable efficiency and honesty, the commercial and political aspects of company administration were separated, with distinct groups of officers for the two functions. In earlier years, private

33. Young, *The Colonial Office in the Early Nineteenth Century*, 172–3.

34. G. D. Bearce, *British Attitudes towards India, 1784–1858* (1961); V. A. Smith, *The Oxford History of India*, 4th edn. (1981), 564–653; P. Spear, *A History of India*, (1979), ii. 106–28.

trading by officials had been a frequent source of corruption; now the practice was forbidden to administrative officials, but in compensation they received substantial salaries from Indian revenues. The existing native systems of taxation were overhauled in ways which, if much less than perfect, at least produced acceptable levels of certainty and stability for many years to come.

Elsewhere in the subcontinent, the native rulers continued to enjoy a nominal sovereignty, but under conditions which effectively rendered them subservient to British control. Under the normal treaty arrangements, the native ruler accepted at his court a British resident, or adviser, sometimes backed by a garrison from the company's Indian army. In effect, the Indian princely states became client states of British India. British rule in the subcontinent still depended heavily upon the exploitation of Indian resources, including the native troops, who provided the majority of the company's army, but British domination seemed increasingly solidly based.

A disproportionate number of company employees were Scots. As a recent study of the British Empire has pointed out, 'In the 1750s little more than a tenth of the population of the British Isles lived in Scotland. Yet the East India Company was at the very least half-Scottish.'[35] Not that this was necessarily unjustified, for Scots made hardy, efficient, and determined colonial administrators as well as adventurous traders, settlers, financiers, engineers, and soldiers. Warren Hastings was English but during his time as Governor of Bengal and then Governor of India nearly fifty per cent of those appointed to Bengal were Scots as were his inner circle of confidants. The influence of Henry Dundas, Viscount Melville, controller of government influence and patronage in Scotland under Pitt, who helped draft the India Bill of 1784 and became President of the Board of Control in 1793, resulted in even more Scots being appointed to writerships and cadetships in the company, an early indication of the central role of Scots in the administration of the Empire as a whole.

Nothing was, indeed, more British, in the sense of not just English, than the Empire. The Union with Scotland had flourished, it has been argued, on the basis of a common Protestantism, enjoyment of economic growth, and the opportunities these developments afforded in Scotland itself, in England, and in Britain's overseas possessions. It was the latter which best exemplifies the role of Scots[36] and they would be at the centre of Britain's empire as it developed during the nineteenth century. As well as playing a central role in the East India Company, Scots already made up a large proportion of the settlers in the Canadian colonies; Nova Scotia adopted a version of the flag of St Andrew as its provincial flag in 1829. If Scots played a part disproportionate to their numbers in the Empire's development, so did the Irish. The stereotype of both Scottish and Irish emigrants to the Empire tends to be that of the poor and dispossessed: Scottish

35. Niall Ferguson, *Empire: How Britain Made the Modern World* (2003), 40.
36. L. Colley, *Britons: Forging the Nation 1707–1837* (1992).

highlanders cleared from their glens or of the Irish seeking escape from near sub-sistence farming. In fact many came from relatively prosperous and educated backgrounds and not a few were the younger sons of minor gentry families. They came from the lowlands of Scotland as well as the highlands and from the north as well as the south of Ireland. Such emigrants provided army officers, adminis-trators, and engineers as well as farmers for the developing empire.[37]

Parliament

Governments, even though they enjoyed the support of the monarch, had always to recognize the need for the support of Parliament. During these years, govern-ments found the management of the legislature one of their most difficult and laborious tasks, despite obvious links between the executive ministry and the groups which provided the majority of both Houses of Parliament. Ministers were normally drawn from the social groups which also provided the majority of the legislature, and both Houses would have a group of ministers sitting on their benches.

The problem was not simply that of maintaining a parliamentary majority for the enactment of the Acts of Parliament which the government needed. The volume of legislation passed in the years after 1815 remained small in contrast to what was to come. There was no doubt about the legal supremacy of parliamen-tary statutes, but the full potential of Acts of Parliament as agents of change was little realized in practice in these early years. Most of the legislation passed was local or personal rather than public and general. The legal supremacy of Parliament was more commonly employed to authorize a canal, to enclose a village's fields, or to cut through legal problems affecting the disposition of a great estate, than to introduce general changes affecting the whole country.

Ministers did sometimes find it difficult to push legislation through Parliament, but a defeat in either House, even on important measures, did not matter too much. The king's ministers could swallow such rebuffs and remain in office, provided that Parliament, and especially the House of Commons, was prepared to extend to them a kind of general confidence. In practice, it was not legislation which provided the most troublesome problems in the relationship between executive and legislature. Much more wearing was the constant pressure exerted on government by MPs and peers who saw it as one of their main func-tions to act as a kind of permanent watchdog over the work of the executive.

In part this attitude reflected the presence within Parliament of a variety of special-interest groups personally involved with some particular aspect of the government's work. In the early nineteenth century, it was normal for 6 or 7 per cent of MPs to have personal interests connected with India, which might

37. Ged Martin and Benjamin E. Kline, 'British Emigration and New Identities', in P. J. Marshall (ed.), *The Cambridge Illustrated History of the British Empire*, 254–79.

not always fit in well with the Indian policies of the government of the day. Similarly, another group would be closely attached to the West Indies interest, others to shipping or other sectors of the economy; the dominant landed interest always provided a high proportion of the members of both Houses. There were also groups of military and naval officers, capable of taking a critical interest in the government's handling of the armed forces.

More important than most of these special-interest groups within Parliament were two other sources of potential trouble for ministers. The social groups which dominated British society were not politically united. Both Houses of Parliament included substantial opposition elements seeking to trip up government, with the intention of defeating and replacing it. This opposition invariably included men of personal wealth and independent influence, and this was something which ministries could not destroy. Opposition politicians were well placed to exploit the second major parliamentary problem facing ministers after 1815, the question of public expenditure. There was a pervasive belief in the country at large, well represented in Parliament, that the executive government was extravagant, wasteful, and at least potentially corrupt. The taxpaying electorate had acquiesced with reluctance in the increases in taxation, and the enormous growth in public borrowing, which the wars of 1793–1815 had entailed, and was now determined to see a major reduction in these burdens. Nor was this public and parliamentary rage for economy in official expenditure without reasonable foundation. Nineteenth-century governments inherited a reputation tarnished by the record of previous generations in the manipulation of public resources for politically partisan purposes or personal gain. The use of official patronage to cement political support or confer favours on relatives and friends still went on in ways which could scarcely be concealed, with the loyalty of most of the forty-five Scottish MPs, so important to administrations, being largely maintained by government patronage. Moreover, the general level of efficiency which public administration had achieved by this time was not high and there were recurring scandals of dereliction of duty in both central and local government. If the extent of official skill and attainment was improving in these years, the process began from a very low level and still had far to go.

In these circumstances, every request for money by government was subject to searching and often hostile scrutiny. Much of the national revenue was mortgaged to pay the interest on the swollen National Debt. Governments found that one of their most difficult problems lay in persuading Parliament to sanction taxation sufficient to keep a minimum of essential services in operation. As is not uncommon in times of peace, the armed forces became a particular target of demands for reduced public spending. Early nineteenth-century governments found it difficult or impossible to obtain the money for national defences adequate to ensure security for Britain, her sea routes, and her empire, in an often uncertain world. Even where ministers had reason to believe that their proposals were sensible and calculated to serve the public interest, their ability to implement these policies was often restricted by the parliamentary passion for reduced expenditure. Moreover, ministers were uncomfortably aware that this was not simply a foible of wayward legislators. The parliamentary campaign for cuts in spending was backed by the bulk of the electorate, and indeed by the wider public, including the vociferous radical campaigners of the years after 1815. The continuous pressure on government spending may have helped towards greater administrative efficiency, but this was little comfort to governments whose revenue was incapable of meeting necessary expenditure.

It was some consolation to ministers who found the managing of Parliament one of their most difficult chores that the legislature did not normally sit for much of the year. In 1816 Parliament was in session only from 1 February until 2 July, in 1817 from 28 January to 12 July, in 1823 from 4 February until 19 July. Even sessions of this length brought grumbling from members of both Houses, and during the parliamentary sittings the level of interest and attendance fluctuated a great deal. However, ministers knew only too well that when questions of taxation or official expenditure were the main business there would certainly be a good attendance. If the MPs' own predilections were not enough to ensure this, then the watchful pressures of a taxpaying electorate could do much to keep their representatives up to the mark.

The House of Lords

In 1820 the House of Lords consisted of 339 peers, mostly hereditary, but including 16 representatives of the peerage of Scotland created before the Act of Union of 1707 (elected for each Parliament), and 28 representatives of the peerage of Ireland created before the Act of Union of 1801 (elected for life as vacancies occurred). Archbishops and bishops of the Church of England contributed 26 spiritual peers; from the Union of 1801 until the Disestablishment of 1869, the sister Church of Ireland was represented by 1 archbishop and 3 bishops, selected by rotation. During the ten years of George IV's reign, membership of the Upper House rose to almost 400, as new creations outstripped the extinction of older peerages.

Peers enjoyed a considerable measure of independence in their legislative role, but this was not an untrammelled freedom for many of them. Their parliamentary tenure might not depend upon electoral vagaries, but their own local prestige and status were much involved in electoral control in their own districts. A substantial number of peers were active political partisans, whether in support of ministers or on the opposition benches. Many also were ambitious, and their ambitions might include promotions within the peerage, admission to the prestigious orders of chivalry, or the attainment of office in court or government. A public test of an aristocratic magnate's power was his ability to obtain favours for his dependants or allies. Such factors provided ministers with leverage in influencing members of the Upper House, apart from political loyalties, although few peers were susceptible to government coercion. The attachment of the overwhelming majority of peers to the existing social order was naturally strong, and tended to provide a comfortable majority for most conservative causes. Although the power of the Lords relative to that of the Commons had declined, the prestige of the Upper House remained high. To achieve a peerage remained a great public honour, and the majority of the king's ministers still sat in the House of Lords.

The House of Commons

The House of Commons contained 658 members.[38] They included 82 members for English counties and 403 members for English boroughs. England also sent 4 university members, 2 each from Oxford and Cambridge, where Anglican clergymen formed a major part of the electorate. Wales contributed 12 county and 12 borough MPs, Scotland 15 burgh members and 30 county members; the Scottish representative system especially was much open to manipulation by the government's Scottish agents before 1832. Since the 1801 Union, Ireland had returned 35 borough and 64 county members, with a single MP from Trinity College, Dublin.

Although each MP nominally had equal weight in voting in the House, there were differences in the prestige attaching to various kinds of constituency. To sit for a county, or for the City of London or some other particularly important urban centre, invested an MP with more prestige than the representation of any of the many minor borough seats. Although the county members only composed a small minority of the House, the members for the English counties formed an especially important group. As Lord Liverpool once put it, the county members, 'if not generally the ablest members in the house, are certainly those who have the greatest stake in the country, and may be trusted for the most part in periods of difficulty and danger'.[39]

These men were seen as the special representatives of that great landed interest which dominated British society. Even a government possessing an apparently secure parliamentary majority might feel endangered if the county members ceased to support it. The results of county elections could usually be calculated not in terms of the reactions of individual voters to national political questions or particular government policies, but in terms of the views of the principal local landowners. For tenants and other dependants to follow the political lead of their landlords was a normal feature of the electoral system. There remained among most county MPs a modest predilection to give a general support to the king's government; this did not, of course, apply to those county members who were closely tied as partisan supporters of the opposition. Nor was the loyalty of

38. E. and A. C. Porritt, *The Unreformed House of Commons*, 2 vols. (1903, 1909); C. Seymour, *Electoral Reform in England and Wales* (1915), 9–28; M. Brock, *The Great Reform Act* (1973), 15–25.
39. Gash, *Aristocracy and People*, 124.

county MPs who were prepared to give a general support to ministers always reliable when matters of taxation and government spending were in question.

In both Houses of Parliament, most members could be listed in terms of party allegiance, though party leaders, whether in office or in opposition, possessed only limited sanctions for enforcing party discipline. The hereditary legislators of the Upper House obviously enjoyed a special kind of personal independence, but many members of the elected House were almost as secure in their parliamentary tenure. Most MPs did not sit as mere representatives of a given political party, but primarily because of their own personal position and influence. Many MPs belonged to families who either virtually owned a constituency or enjoyed a considerable and independent influence within it. The MP who sat as a patron's nominee for a pocket borough might be less independent, but his dependence was on his patron rather than on a party leadership. In the larger county constituencies, where the electorate might be numbered in thousands, a successful candidate was usually someone who enjoyed such a significant personal prestige and local backing that he was not amenable to outside control as long as he did not outrage the susceptibilities of his more important constituents. Interference in constituency affairs by any kind of outside agencies was often hotly resented. By whatever route they reached Parliament, the majority of early nineteenth-century MPs were not easily controlled by government or by party leaders. A party allegiance inspired by strong personal belief could be a powerful constraining force, while ambition in various forms might counsel loyalty to leaders who either then or later might be in a position to distribute valuable favours.

The parliamentary boroughs

The majority of MPs sat for the English boroughs, a very diverse category. Some large cities—the City of London and Liverpool, for example—returned their own members because they were ancient boroughs which had long possessed that privilege. Other places which had developed more recently into major urban areas—like Manchester, Leeds, or Birmingham—had never acquired their own MPs, but this did not mean that they were wholly unrepresented, for they contained a mass of property which could contribute a substantial bloc of votes for the surrounding county; Manchester held many Lancashire voters, and Birmingham could not be ignored in the electoral politics of Warwickshire. Owners of property worth 40s. a year were entitled to a county vote; in Yorkshire the industrial towns of the West Riding were an electoral force in county politics long before they received their own borough members.

Some of the ancient parliamentary boroughs remained important towns, such as Norwich, Newcastle, and York. On the other hand, many ancient boroughs had been reduced by economic and social change to insignificant communities, while yet retaining their electoral privileges. Not surprisingly, the majority of the old boroughs lay in those southern counties which had contained the most important areas of England before the electoral system atrophied. A majority of the 203 English borough constituencies lay in the counties fringing the south coast; the 22 counties north of the Thames–Mersey line possessed only 68 parliamentary boroughs. Thanks to this anomaly, the 2 counties of Wiltshire and Cornwall returned more MPs than the 8 northernmost counties of England. Some of the decayed boroughs have acquired a considerable notoriety, such as Old Sarum with its 7 voters qualified to return 2 MPs because of their possession of specific fields, and Dunwich, where erosion by the sea led to an electorate which never exceeded 32 in number during the last thirty years of the borough's existence. More typical were places where the decay, though real, was less complete. In Sussex the 2 boroughs of Steyning and Bramber had evolved until they formed virtually a single small country town, and it was difficult to know where one ended and the other began; the district nevertheless still returned its 4 members from the 2 ancient boroughs.

Voting rights in the borough constituencies varied haphazardly. Of the 203 parliamentary boroughs, in 59 cases the vote was conferred on the basis of 'scot and lot'—in effect the entire body of ratepayers. In a few urban constituencies, this could enfranchise virtually all of the householders; Westminster, for example, could muster some 8,000 electors. In Gatton, with a theoretically similar franchise, there were so few ratepayers that in 1831 there were only 7 electors. In another 39 boroughs the franchise was attached to specific pieces of property; if someone could acquire a majority of these burgages he was in a position to control elections there. The town council provided the electorate in 43 boroughs, the freemen of the borough in 62. Within this last group, in some boroughs the corporation could create new freemen at will, and exploit this power for electoral purposes; in others the creation of new freemen was restricted and entry might require a hereditary claim or genuine membership of a specific trade within the town. In short, there was no uniformity at all in the ways in which boroughs selected their MPs. For those who were attached to the existing pattern, this diversity and breadth of representative devices could be seen as a strength rather than a weakness.

The smaller boroughs provided ample opportunity both for the venality of limited electorates and for the ambition of men of means. By 1830, 18 of Cornwall's 28 seats had fallen into the hands of individual patrons, while in most of the remaining 10 bribery was common. At Lyme Regis in Dorset, with an electorate of fewer than 40, the Earls of Westmorland controlled the constituency, which returned members of that noble family without a single contest for the first thirty years of the century. At Reigate in Surrey, with about 60 voters, the representation was amicably shared for many years between two patrons, Lord Hardwicke and Lord Somers, each nominating one of the borough's two MPs. At traditionally venal boroughs like Grampound, voters were often open in their quest for bribes from potential members. Even in a large urban constituency, bribery could be significant; in the last by-election at Liverpool before the 1832 reforms, it was estimated that something like £100,000 had been spent in manipulating the voting of the electorate of about 4,400, with exceptionally high prices paid for the key remaining votes in a close finish.

In Scotland the 15 borough members were chosen by close corporations, while in the counties the electors were 'not even necessarily the landowners, but the possibly non-resident holders of certain feudal rights, known as "superiorities", roughly corresponding to the lordship of a manor in England'.[40] The 45 Scottish MPs were perennially firm supporters of the government largely because, while in England it was usually local patronage, influence, and financial inducements which gained votes, in Scotland the members depended on government patronage for their seats.

The Scottish electorate was small, fewer than 5,000, but the electorate of England and Wales was somewhat larger than used to be thought and was around 439,200. Previous estimates were based on the numbers who voted rather than were registered to vote.[41]

Electoral influence

Accounts of the bribery and intimidation which occurred in the electoral politics of these years can be interesting and even entertaining, but another factor was much more telling. Where bribery or simple nomination was not the decisive factor, electoral politics were determined by local considerations and local interests. The nature of the local society and economy, and the distribution of influence within them, were usually crucial in determining results. Even where an aristocratic patron did not actually control a borough, the limited electorate might sensibly choose to defer to the wishes of a neighbouring magnate capable of conferring favours on such a helpful constituency, and capable also of cutting off benefits which seemed unappreciated on polling day. Elections were a form of negotiation between local elites and between them and the electorate with even non-electors having some influence.[42]

In a society in which the greatest fortunes, and most of the country's wealth, were still to be found within the landed interest, the complex nature of borough representation meant that the aristocracy controlled a larger proportion of the House of Commons than the relatively small number of county members might suggest. If the aristocracy of the early nineteenth century was united, or largely agreed, in resisting any measure, there was no possibility of its passing in either of the two Houses. That the members of the Upper House exercised so much influence on the composition of the Commons produced a multiplicity of personal as well as political links between the two chambers, and lessened the

40. J. R. M. Butler, *The Passing of the Great Reform Bill* (1914), 175.
41. Frank O'Gorman, *Voters, Patrons and Parties: The Unreformed Electorate of Hanoverian England, 1734–1832*, 179.
42. Ibid. 384–90.

risk of disagreements between them. It was normal for the heir to a peerage to sit in the House of Commons until he inherited the family honours. The back benches of both major parties in the Commons included many sons, brothers, uncles, cousins of members of the House of Lords.

The seriousness with which elected members took their parliamentary duties varied. This was true both of attendance during parliamentary sessions, and of participation in parliamentary business. C. R. M. Talbot, who was returned by the county of Glamorgan for fifty-five years, seems never to have taken any part in any debate.[43] There were some MPs who possessed a powerful interest in politics which made them assiduous attenders; there were others for whom their parliamentary role might be only one, and that not the most interesting, of a number of commitments. For many aristocratic MPs, social engagements or sporting activities might be more compelling attractions than parliamentary debates. Party leaders always found it difficult to persuade some supporters to come to London in time for the early part of the session, or to remain there after the main social season had ended. The coming of summer beckoned less committed legislators to more beguiling country pursuits. Even when Parliament was in session, the hours of meeting were restricted. Sittings usually began at about 4 p.m., while debates which continued late into the night were rare, and resented by many MPs.

Like government, Parliament accepted a more restricted concept of its role than later generations were to acquire. Already, however, there were some developments which were making this relative detachment more difficult to maintain. The relationship between executive and legislature was involving a greater use of devices which were to lead to wider commitments in future years. The enduring tussle between ministers and Parliament about taxation and the level of public spending, for instance, led to an increase in parliamentary inquiries into such matters, and a more extended use of select committees and royal commissions. Advocates of strict official parsimony would press for searching inquiries into public expenditure. Ministers striving for parliamentary approval for controversial measures might seek to manipulate an inquiry into a source of ostensibly unbiased support. Such tactical moves paved the way for a wider use of such inquiries in years to come. There was not, however, any widespread belief that the official machinery of the State provided a suitable instrument for beneficial intervention.

Local government

Most of the local government activity of these years was carried on with little supervision by national authority. One reason was the absence of substantial

---

43. D. J. Martin, 'The Kidderminster Paving Commission, 1813–56', MA thesis, Wolverhampton Polytechnic, 1985, 35.

disagreement between those who effectively controlled the two areas of public administration. Those who were prominent in Westminster and Whitehall usually came from much the same social groups as those who controlled such machinery of local government as actually existed. In local matters, most ratepayers were as suspicious and distrustful of official spending as most taxpayers were of the efficiency and the probity of the national administration. They were, of course, very often the same people.

Throughout the United Kingdom the pattern of local government varied according to whether the district concerned was administratively part of a county or had been given the status of a borough. In any event, the distinction was not a reliable guide to the difference between rural and urban areas. Some ancient boroughs were by now places of no great importance, essentially rural in character. Some of the country's largest towns, like Manchester, Leeds, or Birmingham, had never achieved municipal status and institutions. It was not until 1848, for example, that Wolverhampton elected its first town council. In the earlier part of the century, it was not very clear just what did constitute a borough; early nineteenth-century estimates of their number varied between 250 and 350 according to the criteria chosen.[44]

The counties

For many years after 1815, the boroughs contained a minority of the population, and most people lived within the jurisdiction of the county authorities. County local government was primarily vested in the unpaid magistracy, the Justices of the Peace. The JPs possessed judicial functions, but also a varied range of administrative duties, including, for instance, supervision of the local Poor Law. At their head in each county stood the Lord Lieutenant; both for that high dignity, and for the magistracy itself, eligibility was derived from individual social position. Lords Lieutenant were drawn from the restricted category of the greatest local landowners. The honour represented at once a formal recognition of the individual's primacy within the county, and also the conferment of considerable powers of local patronage, such as the nomination of county magistrates and the granting of commissions in the local militia and yeomanry regiments. In practice, these powers were constrained by conventional guidelines, which conferred upon certain groups in county society a prescriptive right to the magistracy. To those who are acquainted with the concept of *auctoritas* in republican Rome the situation will have its parallels.

Personal standing was a prerequisite and a qualification for enrolment in a county's magistracy. Members of the aristocracy, the leading gentry, and prominent Anglican clergymen were the principal sources of county magistrates. A survey in early-Victorian times disclosed a pattern which cannot have been

44. J. West, *Town Records* (1983), 166.

very different earlier in the century. In a large sample of fifty counties, landowners provided 86.5 per cent of the JPs, with Anglican clergymen contributing a further 13.4 per cent.[45] Even in the Black Country with its important industrial elements, a recent study found that in the early nineteenth century three-quarters of the local magistrates were drawn from the landowners and clergy.[46]

The exclusive nature of the county magistracy was enshrined in tradition, and also in legal restrictions. An Act of 1744 prescribed a minimum qualification for the county bench of ownership of land worth at least £100 per annum.[47] Appointments were formally made by the Lord Chancellor on the nomination of the Lord Lieutenant. The Lord Lieutenant of Flintshire from 1802 to 1845 was Earl Grosvenor, widely regarded as an enlightened member of the aristocracy. Between 1802 and 1830 he made forty-three nominations to the county magistracy. Nearly half of them were landowners, and well over a third clergymen. Only one of them had a close involvement with manufacturing, although the county's industrial interests were expanding during these years.[48] Nationally accepted conventions governing eligibility for the magistracy were sometimes supplemented by long-standing local conventions which effectively excluded certain categories from consideration. Catholic emancipation enabled a hitherto disbarred religious category to become magistrates but the new Catholic county justices were normally landowners with similar social positions to their Anglican colleagues.

Appointment to the county magistracy represented a formal official recognition of an individual's local importance, but this did not mean that all JPs played an important role in the government of the county. In practice, a minority of the magistrates shouldered the main burden of county administration; contemporary usage often referred to this group as the county's 'acting' magistrates, using that word in the sense of 'active' rather than the more modern sense of 'provisional'. The county's administrative work was centred in Quarter Sessions; lists of attendance at these meetings commonly show that only a minority of interested magistrates took part in these proceedings. These 'acting' JPs dominated both the administrative and the judicial work of the Court of Quarter Sessions; the majority of the county's magistrates would either not attend at all or do so only sporadically.

Many more magistrates were active on their own local stage where, at a time of limited education and limited communications, they provided the main repository of official power. Both as judges at Petty Sessions and in such administrative functions as their supervision of the local Poor Law, magistrates were the key

45. C. H. E. Zangerl, 'The social composition of the county magistracy in England and Wales, 1831–1887', *Journal of British Studies*, vol. 11, no. 1 (1971), 113–25.

46. D. Philips, 'The Black Country magistracy, 1835–60: a changing local elite and the exercise of its power', *Midland History*, 3 (1976), 161–90.

47. 18 Geo. II, c. 20. An alternative qualification was an immediate reversionary claim to land worth £300 p.a.

48. P. F. Nolan, 'The Flintshire magistracy, 1830–1870', MA thesis, Wolverhampton Polytechnic, 1985, 33–5.

element in the limited range of local government activity. It was often unclear whether an individual JP acting in local affairs did so as a magistrate or because of the informal influence arising from his personal status within the local community. Some county magistrates, like some MPs, became enthusiasts, either devoting themselves to county administration generally or fastening on some particular aspects of it which fired their interest. For example, prison reform in the early nineteenth century owed much to the work of a group of enthusiastic county magistrates which included James Neild of Buckinghamshire and Sir George Onesiphorus Paul of Gloucestershire.[49]

The key group of magistrates who formed the regular Court of Quarter Sessions was responsible for levying the county rate to meet the cost of shire government, which could include the building, maintenance, and repair of roads and bridges, the conduct of trials, the maintenance of law and order, the construction and maintenance of prisons and asylums. In this work they were subject to little interference from central government. The magistracy also exercised the patronage of the county over a range of minor local government posts. By contemporary standards, this was an important part of their work; the need to ensure that this patronage rested in the hands of men whose personal position raised them above the temptations of petty corruption was an argument often adduced in favour of the exclusive nature of the magistracy. Magistrates received no formal training and no payment for their services, but to be included in their select ranks was to occupy an important position in local society.

The municipal boroughs

In the boroughs the pattern and quality of local government varied widely. Its form depended largely on the terms of individual charters of the medieval or early modern periods. Usually, town government was firmly in the hands of an oligarchy of 'principal inhabitants'. There were some instances of serious abuse and corruption, as in the case of Joseph Merceron, who was a kind of 'town boss' of Bethnal Green for many years in the late eighteenth and early nineteenth centuries.[50] Inaction or inefficiency were more frequent than corruption; as the Webbs put it, 'the complaint was not so much that the Corporations performed the Municipal functions badly, as that they did not, in the great majority of cases, perform them at all.'[51] Newcastle upon Tyne was an old borough with a cumbrous constitution theoretically working through the old town guilds; in practice, local power rested with a group of leading local families, and a modern verdict is that 'It was highly oligarchical but, though its accounting system was not such as would satisfy a District Auditor today, its members do not appear to have been seriously corrupt by the standards of their day or very seriously at fault

49. *ODNB.*   50. K. B. Smellie, *A History of Local Government*, (1946), 15.
51. Quoted by Martin, 'The Kidderminster Paving Commission', 2.

by ours.'[52] This was a reasonably typical situation in the old boroughs, though there were enough examples of worse practice to provide ammunition for radical advocates of municipal reform.

The burgh was central to Scottish local government and in the eighteenth century there were supposedly some 300 of them, though some were small and inactive. Royal burghs were the most powerful while free burghs held special trading privileges. Burgh councils were, even more than their English counterparts, in the hands of urban oligarchies.

In the early nineteenth century, as later, many borough councils were faced with an influential body of ratepayers who kept a watchful eye on municipal spending. The main reason why the police resources of the towns in these years were so defective was that to provide an effective police would involve a rise in official spending which would all have to come from the local rates. In addition, the actual experiences of towns which had created modest police forces, often financed on a shoestring, did nothing to persuade other ratepayers that municipal policing at their expense was an effective agency which ought to be encouraged and imitated. Of the 46 nightwatchmen employed at a tiny wage in Kidderminster during the twelve years after 1823, half were dismissed: 11 for drunkenness, 2 for inefficiency, 2 for disobedience, 2 for misconduct, 1 for theft, and 5 for unknown causes.[53]

Improvement commissions

Faced with the limited effectiveness of many established borough councils, and the absence of municipal institutions in newer urban areas, a growing number of communities resorted to another local government device, the statutory improvement commission. More than 450 local Acts of Parliament for this purpose were obtained between 1800 and 1840. The patchwork nature of this development meant that the local improvement commissions exhibited as much variety as the boroughs which they supplemented. Some of them had commissioners elected by the local ratepayers, sometimes for life, others had the first commissioners named in the original local Act, with provision for filling future vacancies by co-option. The usual pattern gave the commission limited rate-raising powers to be employed on a stipulated range of activities, which might include road or bridge building and maintenance, power to regulate new buildings, flood control measures, providing sewers or a water supply, street lighting, scavenging, or the creation of some kind of police force.[54]

The membership of local commissions reflected the pattern of social and economic leadership in local society, and the day-to-day management of affairs was

52. W. L. Burn, 'Newcastle upon Tyne in the early nineteenth century', *Archaeologia Aeliana*, 4th ser., 34, (1956), 3.

53. Martin, 'The Kidderminster Paving Commission', 41.

54. West, *Town Records*, ch. 8.

usually left to an active minority of commissioners. The creation of a commission was invariably the result of local initiative, rather than any intervention by central government or Parliament. Local oligarchies exploited the legislative supremacy of Parliament to obtain the establishment under their own control of a form of local government capable of carrying out any local improvements which they thought necessary and practicable. The efficiency and energy of the improvement commissions varied from time to time and from place to place; a recent verdict on a typical example is that 'It was a valuable stage in the evolution of local government; whilst oligarchical in character, its members were public spirited.'[55]

Whether in municipality or in improvement commission, local government in the towns had much in common with official life elsewhere. Formal public authority reflected patterns of social and economic influence derived from unofficial status within the community. Patronage was a major preoccupation, with the conferment of jobs and the awarding of contracts often more controversial and divisive than any policy issues. The links between formal and informal influences were close, in urban government as in the county magistracy. At Exeter, for example, the town authorities were perfectly willing to use the municipal gaol as a device to buttress family discipline:

William Ebbes, an idle and disorderly boy, was sent here by the Mayor at the desire of his parents for a month in solitary confinement ... J. Taylow brought a boy named Hendry at the desire of his parents and by leave of the Mayor and aldermen ... to be flogged with the birch ... John Moore privately whipped at the desire of his mother.[56]

The Poor Law

One function of local government—and only one—covered the whole of England and Wales in reasonably systematic form. This was provision for the poor through the Poor Law. It did not exist in Scotland in anything like the same formal shape until much later in the century. Until 1834, and to some extent until 1930, the Poor Law system was based on legislation at the end of Elizabeth I's reign. This stipulated that in each parish a local tax was to be raised from the occupiers of property, from which local expenditure on the poor was to be met. An assessment was made of the value of the different properties in the district; the amount of money needed for Poor Law purposes was calculated annually, and this total was then levied as a proportion of these assessments, at a rate of a fixed sum for each pound. This rate income was to be used, through the agency of an unpaid annual parish officer, the overseer of the poor, in caring for the impotent poor, setting the able-bodied poor to productive work, and taking punitive action against the idle and disorderly. In the north of England, where

55. Martin, 'The Kidderminster Paving Commission', p. v.
56. W. J. Forsythe, *A System of Discipline: Exeter Borough Prison, 1819–1863* (1983), 40–1.

parishes were often very large and thinly populated, an Act of 1662 empowered individual townships within a parish to operate their own Poor Law arrangements.[57] In Lancashire, this led by the early nineteenth century to the existence of nearly 500 Poor Law units, even though the county possessed only 69 parishes.[58] Not surprisingly, in the absence of any effective supervision of local Poor Law administration by national authority, local practices developed great diversity.

This diversity was reflected in differences in the level of the rates and in the adaptation of relief practices to local conditions. Within a single county, and even over much smaller areas, there were variations as local experiences had evolved over many generations. Within Lancashire, the level of poor rates in neighbouring villages could vary from 10½*d.* to 6*s.* in the pound in the early nineteenth century; expenditure per head of population might amount to 2*s.* 1*d.* in one community, but reach 17*s.* 2*d.* in another village a little distance away.[59] In the 1820s the poorhouses of two adjacent parishes in Newcastle upon Tyne were described very differently; at St Nicholas's the poorhouse 'certainly possesses few attractions, even for those who are steeped in poverty and acquainted with misfortune', while at All Saints' 'The food is of the best, and those who prefer it may have good table-beer at supper instead of milk.'[60]

It is probable that in most places the Poor Law was administered with a reasonable level of competence by contemporary standards. Overseers whose incompetence, cruelty, or corruption caused scandal and suffering were probably less common than those who adequately discharged the duties laid on them, though understandably the former group stands more prominently in the historical record of these years.[61] Given the modest level of administrative attainments displayed by the full-time salaried officials of central government, high standards of competence among overseers were scarcely to be expected.

A recurring source of difficulty in Poor Law administration lay in the fact that hard times in a given district could produce soaring demands on the poor rates and at the same time adversely affect the finances of many ratepayers. Such circumstances were the usual cause of the sporadic campaigns for economy in expenditure which punctuated the history of poor relief in many communities. At Gateshead, for instance, the poor rates rose from £568 in 1780 to £4,500 in 1820. The predictable result was a special meeting of the parish vestry which

57. 14 Cha. II, c. 12. A short account of the working of the pre-1834 Poor Law is given in J. D. Marshall, *The Old Poor Law, 1795–1834* (1968) (Historical Association pamphlet). Fuller accounts are given in G. W. Oxley, *Poor Relief in England and Wales, 1601–1834* (1974) and M. E. Rose, *The English Poor Law, 1780–1930* (1971), Pt. 1.

58. E. C. Midwinter, *Social Administration in Lancashire, 1830–1860: Poor Law, Public Health, and Police* (1969), 16.

59. Ibid. 11.

60. N. McCord, *North East England: The Region's Development, 1760–1960* (1979), 88.

61. Oxley, *Poor Relief in England and Wales*, 44.

resolved that 'on account of the enormous increase of the expenditure of the Parish it is highly expedient that a system of strict economy be appointed in the disposition of the funds, and particularly in the relief of the poor.'[62]

In the summer of 1821 stringent new rules for poor relief were duly adopted by this parish, and in 1822 expenditure dropped to £3,040, 'partly owing to the strict investigation which takes place previous to granting any relief, which, while it does not prevent those from applying who are really the objects of parochial aid, prevents applications from the idle and profligate, whose wants principally arise from their own indolence and improvident habits'. Able-bodied male applicants were now obliged to perform a task of stone-breaking in return for relief payments; this was said to have greatly reduced the number of applications.

At neighbouring Sunderland, a similar reaction included a public invitation from the parish authorities to ratepayers 'to send them the names of paupers having means not disclosed, but they need not sign their own names'. In addition the parish published a printed list of the recipients of poor relief, 'with the object of awakening a decent and becoming pride, to stimulate industry ... in opposition to a lazy and despicable habit—that of existing on the industry of more provident neighbours'.[63]

Such sentiments were widespread, and could be shared by many who were by prevailing standards unquestionably radical in their political views. The distinguished engraver, Thomas Bewick, certainly came into that category, but his views on this matter were trenchant enough:

All men ought to provide for the necessities of old age, & be made sensible of the manly pleasures of being independent—it is degrading and in most cases disgraceful to those who look for parish assistance after a life spent in laziness & mismanagement ... if savings banks and benefit societies were encouraged by every possible means, there would be little occasion for poor Laws, except as a provision for helpless children & the lame & the blind—By such means as these, perhaps this national evil might be done away.[64]

Although in most cases the pattern of poor relief reflected the local adaptation of the Elizabethan legislation over time, there were two innovations which affected practices in some areas. Both measures were the work of interested MPs, rather than considered proposals by central government. Gilbert's Act of 1782 provided that parishes which chose to do so might combine in unions which could provide larger and hopefully more efficient administrative units; for example, such a union could provide one large residential institution for the poor instead of a multiplicity of small parish poorhouses. These optional provisions, foreshadowing the major changes of 1834, were adopted by only a minority of parishes—fewer than 1,000 of the 15,000 or so which existed. Gilbert's Act itself was not original in this matter, for some areas had already introduced

62. McCord, *North East England: The Region's Development*, 89.
63. Ibid. 90.   64. T. Bewick, *A Memoir Written by Himself*, ed. I. Bain (1975), 3.

similar unions of parishes by procuring local Acts of Parliament for that purpose. In East Anglia, eight unions had been formed in this way in 1764–6; Lancashire, Cheshire, Derbyshire, Nottinghamshire, and the West Riding of Yorkshire were among other areas which saw the partial adoption of Poor Law unions long before the general changes of 1834.[65]

The Sturges Bourne Act of 1819 allowed parishes to entrust the management of their Poor Law responsibilities to a standing committee of substantial local ratepayers, known as a select vestry. It also legalized a practice which had already been adopted in many communities where the volume of Poor Law business had outstripped the capacity of an amateur annual unpaid overseer. The legal responsibility attached to the time-hallowed parish overseer remained, but parishes might now appoint a paid assistant overseer to carry out the routine Poor Law work. It would be a mistake to see in this growing body of paid assistant overseers a corps of professional Poor Law officers; for most of them this was only a part-time job, held in addition to other employment.

In a few areas Poor Law administration was exceptionally sophisticated by the early nineteenth century. In Manchester, for instance, the growing population and the growing volume of Poor Law business had led to a series of local Acts regulating the system. This had led to the establishment of a carefully planned system of committees supervising as many as eighty-two paid staff.[66] This was exceptional, and Poor Law administration over most of the country was carried on in a much simpler fashion, operated by amateur unpaid officials and tailored to the needs of the particular community concerned. In small communities, where there were few applicants for relief, the cost might be met by an informal local collection among local farmers rather than go to the trouble of levying a formal rate.

Much the most common form of poor relief was a small pension granted to the aged or infirm poor, the out-relief system. It was also a frequent practice for occasional grants in kind of food, clothing, medicine, or household equipment to be given when needed. Some areas, but by no means all, had developed formal scales for the supplementation of inadequate wages by payments from the poor rates; the most famous of these, but neither the earliest nor the most widespread, was the Speenhamland plan adopted by Berkshire magistrates in 1795. Such schemes were designed to cope with social problems in hard times, by establishing a scale of subsidies from the rates in aid of low wages, with the amount granted varying according to the price of bread and the size of the families involved.

Many other schemes were tried from time to time on a local basis. Some parishes paid for unemployed workers to emigrate, others operated workhouses in which paupers actually did work, perhaps in handloom weaving or some such

---

65. A. Digby, *Pauper Palaces* (1978), ch. 3, describes these developments in East Anglia.
66. Rose, *The English Poor Law*, 64–7.

trade, producing goods which were then sold to reduce the burden of the poor rates. Overall, the Poor Law by the early nineteenth century exhibited an untidy and haphazard range of expedients. No doubt these were often well matched to specific local needs, but the system was increasingly the focus of criticisms, as the cost of poor relief continued to mount, reaching a national peak of nearly £9 million in 1818–19.[67]

These attacks came from a variety of sources. The apparent untidiness and confusion in relief practices seemed inefficient to those who found in the developing study of political economy the germ of a 'scientific' response to social problems. Disciples of Jeremy Bentham and Thomas Malthus came to believe that the existing Poor Law might be doing more harm than good, even to its ostensible beneficiaries. Schemes like the Speenhamland system might encourage the payment of low wages and even the production of larger families by the poor, leading to population growth outstripping the means of subsistence. In the early years of the century there was no certainty that continuing economic growth could supply the means to support a larger population. Moreover, 'indiscriminate giving' encouraged idleness and improvidence, qualities obviously inimical to the poor themselves.

Malthusian fears of over-population and Benthamite belief in scientific responses to social problems were not the only sources of hostility to the old Poor Law. Many ratepayers facing mounting rate demands for poor relief purposes could find simpler and more obvious motives for changes in the system. These varied pressures were not to come to fruition until 1834, but the major changes of that year were foreshadowed both by many local efforts to reform and tighten up Poor Law administration, and by repeated parliamentary inquiries into the working of the system; after all, the members of both Houses of Parliament were ratepayers as well as taxpayers.

Many people in early nineteenth-century Britain believed that they were the victims of a wholly excessive burden of central and local government, marked by official wastefulness and extravagance, if not positive corruption. These views were held by many taxpayers and ratepayers, and shared by most of the radical political activists of these years, who understandably had little confidence in the power for good of the contemporary State and its officials. A typical example of the radical propaganda of the early post-war years complained of 'the people all tatter'd and torn; who curse the day wherein they were born; On account of Taxation too great to be borne'.[68] One of the principal motives underlying campaigns for parliamentary reform in the early nineteenth century was the belief that a reformed House of Commons would be more effective in checking government extravagance at the taxpayers' expense.

67. Ibid. 40–1.
68. E. J. Evans, *The Forging of the Modern State: Early Industrial Britain, 1783–1870* (1983), 186, quoting from 'The political house that Jack built', published by the militant radical William Hone in 1819.

In reality the sum total of official activities did not impinge very much upon the lives of the majority of the British people. Compared with what was to come in later generations, the governments which held office in the years after 1815 possessed only relatively rudimentary resources. Nor was there any popular perception that official administrative machinery provided a trustworthy and efficient means by which beneficial improvement might be effected. The basis for the growth of the modern State was still only dimly discernible.

3

Economy and society

c.1815–1830

In some ways the year 1815 marked a clear break, especially as the end of the long war. From other points of view, the year fell within continuing processes of change which were far from complete. Among these prolonged developments were the growth in population and the changes in its distribution, the economic shift traditionally summarized as the Industrial Revolution, and developments in science and technology, in architecture and the arts. We can look back at these with a fuller knowledge than could possibly have been available to those living through them. Changes which puzzled or alarmed contemporaries can be better understood in a longer perspective. We can view the unprecedented and unforeseeable growth of the population of the United Kingdom from about 16 millions in 1801 to over 41 millions in 1901 with an equanimity denied to contemporaries, and especially to those whose position entailed responsibility for the support and welfare of this fast-growing population.

Population

The extent of the population growth, and the potential problems which it posed, had only become clear a few years before 1815. The first national census, held in 1801, did much to resolve doubts about broad movements in population, however imperfect its procedures (see pp. 53–4 above).[1] It suggested that the population of England and Wales had grown by about a million in the last decades of the eighteenth century. Successive censuses provided surer ground, with the population of the United Kingdom calculated as over 18 millions in 1811, nearly 21 millions in 1821, and over 24 millions in 1831. As Table 1 shows, it was now clear that population growth was accelerating, and that Ireland, with its overwhelmingly rural population, was experiencing an increase similar to that of Great Britain.

1. D. V. Glass, *Numbering the People* (1973), 91, 97. A general guide to the census is *Census of Great Britain, 1801–1931*, published as *Guide to Official Sources No. 2* by the Interdepartmental Committee on Social and Economic Research (1951). For a recent study of much population material, N. L. Tranter, *Population and Society, 1750–1940* (1985). For Ireland, K. H. Connell, *The Population of Ireland, 1750–1845* (1950).

Table 1 Population of the United Kingdom, 1801–1831 (millions)

	1801	1811	1821	1831
England and Wales	9.0	10.2	12.0	13.9
Scotland	1.6	1.8	2.1	2.4
Ireland	5.2[a]	5.9[a]	6.8	7.8
TOTAL	15.8	17.9	20.9	24.1

[a] These are estimates, as the first full Irish census was not attempted until 1821.

The causes of this increase have been much debated. There now seems substantial agreement that the main ones were a reduction in the average age of marriage, an increase in the proportion of the population marrying, and an increase in the average number of children per marriage, associated with the earlier marriage age. More births from younger mothers probably resulted in a higher rate of survival. One of the most influential contemporary writers on population, Malthus, believed that postponement of marriage would be effective in reducing the rate of population growth.[2] Modern population experts have concluded that he was probably right in thinking that marriage patterns in western Europe did much to maintain a balance between the numbers of the population and their means of support before higher rates of aggregate economic growth enabled earlier marriages without falls in real incomes.[3] Malthus made an intelligent analysis of the possibilities of population growth within the constraints that had limited growth in pre-industrial economies but, like most commentators, failed to appreciate the degree to which such constraints no longer applied. Improvements in agricultural productivity had already by the late eighteenth century led to a considerable increase in population, a growing proportion of which was not engaged in agriculture, while developments in services and communications had improved food supplies. Population growth in Ireland owed something to a dietary change, the increase in potato cultivation and consumption; an increased dependence on a single crop could be dangerous, as the partial famines in 1817–18 and 1822 demonstrated.

By 1815 it was also clear that there were changes under way in the distribution of this expanding population, although their extent in the years around 1815 should not be exaggerated. The 1851 census was the first which showed a majority living in towns, and even then many of these were small rural market towns rather than industrial centres. Earlier in the century most towns remained small. The 1821 census credited Cardiff with a population of about 4,000 and the great northern city of York with less than 30,000. In 1831 the three biggest towns in

2. P. Mathias, *The First Industrial Nation*, 2nd edn. (1983), 166–7.
3. E. A. Wrigley, 'The means to marry: population and economy in pre-industrial England', *Quarterly Journal of Social Affairs*, I (1985).

Table 2 Population of major industrial towns, 1801–1831 (thousands)

	1801	1811	1821	1831
Birmingham	71	83	102	144
Blackburn	12	15	22	27
Bradford	13	16	26	44
Glasgow	77	101	147	202
Liverpool	82	104	138	202
Manchester	75	89	126	182
Merthyr Tydfil	8	11	17	22

Bedfordshire—Bedford, Luton, and Leighton Buzzard—mustered only 14,000 between them.[4] In 1821 a substantial majority on the greatest coalfield, that of Northumberland and Durham, lived in communities of less than 2,000 people.[5] The 1831 census showed that not much more than a third of the population lived in towns of any kind.

Small localized communities possessed a greater intimacy and cohesion than the urban society of later years. Within them, individual privacy was—as it always had been—the prerogative of a wealthy minority, and social pressures limited individual freedom. Interdependence within families or small local groups—between people who knew each other—was normal. Local affairs and local interests mattered more than broader considerations affecting the nation or the wider world beyond. This local outlook naturally existed in old established and stable village communities, but it was not confined to them. A study of a squatter settlement on the Shropshire coalfield has shown how continuity of occupancy and intermarriage between local families rapidly became normal even in an industrial hamlet.[6]

Although this scattered and decentralized population distribution, with its local preoccupations, remained typical, the exceptions were increasing. As early as 1780, in his *Essay on the Population of England*, Dr Richard Price had noted that it was 'allowed on all hands, that the principal manufacturing and trading towns have increased, and some of them, as Manchester, Leeds, Birmingham, Sheffield, Liverpool, and Bristol, most amazingly'. Price died in 1791, but if he had survived much into the next century his cause for amazement would have been even greater, as Table 2 suggests.[7]

4. J. H. Clapham, *An Economic History of Modern Britain: The Early Railway Age, 1820–1850* (1930), 66n.
5. N. McCord and D. J. Rowe, 'Industrialization and urban growth in north-east England', *International Review of Social History*, 22 (1977), 31.
6. K. Jones, M. Hunt, J. Malan, and B. Trinder, 'Holywell Lane: a squatter community in the Shropshire coalfield', *Industrial Archaeology Review*, 6 (1982), 163–4.
7. E. J. Evans, *The Forging of the Modern State* (1983), 407–8, gives a selection of population figures for various types of town, as well as a convenient range of other statistics.

Major industrial and commercial centres were outstripping the national rates of increase. In the first half of the nineteenth century the United Kingdom population grew by about 73 per cent. A representative group of old county towns and watering places grew by 139 per cent, a group of ports by 214 per cent, and a group of textile-manufacturing centres by almost 300 per cent.

It was the size and speed of growth of manufacturing towns that most impressed contemporaries but Edinburgh demonstrates how a town that was a centre for administration, law, financial services, and religion with a number of light industries, mostly conducted on a small scale, could flourish. The population of Edinburgh and Leith grew from 83,000 in 1801 to 162,000 in 1831. The Scottish capital was, nevertheless, outstripped by Glasgow. For long important for its overseas trade, Glasgow had already become a manufacturing centre during the eighteenth century with linen and then cotton as its basis. As Table 2 demonstrates, the city's population grew even faster than those of Manchester and Liverpool.

Even the provincial manufacturing centres were small in comparison with London, the most prodigious instance of urban growth. Its population was well over a million by 1801, and almost doubled by 1831. As well as being the national capital, London was a social and economic centre; it was one of the world's greatest ports, employing an army of waterfront labour, and also had a concentration of industry. Some of the city's enterprises were in the forefront of mechanization, as in the use of steam power in the great metropolitan breweries. London workshops were a nursery of advanced technology, in, for example, the development of lathes and other machine tools by engineers like Maudslay and Bramah. Some London factories and shipyards were large for those years, and by the 1820s the building contractor Thomas Cubitt was employing more than a thousand workers from his headquarters in Gray's Inn Road.

Yet of the 16,500 industrial enterprises listed in the *London Directory* of 1837, the overwhelming majority were much smaller than this, as were most of the commercial undertakings which employed the thousands of London clerical workers.[8] The enumerators for the 1831 census found 400 different kinds of London workman whom they preferred to assign to 'Trades and Handicrafts' rather than 'Manufactures'. The small workshop, office, or shop was a pervasive feature of this great city, which in 1831 held more than a tenth of the country's population. Employment in London covered a kaleidoscopic variety of callings and conditions. It included many domestic servants, many casually employed porters, dockers, and labourers, and also some of the country's most highly paid workmen, whether in the luxury trades, such as fashionable cabinet-making, or among the exceptionally skilled men of the advanced engineering workshops.

No other city could rival London in size or in the variety of its enterprises. Yet all industrial towns were similarly dominated by small units. Even in the

8. R. M. Reeve, *The Industrial Revolution, 1750–1850* (1971), 105.

expanding manufacturing centres, the factory employing 500 or 1,000 was still unusual. In Manchester and Leeds most workers were employed in smaller concerns. Much industrial activity was carried on in industrial villages or hamlets. Water power was still more important than steam power, and older towns were not always well placed for this. Mining, whether for coal or other minerals, was often carried on in areas remote from towns.

British society was, then, neither predominantly urban nor industrial, but it was experiencing accelerating population increase. In his novel *Sybil* Disraeli expressed the situation graphically:

I speak of the annual arrival of more than three hundred thousand strangers in this island. How will you feed them? How will you clothe them? Why, go to your history... and see the fall of the great Roman Empire—what was that?...What are your invasions of the barbarous nations, your Goths and Visigoths, your Lombards and Huns, to our Population Returns?

National identity

Britain was becoming more English at least in numerical terms for, although the population in general was increasing, that of England was increasing faster. The same was not true of the United Kingdom as the Irish population was increasing at an astonishing rate, 50 per cent in thirty years.

Census returns tell us about the geographic spread of the population but not about identity. Britain was experiencing considerable internal migration and it is impossible to estimate how many generations it took for Welsh or Scottish migrants to England or English migrants to Wales to shake off one form of identity and take on another. Nevertheless, geographic mobility must, along with a more national, in the sense of British, economy and more rapid communications, have added to a growing sense of 'Britishness', though the word itself appears to have only come into use later in the nineteenth century.[9]

The development of a common British identity in the late eighteenth century had been assisted by economic growth and the opportunities afforded by the Empire together with the cohesive effects of facing common enemies, particularly France, a Catholic and then a revolutionary power. Eventual success in 1815 after decades of war with France consolidated this process.[10] The great size of the armed forces was in itself a factor. By 1815 about half a million men were serving in the army and navy and another 400,000 in the Volunteers. The 1813 inspection returns demonstrated that the army had become one half English, one third Irish, and one sixth Scottish and that in the officer corps Scots and Irish were the majority. 'Armed service did much to dissolve national loyalties.'[11]

There were, however, other developments which encouraged, not just the perseverance of other national identities but reinterpreted them. The growth of

9. Paul Langford, *Englishness Identified: Manners and Character 1650–1850* (2000), 13.
10. Linda Colley, *Britons*, 7.   11. Frank O'Gorman, *The Long Eighteenth Century*, 310.

literacy and the expansion of print made possible what have been called 'imagined communities' and played a great part in the growth of nineteenth-century nationalisms. When it came to national identity in Britain, their impact cut both ways: they could accelerate a common British identity or reinforce, to some extent reinvent, Scottish or Welsh identities. Newspapers and journals catering for the well-educated and those catering for a popular audience were able to attain national circulations, while novels and non-fiction increasingly published in London and Edinburgh had a readership throughout Britain. The influence of romanticism transmitted via the printed word found in Britain as elsewhere a readership interested in the past glories of nations and even regions. The result was a relatively easy accommodation of multiple identities and even a sense that differences could enhance an essential unity. The monarchy could lay claim to all constituent parts, while easier travel meant that monarchs could for the first time burnish associations with visits; George IV's visits to Dublin and Edinburgh were early indications of this. The Hanoverian dynasty found it convenient to emphasize its Stuart blood in the interests of the link with Scotland, despite the fact that such an association would have horrified its dominant Scottish supporters a half century earlier, but now the Stuarts were no longer a threat and had become a romance.

Early nineteenth-century Scotland portrayed many paradoxes and, indeed, the strands that were to make for a Scottish identity, whether separate from or within a British identity, were and were to remain contradictory. As well as the strange acceptance of Highland dress and Celtic pageantry as national by Lowland Scots, there was the legacy of the eighteenth-century Enlightenment, a mode of thought which emphasized reason and often led to deism if not to atheism; this secularization of Calvinist energy had led to Edinburgh becoming as much the intellectual centre of Britain as London and a publishing centre for books and intellectual journals such as the *Edinburgh Review* and the *Quarterly Review*. Along with this went a lifestyle for the elite of debating and dining clubs, sophisticated conversation, and good claret. Rather different was the way in which Scotland could almost be seen as a Presbyterian theocracy with local government and education dominated by the Kirk. Neither the rationalist philosophical outlook nor Calvinism presided easily over the developing industrial areas of Scotland concentrated in a narrow central belt with its rich coalfield between the rivers Forth and Clyde. Industrial Scotland failed to fulfil the aims of those of the '*literati* of the "Enlightenment" [who] had wanted to promote a balanced social development based on agriculture and rural industries'[12] and was a scarcely suitable context for a godly society. The beginning of large-scale Irish immigration brought new problems for Scottish identity including an increasing Catholic population. Perhaps one should say Scotch rather than Scottish identity for the former term passed only gradually into abeyance. Lord Cockburn, Whig

---

12. Christopher Harvie, *Scotland: A Short History* (2002), 157.

Solicitor General, wrote: 'Scots is the affected pronunciation and spelling of a paltry, lisping, puppy Englishman. A good Caledonian calls himself a Skotchman.'[13]

National consciousness and language are usually seen as closely associated. The great majority of Welsh people spoke Welsh at the beginning of the nineteenth century though a great many of this majority spoke English as well. In Scotland, by contrast, Gaelic was only just surviving in outlying areas. The reasons for this are fundamental. Welsh had been the language of the Welsh, while Gaelic was probably never the language of the majority in Scotland. Lowland Scots may have relished adopting Highland dress for high days and holidays but drew the line at learning more than a few words of Gaelic. Yet, despite the language factor, Scots had a much clearer sense of national identity than the Welsh.

Scotland had been a separate state under a different monarch to England's until 1603 and a separate state under the same monarch until the Act of Union of 1706–7, while after the union it retained separate institutions and laws. Wales had been securely united with England since 1536 and in contrast to Scotland, which retained its own legal system and institutions, was in legal and governmental terms at one with England.

The Romantic Movement led to a search for the Welsh past, which was at first largely pursued by the Welsh gentry. A largely mythical world of bards and druids was discovered that was entirely compatible with Britishness for, after all, the Welsh could claim to be the true Britons. What was far from foreseeable was the way that a further development, the rise of nonconformity in Wales, would lead to a welding together of disparate strands of historicism, language, and salvationism into a new national ethos.

Until after the mid-eighteenth century, the religion of the majority in Wales had been that of the Anglican Church of Wales and its clergy had been prominent in the revival and invention of Welsh traditions. By the 1820s, the old dissent of Congregationalists and Baptists had revived and that peculiarly Welsh denomination, the Calvinist Methodists, had attracted numerous adherents in rural areas with the result that, in contrast with England, nonconformity was rapidly becoming the religion of the majority. The growth of nonconformity did not at first seem to imply an association with Welsh identity and, indeed, the lack of sympathy of pastors with old rural customs, such as well-dressing or other rites connected with the desire to encourage fertility, suggested that Welsh nonconformity was more inclined to eradicate cultural difference, even including the Welsh language, than support it. But Welsh nonconformity was a popular movement and found it necessary to create a sense of Welshness that included reformed bards, teetotalism, support for the language, and a protestant version of Welsh history. As yet, however, Welsh national consciousness was apolitical.

A largely agrarian economy and society at the beginning of the nineteenth century, Wales industrialized later than Scotland. The industrial economy was

13. Alan Bell (ed.), *Lord Cockburn: Selected Letters*, 7.

also narrower than that of England or Scotland, being largely based on iron and coal. To some extent this widened the divide between rural north and industrializing south Wales, but at the same time, while many north Welshman made their way to Liverpool or the Midlands in search of employment, others were attracted to the burgeoning economies of Glamorgan and Monmouth, though the latter was at the time an English county. At this stage, population movement posed little threat to the Welsh language and even strengthened it as immigrants from the north brought the language with them.

The English, the most powerful nation, found it easiest to come to terms with Britain, seeing it largely as a greater England, but more difficult to define 'Englishness', though the negative 'un-English' was easier and had been in use since the seventeenth century.[14] Scots, however inaccurately, could just about manage to persuade themselves that they were all Celts and the tartan their common heritage, while the Welsh had a language, still spoken by the majority of the population and not shared with the island as a whole, and were beginning the hunt for the Welsh past.[15] The English had several disadvantages, no national dress, invented or extant, and an early history of being successively conquered with obvious implications for any claim to racial distinctiveness but, as the largest and dominant nation, they could claim success and put it down to character, which is by and large what they did.

Economic growth

Few historians now use, without qualification, the once popular term 'Industrial Revolution' though as one authority has concluded, 'The term is so deeply embedded in both popular and academic usage that it may be too much to hope that it will be superseded.'[16] Most continue to use the term 'Industrialization' emphasizing a gradual process rather than a sudden leap. Older views gave pride of place to a series of great inventions and inventors by which steam power and factory systems transformed productive capacity and led to an industrial revolution starting with the cotton industry. The highly influential work of the American economic historian, Walt Rostow, retained the concept of a short period of rapid change in the economy beginning in the 1780s but placed the emphasis upon economic growth rather than new methods of production. Drawing upon the analogy of the aeroplane on the runway, he wrote of the British economy 'taking off' and achieving the feat of sustained economic growth. Cotton was the lead sector but it stimulated other sectors of the economy and by the 1830s the first stage of industrialization was complete.[17] More attention was perhaps paid to Rostow's

---

14. Langford, 13.
15. Prys Morgan, 'From a Death to a View: The Hunt for the Welsh Past in the Romantic Period', in Eric Hobsbawm and Terence Ranger (eds.), *The Invention of Tradition* (1983), 43–100.
16. E. A. Wrigley, *People, Cities and Wealth* (1987), 2.
17. W. Rostow, *The Stages of Economic Growth* (1960).

reinforcement of the 'Industrial Revolution' and the spectacularly short period (1783–1802) in which he thought 'take off' occurred than to the long trundle along the runway which provided the thrust for it. More recently some historians have questioned the whole idea of an industrial revolution with its emphasis upon factory systems and steam power, pointing to the facts that only a minority of cotton mills were worked by steam power as late as the 1830s while in most manufacturing centres small workshops rather than large factories remained the norm.[18]

It is clear that a spectacular change came over the British economy but less clear that it was rapid or confined to the period after 1780. The vigour of the seventeenth- and early eighteenth-century commercial and manufacturing economies together with the strength of the non-industrialized sectors of the mid-nineteenth century economy point to a long process rather than a sudden leap as characterizing the economic change. Probably the main determinant of economic growth is the strength of the existing economy. That economy expands first within traditional parameters and then the parameters themselves change. In that the late eighteenth-century British economy was an agricultural and trading economy with agriculture providing its base, changes in agriculture were central to its development.

Agriculture

The resources with which to support the additional population had to be found within the national economy. Agriculture was still the most important element, not only the biggest source of direct employment, but also the basis of many dependent economic activities. The ability of British agriculture to feed the growing population was crucial.

During the eighteenth century, contemporaries had been impressed by technical changes in farming. This led future generations to conceive of an Agricultural Revolution comparable to the Industrial Revolution. In the case of both 'revolutions', modern studies have tended to modify generalizations about the rapidity and the extent of the shift in forms of production.[19] Although there was agricultural improvement, the process was patchy rather than general. North-East England provided celebrated examples of improved farming techniques, and the success of men like John Grey of Dilston or the Culley brothers earned them national reputations.[20] As late as 1851, however, *The Times* had this

---

18. One of the first examples of this revisionism is Michael Forbes, 'The Myth of a British Industrial Revolution', *History*, vol. 66, 217, June 1981, 181–98. A counter view is expressed by M. Berg and P. Hudson, 'Rehabilitating the Industrial Revolution', *Economic History Review*, 2nd ser., 45 (1992), 24–50.

19. A. E. Musson, 'Industrial Motive Power in the United Kingdom, 1800–1870', *Economic History Review*, 2nd ser., 29 (1976) provides an excellent example of such revisions.

20. J. Butler, *John Grey of Dilston* (1869); D. J. Rowe, 'The Culleys, Northumberland farmers', *Agricultural History Review*, 19 (1971), 156–74; S. Macdonald, 'The role of George Culley in the development of Northumberland agriculture', *Archaeologia Aeliana*, 5th ser., 3 (1975), 131–41; *Matthew and George Culley: Farming letters 1798–1804*, ed. by Anne Orde, Surtees Society, 2006.

to say of the area concerned:

It must surprise many who have hitherto been led to consider the agriculture of Northumberland as a model for the rest of the kingdom, to learn that a great portion of the county … is as little drained and as badly farmed as any district we have yet seen in England, and that the occupiers of the small farms can only eke out a scanty subsistence by careful parsimony, and by employing no labour except that of themselves and their families.[21]

In 1815, Scotland, Wales, and Ireland possessed wide areas which were still little affected by improved farming techniques, if they were affected at all. Scotland provided an example of both cases: the rapid improvement with agriculture in the Lowlands being admired for its efficiency in sharp contrast to the north and west where many farms provided bare subsistence and only large-scale sheep-farming prospered.

Yet enough British landowners and farmers were gripped by enthusiasm for innovation to ensure big increases in the production of food and fodder. This played a crucial role in feeding the growing population and facilitating the expansion of industry and commerce. As late as 1868 it was estimated that four-fifths of the food supply of an increased population was provided by home production.[22] Improvement took place, however unevenly, in the quality of cultivated crops, the breeding of cattle, sheep, and other livestock, and the application of fertilizers and machinery.

In a society dominated by the landed interest such developments attracted much comment, but their causes were often imperfectly understood. Some observers conjectured that improvement was associated with areas in which large estates and large farms predominated, others saw a spur to progress in greater security to tenant farmers by granting leases rather than a precarious annual tenure. For some the process of enclosure, largely completed by 1815, itself provided the explanation for change in farming. In fact, it is not easy to correlate the known centres of improvement with any of these hypotheses, even if enclosure was often a prerequisite for improvement. Security of tenure did not always lead to better farming, nor were larger estates always in the vanguard of progress—in Ireland, for instance, some large estates were far from being models of progressive agriculture.

While many farmers continued to apply traditional methods, the rewards for the successful innovator could be substantial. The aristocracy which dominated British society had an obvious interest in agricultural prosperity, and good farming could bring distinction and advancement. The farmer who introduced profitable innovations could increase his own income and his family's status.

---

21. Quoted by D. J. Rowe in his 1972 edition of J. Bailey and G. Culley, *General View of the Agriculture of Northumberland, etc.*, p. xxii.
22. J. D. Chambers and G. E. Mingay, *The Agricultural Revolution, 1750–1880* (1966), 208.

A reputation for skilful farming could bring enhanced prices for improved breeding stock or substantial premiums for taking pupils. For the fortunate few, improvement could make it possible to buy land instead of renting it. This meant not only individual success, but the endowment of a family with the multiple economic, social, and political advantages which landownership conferred in that society. Equally the unsuccessful farmer might sink into bankruptcy, disgrace, and obscurity. For those who won, the prizes were considerable. At the beginning of our period, shortly before his death, one such successful farmer could reflect, 'To think of my son, now inhabiting *a Palace*! altho' his father in less than 50 years since worked harder than any servant we now have, and even drove a coal cart.'[23] The writer was born the younger son of a tenant farmer, but ended his life as head of a family owning a landed estate capable of sustaining gentry status, with a large country house as its centre. Such transitions were not common, but they were sufficiently celebrated to provide a spur both to ambition and to economic growth. Parallels could readily be found in other sectors of the economy.

Trade and consumption

The prosperity of British agriculture had important effects on the consumption patterns of the middle orders of society. Not only farmers but millers, corn merchants, and brewers benefited directly, while a host of other trades and professions in market towns expanded and became prosperous. Another factor was the increase in overseas trade, particularly trade across the Atlantic, which provided profits for merchants and manufacturers. This new spending power stimulated a wider economy as more of the middle orders began to buy new furniture, china, mirrors, and fashionable clothes which manufacturers hastened to provide.[24] This development was not universally approved of: to some it seemed an unseemly and materialist phenomenon while others discerned a spirit of emulation which threatened the social fabric. The conservative radical William Cobbett railed against the passing of the old farmhouse way of life and the coming of farmers who aped the gentry with 'the mahogany table, and the fine chairs, and the fine glass'.[25] Yet such consumption led to an expansion of manufacturing and to the growth of both internal and overseas trade. It may have been modest in comparison with the enormous expansion of consumerism in the Victorian period but it did much to provide the foundations of the economy which made the latter possible.

23. Rowe, 'The Culleys', 174.

24. Paul Langford, *A Polite and Commercial People: England 1727–1783* (1989), 69–76; see also, N. McKendrick, J. Brewer and J. H. Plumb, *The Birth of a Consumer Society: The Commercialisation of Eighteenth Century England* (1982).

25. William Cobbett, *Rural Rides*, Penguin edn. (1967), 266.

Industry

The technology applied to most industrial processes would present no real mystery to rural craftsmen. One informed study offers these cautionary words:

It is not generally appreciated that in 1800 steam power was still in its infancy, that in the vast majority of manufactures there had been little or no power-driven mechanisation, and that where such mechanisation had occurred water power was still much more widespread and important than steam. And after 1800, 'the triumph of the factory system' took place much more gradually than has generally been realised.[26]

The application of steam power to a narrow range of functions, including pumping out water from mines, was already established, but early steam engines were relatively simple devices. In industry as in farming, most processes were carried out with simple hand tools. An early nineteenth-century illustration of 'Draughts of the several Instruments necessary for the Dressing of Lead Ore so as to fit it for Smelting' depicts items which could easily be mistaken for gardening implements.[27] A millwright might be concerned with rural watermills or windmills as well as with an early nineteenth-century industrial plant. It has recently been noted that in Essex the peak period of windmill operation came as late as the 1830s, when the county had some 280 working.[28] Shipbuilding was for the most part a small-scale activity dependent on traditional woodworking techniques. When Queen Victoria came to the throne in 1837, only a small proportion of British workers had ever seen the inside of a 'dark satanic mill'. The most numerous occupational groups were agricultural labourers and domestic servants. Many years ago, Sir John Clapham demonstrated that 'the man of the crowded countryside was still the typical Englishman'.[29]

Although the cotton industry employed around 450,000 'hands' in the early 1830s, many of these were women and children. Agriculture supported many more families. The building industry employed about 350,000 male workers, overwhelmingly in small-scale concerns rather than the huge firms controlled by such exceptional contractors as Thomas Cubitt. Coalmining employed less than 100,000, in contexts ranging from a few large advanced collieries with perhaps as many as 500 workers through to many small drift mines employing only a handful of workers with little if any machinery. A variety of crafts carried on individually or in small workshops provided more typical forms of work than factory employment.

Mixed occupations remained common. In many parts of the country, families partly employed in farming could also be involved in carrying out at home work put out to them in connection with textile manufacture. In the northern lead-mining dales, a combination of mining with small-scale farming was normal

26. Musson, 'Industrial motive power', 416.

27. MS by James Mulcaster in the library of the Literary and Philosophical Society of Newcastle upon Tyne.

28. K. G. Farries, *Essex Windmills, Millers and Millwrights* (1984).   29. Clapham 66.

practice. A study of a Midland estate observes that 'the holder of 15 acres plus another job which provided most of his cash income may well have been better off than the holder of 50 acres who had no other occupation than farming: hence the rise of the former at the expense of the latter from 1815 to 1832.'[30]

An even clearer example of the connections between industry and agriculture occurs in their continued dependence on the horse. Consider the groups of workers involved here:

smiths, farriers, saddlery and harness makers: whipmakers, stirrup, bit and spur makers; wheelwrights, carriage- and coach-builders, fitters, painters, upholsterers, and trimmers; cart, van, and waggon makers; coachmen, grooms, cabmen, flymen, carmen, carriers, carters, and hauliers; horse-keepers, horse-breakers, horse-dealers, jobmasters and livery-stable keepers—not forgetting the knackers.[31]

The skills needed for many of these jobs could be deployed in many contexts—a farm or a country house, a colliery or a factory, road haulage or the army—without great variation in the training or the work involved.

An industrial revolution?

Yet when all due reservations are made about the concept of an 'Industrial Revolution' in the early decades of the nineteenth century—and, as we have seen, the term can be misleading—the growth of manufacturing appears prodigious when compared with any earlier age. Such growth was increasingly important in providing the additional resources with which the growing population could be supported, although it is premature to talk of a predominantly industrial society.

The most remarkable growth was in cotton, where imports of raw cotton trebled between 1815 and 1830, while the prices of some of the principal varieties of yarn were halved. Over the same period coal production rose from around 16 million to just under 30 million tons. At the beginning of the century it took 8 tons of coal to produce 1 ton of pig iron; by 1830 this figure was down to 3.5 tons. In the early 1830s Charles Babbage, one of the leading scientists of the day, embarked upon a tour of factories in Britain and on the Continent. In his book *The Economy of Manufactures*, published in 1832, he set out his findings. Between 1818 and 1830 British pig iron had fallen in price from £6. 7s. 6d. to £4. 10s. per ton, and bar iron from £10. 10s. to £6. In 1830 the larger sizes of British plate glass cost less than half their 1800 prices, but no such drop had occurred in either French or German glass. Overall, Babbage had no doubt that manufactured products in Britain were much cheaper than their equivalents elsewhere.[32]

30. J. M. Wordie, 'Social change on the Leveson-Gower estates, 1714–1832', *Economic History Review*, 2nd ser., 27 (1974), 602.

31. F. M. L. Thompson, 'Some nineteenth century horse sense', *Economic History Review*, 2nd ser., 29 (1976), 78–9. This short article is an admirable account of the continued dependence on the horse.

32. A. F. Burstall, *A History of Mechanical Engineering*, 2nd edn. (1965), 281.

Britain also led the improvement of power sources. By 1820 the waterwheel had been refined to make it a more efficient prime mover than the cruder versions of earlier years.[33] For example, in 1817 a new waterwheel, capable of generating 100 h.p., was installed at the Quarry Bank Mill at Styal in Cheshire, where it continued at work until 1904. Although the full potential of steam power still lay in the future, the steam engine's efficiency was improved by a series of refinements devised and applied in Britain.[34]

The increasingly competitive nature of many British products was reflected in export growth from about £35 million in 1815 to about £47 million in 1830.[35] The effect on employment can be illustrated by the leap in the number of cotton mills in Manchester from 66 in 1820 to 96 in 1832.

The British economy in the first decades of the nineteenth century was preponderantly a 'modernized organic' economy with pockets of an economy based upon 'inorganic' power. It may well be that the spectacular expansion of the organic economy had the very limits which Malthus had described and that it was the, as yet hardly discernible, development of those characteristics which economic historians for long described as an 'Industrial Revolution', the use of steam power and a 'factory system', which, *after* c.1830, enabled those limits to be exceeded.[36]

Transport and communications

Economic development was aided by improved communications. The railway and the steamship were the most spectacular of these, but had produced little effect by 1830, except in the increased use of relatively short wagonways, especially in mining areas or other contexts where it was necessary to carry bulky products to shipping points. In other forms of transport, though, there were improvements before the Age of Steam was well under way. In his book *The Progress of the Nation*, the political economist G. R. Porter estimated in 1851 that Britain possessed something like 4,000 miles of navigable rivers and canals. An increasingly sophisticated system of coastal shipping was tied in not only to river- and canal-borne traffic but also to a network of arrangements for collection and distribution by road. Roads had been much improved, primarily by turnpikes,[37] during the later eighteenth century, but the fruits were now more obvious. A striking illustration was the reduced journey times by stagecoach. By 1832, it was possible to go from London to Edinburgh in 42 hours, instead of taking the 10 or 12 days needed in the mid-eighteenth century. The stagecoach could only be used by the relatively wealthy, or for the carriage of small amounts

33. D. L. S. Cardwell, *Technology, Science and History* (1972), 103.
34. Burstall, *History of Mechanical Engineering*, 279.
35. Mathias, *The First Industrial Nation*, 432.
36. This is essentially the thesis argued by E. A. Wrigley, *People, Cities and Wealth*.
37. H. C. B. Rogers, *Turnpike to Iron Road* (1961) chs. 1 and 2.

of expensive goods. The improvement and the cheapening of other forms of road transport were more important. Telford's work introduced advances in road construction; McAdam added refinements which produced a metalled road which cost much less.[38] By the 1830s, except in remote and thinly populated areas (which included much of Ireland, Scotland, and Wales), the United Kingdom was served by an intricate system of road freight services, mainly using the rugged but slow stage wagons. These were heavy vehicles with broad wheels to minimize road wear. Local directories of the early nineteenth century (in themselves an indication of more sophisticated commercial organization) published the timetables for these services, with the number of regular journeys matched to the volume of business expected between the places served. These services connected with coastal shipping lines, and in addition to economical carriage of goods they provided cheap if slow travel for a limited number of passengers.

There is no mystery in the motivation which brought about these changes, even before the railway age. The early railways do, however, provide an admirable example. The building of the Stockton and Darlington Railway in 1825 has always been seen as an important event in the evolution of transport facilities, but it is not always clear just what kind of a 'first' it was. It was not the first railway, or the first railway to use locomotives. It ought to be celebrated as an influential demonstration that a railway could be profitable. Earlier, a ton of coal, which cost 4s. at an inland colliery, doubled in price when carted to Darlington and tripled by the time it reached Stockton, a total distance o£ about twenty miles. The building of the early coal-carrying railways reduced the cost of overland carriage of coal by almost three-quarters. This saving transformed the competitive position of the collieries served, and also the profits of the coal-owners. The high dividends paid by the Stockton and Darlington line had more influence on railway development than any technical innovations. Similar inducements underlay earlier transport improvements. On a reasonably well-metalled road a horse could pull a load three times as heavy as on an unmade surface. If a load of 2 tons was as much as a horse might be expected to move on even a decent road, a single horse on a canal towpath might pull a boat of 50 tons.

Supply and distribution

Increased production, improved productivity, and better communications were beginning to provide a range of goods and services which would have amazed earlier ages. The supply arrangements which provided the metropolis of London with food and other necessities were in themselves a remarkable achievement, but the improvement in services and supplies reached smaller places too.[39] In 1830 Aldeburgh in Suffolk was primarily a fishing village with a population of

38. P. W. Kingsford, *Engineers, Inventors and Workers* (1964), 72.

39. Clapham, *Economic History of Modern Britain*, ch. 7. The examples from Aldeburgh and Thirsk are taken from D. Davis, *A History of Shopping* (1966), 265–6.

about 1,300. It had markets twice a week, large fairs twice a year. A carrier from Ipswich provided goods carriage twice a week. Aldeburgh then had 8 inns, 6 shoe-makers, 4 grocers, 3 bakers, 2 chemists, 4 tailors, 3 milliners, 5 blacksmiths, a sad-dler, and a hairdresser. Thirsk, a Yorkshire country town of some 5,000 inhabitants, possessed 30 public houses, 12 butchers, 2 fishmongers, 4 bakers, 25 shoe shops, 12 grocers, 3 confectioners, 2 candlemakers, 4 chemists, 18 general shops, 15 tailors, 8 drapers, 9 milliners, 5 hairdressers, 4 hatters, 2 clog-makers, 6 cabinet-makers, 2 china shops, 4 booksellers, 3 ironmongers, 4 clock-makers, 3 blacksmiths, and a coal merchant. These services were not only providing for their host communities; Thirsk and even Aldeburgh served as local centres for the surrounding countryside. Long before the pace of industrialization and urbanization had reached its peak, even in rural areas services were increasingly sophisticated.

In remote and thinly populated areas like much of southern and western Ireland, much of highland Scotland, and large parts of inland Wales, the retail and distributive services were more primitive, and higher levels of self-sufficiency were essential. In the northern lead-mining dales, it was well into the new century before packhorses were supplanted by wheeled vehicles. Increasingly, though, the majority of Britain's inhabitants had an expanding range of goods and services available.

Science and technology

The improvement in productivity and the extension of services owed something to enhanced understanding of science and the application of improved technol-ogy. Contemporaries were well aware of this. At the beginning of the century, the Royal Institution had been founded to promote scientific progress, and its early employees included Humphry Davy and Michael Faraday. From its inception the Institution's aims indicated a practical emphasis; its main objective was

diffusing the knowledge and facilitating the general and speedy introduction of new and useful mechanical inventions and improvements and also for teaching by regular courses of philosophical lectures and experiments, the applications of new discoveries in science to the improvement of arts and manufactures and in facilitating the means of procuring the comforts and conveniences of life.[40]

Where individuals were involved in the invention and application of improved techniques, though, the principal motive was to improve the position of those individuals and their families, rather than a disinterested zeal for scientific advancement. When Robert Stephenson was born in 1803, his father George was a colliery worker, unknown outside a limited local circle. In the latter years of his life, because of his engineering successes, especially in railways, George Stephenson was a respected national figure, and the family address became Tapton House, near Chesterfield. This transition had not been easy, and sometimes involved

40. Burstall, *History of Mechanical Engineering*, 203.

considerable risks, as in the experiments leading to the invention of a practicable safety lamp for miners.[41] Stephenson's success established not only his own position, but a dynasty. By 1850 his son Robert enjoyed an income of £50,000 per annum, equal to that of many aristocratic families. It was possible—indeed common—for the innovator and the adventurer to come to grief. It was also obvious that, for those who succeeded, this highly unequal society had much to offer.

There was nothing new about these inequalities. As far back as history will take us, society had been marked by disparities of status, wealth, power, and opportunity. No one alive in early nineteenth-century Britain had experienced a situation in which social, economic, or political equality had been generally accepted; those European societies which had seen revolutionary outbreaks in the recent past did not offer models which most people in Britain found attractive.

The royal family

At the top of the social pyramid stood the monarchy and the aristocracy, as they had done for countless generations. The sovereign himself, as in the case of George IV, may not have been held in high regard by those closely associated with him, but this degree of association was rare. More widely, despite such unsavoury episodes as the Queen Caroline affair (see pp. 29–31 above), the Crown was still invested with a high degree of respect. Popular petitions were commonly offered to the monarch as well as to the two Houses of Parliament or other sources of authority; there was a widespread belief that this could be an effective course of action. The relatively small ruling groups in Britain were aware that the actual power of the sovereign had diminished markedly by 1815, but this decline was not generally appreciated among the less sophisticated elements in society. While it remained true that the royal family did not always present the most edifying spectacle to public gaze, there remained a residual strength in the monarchy which enabled it to survive changes in British society.

If George IV could be irritating to those responsible for governing in his name, in other ways he fulfilled monarchical functions with some skill. In contrast to his denigration by previous generations of historians, there has of late been a partial rehabilitation of George IV, a rehabilitation which recognizes his obvious faults but warms to his zest for life, his artistic sensibility, and his innate kindness.[42] The aristocracy dominated Britain in these years, and George, both as Prince Regent and as King, provided an active lead in aristocratic society. To a greater extent than his more virtuous father, he succeeded in establishing the influence of the monarchy in many of the tastes and the activities of the aristocracy.

The King also understood the need for the monarchy to project itself to wider sections of society. He realized that much of the population appreciated the

41. Kingsford, *Engineers, Inventors and Workers*, 101–2.
42. See Steven Parissien, *George IV: The Grand Entertainment* (2001); E. A. Smith, *George IV* (1999); David Saul, *Prince of Pleasure: The Prince of Wales and the Making of the Regency* (1998).

glitter of kingship. His coronation was an opulent, carefully staged, and popular affair and he then embarked upon visits to Hanover, Dublin, and Edinburgh which were great successes. As King of Hanover, George was theoretically independent of the British government, and he had a second coronation there and was greeted with much adulation. Although we know with hindsight that the Union of Britain and Ireland was to fail, in the 1820s there seemed still much to hope for it. There seems no doubt that George's visit to Dublin was well received. When he wanted to please, the King could draw on great social skills.

The visit to Edinburgh was to have the most beneficent consequences. It came at a time when a number of favourable, if diverse and even contradictory, factors were in conjunction. Scotland and especially Edinburgh had acquired a confidence due to the 'Scottish Enlightenment', which had given Edinburgh a justified reputation as a city of learning and sophistication; the development of Edinburgh's New Town embellished its claim to be a city of consequence and taste. The Romantic Movement had enabled the Lowlands to exchange a supercilious attitude to the Highlands for one of appropriation for things tartan and castellated, however bogus much of this might be, and this new image of Scotland was very fashionable.[43] Above all Scotland was enjoying substantial fruits from the Union and, as we have seen, scenting the rewards that Scots could find in England and in Britain's overseas empire. The visit was orchestrated by Sir Walter Scott, who had originally suggested it. George added his bit to the tartanization of Scotland by wearing the newly invented—indeed his wearing of it played a part in the invention—kilt under which he wore pink tights. George was at his best and the first visit of a monarch to Scotland since the seventeenth century was a resounding success. The King had done something towards cementing relations between the Crown and Scotland and contributed to a new sense of Scottish identity, one which later monarchs would enthusiastically acclaim. His visits to the outlying parts of his realms demonstrated a flair for public relations. It was George's tragedy that he came to the throne when his health was beginning to fail and that, rather than build on these achievements, he had gradually to withdraw from the public gaze.

So far as the higher echelons of society were concerned, George IV's influence was not confined to his conspicuous participation during the regency and in the first years of his reign in the round of social activities which marked the London season. In a variety of spheres his own tastes enabled him to act as a leading cultural patron. Architects, artists, and writers learned that royal appreciation and patronage were available to those who made contributions to that cultural flowering which marked the early decades of the century. Authors like Jane Austen and Walter Scott, artists like Lawrence and Wilkie, architects like Nash and Wyattville, illustrate the breadth of royal interest and encouragement.[44] Though

---

43. See H. Trevor Roper, 'The Highland Tradition of Scotland', in E. Hobsbawm and T. Ranger (eds.), *The Invention of Tradition* (1983).

44. J. Stigman, *The Rule of Taste from George I to George IV*, 174.

popular memory sees his taste as exemplified in the fantasy of the Brighton Pavilion, London owes to him and Nash the grand though only half-realized development of Regent's Park itself and the whole area down to St James's. George rebuilt 'the public face of the West End of London'.[45] His tastes accorded admirably with those of many (though not all) of his more powerful subjects, and his role in such matters played a part in vindicating the position of the monarch at the head of Britain's aristocratic society.

Other members of the royal family played analogous roles in other spheres. If HRH the Duke of Cumberland provided royal encouragement for conservative or reactionary causes, HRH the Duke of Sussex was a distinctly liberal figure. He and one of his royal cousins were among the peers who entered a formal protest against the 1815 Corn Law in the journals of the House of Lords. The Duke of Sussex also took an interest in scientific research and encouraged the development of literary and philosophical societies in the provinces. A number of the members of the royal family were more than nominal members of the Royal Society. Several royal princes were involved in freemasonry, a movement attracting increasing numbers of adherents from a broad social range. Most of the royal family were not conspicuously devout, but HRH the Duke of Kent was much under evangelical influence, something which helped to direct the upbringing of the future Queen Victoria.[46] George IV, for all his faults, was a kindly man and his support for philanthropy and charity allowed sections of society who disapproved of sexual licence to overlook his private life. 'Religious reformers and charitable campaigners drew on a deep well of Christian forgiveness where the monarchy was concerned.' Even Hannah More wrote of 'his unimpeachable honour'.[47] The royal family's interests, while not always pursued with wisdom, were sufficiently varied to maintain a position of patronage and leadership in a range of activities within influential elements of society.

The aristocracy

The political dominance of the aristocracy was not to be substantially eroded for many years after 1815. There was nothing extraordinary in this. The eminence of the nobility was traditional in British society, and was present, sometimes to an even greater degree, in most contemporary States. The aristocracy controlled the political system and provided most Cabinet ministers.

The aristocracy was small in numbers and linked together by a variety of ties. It was the most completely British layer of society. Aristocrats might be proud of their regional or Scottish or Welsh associations and history but they were a caste that transcended these, while Irish landowners were also part of the unified aristocratic order. Many of the great landowners had estates in several parts of the

---

45. E. A. Smith, *George IV* (1999), 244.
46. I. Bradley, *The Call to Seriousness* (1976), 35–6.
47. Frank Prochaska, *Royal Bounty: The Making of a Welfare Monarchy* (1995), 39.

kingdom while a townhouse in London was a necessity. Although there were a few widely publicized marriages with heiresses from outside the nobility, the majority of aristocratic marriages were naturally enough at the same social level. A complex network of family relationships helped to hold together the great 'cousinhood' of the aristocracy. Other bonds were a common culture, education, and recreation.

The universities

Many sons of noble families attended the universities of Oxford and Cambridge. These institutions were themselves small in the early nineteenth century, each admitting something like 300–400 students each year. In these universities the scions of noble families were accorded a special status, manifested in such matters as the trimmings of their academic gowns and the privileges they enjoyed under the university regulations.

In England, university was still largely synonymous with Oxford and Cambridge, although University College, London, founded in 1828, was characterized by its openness to non-Anglicans. Scotland had four long-established universities, St Andrews, Glasgow, Aberdeen, and Edinburgh, whose high reputations and lack of religious affiliations attracted many English as well as Scottish students. Edinburgh produced over 200 medical graduates a year, which made it the centre of British medical education.

Already by 1815 there were signs that the old English universities were emerging from a period of decay. In 1800 Oxford had followed Cambridge in instituting genuine examinations for degrees, and by 1815 both universities provided better educational opportunities than in the previous century. Perhaps a third to a quarter of undergraduates now belonged to the category of those who were sometimes called 'reading' students, that is those who took their education seriously. Individual colleges earned special reputations: 'Christchurch became a school for Tory statesmen, first Oriel and then Balliol attracted intellectual men, Trinity College, Cambridge, attracted the sons of Whig noblemen, gradually displacing its neighbour St. John's in that service, first Magdalene, Cambridge, and then Queens', Cambridge, attracting Evangelicals, and so on.'[48]

Such specialization did not, of course, prevent the existence of shared interests among students across the university. Most undergraduates could get to know a substantial number of the young men of the same age and from broadly the same social status. Links formed at university, whether or not they had any specifically intellectual content, often continued into later life. Moreover, the performance of the young men at the English universities, whether academical, sporting, or

---

48. G. Kitson Clark, *The Making of Victorian England* (1962), 256–7. For the universities more generally, A. I. Tillyard, *A History of University Reform, from 1800 to the Present Time* (1913); M. Sanderson (ed.), *The Universities in the Nineteenth Century* (1975); a good example of a 'reading' student is given by N. Gash, *Mr. Secretary Peel* (1961), 347–59, which also describes the way in which the political world was well aware of the young man's promise.

merely social, was likely to be known to their predecessors and relatives occupying positions of importance in society or the State. The emergence of the young
Robert Peel from Oxford after a distinguished career there was anticipated by
ministers anxious to enlist able recruits for their party. Apart from shared experiences in school and university, most of the aristocracy shared similar tastes in
culture, sport, and recreation. In addition, of course, they shared a powerful
common interest in the prosperity of their landed interests.

The landed interest

The aristocracy's basic strength lay in its ownership of land. Land seemed, and
usually was, a safe and permanent form of wealth. In contrast, incomes derived
from commercial and industrial sources could be precarious, as the contemporary lists of bankruptcies demonstrated. Ownership of a landed estate conferred
independence, likely to be jeopardized only by a feckless course of incompetence
or extravagance. Acquisition of a landed estate promised a secure base for an
individual and his family, and it signalled arrival into the higher reaches of
British society. It also involved responsibilities for the ethos of landowning was
only in part about economics and involved the leadership of county society and
of a wider agricultural interest which included farmers, millers, corn merchants,
and even farm workers.

The advantages derived from the ownership of land were appreciated by successful men engaged in industry and commerce, however proud they might be of
their own achievements. Industrialists could be critical of the attitudes, policies,
and advantages of the landed aristocracy, while fully appreciating how powerful,
how privileged, and how desirable these attributes were. There was a procession
of successful manufacturers, merchants, and bankers into the ranks of the landed
aristocracy.[49] The motivation behind it was often clear enough, as a political
economist pointed out in 1820:

It is not the most pleasant enjoyment to spend eight hours a day in a countinghouse. Nor
will it be submitted to after the common necessaries of life are attained, unless adequate
motives are presented to the man of business. Among those motives is undoubtedly the
desire of advancing his rank, and contending with the landlords in the enjoyment of
leisure, as well as of foreign and domestic luxuries. But the desire to realise a fortune as a
permanent provision for a family is perhaps the most general motive for the continued
exertions of those whose incomes depend upon their own skill and efforts.[50]

---

49. H. Perkin, *The Origins of Modern English Society, 1780–1880* (1969), 88–9. The degree of 'openness' within the aristocracy has been a matter of controversy among historians. Lawrence Stone and
Jeanne C. Fawtier Stone, *An Open Elite? England 1540–1880* (1984), initiated a lively debate with their
argument that upward mobility into the aristocracy had been much exaggerated. For a recent contribution, which conveniently gives references to earlier contributions to the debate, D. and E. Spring,
'Social history and the English landed elite', *Canadian Journal of History*, 21 (1986), 333–51. A major
study is J. V. Beckett, *The Aristocracy in England, 1660–1914* (1986).

50. Malthus, quoted by Perkin, *The Origins of Modern English Society*, 89.

There was no better 'permanent provision for a family' than landownership, and there was never any lack of candidates for this beneficial transition. There were, however, only a limited number of places at the very top of the social pyramid, even though the peerage expanded rapidly from the late eighteenth to the mid-nineteenth century from 179 peers in 1780 to 383 in 1840.[51] Only a minority of new creations went to men who had made their fortunes in commerce, industry, or banking though bankers did better than merchants or industrialists; a fifth went to established gentry families but the greater part, about half, went to politicians, diplomats, judges, and generals and admirals. A Duke of Wellington or an Earl Nelson displayed the rewards given to national heroes. For centuries the law had provided a route to social advancement; the Earl of Eldon and Lord Stowell, sons of a Newcastle coal merchant, demonstrated in 1815 that this avenue still existed. More modest titles were, nevertheless, available and even the successful architect, doctor, artist, or scientist might hope for a knighthood or baronetcy and the modest estate which could support such lesser dignities. The mere ownership of sufficient acres was enough over time to give gentry status.

There was nothing new about such advancement. Among the established aristocracy in 1815 there were few who could credibly trace their ancestry to a companion of William the Conqueror. Many of the peerages created in the late eighteenth and early nineteenth century were given to landed families, but those families had often emerged in earlier generations from the ranks of the successful in other occupations. Although the continuing movement of new wealth into the aristocracy aroused comment in the early nineteenth century, such comments had many precedents, and the process represented continuity rather than innovation. The number of cases of spectacular advancement may not have been large, but they were sufficient, and sufficiently publicized, to provide a continuing spur to the ambitious.

Industrialists were sometimes frank about this. In 1845–6, when industry already counted for more than it had done in 1815, there was a public subscription for a radical politician; one of the fund's trustees, himself a manufacturer, remarked:

> Nor have I any notion of its being desirable that the public man whom his country shall have qualified to sit down on his own broad acres, should remain subject to the contingencies of an anxious trade, of watching, either personally, or by deputy, the processes by which 6*d*. a piece is to be gained or 2/6 to be lost, in the production of beggarly printed calicoes.[52]

Landowning was not necessarily a restricted form of economic activity. Other kinds of business were often profitably combined with the management of a landed estate and attempts to establish a distinction between landowners and those involved in commerce and industry must soon founder on the links

51. Beckett, *The Aristocracy in England*, 487.
52. N. McCord, *The Anti-Corn Law League* (1958), 31.

between these interests. The production of agricultural commodities involved attention to their marketing; even in agricultural affairs landowners needed services from the commercial and financial sectors in the management of their estates. The links went further than this, and the exploitation of many estates involved interests other than farming.[53] Direct aristocratic involvement in non-agricultural economic activity reached something of a peak in the late eighteenth and early nineteenth centuries. Most economic developments made some demand on land, whether for house-building or railway-building, mining or the erection of factories. Coalmining provided one of the clearest links between the aristocracy and industry. On the Great Northern Coalfield of Northumberland and Durham, a list of coal-owners contained a high proportion of the nobility and gentry of the two counties, not forgetting such associated parties as the Bishop (and the Dean and Chapter) of Durham. Coal laid the foundations of a number of landed estates in that region, and coal also brought some substantial families to ruin in a situation where an incautious investment could result in the loss of an entire fortune. Mining magnates included the Dukes of Portland, Rutland, Cleveland, Buccleuch, Devonshire, Sutherland, and Bedford, as well as many other noble and gentry families. It was common to find a great aristocratic landowner as owner or part-owner of towns, mines, quarries, brickworks, ports, shipping, wagonways, railways, and a variety of other enterprises, according to the opportunities offered by his estates.

Aristocratic patronage

Another feature of the aristocracy's strength was the varied nature of its influence. It is difficult to find any important aspect of society in which the aristocracy did not play some part. They provided the top echelons of polite society, whether in the London season or in dispensing the sought-after invitations to social functions at their country seats. The developing provincial Press regarded the chronicling of the activities of local aristocratic families as an important part of their coverage, and nothing suggests that this was unwelcome to the majority of their readers. The patronage of the aristocracy was also of the first importance in a wide range of cultural, artistic, and scientific activities.

The literary flowering of these years was not primarily directed to a wide popular reading public, but rather to discriminating minorities which included those who could effectively reward literary achievement. Time and again writers sought the countenance, encouragement, and the largess of aristocratic patrons, as their predecessors had done over the centuries. Wordsworth owed his secure income from a government post, together with a private pension, to the Earl of Lonsdale. Southey was helped by the Earl of Radnor, and later granted a

---

53. For a discussion of such links see the first two essays, by D. Spring and J. T. Ward, in J. T. Ward and R. G. Wilson (eds.), *Land and Industry* (1971), 16–116.

government pension. Some of the writers who attacked the Tory government depended upon support from Whig aristocrats. Thomas Moore was a friend of Lord John Russell, and was to receive a pension from the grateful Whigs in 1835. Leigh Hunt was another opposition writer who was encouraged by opposition aristocrats and eventually received a government pension from them. On the other hand, the romantic rebel within the arts, as elsewhere, was unlikely to provide for himself and his family success, comfort, or security. William Blake was not widely admired in his own day. The readership which appreciated the works of Wordsworth, Southey, Keats, Shelley, Byron, Jane Austen, Sir Walter Scott, Charles Lamb, Hazlitt, and Leigh Hunt was primarily drawn from influential minority groups. The same readership supported the three major literary and political magazines, the Whig *Edinburgh Review*, founded in 1802, the Tory *Quarterly Review* of 1809, and the radical *Westminster Review* of 1824.

Similar relationships existed in art and architecture. The building, rebuilding, or embellishment of country houses offered prestigious and rewarding opportunities. Sir Geoffrey Wyattville enjoyed, in addition to commissions from George IV, patronage from the Dukes of Beaufort, Bedford, and Devonshire, the Marquis of Bath, the Earls of Bridgewater, Cawdor, Chesterfield, and Clarendon, and many lesser noblemen and gentry. John Nash's commissions included Killymore Castle, Childwall Hall, Corsham House, and Hale Hall, in addition to much royal patronage. Benjamin Wyatt worked for the Duke of Wellington at Apsley House, designed Londonderry House in London, and the clubhouse of the aristocratic Crockford's Club. Artists and sculptors, too, depended upon the sale of their works to aristocratic patrons or upon subsidies on which to live. Not all of the aristocracy took a keen interest in the arts, but enough of them did to leave a legacy of discriminating taste to future generations. The third Earl of Egremont practically employed the sculptor John Carew full-time for years, and patronized a considerable range of painters. He was especially indulgent to Turner, who was allocated a studio at the earl's country seat at Petworth; it was understood between them that the earl would only enter this apartment after giving an agreed code knock.[54] Sir Robert Peel was a collector on a large scale. In addition to buying paintings from Benjamin Haydon, he provided the money to release that artist from a debtors' prison in 1830.[55] Others who patronized that prickly and difficult painter included the Duke of Sutherland and Earl Grey. The successful career of Sir Thomas Lawrence showed what a more equable temperament allied to artistic ability could achieve through aristocratic patronage. Even where personal interest in the arts was not as deep as that of such men as Egremont and Peel, a sense of what was right and fashionable could arouse emulation. The third Marquis of Londonderry was not primarily noted for cultural attainments, but he was proud of his Correggios.

Aristocratic leadership and patronage also extended to science and technology. In the Royal Society, the Royal Institution, and the British Association for

54. DNB.   55. Ibid.

the Advancement of Science, interested noblemen did much to invest those bodies with a prestige unlikely to have been obtained by scientific attainments alone. When the Royal Institution was founded in 1799, Earl Spencer and the Earl of Morton were among its principal sponsors; dukes and earls continued to provide influential members in the Institution's work as a pressure group for scientific progress. Even if few aristocrats could equal the ninth Earl of Dundonald, the third Earl of Rosse, or Sir George Cayley, Bt, all distinguished scientists, the intellectual interests of the aristocracy were sufficiently diverse to give the nobility a role in the contemporary world of scientific discovery. As with writers, painters, sculptors, musicians, and architects, scientists like Sir Humphry Davy, John Dalton, and Michael Faraday were dependent upon the encouragement and support of aristocratic patrons. This was not a negligible activity, given the significance of Dalton's contribution to atomic theory, Faraday's discoveries in electrical generation, or Cayley's role as a pioneer in aviation. On a more mundane and immediate level, experimenters in such useful fields as railway development or mining techniques might receive flattering notice and advancement at the hands of interested aristocrats.

There were many other channels of noble influence, too. In field sports, boxing, horse racing, and the gambling which was associated with much sporting activity, noblemen often took the lead. Lord George Bentinck, wealthy younger son of a Duke of Portland, had a national reputation as a leading sportsman and successful gambler long before he became an important political figure in the 1840s.[56] Such activities could do as much to consolidate the primacy of the aristocracy as attainments of more obvious public utility. There were many other spheres—philanthropy or the theatre, fashion, or contacts with other countries—in which the nobility's eminence was unmistakable.

For many years much of the writing on the history of art in this period embodied a curious myth. This was the belief that changes in taste, culture, and manners owed their origin to the rise of a new 'middle-class' source of patronage. The error was an odd one, for only a slight acquaintance with the actual timing of these changes, and the nature of their earlier manifestations, would show that what actually happened was an autonomous change in aristocratic taste, obediently imitated lower down the social spectrum. In architecture, Fonthill and Strawberry Hill exemplified growing aristocratic enthusiasm for the Gothic long before suburban villas followed in their train; William Beckford and Horace Walpole would have indignantly repudiated any suggestion that they were merely imitating the tastes of the contemporary bourgeoisie. George Gordon, the sixth Lord Byron, was one of the greatest representatives of the romantic movement in literature.

Given the pre-eminence of the landed aristocracy and its solid base in social, economic, and political influence, it is important to remember the existence

56. The *ODNB* entry on Bentinck is lyrical in its praise of his sporting distinction.

of some practical checks on their freedom of action. While, for instance, a landowner could in theory dispose of the farming and other tenancies on his estate as he wished, in practice he (or his agent) needed to attract and keep good tenants, and this necessitated attention to their interests and their opinions. It was common for landowners to give remissions of rent to help tide tenants over bad seasons, and to provide food, fuel, and fodder for poorer dependants in hard times. Harshness towards dependants could be damaging to reputations. Even the greatest aristocratic magnate would find life more comfortable if he used his wealth and influence in ways which matched the accepted traditions and conventions of the communities whose leadership he claimed. It was rare for one family to have complete dominance in any region. Commonly even a great ducal magnate found it expedient to cultivate and generally to work with the lesser landowners in his own area. In Northumberland parliamentary elections, it was normal for the Duke of Northumberland to content himself with the nomination of one of the county's two Tory candidates, acquiescing for the other in the choice favoured by the county's lesser Tory landowners.

Problems of definition

It is not possible to define the limits of the aristocracy with any precision. Any definition which confined the aristocracy to peers would be too narrow. At the death of George III in 1820, the House of Lords had 339 members. This was an important part of the aristocracy, but by no means the whole of it. Their immediate families would have to be included, and it would not be easy to decide just how far 'immediate' could reasonably be taken to extend. Moreover, although possession of a peerage, especially one which carried a hereditary seat in the House of Lords, was an unmistakable claim to aristocratic distinction, there were baronets and knights, and even untitled individuals, whose wealth and influence exceeded those of many peers. In the Welsh county of Denbigh, Sir Watkin Williams Wynn, Bt was as much a local potentate as any ducal Lord Lieutenant of an English county. In the Irish county of Connemara, Richard Martin, Esq., MP—nicknamed 'Humanity' Martin because of his philanthropic crusades— was perhaps even more pre-eminent: 'he dwelt at the castle of Ballinahinch, and practically ruled over the district of Connemara. His property at Connemara alone comprised two hundred thousand acres in extent, stretching for a distance of thirty Irish miles from his house door.'[57] Formidable landowning ladies such as Miss Lawrence of Ripon or Miss Peirse of Northallerton, though untitled, were aristocrats in all other significant respects.[58] Similarly, the owner of a relatively

---

57. *ODNB.*
58. N. Gash, *Politics in the Age of Peel* (1953), 219–23. Professor Gash suggested here that the magnificent funeral of Miss Lawrence was 'perhaps one of the last of its kind'; there were, however, many magnificent aristocratic funerals still to come such as that of the third Duke of Northumberland in

small but innately valuable estate in England might well, even if untitled, be more influential than many an Irish peer who owned extensive but poor estates in the sister island.

The gentry

There is therefore no definite break-point at which we can draw a line between aristocratic landowners and the lesser landowners, commonly described as the squirearchy or gentry. Acreage and wealth are two yardsticks and it has been suggested that the possession of more than ten thousand acres and an income over £10,000 per annum separated great landowners from richer gentry.[59] The expression 'aristocracy and gentry' was in common use, but no precise boundary existed between them; instead they shaded imperceptibly into one another. The Beaumont family of Northumberland and Yorkshire who had large estates and owned lead mines were known as the 'richest commoners' in England but can be seen as either aristocrats or greater gentry. The role of the aristocracy was reproduced further down the social scale, and, to a more limited extent, by lesser landowners. Their individual influence was smaller but their cumulative power was considerable. Collectively, the 'principal inhabitants', the men of significant influence within a county, were a group to be reckoned with. As with the nobility, their basic strength usually derived from the ownership of land, and they often shared the mixed economic interests associated with many aristocrats.

A good example of a gentry dynasty is provided by the Ridleys of Blagdon, Northumberland. By the early nineteenth century this family had built up a modest landed estate of about 10,000 acres, beginning with the purchase from mercantile profits of estates confiscated from Jacobite rebels after the 1715 rising. By 1815 the head of the family had been for many years a baronet and an MP, but these dignities made no difference to his business enterprise. Sir Matthew Ridley was a partner in an important local bank, and he was careful to see to it that his collieries and his urban property (which included shops and a brewery) made adequate contributions to his income, as well as ensuring that his farms were profitably worked. He also took a prominent part in local cultural activities, including the patronage of local artists such as the sculptor John Lough.[60] There were lesser landowners whose income depended entirely on agricultural rents, but mixed resources were as common here as among the greater landowners. The gentry had their corps of dependants and their own local influence was multifarious, combining economic, social, and political elements.

1847 and that of the third earl FitzWilliam in 1857 described by F. M. L. Thompson, *English Landed Society in the Nineteenth Century* (1963), 80–1.

59. F. M. L. Thompson, ibid., ch.1.

60. Lough has a notice in the *ODNB*. The Ridley Papers are in Northumberland County Record Office; a selection of them with a commentary is given in W. R. Sullivan, *Blyth in the Eighteenth Century* (1971).

Social class

The absence of clear differentiation between aristocracy and gentry introduces one of the most paradoxical aspects of British society in the nineteenth and twentieth centuries. Increasingly, analysis and discussion of society were expressed in terms of broad social classes such as the middle class or the working class, or, slightly more circumspectly, the middle classes or the working classes. The basis for a belief in the existence of such discrete classes consists of a multitude of assertions to that effect, from many different sources. However numerous these assertions may be, their validity essentially depends upon the identification of discontinuities within the social fabric—break-points where one class ends and another begins, with something significantly different on either side of the boundary. Despite a formidable concentration of interest extending over many years, such divisions have never been credibly identified. Instead, the evidence demonstrates the ineffectiveness of associations conceived in terms of broad classes, and the vigour of motivations derived from personal, family, local, sectional, and even national interests.

That there were numerous horizontal social divides loosely based upon wealth and status is incontestable but the social hierarchy resembled a spectrum with the colours blurring into each other rather than neatly separated and cohesive entities. Even then, vertical divides such as those which divided the religious, and drew a line between the religious and the not religious, or that important divide which separated the respectable from the not respectable, could be as, if not more, important than horizontal divisions.

The 'middle class'

There are serious problems in identifying a coherent middle class within nineteenth-century society. This is at first sight surprising, for contemporaries had no doubt of the existence of a powerful, articulate, and coherent middle class. The concept is common in contemporary descriptions and discussions of society, and it has been much employed by subsequent generations. As early as 1799, Canning attributed the weaknesses of Irish society to the absence of 'those classes of men, who connect the upper and lower orders of men, and who thereby blend together and harmonise the whole . . . that middle class of men, of whom skill and enterprise, and sober orderly habits, are the peculiar characteristics'. A quarter of a century later the political economist James Mill equally had no doubts of the solidity of this class; 'It is the strength of the community. It contains, beyond all comparison, the greatest proportion of the intelligence, industry and wealth of the state.'[61] An attempt to test this pervasive belief, by considering its relationship to identifiable social groups, indicates that we are dealing here with the mythology of the nineteenth century rather than the reality.

61. N. McCord, 'Some difficulties of parliamentary reform', *Historical Journal*, 10 (1967), 377–8.

Ministers of religion formed an influential group, but it is not possible to use this category to illustrate a coherent middle class. Within the Anglican Church there were enormous disparities in income and status between on the one hand the high-ranking clergy and the holders of well-endowed livings, and on the other the often poorly paid curates. This difference between the rich and the poor among the clergy has often been noted; it is less often remarked that it represents extremes on a broad scale which covered an immense variation of income and social status. Before the reforms of the 1830s the income of the Bishop of Durham was more than fourteen times that of the Bishop of Oxford. At Stanhope in 1830, the Rector enjoyed an income of nearly £5,000 per annum, swollen by lead-mining royalties and equal to the patrimony of many gentry families. To carry out the actual work of the parish, the Rector paid two curates a total of £270 per annum—and this was a generous stipend for curates.[62] This pair were certainly better off than the Vicar of Norton, Hertfordshire, whose parishioners, 'resolved that their parson would not starve', gave him midday meals by rota.[63] The poorest clergymen might be expected to live on an income no higher than the wages earned by many working men, and sometimes lower. Many clergymen held positions which allowed modest comfort, some were wealthy. The varied ministers of other Churches offered additional variations, including the broad spectrum of the Catholic priesthood in Ireland or the early Primitive Methodist missionaries. Generally, ministers of religion were important members of society for whom the concept of a distinct middle class has little relevance.

Farmers provide a similar example. Their absence from contemporary and later discussions of the middle class presents a surprising anomaly. When observers in the early nineteenth century made use of the concept of a middle class they usually ignored the farmers. Farmers covered a varied social range, from the successful and relatively rich tenant who might be moving towards landownership, to the Welsh hill farmer, the Scottish crofter, or the poor Irish tenant, all of whom might well be worse off than many a miner or factory worker. The differing conditions of British farmers covered a complex gradient of situations rather than any neat categories. Given what we know of the distribution of population and occupation in these years, any mode of categorizing that society which does not comfortably accommodate the farmers is unsatisfactory. The same difficulty arises in exploring any of the other groups commonly attributed to the middle class. Doctors, lawyers, bankers, factory-owners, or mine-owners, to take a few typical examples, covered far too wide a social spectrum to be comprehended within a unitary middle class, while such euphemisms as the middle 'classes' or the 'middling' class do not solve the problem.

62. A principal source for the discussion of the Churches in this period is A. D. Gilbert, *Religion and Society in Industrial England* (1976), which has been drawn on heavily for the account offered in this chapter.

63. R. L. Hine, *Confessions of an Un-Common Attorney* (1946), 227.

There was little in common between many of the unqualified doctors practising in remote provincial areas and the London members of the Royal Colleges of Physicians and Surgeons with their sprinkling of baronets and knights. It is unlikely that a successful and fashionable London doctor like Sir William Knighton, Bt was aware of any class consciousness shared with those doctors without any kind of recognizable professional training, often working in thinly populated rural areas, who were to prove such a thorn in the side of the Poor Law Commission after 1834. Moreover, this was not a matter of simple polarization, for a multitude of intermediate medical situations lay between these extremes. Similarly, there was little in common between a country attorney and the lawyer brothers John and William Scott, who became Earl of Eldon and Lord Stowell, and acquired substantial fortunes and estates. Again the distance between the two extremes was occupied by a varied range of intermediate positions within the legal profession. Bankers like Nathan Rothschild (an Austrian baron) and Alexander Baring (the future Lord Ashburton) cannot be accommodated within merely middle-class status, and were far removed in importance, wealth, influence, and social status from partners in local country banks.

Among the owners of factories, dynasties like the Strutts of Belper were already beyond 'middle-class' status by any reasonable test. Their peerage did not come until 1856, but early in the century the son of the house, who was to become the first Baron Belper, was educated at Trinity College, Cambridge, and served as President of the Cambridge Union. The family continued to own factories, but they were poles apart from the young Richard Cobden who, after working as a commercial traveller and a clerk, managed to scrape together the money to set up a calico-printing business in 1828. Other industrialists occupied a wide spread of positions between these two examples. Ownership of a factory does not prove a satisfactory basis for allocation to a coherent social class. Mine-owning is, as has been shown, an even clearer case, for a substantial body of the aristocracy was much involved in it, as well as the proprietors of small mines serving a purely local market, perhaps operated as a minor part of a farm's business.[64]

There is a disparity between the belief in the existence of a coherent middle class and the complex realities of that society. The attempt to reconcile the two may seem more promising if we accept a more limited aim than a middle class into which we thrust everyone who cannot be credibly assigned to a working class or an upper class. The contemporary concept of a middle class may have reflected a largely urban phenomenon, even if only a minority of the population actually lived in towns. There does seem to be a sketchy link between contemporary concepts of the middle class and the professional, commercial, and industrial groups in the towns. Even here, though, closer inspection soon undermines the concept. If a coherent middle class actually existed, then surely the merchants

---

64. An example of a small mine-owner is given in T. C. Smout, *A Century of the Scottish People, 1830–1950* (1986), 19. He cites the autobiography of Thomas Stewart whose father was a self-employed man with his own little pit in Lanarkshire where he worked the coal with family labour.

and manufacturers of Glasgow would provide a good example. One perceptive observer of that circle was Sir Archibald Alison, who arrived there as Sheriff of Lanarkshire in the early 1830s, and noted on this 'class' that 'I had not been long in Lanarkshire before I discovered that society in its commercial community was split into more divisions and coteries, which were actuated by a stronger feeling of jealousy towards each other, than the most aristocratic circles in London.'[65]

He described these divisions in detail, and then went on to adduce reasons for this disunity. They included matters of shared upbringing among the longer-established groups and their easy comprehension of the habits and conventions of polite society. Those accustomed to settled wealth and the workings of the city's upper society did not find it easy or agreeable to mingle with those whose newly acquired wealth had not been accompanied by the acquisition of polished education or social graces, nor were they conscious of any shared class identity here.

For a variety of reasons, then, it is sensible to accept that the common contemporary belief in the existence of a coherent middle class represents a widely accepted and influential intellectual invention or social myth rather than a reflection of contemporary realities. There was a middle to society and the term 'middle classes' has some utility provided it is recognized that the concepts of 'lower-' or 'upper-middle class' are subject to the same qualifications as 'middle class' itself.

Urban oligarchies

British towns were normally dominated by minorities who, like the landed interest in the counties, enjoyed a mixed pattern of economic, social, and political influences. These groups were of varied social status. They also differed in such matters as affiliation to different Churches and political parties. Although they dominated urban local government, this was not the basis of their power, which derived more from unofficial attributes such as personal status and property. Election as mayor did not make a man a 'principal inhabitant': only the 'principal inhabitants' were eligible for election as mayor.

Towns provided many of the available opportunities for social advancement, but the 'sober orderly habits' which Canning assigned to his middle class were not the prerogative of any particular social group. Examples of the industrialist or engineer who from lowly beginnings raised himself to great wealth and respectability provided a mainstay of nineteenth-century edifying literature, as exemplified in the best-selling works of Samuel Smiles. Such models existed in reality, and their success usually involved hard work. The early nineteenth-century industrial entrepreneur striving to establish himself had to play many parts—perhaps an innovator in technology, an industrial relations manager, an accountant, a market analyst, a salesman, a managing director, and a company

---

65. A. Alison, *Autobiography*, vol. i (1883), 344–8. I owe this reference to Dr J. M. Milne.

chairman, all rolled into one. Some of these men had great ambitions, which a few of them were able to translate into reality. Others set their sights lower. The engineer Joseph Clement described one of his early employers as 'only a mouthing common-council man, the height of whose ambition was to be an alderman'.[66] Clement himself was determined to do better than this, and did, but the less bright Mr Galloway, who would only pay him a guinea a week, and whose ambition was so limited, was far from unique. The high-flyers in industry and commerce existed in limited numbers, but behind them trailed a larger cohort of diminishing but real ambition and achievement. We have already seen that British agriculture improved, not because farmers were uniformly actuated by progressive zeal, but because in a varied situation enough of them were for the overall effect to be a rise in agricultural efficiency and output. The situation was similar in other economic sectors.

Despite claims made for the existence of a high level of virtue among the 'middle class', merchants, bankers, and manufacturers were not uniformly imbued with skill, application, honesty, or success.[67] Canning's faith in the 'sober, orderly habits' of his middle class induces scepticism. If we are to take 'sober' in a restricted sense, it is clear that hard drinking was not limited to any particular social group. The records of banks, schools, factories, builders, shipbuilders, and many other areas reveal instances of individuals—and families—ruined by excessive drinking. The Newcastle branch of the Bank of England was founded in 1828. During its early years members of its small staff were dismissed because of drunkenness; others were discarded because of adultery, embezzlement, and gambling.[68] In this period, as in others, 'skill and enterprise, and sober, orderly habits' were not the 'peculiar characteristics' of any distinct social class.

The 'working class'

The difficulties encountered in trying to match reality to the contemporary belief in the existence of a coherent middle class, endowed with its own peculiar characteristics, are repeated when we try to distinguish a working class. This problem exists even for historians convinced of the reality of discrete and separate social classes.[69] There is no difficulty in describing the condition of a banker and a labourer and deducing that they belonged to different positions in society. This difference does not lie in the fact that they belonged to discrete and separate social classes, but in the way in which they occupied different positions on a complicated social gradient, with a multitude of intermediate positions between them.

66. Kingsford, *Engineers, Inventors and Workers*, 83–5.
67. Cardwell, *Technology, Science and History*, 145, gives a good example of industrial sharp practice.
68. N. McCord is grateful to the Bank of England for allowing the use of correspondence of the Newcastle branch, held in the Bank's Record Office.
69. A good example of this difficulty will be found in D. Thompson, *The Chartists* (1984), 152.

In spite of the widespread belief that the development of industrial society produced a sharpening of social demarcations, the reverse is actually the case. In a pre-industrial context, when occupational patterns were simpler—with indeed the majority of workers involved in relatively uniform agricultural work—the concept of a working class may be easier to employ. One of the corollaries of the more complex economy which was emerging in the early nineteenth century, especially the expansion of commerce and industry, was a proliferation of different kinds of employment. Although the main effects of this were to come later, the trend already existed in 1815.

In the eighteenth century, the work of erecting a primitive steam engine had involved only three established trades—blacksmith, carpenter, millwright. Of these the millwright in particular possessed skills which were soon to be divided among a variety of new specialized trades.[70] If we believe that these variations mattered a great deal to those involved, the concept of an increasingly homogeneous working class will be difficult to accept. Consider the experience of the engineer James Nasmyth when he first encountered the workforce of a naval dockyard early in the nineteenth century:

The first Sunday that I spent at Devonport I went to the dockyard church—the church appointed for officials and men employed by the Government. The seats were appointed in the order of rank, employment and rate of pay. The rows of seats were all marked with the class of employees that were expected to sit in them. Labourers were near the door … No doubt the love of distinction, within reasonable limits, is a great social prime mover, but at Devonport, with the splitting up into ranks and dignities even amongst the workmen, I found it simply amusing.[71]

It is unlikely that this amusement was shared by the congregation, or that the distinctions meant little to those involved. An engineering worker operating a planing machine in routine work might be paid less than £1 weekly by 1830. There remained a small core of exceptionally skilled mechanics in advanced workshops who could command over £3 a week, more than six times the pay of many agricultural workers and appreciably more than the income of many Anglican clergymen and small business men.[72]

The expanding requirements of industrial work in fact produced an increasingly complicated division of labour. Joseph Clement's career before he became an engineering employer shows something of the variation which could be involved for an individual. We need not suppose that at his various stages he evinced much common feeling for those who failed to seize opportunities as he did. Beginning as a handloom weaver in Westmorland, he was promoted to thatcher and slater before obtaining better-paid work in a small Kirkby Stephen factory which manufactured power looms. When he was 28 he moved to

70. Kingsford, *Engineers, Inventors and Workers*, 49–50, gives an account of the multiple skills of the millwright.
71. Ibid. 142.   72. Ibid. 86–7.

Glasgow, by now a fully fledged turner by trade. By the time he was 34 he was earning more than £3 a week as a draughtsman in Aberdeen, having achieved this transition partly by his own efforts in self-education, partly by saving the money needed for drawing lessons. He later moved to London where he became super-intendent of Bramah's Pimlico works, accumulating there the savings with which to set himself up as an engineering employer. One of his early successes in his own business was to develop a planing machine which could earn him £20 a day when in full operation.[73]

As a consequence of the emergence of new specialized skills, an earlier pattern of relatively simple social divisions was being increasingly replaced by more complex hierarchies of occupation. These were often obvious in the developing industries, as in this account of a Welsh coal- and iron-working context:

At Hirwaun, for example, with its five furnaces, forge and mill, out of a total force of 1200, some 150 were skilled men, classified in eight different grades. Among the semi-skilled firemen, there were no fewer than 17 trades and even in the mass-occupations of miners and colliers, four or five categories can be distinguished.[74]

Similar, and sometimes more complicated, hierarchies existed in other occu-pational sectors, including domestic servants. There was a world of difference between a butler or a housekeeper in a great mansion and either the lower domestic ranks there or the single servant kept by an urban family in modest circumstances. It is unlikely that the Duke of Bedford's butler at Woburn Abbey would think of himself as occupying a position inferior to that of many shop-keepers or owners of workshops, probable that such a dignitary would himself have begun his career in lowly positions within the hierarchy below stairs. Nor was there much homogeneity to be found in the incomes, status, or conditions of various groups of workers. Some earned weekly or fortnightly pay, while for many engagements and wages were still on an annual basis. Wages for domestic servants were usually expressed as an annual sum; many farm workers and miners were tied to a binding annual engagement.

In a society still largely living in small, localized communities, with limited even if improving communications, opportunities for widespread contacts and organization between different groups of workers were weaker than they were to be in later periods. There were some, though, as can be seen from a variety of evidence. The working population was not completely immobile, even if the majority did not move far, if they moved at all. There was continuing movement in search of new or better employment, as Joseph Clement's career shows. Each year saw a migration of seasonal labour, much of it Irish, for harvesting crops. Major construction projects, such as the building of Waterloo Bridge in London, completed in 1817, involved the bringing together of many imported workers.

73. Kingsford, *Engineers Inventors and Workers*, 84.
74. G. A. Williams, 'The emergence of a working-class movement', in A. J. Roderick (ed.), *Wales Through the Ages* (1960), 142.

There is some evidence from early trade unionism of more than local contacts and cooperation, even if this was often sporadic.

The extent to which such contacts reflected the existence of a coherent 'working class' in early nineteenth-century Britain is still a matter of controversy. As in the case of the arguments about the standard of living in these years, the energy devoted to the problem is not derived solely from a desire to understand that society. In one of the twentieth century's most influential history books, E. P. Thompson's *The Making of the English Working Class*, an eloquent case was put forward for the existence of such a coherent class by 1830, citing a criterion which may not be immediately obvious:

class happens when some men, as a result of common experience (inherited or shared) feel and articulate the identity of their interests as between themselves, and as against other men whose interests are different from (and usually opposed to) theirs. The class experience is largely determined by the productive relations into which men are born—or enter involuntarily.[75]

It is easy to find some people who thought of themselves as part of a coherent working class in something like this sense. The difficulties arise in trying to determine how widespread such ideas may have been. On the whole, it seems that such concepts were not widely entertained. In a society in which farm labourers and domestic servants provided the largest elements among the workers, in which most people lived in small, locally orientated communities, in which many workers worked long hours for low wages, and in which communications and the level of literacy were still limited, there was not much in the way of promising material for class conflict on a broad scale.

If we look at specific groups which at first sight might offer greater promise for the implementation of E. P. Thompson's definition of the working class, there is some awkward evidence in the way. The handloom weavers, their position threatened by increasing competition from factory textile production, surely provide some of the best candidates here. However, an examination of the evidence relating to their condition, or rather conditions, has demonstrated a lack of uniformity. Even when handloom weavers in cotton alone are considered the results are clear:

This lack of homogeneity among the cotton handloom weavers was to crop up again and again among other groups of outworkers, and was to have many important consequences, not the least of which is the impossibility of making generalisations about large groups which had such diverse experiences and values.[76]

Even in cotton alone, handloom weaving was a varied occupation. There were different levels of work, entailing different levels of skill and offering different

75. E. P. Thompson, *The Making of the English Working Class* (1963), 193.

76. D. Bythell, *The Sweated Trades* (1978), 41. The standard study of the cotton handloom weavers is D. Bythell, *The Handloom Weavers: A Study in the English Cotton Industry during the Industrial Revolution* (1969). In *The Sweated Trades*, Dr Bythell widened the account to a perceptive study of outworkers in general.

technical problems for the introduction of mechanized production. In the finer grades, handloom weavers could be immune to competition from power-loom weaving for many years after the less skilled grades had been hard hit. If, however, we are told that we cannot make valid generalizations about such a limited group as handloom weavers in cotton, there seems little point in trying to argue for them within the concept of a broad working class.

As with that other contemporary concept, the middle class, the existence of the idea of the working class as an article of faith for deeply committed individuals in that day and later need not be doubted. If it is realized that entities such as the middle class and the working class represent a mode of thought rather than an objective representation of social realities, it may be possible to avoid the conceptual straitjacket which thinking in broad class terms often entails.

Class terminology was, nevertheless, to become, increasingly from the 1830s, part of everyday speech and 'common sense'. A resolve by a historian to refrain from it altogether would be ponderous and awkward. In what follows, class terminology will sometimes have to be used, subject to the doubts and caveats described. Where it is possible, the plural ('middle classes' and 'working classes'), which is less misleading than the singular, will be employed.

Rural conditions

What then motivated early nineteenth-century protest movements in the absence of class and 'class-consciousness'? Clearly, reductions in wages and threats to employment were the general and the particular causes but protesters usually have some ideological concept, however hazy. Recent studies have turned to the concept of 'populism' and emphasized the importance of attachment to tradition and community as well as to a largely oral historical memory of their rights. The notion of a 'moral economy' rather than a free market economy died hard especially amongst groups of workers who were threatened by economic change. One historian has argued that: 'Many craftsmen and village labourers continued long traditions of rebellion against an economic and social dislocation that had been going for five hundred years' and has termed the radicalism of the first decades of the century as a 'reactionary radicalism' shaped by 'present experience as well as "real" history'.[77]

Different groups of workers exhibited varying capacities for mutual support. Not surprisingly, organized protest by the rural worker was rare on anything more than a local basis. There were never any nationwide manifestations of rural discontent. The relatively widespread disturbances of the early 1830s, sparked off by attempts to introduce laboursaving machinery at a time of rising population and underemployment, showed that the long tradition of protest and demonstration was still alive in the British countryside. The scale of trouble in these years was exceptional rather than typical.

77. Craig Calhoun, *The Question of Class Struggle: Social Foundations of Popular Radicalism during the Industrial Revolution* (1982), 9 and 43.

The 'Highland Clearances' in Scotland, which occurred in two waves, 1785–1820 and 1820–50, the first marked by the eviction of tenants to make way for large-scale sheep farming and the second by the removal from coastal farms of tenants, who due to a decline in the prices for cattle and for kelp could not pay their rents, were met with widespread opposition, some of it violent and some of it repressed with violence. Essentially, the clearances, like the emigration from the Highlands, were caused by over-population and pressure upon the land combined with a more economic approach to estate management by landlords.[78]

The relative quiescence of the countryside should not be interpreted as reflecting a rural idyll. Conditions of farm workers varied. Better wages were paid where alternative employment was available in industry or mining. Farm workers adept in improved farming techniques could command higher wages if they made timely moves.[79] There were variations between wages and conditions in different regions, too. Housing for farm labourers was often poor—cottages without proper windows, ceilings, or internal divisions—partly because the considerable volume of short-distance migration which regularly took place after hiring fairs limited continuity of occupation. Prudent labourers might carry window frames with them on their moves, and invest in the box-beds which could provide storage space, substitutes for internal walls, possibly even some semblance of individual privacy. Some reforming landowners were already constructing better housing, but rural slums were still common.[80] On the whole, wages for farm labourers in the north were better than in much of the south. Dorset came to have something of a reputation for very poor conditions among farm labourers; in the late 1830s, the Anti-Corn Law League fastened on this to fight back against aristocratic criticisms of factory conditions. The variations to be found in rural areas were another factor militating against any concerted action by farm workers. Moreover, the small, close communities of the countryside were often much under the eye of local landowners, clergymen, and farmers.

Trade unions

Possession of a scarce skill could give workers some influence over their conditions of employment. Printers had tight apprenticeship regulations and a considerable coherence within the trade, even if their early trade unions were maintained on only a local basis. By 1827 the Printers' Pension Society had been placed on a firm footing, well before such facilities became available in other sectors of employment. Engineering workers were also early in the field in creating local unions of some influence and stability. Before the strong position of the millwrights was eroded, they had shown a capacity for coherent organization. William Fairbairn, later to become a distinguished Victorian engineer, recalled

78. J. D. Mackie, *A History of Scotland* (1964), 316.
79. Butler, *John Grey of Dilston*, 167.
80. W. S. Gilley, *The Peasantry of the Border: An Appeal on their Behalf* (1842), 14–15.

his experiences on coming to London in search of work in 1810. He and a friend were offered jobs by John Rennie, who was about to build Waterloo Bridge, but the foreman, Walker, explained to them that they would have to join the Millwrights' Society before they could take up the job offer, as a closed shop was in operation. On applying to the union secretary, the two applicants were told that they must wait for nearly a month until the union committee met. In the meantime they forged appropriate indentures, but used stamped paper with a watermark which had a later date than that in the forged documents. An attempt to erase the dates proved unconvincing. When the committee met they 'were at once declared illegitimate, and sent adrift to seek our fortunes elsewhere'.[81] Such workers' control was not always suffered to continue unchallenged. James Nasmyth was one engineer who insisted on choosing and training his own workers, preferring to select able and ambitious candidates from among the unskilled, rather than be obliged to take men approved by the union. The union called a strike to enforce the sacking of the promoted workmen and their replacement by union members.[82] These incidents also cast their own light upon the question of class unity among a particularly sophisticated group of workers.[83]

By the 1820s, despite the erosion of the privileged position formerly held by the millwrights, unionism among the skilled engineering workers had made progress. The biggest of their unions—the Journeymen Steam Engine and Machine Maker's Friendly Society—founded in 1826, which became known as the 'Old Mechanics', had thousands of members, even though it was far from incorporating all those eligible to join it. In the provinces, the main engineering centres preferred to rely on their own local unions, like the Mechanics' Friendly Union Institution in Bradford, the Steam Engine Makers' Society in Liverpool, or the Manchester Friendly Union of Mechanics. The coverage of such societies was modest, either restricted to a specific locality or to precise groups of workers—like the Amalgamated Society of Metal Planers or the Society of Friendly Boilermakers. Some of these early societies, and notably the Old Mechanics, survived to play a part in trade union development during the Victorian period. In these earlier years, they were small in relation to the growing numbers of skilled workers, and highly exclusive in their attitudes towards 'illegal' workers seeking to enter the skilled trades. They did, however, represent one of the areas in which trade unionism was entrenched. For many other groups of workers, union organization was either weaker or non-existent.

Friendly societies

Apart from trade unions, or sometimes combined with them, were various forms of 'self-help' agencies, of which the friendly societies were the most important.

81. Kingsford, *Engineers, Inventors and Workers*, 53–4.
82. Ibid. 138–9.
83. For a further illustration of Nasmyth's reactions to union activities, ibid. 86–7.

The typical friendly society provided, in return for regular subscriptions, support in time of sickness or death within a family. Many of them were purely local bodies, and some of them were short-lived, but a few acquired a more than local coverage. Some provided social activities, often on a quasi-masonic basis, as in the Ancient Order of Foresters for men or the Loyal Order of Ancient Shepherdesses for women. The merely local friendly society was more common. A typical situation was described by a local Tyneside directory of the 1820s, which noted that there were about 165 friendly societies in the district, with more than 10,000 members. This excluded many smaller societies, often based in a public house, and the 'Annual Benefit Societies', which offered only small welfare payments and distributed most of their funds in annual lotteries among members.[84] Local societies existed for diverse purposes. In the early 1830s the little northern village of Ford, like similar communities, possessed an 'Insurance Club' to insure the cows owned by the local farm labourers; local farmers valued the beasts involved in claims for compensation from the club's funds.[85]

Benefits of the kind offered by friendly societies were also available from other agencies, such as masonic lodges or trade unions. In addition, welfare payments could be made on an individual basis by employers who held paternalistic views. Friendly societies were regarded benevolently by authority; Parliament began a long series of protective and encouraging measures by an Act of 1793. The societies were never regarded with the same degree of suspicion as trade union activities often aroused. This attitude persisted even after it became clear that the respectable nature of friendly societies could be exploited for more dubious purposes, especially during the first quarter of the nineteenth century, when the Combination Acts of 1799–1800 seemed to make overt trade union activities vulnerable.

A well-documented instance of trade union activities under the cover of a friendly society is presented by a contemporary organization among merchant seamen.[86] The accounts of this body for 1826 are preserved among the Home Office papers, probably sent there by a correspondent who was more alarmed than gratified at the sophisticated organization evinced by the Loyal Standard Seamen's Association. That body was based on the seamen of the east coast collier fleet. In 1826 it paid out more than £1,000 in sickness and unemployment benefits, £315 in shipwreck relief, £171 in death grants, and nearly £70 in advances

84. Parson and White, *Directory of Northumberland, etc.*, vol. i (1828), pp. lxxxviii–lxxxix.

85. *Rules of the Ford Insurance Club* (1834) (Northumberland County Record Office).

86. Accounts of the Loyal Standard Seamen's Association, PRO, HO 40/21. Further discussion in N. McCord and D. E. Brewster, 'Some labour troubles of the 1790s in north east England', *International Review of Social History*, 13 (1969), 366–83; N. McCord, 'The seamen's strikes of 1815 in north east England', *Economic History Review*, 2nd ser., 21 (1968), 127–43; D. J. Rowe, 'A seamen's union of the north east coast seamen in 1825', *Economic History Review*, 25 (1972), 81–98; N. McCord, 'The government of Tyneside', *Transactions of the Royal Historical Society*, 5th ser., 20 (1970), 25–8; S. Jones, 'Community and organisation: early seamen's trade unions on the north east coast, 1768–1844', *Maritime History*, 3 (1973), 35–66.

to members against future pay. The association arranged access for its members to local hospital and dispensary facilities by paying collective subscriptions. Its president, Thomas Woodroffe, a leader of considerable dexterity, was a paid full-time officer (it was not until 1843 that the 'Old Mechanics' acquired a full-time general secretary). Other documents show the association soliciting donations and backing from influential quarters, operating a library, and disciplining seamen who either obtained grants from its funds on false pretences or disobeyed association orders during an industrial dispute. Another activity consisted of feeding selective evidence and primed witnesses—Woodroffe was one of these—to the parliamentary inquiry which preceded the repeal of the Combination Acts in 1824. Ostensibly a friendly society, this association was in reality an effective trade union too. In the great strikes of 1815, to give only one example, its seamen paralysed the north-east coal-shipping ports and the east coast coal trade; that strike ended with some gains for the seamen and limited retaliation by the authorities.

In the early nineteenth century, such activities were unusually advanced and sophisticated. At the same time, the association's attitude towards other workers seems to have been ambivalent. The 1826 accounts include an item '£50 to the Artisans at Bradford', representing a donation to workers in another part of the country. Other evidence suggests that too much should not be made of this instance of solidarity.[87] In 1831 the north-east miners struck for better wages and conditions, and this stoppage meant that the seamen of the collier fleet were laid idle. Instead of making common cause with the miners, Woodroffe negotiated an agreement with the local authorities whereby his members would remain quiescent in return for a semi-official collection for the relief of distressed seamen. The Mayor of Newcastle sponsored this appeal, and the proceeds were handed over to the Seamen's Loyal Standard Association for distribution at its discretion. The Home Office was kept fully informed, and the Duke of Northumberland thought that 'the seamen of this port are behaving in a very creditable manner.' When the miners' strike ended, the seamen's leaders refused to man the collier fleet unless they were promised a wage increase. During these troubles, Woodroffe assiduously cultivated the local magistrates and the senior military and naval officers in the area. In the unequal society of these years, this kind of leadership was sagacious.

Popular discontent

Industrial disputes of this kind had many precedents, and long before the opening of the nineteenth century Britain's rulers had accumulated a great deal of experience in dealing with popular discontent.[88] Local magistrates had to go on

---

87. N. McCord, *North East England: The Region's Development, 1760–1960* (1979), 84–7.
88. PRO, SP 70/5, for example, provides illuminating insights into the official reaction to an important miners' strike in 1765.

living in their communities after any eruption had subsided, and most of them appreciated that life might be more comfortable if they behaved reasonably. Magistrates were therefore often lenient in the sentences inflicted in trials arising out of local troubles, especially if no overtly subversive element was involved. Such restraint could be contrasted with the often draconian nature of the contemporary penal code. In a society which might hang a man for forging a cheque, the frequently mild response to strikes and other manifestations of discontent is illuminating.

In other ways, too, local authorities often sought to appease discontent. There was a tradition of mediation in industrial disputes, and in many parts of the country prominent individuals acquired reputations for patient negotiations to settle strikes and other local disputes. It was also common practice for the spokesmen of the discontented to seek countenance, support, and mediation from influential groups. In practice this approach could be more profitable than overt defiance of the established order.

The recorded demonstrations, riots, strikes, and other clashes of these years present to us only some of the cases in which pressure was exerted on those in authority, whether the latter were employers or magistrates. It is not at all clear, however, that the early nineteenth century exhibited any escalation even in the more obtrusive methods of exercising such pressures. No collision between crowds and the army during the early nineteenth century equalled the bloodshed of the militia riots of 1761, when the country town of Hexham saw a battle between troops and rioters, in which as many as fifty-two may have been killed and women and children were among the dead and wounded.[89] One of the leaders of a previous disturbance at Morpeth, also arising out of militia balloting, 'a yeoman farmer worth some £4,000, and well over seventy years of age', was subsequently executed for high treason. Nothing in the nineteenth century approached in scale the Gordon Riots of June 1780, which caused hundreds of deaths and widespread destruction in London.[90]

In these matters, as in some others, a fuller survival of evidence has tended to exaggerate the extent to which the population of the early decades of the century was more volatile and disaffected than earlier generations. Only a small minority of workers was involved in trade union activity. Attempts to found broad unions covering wide ranges of employment all foundered. The most famous, Robert Owen's Grand National Consolidated Trades Union of the 1830s, reached during its short life a maximum paying membership of only about 16,000, though no doubt many more sympathized with its aims.[91] Most popular demonstrations of discontent during these years were attempts to seek redress of practical grievances rather than any deliberate challenge to the existing patterns of authority.

89. T. Corfe, *Riot: The Hexham Militia Riot, 1761* (2004), 40.
90. J. Stevenson, *Popular Disturbances in England, 1700–1870* (1979), 76–90.
91. A. E. Musson, *Trade Union and Social History* (1974), 16–17.

The standard of living

One of the historical controversies of the twentieth century has been the 'standard of living' debate. This involved in the 1960s and 1970s a series of exchanges between 'optimists' and 'pessimists' in relation to the effects of the 'Industrial Revolution' on living standards in Britain, especially those of the poorer sections of society.[92] An ironic twist underlies the whole debate, which concentrated on the imperfect evidence relating to the late eighteenth and early nineteenth centuries. Much of the heat engendered in the exchanges was derived from conflicting views of the impact of 'capitalist' industry on the working population and the poor. The irony lies in the fact that most of these broadsides were aimed at the wrong targets. The principal contestants concentrated their fire on the early nineteenth century. However, to appreciate the real impact of industrialization it is to the Victorian period and later that attention should be directed. The factory system and the mechanization of production exerted only a limited effect by 1830; it was only in the second half of the century that industry came to affect directly a large proportion of the population. There is substantial agreement that during the later period, despite the huge increase in population, there was overall improvement in the standard of living.

The surviving evidence cannot provide anything like a complete answer to questions about the British standard of living in the early nineteenth century. To talk in terms of a single standard of living is a grotesque over-simplification, for conditions varied in both time and place. Some groups of skilled workmen could obtain wages of more than £3 a week; many farm labourers in low-wage areas might receive only an eighth of this. In 1805 some handloom weavers of a not particularly skilled kind might have been paid 23s. a week; as competition from factory production spread in the cotton industry, they might have been hard put to it to earn 8s. 6d. by 1818 and as little as 6s. by 1831. On the other hand it was not until after 1835 that competition from power-loom weaving began to bite in the worsted trade and not until after 1850 in much of the woollen trade, so that handloom weavers' wages held up for longer in those sectors.[93] There was not even any uniformity in the relationship between wages paid to men and women. In some groups of textile workers, men and women doing the same job received at least nominally the same wages, in others men were paid more highly. In many other contexts, men were paid much more than women doing comparable work.[94]

Two investigations which quantified the evidence resulted in a modest divergence. In 1974 Professor Michael Flinn compared the various indices of wages which had been computed for 1780 to 1830.[95] He demonstrated a correlation

---

92. The main contributions to the debate are conveniently listed in M. W. Flinn, 'Trends in real wages, 1750–1850', *Economic History Review*, 2nd ser., 27 (1974), 412–13.

93. Bythell, *The Sweated Trades*, 49–50.

94 E. H. Hunt, *British Labour History, 1815–1914* (1981), 102–3.

95. Flinn, 'Trends in real wages', 395–413.

between the various calculations, and that this indicated a slow rise in wages over the fifty years in national aggregate terms. Another investigation by G. N. Von Tunzelmann five years later found that during the same period the trend in real wages was flat.[96] That the question can ever be definitively resolved is doubtful for there are still serious gaps in our knowledge. It is difficult to equate wage rates with actual earnings, because of factors like irregular hours or weeks of working, family earnings, or the incidence of sickness. Another problem is that our knowledge of retail prices in these years is defective.

Even if it is accepted, as now seems likely, that there was on average a slow improvement in these years, this will be an average of limited significance because of the variations which it conceals. There can be no simple or uniform answer to questions about the standard of living. We know that there *were* marked fluctuations in prices, and that temporary depressions could hit employment and earnings hard in some parts of the country. Even if we had more reliable indications of movements in wages, earnings, and prices, there are other variables to be taken into account in considering the condition of the people—housing, health, diet, levels of education, and opportunity, for example. At the Quarry Bank Mill at Styal in Cheshire, the Greg family paid wages which were much the same as levels in comparable factories elsewhere. However, their provision of housing, education, and medical services was remarkably generous for those years. Despite the limitations of the surviving evidence for standards of living in early nineteenth-century Britain, to show any improvement at all in a context of accelerating population growth was an achievement.

Poverty

Economic change brought enhanced opportunities for some workers and disastrous competition from new modes of production for others. Throughout the period covered by this book there remained a mass of poverty and suffering. Early in Victoria's reign, Macaulay noted that roughly a tenth of the British population might need help from the Poor Law in a bad year, perhaps only a fifteenth when times were better. He took comfort from his probably well-founded calculation that these proportions were appreciably smaller than had been the case in earlier periods, and reflected that

The more carefully we examine the history of the past; the more reason shall we find to dissent from those who imagine that our age has been fruitful of new evils. The truth is that the evils are, with scarcely an exception, old. That which is new is the intelligence which discerns and the humanity which remedies them ... the more we study the annals of the past the more shall we rejoice that we live in a merciful age, in an age in which cruelty is abhorred, and in which pain, even when deserved, is inflicted reluctantly and from a sense

96. G. N. Von Tunzelmann, 'Trends in Real Wages, 1750–1850, revisited', *Economic History Review*, 2nd ser., 32 (1979), 33–49.

of duty. Every class doubtless has gained largely by this great moral change; but the class which has gained most is the poorest, the most dependent, and the most helpless.[97]

To support these comforting reflections, Macaulay noted that practices such as child labour were not a recent innovation, but long established, and he commended the way in which Parliament had recently begun to restrict this practice. His claims for the ability of the society of the early nineteenth century to discern and remedy social evils must rely upon a number of factors. Part of this lies in the working of the Poor Law and other instances of official activity in the relief of poverty and associated problems, already discussed in the previous chapter. In these matters, however, as in others, the formal agencies of central and local government played a restricted role in these years; unofficial activity was more extensive. In that unequal society, official and unofficial agencies were commonly controlled by the same influential groups.

Philanthropy

The historical record will not preserve the full account of individual suffering during these years, much of which must have gone unrecorded. On the other hand, much of the help extended to those in need will have come in personal responses by individuals, and most of this will also be missing from the historical record. Chance mention will supply examples, but there can be no reliable quantitative assessment of either suffering or its alleviation. The distinguished engraver Thomas Bewick happened to mention in his autobiography the case of the bookbinder Gilbert Gray; after noting other virtues of 'this remarkable, singular & worthy man', Bewick remarked

I have often discovered that he did not overlook ingenious Mechanics, whose misfortune, perhaps mismanagement, had led them to a lodging in Newgate—to these he directed his compassionate eye, & to the deserving (in his estimation) he paid the debt & set them at liberty—he felt hurt at seeing the hands of an ingenious man tied up in a prison, where they were of no use, either to themselves or to the community.[98]

Obituaries and memorials can provide other evidence of a kind. Here is part of the epitaph on William Colling, Esq., a Durham landowner, in St Michael's Church, Heighington; there are many parallels elsewhere.

In this village and neighbourhood his exemplary regard to the claims of helpless age, or orphan destitution, of struggling industry, and faithful service, will long be gratefully remembered. Nor can it be forgotten how constantly the cheerfulness of habitual benevolence, and of a conscience void of offence, which shone forth in his countenance and brightened his path in life, shed its kindly influence on others, endeared him to his friends and the poor, and deepened the regret universally felt at his loss.

97. The passage is in the celebrated third chapter of the *History of England*. Macaulay began to write his history in the spring of 1839; the first two volumes were published in 1848.
98. T. Bewick, *A Memoir Written by Himself*, ed. I. Bain (1975), 43–4.

There may be hyperbole here, but the account is unlikely to be a serious distortion of reality.

Charitable activity and expenditure were an obligation laid by convention, and also by religious duty, on those who were able to help others. An example was set by the royal family who from the time of George III onwards were strenuous in their support for charitable causes. We know of many recorded demonstrations of personal philanthropy.[99] The third Earl of Egremont, whom we have met as Turner's patron, regularly devoted £20,000 per annum to charitable expenditure. It was normal for aristocrats to be major subscribers to a range of philanthropic activities within their own area of influence. It was conventionally accepted that a wealthy landowner would provide for his own dependants, as can be seen in surviving examples of almshouses. Pensions to retired servants were common. If charity was expected to begin at home, it was not expected to end there. Personal philanthropy was necessarily patchy, with individuals embracing causes which they found attractive, while taking little interest in others. Richard 'Humanity' Martin, already encountered as an Irish landlord, provides a good example.[100] As a well-connected member of the House of Commons, and a personal friend of George IV, he could make his wishes count, and his reputation as a duellist did not detract from his ability to exert influence. One of his interests was a crusade against cruelty to animals. In 1822 he was the sponsor of the first legislation on this subject, and he did his best to secure successful prosecutions for breaches of that Act. He was also involved in the campaign for mitigating the severity of the penal code. In his native Ireland he was regarded as a benevolent landlord.

A second category of philanthropic activity took the form of collective responses to local tragedies or catastrophes; it is an illuminating reflection on the limited role of the State that this was a field for unofficial rather than official exertions. Activities of this kind were a normal responsibility of the 'principal inhabitants' of the affected area. A hard winter, a colliery disaster, an epidemic, depression in local industry, events of this kind normally sparked off local collections of money and the establishment of ad hoc organizations for relief work. Collections were not confined to money; gifts of food, fuel, or clothing might also be made on suitable occasions. As the country's banking system developed, it became standard practice for local banks to provide unpaid facilities for the administration of relief funds as well as making their own donations.

The financing of public works in times of unemployment was an activity often embarked upon by such agencies, while the setting up of soup kitchens or other emergency feeding arrangements was equally common. A couple of examples of such operations may serve as illustrations. In January 1805, five fishing boats carrying nineteen men were lost in a storm off the north-east coast. There

99. One good example is the list of Peel's personal donations given in N. Gash, *Sir Robert Peel* (1972), 185–6.
100. DNB.

followed an appeal for subscriptions to aid the bereaved families, which raised a total of £1,701. Most of this came in donations from the wealthier sectors of local society, including both old-established landed wealth and newer fortunes derived from coal and commerce. The hard winter of 1816 saw public subscriptions set on foot in many places to provide employment and relief for the poor. At Sunderland the collection of 1816 raised £2,437. A similar effort there three years later received the blessing of the Home Secretary, Lord Sidmouth, who expressed his warm approval of these voluntary efforts 'for the purpose of finding Employment for poor Persons who have been deprived of it, in consequence of the peculiar Circumstances and Pressures of the Times'.[101] The extent of this kind of activity was impressive, the more so since in many cases, as, for example, a slump in the local economy, the causes of the distress also made it more difficult for some of the potential donors to contribute to relief funds.

A third element in contemporary philanthropic activity was the creation of lasting charitable institutions. This development was under way before the nineteenth century began. By 1815 more energy and money were deployed in these ameliorative measures than by the official Poor Law machinery. There were parallels between charitable institutions in various parts of the country, and imitation and even rivalry in provision. Many of the new institutions were established in the principal towns. One of the best examples was provided by the work of the great voluntary hospitals. In London, Guy's Hospital had been founded in 1721, but received a major fillip from a legacy of almost £200,000 in 1829, among many lesser gifts and bequests. Charing Cross Hospital was established in 1818 and received new premises in 1831. Such metropolitan examples were imitated in developing provincial centres. The Newcastle Infirmary had been established in 1751 by a group of that town's 'principal inhabitants' in imitation of a slightly earlier example at Northampton. New premises were acquired in 1802 after a public appeal netted more than £5,000, nearly half of it in donations from local peers and baronets. A further appeal in 1817 financed the addition of 'warm baths, on an approved pattern'. Just as Newcastle had imitated Northampton, so Sunderland imitated the regional capital; in 1822 Lord Londonderry laid the foundation stone of the first voluntary hospital there.

The growing number of voluntary hospitals was accompanied by dispensaries for the provision of free medicines and treatment for minor afflictions. In practice, conditions in early nineteenth-century hospitals did not always match the good intentions of their founders, while the limitations of contemporary medical science meant that hospital treatments remained primitive as far as curative potential was concerned.

Charities like these were usually operated on a patronage basis, which reflected the nature of contemporary society. Apart from emergency cases, it was normal

---

101. These voluntary philanthropic efforts are mentioned in several letters in PRO, HO 41/5, 42/196, and 42/197.

for subscribers to possess pro rata rights to introduce patients for treatment. Town councils, friendly societies, and other corporate bodies might equip themselves with rights of nomination by paying an appropriate annual subscription. Regulations often stipulated that patients must express thanks to the institution for the help given, and also give thanks to God. The number and variety of charitable institutions continued to grow, including orphanages, asylums, and specialist facilities for such categories as maternity cases, the blind, the deaf and dumb, and even for prostitutes.

They were only one facet of a more varied pattern of philanthropy.[102] The toll of death and injury among merchant seamen was for most of the century greater than that among coal-miners, and by 1800 the principal ports possessed a chain of Shipwrecked Mariners' Societies, linked so that a seaman of one port could claim assistance in another if shipwrecked away from home. From similar motives the National Lifeboat Institution was founded in 1824, and in its first year managed to save 124 lives. Ten years later the annual figure had risen to 214, but many more seamen were still lost; in 1830 for instance 677 British vessels were lost at sea. A new Destitute Sailors' Fund was established on a national basis in 1827, while there were also many local charities for seamen and their families, such as the Hull Sailors' Children's Society founded in 1821.

The philanthropic movement continued to grow despite doubts about the wisdom of some of its manifestations. A fear was sometimes voiced that if charity became too readily available it might stultify the incentives to individual effort, sap healthy independence, and discourage attempts at self-improvement. A principal reason why such doubts failed to stem the increasing level of charitable provision was that charity was seen as a Christian duty in a society in which religion was a powerful force. There was, nevertheless, a tendency to greater discrimination between the deserving and the undeserving poor and a new view that charity should aim to help eradicate social problems rather them ameliorate them; here utilitarianism and evangelicalism came together.

Religion

Another indication of the strength of this Christian influence was the increase in school provision in these years. One major motive for this was the desire to spread literacy in order that religious works, and especially the Bible, could be read, and more children reared in an atmosphere which emphasized the duties of a Christian. Religious education was widely seen as the most important topic in the expansion of schooling. Education was not to be given in any detached sense; even apart from specifically religious instruction, education should be directed

---

102. For a general discussion of this theme, D. Owen, *English Philanthropy, 1660–1960* (1965). For a regional example, N. McCord, 'The Poor Law and philanthropy', in D. Fraser (ed.), *The New Poor Law in the Nineteenth Century* (1976), 87–110.

to character-building and the inculcation of virtue. Children should be taught to do their duty in whatever station they had been called to by Divine Providence. A good example of this kind of educational expansion was given by the numerous Jubilee Schools which were built after the Jubilee of George III in 1810, and the aged monarch's much publicized wish that all of the children in his dominions should be able to read the Bible.

An important impetus behind medical relief agencies was not only general Christian charity, but the belief that sick people could scarcely be expected to perform religious duties. Charities which aimed at improving social conditions often had as their ultimate aim the provision of an environment in which devoutness could flourish. Many people believed, not unreasonably, that the profoundest charity of all was that which sought the salvation of immortal souls. For them, organizations like the British and Foreign Bible Society, of 1804, the London Society for Promoting Christianity among the Jews, of 1809, the National Society for Promoting Religious Education in Accordance with the Principles of the Church of England, of 1811, and the Lord's Day Observance Society, of 1831, were every bit as much philanthropic endeavours as hospitals and dispensaries, maternity institutions, and eye infirmaries.

It is difficult for our generation, living in a largely secularized society, to appreciate the importance of religion within the society with which this book is concerned. The Christian religion, in its various sects, occupied the energies and the devotion of many people, including a high proportion of those who possessed effective influence. Religious devotion was not the prerogative of any particular sector of society; it recruited large numbers of adherents at all social levels, without achieving complete dominance in any.

Religion, nevertheless, permeated almost every aspect of life to the extent that one study of the early nineteenth century has described the period as 'The Age of Atonement', arguing that even economic thought was not just a secular matter and that for Evangelicals economic developments were invested with moral and religious meaning, with depressions being seen as punishments from on high rather than blips in the trade cycle.[103]

In 1815 a religious revival was already under way, exemplified both by the Evangelical movement within the Church of England and by an expansion and reinvigoration of the Nonconformist Protestant sects. The relative pre-eminence of the Established Church of England was to decline during the early nineteenth century, but it remained the biggest single Church and the Church of the majority of the devout members of the most influential groups in society. In recent years, historians have devoted much attention to the role of evangelical religion among society's poorer groups. Where there has been any sustained investigation of the role of religion among the most powerful groups within that

---

103. Boyd Hilton, *The Age of Atonement: The Influence of Evangelicalism on Social and Economic Thought 1785–1865* (1988).

unequal society the evidence for widespread conversions and genuine devotion is impressive.[104]

The Anglican Church in 1815 possessed a traditional organization which could not be easily altered; the creation of a new parish required a special Act of Parliament. Even before industrial and urban growth had distorted the older distribution of population, in some areas the parochial organization did not fit demographic patterns. Other weaknesses included disparities in clerical incomes, clerical absenteeism, and the plural holding of benefices. In the early nineteenth century, as many as a thousand parishes could be without a resident clergyman, although this amounted to only about 10 per cent of the total. In many cases the problem of non-residence was mitigated by arrangements made outside the parochial system; a parish would be counted in the 'non-resident' total even if it was served by a clergyman who lived just outside its boundary. However, the Established Church was failing to reach a substantial part of the population, especially in areas of concentrated population growth. When Charles Blomfield became Bishop of London in 1828, he advocated the immediate construction of fifty new churches, in order to make some headway in the formidable task of matching accommodation to inhabitants in the capital alone.

Both then and later the shortcomings of the Church of England attracted description and comment. Here as elsewhere there is an inherent bias in the historical record, which tends to record things which have gone awry, while neglecting the continuance of relatively satisfactory normality. In a Britain which was still largely rural, the traditional Anglican organization was not as badly out of tune with the times as it appeared to be in the principal areas of economic and social change. If there were notorious cases of nepotism, pluralism, and absenteeism among the clergy, there were many conscientious and humane parsons, too.

It is also instructive to consider some of the more notorious cases of nepotism in high ecclesiastical appointments.[105] Richard Bagot was the sixth son of Lord Bagot; after taking holy orders in 1806 he was at once presented to two livings of which his father was the patron. In 1812 he became a prebendary of Lichfield, in 1817 a canon of Windsor, in 1827 Dean of Canterbury, and in 1829 Bishop of Oxford, continuing to hold his deanery with that see. No doubt much of this preferment, perhaps all of it, was owed to his influential connections, but he proved a conscientious and competent bishop. Charles Manners Sutton, Archbishop of Canterbury from 1805 to 1828, may have owed his rapid rise in the Church to his being a grandson of the third Duke of Rutland. He was an active and conscientious prelate long before the main period of Church reform; he

104. Gilbert, *Religion and Society in Industrial England*, gives a general discussion of religion in these years, drawn on heavily for the account here; Bradley, *The Call to Seriousness*, specifically discusses the impact of evangelical religion on the aristocracy. The religious revival of these years was not a specifically British phenomenon, but part of a wider development; other European countries and America provide parallels.
105. DNB.

played a useful role in laying the foundations for the ecclesiastical reforms of the 1830s, energetically supported the building of Anglican schools, and facilitated the rise of many of the most able clergymen of the next generation. Edward Harcourt, Archbishop of York from 1807 to 1847, was the younger son of Lord Vernon, and inherited the fortune of the third Earl Harcourt; he used his influence to further the clerical career of one of his sons. He also regularly spent more than his clerical income on the needs of his diocese. Bishops and rectors appointed because of their birth and connections were not necessarily careless or incompetent; the influence which their personal position entailed could often be deployed to serve the purposes of the Church. By the early nineteenth century, clergymen were generally exposed to more pressures for the effective discharge of their duties than had been the case in the previous century.

During the late eighteenth and early nineteenth centuries, Parliament passed a series of Acts dealing with clerical residence, pluralism, and provisions to increase the scandalously low income of the poorest clergy. In 1818 a clutch of new statutes appeared; Parliament not only voted the considerable sum of £1 million of public money for church building (to be followed by another half million six years later), but also provided for the easier creation of new parishes.

Nevertheless, the Established Church faced a difficult situation in these years. The number of Anglican churches rose only from 11,444 in 1811 to 11,558 in 1821 and 11,883 in 1831, while over the same period the population increased by almost a half. In Ireland, the sister Church of Ireland served only a small minority within a predominantly Roman Catholic population. In Wales the Established Church faced a strong Nonconformist challenge.

Scotland was a mirror-image of the religious face of England. The established church was Presbyterian, disavowing bishops and governed by a hierarchy of courts culminating in a General Assembly. The Episcopal Church of Scotland, a member of the Anglican Communion, had been close to extinction in the early eighteenth century but had revived as an independent and disestablished church. A desire for Calvinistic doctrinal purity made the Presbyterian church the focus for disagreements and consequent splits, the most important of which was to be the 'Disruption' of 1843, the result of dissension over the question of patronage in ministerial settlements.

Throughout Britain the Nonconformist sects were making progress in the early nineteenth century. The Methodist Churches saw their membership rise from 143,311 in 1811 to 288,182 in 1831. The other dissenting sects, some of which had been in existence for many years, experienced a comparable revival in enthusiasm and membership. The Congregational connection grew from 35,000 members in 1800 to 127,000 in 1837, while over the same period the two main Baptist sects grew from 27,000 to just under 100,000. But the Methodists provided the most prodigious example of expansion. Their early growth was concentrated in the original Wesleyan Methodist Connection, which grew from 135,863 members in 1811 to 232,883 in 1831. In 1811 the numbers enrolled in breakaway Methodist sects were negligible, but from the separation of the Primitive Methodist Connection during the years 1807–12, the older communion was challenged by vigorous secessionist groups. These were to prove especially successful in penetrating areas such as the northern mining districts, as well as making many converts in rural areas. The divisions among Methodists arose partly over authority within the sect, and partly over differing attitudes towards evangelical activities. The original Wesleyan Connection had given its ministers a prominent place in Church government, and established a relatively tight discipline. At the same time its leaders were sceptical about both the spiritual validity and the practical utility of the emotional revivalist modes of worship and conversion increasingly advocated by ginger groups within the Connection.

The two main founders of Primitive Methodism were Hugh Bourne, a carpenter, and William Clowes, a potter. Clowes had been a wild youth and a champion dancer, but in his twenties he experienced the spiritual experience of personal conversion. In 1807 Bourne refused to accept the Wesleyan Conference's ban on 'camp meetings'—emotional open-air revivalist occasions following American models. After his subsequent expulsion from the Wesleyan Connection, he was instrumental in forming the new Primitive Methodist Connection. For many years Bourne made no claim on the tiny resources of his Church, supporting himself by his work as a carpenter while continuing missionary activity.

The secession of the Primitive Methodists—often known as 'the ranters'—was imitated by other breakaway Methodist groups, such as the Bible Christians and the New Connection Methodists. Although the original Wesleyan Connection remained the largest element within this branch of dissent, the Primitive Methodists were particularly active among the poorer sectors of society. Its early agents were workers who, like William Clowes, had themselves undergone the transforming experience of spiritual conversion and now sought to bring others to it. Often travelling on foot in all kinds of weather, frequently greeted with vigorous and sometimes with violent opposition, they achieved a degree of success in penetrating sections of society who had often been virtually immune to religious influences during the recent past.

Some idea of the atmosphere of these crusades is suggested by a description of an early Primitive Methodist mission in a northern mining district:

The most impressive scenes were witnessed. Fallings were common, as many as fourteen being seen on the floor at once. At a love-feast at Bishop Auckland the people fell in all directions and there was a strange mingling of shouts, groans and hallelujahs. During the revival at South Side, centres of gambling were broken up; confirmed gamblers burnt their dice, cards and books of enchantment; drunkards, hopeless, incurable sots, were freed from the dread tyranny of fiery appetite; pugilists, practiced and professional, and cock-fighters of terrible experience, turned from their brutalities. The miracle was repeated at Evenwood, West Auckland, and elsewhere, and at each place the converts became church workers and several of them local preachers.[106]

106. W. M. Patterson, *Northern Primitive Methodism* (1909), 70.

Future generations believed that the missionaries of these years played an important role in reforming the morals and manners of the groups they penetrated, as well as effecting many conversions. By the early 1830s, a visitor to the northern lead-mining dales said of the Methodist missionaries that

They have been the principal engine in effecting a change in this wild district, and instead of insult and a volley of stones, strangers are met with civility and good behaviour ... They have reclaimed and reformed individuals who were enemies to their families and themselves, as well as a perfect pest and disgrace to the neighbourhood.[107]

Such achievements no doubt occurred, but they were far from universal. These crusades did not convert Britain in general to a vigorous Christianity even if they did convert many individuals. Works of Nonconformist hagiography show that if some communities early acquired and long retained a strong religious vocation, others required repeated doses of missionary zeal to keep them up to the mark, and some successfully resisted all crusading efforts.[108] Later in the century it was found necessary to mount repeated campaigns of large-scale missionary activity; great missions on a national scale took place in 1849, 1859–60, 1874–6, and 1881–3, with the last great campaign of our period coming in 1904–6.[109] Even with these repeated efforts, though, success was always far from complete. It was said of one group of northern workers that 'A few of these men were deeply religious and attached to the Wesleyan or Primitive Methodist Churches, but the great bulk kept outside the boundaries of ecclesiastical influence. Their principal hobbies were dogs, rabbit-coursing and bowling on the sands by the sea.'[110]

Even the limited success attained by the Churches had important consequences. Religious zeal was a factor not only in the spread of charitable activities, but also in the accelerating course of social reform, and the increasing pressure for official action to ameliorate the ills of contemporary society. Factory reform, mines reform, protection of children and animals, the campaigns against slavery, all these and others owed much to the support of the devout. At all points on the social spectrum there were individuals who shared a belief in the paramount importance of salvation. Evangelical fervour linked a devout Tory peer, like the philanthropic Lord Shaftesbury, with devout manufacturers like the Huntley and Palmer families of Reading, and the converted miners of Bishop Auckland who took to local preaching. The successes of the evangelical revival at all levels of society were matched by their failures. If there were devout members of the peerage, there were also those there whose manners and morals were far from meeting evangelical prescriptions. If there were genuinely devout bankers, merchants, and industrialists, there were also others whose commercial morality, to take only one aspect, was far from conforming to Christian ethics. If there were many

107. C. J. Hunt, *The Lead Miners of the Northern Pennines* (1970), 221.
108. Patterson, *Northern Primitive Methodism*, provides good examples of all three categories.
109. Gilbert, *Religion and Society in Industrial England*, 192.
110. W. Runciman, *Collier Brigs and their Sailors* (1926), 80. The men involved were the keelmen who manned the coal-carrying barges of the northern rivers.

devout coal-miners and farm labourers, there were others who remained rough and barbaric in their behaviour.

Women

The evangelical movement also played a part in redefining the role of women in society. As one historian has put it: 'Evangelicalism was above else the religion of the home. It idealised and sanctified family life.'[111] Enormous importance was placed upon the wife as the guardian of the hearth and the custodian of a paradise withdrawn from worldly corruptions.

The position and role of women in the early nineteenth century is hotly contested by historians. Recent work on women's history has greatly extended our knowledge of the lives and positions of women in this period but has exposed the difficulty of distinguishing between what women had in common and what they had in variance. As a historian of aristocratic women has written: 'A duchess had only as much in common with the wife of a factory worker as their respective husbands had with each other.'[112] Whether in terms of the social order, the commonalities of interest groups, or religious divisions, it is obvious that the experience of diverse groups of women fractured if it did not transcend sex and gender.

Many writers of women's history have seen the late eighteenth and early nineteenth century as a period in which women were increasingly cut off from the world of work and business as the home and workplace became separate spheres,[113] while even aristocratic ladies and gentlewomen withdrew from the active management of estates and households and an active interest in public life. As Amanda Vickery has remarked, the problem with this thesis is that, as with the famous rise of the middle class, the development has been discerned by historians of many different centuries: 'So, if the literature is read as a whole, it is hard to avoid the impression that the spheres definitely separated and the new domestic woman was born in every century since the end of the Middle Ages.'[114]

Although interpretations of changes in the position of women during the early nineteenth century may have compressed developments into too narrow a timescale and discounted continuities, we can, nevertheless, point to a greater emphasis upon women's separate and domestic role due in part to economic developments and in part to religious revival.

For those sectors of society experiencing greater prosperity, the removal or distancing of wives and daughters from a wider society with all its brutalities and

111. Bradley, *The Call to Seriousness*, 179.

112. Kim Reynolds, *Aristocratic Women and Political Society in Victorian Britain* (1998), 4.

113. Leonore Davidoff and Catherine Hall, *Family Fortunes: Men and Women of the English Middle Class 1780–1850* (1987), argue that 'separate spheres' was the outcome of the development of capitalism which separated home from work.

114. Amanda Vickery, *The Gentleman's Daughter: Women's Lives in Georgian England* (1998), 3. See also her historiographical review, 'Golden Age to Separate Spheres? A Review of the Categories and Chronology of English Women's History', *Historical Journal*, 36, 2 (1993), 383–414.

poverty could be a mark of status, while a sentimentalism as to female purity and otherworldliness fitted in with both one strain of romanticism and that aspect of evangelicalism which emphasized patriarchy, duty, and a subjugation of sensual appetites. Whereas previous ages had often seen women as sexually insatiable and thus a potential threat to men and the social order, the early nineteenth century increasingly represented women, or at any rate 'respectable' women, as without sexual desire.

The eighteenth century had seen alternative models for the woman who was independent, either by status or inclination: that emanating from the Enlightenment pointed towards intellectual independence and free thinking, while that provided by religious revival stressed pure-mindedness and the importance of 'female' qualities such as humanity, benevolence, and compassion. Hannah More exemplifies the transition from one to the other as she moved from being a member of the fashionable literary circles of London in the 1770s to become a polemicist in the evangelical interest in later life. It must be emphasized, however, that this transition did not mark a withdrawal from public life but rather a change in the nature of the claim to participate in that life. While the Georgian 'blue-stocking' claimed equality based upon similar intellectual powers to men, it became more common in the 1820s to make the case for women's activities in the areas of charity and social and moral reform in the name of the special insights and sympathies that women had by virtue of their moral and domestic positions.

One problem is the gap between the discourse of a period and the practice. Even a growing insistence in publications as to what correct conduct should be did not necessarily lead to such conduct in practice. Even the new emphasis upon the pleasures and merits of the home did not prevent the growth of the gentlemen's clubs. There can be little doubt, however, that, although there was plenty of moral seriousness and censoriousness in the publications of the late eighteenth century, the early nineteenth century witnessed a change of tone. Thackeray writing in the 1840s had frequently to apologize to his readers for the manners he illustrated and the words he put into the mouths of the female characters he depicted in his novels set earlier in the century. The 1820s saw a juxtaposition of Regency and what would later be called 'Victorian' attitudes towards women, what was expected from them and what was due to them. We must remember, nevertheless, that, if the 'Angel of the Hearth' was emergent, she was emerging as an ideal rather than as everyman's wife.

In the rural world the position of the great majority of women did not change very much. Farmers' wives retained major roles in administering household economies which included important sections of the family business, looking after the dairy and sometimes calves and pigs, and in the evenings 'mistress and maids would frequently spin flax and wool to provide yarn for linen, blankets and clothing for the family.'[115] The wives of farm labourers supplemented their

---

115. Pamela Horn, *The Rural World, 1750–1850* (1980), 30.

husbands' wages by taking in work and, despite a decline in cottage industries after 1815, activities like glove-making, lace-making, and straw-plaiting were to remain important to the rural poor for much of the century. Large numbers of women continued to be employed on the land though their work was mainly seasonal. In Northumberland and the Scottish border counties farm workers were expected to provide a female worker, a bondager.

Aristocratic and gentry women also continued with their traditional roles of administering the complex worlds of country houses and town houses with often a wider role in looking after estates, while they concerned themselves with parish affairs, exercising authority and promoting charities. A recent study has concluded that for most of the nineteenth century, 'aristocratic women had a considerable voice in the political affairs of the nation, in part through their engagement with the political careers of the men in their families, and in part because of the nature of aristocratic culture which blended politics and society inexorably.'[116] One aristocrat who certainly felt that she wielded considerable influence was not only a woman but a foreigner. Princess Lieven, the wife of the Russian Ambassador, used her close relationships and love affairs with the leading politicians of the 1820s to attempt to further Russian foreign policy.[117]

Contemporaries and many historians have seen the main changes to women's positions as taking place within the 'middle classes'.[118] As has been suggested, this term encompasses too wide and varied a section of society to be of much utility but it was among the merchant, business, and professional classes that the tendency towards separate spheres was most marked. In early eighteenth-century London, a third of women of property had run some sort of business, a figure which had declined substantially a century later. Where husbands and wives had previously often been effectively business partners the tendency to move the home away from the place of business led to a firmer separation of roles.[119] That the lifestyle for women which resulted was necessarily resented or that 'wives of the middle and upper classes became idle drones',[120] has been challenged.[121]

Increasingly the vast majority of working-class women worked before marriage but only a minority went out to work afterwards. Female apprenticeships declined sharply and an insignificant number of women were skilled artisans. Ivy Pinchbeck's pioneering study of female employment placed rather too great an emphasis upon the relatively small percentage of employed women who worked in factories.[122] Even though women made up the largest group of workers in

116. Reynolds, *Aristocratic Women*, 187.

117. J. Charmley, *The Princess and the Politicians: Sex, Intrigue and Diplomacy* (2005).

118. A restatement of the view that separate spheres developed as a powerful ideology amongst the middle class in the late eighteenth and early nineteenth century is contained in Davidoff and Hall, *Family Fortunes*.

119. Frank O'Gorman, *The Long Eighteenth Century*, 347.

120. Stone, *The Family, Sex and Marriage in England, 1500–1800* (1977), 396.

121. See P. Branca, *Silent Sisterhood: Middle Class Women and the Victorian Home* (1975).

122. I. Pinchbeck, *Women Workers and the Industrial Revolution, 1750–1850* (1930).

cotton and woollen factories by 1835,[123] many more worked in domestic manufacturing. By far the greatest number of employed women worked in domestic
service, an occupation which not only grew absolutely in this period but was
increasingly feminized; by 1841 there were to be nearly a million female servants.
Statistics tend to record paid work outside the home and the figures for female
employment are clearly under-estimates if we consider the part-time work many
women did in their homes, taking in washing, dress-making, and all kinds of
stitching-work which was rarely recorded.

An overestimation of the extent of the change in women's position and of the
speed of change has much to do with the lingering concept of a rapid 'Industrial
Revolution' which led to concomitant belief in a social and cultural transformation as a result of it.

Sport and recreation

Another result of the long-held concept of an 'Industrial Revolution', a radical
change in economy and society within a short timescale rather than a process
extending over a longer period, has been the extension of the idea of a sharp
break and a discontinuity to sport and recreation and the wider category of
popular culture of which they are part.

A long succession of cultural theorists from the conservative Matthew Arnold
to twentieth-century Marxists conceived of a great divide between a rural culture, a 'folk' culture that was of the people, and a new urban, commercial, popular culture that was provided for the people; the one was worthy and vital, the
other shallow and unfulfilling. This scenario of a 'fall' fitted in with the works of
some early twentieth-century historians such as J. L. and Barbara Hammond[124]
and those of socialist historians of the 1960s. Changes to popular culture were
held to have resulted in a dislocation as the older rural culture disappeared and
was replaced by a commercial culture. The older popular culture, it was argued,
did not just decay but was actively suppressed because it was bawdy and brutal,
because the efficiency of industrial capitalism depended upon a workforce that
was disciplined, and because earnest evangelicals and their converts considered
popular recreations immoral and degrading. Such views disregarded continuities, the perseverance of many older forms of recreation, and the degree to
which traditional popular culture had always been commercial. Popular culture
did indeed come under attack but that the attack met strong opposition is a
tribute to the resilience of popular resistance to indoctrination which has been a
pervasive feature of modern British history.[125]

123. E. J. Evans, *The Forging of the Modern State*, 400.
124. J. L. and Barbara Hammond, *The Bleak Age* (1934).
125. See: Robert W. Malcomson, *Popular Recreations in English Society, 1700–1850* (1973);
J. M. Golby and A. W. Purdue, *The Civilisation of the Crowd* (1984); H. Cunningham, *Leisure in the
Industrial Revolution* (1980).

Aspects of popular culture in the early nineteenth century challenged both the rationalism of the Enlightenment and the moral seriousness of Evangelicalism. Many sports were characterized by the three Bs, blood, beer, and betting, while much the same could be said of popular festivals such as bull-runnings and fairs. The result was to be a protracted tussle between those who sought to reform the lifestyle and the recreations of the population and those who resisted such reform. This was by no means a class against class dispute, nor were the reformers universally victorious.

Cock-fighting, bear-baiting, and bull-baiting remained common long after legislation was passed forbidding them and their following and that of bare-fisted boxing was not confined to any particular social groups.

The popular heroes within British society included not only the victors of Trafalgar or Waterloo, but also such prize-fighters as Tom Cribb and John Gully. One of Cribb's most famous victories took place in Leicestershire in 1811, but failed to satisfy the vast audience:

The match was witnessed by upwards of twenty thousand persons, one-fourth of whom belonged to the upper classes. The fight much disappointed the spectators, as in the ninth round Molineaux's jaw was fractured, and in the event he was unable to stand, and the contest only lasted twenty minutes. On the champion's arrival in London...he was received with a public ovation, and Holborn was rendered almost impassable by the assembled crowds.[126]

At George IV's coronation, Cribb was one of a group of boxers on duty, nominally as pages, at the entrance to Westminster Hall during the coronation banquet. His contemporary, John Gully, who had retired from the ring in 1808, turned instead to horse racing and especially to the accompanying gambling. These were widely shared interests and, like Lord George Bentinck, Gully was one of the lucky few to make this pastime highly profitable. His successful betting career led to the purchase of a landed estate, and then to investment in the expanding coal industry (something which in the circumstances of the time could perhaps be seen as another form of gambling). Gully sat in the House of Commons in the first two Parliaments after the 1832 Reform Act. In 1832 his horses won both the Derby and the St Leger, in 1834 both the Derby and the 2,000 Guineas. He died in 1863 at the age of 80. Men like Tom Cribb and John Gully were better known than many political activists who have figured more prominently in the received historical record.

In a country which was still largely rural, or closely associated with rural life, the field sports of the countryside continued to attract wide interest, participation, and support. So did such related illicit activities as poaching, despite the ferocity of the Game Laws by which a landowning legislature sought to protect living property. Violent affrays between poachers and gamekeepers occurred throughout the period covered by this book, and indeed much later. If poaching

126. DNB.

and the Game Laws were a source of social division in the countryside, the field sports, including the varied forms of hunting, provided a widely shared interest, even among those who might only be enrolled among the 'foot followers' on such occasions.

In the expanding urban environment, the 'fancy' continued to patronize sports with their roots in the countryside while a vital urban popular culture arose which was no more edifying from the viewpoint of the serious-minded than the rural tradition with which it maintained strong links. The public house remained at the heart of popular culture in the town as in the village. A minority of large employers sought to impose the discipline of the clock but most small workshops had to accept the cult of St Monday, which extended the drunken weekend into the next week, and the habit of breaking off from work when the hunt came past.

Whether we consider the printed word, the entertainment provided by panto-mimes or hippodromes, the racecourse or the rat pit, the visit to a fair or the comforts of the public house, there is good reason to believe that there was a vital popular culture to excite a very broad cross-section of society.[127]

The United Kingdom over which the aristocratic governments of the early nineteenth century presided was not a simple, uniform, or completely tranquil society. The formal agencies of central and local government played only a lim-ited role. Most of the energies and most of the achievements in that society emanated from individuals and groups pursuing their own aims and ambitions.

It was not just posterity which saw early nineteenth-century British society as unregulated and with a tendency to disorderly behaviour. Foreign visitors often contrasted Britain with the more orderly and less violent societies they came from:

The streets [of London] remained busy until midnight: nay I even saw a boy of eight years old at the utmost, perfectly alone in a little child's carriage drawn by a large dog, driving along full trot, and without the slightest fear, among the latest carriages and stage-coaches. Such a thing can only be seen in England where children are independent at eight and hanged at twelve.[128]

Disorderly British society may have been, but the disorder was part of its freedom, boldness, and dynamism.

---

127. See: Cunningham, *Leisure in the Industrial Revolution*; Golby and Purdue, *The Civilisation of the Crowd*; and J. K. Walton and J. Walvin (eds.), *Leisure in Britain 1780–1939* (1983).

128. E. M. Butler (ed.), *A Regency Visitor: The English Tour of Prince Puckler-Mushau described in his letters 1826–28*. From the original translation by Sarah Austen (1957).

Part II

4

Political developments

1830–1852

The government formed by Earl Grey[1] after the fall of the Tories in 1830 was responsible for some of the most important reforms within the period covered by this book. At first sight this might not appear a likely development. The Tories had carried notable reforms, such as Catholic emancipation, and the new Cabinet scarcely wore a radical aspect. It was not simply a Whig ministry, but a new coalition including men who had worked comfortably under Lord Liverpool. The Canningite Tories did not bring to Grey's government a numerous parliamentary following, but their leaders' administrative experience was welcome to a Whig Party which had been excluded from office for many years. The importance of the Canningites' entry into the coalition was illustrated by the major offices which they received. Melbourne took the Home Office, Palmerston the Foreign Office, Goderich the Colonial Office, and Charles Grant became President of the Board of Control for India.

Otherwise, the composition of the new government, with one significant exception, was obviously aristocratic, bearing out Asa Briggs's judgement that 'The leading Whigs were born, not made; only a few outstanding individuals... ever penetrated the inner citadel of Whiggery after starting as complete "outsiders".'[2] Not only were the remaining members of the Cabinet drawn from the Whig aristocracy, but it was a matter of comment how many ministers were close relatives or associates of the new premier. Henry Brougham offered the only exception. In contemporary estimate he was a radical who had made his own way in the world. His rise to prominence had been due to the energy with which he had championed a variety of reform causes in the recent past.[3]

Although in some respects a skilful parliamentarian, he had also appealed to out-of-doors opinion. By 1830 he had made such a name for himself that he was

---

1. There were few more pure Whigs than Grey, who had spent most of his political life in opposition. E. A. Smith, *Lord Grey 1764–1845* (1990).

2. A. Briggs, *The Age of Improvement, 1783–1867*, 2nd edn. (1979), 237.

3. W. H. Hay, *The Whig Revival, 1808–1830* (2005) follows Arthur Aspinall, *Lord Brougham and the Whig Party* (1927) in giving a central role to Brougham in the success of the Whig revival. R. Stewart, *Henry Brougham: His Public Career, 1778–1868* (1985) gives a full account of his shortcomings as a ministerial colleague.

an obvious candidate for office. It was dangerous to try to fob him off with some minor post, for an aggrieved Brougham could be a damaging enemy to the new ministry. At the same time neither Grey nor his closest colleagues felt any confidence in Brougham's reliability. Grey first offered Brougham the post of Attorney General, normally a considerable recognition for a lawyer who had never held office. Brougham saw this as an inadequate reward for his services to the Whigs in opposition, and indignantly refused the offer. With difficulty he was persuaded instead to accept the senior position of Lord Chancellor. For Grey this had the advantage that it involved Brougham's removal to the House of Lords, and from effective participation in popular politics. The decision proved shrewd. Although Brougham gave some good service in the next few years, especially in piloting legislation through the Upper House, he was unable to restrain a penchant for intrigue and disloyalty. By 1836 his behaviour had so alienated his colleagues that he was dropped from the government altogether. In Grey's aristocratic Cabinet, Brougham was the most obvious outsider. Experience of his behaviour as a minister might well have confirmed aristocratic doubts about the wisdom of admitting such men to high office.

Law and order

The new government soon showed that it was not wholly influenced by liberal sentiments. It took office at a time when disturbances in rural southern England were spreading.[4] November 1830 marked the peak of the troubles, which affected sixteen counties with varying degrees of seriousness and continued into 1831. They were much more examples of traditional protest than of revolutionary danger in the English countryside. There was little violence against people, and no evidence that the rioters were responsible for a single death. Verbal violence there certainly was, with blood-curdling threats against those who were seen as oppressors. There was little sign of radical political motivation in the recorded sentiments of local leaders, who were often ignorant about matters outside their own local concerns.

The causes of the outbreaks varied from place to place, but seem to have been for the most part local grievances. Rising population had not been matched by increased employment in rural areas. The objectives of the rioters of 1830–1 were usually higher wages, better Poor Law payments, and destruction or abandonment of labour-saving threshing machines. Melbourne took over the Home Office when the disturbances were at their peak. By the end of 1830 his orders had led to the arrest of nearly 2,000 men and women. The new Home Secretary found that some of the local magistrates were treating the defendants with what he considered unjustifiable leniency, and therefore special judicial commissions

---

4. E. J. Hobsbawm and G. Rude, *Captain Swing* (1969) is the standard source for the rural disturbances of 1830–1.

were dispatched to the worst-affected areas. More than half of those arrested were brought to trial; there were more than 250 death sentences, although only 19 of these were carried out. More than 450 of the prisoners were transported, and about 600 imprisoned.

It was not only rural districts which experienced the new government's determination to preserve law and order. During the crisis over the parliamentary Reform Bill, in October 1831, there was rioting in a number of towns, and again the government responded forcibly.[5] The worst incidents were at Bristol, where the authorities mishandled a situation which had as much to do with looting as with politics; the military commander involved later committed suicide rather than face a court martial. Rioting escalated in face of official inaction; there were 12 deaths and nearly 100 serious injuries. More than 100 arrests were made subsequently, and 31 rioters were sentenced to death; 4 of these were executed. Similarly, the government's 1833 coercive legislation for Ireland was a tough police measure.

In considering the priorities of the Whig ministers when they took office, a useful guide is the slogan which was often described as Lord Grey's motto. 'Peace, Retrenchment and Reform' was a much-used Whig campaign message. A principal aspect of 'Peace' was a reduction in the cost of the armed forces, 'Retrenchment' meant what it said, and 'Reform' was seen as a method of cutting down the extravagance and corruption frequently associated with the unreformed system of government. The reforms of the 1830s owed much to the continuing demands for cheap government. During their first years in office, the Whigs succeeded in reducing the level of government spending by some 10 per cent. This may have done as much to keep them in office as any of the reforms for which they are better known. Reductions in defence expenditure provided a major part of the savings, but also reduced the operational readiness of the armed forces in an often uncertain international situation.

The genesis of parliamentary reform

While the Home Office was cracking down on the 'Swing' riots in the countryside, the ministers were formulating the piece of legislation which was to constitute their biggest claim to fame. The reform of the representative system in 1832 was not a hastily planned device improvised to meet a crisis. It embodied conceptions of reform which had been discussed for many years. Nor did the Whig ministers embrace the cause of reform because of popular pressures. Grey and Russell, and other ministers, had been committed to a measure of parliamentary reform for many years. Support for reform in the recent past had come from unexpected quarters. Right-wing Tories, outraged at the concession of

5. J. Stevenson, *Popular Disturbances in England, 1700–1870* (1979), 221–3. For the Bristol riots, see also J. H. Bettey, *Wessex from A.D. 1000* (1986), 269.

Catholic emancipation, claimed that a House of Commons more representative of public opinion would never have conceded that measure, and in this they were no doubt correct. They argued that it was the weight of the pocket and rotten boroughs which had enabled the Wellington government to flout public opinion in 1829. In the last months of Tory rule, right-wingers in Parliament advocated the elimination of decayed constituencies and the transfer of their seats to the more healthy county constituencies.

Grey had made his acceptance of William IV's invitation to form an administration conditional on the King's acceptance of a Reform Bill. Parliamentary reform was now government policy for the first time in half a century. The task of framing a bill was entrusted to a government committee, selected by Grey and composed of decided reformers. The members were Lord Durham (Lord Grey's son-in-law), Lord John Russell (the younger son of a duke), Sir James Graham (a baronet who headed an important northern landed family), and J. W. Ponsonby (member of an Anglo-Irish aristocratic family and heir to an earldom). The Reform Bill was created by the Whig aristocracy, and represented ideas well established there. The brief given the committee was a simple one. They were to devise a practical measure which would satisfy all legitimate objections to the existing system, while securing the State from any threat of future revolutionary change. The injunction was somewhat nebulous, perhaps, but then the issues had been discussed for many years. The ministry did not think it necessary to embark upon any preliminary inquiry by royal commission or other agency. The government's interpretation of 'reform' was changes that would strengthen the existing system, rather than radical change towards a democratic system.

Prime Minister and Cabinet left the drafting of the measure to the committee, serving rather as arbiters on points of disagreement and bestowing a final approval on the committee's proposals. Lord Durham advocated the secret ballot in the committee's discussions, but both Grey and the majority of the Cabinet rejected an innovation which might restrict the deployment of legitimate influence in electoral matters. By contemporary standards, arguments against the secret exercise of political privileges were strong; apart from the need to maintain the legitimate influence of property and status, there was much to be said for the voter being obliged to employ his constitutional privileges openly and honestly rather than skulking to the ballot box.[6] In general, the Cabinet endorsed the proposals of its committee, which were broadly the same as those which finally emerged in the Act of 1832. There were a number of relatively minor changes during the parliamentary battle on the measure, but none which seriously altered the main shape of the original bill.

---

6. B. L. Kinzer, *The Ballot Question in Nineteenth-Century British Politics* (1983) gives a lucid account of its subject, including the contemporary arguments for and against the ballot, and details of the various occasions in which the ballot became a matter of active political interest. For the reform crisis of 1831–2 see M. Brock, *The Great Reform Act* (1973). The best detailed examination of the changes introduced by the 1832 Reform Act remains N. Gash, *Politics in the Age of Peel* (1953).

The cause of opposition to the Reform Bill was lost before the parliamentary and electoral battle began. Catholic emancipation and the abolition of the Test and Corporations Act had fatally weakened defence of the existing order, created divisions in Tory ranks, and compromised the major Tory leaders, Peel and Wellington. Peel kept a relatively low profile during the developments of 1830–2, perhaps biding his time, while Wellington, disturbed as he was by the implications of reform, was no ultra, believing that it was essential that the business of His Majesty's government be carried on and that there was much to play for in safeguarding the powers of the Lords and the number of MPs representing county divisions. The somewhat confused and half-regretted support for the Whig ministers by the King also denied the Tories the usual anchor in opposition to constitutional change. It was left to a man like the fourth Duke of Newcastle, who hated public speaking, to carry on with forthright opposition to parliamentary reform.[7]

In the end what mattered was the combination of an irresistible tide for reform and the fact that the leadership of both parties was aristocratic. The Whigs wanted change, but not change which would threaten their own interests. The Tories opposed change but their leaders were realistic enough to recognize that they could save much that was to their advantage from defeat.[8]

Reform crisis, 1831–1832

The drafting committee worked quickly, and, after consideration by the Cabinet, the Reform Bill was ready for presentation to Parliament on 1 March 1831. Its introduction sparked off one of the century's major political crises. The House of Commons into which Russell introduced the Reform Bill had not been elected in an atmosphere of reform enthusiasm, even if it had proved unwilling to sustain the Tories in office. The scope of the proposed reform filled many MPs with incredulity, and there was widespread scepticism about the government's chances of success. After a spirited debate, the second reading of the bill was carried on 22 March by the narrowest of margins, 302 votes to 301. It was obvious that ministers would be in difficulty during the committee stage. When the House in committee passed by 8 votes an Opposition amendment stipulating no change in the size of the House of Commons, it became clear that the opposition intended to mutilate the bill by detailed amendments. The Cabinet decided that the only solution was an immediate dissolution and an appeal to the existing electorate on the issue of reform. The King was unhappy at the prospect, with Parliament less than a year old, but yielded to Grey's pressure.

7. R. A. Gaunt (ed.), *Unhappy Reactionary: The Diaries of the Fourth Duke of Newcastle-under-Lyme 1822–50* (2003).

8. Robert Stewart, *The Foundation of the Conservative Party, 1830–1867* (1978) provides a perceptive account of the attitudes and policies of the Conservative leadership during the reform crisis.

The general election of 1831, unlike that of the previous year, was fought on the government's reform proposals and produced a clear-cut response. It was fought on the old distribution of seats, and the old franchise. In some areas the returns were influenced by popular pressure. In Liverpool, for example, an ancient two-member borough which would merely retain its existing seats under the bill, reform enthusiasm ensured the defeat of a long-serving MP who had moved the hostile amendment which precipitated the election. The City of London returned four committed supporters of the bill. Most striking of all were the returns from the county constituencies. They provided unmistakable evidence that in opposing this kind of reform the Tories were not supported by the bulk of county voters and those who influenced county voters. Only a tiny handful of the counties returned anti-reformers in 1831.

The unequivocal result gave ministers an overwhelming majority in the new House of Commons. Nor was this all. The election had shown the Whigs that they enjoyed the support, not only of the noisy and even embarrassing crowds of the towns, but also of the majority of 'respectable' opinion. The Tories knew that in opposing reform they had lost many of their former supporters among influential groups in society. The second reading of the reintroduced reform proposals was carried in June by the convincing majority of 136. The Opposition fought every step of the way during the committee stage, but the government majority held together; by September the bill had completed all of its stages in the House of Commons.

On 8 October the second reading of the Reform Bill was rejected in the Lords by 199 votes to 158. It was in response to this that the Bristol riots already referred to took place, as well as serious disturbances at Derby and Nottingham, and a rash of less alarming demonstrations in other places. The organized nature of some of the pro-reform agitation worried Whigs as well as Tories. On the model of the 'Political Union of the Lower and Middle Classes of the People', established at Birmingham in 1829 to work for reform, similar bodies multiplied, and seemed to offer a dangerous alternative to traditional political interests. The element of danger was perceived to lie primarily in the extent to which men of influence lent their support to such activities; this was much more worrying than signs of restlessness confined to the lower orders.

The Whig reformers had as one of their aims the conciliation of that respectable element in society which they thought of as the middle class or the middle classes, however nebulous and inaccurate their conception. The pro-reform speeches of 1831–2 stressed the need to conciliate this element, and ensure its adherence to the existing order. The danger that a failure to reform the electoral system might alienate so important a sector of society made the Whigs stand firm during the reform crisis. The Tories feared the consequences of yielding to popular pressures; such a surrender could pave the way to the eventual loss of all of the safeguards of order and property. The Whigs drew a different conclusion. By conceding moderate reform, they could leave the dangerous elements isolated and weak, since respectable opinion would rally to a constitution purged of its indefensible features. The experience of Chartism a few years later suggested that the Whigs had the best of the arguments here.

The reform offered did not 'give the vote to the middle class'. However such a social grouping might be imagined, many of its members were, or could have been, voters before 1832, as forty-shilling freeholders, for example. What was being offered now was a diminution in the number of pocket and rotten boroughs, and an extended representation of the growing towns. Such proposals had attractions for the local urban oligarchies, but the increase in county seats was also attractive to rural electors. Moreover, the elimination of decayed borough constituencies pleased the large proportion of the tax-paying electorate who saw in them the corrupt agency which enabled extravagant governments to remain in office.

It was difficult for ministers to have any clear perception of the dangers proffered by the out-of-doors agitation in support of reform in 1831–2. Nor is it now at all easy to gauge just how significant the political element in the disturbances of these months actually was. Certainly, the troubles of 1831–2 did not all stem from parliamentary reform. The first great cholera epidemic, major industrial disputes marked by some serious violence, and a variety of local grievances all contributed to the ferment. Some of the disorder was plainly not prompted by political reform. The miners' strikes of 1831–2 began shortly after the first Reform Bill was introduced, but the grievances complained of all related to specifically mining matters. Merthyr Tydfil was one of the worst trouble centres, with considerable bloodshed, but a mid-Victorian recollection there was that

In the summer of 1831 times were excessively bad... Politics had little to do with the matter, though it was natural that a suffering people should attribute their condition to many causes and think that 'Reform' would bring them better times. As it was, Reform cries were occasionally heard, and, in the sack of Coffin's house, women carrying away sides of bacon and other things cried out, in Welsh, 'Here's Reform', thus misleading some to think it a political riot.[9]

If ministers were uncertain of the extent of the dangers confronting them, they were clear that there could be no question of accepting the Lords' rejection of reform. It was more difficult to know what to do about it. In December 1831 the government introduced a third Reform Bill, modified in some slight respects to conciliate moderate critics, but essentially on the same lines as its predecessors. There was one obvious device which might be used to coerce the Upper House, the use of the royal prerogative to create new peers. Grey himself viewed such a prospect with distaste, and it was with great difficulty that William IV was brought to accept in January that such a step might be necessary.

9. C. Wilkins, *History of Merthyr Tydfil* (1867), quoted by D. Smith, 'Breaking silence: Gwyn Thomas and the "prehistory" of Welsh working class fiction', in C. Emsley and J. Walvin (eds.), *Artisans, Peasants & Proletarians, 1760–1860: Essays Presented to Gwyn A. Williams* (1985), 104.

Faced with the unpalatable reality that to persist in frustrating the will of the House of Commons and the electorate could lead to the flooding of their House with new Whig peers, enough of the Tory majority yielded to see the Reform Bill pass its second reading in the Lords by 184 votes to 175 on 13 April. Any rejoicing was premature, for it became clear that the committee stage might be used to weaken the bill's provisions. The Cabinet once again put pressure on the King, with a threat of resignation if William IV refused the immediate creation of fifty new peers as a sign of his support for ministers. The King's acquiescence in his ministers' policies had been weakening; he too was unhappy at the idea of yielding to popular agitation. Misjudging the situation, he chose to accept Grey's resignation, and attempted to install a Tory administration which would carry a more moderate reform proposal.[10] In response, the reform agitation out of doors became more strident, while the House of Commons formally resolved its opposition to any ministry which would not implement the existing reform proposals. Peel, who had led the Tory opposition to parliamentary reform in the Commons, refused to join the kind of Tory ministry envisaged. After a week of uncertainty, on 14 May Wellington abandoned the attempt to take office. He knew that such an administration could not stand in the existing House of Commons, and that there was no chance of an election producing a more favourable result. The King now had to turn to Grey and promise to place the royal prerogative of creating peers at his disposal. Faced with this pressure, the Tory majority in the Lords crumbled; the committee stage of the Reform Bill was completed in six days. Most Tory peers absented themselves from the final divisions, and on 7 June the Great Reform Act received the royal assent.

A central question is the degree to which the passing of the Great Reform Act was largely a matter of 'high politics', though few would argue that extra-parliamentary agitation did not play a part, or that the Act might not have passed without the demonstrations and the disorder that accompanied its process. Even its proponents were worried by the demonstrations of support for the bill. Lord Cockburn, a leading Scottish Whig, thought the thousands who paraded peacefully through Glasgow in favour of the Scottish Reform Bill a 'gratifying yet fearful spectacle'.[11] Parliamentary reform which had been far from the top of the political agenda a few years earlier had become the 'common sense' of the day, had gained the support of the existing electorate, and was acclaimed by the popular support of many who would not gain from it. Yet, however much events outside the parliamentary arena influenced its passing and however much the politicians had to adjust their policies to accommodate popular feeling, the result

10. Queen Adelaide was widely held responsible for stiffening King William's resistance to the creation of peers. This was probably true as her experience of radicalism and revolution in Germany had given her a pronounced apprehension of the consequences of giving way to popular agitation. A.W. Purdue, 'Queen Adelaide: malign influence or consort maligned?', in Clarissa Campbell Orr (ed.), *Queenship in Britain 1660–1837* (2002), 237–67.

11. T. C. Smout, *A Century of the Scottish People*, 233.

can be seen as a shrewd modification of the existing parliamentary system and as a triumph for the Whigs which, nevertheless, left much for the temporarily subdued Tories to build on.

The Great Reform Act

This was one of the century's most important political events. The main aim of its aristocratic creators was to rid the representative system of indefensible features, and to produce a better representation in the House of Commons of the property and intelligence of the nation. In the 1830s the word 'intelligence' was not used in its modern sense of a natural gift, but in its older meaning of 'information', which survives in such expressions as 'intelligence work' today. In the 1830s, education and knowledge were largely the prerogative of social groups which could pay for schooling and access to reading material. The association of property and intelligence was not absurd in 1832; the reformers aimed to confer political rights on those who could be expected to use that privilege in an informed and responsible way.

At the same time, they did not see society as simply an aggregation of individuals, but as a more organic and complex entity, in which individuals and property were bound together in 'interests'. These included the cotton industry, shipping, or the greatest of them all, the landed interest which embraced everyone who depended on the land for their livelihood. The Whigs aimed at a more balanced representation of these interests—not anything like a mathematically accurate share-out, which would be impossible—but an arrangement which would give every important interest a hearing in the legislature.

The translation of these aims into a workable scheme posed practical problems, exemplified in the property qualifications used to define the reformed electorate. None of those responsible for the 1832 Act saw the vote as a natural right; the public interest required that the electorate be limited to those who deserved the vote and could be trusted to use it responsibly. Preferably they should be those who had something to lose if the nation's affairs were mismanaged, and those who could be expected to appreciate the issues at stake during elections. A selective exercise was therefore imperative. But how, in the Britain of 1831–2, was this to be managed? It was not easy to discover appropriate tests. Age was not available, in the absence of any system of public registration of births, nor was age in itself a satisfactory test for suitability.

The most admired constituencies of the old system were the counties, with their substantial electorates of forty-shilling freeholders. By contemporary standards, the county electoral system had not worked badly, so the forty-shilling freehold qualification was retained there, with the addition of leaseholders and copyholders who could be seen as equivalent in economic status. The Whig acceptance of an opposition amendment which added tenants-at-will paying at least £50 in annual rent could be justified on the same grounds.

The boroughs presented a greater problem. Here the Whigs wanted to replace kaleidoscopic variety with a more uniform system of representation. The drafting committee found a tolerably neat solution here, apparently by appropriating an existing test from another area of administration. The house tax was levied on a selective basis, and as recently as 1825 the level at which this tax began had been set at the occupier of property valued at £10 per annum. This tax discriminator was now borrowed as the basic borough franchise qualification.

The property qualifications of the 1832 Reform Act owed something to the prevailing respect for property and the belief that its possession usually entailed qualities of stability and respectability. They owed much also to the practical problem of devising selective qualifications in a little-governed and little-measured society. All of them had this in common—they used existing materials and they could be readily checked by existing evidence. The forty-shilling freeholder could establish his voting claim by a land tax receipt; leaseholders and copyholders could produce leases or copyhold certificates; a tenant-at-will could submit a rent receipt. In the boroughs the claims of £10 householders could be checked by reference to the borough's rate-book; in some boroughs the 1832 Act continued the voting rights of existing freemen, and their claims could be checked by inspection of the borough's register of freemen. Neither the drafting committee nor the Whig Cabinet was foolish enough to suppose that these franchises represented the attainment of constitutional perfection; instead they embodied a practical response to practical problems.

Although at first sight the franchise arrangements seemed uniform, in practice the results varied greatly, mainly because property varied in value between different areas. In the London borough constituencies created by the Act, the £10 household level produced a wide electorate; in northern centres like Leeds, and in many country towns, lower property values produced a proportionally reduced electorate. This discrepancy was obvious at the time; during the reform debates the government's champions tried to turn this into a virtue by emphasizing the absence of any rigid uniformity.

A similar rough-and-ready result was seen in the redistribution of parliamentary seats. The main aims were to suppress constituencies too small to be either independent or significant within national counsels, and the transfer of seats to places and interests worthy of the privilege. A rough arithmetical guideline was used as a yardstick for disfranchisement. A borough with fewer than 2,000 inhabitants lost all separate representation; boroughs of between 2,000 and 4,000 population lost one of their two seats. Fifty-six boroughs were disfranchised and thirty reduced to single-member status. In a number of other cases small borough constituencies were retained with widened boundaries.

The beneficiaries of this wholesale extinction of ancient rights, without any compensation, fell into a number of groups. Most attention has been focused on the urban areas which benefited. Twenty-two new borough constituencies received two MPs, and another twenty received one. The rough-and-ready element was clear here. No matter how important a borough was, it received no more than two members; Manchester was given the same as Sunderland, although the population and the wealth of the two communities differed widely. The reformers were not obsessed with a counting of heads, but with something more subtle. Manchester received two seats, not simply to reflect the town's size and importance, but to give the cotton interest a parliamentary voice, while Sunderland's MPs could be expected to represent not just that town but the important north-east coal and shipping interests. Merthyr Tydfil received a single member as a centre of the South Wales iron industry (and duly returned the iron-master John Guest to Parliament for the next twenty years).

The Whig aim of representing national interests did not work out too badly in practice. The greatest interest in 1832 was that of the land and agriculture, and the 1832 Act improved the position here, at least in part. After 1832, borough MPs still made up nearly two-thirds of the House of Commons, a preponderance still out of tune with the distribution of wealth, electors, and population, but less so than before. A substantial proportion of the surviving borough constituencies was made up of country towns; in addition the counties received a total gain of sixty-five seats in the redistribution. Twenty-five counties saw their representation doubled. Before 1832, for example, Kent returned two MPs; after 1832 East Kent and West Kent each returned two members. The three Ridings of Yorkshire and the three Parts of Lincolnshire became separate two-member constituencies. Seven smaller counties received one additional member.

This expansion in county members was a reform which had been advocated for many decades, and did much to facilitate the rallying of influential opinion which made the carrying of the Act possible. Overall the balance of electoral strength saw a considerable shift, with the areas north of the Trent gaining 110 additional seats. In terms of population and wealth, however, the south was still over-represented, if to a lesser extent than before.

The main Reform Act for England and Wales was accompanied by separate measures for Scotland and Ireland. The impact on Ireland was less striking than elsewhere, because the Irish representation had been overhauled at the time of the Union in 1800. The 1832 legislation gave Ireland five additional MPs: a second member for Trinity College, Dublin, and four more for Irish boroughs. The Whigs made no attempt to reverse the raising of the Irish county franchise effected in 1829. The Scottish Act was more important, inaugurating a major change in Scottish politics. North of the border, electoral politics had been tightly controlled by dominant minorities and government influence; the total Scottish electorate had been little more than 5,000. At a stroke the 1832 Act raised this to 65,000. There was a radical redistribution of Scottish seats, and new franchises were introduced, broadly similar to the English model. After 1832 Edinburgh and Glasgow were two-member burghs, Dundee, Aberdeen, Perth, Paisley, and Greenock single-member burghs, with a new £10 voting qualification. Smaller towns were grouped into fourteen districts with single members;

overall the burghs received eight more seats. The number of Scottish county seats was held at thirty, but with a wider electorate. The 1832 changes brought a more open and free electoral pattern to Scotland. It should not be imagined, however, that reform brought an end to patronage in Scotland any more than England. The new Whig Solicitor General for Scotland, Lord Cockburn, wrote to his friend the Lord Advocate, Francis Jeffrey, on a matter concerning the vacancy in a Crown living: 'I am for adhering to patronage; tho' not against checking its abuses.'[12] These changes destroyed the Tory grip on Scotland and the Conservative Party was never again to win half the Scottish seats until 1900.

There was nothing democratic about the Whig reforms, nor is there any reason why they should have been so. Yet at the time, the reforms were seen as far-reaching, even unexpectedly radical, by most influential people. Once the legislation was implemented, and the representative system settled down, it became clear that the Great Reform Act had not effected any revolutionary changes in the distribution of power. The aristocracy still held a dominant position within society and the State; the influence of property and rank was consolidated rather than destroyed. However, the reform crisis had implications which were less obvious.

Nothing in the legislation affected the rights of the sovereign or the House of Lords, but the circumstances of the Act's passing inevitably involved changes in constitutional relationships. In effect, the will of the majority of the electorate and the House of Commons, backed by a wider public opinion, had forced both king and peers to acquiesce in measures they opposed. After these events, the relationship between the three elements in Parliament could never be the same again. The supremacy of the elected chamber had been demonstrated, even if there was no specific legislative statement of this.

In the light of subsequent changes, the actual provisions enacted in 1832 may appear meagre—though they did not seem so at the time—but the symbolic importance of the Great Reform Act was immense. The dominant aristocracy, still in control of the State, had acted, in some respects against its own sectional interests, to reform the Constitution by Act of Parliament, without revolution or civil war. It seemed that in Britain the desire of the people and the triumph of right could succeed by peaceful constitutional means. If outside pressure played a part in securing parliamentary reform, the framing of the legislation and its championing in Parliament had been the work of the Whig aristocracy. Even the Tory peers had yielded rather than be responsible for further strains in the political fabric of the nation. This aspect of the success of reform in 1832 was to have profound implications for later British history.

The reformed parliament

After the triumph of parliamentary reform, the Whigs went on to consolidate their victory. A new House of Commons would have to be elected under the new

12. Alan Bell (ed.), *Lord Cockburn: Selected Letters* (2005), 45.

dispensation. Time was needed to make the necessary alterations. The 1832 Act prescribed the compilation for the first time of formal lists of electors. In default of any other available official agency, these had to be drawn up by the local Poor Law overseers. Since overseers notoriously varied in diligence, competence, and even literacy, a system of revision courts, under part-time electoral judges known as revising barristers, was set up to hear appeals against the overseers' decisions. All of this took time, and it was not until December 1832 that Parliament could be dissolved.

The first reformed election was a disaster for the Tories. The reforms had deprived them of a large number of pocket and rotten boroughs, and their successes in the more open constituencies were limited. There were still about 50 seats which were effectively controlled by individual patrons, but not all of these were in Tory hands. Even in the counties the Tories did badly, winning only 42 of the 144 seats. Altogether, in the new House of Commons the Opposition held only 185 of the 658 seats.

The supporters of reform enjoyed a huge majority, and within that majority the more radical elements seemed to have done well. There were about 100 MPs whom contemporary opinion would have classed as radicals, and these included individuals who would not normally have been thought of as parliamentary material. The new borough of Oldham sent William Cobbett, the veteran radical journalist and politician. Pontefract returned John Gully, ex-prize-fighter, now racehorse-owner and landowner. None of the radical MPs returned in 1832 succeeded in making much of a mark in a legislature still dominated by the Whig and Tory aristocracy and gentry. There were soon signs not only of tensions between Whigs and radicals but also of the inability of the various groups of radicals to present a united front.

The Whig ministry, despite prickly relations with its radical followers, and its own internal problems with troublemakers like Lords Brougham and Durham, continued on its reforming career. The reform of local government was a natural corollary to parliamentary reform, but legislation here awaited the reports of royal commissions set up to inquire into the Poor Law and municipal corporations. In 1833 there was an innovative Factory Act (see pp. 203–6 below). In the same year a lengthy campaign, fuelled by religious and philanthropic energies of a non-party kind, came to fruition with the abolition of slavery throughout the British dominions. The legislation provided for an interim period of 'apprenticeship' for slaves over the age of 6, to be followed by complete emancipation. A Parliament much under the influence of 'cheap government' ideas was prepared on this issue to spend on a large scale; a special fund of £20 million was set aside as compensation to the slave-owners whose human property was involved. Reform in local government included the 1834 Poor Law Amendment Act (see pp. 206–11 below), and the 1835 Municipal Corporations Act (see pp. 216–17). With the creation of the revised system for the Poor Law, the way was open for the introduction of civil registration of births, deaths, and marriages, using this refurbished administrative apparatus. Although such measures as these figure prominently in modern accounts of the ministry's work, other matters often posed more serious problems at the time.

Religious affairs, for example, still produced a great deal of heat, though the continued reform of the Church of England through such devices as the new Ecclesiastical Commission, which supervised the Church's revenues, could command support from both major parties. Matters were more difficult in Ireland, where politics and religion were inextricably mixed. The Established Church of Ireland ministered to only a minority, but supported a large clerical establishment and taxed the whole community for its maintenance. The Whig government proposed to reform the Irish tithe system, and to abolish a number of Irish bishoprics. The intention of using the revenues of suppressed sees, at least in part, for secular purposes—'lay appropriation' as it was called—brought serious difficulties. Cabinet agreement to the alienation of part of the revenue of an Established Church was achieved only after lengthy argument. When the proposals reached Parliament, the level of opposition, including that of the more conservative of the ministry's supporters, was so strong that the appropriation clauses had to be dropped. The Irish nationalists were, in consequence, disappointed, while the defenders of the Established Churches had been put on their guard. Within the ministry, more liberal members like Russell were anxious to renew the battle for lay appropriation, while the government's right wing was as strongly opposed.

In the early summer of 1834, quarrels over lay appropriation led to the resignation of four Cabinet ministers, Stanley, Graham, Ripon, and Richmond. Stanley and Graham, especially, were serious losses from a team not overly endowed with administrative talent. Stanley was also the heir to the earldom of Derby, an important aristocratic influence in north-west England. Sir James Graham was the head of a long-established and influential landed family. The Earl of Ripon was the former Lord Goderich, briefly Prime Minister in 1828, while the Duke of Richmond represented another important block of aristocratic influence. Grey himself sympathized with these dissidents, and this was well known.

In 1833 the majority of the Cabinet had insisted on a tough Coercion Act to combat Irish disorders. The more liberal ministers had always disliked this measure, preferring a working alliance with the Irish nationalists led by Daniel O'Connell. Disputes over tithe and other grievances were still creating disturbances in Ireland when the year's duration of the Coercion Act neared its end. Grey was convinced that the Act should be renewed. In July 1834 he discovered that, behind his back, some of his colleagues were discussing with O'Connell schemes for weakening the Coercion Act. Understandably angered, Grey now insisted on resigning himself. The Home Secretary, Lord Melbourne,[13] only a few

13. A recent biography is L. G. Mitchell, *Lord Melbourne, 1779–1848* (1997).

years earlier a member of a Tory administration, took over the leadership of a government weakened by these events.

William IV had become increasingly hostile to the behaviour of some of his ministers in religious and Irish affairs; his sympathies lay with those who had left the government on these issues. Never gifted with great political insight, he now entertained ideas of a coalition government which would bring together the more acceptable elements within both Whig and Tory groupings. Apart from this, he was determined to oppose any further strengthening of the influence of the more liberal element within the ministry. In November 1834, the death of Earl Spencer elevated Althorp, the Chancellor of the Exchequer, to the House of Lords. While no great orator, Althorp had been an asset to the ministry in the House of Commons, where he was widely respected and trusted. His departure weakened the government team there, as well as necessitating some ministerial changes. Lord John Russell had a strong claim for promotion to the Exchequer, but his recent efforts in favour of lay appropriation and other concessions to Irish nationalism had aroused suspicion and hostility. Melbourne would not pass him over, even though he was not enthusiastic about the appointment. The King was determined not to accept this nomination, and instead dismissed the government, claiming that it was too weak to continue as a viable administration.

Peel's first ministry

Melbourne made no serious effort to resist this royal decision, and indeed anyone who had endured the recent bickerings within the ministry might well greet the intervention with relief. The King had made his move while his choice as the new Prime Minister, Peel, was absent on holiday in Italy; in the meantime Wellington acted as interim head of government. Peel hurried home and constructed a minority administration.

These events were unwelcome, even bewildering, to supporters of the reform government, who now saw the Tories in office again, only two years after the triumph of reform in 1832. The Queen's known Tory sympathies made her once again the object of suspicion and *The Times* declared, on little evidence, 'The Queen has done it all.' The radicals in particular were outraged, and began a campaign to unseat the new ministers. Peel's government could not survive in the House of Commons elected in 1832. A general election would be necessary. Many radicals were convinced that the events of 1834 demonstrated that the electoral changes of 1832 had not gone far enough, that further parliamentary reform was essential. In the north, Lord Durham headed a campaign aiming at household suffrage, vote by ballot, and a maximum duration of Parliament of three years. Even more moderate supporters of the Whig ministry expressed indignation at the way in which the change of government had been effected.

Although Peel had not thought the time ripe for such an experiment, he was willing to accept responsibility for the King's action, and determined to make a fight of the election. His preparations included the composition of one of the most celebrated political documents of the century, the Tamworth Manifesto. Ostensibly this was Sir Robert Peel's address to the electors of the borough of Tamworth. It was in reality an early example of a party manifesto. Its text was discussed by the Cabinet, and steps were taken to give the statement the widest possible publicity. The Manifesto was a rallying call to Peel's followers, who were now to be given the designation of Conservatives rather than the somewhat tarnished Tory label. The new name expressed the core of the party's philosophy. For the remainder of the decade, Peel's case was that there were two main forces at work in British society, the Conservative and the Destructive. The former, under reliable leaders like Peel and Wellington, were concerned to conserve all that was essential and useful, while the Destructive faction, exemplified by extreme radicals and Irish nationalists, were dangerous foes to the established order. It was not easy to portray men like Lord Melbourne or Lord Palmerston as militant radicals. It was easier to portray the Whigs, increasingly dependent for their Commons majority on Irish and radical votes, as the unwitting tools of more dangerous men.

Moreover, it was not to be supposed that Peel's Conservatives were reactionary Tories. Instead, the Reform Act was accepted as the final and irrevocable settlement of a great constitutional question; there was to be no Conservative attempt to undo the verdict of 1832. In addition, while doing everything necessary to conserve vital national institutions such as the monarchy and the Established Church, the Conservative Party would be no enemy to a judicious review of the institutions of both Church and State, with a view to effecting necessary improvements.

This proved an admirable means of winning new friends during the 1830s. The enfranchised minority after the 1832 changes showed little enthusiasm for sharing their privileges more widely. As the post-1832 electoral system settled down, the influence of position and property re-established themselves. From a long-term point of view, though, the Tamworth Manifesto concealed dangers. These Peelite ideas demonstrated that they could win a wide range of support, but the Conservative case offered in 1834 had much that was vague about it. Opinions could differ about what constituted essential national interests, and what represented judicious improvement in Church and State. In the short term, however, the Tamworth Manifesto proved a major political success.

The fruits of this success were not all to be gathered immediately. In the general election at the beginning of 1835, the Conservatives won about 100 additional seats, but this was not enough to allow the Peel ministry to hold on in face of the hostile coalition of Whigs, radicals, and Irish. The opposition soon showed that they were determined to oust the minority government. The official nominee as Speaker was rejected in favour of a Whig candidate, and there followed a series of government defeats. In April Peel bowed to the inevitable and resigned. These political events of 1834–5 showed the working out of some of the hidden implications of the 1832 reform. For the first time, a government possessing the confidence of the sovereign had been beaten at the polls and forced into resignation; royal favour could no longer sustain in office a ministry which could not win from the electorate the support of a Commons majority.

Decline of the Whigs

On Peel's resignation, Melbourne returned to office, but in a weaker position than before. His strength in the new House of Commons was diminished, and his dependence on radical and Irish votes more obvious. In the campaign against the minority Conservative government, Russell had negotiated with the Irish leader Daniel O'Connell an understanding known as the Lichfield House Compact. This ensured Irish support for the Whigs in Parliament, in return for a promise of Irish reforms when the Whigs returned to office. This was useful for immediate tactics, but the alliance between the Whig leaders and the Irish nationalists played into the hands of Conservative propagandists. The commitment of the Whigs to such measures as a Tithe Commutation Act for Ireland, and their allotting a share of government patronage in Ireland to moderate nationalists, were obvious developments. As the nationalists increased their agitation against the Anglo-Irish Union, Melbourne's ministry could easily be pilloried as allied with one of the most obviously destructive forces in the politics of the United Kingdom.

In other ways, the majority behind the renewed Whig ministry was far from solid. Bickering intensified in increasingly difficult political circumstances. Radicals blamed Whigs for losing support because of supineness in the cause of further reform; Whigs blamed radicals for alienating moderate support by their extreme policies. Radicals themselves were incapable of presenting a united front; they differed openly on the Poor Law, factory reform, and further parliamentary reform.

Meanwhile the Conservative leaders, and especially Peel, were consolidating a reputation for statesmanlike and constructive behaviour in opposition. Instead of trying to defeat the Municipal Corporations Act in 1835, the Opposition gave it a general support, and indeed in both Houses of Parliament introduced what could be seen as improvements to the government proposals. Similarly, the creation in 1836 of a permanent Ecclesiastical Commission to supervise the revenues of the Church of England was treated as a non-partisan measure. On this issue the role of Peel was so prominent that he received much of the credit for the reform. The Tithe Act of 1836, replacing the old obligation to the Church by a standardized money payment, was also accepted by the Opposition with little demur.

Church affairs played an important role in altering political alignments in the later 1830s. Leading politicians like Stanley and Graham, who had broken with the Whigs over Church matters earlier, were impressed by Peel's emergence as the judicious champion of the Established Church, while the Whigs continued to feed the suspicion of the Church's supporters. In 1837 the ministry introduced a bill to extinguish church rates and replace them by a modest subsidy derived from pew rents in parish churches and minor additional elements in Church income. There was increasing hostility to church rates, levied for the maintenance of the Anglican parish churches, from Nonconformists, but the government's initiative did it no good in more influential quarters. Although a majority of twenty votes was scraped together in the House of Commons, the Opposition well knew that this was a proposal without formidable backing and the House of Lords rejected it with impunity.

Another general election took place in 1837 as a result of the death of William IV and the accession of the young Queen Victoria. Nothing had happened to strengthen the Whig administration, and the 1837 results saw a further erosion of the ministerial majority. Radicals suffered disproportionately high losses, which did not improve their opinion of the Whig leadership. After 1837 Melbourne had only a shaky Commons majority; the most favourable calculation gave the ministry only twenty-four more seats than the Conservative Opposition, and in practice the situation was less encouraging. Even if the Government had tried to embark upon major reforming legislation, failure seemed certain, with a powerful Commons opposition and a hostile majority in the Lords. In fact the Melbourne ministry had little in the way of constructive ideas to offer in these years.

Queen Victoria

The Whigs did acquire one new source of support in 1837, but it was no longer capable of buttressing their hold on office to any decisive extent. William IV had come to care little for his Whig ministers, but the young Queen Victoria, inexperienced at her accession, leaned heavily on the advice of the avuncular Lord Melbourne. In contrast, Peel appeared to her as a cold and unhelpful personality, and these personal reactions were to blow up into political crisis.

In the West Indies the implementation of the emancipation of the slaves enacted in 1833 had run into difficulties. By 1839 the home government was so frustrated by the obstructive tactics of the planter-dominated Assembly of Jamaica that the Cabinet decided to suspend the island's constitution. This was the kind of issue on which a government possessed of the confidence of the legislature might expect a secure margin of votes. When on the key division the ministerial majority sank to only five, accompanied by a display of disunity on the government benches, this amounted to a demonstration of weakness. Melbourne chose to accept the vote as a sign of want of confidence, and resigned.

Unwillingly, the Queen accepted her government's resignation and sent for Peel. The Conservative leader accepted the commission to form an administration, but without enthusiasm, since he would have preferred to see the Whig decline allowed to go even further. A difficulty then arose in relation to the royal household, which included a high proportion of members drawn from the Whig aristocracy. Peel insisted that to demonstrate her confidence in her new advisers, the Queen should introduce some changes among the ladies of her household, to the benefit of the Conservative section of the aristocracy. So began the 'Bedchamber Crisis'. The Queen indignantly refused, and when Peel persisted she turned to Melbourne for support. The Whig leaders decided to stand by the Queen, who then persisted in her refusal of Peel's demand. Peel thereupon refused to form a government, and the Whigs returned to office, but without any real improvement in their position.

The affair demonstrated a possible danger for the monarchy. Queen Victoria had acted in a politically partisan fashion during the episode, and for a while it appeared as if the sovereign was the ally of one party in the State. The arguments over whether she was acting constitutionally, or indeed whether William IV had done so in dismissing Melbourne's administration in 1834, rather miss the point. The constitution had not changed but the context within which it operated was changing. The danger here was averted by the Queen's marriage to Prince Albert in 1840; this provided her with an alternative source of wise advice, and removed her personal dependence on Melbourne. In subsequent years the work of the Prince Consort did much to mark out for the monarchy a role of continuing importance which could be reconciled with the accelerating changes within Britain. If contemporary opinion did not always appreciate his great services to his adopted country, modern historical research has produced a more perceptive analysis.

Chartism and the Anti-Corn Law League

From 1837 Britain faced a deepening economic depression, with bad harvests, an industrial slump, and increasing unemployment and privation. Declining trade meant reduced income from tariffs, still a crucial element in national revenue. Year after year the Whig ministers faced Parliament and country with unbalanced Budgets. Even if the role of government was not rated very highly in these years, ministries were expected to manage the national finances competently, and failure to do so was regarded as evidence of ineptitude. Again and again financial debates saw ministers in a poor light, while Peel and his colleagues made the most of the debating opportunities offered. Other developments added to the ministry's weakness. The early Victorian years saw the arrival on the political scene of two major radical agitations, the Chartist Movement and the Anti-Corn Law League.[14] The government's handling of these did not improve its chances of survival.

14. For the Chartists an invaluable guide is D. Thompson and J. F. C. Harrison, *Bibliography of the Chartist Movement* (1978). Two modern studies of contrasting approach are J. T. Ward, *Chartism* (1973), and D. Thompson, *The Chartists* (1984). Most of the details of individual Chartists which follow are taken from the latter source. For the Anti-Corn Law League, N. McCord, *The Anti-Corn Law League, 1838–1846* (1958) and Paul A. Pickering and Alex Tyrrell, *The People's Bread: A History of the Anti-Corn Law League* (2000).

These movements have received a disproportionate amount of historical attention in relation to their significance in their own day. In both cases this attention has been largely due to their presumed relevance to later political battles, rather than a simple desire to understand early-Victorian Britain. The aims of both movements were far from new. Objections to the Corn Laws had been vehemently expressed since the time of the enactment of the 1815 Corn Law, while the six points usually associated with Chartist demands—universal manhood suffrage, vote by secret ballot, equal electoral districts, annual parliamentary elections, payment of MPs, abolition of the property qualifications for MPs—had been advocated by radical groups since the late eighteenth century at least. The land settlement scheme, which Feargus O'Connor was to graft on to Chartism, was equally no new concept. Ideas for resettling workers in idyllic rural communities had been tried before, and were to resurface at intervals in the nineteenth and twentieth centuries; nor was O'Connor the only one to claim that by such means he 'would make a paradise of England in less than five years'.[15]

Moreover, the ten years 1838–48, which marked the peak years of Chartism, were only a small part of the active lives of most Chartists. Many of them had been radicals long before the People's Charter was drawn up in 1838; many of them continued as active radicals after the Chartist movement had faded into obscurity. At Sheffield two of the local Chartist leaders, Booth and Kirk, had taken part in radical activities since the days of Peterloo.[16] Many Chartists had been active in opposition to the post-1834 Poor Law. At Bury one of the leading radicals, the surgeon Matthew Fletcher, had been prominent during the 1831–2 reform campaign and subsequent years; at first dubious about the value of the Chartist agitation he later became a keen local supporter of it.

Like some leaders of the radical agitation in the post-1815 years, some of the Chartist leaders were of dubious quality. The most prominent of them all, Feargus O'Connor, provided the movement with a kind of personal national focus, an important contribution to a movement composed of varied sectional and local groups.[17] On the other hand his flamboyant egotism, unscrupulous pursuit of his own aggrandizement, and shaky nerve were undoubtedly harmful. There were other recruits who in one way or another proved to be liabilities. Immediately after the suppression of a Chartist uprising at Newport in 1839, when it was notorious that the authorities were opening the letters of suspected subversives, Dr John Taylor wrote to the Dundee Chartists to offer suggestions for the manufacture of explosives.[18] An even less helpful recruit was Israel

15. Quoted by P. Mathias, *The First Industrial Nation*, 2nd edn. (1983), 332.
16. S. Pollard and C. Holmes (eds.), *Essays in the Economic and Social History of South Yorkshire* (1976), 154.
17. For O'Connor see, J. Epstein, *The Lion of Freedom: Feargus O'Connor and the Chartist Movement, 1832–42* (1982).
18. D. Vincent, 'Communication, community and the State', in C. Emsley and J. Walvin (eds.), *Artisans, Peasants & Proletarians*, 180.

Ferment, or Firman. In practice as a quack doctor and astrologer for many years, he joined the Chartist movement in its early years, only to turn Queen's Evidence after the Newport Rising, at the age of 91. After contributing, in part by false testimony, to the conviction of some of his Chartist comrades, he reverted to his earlier trades.[19]

Such dubious assets were not an uncommon experience in Victorian political movements, though they were damaging. The Chartist movement also attracted and retained the devotion of men and women who fought hard for the cause, often making tremendous personal sacrifices. The fate of some of those who openly identified themselves with the democratic movement was hard. George White died in the Sheffield workhouse and Bronterre O'Brien also fell on hard times. Other ex-Chartists contrived to become respectable and successful figures in later years.

A feature of the Chartist movement was its episodic character. There were peaks of activity, such as the first and most impressive phase lasting from 1838 to the early part of 1840; other peaks came in the summer of 1842 and February–August 1848. Another feature is the way its strength and nature varied between towns and regions. It has been argued that Chartism is a term 'which imposes a misleading sense of unity on a conglomerate of individuals, groups and regions'.[20] Sometimes concentrated activity appeared in one area while others were quiescent, as in Wales in 1843.

What is certain is that it drew upon a deep and wide well of disparate griev-ances: those of the dispossessed such as the archetype for the redundant, the handloom weavers; emergent factory workers subject to economic fluctuation and work-discipline; and even skilled workers, for tailors and shoemakers formed the avant-garde of radicalism. These coalesced with the disappointment of many who had demonstrated for parliamentary reform but remained unenfranchised. Chartism had many faces: 'moral force' as it mainly was in Scotland and more inclined to 'physical force' in Wales, Nottinghamshire, and Leicestershire, though everywhere both tendencies were present; and a manifest-ation of secular radicalism in London and close to radical nonconformity in much of the north of England. It has been seen as both proto-socialist and nos-talgically populist with its language, flags, and ceremonies being expressions of traditional popular culture. Certainly, if the back-to-the-land ethos of the Chartist Land Plan resulted in an economically unviable enterprise that brought Chartism into discredit when it collapsed, it touched a chord in the popular imagination that would surface again and again throughout the century.[21]

It has often been noted that the high points of Chartist agitation coincided with periods of economic and social distress, although the implications of this

---

19. F. B. Smith, *The People's Health, 1830–1910* (1979), 334.
20. Williams and Ramsden, *Ruling Britannia*, 216.
21. Malcolm Chase, ' "Wholesome Object Lessons": The Chartist Land Plan in Retrospect', *English Historical Review*, vol. cxvii, no. 475 (2003), 59–85.

have not always been appreciated. Throughout the Chartist years there was a core of dedicated and intellectually convinced champions of the democratic cause, Chartists in good times and bad. Mass support for the movement only surfaced in times of depression, when thousands of deprived men and women were likely to grasp any prescription which promised an end to hardship. When times improved, this kind of 'foul weather' support melted away, with the inescapable implication that for this mass following the commitment to Chartism was shallow as well as transient. This trend was obvious enough at the time, and contributed to the confidence with which established authority confronted the threat of Chartism.

In the context of 1838, the demands of the Chartists were extreme. Many people found it impossible to believe that Britain's problems were of a kind which could be solved by an immediate transition to democracy, given the widespread illiteracy and ignorance and the pervasive inequalities which had always existed. The Chartists faced a powerful aristocratic oligarchy which was not much given to agonizing reappraisals of its right and duty to rule. The way in which the early-Victorian authorities reacted to Chartism reflects the movement's essential failure. One of the repeatedly employed expedients of Chartism was the great national petition. Repeated resort to this device was in itself an indication that the movement lacked any means of exerting effective pressure on the State. Like many other petitions, including those of the Anti-Corn Law League, there were dubious signatures to be found on these petitions, but there can be no doubt that the Chartist petitions contained the genuine signatures of hundreds of thousands of people.

The authorities never entertained the idea of yielding to these demands. Instead, the House of Commons, by large majorities, repeatedly refused even to consider the mass Chartist petitions, usually with only about half of the MPs troubling to attend the divisions. For example, the first great petition was denied a hearing in 1839 by 235 votes to 46. Of the handful of MPs prepared to support the debating of the petitions, few if any would have voted for their demands. Radical MPs prepared to argue that the petitions should be considered often accompanied their arguments with denunciations of Chartist methods and Chartist personalities. On one celebrated occasion a leading radical MP, J. A. Roebuck, described Feargus O'Connor as 'a malignant and cowardly demagogue', a view shared not only by many respectable observers but also by some of O'Connor's rivals within the Chartist leadership.

Instead of any thought of surrender to Chartism, the reaction of early-Victorian governments was to deploy their substantial resources in displays of strength. There were, however, differences in emphasis. During the first great upsurge of the agitation in the later 1830s the Whig government responded with restraint. As deliberate policy, prosecutions for political offences were normally based on charges carrying relatively minor punishments. There were exceptions; three of the ringleaders of the Newport Rising of 1839 were charged with high treason and sentenced to death, proceedings which were undoubtedly perfectly legal. The Whig Cabinet would have been prepared to carry out the sentences, but a successful intervention by the judges involved brought about the substitution of transportation for life.[22] In general, the Whigs sedulously avoided the making of credible Chartist martyrs. As Lord John Russell put it, 'As long as mere violence of language is employed without effect it is better, I believe, not to add to the importance of these mob leaders by prosecution.'[23] Often attempts were made to persuade Chartist leaders to give undertakings of future good behaviour in return for the abandonment of prosecutions or the remission of punishments.

When the Conservatives took office in 1841 there was some change. This was due not so much to such tactical considerations, for there the Conservatives could be cautious too; for example, in 1842 the Chartists were allowed to take a great petition to Westminster from a preliminary mass meeting in Lincoln's Inn Fields. Here, however, there had been no large-scale overt defiance of the law. In the same year, faced with serious disturbances in some industrial districts, the Peel government showed its determination to uphold the rule of law. There had been illegal pressures and intimidation, with some violence involved.[24] Peel's Home Secretary, Sir James Graham, had been at his post throughout the summer's troubles (an unusual experience for an early-Victorian Cabinet minister), and finally took drastic action. There were more than 1,000 arrests, and three-quarters of those arrested received prison sentences of some kind. The sentences handed down by the special judicial commissions dispatched to the affected areas included five of transportation for life.

Both Whig and Conservative governments could respond confidently because they were much stronger than Chartism. Despite the extension of urbanization and industrialization, most people still lived in small and relatively isolated communities. The groups which provided some of the core support for Chartism, such as some of the handloom weavers, were poor and relatively impotent. The great National Convention of the Labouring Classes of 1839, the first Chartist quasi-parliament, could not scrape together the few pounds needed to meet postal expenses. A few months later, a Manchester landlady admitted police agents to a Chartist meeting held at her house, because her Chartist lodgers had failed to pay their rent.[25]

The dominant aristocracy retained that powerful combination of political, economic, and social powers which underpinned their control. Moreover, the armed forces, the ultimate repository of physical force within the kingdom, were loyal. A tiny force of twenty-eight soldiers repulsed the Chartist rising at Newport in November 1839—the biggest single act of political violence in these years—with fifteen of the assailants shot dead. If there were doubts about the

22. Thompson, *The Chartists*, 81–2.
23. Quoted by E. H. Hunt, *British Labour History, 1815–1914* (1981), 235.
24. G. Kitson Clark, 'Hunger and politics in 1842', *Journal of Modern History*, 25 (1953), 355–74.
25. Vincent, 'Communication, Community and the State', 178. Hunt, *British Labour History*, 236.

possible loyalty of some units when ordered to act in support of the civil power, there seems to have been no fear of disloyalty as far as the Irish regiments were concerned, and General Napier frequently used them to cope with Chartist activities.[26] The development of the railway and telegraph systems made the effective deployment of the army much easier.

The most convincing demonstration of the comparative strength of government and Chartism came in April 1848. The Whig government, ignoring the precedent of 1842, determined to prevent any mass procession from carrying the great Chartist petition to Parliament. To enforce their ban, they concentrated more than 8,000 troops, more than 4,000 London policemen, and a reserve force of special constables so numerous that their actual number remains doubtful, though at least 100,000 were enrolled. At the Tower 30 guns were held ready, with steamers ready to transport them if necessary. Characteristically, O'Connor claimed that almost half a million Chartists assembled on Kennington Common, but a modern computation has shown that the space available could scarcely have held a tenth of this number.[27] Many of those present seem to have been casual spectators, and the mass meeting itself probably numbered no more than 20,000; the Chartists were certainly hopelessly outnumbered by those who had rallied to the authorities.

Even the most sympathetic of historians have found themselves unable to credit the Chartists with any great strength in the adverse conditions offered by early-Victorian Britain. For example, Professor E. J. Hobsbawm has concluded that 'the historian of Chartism . . . can hardly fail to be saddened by the extraordinary feebleness of this greatest of all the mass movements of British labour.'[28] Given this feebleness, it is not surprising that the Melbourne government, despite its own growing problems, was able to respond effectively to the first and greatest period of Chartist activity in 1838–40. This success owed something to their prescience in pressing in 1831–2 for the kind of parliamentary reform they had enacted, and in following this up by reforms in Poor Law and municipal administration. The Chartists faced a reinforced garrison for the status quo. Many men of local influence who had been hostile to the unreformed State might now be Poor Law guardians, town councillors, or borough magistrates (or very probably all three), and understandably hostile to the extreme demands for power-sharing made by the Chartists. Men who in 1832 had been active in threatening opponents of reform with warnings of revolution could in 1839 be found busily swearing in special constables and calling for military support to overawe Chartist activities. A good example is Sir John Fife, a Newcastle doctor who took a prominent part in the reform agitation of 1831–2 on Tyneside. As Mayor of the reformed Newcastle Corporation, he vigorously opposed the local Chartists in 1839 and was knighted soon afterwards.

26. Hunt, *British Labour History*, 168.
27. D. Large, 'London in the year of revolutions', in J. Stevenson (ed.), *London in the Age of Reform* (1977), 192.
28. E. J. Hobsbawm, *Labouring Men: Studies in the History of Labour* (1968), 381.

It is plainly incorrect to say that Chartism died out after the 1848 Kennington Common fiasco, but it ceased to attract the same amount of attention in future years. For many people in the third quarter of the century, Chartism represented a kind of false start or a digression in the general flow of development in Britain. Here, for instance, is how its story was concluded in a history book of 1873:

Hardly any person of knowledge or observation can imagine that the extreme changes thus proposed could be productive of real benefit to any rank or order of men. But still this Charter was espoused … very extensively among the working classes, and was afterwards brought the more before the public eye by the example of the revolution in France of 1848. It resembles also the constitution of the United States of America.[29]

The picture of Chartism which received the most widespread credence in these years was an unflattering one, although there was always an opposing tradition in existence. Later in the nineteenth century, and even more in the twentieth, there was a change. Chartism became a source of inspiration to socialist pioneers and a topic of intense interest. The fact that by 1918 at least four of the six points of the Charter had been realized[30] also contributed to a revaluation of the movement, often without much consideration of how far the Chartists themselves bore any responsibility for that development. Less attention has probably been given to those who were actually responsible for the abolition of the property qualification for MPs as early as 1858, or the enactment of the secret ballot in 1872.

The Anti-Corn Law League

In the first years of Victoria's reign, the radical campaign against the Corn Laws could also be met by those in power without undue difficulty. In the 1840s the situation changed; the Anti-Corn Law League grew to considerable size, and proved capable of matching the Chartists in nuisance value to the authorities. After disastrous early years, it contrived to bring together a wide and varied array of interests in a crusade against agricultural protection. Economic, political, social, humanitarian, and even religious arguments were marshalled against 'the Bread Tax'. Industrialists were persuaded that repeal of the Corn Laws would bring cheaper labour costs, and a greater ability for food-producing countries to buy British manufactured products. Nonconformists, aggrieved at tithe payments to the Established Church, might make much of texts like 'Give us this day our daily bread.' Radicals of various shades of opinion were happy to portray the aristocracy as men who inflicted artificially high food prices to safeguard their agricultural rent-rolls. The general tenor both of economic doctrines and of

29. Mrs Markham, *A History of England … For the Use of Young Persons* (1873), 481. The contemporary *Journal of Education* described this work as 'deservedly popular'.

30. It is usually stated that five had been realized, the unrealized point being annual parliaments, but, although electoral districts were much more even than in the 1830s, they were in 1918 and remain today far from equal.

government policies in recent decades had been towards free trade and the removal of fiscal impediments to commerce. Even the landed interest itself was not wholly united in defence of the Corn Laws; landowners acquiring a substantial part of their incomes from urban rents or mineral royalties were not always concerned to defend agricultural protection.

Yet nothing which the League did in its first years from 1838 to 1840 proved effective. Then, early in 1841 it turned to active involvement in electoral politics. This developed into a large-scale manipulation of the post-1832 franchise categories by the multiplication of property qualifications for supporters. This gave it more muscle on the contemporary political scene, and by 1843 *The Times* was brought to describe the League as a 'great fact'. Economic recovery after 1842 helped to swell its coffers, and from 1843 the League raised funds of £50,000, £100,000, and eventually in 1846 £250,000 (not all of which was actually collected). The League's financial backing, much of it coming directly from industrialists, was much greater than that of the Chartists. In addition, the League had more effective parliamentary spokesmen than the Chartists ever had, especially after Richard Cobden's election for Stockport in 1841. Even so, the actual power of the League in the context of early-Victorian Britain remained meagre, although like the Chartists it was capable of making a great deal of noise. The number of constituencies amenable to the League's manipulation remained small in relation to the massed ranks of Conservative and Whig MPs. Neither of the great radical agitations came even reasonably close to the exercise of effective power.

The fall of the Whigs

The fortunes of Melbourne's declining government were not enhanced by its response to these radical challenges. The restraint it showed in dealing with the Chartists in 1837–41 may have earned the praise of later historians, but it was an electoral liability at the time. Many of those enfranchised after 1832 would have welcomed a tougher reaction. The existence of the Anti-Corn Law League added to the friction between Whigs and radicals. Free traders were disappointed at the Whig refusal to embrace repeal of the Corn Laws, while the Manchester-based League was disliked by more conservative Whigs, including many of the government's followers within the landed interest. The irruption of the League into the electoral scene was not always helpful to the Whigs; the League's first electoral adventure, at Walsall in early 1841, split the liberal vote and so let in a Conservative.

Circumstances were to bring about a change. As the failure of the Melbourne government's financial policies became evident, the more liberal members of the ministry began to urge the need for new initiatives here. There was little support for an attempt to reintroduce an income tax, because such a move would be unpopular and beyond the government's strength to carry, but there was an increasing belief that the only way to economic recovery and government solvency lay in cutting indirect taxation. Although this would mean an increased deficit in the short run, it was hoped that the stimulus to trade given by reduced duties would soon promote economic recovery and increase revenue again. These ideas were encouraged by the report of an influential Select Committee on Import Duties in 1840, which was in favour of further tariff reductions. The committee's sponsor was the radical MP Joseph Hume, and the evidence adduced was heavily weighted by Board of Trade officials who were partisan free traders. In 1841, after it was clear that increasing duties actually reduced revenue by discouraging trade, the Melbourne government decided to change its policy. New proposals were produced which included reductions in the levels of duties on a variety of articles, the most controversial of which were likely to be sugar, timber, and corn. These guaranteed opposition. A reduction in duties on foreign timber was to be accompanied by a rise in duties on colonial timber; both would aggrieve vested interests. The sugar proposals involved no change for colonial sugar, but a decrease of nearly half in the tariff on foreign sugar, something which would annoy anti-slavery crusaders as well as West India sugar interests. The sliding scale of the 1828 Corn Law was to be replaced by a moderate fixed duty on the import of foreign corn, unacceptable to the bulk of the agricultural interest.

These adventurous proposals were nevertheless introduced into Parliament by Baring, the Chancellor of the Exchequer, at the end of April 1841. Peel now felt that the time had come to deal the Whig government a fatal blow. Tactically, the Conservatives chose to fasten on the general weakness of the Whigs' recent financial record, and on the specific proposals on sugar. In a memorable contribution to the debate on 18 May Peel asked, 'Can there be a more lamentable picture than that of a Chancellor of the Exchequer seated on an empty chest—by the pool of a bottomless deficiency—fishing for a Budget?' The tactical decision to attack the Whigs on sugar was clever. The implication of favouring slave-grown foreign sugar could be used to rally more opposition than the other proposed tariff changes. The Conservative tactics paid off, and the sugar proposal was defeated by a stinging 36 votes before the proposed corn duties had been debated at all. The Whigs still cherished some hopes of hanging on, but early in June, forestalling any full debate on the Corn Laws, Peel moved a vote of want of confidence which was carried by 312 votes to 311.

The Whigs now had no choices other than resignation or an appeal to the electorate. They decided to dissolve Parliament, though privately the ministers had little hope of victory. The Conservatives were better prepared for a general election than the Whigs. Since 1832, under the guidance of their principal electoral agent, F. R. Bonham, there had been vigorous Conservative electoral activity. Much attention had been given to the state of the new electoral registers, and a good deal of preparatory work in the constituencies had been carried out, such as the advance selection of suitable candidates.[31] More important than this,

31. For Bonham, see N. Gash, *Politics in the Age of Peel* (1953), 413–18.

however, was the decline in the reputation of the Whig government, and the concurrent rise in Peel's stature in public estimation.

The events of 1834–5 and the failure of Peel's minority administration had already shown some of the effects of 1832; now, the general election of 1841 illuminated others.[32] Queen Victoria's confidence in her Whig ministers could not preserve them from defeat, while the election result was a clear demonstration of the effect of a shift in the opinion of the electorate. For the first time a disciplined opposition party succeeded in reversing the decision of the previous general election.

In 1841 the Conservatives returned 367 MPs, and the distribution of their victories was as striking as their total. Two of the seats for the City of London were won, while Leeds and Bristol were among the large towns which added to Peel's majority. At Reading 2 Conservatives who stressed the Whig threat to the Corn Laws were returned, the first such victory there for forty years. In the smaller boroughs the Conservatives made a useful gain of 13 seats over their 1837 count, more than balancing a net loss of 2 seats in the larger boroughs with more than 2,000 electors. Overall the Conservatives won 155 of the 323 borough seats. In Scotland they won 22 out of 53, in Ireland 43 out of 105, and in Wales 19 out of 29.

The decisive theatre, though, was the English counties. There, in the disaster of 1832, the Conservatives had held only 42 out of the 144 seats, but now in 1841 the day of revenge came; 124 Conservative MPs were returned by the English counties. This was not only a crucial numerical victory, but also a great boost to party morale, in view of the prestige attached to these seats; equally it was a disastrous blow to the Whigs, who suffered notable casualties. Lord Grey's heir, Viscount Howick, lost in North Northumberland, and the Duke of Norfolk's heir, Lord Surrey, in West Sussex. The most serious reverse came in that especially prestigious constituency, the West Riding of Yorkshire; Viscount Morpeth and Viscount Milton, heirs to two great Whig aristocratic dynasties, were beaten by two good Conservative candidates. The Conservative victory here, a narrow one, owed something both to local opposition to a weakening of the Corn Laws and to anti-Poor Law feeling, though the national trend to loss of confidence in the Whigs and growing confidence in Peel also played a part. The Conservatives had done very well in the most prestigious constituencies, and they came to Westminster as a relatively united body; their victory owed much to the ideas set out in the Tamworth Manifesto, which had succeeded in marshalling behind Peel a wide and varied following. The Whigs' defeat, on the other hand, was accompanied by recriminations between them and the radicals about responsibility

32. T. L. Crosby, *Sir Robert Peel's Administration, 1841–46* (1976), 20–34; N. Gash, *Sir Robert Peel* (1972), 264–6. The following account of Peel's second ministry is also largely based on these sources. A recent reassessment of Conservative opposition to Peel's policies is A. Macintyre, 'Lord George Bentinck and the protectionists: a lost cause?', *Transactions of the Royal Historical Society*, 5th ser., 39 (1989), 141–65.

for the disaster. The new opposition was not to show much ability to unite against the victors.

Peel's second ministry

When the new Parliament met in August, the Whigs were speedily defeated on the Address and resigned. In constructing his new Cabinet, Peel had to take account of the wide nature of his support. Some of the new government's most important members had been recruited by the Conservative policies of the 1830s. Peel's closest colleague was to be the new Home Secretary, Sir James Graham, who had been a successful member of Grey's reform ministry as First Lord of the Admiralty, and had actually served on the drafting committee for the 1832 parliamentary reform. Graham had been an important early defector from the reform ministry, and after a period of some hesitation had moved into Peel's following in the later 1830s. The new Colonial Secretary was Stanley (the future Earl of Derby), who, like Graham, was a valuable recruit from the ranks of the more conservative Whigs. He had broken with the Whigs at the same time as Graham because he would not accept liberal proposals on such matters as the Established Church of Ireland. After a few years' experience of being overshadowed in the Commons by Peel himself, Stanley was willingly elevated to the Lords in 1843, with the intention that he should serve there as a leading spokesman for the government. This move had important and unforeseen consequences during the political crisis of 1846.

Some of Peel's other colleagues had longer credentials as party members. Wellington's unique position, at once national hero and ex-premier, was recognized by his inclusion within the new Cabinet as a minister without portfolio. He was not the easiest of colleagues, being elderly, deaf, and somewhat irascible, but any resulting problems and misunderstandings could be ironed out because Wellington had a considerable respect for Peel's gifts as a leader.

Others of the new Cabinet had already served in the brief minority administration of 1834–5. Apart from Peel and Wellington, they included Lord Lyndhurst, the Lord Chancellor; Lord Ripon, President of the Board of Trade; Henry Goulburn, Chancellor of the Exchequer; and the two armed forces ministers, Sir Henry Hardinge at the War Office and Lord Haddington at the Admiralty. The Foreign Office went to Lord Aberdeen, who had occupied that post under Wellington in the late 1820s.

There were also other elements in the Conservative Party which Peel was obliged to recognize. The victory of 1841 owed something to a marked right-wing reaction against the Whigs. Many Conservative MPs owed their returns to a trenchant support for the Corn Laws, and some had also benefited from attacks on the post-1834 Poor Law administration. It was necessary to give this right wing some recognition in the new Cabinet, but not easy to find men of ministerial calibre in that quarter. The choice eventually fell on the Duke of Buckingham and

Sir Edward Knatchbull, who did not prove useful assets. Buckingham refused to accept Peel's modification of the Corn Laws in 1842, and promptly resigned, without his colleagues feeling any great sense of loss. Knatchbull was to hang on until early 1845, increasingly conscious of the growing gap between Peel's policies and the views of the right-wingers with whom he felt most at home.

Was it Peel who won in 1841 or the Conservative Party he led? One view is that Peel had since the Tamworth Manifesto done much to make the party electable. Another is that Peel's managerial view of politics and his sympathy with the manufacturing and commercial interests was at odds with much of the party he led. One historian has commented that: 'It was not Peel who won in 1841, but the reactionary forces which deeply offended him.'[33] This is perhaps to read the events of 1841 in the light of the events of 1846 and to underestimate Peel's contribution to the electoral victory but it is arguable that the Conservative victory was as much a reaction against a decade of reform as a vote for a reformist leader. The victory was won in the counties and smaller boroughs with most of the larger towns returning Liberals. The causes on which the party campaigned were protection of the Anglican Church and the maintenance of the duties on corn. Feelings towards Peel by his party were those of mixed discontent and admiration for a leader whom it felt was distant from party feeling but was strong and capable. It was soon to become clear that Peel was no great defender of the Church and had become sceptical of the efficacy of the Corn Laws.

Peel's second government took office at a time of grave difficulty. The failures of the previous administration had weakened public confidence in the ability of its rulers to face up to the economic and social problems of these years. The winter of 1841–2 brought deepening economic depression, and serious hardship. The situation, as far as those now responsible for government were concerned, was not helped by the attitude of many radicals who, bitterly disappointed in the election results, sought to impugn the validity of the decision by attacking the new legislature as the 'Bribery Parliament'. There had of course been some electoral corruption in 1841, though it was no worse than that of the previous two elections, or of some which were to follow.

Some of the new government's most important work was to be in economic policy. Peel himself was the dominating figure here, at the head of a small ministerial group which included Ripon and Goulburn, and also W. E. Gladstone, the new Vice-President of the Board of Trade and that department's spokesman in the House of Commons. The problem of public order was primarily Graham's sphere, though he and Peel saw eye to eye on such matters. The main responsibility for deciding how to respond to the domestic crisis he had inherited rested on Peel, and it bore heavily upon him during these months. Under pressure to take some kind of immediate emergency action to deal with the pressing problems, he refused to take hasty, ill-considered initiatives. Instead, only too

33. Ian Newbould, *Whiggery and Reform 1830–41* (1990), 321.

well aware of the social consequences of his choice, he determined to spend the first months in office in preparing a carefully considered plan of action. A brief parliamentary session in September 1841 dealt with essential matters, but Peel intended to meet Parliament in early 1842 with far-reaching proposals for which he had obtained the support of his colleagues.

The immediate results of this hard decision seemed to justify the delay, for Peel's financial proposals of 1842 proved a considerable political and economic success. There was nothing very original about them, for they were based on ideas which had been in the air at least since 1815. In order to stimulate the economy there ought to be a significant cut in the indirect taxation imposed on commerce. To do this without more serious revenue deficits, resort must be had to direct taxation, at least until economic recovery produced matching revenue from the lower scales of tariff. Such policies had been desired by the Tory governments of the 1820s, but they only became politically practicable when there was a strong and determined government in office, and when a spell of severe depression and repeated deficits in revenue had brought influential opinion to accept the need for such drastic action.

It took time for Peel to persuade some of his colleagues that income tax should be brought back in order to obtain a freer hand for tariff reductions. There were also special difficulties in altering duties on such products as sugar, timber, and corn, as the previous administration had discovered. Predictably, within the government and within the party, the Corn Laws proved the most awkward instance. Peel was determined to embark upon a revision of the whole tariff system, and was not prepared to see agricultural protection as a sacred exception. There were in any case good practical reasons for Corn Law revision. The sliding scale of the 1828 Corn Law, itself the result of a patched-up political compromise, had not worked well. Peel now aimed at an improved sliding scale which would maintain the price of wheat at about the 50–60s. per quarter price range, and at the same time prove more effective in smoothing out price fluctuations than the 1828 scale, which had tended to jump rather than slide. The projected price bracket was too low for the devoted champions of agricultural protection; at some points on the new scale the duty charged on corn imports was less than half that imposed in 1828. The Duke of Buckingham, expressing the reaction of many right-wing Tories, refused to accept the reductions; however, the proposed alterations in the Corn Laws, and the reasoned arguments behind them, attracted such substantial support that his departure from the government was of little moment. There was predictably a great deal of grumbling from the agricultural interest, but this did not amount to a serious challenge to Peel's authority.

The new Corn Law was the first major business of the 1842 parliamentary session, although it was made clear that it was only one component within a wider plan. The next instalment came in March, with the debates on the income tax. This initiative had been successfully kept as a Cabinet secret until Peel was ready to unveil it in Parliament. He pointed to the series of Whig budget deficits in previous years as an unmistakable justification for taking decisive action to restore the finances of the State. The proposed tax was proffered as a temporary expedient, authorized for three years only. It would only be paid by those able to afford it, and the level was low. On taxable incomes over £150 per annum a flat rate of 7*d*. in the pound would be levied.[34] The overwhelming majority of the population would be unaffected (and was indeed to remain untouched by income tax until well into the twentieth century).

Apart from solving the immediate financial pressures, the new income tax was to provide the leeway for the rest of the government's economic proposals. Opposition proved more muted than might have been expected. This was partly due to the skilful way in which Peel sugared the pill. His income tax scheme embodied special concessions for farmers, and also for Scotland and Ireland. Some strenuous resistance was offered to the measure, but there was enough acceptance of the need for it in both Parliament and country for it to pass in June 1842 with little difficulty.

Before then, early in May, Peel had introduced the remainder of the package, lucidly expounding the principles which the Cabinet had accepted. First, prohibition of any imports was seen as unwise and any barriers of that kind were to go. Secondly, the imposition of high import duties on raw materials needed by British industry was patently unsound, and a maximum figure of 5 per cent had been agreed here. Even for the import of foreign manufactured goods, a maximum levy of 20 per cent was reckoned to give British producers adequate protection. The implementation of these principles involved a revision of well over half of the existing duties.

In general the tariff proposals were enacted easily. The main opposition party was already committed to a policy of tariff reduction, which made it hard for it to resist the new proposals. The most substantial hostility came from among the government's followers. The grand scheme of tariff reduction included several categories of agricultural produce not covered by the main Corn Laws, especially the import of meat and live cattle. Faced with pleas for concessions here by the vocal representatives of the agricultural interest, Peel refused to compromise, basing his refusal on the argument that the food supply for an increasing population must be a paramount consideration. Although about a quarter of the Conservative MPs opposed Peel on this issue, the government mustered enough votes from moderate members of the opposition to beat off the rebellion by a convincing majority.

It may well be that Peel's 1842 Budget was more important for its effect on national morale than for any direct economic impact. The sweeping nature of the proposals, and the impression given of well-thought-out and competent policies, made a great effect in the country. In the restoration of national confidence after the recent economic setbacks and the unimpressive performance of

---

34. This is of course the pre-decimal £ of 240*d*.

the previous ministry, Peel's apparent mastery of the situation was important. More generally, Peel's second government contrived to give the impression of an administration which could be trusted to govern competently and in the national interest. This enhanced confidence in government was maintained not only by the remaining budgetary innovations, but also by reforms in banking and company law, which helped to build confidence in the country's financial institutions (see pp. 200–2 below). This changed situation was well exemplified in 1844, in a financial operation whereby the interest on about £250 million of the National Debt was reduced by 0.25 per cent; the overwhelming majority of the stockholders concerned accepted the government's proposal for conversion, and there was an immediate saving of £625,000 per annum in debt charges. The previous administration had cut defence expenditure to the point where the operational strength of the Royal Navy was probably inferior to that of the French Navy. As revenue improved in 1844 and subsequent years, Peel increased spending on the armed forces, especially the navy, remedying some of the more obvious deficiencies, and showing that the Conservative government was more capable than its predecessors in safeguarding national security.

An impression was given of a higher level of administration than had been the case before 1841. It is not altogether clear how this impression came about. The departmental ministers probably did display more vigour and application than their predecessors, and Peel was certainly a much more watchful supervisor of the government than Melbourne, but there is little sign of any significant changes in administrative techniques at the centre between 1841 and 1846. It is clear, though, that Peel's personal standing had much to do with his government's reputation. The election victory in 1841 had been, many thought, a Peelite victory; the tactics which Peel had advocated had swept his party to power. Thereafter Peel dominated the policies of his government. Although he had on the whole an able team of ministers, Peel played a key role in the formation of all major policies, and exhibited considerable skill in manipulating his colleagues into accepting his own views. A successor in the premiership said of him that Peel was 'the model of all prime ministers'.[35] In one respect this tribute ought to be qualified, since Peel seriously overworked himself during the 1841–6 administration. However, his industry, his obvious ability, and his capacity for seeming to rise above sectional or party advantage and govern in the national interest raised him in these years to an unequalled position in public esteem. This is not to say that everyone admired him, but to claim that, in comparison with other contemporary politicians, Peel appeared to a broad range of public opinion as a figure of different stature from his predecessors or colleagues.

In succeeding years Peel propelled the ministry further along the lines laid in 1842. There was not much opportunity for further financial initiatives in 1843, because the revenue did not recover as rapidly as Peel had hoped. Reduced levels

35. Lord Rosebery, *Miscellanies*, vol. i (1927), 197.

of trade in many articles brought a deficit of over £3 million, despite the contribution from income tax. There was, however, one notable innovation in 1843, the Canada Corn Act, which allowed Canadian corn on to the British market at a greatly reduced duty. Stanley, the responsible minister, argued that this was not a mere matter of tariffs, but much more intended to extend imperial preference to ensure that Canada remained tied to Britain and resisted any economic blandishments which the United States might offer. This further erosion of the system of agricultural protection brought complaints from protectionists within the Conservative Party, but again the government beat off the attacks with relative ease.

In 1844 the situation changed. Revenue was even more buoyant than ministers had estimated. There was now scope for further reductions in tariffs, even with some increase in defence spending. There was, too, a general impression that Peel's prescription for curing the country's ills was working. It was natural that Peel and his colleagues should ascribe the economic recovery to their enlightened policies, and not surprising that such assumptions were widely accepted. The Cabinet agreed to another sweeping round of tariff reductions in the 1845 Budget, amounting to an estimated total cut of well over £3 million per annum, to be offset by prolonging the income tax for a further three years.

Conservative discontent

The 1845 financial proposals included one which was potentially dangerous, a halving of the duty on sugar imports. This could not be confined to merely economic arguments, since slavery and imperial preference were also involved. The ministry's critics within its own party began to show signs of political organization. They produced a motion which inflicted on the government its first serious rebuff, an ingenious resolution retaining the proposed new duty on foreign sugar, but inserting a lower figure for colonial sugar than the ministry's own proposition, something which might be expected to attract anti-slavery votes. In a confused parliamentary situation, a motley coalition defeated the government by twenty votes. Peel was furious, as much at the factious motives he detected as by the defeat itself. He contemplated resignation, but second thoughts prevailed; instead, it was made clear to the House of Commons that persistence in the vote might result in the ministry's resignation. Faced with this ultimatum, a second vote cancelled the rebellious resolution's effect.

This kind of knuckling under to the executive was not something which the early-Victorian House of Commons found palatable, and the incident played a part in the deteriorating relationships between Peel and a sizeable section of his following. With all his great qualities, the Conservative leader was not able to imbue the backbenchers of his party with a sense that he was a friendly and sympathetic colleague. Although in private life, with family and with friends, he was both devoted and popular, Peel's public demeanour often seemed aloof and austere. Other matters also strained relations between Peel and many of his followers. Some of the Conservative MPs had won their seats in 1841, at least in part, by joining in the attacks on the post-1834 Poor Law administration. On this issue Peel had preserved during the election what might be politely termed a dignified reserve, although privately he was clear about the correct course to pursue. In 1834 he had supported the Poor Law Amendment Act, and he now intended to prolong its life. In 1842, with criticisms from some Conservatives having been beaten off, the Poor Law Commission was given another five-year term, and the Conservative Poor Law legislation of 1844 was confined to making detailed improvements in the 1834 system. Alike for humanitarian reasons, and on grounds of local autonomy, this policy was disliked by many Conservatives both in Parliament and in the country.

Similarly, the government's cautious approach to factory reform was not popular with some of its followers. The ministry's first proposals here were wrecked by sectarian religious controversy (p. 196 below). The amended measure which reached the statute book in 1844 was too limited to satisfy keen Conservative social reformers like Lord Ashley. The decision to appoint only one inspector of mines after the 1842 Mines Act fell into the same category. It was not until some years after the fall of Peel's second government that mines inspection was put into a more practicable shape.[36]

Ireland

One of the priorities which Peel always had in mind was the conciliation of Ireland. During the ministry's early days, with pressing problems of public order and economic recovery, little could be done to work out a constructive Irish policy, although the need for it was appreciated from the beginning. The situation was not eased by the fact that Daniel O'Connell retained his old alliance with the Whigs, and showed no inclination to respond to attempts by the Conservative government to enlist his cooperation. At the same time, the election of 1841 had seen O'Connell's parliamentary 'tail' drop to a mere eighteen MPs, less than half the high point reached in 1832. However, it was misleading to build too much on this apparent loss of support for the nationalist cause.

During the early 1840s O'Connell intensified his campaign for the repeal of the Anglo-Irish legislative Union. In February 1843 the corporation of the city of Dublin passed a pro-repeal motion by a large majority. Enormous audiences were brought to mass meetings in Ireland, and some important figures in the Roman Catholic Church in Ireland backed the agitation. These developments brought an anti-Catholic and anti-Irish backlash in Great Britain. Ministers were under pressure to take action to crush the repeal movement before it became too

---

36. O. MacDonagh, 'Coal mines regulation: the first decade', in R. Robson (ed.), *Ideas and Institutions of Victorian Britain: Essays Presented to G. Kitson Clark* (1967), 58–86.

strong. O'Connell and his associates tried to head this off by stressing the legal and explicitly non-violent nature of the repeal campaign. The government's stance was not helped by the action of the Irish Lord Chancellor, Sugden, who on his own responsibility took to dismissing from the bench Irish magistrates who attended repeal meetings. In 1843 the government legislated to improve the control of weapons in Ireland, and went on to reinforce the Irish garrison, so that by the end of 1843 there were 34,000 regular troops there (a change made easier by a quietening of Chartist activities in Great Britain).

Fortunately for ministers, Irish political rhetoric provided a pretext for intervention. As the programme of mass meetings continued, the legality of the proceedings became increasingly dubious. The main nationalist orators were drawn into more adventurous flights of language which could be considered seditious. In October 1843 the government acted, prohibiting a planned mass meeting at Clontarf, and authorizing the arrest and prosecution of O'Connell and some of his principal followers. Faced with this challenge, O'Connell accepted the situation, calling off the Clontarf meeting and submitting to arrest. The apparent threat of immediate danger in Ireland seemed to have been averted. Yet though the ministry genuinely wanted to introduce conciliatory measures for Ireland, its freedom of manoeuvre was limited. Unwilling to introduce drastic changes in the Irish land laws (which were unlikely to be acceptable to Parliament) neither the Cabinet nor Parliament would accept any significant change in the status of the Established Church of Ireland. It was difficult, therefore, to find a basis for conciliatory moves. Peel tried to induce the Irish administration to adopt a less partisan attitude to the distribution of official patronage, without any great success.

Like many would-be reformers of Anglo-Irish affairs, Peel believed that the blessings of the connection were real and ought to be obvious to all well-intentioned men. If, especially, the Irish Roman Catholic priests could be brought to see the advantages of Anglo-Irish unity, that would be a major step forward. However, the Roman Catholic Church in Ireland was not rich, and if there was to be an improvement in the quality and the outlook of the priesthood some public expenditure would be required. Hopeful precedents existed. During the great French wars the main Irish seminary had been established at Maynooth, and subsidized by a modest grant of public funds voted annually by Parliament; by the 1840s this was a routine vote, the figure of £9,250 per annum fixed in 1808 being still in 1844 the current award. Peel considered that a reform of Maynooth might play a useful part in the ministry's Irish policy. While this was being considered, an Act of 1844 reformed the law affecting voluntary endowments of Catholic religious activities in Ireland, making donations and bequests for such purposes easier. After some initial doubts, the Irish Catholic bishops agreed to cooperate in this modest reform. But the spectacle of a Conservative administration anxiously engaged in moves to conciliate Irish Catholics was not calculated to be popular in Great Britain, and hostile feelings erupted with the introduction in April 1845 of Peel's scheme for the improvement of Maynooth.

The plan involved an increase in the annual parliamentary grant to £26,000, and an immediate capital grant of £30,000 for urgently needed building work at the college. Peel also decided to make the subsidy a permanent charge on the Exchequer rather than an annual grant. The government appreciated that there would be opposition, but they were surprised and taken aback by its nature and extent, in their own party as elsewhere. In the key division on the Maynooth proposals, fewer than half of the Conservative votes were cast for the government. With some opposition support the scheme passed with an apparently safe majority, but the storm signals were clear enough. Ministers nevertheless succeeded in adding one further Irish reform before the crisis which destroyed the government. In July 1845 an Act establishing colleges for higher education at Belfast, Cork, and Galway was passed. Again careful negotiations succeeded in overcoming the initial doubts of the Irish Catholic bishops about the proposal.

Peel's desire to conciliate Ireland had been genuine, but the actual results of this determination had not been very substantial. The concessions made had not been sufficient to disarm Irish opposition, while they were enough to add to existing suspicions of their leaders among right-wing Conservatives. The memory of Peel's part in Catholic emancipation in 1829 was still there, and concessions to Irish Catholics served to revive old doubts.

The repeal of the Corn Laws

Late in the summer of 1845 there were rumours of a failure of the potato crop in Ireland. Not until October was the extent of the disaster confirmed. Peel was well able to appreciate its implications, because he had been Chief Secretary for Ireland during the severe famine there in 1817 and had seen the consequences at first hand. The 1845 potato failure represented an even worse threat; the blight also affected the potato crop on the Continent, while a generally bad harvest for other crops meant that alternative food supplies would not be easily available.

Peel decided that a sensible response must include the repeal of the Corn Laws which taxed the import of the food which was going to be so desperately needed. Graham, who as Home Secretary also had important Irish responsibilities, came to the same conclusion. Peel had privately made up his mind some years earlier that the Corn Laws were not a necessary support for British farming, while they were harmful to other sectors of the economy. In 1842 over his new Corn Law, and in 1843 over the Canada Corn Act, the vocal agricultural lobby had forecast disaster for British farming. Peel believed that subsequent experience had shown these fears to be groundless; the Corn Laws could be safely repealed, and the Irish crisis offered an obvious occasion for doing so.

The conclusion was not nearly so obvious to most of his Cabinet colleagues: was it not possible to meet the current emergency by a temporary suspension of the Corn Laws? Peel and Graham argued against this, on the grounds that the need was so urgent that the ports must be seen to be wholly open to food imports. To keep the Corn Laws on the statute book would expose the government to attack as the maintainer of scarcity. Peel encountered little difficulty in persuading his colleagues of the need to set up an emergency supply organization for Ireland, but over Corn Law repeal he met stiff resistance.

It was obvious that for Peel to come to the Parliament elected in 1841 with a proposal for the repeal of the Corn Laws would be seen by the right wing, already angry and suspicious on other issues, as a betrayal of Conservative principles. Some ministers, notably Stanley, were adamant in refusing to accept Peel's view of the situation. More were distinctly unhappy at the prospect. At a lengthy series of Cabinet meetings in November and early December 1845, Peel fought for his proposals. He offered some concessions to try to win support, including a modified scheme whereby eight years would elapse before the tariffs on imported grain effectively disappeared (with of course some immediate emergency action to cope with the Irish situation). The Cabinet was still unconvinced, and it was made clear that if Peel persisted there would be important resignations, including those of Stanley and the Duke of Buccleuch. Peel felt that this was a vital matter on which he could not yield further, and on 5 December the breach led to the resignation of the ministry.

Meanwhile the Whigs had not been idle. The prolonged series of Cabinet meetings without any announcements of decisions had indicated divisions within the ministry. In late November, Lord John Russell, increasingly seen as the successor of the ailing Lord Melbourne in the Whig leadership, declared that he thought the Corn Laws should go. This made it appear that the only alternative government had accepted that policy. On Peel's resignation, the Queen summoned Russell and commissioned him to form a new administration. The attempt only lasted a fortnight, because Russell found problems on two fronts. Such a new government would be in a minority in both Houses of Parliament, but a general election in the midst of the Irish crisis was not an attractive expedient. Russell tried to extract from Peel an undertaking of support for the new administration's policy. Peel would not go beyond a vague general undertaking to support Corn Law repeal. Russell was understandably uncomfortable at the prospect of forming a minority government in these circumstances.

Moreover, he had to deal with friction among his own colleagues. Palmerston's spirited handling of foreign policy under the previous Whig administration had not won general support from other leading Whigs. In particular, Lord Grey (son of the Lord Grey of the Reform Act, who had died in 1845) refused to join the new Cabinet if Palmerston returned to the Foreign Office. Learning of this, Palmerston refused to join a Cabinet in which he went anywhere else. Faced with these problems, Russell decided against the formation of a government and, in Disraeli's words, 'handed back the poisoned chalice to Sir Robert'. The Queen now sent for Peel again. It seemed clear that repeal of the Corn Laws was inevitable, and therefore the majority of his senior colleagues were now prepared to accept Peel's proposals. The only major defector at the end of 1845 was

Lord Stanley; the other ministerial changes which proved necessary seemed to produce, if anything, a strengthened team.

As the parliamentary session of 1846 approached, Peel sought to put his proposals in an acceptable form, but growing hostility was already evident in a spate of meetings and publications designed to oppose repeal. By-elections in such agricultural constituencies as Buckinghamshire and Nottinghamshire went badly for government supporters. Peel made no determined attempt to conciliate his aggrieved followers, but the manner in which he introduced his 1846 proposals was skilful. The tariff proposals, including the repeal of the Corn Laws, were presented as another instalment of the beneficial policies which had been followed since 1841. Now, however, Peel was prepared to argue the general point that protective duties were in principle unwise. Repeal of the Corn Laws was to be only one major element within a package which also abolished or reduced duties on other food imports and on other articles such as shoes, soap, and timber.

The scheme was proffered not only as a further instalment of freer trade, but as a kind of national compact, under which the landed interest would be given compensation for the loss of the Corn Laws. Animal feeding stuffs would be included in the tariff reductions, farmers would be given increased access to public loans at low interest for farm improvements. The Treasury would take over responsibility for a number of items of local official expenditure, lowering the burden of local taxation on property occupiers.

Any hope that this mode of presentation would mollify opponents proved unfounded, although this did not become clear until well into 1846. No one could suppose that the right wing of the Conservative Party would meekly accept the repeal of the Corn Laws, but it was by no means obvious that their hostility could be made effective. Peel himself had no high opinion of the political abilities of many of the Conservative backbenchers, while with the exception of Stanley, safely out of the way in the House of Lords, Peel knew that he had the support of all of the ablest leaders of the party. For a while it seemed possible that the opposition within the Conservative Party would be confined to impotent grumbling, while for repeal of the Corn Laws opposition votes would give Peel a comfortable Commons majority. The issue of the debates of 1846, as far as Peel's political future was concerned, turned on whether or not the recalcitrant Conservative backbenchers could develop effective cohesion.

There were some men of ability among Peel's Conservative opponents. Benjamin Disraeli, an eccentric and flamboyant backbencher who had scrambled into Parliament in 1837 after earlier defeats, had made something of a name for himself in recent months by his waspish attacks on Peel. The increasingly disgruntled right-wingers had come to listen to these with some approbation. Disraeli had emphasized the possibility that Peel, the man of 1829 and Catholic emancipation, was contemplating a second betrayal of the party and the principles which had raised him to power.

None the less, the Conservative country gentlemen in Parliament were not likely to see their salvation in a Jewish adventurer of dubious reputation. It was widely believed that Disraeli had married his wife for her money, which had made his return for venal borough constituencies in 1837 and 1841 possible. His early life and his novels had left him with a tarnished reputation.[37] Whatever his abilities, he was not the stuff of which early-Victorian Conservative leaders were made. The key political development of 1846 lay elsewhere; it was unforeseeable, but involved the emergence of a more satisfactory focus for Conservative rebellion. Lord George Bentinck, younger son of a duke and a leading figure in country sports and on the turf, was among the Conservative MPs who felt betrayed by Peel's change of front on the Corn Laws. His resentment was so powerful that he came forward as a possible leader and organizer of the opposition to the Prime Minister. Moreover, despite their different origins and characters, he and Disraeli proved capable of cooperating in an effective partnership.

The fall of Peel

If Peel were to retain office it was crucial that his proposals should be accepted in Parliament before hostility within his own party had time to crystallize into a formed opposition. The new leadership emerging among the protectionists prevented this from happening, dragging out the debates by moving hostile resolutions and keeping discussion going for night after night. The government continued to carry its proposals by what seemed adequate majorities, but on a number of key divisions most of the Conservative votes were in the opposition lobby, and only Whig and radical votes saved the ministry's free trade policies. The protectionists sometimes marshalled as many as two-thirds of the Conservative MPs against the measures of the Conservative government. In January 1846 it had been by no means certain that trouble on this scale would develop. The unexpected success of the protectionists under Bentinck and Disraeli in dragging out the Corn Law debates led to a situation in which Peel, generally regarded as a master of parliamentary tactics, found himself trapped in a dilemma which precipitated his downfall.

Meanwhile, the crisis in Ireland was deepening. Ministers had succeeded in enacting some remedial measures, including the provision of emergency medical services, but famine was leading to an increase of crime and violence in Ireland. The Lord Lieutenant pressed for the grant of emergency police powers to contain the situation, and early in 1846 the Cabinet agreed on a Protection of Life Bill, which was introduced into the House of Lords in February. This 'Coercion Bill' passed through all of its stages in the Upper House without difficulty, and moved to the Commons in late March. At its first reading there, the bill encountered

---

37. Disraeli's early life is analysed from a number of angles in C. Richmond and P. Smith (eds.), *The Self-Fashioning of Disraeli 1818–51* (1998).

vociferous opposition from Irish nationalist MPs, but acceptance from all of the major groups. Peel's own followers of course accepted it, while the dissentient right-wing Conservatives were not likely to oppose such a measure in principle, and might even welcome any proposal which would absorb more debating time and postpone Corn Law repeal. Russell too supported the first reading, while giving no pledges about the Coercion Bill's later stages. Disraeli had already scented an opportunity to damage the government, and warned Bentinck not to commit himself too far.

Peel's opponents could not prevent the repeal of the Corn Laws. In May the new Corn Bill passed its third reading in the Commons, amidst vituperative attacks on Peel by protectionists. As a financial measure, this legislation was primarily Commons business, and its progress through the Lords was helped by other factors too. Russell put pressure on Whig peers to give the Corn Bill a steady support, while Wellington used his considerable influence to the same end. However, on the same day that the Corn Bill completed its progress through the House of Lords, more dramatic scenes had been enacted in the Lower House. With Corn Law repeal now safe, the Whigs had no further motive for preserving Peel's ministry, while the protectionists were bent on revenge. Both groups found ground on which they could wriggle out of their early support for the Irish Coercion Bill. The government had claimed that the measure was urgently necessary, but had then given the Corn Bill priority in the allocation of debating time. This provided at least a colourable excuse for an official opposition party to withdraw its support of the bill. There seemed much less likelihood that many right-wing Conservatives could be brought to vote against the Protection of Life Bill, even though Bentinck and Disraeli had determined to oppose the second reading. There followed one of the great parliamentary occasions of the century, and one in which the issue of the vote was uncertain until the counting was over. Most Conservative MPs rallied to support the Coercion Bill, but Bentinck and Disraeli led a sufficient minority into the opposition lobby with the Whigs to ensure Peel's defeat by 292 votes to 219. Ministers were not perhaps in the end surprised to be beaten, but to be beaten by such a convincing margin was unexpected.

In the circumstances there was no alternative to resignation. Peel heightened the breach between himself and the protectionists, partly by virtually accusing the dissident Conservatives of being the party of high food prices for the poorer sectors of society, and partly by paying an unexpected and exaggerated tribute to Richard Cobden, the leader of the Anti-Corn Law League. In fact the timing of the Corn Law repeal owed most to Peel. The Anti-Corn Law League, despite the noise which it made, was unable to exercise any effective influence upon the course of events in 1846, though no doubt the League's agitation had played some part in keeping the issue of Corn Law repeal prominently before the public in previous years. Peel's statements added to the growth of a myth which exaggerated the contribution of the League to the adoption of free trade.

Although Peel never held office again, he retained great influence until his death in 1850. The Whig government which followed his second ministry seemed an inferior replacement. It never had a safe parliamentary majority, and it owed much to Peel's general support in the years after 1846. On a number of crucial issues, including commercial policy and Irish affairs, the new government depended heavily on him as an unofficial adviser. After the general election of 1847, the support of the Peelites in the House of Commons was necessary to the Whig government, and on occasion Peelite votes saved it from defeat on vital issues. Peel himself made no attempt to consolidate a party following, and although a 'Peelite' party did establish itself for some years it was not in the end to achieve a long-term position of importance. By the 1860s it had ceased to have any meaningful existence, while those party members who had broken with Peel in 1846 appropriated the Conservative label.

Peel's reputation and the respect given to him owed much to the work of the 1841–6 administration. Taking office at a time of distress and depression, with radical agitations apparently threatening the established order, and with the previous ministry unable to cope with the crisis, his second government had taken decisive action. When, after 1843, conditions improved, this seemed to be the result of its enlightened administration. The repeal of the Corn Laws, against the opposition of the articulate agricultural lobby, seemed to be the work of a statesman who was prepared to court political ruin in order to rule justly in the national interest. The belief that Peel had placed country before party, national duty before personal and sectional interests, was widely shared in the years after 1846. After his death following a riding accident in 1850, the mourning for Peel was both widespread and sincere, summed up by that sentence in the *Times* obituary which credited him with the major share in the responsibility for the transformation from 'the confusions and darkness which hung round the beginning of the century to the comparatively quiet haven in which we are now embayed'.[38] The almost hagiographical nature of the mourning on the death of a politician with an aloof and austere public personality reflects the seriousness and reason with which many early-Victorians viewed political life. There followed the erection of an unprecedented number of memorial statues, and a variety of other memorial activities, many specifically financed by collections from working men, which may have irritated old Chartists who remembered the poverty which had dogged that movement. Such commemorative tributes were part of a changing historical perception. The bad old days of Peterloo and the Tolpuddle Martyrs, of the Newport Rising, the terrible winter of 1841–2 and the 'Hungry Forties' had now passed away as Britain entered a new world of free trade and social reconciliation. Of those who had helped to secure this shift, Sir Robert Peel was selected as the pre-eminent heroic figure; the mourning at his death epitomized this belief.[39]

38. *The Times*, 4 July 1850.
39. Donald Read, *Peel and the Victorians* (1987), 266–320, gives a full account of the mourning, the tributes, and the commemorative statues, busts, and figurines that followed on Peel's death.

Russell's first ministry

Successes by Russell's government were often seen as simply a continuation of the policies associated with Peel. Free trade was taken further by such measures as the modification of the Navigation Laws protecting British shipping. The 'sanitary' (public health) legislation of 1847–8 could be reconciled with Peelite support of judicious State intervention when clearly required. The course of the Russell government's tenure was not marked by any growth of public support, and in some respects the record of the 1846–52 ministry was inferior to that of its Conservative predecessor. A recent study of defence policy in these years has demonstrated that the Whigs once again subordinated national security to political expediency.[40] Although a new Napoleonic regime was ruling France from 1851, Russell's Cabinet failed to maintain Peel's earlier care for national defence. Not only did it fail to mount an effective resistance to public and parliamentary demands for cuts in public expenditure, but it missed real political opportunities for securing adequate spending on the armed forces.

The government's own following remained diffuse; a Whig Cabinet presided over a motley following of Whigs, Irish, and various brands of radicals. On a number of issues the diversity of this loose coalition became painfully obvious. Palmerston's handling of British foreign affairs aroused hostility both from high-minded Peelites and from internationalist radicals like Richard Cobden. In 1850 his bellicose backing of the dubious claims of Don Pacifico, a Portuguese Jew who claimed British citizenship because he had been born in Gibraltar, led to an international crisis. Palmerston pushed this adventurer's inflated claims against the Greek government to the extent of a naval blockade which aroused strong protests from other European powers. A dangerous attack in the House of Commons on the issue was only beaten off by Palmerston's famous 'Civis Romanus Sum' speech, a rousing defence of British institutions and the need to protect British citizens anywhere in the world.[41] Despite this defensive success, an alarming number of the government's usual supporters went into the hostile lobby.

A second crisis erupted in the 'Papal Aggression' uproar of 1851. The reintroduction of a diocesan system for the Roman Catholic Church in Great Britain produced an explosion of anti-Catholic feeling even greater than the Maynooth uproar of 1845. Russell himself chose to lead the cries of outrage, referring to Catholic ceremonies as 'mummeries of superstition'. An Ecclesiastical Titles Act was passed, which imposed criminal sanctions against members of Churches other than the Established Church who had the temerity to adopt territorial titles in Britain. There was a majority of 438 votes to 95 for it in the House of Commons. The minority included a high proportion of the more talented MPs, and the measure earned the ministry the hostility of the Irish Catholic MPs,

40. M. S. Partridge, 'The Russell Cabinet and national defence, 1846–1852', *History*, 72 (1987), 231–50.
41. A recent biography of Palmerston is, J. Chambers, *Palmerston, 'The People's Darling'* (2004).

normally an important group among its supporters. The Act was effectively a dead letter, and was quietly repealed a few years later.

With this kind of leadership, it was not surprising that Russell's first ministry soon collapsed. Early in 1851 its weakness had been shown when in a poorly attended Commons session the government was defeated on a radical motion for parliamentary reform. This demonstrated the absence of enthusiasm for the administration's survival. The Queen sent for Lord Stanley, who, surveying the material for Cabinet-making among the protectionists, decided, to Disraeli's annoyance, that he could not form a viable administration. Russell returned to office, but at the end of 1851 his ministry lost its most valuable asset. Palmerston's habit of acting first in foreign affairs, and seeking approval from Queen and Cabinet afterwards, had already caused disputes and reprimands; renewed complaints now led Russell to demand his resignation. The Foreign Secretary departed angrily. In February 1852 he took his revenge by playing a leading part in ensuring the defeat of a poorly drafted Militia Bill which the government had introduced in belated acknowledgement of the serious weaknesses in national defences. This time, Russell resigned.

Derby's first ministry

Lord Derby (Stanley became the fourteenth Earl of Derby in 1851) saw that if his party was to be seen as a potentially governing group he must now take office. After the Militia Bill debates, therefore, a weak Conservative minority government was formed, in which Disraeli became Chancellor of the Exchequer. In previous years, the Conservatives who had broken with Peel in 1846 had difficulty in finding adequate leadership in the House of Commons. There was no doubt about the principal party leader; Lord Stanley held that position unchallenged. Yet it was not easy to organize effective leadership in the Commons, especially after Bentinck's sudden death in 1848. Only after trying a variety of other expedients, including some distinctly unpromising devices, could the Conservative backbenchers reconcile themselves to Disraeli's leadership. Even then, the decision was unwelcome to many of his followers.[42]

The new Conservative ministry was in a minority in the existing House of Commons, and a general election could not be postponed for long. The tenure of Derby's first ministry was largely taken up with electioneering. As yet the Conservatives had not openly swallowed the 1846 decision on the Corn Laws. Disraeli privately believed that any return to agricultural protection was politically impossible, but Derby and many of the others who had broken with Peel on the issue did not share his flexibility of principle. The Conservatives therefore entered the general election of 1852 without any clear indication of their policy in

42. R. Blake, *Disraeli* (1966) is the standard work on Disraeli's career. The tale of the Conservatives' search for a Commons leader is told at pp. 247–8.

this key area. Critics remarked that a Derbyite was a protectionist in an agricultural constituency, neutral in a small town, and a free trader in a large town.

With the question of Corn Laws again in the air, the various opposition groups could make common cause. This was perhaps the one issue which could unite Whigs and all shades of radicals. The Anti-Corn Law League was nominally resurrected; in many constituencies bickering between Whigs and radicals was subordinated in the fight to sustain the verdict of 1846. At the general election in July the ministry made gains, but still faced the new Parliament in a minority of about twenty. The Conservative government survived for a little while. The triumphant free traders produced a motion praising the repeal of the Corn Laws in 1846 in terms which the ministry could not accept, but here an amendment moved by Palmerston provided them with a slightly more palatable alternative which they could swallow, even if it meant abandoning any idea of a return to protection.

Disraeli, an inexperienced minister, faced difficult budgetary problems. The change of government had postponed the main Budget to an awkward time of year, and in addition he had to try to cobble together something which would give some concessions to agriculture while remaining acceptable to the new Parliament. The Opposition was not in a mood for tolerance. The Peelites, and Gladstone in particular, never forgot the unscrupulous and wounding attacks which Disraeli had made on Peel in 1845–6. In the 1852 Budget debates, Gladstone took revenge by powerful attacks on the vulnerable elements in the Chancellor's proposals. After less than a year in office the ministry was defeated on the Budget by nineteen votes on 16 December, and Derby promptly resigned. It was not at first clear who his successor would be, but in the last days of 1852 agreement was reached on the formation of a Cabinet under the Peelite Lord Aberdeen,[43] representing a coalition of Whigs, moderate radicals, and Peelites. At first sight this coalition seemed to promise a return to a greater degree of political stability, for the new ministry enjoyed the support of political groups commanding a clear majority in the House of Commons elected in 1852. As 1853 opened, there seemed nothing to indicate that trouble lay ahead. Yet the Aberdeen administration's tenure was destined to be both short and inglorious.

Foreign policy

The European backdrop to the British 'Reform Crisis' of 1831–32 was one of revolution: successful revolutions in France and Belgium and unsuccessful revolutions in the Italian states and Poland. The conjuncture of these revolutions was important for had Austria and Russia not been busy putting down, respectively, the revolutions in Italy and Poland, then the major challenge to the Vienna Settlement that events in France and Belgium represented might have resulted in

43. M. E. Chamberlain, *Lord Aberdeen: A Political Biography* (1983).

their, and particularly Russia's, intervention. As it was, the division that had been incipient between the autocratic Russian and Austrian Empires on the one hand and western Europe on the other hardened as France acquired a more liberal monarchy and Belgium eventually became an independent state with an equally liberal monarchical constitution.

There was considerable continuity in British foreign policy with that of the 1820s. A support for liberal causes was combined with but subordinated to a pragmatic support for British interests. Continuity was ensured by the fact that the ex-Canningite Lord Palmerston was Foreign Secretary from 1830 to 1841 (except for the brief interlude of Peel's 1834 administration) and again from 1846 to 1851.

Thus support for the constitutional queens of Spain and Portugal against the more conservative claimants to their thrones continued, though Britain was wary of French influence, and in 1834 a Quadruple Alliance of Britain, France, and the two Iberian states bound Britain and France to uphold the interests of the queens. In the mid-1840s Anglo-French relations were embittered over the question of the 'Spanish Marrriages'; should Queen Isabella of Spain marry a Coburg, an Orleanist of the French royal house, or a Bourbon? The unfortunate woman eventually married the unattractive Duke of Cadiz.

The Greek War of Independence had created a number of problems. It had given Russia opportunities to extend territory and influence and it had unleashed the Ottoman Sultan's nominal satrap, Mehemet Ali, the effective ruler of Egypt, who controlled rather more effective military forces than those of the Sultan, and was by the late 1830s taking control of Syria. British policy was to preserve the Ottoman Empire, keep Russia away from the Straits, and make sure that the French, who had economic interests and military influence there, didn't increase their influence in the Near East. Palmerston achieved a temporary accord with Russia and Mehemet Ali's ambitions were thwarted. A month before the Melbourne government fell, he seemed to have secured British interests and Turkish independence by the Convention of the Straits of July 1841 by which the great powers guaranteed Turkish independence and accepted that the Bosphorus and the Dardanelles should be closed to the warships of all nations in time of war. Palmerston had adroitly played off Russia against France. War with France had seemed possible in 1840–1 but Palmerston's belligerency had been tempered by caution.

During the year of revolutions, 1848, Britain seemed, despite the last great Chartist petition and demonstration, to be, relatively, an oasis of calm but threats to European stability posed problems for British foreign policy. The new Republican government in France might well, despite its assurances that it sought no modifications to the Vienna Settlement, prove expansionist, while turmoil in the Italian states and the declaration of war on Austria by Piedmont threatened the balance of power. Palmerston's moderate support for liberalism abroad had always come second to his determination to safeguard British interests and he had no desire to see Austria weakened and France resurgent. He offered mediation between Piedmont and Austria in conjunction with France and, though he had some sympathy with Italian nationalism, was probably relieved when the Austrians defeated Piedmont in 1848 and again in 1849. Liberalism and nationalism seemed allied in 1848 but Palmerston worried that in Germany, even more than in Italy, major changes to the existing boundaries of states might upset the balance of power and be inimical to Britain's interests. Again in the case of the Hungarian revolution, he put aside his proclaimed liberal sympathies and did not demur when Russia put down the revolt for the Austrians and only later protested against the severity with which this was done.

That Palmerston, despite his sometimes intemperate language, managed to steer Britain clear of wars was just as well for economical governments dedicated to low taxation had left British military and naval forces in a poor state. Just how unprepared the army and navy were for a major war was to be revealed in 1854 when Britain and France would declare war against Russia. Public reaction to the parlous state of British arms would bring down the Aberdeen government.

5

Government and administration

c.1830–1850

In these years British government expanded but remained, both in scope and efficiency, undeveloped in comparison with later periods. Yet, if the achievements of other contemporary governments are considered, those of the British State may appear more substantial. No other State, for instance, intervened to help the poor as much as did the much criticized English Poor Law system.[1] Official activity grew, in the teeth of continuing demands for cheap government, fuelled by popular hostility to higher taxes.

Taxation

In the late eighteenth century, national taxation normally raised about £11 million a year, local taxation as little as £1.7 million. By 1830 central taxation had already risen to produce £55 million, and local taxes (poor rates by far the largest item) more than £8 million. A short-lived drop in local taxation after the Poor Law Amendment Act of 1834 was followed by a further and sustained rise; by the end of the century local revenue was equivalent to one-third of the sum raised by national taxation.[2]

Most of the central revenues came from a complex system of indirect taxes. Duties on commerce provided the lion's share, but in 1840, for instance, 15 per cent came from stamp duties imposed on legal transactions.[3] The reimposition of income tax by Peel in 1842 raised the proportion of the national revenue provided by direct taxation on the richer and more influential sections of society from about 8 per cent to about 18–20 per cent.[4] A much larger proportion of British society paid the rates levied to meet the cost of local government. All occupiers of property were affected either directly or indirectly by the rates, and were likely to take a more personal interest in local administration than in the limited functions of the central departments of State. Rating was already a

1. E. H. Hunt, *British Labour History, 1815–1914* (1981), 366 n. 57.
2. P. Mathias, *The Transformation of England: Essays in the Economic and Social History of England in the Eighteenth Century* (1979), 117.
3. Ibid. 127.   4. Ibid. 126.

matter of considerable controversy. The level of rates demanded, the availability of other forms of local revenue, and local conventions governing rating assessments all varied greatly. After 1830, governments tried to tidy up some of the principal areas of confusion, with little success. The Parochial Assessments Act of 1836 attempted to establish standardized rating procedures throughout England and Wales, but was ineffective.[5] One specific area of uncertainty was whether or not stock in trade was a rateable asset. After many local disputes on this issue, the Whig government enacted the Poor Rate Exemption Act of 1840, which exempted business stock from the rates. This measure was introduced avowedly as a stopgap, pending a thorough review of the system of local taxation; the temporary 1840 Act was renewed every year until 1932, when it was made permanent. The centuries-old rating system, with all its weaknesses and injustices, remained in existence as the main source of local revenue. Early in the twentieth century, a royal commission noted the continuance of great diversity in local taxation.[6] The failure of early-Victorian attempts to reform local taxation effectively (a failure repeated by later generations) illustrates the limited efficiency of the State in these years. In some respects, however, the second quarter of the nineteenth century saw a continuing improvement in the quality of official administration.

The Civil Service

One factor governing the competence of government was the quality of its officials. These years saw continued improvement in this respect, but improvement from a low level. When the Whig reforms of the 1830s established new official agencies, it was often necessary to recruit from outside the existing administration to obtain suitable officials. The nature of the new posts involved owed much to examples existing outside the ambit of government. By 1830, before official inspection was applied to schools, the Poor Law, factories, or mines, the principal voluntary school-building societies had already evolved their own system of paid school inspectors.

The available pool of administrative and professional expertise was limited. During the cholera epidemic of 1831–2, the government turned to leading doctors for help and advice, including the President of the Royal College of Physicians. In doing so, ministers made an understandable error. While they failed to enlist the services of doctors with actual experience of cholera in India, the eminent doctors they did recruit (and paid £500 a year for this purpose) proved worse than useless. One modern critic has described them as 'notorious incompetents', but then the Whig ministers were not medical experts.[7]

Traditions of patronage in public appointments proved tenacious, and governments were under pressure, especially from their own political supporters, to

5. H. Finer, *English Local Government* (1933), 418.
6. Ibid. 391; see also p. 398 for difficulties encountered in assessing railways for rating purposes.
7. F. B. Smith, *The People's Health, 1830–1910* (1979), 199.

reward loyal support by official favours. In December 1835, Lord Howick, by no means the least scrupulous of the leading Whigs, wrote to the Prime Minister to stress 'the necessity of losing no time in getting steady friends of our own into the most important of the permanent official positions'.[8] The staff recruited to man the Poor Law Commission's headquarters after 1834 has been described as 'idle aristocrats and pushy briefless barristers'.[9] More generally, the expansion of the Civil Service involved in the Whig reforms of the 1830s provided a useful opportunity for that party, excluded from government for many years, to distribute some of the sweets of office to their hungry following. There were always more applicants than vacancies. The partisan uses of patronage in these years could scarcely be concealed, and did nothing to increase public confidence in the impartial nature of the Civil Service.

Government and social problems

The failure of government and Parliament to deal effectively with public health problems during this period has provided ammunition for those who believe that the past ought to have been different. This failure was not solely due to the shortcomings of the State, for other aspects of the contemporary world made success impossible in this sphere. In considering the horrific record of infant mortality, it is worth remembering that, until late in the century, conception, menstruation, foetal development, and birth were not fully understood even by competent doctors. Traditional views of medicine, still largely accepted, gave a low priority to such matters. Sir Henry Halford, President of the Royal College of Physicians, thought in 1841 that 'midwifery was an occupation degrading to a gentleman'.[10] With specialist opinion set in such a mould, it is difficult to see how government could be expected to produce effective answers to the prevailing problems of infant mortality.

In other respects too, efforts by official agencies to improve social conditions were beset by problems. Although sanitary improvements were clearly needed, for many years there were professional disagreements about such matters as the most effective kind of sewers, with disputing engineers sincerely holding opposed views. Moreover, it was not within the power of contemporary governments to transform the available contractors into paragons of honesty and competence; 'Throughout the century drains were laid which did not flow, joints were made which did not meet or were not concreted, materials were used, crumbling brick, over-thin lead, and lightweight tin sheet, which did not last.'[11] Contemporary technology, even without such malpractices, could allow situations which might reasonably induce scepticism about the value of expensive improvements. Before the provision of a continuous water supply, and the invention of an efficient sewer

8. R. C. Snelling and T. J. Barron, 'The Colonial Office: its permanent officials, 1801–1914', in G. Sutherland (ed.), *Studies in the Growth of Nineteenth-Century Government* (1972), 147.
9. Smith, *The People's Health*, 360.   10. Ibid. 16, 23.   11. Ibid. 223.

trap, it was possible for sewer gas to rise through the water closets of houses which had been equipped with those expensive devices. When that happened, it was difficult to persuade householders of the advantages of spending money on such sanitary improvements.[12] And there were always preachers who would explain epidemics as visitations by God in punishment for human sinfulness rather than social disasters to be energetically combated.

If the great proponent of proper drainage was Edwin Chadwick, the crucial determinant in giving urgency to the cause was the proof that many diseases were waterborne. A great battle raged for decades between those scientists and medical practitioners who considered that diseases like typhoid and cholera were carried in the air by miasma and those who claimed that they were carried by polluted water supplies. Dr John Snow made the case for waterborne contagion as early as 1849 with his book, *On the Mode of Communication of Cholera*. It was not until 1883, when the cholera microbe was isolated, that the medical profession as a whole accepted his findings.

In these circumstances reformers, on both the national and the local scene, sought statistics to persuade taxpayers and ratepayers that the financial benefits of public health improvement exceeded their cost. Edwin Chadwick, one of the most energetic advocates of sanitary reform, exemplifies this in his 1842 *Report on the Sanitary Condition of the Labouring Population*. He was perfectly sincere in this approach, but also appreciated the tactical value of chapter headings such as 'Pecuniary Burdens Created by the Neglect of Sanitary Measures', 'Cost of Disease as Compared with the Cost of Prevention', and 'Cost of Remedies for Sickness and of Mortality which is Preventable'.

Government and education

In the field of education, too, official activity increased during the 1830s and 1840s. The expansion was a matter of gradual accretion rather than dramatic innovation. In 1833 the Whig government carried an annual grant of £20,000 to subsidize the work of the voluntary school-building societies. Given the contemporary attitude towards public expenditure, even such paltry sums could not be sanctioned without some kind of check on how the money was spent. For the first few years this was unsystematic; grant-aided schools were required to submit an annual account, which might be followed up by supplementary queries from the Treasury. When an increase in the annual grant to £30,000 was approved in 1839, a further device was tried. The Privy Council was entrusted with the oversight of the State contribution, and an Order in Council set up a standing Council Committee for that purpose. Over the next few years, by a process of trial and error, this committee gradually evolved its own procedures, starting from the premise that all schools receiving grant aid must be open to inspection by the

12. Ibid. 222.

committee's salaried inspectors. By 1846 the Council Committee was trying to enforce standards of qualification for teachers employed in grant-aided schools. It waged a campaign to obtain from Parliament sufficient resources to set up a national system of teacher training, but this ambitious project was wrecked by the opponents of additional government spending.

A more spectacular defeat was inflicted on Peel's Government in 1843, when the educational provisions in the scheme for factory reform produced by the Home Secretary, Sir James Graham, fell foul of sectarian religious rivalries. The proposals for compulsory schooling for factory children either in the mornings or in the afternoons might have proved acceptable, but the proposed arrangements for the management of the schools proved a serious political miscalculation. Teachers were to be Anglicans, and the parish clergyman and churchwardens were to be given an *ex officio* position in the schools' administration. The reaction from Nonconformists had been underestimated (in itself an indication of government's limited competence). Vociferous Nonconformist opposition forced even this strong government to abandon its education proposals in order to obtain the enactment of some of its other factory proposals in the following year.

Provision for the mentally ill

Other areas revealed a similarly mixed pattern of achievements and setbacks, with on balance the creation of a higher level of public regulation. The care of the mentally ill was another topic which intermittently erupted into public attention, usually when some serious scandal had been uncovered. From the late eighteenth century, statutory provision had provided for the inspection of lunatic asylums by members of a panel appointed from among its own members by the Royal College of Physicians. In 1808 this unsuccessful experiment was replaced by a system of regular visits by magistrates. At the same time, county magistrates were given permissive powers to set up county asylums at the ratepayers' expense. The cost of this was enough to discourage most counties from implementing the suggestion. Private asylums, often established by doctors, provided most of the available accommodation, although local Poor Law authorities might send individual patients there and pay the fees.

In 1828 public concern about the treatment of lunatics produced yet another experimental control system. Under the Madhouse Act of that year, the government appointed a commission of sixteen members, ten concerned laymen and six doctors; the former were unpaid, the latter could draw a fee of £1 per hour while engaged in the work of visiting asylums. This expedient did not work well, and in 1845 the system was overhauled again, with the establishment of a more powerful standing Lunacy Commission, which was given considerable powers over private asylums, including licensing and inspection. Because of a continuing shortage of asylum space, the scope for using these new powers to enforce acceptable standards remained limited. The slowly growing number of public county asylums did not necessarily ensure adequate conditions; in the autumn of 1849, 226 of the 601 inmates of the West Yorkshire Lunatic Asylum died in appalling conditions during a cholera epidemic.[13] It was not until after mid-century that legislation enforced a complete public system of county asylums, and still further reforms were to be needed before these institutions could be made reasonably effective agencies of care and treatment.[14]

The penny post

In reforming the national postal system, as in other spheres, the initiative came from crusading individuals rather than from government itself. The campaign for the penny post, led by Rowland Hill, achieved success in 1839, but the immediate results were mixed. The average price of sending a letter before 1839 had been sixpence, so the reduction was substantial. The average number of letters posted doubled from four to eight per head of the population during the first full year of the new scheme's operation. The postal reformers had confidently prophesied a five- or sixfold expansion. The acceptance of the penny post scheme by government and Parliament had been largely based on such optimistic calculations. When a mere doubling in the volume of letters occurred, this had awkward implications. Before 1839, Post Office revenue had been an important item in the national accounts; in 1839, under the last year of the old system, these profits had contributed about £1.5 million to the Exchequer—covering, for instance, the annual education grant fifty times over. The introduction of the penny post meant in the short term an annual loss of something like £1.2 million to a Treasury struggling to make ends meet in a deteriorating economic situation.

Other factors made it impossible for the new postal system to realize all the hopes of its advocates. Limited levels of literacy and understanding of the system hampered its efficiency. In one day in 1843 the Post Office had to cope with 3,557 letters addressed only to an individual's name and 'London'. By the 1850s the forecast massive increase in postal business was well on the way, though it took another twenty years before the subsidy to the Treasury from postal profits reached pre-1839 levels. By the 1880s the Post Office was able to express satisfaction at the drop in the number of badly addressed letters.[15]

Legislation

During the second quarter of the century, the legislative supremacy of Parliament, legally unchallenged for many years, was actually exploited more

13. A. Sims, 'Why the excess mortality from psychiatric illness?', *British Medical Journal*, 18 April 1987, 986.

14. U. Henriques, 'Jeremy Bentham and the machinery of social reform', in H. Hearder and H. R. Loyn (eds.), *British Government and Administration: Studies Presented to S. B. Chrimes* (1974), 173, 177.

15. D. Vincent, 'Communication, community and the State', in C. Emsley and J. Walvin (eds.), *Artisans, Peasants & Proletarians, 1760–1860: Essays Presented to Gwyn A. Williams* (1985), 166–85.

and more to introduce beneficial change. The most important single instance of this came in 1832, when Parliament used this overriding power to reform itself.[16] The reformed Parliament saw a quickening of legislative intervention in many aspects of national life. The legislature did not always appear as an unflawed embodiment of the general interest of the nation. Many members of both Houses had private interests which might be affected by legislation. This aroused suspicions concerning how far Parliament could be seen as simply the guardian of the general welfare, even after the 1832 reforms. At mid-century, many MPs owned railway shares; about 100 MPs were railway company directors. There was some involvement by interested politicians in the business of railway legislation, suspicion of manipulation, and rumours of corruption in such matters.[17]

Despite such fears, Parliament was far from being simply the agent of vested interests, as the increasing amount of interventionist legislation demonstrated. Vested interests might impede or slow down the process of change; they were never able to frustrate it entirely. Much of the legislation of these years embodied a disregard for existing interests, and a willingness to suppress them when they seemed to stand in the way of progress. The Slavery Abolition Act, 1833, the Municipal Corporations Act, 1835, the Ecclesiastical Commission Acts of 1836 and 1840, and especially the Great Reform Act, 1832, are all examples of statutes which destroyed long-standing, traditional, or chartered, rights. The inability of all of the vested interests bound up with the supremacy of the horse in transport to frustrate railway development is another example of the limited defensive capacity of vested interests.

The increasing volume of national legislation produced some improvement in drafting techniques, but still Acts of Parliament were often defective in achieving their desired objectives. In 1844 there were two Eastern Counties Railway Bills before Parliament, one of them incomplete. In error the royal assent was given to the latter, and the mischief required a special Act to remedy the situation. It was common for a major piece of legislation to be followed to the statute book during the following years by a series of supplementary measures needed to clarify or improve the original statute.

There were, however, indications of greater competence in the art of legislation. One aspect of this was the increasing use of 'Clauses' Acts, intended to facilitate the passage of statutes of a repetitive nature. A self-explanatory example is given by the formal title of the Town Improvement Clauses Act, 1847—An Act for Consolidating in One Act Certain Provisions Usually Contained in Acts for Paving, Draining, Cleansing, Lighting and Improving Towns. In these statutes

16. The best account of the effects of the 1832 reform settlement remains N. Gash, *Politics in the Age of Peel* (1953). A more recent account of the 1831–2 crisis and the nature of the reform legislation is M. Brock, *The Great Reform Act* (1973).

17. P. Mathias, *The First Industrial Nation: An Economic History of Britain, 1700–1914*, 2nd edn. (1983), 258–9.

provision was made for their key elements to be incorporated in relevant Local Acts by a simple citation there of the authority of the Clauses Act. The middle years of the century saw this device repeated for many purposes, including markets and fairs, gasworks, waterworks, cemeteries, police, as well as town improvements; the single year 1847 saw a large batch of this enabling legislation put on the statute book.

Even when there were no major problems with the wording of legislation a major bill could take time to implement. The Tithe Commutation Act was passed in 1836 but agreements as to the new money rents had to be agreed acre by acre with the assistance of surveyors; the process was still underway well into the 1840s.

By mid-century the volume of legislation had already grown considerably, and the share of public general statutes, as against local and private Acts, was now much greater. Much of this legislation did not create any high level of political noise at the time of its enactment, nor has it left much mark on the historical record, but cumulatively the increased volume was impressive. We have seen that 1847 produced a major crop of 'Clauses' legislation; there was also a variety of other interventionist legislation in that year, including a Nuisances Removal Act of some importance in strengthening public health law. The next year saw an important Public Health Act, reforms in the legal system, and the first of a group of mid-century changes in the Irish land law. In 1849 came the second, very innovative, Encumbered Estates Act for Ireland, and an Act reforming Irish lunatic asylums (as well as the temporary suspension of habeas corpus in Ireland because of a short-lived and unsuccessful rising there); 1849 also saw Acts for advancing money for famine relief in Ireland, and for providing cheap loans for public works there. Apart from Irish concerns, the 1849 session saw legislation relating to enclosure of common lands, the law of larceny, highways, Greenwich Hospital reform, Scottish turnpikes, merchant shipping, the law relating to small debts, drainage and improvement of land, prison reform, municipal corporations, bankruptcy law, suppression of the slave trade, cruelty to animals, metropolitan sewers, the law of marriage, nuisances removal, burial law. Nor is this a complete list, but merely exemplifies a trend.

Not only had the volume of law-making changed; the meticulous nature of some of the interventionist statutes showed new attitudes. The Gasworks Clauses Act of 1847 instituted a code whereby gas companies were forbidden to pay more than a 10 per cent dividend to their shareholders; any additional profits must be held in a reserve account compulsorily invested in government stock. Any two of a gas company's customers could apply to the Court of Quarter Sessions for the appointment of accountants to check the company's accounts and report their findings to the court. Apart from this, a copy of every gas company's accounts must be laid before Quarter Sessions annually. The Waterworks Clauses Act contained similar stipulations. The Town Police Clauses Act saw the national legislature providing for such matters as furious driving or riding, leaving or placing a basket or bucket on the highway, hanging clothes lines across streets, the erection of awnings, flying kites, and a variety of similar minutiae.[18]

Another instance of innovation in the legislation of these years is provided by the Encumbered Estates Acts for Ireland, designed to assist economic recovery in the aftermath of the great famine of the mid-1840s.[19] The 1848 Act sought to facilitate the sale of Irish estates to purchasers able to work them more efficiently, using the existing machinery of the Irish Court of Chancery for that purpose. When it appeared that this route was proving slow and expensive, a second Act in the following year created a special court of three paid commissioners, with wide powers to authorize the sale of estates in Ireland and divide the proceeds equitably among those with an interest in the property. Within ten years something like 10 per cent of all Irish land changed hands under these provisions. It is a commonplace of British history later in the century that the urgency of Irish problems provided there a kind of social laboratory in which new ideas were tried out before public opinion was ready to see them introduced into Great Britain. It would be more accurate to see this as a long-established habit, already evident in the late eighteenth and earlier nineteenth centuries. Ireland possessed a network of publicly supported dispensaries and relatively advanced systems of school and prison inspection well before such arrangements were set up in Great Britain.[20]

Banking

A more sophisticated economy required increasing regulation. Acts of Parliament interfering with and prescribing regulations for banks, companies, and factories provided repeated examples of official intervention in economic activities. They were, however, less the result of a continuing legislative preoccupation than intermittent responses to particular crises. The banking legislation of 1826, which allowed the formation of joint-stock banks outside a 65-mile radius from central London, was a response to a banking crisis which involved the collapse of about sixty banks. Complaints about the unfairness of the restriction led in 1833 to the legalizing by the Whigs of such banks in the London area, though without the privilege of note issue. The Bank of England's first reaction was one of animosity towards these rivals, but wiser counsels soon prevailed. The 1826 legislation had also allowed the Bank of England to establish provincial branches, and after an initial period of local infighting between banks a more cooperative atmosphere prevailed both in the City and the provinces.

The 1826 legislation was far from a complete success, as was shown by the continued existence of dubious banking practices. Indeed the aftermath of 1826

18. W. L. Burn, *The Age of Equipoise: A Study of the Mid-Victorian Generation* (1964), 153–5.

19. Ibid. 149.

20. Henriques, 'Jeremy Bentham and the machinery of social reform', 176; Smith, *The People's Health*, 11.

saw new elements of instability introduced, as the new joint-stock banks fought to capture a substantial slice of banking business, often taking excessive risks. Between 1826 and 1844 there were about 100 bank failures. A clause in the banking legislation of 1833 which provided for a reconsideration of the status of the Bank of England after ten years gave Peel's ministry an opportunity to introduce further regulations. A main objective of the Bank Charter Act of 1844 was to control the issue of notes by banks other than the Bank of England, and also to ensure that the Bank's own note issues remained at a safe level. Banks created in future would not be given the right to issue their own notes; any existing bank which suspended issue for any reason was now forbidden to resume the practice. In any event, the maximum issue allowed was fixed at the level in operation during the early months of 1844. This was accompanied by a campaign by the Bank of England to persuade other banks to stop issuing their own banknotes and to act instead as agents for the supply of Bank of England notes; banks which accepted these proposals were granted favourable terms by the national bank. The success of the campaign ensured that, although some banks went on issuing their own notes, Bank of England notes consolidated their primacy.

The Bank of England itself was brought under new restrictions by the 1844 legislation. It was divided into two divisions, one for general banking business and the other for note issue. The Bank was forbidden to issue more than £14 million of notes unbacked by bullion reserves, the fiduciary issue. Well-meaning as these measures were, their limited efficacy was soon revealed. The banking panic of 1847, largely due to the unsoundness of some major provincial banks, brought the Bank of England under heavy pressure to increase its supply of money to the economy. Almost all legally available issues were used, and the government was obliged to give the Bank emergency authority to increase the fiduciary issue. As it happened the knowledge that this facility existed served to dampen the crisis and the exceptional powers were not used. A similar situation occurred in another banking crisis ten years later, but again the Bank of England weathered the storm without too much difficulty. Meanwhile other important changes in banking were taking place informally without legislation. The directors of the Bank of England learned that they must place national responsibilities before the Bank's profits as a financial institution. They soon developed an awareness of the scale of reserves they must keep available, and both in 1847 and 1857 the intervention of the Bank of England limited the damage caused by the failure of other banks. The success of this learning process was shown by the Bank's more confident and skilful responses in 1857 in comparison with ten years earlier.[21]

The dynamic banking sector of the Scottish economy was opposed to control of the Scottish banking system from London. Having successfully opposed the

21. Mathias, *The First Industrial Nation*, 321–9; T. L. Crosby, *Sir Robert Peel's Administration, 1841–46* (1976), 58–60. The Bank of England was generous in giving permission to N. McCord to study the correspondence of the Newcastle branch of the Bank.

abolition of the £1 note in Scotland in the 1820s, Scotland now found that new legislation prevented all but existing banks from issuing notes. No new major banks were to be formed in Scotland although the number of branches of Scottish banks continued to grow as did the volume of lending and deposit taking.[22]

Companies

Banking legislation was accompanied by more regulation of companies. Under the 1844 Joint Stock Companies Act, companies with transferable shares and more than twenty-five members had to register with a new salaried Registrar of Companies, who was also to receive regularly audited balance sheets from every registered company. It was not possible by a single statute to eradicate all the fraud and sharp practice which marked contemporary commercial life, but the 1844 legislation was an important step towards tightening up the legal defences against commercial malpractices. This Act did not cover all important companies. Those created under special Acts of Parliament were excluded from its purview. This meant that most railway companies were not covered, but here Peel's government had alternative plans in mind. State intervention in the railways again illustrates some of the characteristics of statutory regulation in these years.[23] The process was inaugurated with Lord Seymour's Act of 1840, which set up the Railway Department of the Board of Trade. In 1842 the junior minister at that office, Gladstone, extended this provision, giving officials power to inspect railways, authorize their by-laws, collect information about accidents, and take action against companies which flouted the embryonic code of safety regulations.

Gladstone's appetite for intervention had been whetted, and in 1844 he moved to obtain a more thoroughgoing measure, although his freedom of action was limited by Peel's pledge that the existing powers of railway companies would be respected. The first form of the 1844 railway legislation, introduced in June, demonstrated that the government was not under the influence of any principle of non-intervention. The Bill provided that when any future railway had operated for fifteen years, the State could either exercise a power to purchase the line or effectively acquire control of its management. Yet these far-reaching proposals were dropped in the course of the debates in Parliament, after vehement opposition by railway companies and their parliamentary friends. Peel and his senior colleagues, with many other problems facing them, were unwilling to fight on this issue. The period before possible State takeover was extended to twenty-one years, and the alternative control clauses disappeared. No subsequent ministry attempted to implement the takeover provisions.

22. S. G. Checkland, *Scottish Banking, A History 1695–1973* (1975).
23. J. H. Clapham, *An Economic History of Modern Britain: The Early Railway Age*, vol. i (1930), 412–24.

Some of the Bill's other provisions survived, including clauses designed to safeguard at least a minimum service of cheap rail travel for passengers. In other respects the final shape of the legislation treated the railway companies generously, while the powers of the Railway Department were left imprecise. Even with a modest increase to five senior officials, that agency could not cope adequately with a sudden escalation in railway schemes over the next few years. The officials were continuously faced with strident and often unfair attacks from railway companies and their promoters. Their political masters, beset by more pressing concerns, would not provide the tough government backing needed to enable the Railway Department to beat off its assailants. In the course of 1845–6 successive weakenings in the Department's position drastically reduced its effectiveness, and in the late summer of 1846 poorly drafted legislation instituted another experimental system of railway supervision which proved a failure in practice.[24]

Overall, the legislation affecting banks, companies, and railways brought increased official interference in the affairs of private concerns. The degree of competence with which this task was carried out nevertheless limited its effect. In these areas, too, the early-Victorian legislation was an extension of the principle of control rather than a complete innovation.

Factory Acts

The same was true of factory legislation. Earlier Acts of 1802, 1819, and 1826 had depended on the ordinary magistrates, then the normal agents for the enforcement of much legislation, for their implementation. Although the early Factory Acts were by no means a dead letter, the reports of the more active magistrates, together with repeated complaints from humanitarian sources, pointed to the need for more effective provisions. Pressure mounted during the heady days of the parliamentary reform crisis of 1831–2, when a sensational report of a Commons select committee highlighted factory abuses, especially in the field of child labour. A defensive reaction by industrialists and their parliamentary friends brought about the appointment of a royal commission in 1833. Although its findings were less alarming than the 1832 report, the commission none the less produced evidence that further legislation was necessary.

The Whig government responded with the Factory Act of 1833, which exemplified the trial-and-error aspects of contemporary interventionist legislation. The Act had two main elements. It followed and extended earlier statutes in laying down limits on the hours which might be worked by children and 'young persons' in power-driven textile mills, while it also instituted new methods of enforcing factory legislation. In the case of most textile mills, children under 9 were not to be employed. A maximum working day of nine hours, or a total of forty-eight hours a week, was laid down for the 9 to 13 age group; from 13 to 18

24. An Act for Constituting Commissioners of Railways, 9 & 10 Vict., c. 105.

the limits were a twelve-hour day or a sixty-nine-hour week. Night work for those under 18 was prohibited. Children under 13 were to be given at least two hours' schooling in each working day.

These provisions were to be enforced by a new agency, HM Inspectors of Factories. There were to be four salaried inspectors, assisted by subordinates known as Superintendents of Factories (later renamed Sub-Inspectors). The device was not wholly new. The voluntary educational societies already had teams of salaried inspectors of schools; in earlier years paid inspectors had been used to ensure product standards in a variety of trades and survivals of that regulation still existed within the textile industries affected by the 1833 Act. There is some evidence that the new inspectorate was suggested to the 1833 royal commission by witnesses acquainted with the use of inspectors for the supervision of quality in the worsted trade.[25]

The new factory inspectorate was one of the notable experiments in government during these years. The inspectors were in the first instance conceived of as travelling stipendiary magistrates, with powers of deciding cases and inflicting fines for breach of the factory legislation. After some years, this dual inspecting and quasi-judicial role was found unsatisfactory in practice. Subsequent modifications saw the inspectors bringing cases before the ordinary courts. The trial-and-error element in the evolution of factory regulation continued; in the legislation of the 1840s it was enacted that fines for breach of the Factory Acts should go to a special Factories Penalties Fund, from which grants were made by the Home Secretary, on the recommendation of the inspectors, either towards the cost of factory schools or as direct payments to the victims of factory accidents or their dependants.

It was not easy to find the right calibre of officials for the new posts.[26] At inspector level it was possible to enlist a few men of some distinction, such as Leonard Horner, a prominent scientist and university administrator. Some appointments were less happy, as in the case of James Stuart, whose selection for this well-paid position was a reward for his services to the Whig Party in Scotland; his performance proved less than satisfactory. The main problems were encountered at superintendent level, a position of lower salary and status; the records of the early years of the system abound with difficulties here. These range from simple inefficiency or prolonged incapacity to the more sinister behaviour of James Webster, who combined a disinclination to move away from Bath to perform his duties with more than a suspicion of corruption. It was difficult to find competent and disinterested agents of public service in a society little accustomed to such functions.[27]

25. The best account of the factory reform movement generally is J. T. Ward, *The Factory Movement* (1962); see also Clapham, *Economic History of Modern Britain*, 574–5.

26. U. Henriques, *The Early Factory Acts and their Enforcement* (1971); U. Henriques, 'An early factory inspector: James Stuart of Dunearn', *Scottish Historical Review*, 50 (1971), 18–46.

27. The HO 87 series in the PRO contains many examples of these problems; for Webster, HO 87/1, Maule/Webster 24 April 1837 and 27 July 1839.

Another aspect of the 1833 Act is equally illuminating. At first sight the prohibition laid on the employment of children under 9 seems straightforward enough. In 1833 matters were more complicated. Britain did not yet possess any orderly registration of births, so that there was no standard proof of age. The rough-and-ready solution to this practical difficulty was to institute certificates of age for factory children. Surgeons were to issue these, but the best criteria which the government's law officers could offer were 'that the child had the ordinary strength and appearance of a child *at least nine* years of age, or *exceeding* nine years of age, as the case may be'. The problems did not stop there. Who, in the Britain of 1833, was a surgeon? The professional groups had not yet crystallized into a clear identity, and the best the law officers could do here was to rule that 'any person acting as a Surgeon although not a member of any College of Surgeons is a Surgeon entitled under the Factory Act to grant certificates.'[28]

Factory reform was taken further by Peel's government in the 1840s. Although the education elements in the first proposals fell foul of religious sensibilities (see p. 196 above), a revised and reduced measure was piloted through in 1844. Some of its provisions derived from experience already obtained by the factory inspectors. This included the stipulation that dangerous machinery must be fenced in. Protection was now extended to women factory workers, included in the same restrictions as the 'young persons' of 1833. The 1844 Act tried to close loopholes discovered in the working of the 1833 Act, and make the code of regulation more effective.

Parallel legislation extended intervention to other contexts. The melancholy tale of colliery accidents, and fears of immorality among scantily attired underground workers, produced in 1842 an Act which forbade the employment of women in underground work. As in most aspects of social reform by statute, this stipulation was not an official invention, but merely sought to generalize existing best practice. Women had not worked underground on the Great Northern Coalfield for many years, although they still did in some other coalfields. The 1842 Act also forbade the payment of miners' wages in public houses, and authorized the government to appoint inspectors of mines and collieries. In the event Graham chose to appoint only one inspector, H. S. Tremenheere, scion of a Cornish landed family, who had already served in a number of similar government posts since his first appointment to lucrative office by his Whig friends. Tremenheere was an active official, but inevitably his impact was limited. Further experience dictated an expansion in mines regulation, and at mid-century a team of new inspectors was appointed, including some acknowledged mining experts.

Governments still had only woolly ideas of what they expected from new officials; here is part of the letter appointing one mining engineer to the inspectorate in November 1850:

28. The law officers' opinions are given in HO 87/1, 11 and 31 August 1836.

You will keep a record of your visits to all the Collieries you inspect, and of the results of your inspection . . . You will not fail to act with courtesy and forbearance in your official intercourse with all parties, and you will encourage a good feeling and understanding between the miners and their employers. Although it will not fall within your province to take any direct measures for promoting education among the miners, you may usefully avail yourself of any opportunity of pointing out to them its importance and advantages, and lend your influence to the encouragement of any well devised plans for advancing their moral and intellectual improvement.

The District assigned to you will, for the present, comprise the Counties of Durham, Northumberland, Cumberland, and the Mining Districts of Scotland.

Officials appointed from outside interests might be ignorant of the workings of administration; this official's first expenses claim was indignantly referred back by Treasury officials unwilling to accept items like 'sundry expenses about home'.[29]

The new Poor Law

One of the most striking new departures in these years was the remodelling of the Poor Law.[30] In 1832 the Whig government, victorious in the struggle over parliamentary reform, and alarmed at the 'Captain Swing' disturbances in the southern agricultural counties, decided to tackle this area of local government and social policy. A royal commission was set up to inquire into the Poor Law's working and recommend any necessary changes. The commission's chairman was the Bishop of London, C. J. Blomfield. He was widely respected as an expert in such matters; during the 1820s, when he had been Bishop of Chester, he had been one of the government's most trusted advisers on social problems and regional distress. Although the part played in the commission's work by two leading political economists, Edwin Chadwick and Nassau Senior, is well known, Blomfield's role was far from passive. In the 1830s the Bishop of London was a more important figure than any political economist, and Blomfield worked hard in getting the 1834 Poor Law legislation through the House of Lords.

The proceedings of the royal commission have been criticized in modern writings. In some respects its proceedings were defective. One mode of gathering evidence was the dispatch of questionnaires to existing Poor Law authorities to

---

29. R. K. Webb, 'A Whig inspector', *Journal of Modern History*, 27 (1955), 352–64; O. A. O. MacDonagh, 'Coal mines regulation: the first decade', in R. Robson (ed.), *Ideas and Institutions of Victorian Britain: Essays Presented to G. Kitson Clark* (1967), 58–86. For a general consideration of problems of this kind, N. McCord, 'Some limitations of the Age of Reform', in Hearder and Loyn (eds.), *British Government and Administration*, 187–201. Dunn's letter of appointment is quoted in the latter source at p. 198.

30. There is a considerable volume of modern writing on the Poor Law. Two useful examples are M. E. Rose, *The English Poor Law, 1780–1930* (1971) and D. Fraser, *The New Poor Law in the Nineteenth Century* (1976). For the separate course of Poor Law history in Coventry, M. B. Rowlands, *The West Midlands from A.D. 1000* (1987), 292.

ascertain prevailing practice. Since it was known that there were significant diversities in practice, two questionnaires were devised, one for rural and one for urban contexts. Existing knowledge was incapable of ensuring that this distinction was efficiently applied in practice, nor was there any effective method of dealing with those parish authorities who did not bother to reply at all. Some of the commissioners entered the inquiry with settled ideas of what its outcome should be. Nevertheless, the 1832–4 royal commission inquiry into the Poor Law marked an important extension of the technique of preceding legislative innovations by preliminary investigations.

The royal commission's report reflected widespread views on the Poor Law and its proper social function. Outdoor relief to the able-bodied was condemned; such practices, it was alleged, encouraged idleness and thriftlessness. A tightening up of relief practices for the able-bodied generally would be, it was believed, in the interests of the whole country, including the poor themselves. There was no intention to impair the treatment given to the aged and feeble poor who were the majority of the Poor Law's clients. The principal objective was to reduce the excessive cost of the system, and at the same time to rehabilitate the able-bodied poor by making the public provision for them less attractive than honest labour. As advocated by the royal commission, the 'principle of less eligibility' aimed at ensuring that virtuous independence through hard work always appeared a more attractive option than battening upon the subsidies of the ratepayers.

This should be effected by cutting off outdoor relief to the able-bodied, while retaining it unaltered for the aged and the unfit. Where men and women of working age were concerned, if they needed help from the Poor Law they should only be able to obtain it by entering a well-disciplined workhouse, where conditions would be 'less eligible' than honest toil outside. In making these recommendations, the royal commission was not breaking new ground, but echoing criticisms of existing practice which had been heard for many years.

The Poor Law Amendment Act of 1834 resembled the royal commission's recommendations, but there were some significant departures. The commission would have preferred a definite banning of outdoor relief to the able-bodied from a stipulated date; the Act, more cautiously, gave the new administrative Poor Law Commission power to regulate this matter. The powers given to the new three-man central Poor Law Commission in relation to the new local Poor Law unions were, in deference to a continuing belief in local responsibility, much weaker than Chadwick and his associates wanted. In reality the 'New Poor Law' was an amalgam of old and new. The new Poor Law unions were federations of existing parishes and townships rather than a complete redrawing of the administrative map of England and Wales. The parishes elected their own representatives to the union's board of guardians. More importantly, until the 1860s (see p. 332 below) each parish remained responsible for the cost of caring for its own paupers, even if the work was now actually done by union officials. This was a serious weakness. It often happened that within a union poverty was concentrated in one or two parishes; until 1865 the other parishes in the same union were under no obligation to share in the cost of maintaining the poor of hard-hit parishes.

The local magistrates lost most of their old supervisory powers over the Poor Law, but remained *ex officio* members of the local board of guardians; most of the board members were now to be elected by the ratepayers. Voting rights were graduated; property of less than £50 in rateable value gave only one vote, the number rising by £50 stages to six votes for more than £250 rateable value. An owner-occupier could vote in both capacities and might therefore have twelve votes. The realities of local power meant that the new central Poor Law Commission found it difficult or impossible to enforce its policies in the face of recalcitrant boards of guardians. Some places which had reformed the local Poor Law by local Act in previous years continued to go their own way after 1834. Coventry continued under its own 1801 local Act until 1873, and followed policies very different from 'the principles of 1834'. The Poor Law Amendment Act did not introduce a wholesale change in patterns of local influence, and the new Poor Law was effectively controlled at local level by the same men who had controlled the old Poor Law. The cost of the Poor Law continued to be met from the local rates, and this gave local influences a strong position. The results can be seen from the degree of success attained in reducing outdoor relief to the able-bodied. In 1841, of the 345,656 able-bodied adults receiving poor relief, only 65,467 were relieved inside workhouses; very many more continued to receive outdoor relief as in pre-1834 days.

The central Poor Law Commission was another significant administrative experiment. In part it represented an attempt to take the Poor Law out of politics. The new commission was a kind of extra-parliamentary corporation to administer the Poor Law in England and Wales, deriving its powers entirely from the 1834 Act. The commission employed a small headquarters staff at Somerset House, with Edwin Chadwick as its Secretary. In addition, a small team of Assistant Poor Law Commissioners (subsequently renamed Poor Law Inspectors) acted as a link between the London-based commission and the local unions. As with the factory inspectors, government found a number of distinguished recruits from outside official circles to occupy these new positions. In that highly unequal society, it was important that the principal agents of the commission could deal with local dignitaries on equal terms. A good example of the group was Sir John Walsham, Bt, deputy Lord Lieutenant of two counties, with useful family and political connections which materially assisted his official activities.[31] In his correspondence with his official superiors of the Poor Law Commission, Walsham's letters display a mixture of bureaucratic formality and friendly personal exchanges.

31. N. McCord, 'The implementation of the 1834 Poor Law Amendment Act on Tyneside', *International Review of Social History*, 14 (1969).

The Poor Law Commission needed every scrap of additional influence it could muster, for the task it faced was not easy and the materials it had to work with frequently defective. As in other areas of government expansion, it was difficult to recruit and keep satisfactory officials at the local level. There was one obvious source on which to draw, the officials already employed in administering the pre-1834 Poor Law, such as the paid assistant overseers. This corps was of mixed value, and the records of the Poor Law after 1834 abound with incompetent, dishonest, or inefficient workhouse masters, relieving officers, and other staff. These weaker brethren provided only a minority of the Poor Law agents, but they existed in sufficient number and notoriety to perpetuate public suspicions of the efficiency and integrity of the system. Gradually the post-1834 system contrived to establish higher standards, but this proved a slow and difficult process. In many areas ratepayers were unwilling to sanction the payment of substantial salaries, which might be higher than the income of many ratepayers, and this militated against the availability of good candidates.

Another area in which the efficiency of the Poor Law system was limited by contemporary conditions was the provision of medical services. Before 1834 there had been no systematic medical provision for paupers. The larger and more advanced Poor Law authorities had usually retained the services of salaried doctors, and after 1834 the Poor Law Commission sought to regularize this practice on a national basis. Among the difficulties encountered was the absence of any satisfactory definition of what constituted a doctor. It was not until 1858 that the General Medical Register began to provide a clear indication of such professional status. Although the Poor Law Commission refused to accept the appointment on more than a temporary basis of doctors they considered unqualified, the choice was sometimes between accepting an unsatisfactory nomination and having no local Poor Law doctor at all. Even doctors who possessed recognizable medical qualifications might be too dependent on local boards of guardians; until 1847 their tenure was often on a short-term basis, subject to the economical view of local guardians, who often had little respect for undistinguished members of the emerging profession. From 1847 the Poor Law Board which replaced the Poor Law Commission sought to provide Poor Law doctors with more secure tenure, but the emphatic reissue of their orders to this effect in 1855 and 1857 suggests limited success.

Some regions posed particular problems. In thinly populated areas there might be few or no doctors; the Highlands of Scotland were badly served throughout the century as far as medical services for the poor were concerned. In Wales, despite many shortcomings, the post-1834 Poor Law brought medical services, as distinct from quack doctors and folk medicine, to many areas for the first time. In such areas, Poor Law medical salaries were usually very low; many of the medical officers in the Welsh countryside were English-speaking Irish or Scots doctors, sometimes trying to minister to wholly Welsh-speaking communities.[32]

32. Smith, *The People's Health*, 354.

Poor Law medical appointments were usually on a part-time basis, with stipends too low to attract successful doctors. It was common for the district relieving officer to be paid more than the Poor Law doctor. In 1837 the 57 officials employed directly by the central Poor Law Commission cost £52,000, while the 2,000 Poor Law doctors were paid a total of £130,000. One of the early-Victorian members of the Poor Law Commission, himself enjoying a salary of £6,000, explained the relevant background:

medical care is one of those things which each person provides for himself according to his class in society. The higher class provide a better sort... of attendance than the middle class, and the middle class better than the poorer classes. I do not see how it is possible for the State to supply medical relief to the poor of as good a quality, and to as great an extent, as the richer classes enjoy.[33]

The 1834 administrative experiment was not a complete success. The attempt to frame a non-political form of Poor Law administration encountered great obstacles. From the beginning the Poor Law Commission and its agents faced vituperative hostility from both the right and the left of the political spectrum, from paternalistic Tories like John Walter, MP and proprietor of *The Times*, and from humanitarian radicals like William Cobbett. Some of these attacks were exaggerated or unfounded. Where disgraceful abuses were uncovered, as in the case of the notorious Andover workhouse scandal of 1845 (with descriptions of half-starved paupers fighting over the marrow from decaying bones), they were commonly the result of local disregard of the orders of the Poor Law Commission, rather than that body's fault.

There remained a sufficient consensus of political support for the 1834 system for it to endure. Peel generally supported its principles, and after he came to power in 1841 he extended the Poor Law Commission's life for a further five years. He followed up this Act of 1842 with another two years later which made minor changes in such matters as the law of bastardy, the education and apprenticing of pauper children, and the arrangements for electing guardians. The following year brought the Andover scandal already mentioned, and the volume of criticism against the Poor Law administration reached a point which brought the weaker Russell government to enact significant changes.

The extra-parliamentary nature of the Poor Law Commission had proved vulnerable in practice, so from 1847 that body was replaced by a Poor Law Board embodying the fruits of experience since 1834. The new Board resembled the Board of Trade in taking the form of a kind of ministerial committee, with its President a member of the government and usually of the Cabinet. Thereafter the Poor Law system formed a department of State. The change was marked by an increase in the bureaucratic nature of Poor Law procedures; formal regular returns became more dominant. Expressions of personal opinions by Poor Law

33. Smith, *The People's Health*, 360. The passage also provides a good example of the common and loose use of the vocabulary of class.

inspectors, or details of the circumstances of individual paupers, became less common in the surviving records.

The 1834 Act did not extend to Scotland. There the old system instituted, like the Elizabethan system for England and Wales, in the late sixteenth century continued. Relief was seen as a duty of the Kirk and parishes had to maintain lists of the sick and impotent poor whose needs were assessed by church elders. There was no assistance for the able-bodied poor and only outdoor relief. As in England, economic change had made the old system less effective and this was exposed by the Royal Commission of inquiry whose report led to the Poor Law (Scotland) Act of 1845. A major reason for this act was, however, that secessions from the established Presbyterian Church and in particular the 'Great Disruption' of 1843, which had split that church (see pp. 261–2), had weakened the claim of the established church to be responsible for the whole of a parish. The new system provided for Parochial Boards and Inspectors of the Poor in every parish and these were put under the control of a Central Board of Supervision. Permission was given for parishes to build poorhouses but there continued to be no relief for the able-bodied.

As in the case of the original factory inspectorate, the Poor Law Commission had been part of a lengthy and complex process of trial and error in the techniques of government, with the less successful elements discarded or altered as experience suggested. Yet the creation throughout England and Wales of a standardized administrative structure, with a new central authority and more paid officials, produced results which went beyond the Poor Law itself. The reorganized Poor Law machinery provided the administrative framework on which to graft public registration of births, deaths, and marriages. Normally the Clerk of a Poor Law union became Superintendent Registrar for his district, with the relieving officers taking on the additional function of district registrars. The Vaccination Act of 1840 also depended upon the Poor Law administration for its implementation. The Poor Law system, with its corps of local paid agents, could also be used as an information-gathering agency whenever government or Parliament might direct. Despite continued shortcomings as a welfare agency, the revamped Poor Law administration after 1834 equipped the British State with new resources. It remained the most extensive system of its kind; no other European State had anything which could match it.

Information gathering

The information-gathering possibilities of the reformed Poor Law formed only a small part of a kind of early-Victorian information explosion. The decennial censuses provided an indication of improving standards. In the 1801–31 censuses, the actual collection of raw data at household level was carried out by enumerators of mixed quality. By 1841 more sophisticated methods had been devised. The revised Poor Law machinery was now involved, with enumerators appointed and their returns checked by local registrars who were usually the clerks of Poor Law unions. Instructions to enumerators were made clearer. From 1841 onwards only a small minority of census enumerators were unsatisfactory.[34]

The improvement in available information, though real, remained patchy. The regular official returns relating to Britain's foreign trade appeared to be one item in the government's statistical resources which was securely established. Yet these returns were seriously misleading, because of the continuing use of obsolete price levels for both imports and exports. In consequence the official figures depicted a great boom in the value of British exports, while in reality the decline in export prices involved an adverse balance of visible trade. From 1854 the official statistics gave a reasonably reliable indication of the cost of imports.[35]

It was not until 1847 that there were adequate returns of the number of deaths in childbirth. One reason for this was that by social convention a stillborn baby did not require an expensive funeral, so that it was tempting for poorer parents to return as stillborn a child who was born alive but did not survive for long. Although the general arrangements for the registration of births began in 1837, it was not until 1874 that it became effectively compulsory.[36] The registration of deaths was also imperfect during the early years of the public registration system. The cholera epidemics of these years were recorded very unevenly. There are reasonably reliable returns of cholera deaths, but no way of knowing the total numbers attacked by the disease. The Royal Commission on the Poor Laws in 1832–4 noted 'how loosely and imperfectly the means of the independent labourer has usually been inquired into, and how little is really known of their wants by those who order relief'; the data-gathering by that Royal Commission itself has been condemned as muddled and unreliable. A leading authority on the history of local government, writing in 1933, commented that, 'It is to-day possible for the central authority to know the outskirts of England more vividly than in 1835, or even in 1885, it was for the county officers to know the peripheries of their own county.'[37]

Select committees and royal commissions

The increasing range of public inquiries by parliamentary select committees and royal commissions contributed to an improved information flow.[38] In the years after 1815 select committees had been more commonly employed, with more than 500 such inquiries in the first thirty years of the century. At first the composition and working of these committees varied, but from 1836 the House of Commons standardized the device, stipulating the normal membership at fifteen, with a

34. N. L. Tranter, *Population and Society, 1750–1940: Contrasts in Population Growth* (1985), 9–13.
35. Mathias, *The First Industrial Nation*, 277.
36. Smith, *The People's Health*, 13, 65.   37. Finer, *English Local Government*, 14.
38. Henriques, 'Jeremy Bentham', 169–81; H. M. Clokie and J. M. Robinson, *Royal Commissions* (1937).

quorum of five needed to transact business. It remained usual for the MP who successfully proposed a select committee to nominate its members, often taking the chairmanship himself; the House rarely challenged such arrangements.

Select committees, perhaps especially Commons select committees, were open to manipulation. A determined MP who successfully proposed a select committee on an issue which interested him was in a strong position to pack the committee with sympathizers, tailor the witnesses and the evidence, and procure a report in accordance with his own views. Occasionally, an equally skilful ploy by opponents could thwart such schemes. In 1837, as part of his campaign against the revised Poor Law system, John Walter moved for a select committee to investigate the workings of the Poor Law. Although the proposal to appoint a select committee was accepted, Lord John Russell for the government succeeded in passing instructions to the committee which curtailed the scope of the enquiry; he also succeeded in packing the committee with supporters of the Poor Law. In this instance the original proposer was outmanoeuvred, and the committee reported in favour of the new Poor Law.

The opportunities for manipulation of select committees, whether to support or obstruct change, encouraged increased use of the nonparliamentary royal commission as a method of inquiry. This involved the renewed employment of a device which had been common in the seventeenth and earlier eighteenth centuries but had then gone out of fashion. In the early nineteenth century more royal commissions appeared, including the Charity Commission of 1818 and the Common Law Royal Commission of 1829. In the 1830s their use became more frequent, with some important reforms preceded by such inquiries, as in the case of the 1834 Poor Law Amendment Act and the 1835 Municipal Reform Act.

Royal commissions offered some advantages over select committees. They could continue their work independently of the sittings of Parliament, and they could include useful experts who were not MPs or peers. They could appear to be less amenable to political manipulation than parliamentary select committees. This advantage was more apparent than real. The members of royal commissions were appointed by government, and they could be packed as well as select committees. This was true, for instance, of the Factory Commission and the Municipal Corporations Commission, both appointed in 1833. C. J. Blomfield, Bishop of London, dominated the royal commissions appointed in 1833 and 1835 to inquire into Church property. The salaried staffs serving royal commissions also provided hard-pressed ministers with welcome opportunities to reward their own supporters, while influencing commission proceedings. The chairman of the royal commission into municipal corporations which preceded the reform legislation of 1835 was described by the commission's secretary as 'an excellent Rad., Ballot, etc.'; the well-paid secretary was Joseph Parkes, who had earned this patronage plum by loyal service as the principal Whig expert in electoral manipulation. Commissions like this were not likely to produce reports distasteful to those who appointed them.

These reservations have to be made, but do not much undermine the significance of the increased range of official inquiries. With all their shortcomings, the volumes of reports of select committees and royal commissions created a body of evidence on contemporary problems which alike in quantity and quality much exceeded the achievements of any earlier period. This has had one curious result, well expressed in a famous comment by T. S. Ashton: 'a generation that had the enterprise and industry to assemble the facts, the honesty to reveal them, and the energy to set about the task of reform has been held up to obloquy as the author, not of the Blue Books, but of the evils themselves.'[39]

Another contribution to the increasing volume of information and ideas came from the regular reports of new official agencies. Faced with similar problems in various parts of the country, and having to cope with a barrage of attacks by anti-Poor Law campaigners, the team of assistant Poor Law commissioners appointed after 1834 adopted the practice of meeting in London for a week every year. At these meetings they exchanged information and ideas, discussed common problems, and worked out a joint approach for submissions to the Poor Law Commission itself. In this way a kind of corporate identity and policy emerged among this key group of officials, capable of exerting an influence on the course of Poor Law administration.

The factory inspectors at their first appointment had been seen as individual officers, but they too developed a corporate identity, with regular meetings and discussions.[40] Constant pressure eventually produced a grudging Treasury acquiescence in the establishment of a small London office for the factory inspectors collectively, with a single salaried clerk. This led by chance to the establishment of a kind of career hierarchy within the inspectorate. An unexpected vacancy among the sub-inspectors, with no other obvious candidate in sight, resulted in the appointment of the clerk in the inspectors' London office. By mid-century this official had been promoted again to the full inspectorate, an illuminating example of the casual evolution of career structures in the Civil Service.

The emergence of these corporate official identities, certainly an unplanned development, had other results. When the early-Victorian Parliament created new official agencies, it was normal to add an obligation to present regular reports on the performance of the duties entrusted to them. The accumulation of these reports, like the increased volume of reports from select committees and royal commissions, was part of the expanded information on matters of public concern available to government and Parliament.

Many of the new officials entertained strong views on how their roles could be made more effective. The factory inspectors regularly tried to include in their

---

39. In F. A. Hayek (ed.), *Capitalism and the Historians* (1954), 36.
40. The discussion of the factory inspectorate here is based on the relevant correspondence in the Home Office factory letter-books, PRO, HO 87/1–3.

reports not only an account of what they had done but also an expression of opinions on how factory regulation could be improved. The official correspondence involved illustrates a kind of veiled bureaucratic warfare. Regularly the inspectors submitted their reports to the Home Office in readiness for them to be laid before Parliament; with equal regularity the Home Office returned them with a request for revision, on the grounds that they contained controversial matters beyond the scope of a report on the inspectors' performance of their duties. In the early years of the factory inspectorate, the outcome was a drawn battle on the issue.

Overall the years after 1830 saw a considerable expansion of State activities. The move forward was also reflected in a continuing process of legal reform, bringing the law more up to date and where necessary introducing new devices to smooth its working. In 1842 new district courts to deal with bankruptcy were introduced, followed four years later by the creation of county courts to deal with minor civil cases in a more convenient and economical fashion. In the decisions on the siting of the new county courts, the government was subjected to considerable political pressure in favour of various possible towns.

Local government

Governments also moved to strengthen the resources for the maintenance of internal order. The Municipal Corporations Act of 1835 imposed on the reformed borough councils the obligation to create police forces. Like the Metropolitan Police after 1829, these new borough forces often had serious difficulties initially. The newly established police force was usually the most expensive item in municipal spending, and provided a target for economically minded ratepayers. Moreover, it was not at all easy to find and keep good policemen, when wages were low, discipline strict, and public opinion often hostile. However, progress was gradually made, and in the early years it was possible to draw on the more settled Metropolitan Police to stiffen local forces in time of trouble. Permissive legislation of 1839 allowed counties to create their own police forces, but it was not until after 1850 that the national network of 'Peelite' police forces was completed. In 1835 the system of prison inspection was improved by the creation of another salaried inspectorate, replacing the local magistrates as the main check on the prison system.

Local government mirrored many of the features of central administration. On town councils, boards of Poor Law guardians, and county quarter sessions, matters of patronage frequently engendered more heat than any questions of policy.[41] The ability to control appointments to local offices was a symbol of

41. D. Fraser, *Urban Politics in Victorian Britain* (1976) provides a wealth of information illustrating the weaknesses, malpractices, and partisan use of patronage in the more important provincial boroughs in the mid-century decades. Rowlands, *The West Midlands*, 211, 285, provides illuminating regional examples of changes in local government.

pre-eminence in communities still much preoccupied with local concerns. Local authorities often championed their officers when incompetence or more serious failings reached the ears of central officials. This was sometimes due to an appreciation that it might be impossible to find anyone better to fill local offices which were often, because of ratepayers' pressure, ill paid and not highly regarded in the neighbourhood. The quality of some of the local administrators in early-Victorian years comes through clearly in a magisterial rebuke addressed to a Cumbrian Poor Law union by the Poor Law Commission in 1844: 'The Commissioners desire to state that they think it extremely discreditable for a master of a workhouse to be wandering about in a state of drunkenness in the middle of the night so as to be robbed in a public highway by a prostitute.'[42] The general trend in these years was towards higher standards in public office, but this was a long and difficult process. In the years after 1830 the tale of incompetent, drunken, or dishonest local officials continued in sufficient numbers to prevent either central government or local communities from regarding local authorities as ideal agencies for beneficial social transformations.

The Municipal Corporations Act of 1835 illustrates several features of government in these years. At first sight it appears an admirable example of a reform by statute, preceded by an inquiry by royal commission. The reality was more complex. The royal commission into the existing boroughs was chosen by a government determined to change the structure of municipal government, a determination reflected in the choice of commissioners and in the appointment of the commission's paid staff. From its creation, the commission's secretary, the radical electoral expert Joseph Parkes, was in friendly and confidential correspondence with radical leaders within the existing boroughs. Not surprisingly, the commission reported in favour of major change in the government of towns.

The 1835 Act provided two main avenues of municipal reform. Existing municipal constitutions, varying with individual charters, were swept away. In their place there came a standardized system of borough government. Ratepayers elected councillors, who then chose the mayor. During the bill's progress, the Conservative majority in the House of Lords added to the new councils a body of aldermen, chosen by the elected councillors and serving for a longer term, to ensure a higher level of continuity and stability. From 1835, the powers of borough councils were derived from this statute, together with any additional powers which might be conferred by subsequent legislation, whether general or local. In the first instance, the powers of the councils were narrowly limited.

The Act also prescribed a procedure for the creation of new municipalities in towns without adequate local government. If sufficient ratepayer support could be demonstrated, a local petition could lead to the issue of a royal charter of incorporation establishing a new town council on the reformed model. As with

---

42. R. N. Thompson, 'The new Poor Law in Cumberland and Westmorland', Ph.D. thesis, Newcastle University, 1976, 439.

other reforming statutes of these years, the existence of new legislation did not solve all the problems. The new councils in existing boroughs rarely embarked upon any expensive improvements, at the expense of their rate-paying electorate, and in some cases the reformed councils were more tight-fisted than their unreformed predecessors. Campaigns for the incorporation of new boroughs often led to prolonged local struggles; the acquisition of borough status might seem a doubtful asset, since the one thing it certainly involved was the imposition of higher rates. The process of creating new boroughs in urban areas was prolonged; examples include Wolverhampton (1848), Tynemouth (1849), South Shields (1850), Hanley (1856), Dudley (1865), Stoke-on-Trent (1874).

Charters of incorporation issued under the 1835 Act were subjected to legal challenges in some towns, either from older forms of local government or from aggrieved ratepayers. Sunderland and Manchester provided two examples of prolonged wrangling of this kind. During the first great phase of Chartism in the early-Victorian years, Manchester possessed two competing systems of local government, the old manorial authorities and the new borough council; Parliament was forced to make special arrangements for the town's police until these disputes were settled. The Municipal Reform Act of 1835 provided a new foundation for urban government, but it was a long time before the reformed municipalities were accepted as bodies which might be trusted to carry out extensive and expensive schemes of social improvement.

The Scottish Burgh Reform Acts of 1833 followed the Parliamentary Reform Act in instituting a £10 householder franchise in municipal elections and provided for regular elections every November; one third of each council was to retire annually. Burghs were divided into wards and important burghs were able to adopt a new elective authority, the Commissioners of Police (not a police authority in the usual sense) to regulate order, sanitation, and the amenities of urban life.

Grants in aid

The years after 1830 brought an important development in the relationships between central and local government, the invention of grants in aid. The concept, whereby central taxation subsidized the work of local authorities, did not exist in 1830; by 1850 it was well established, although on only a modest scale. The first experiment followed a select committee report of 1834, which highlighted problems associated with the rating system in local finance.[43] The committee noted the complaints that many forms of wealth were untouched by the rates, while ratepayers were saddled with the full costs of local prosecutions, which ought to be a matter of general public responsibility. In response

---

43. Report, HC 542, 1834; Finer, *English Local Government*, 285, 429–31, discusses the early development of the system of grants in aid.

Parliament voted a sum of £30,000 as a subsidy to local spending on transporting prisoners to court, and £80,000 to meet half of the other costs involved in criminal prosecutions. At first these grants were regarded as a stopgap measure, pending that fundamental reform of local taxation which did not occur until the late twentieth century. It was to be more than half a century before an annual vote was replaced by permanent legislation concerning these subsidies. The principle once accepted in this modest fashion was carried appreciably further by Peel. To that statesman, the concept had considerable attraction, especially as he attached to it provisions for ensuring that the subsidies were efficiently employed. Peel used the idea to try to remedy some of the shortcomings of the revised Poor Law system, and his speech outlining this proposal made his motivation explicit:

There is no part of the administration of the poor law which I think has given greater dissatisfaction than the administration of medical relief. There seems to have been great unwillingness on the part of the Guardians of the Poor to afford relief, under the impression that their immediate concern was with the relief of absolute distress, and giving sustenance to those who were in danger of starvation. I am sorry to say there have been, frequently, just grounds of complaint in respect of the administration of medical relief, and for the purpose of meeting the view of those who object to the present system and for the purpose of giving the Executive government a greater degree of control over it and gradually introducing an amended system, we propose to take one-half of the charge of the payment of Medical Officers upon the Treasury. Thus we shall be able to meet the objections of those who demur to the exercise of government control and to the expense by offering on the part of the public to contribute one half.[44]

These new grants were explicitly conditional on reasonable performance, as Peel explained in relation to his parallel proposals relating to workhouse teachers' salaries: 'We require qualifications, we require a right of dismissal and the right of inspection but we are ready at the public charge to provide a competent and decent salary for those who are to have charge of the education of the poor.'

Additional grants in aid devised by Peel accompanied his proposal for the repeal of the Corn Laws in 1846. There was a political objective here; the new grants were offered as compensation to local interests for any disadvantages entailed in the loss of agricultural protection. It is clear, however, that the system of grants in aid, accompanied by checks on efficiency, was something which appealed to the Peelite administrative cast of mind. The package included the taking over by central government of the whole cost of criminal prosecutions, grants towards the maintenance of certain classes of prisoners in local gaols, and grants to meet half of the salaries of Poor Law medical officers, teachers, and industrial trainers. The amount of sophisticated planning involved was limited; the provisions for central inspection and control were not part of Peel's draft scheme, but were added as a useful afterthought.

44. Finer, *English Local Government*, 431; *Hansard*, 3rd ser., 83, 264–5.

A similar development, which also occurred without clear appreciation of long-term consequences, involved the auditing of local government accounts. The Poor Law Amendment Act of 1834 prescribed the compulsory auditing of the accounts of the new Poor Law unions. At first each Board of Guardians appointed its own auditor, a part-time official and often a local banker, paying him a small annual fee for this work. One of Peel's 1844 tidying-up changes in Poor Law administration was to give the Poor Law Commission power to group Poor Law unions into Audit Districts. Since the new District Auditors were still appointed by the chairmen and vice-chairmen of the unions involved, and paid by these unions, the concept of an independent check on the finances of local government was only imperfectly realized. The growth of public confidence in local authorities depended upon their reliability, efficiency, and honesty. The years after 1830 saw some moves in that direction, but the process still had a long way to go.

The Empire

Expansion in official activity was not confined to domestic affairs. The British Empire continued to grow, though less from a definite imperial vision than from unrelated special circumstances. In 1839 the Whig government became embroiled in a war with China, partly because of attempts by the Chinese authorities to impede imports of Indian opium. Although illegal from the Chinese standpoint, this trade was important for India's balance of payments with the Far East. The dangers of opium addiction were imperfectly understood in early-Victorian years, when the consumption of opium, particularly in the form of laudanum, was widespread in Britain for a variety of medicinal or quasi-medicinal purposes. British merchants, both in India and in China, showed no reluctance to continue and expand the trade, and to obstruct Chinese attempts to enforce restrictions. A series of clashes between merchants and the Chinese authorities escalated into the full hostilities known as 'The Opium War' when the British representative on the spot backed up the merchants. After initial setbacks, the British forces succeeded in imposing a settlement on China, which included the ceding to Britain of the island of Hong Kong, the opening to British trade of four 'Treaty Ports' on the Chinese mainland, and the payment by China of a substantial indemnity to compensate Britain for the cost of the war. This victory was celebrated as one of the early achievements of Peel's second government, which had inherited the war on taking office in 1841. Behind the scenes that government was less than happy about the acquisition of a new colony in the Far East. Hong Kong had been seized with the intention of using it as a possible base of operations against China, or at least as a bargaining counter in negotiations. Once occupied, however, Hong Kong attracted a British commercial community. At home the Peel Cabinet would have preferred to abandon this distant commitment, but, as the Foreign Secretary, Lord Aberdeen, told a Cabinet colleague,

'The immense influx of wealth and inhabitants, with the great works in progress undertaken by private persons, must create interests which it will every day become more difficult to abandon.'[45] Vested interests carried the day and the Cabinet reluctantly accepted this new imperial possession. The most famous of British companies involved in the China trade, Jardine Matheson, operated from Hong Kong and the Hong Kong and Shanghai Bank was founded in 1864; both were largely Scottish firms and Hong Kong was to become a very Scottish dominated British colony.

Since 1819 Britain had effectively controlled Singapore. Between Singapore and Hong Kong, a new oriental foothold was created on Borneo. A British adventurer, James Brooke, had become involved in the affairs of northern Borneo in early-Victorian years; his energetic support of the Sultan of Brunei in native conflicts led to his appointment in November 1841 as Rajah of Sarawak, in effective control of an area about the size of Yorkshire. Brooke was keen to have backing from British imperial power, and there were some valid arguments for British intervention in the region, including a long record of piratical attacks on shipping.

The discovery of coal on the island of Labuan, off the north Borneo coast, offered an additional motive, for this seemed to mark out the island as a suitable naval station between Singapore and Hong Kong. Brooke had little difficulty in persuading his Brunei suzerain to offer the island to Britain. The case for intervention was heightened by continued piratical attacks on shipping in the area, and instability in much of Borneo, including the activities of head-hunters among the native tribes. There was less enthusiasm for this further acquisition among the Conservative ministers. In the summer of 1846 Gladstone, briefly Colonial Secretary in these months, expressed the opinion that,

The multiplication of colonies at the other end of the world must at all times be a matter of serious consideration: but especially at a time when we have already land infinite to defend that we cannot occupy, people to reduce to order whom we have not been able to keep in friendly relations, and questions in so many departments of government to manage, the discussion of which has been found embarrassing at home, and which appear to be thought fully equal in the demands they make, to any energies which the Executive Government is able to apply to them.[46]

Neither the Colonial Office nor the Treasury were keen on taking Labuan, but their reluctance was eventually undermined by practical considerations relating to the security of British interests in the area and the need for some policing of the shipping routes there. The gift of Labuan was accepted by the Russell government, which took office on Peel's fall in 1846.

New Zealand provided another instance of ministerial reluctance overcome by practical issues. British colonists began to head for New Zealand in significant

---

45. Crosby, Sir *Robert Peel's Administration*, 120–2. This book gives a convenient summary account of Peel's 1841–6 administration in all its aspects; for a fuller treatment, N. Gash, *Sir Robert Peel* (1972).
   46. Crosby, Sir *Robert Peel's Administration*, 125–6.

numbers from 1839, as part of an emigration and settlement scheme under the aegis of the New Zealand Company, a private concern with some influential backing. The Whig government viewed these activities with suspicion enhanced by reports of dubious practices by company agents both at home and in New Zealand. To forestall trouble, ministers tried to control events by authorizing the signing of a treaty with a number of Maori chiefs, the 1840 Treaty of Waitangi. In return for a British guarantee of secure possession of their lands, the chiefs acknowledged British sovereignty in the islands. This policy was inherited and accepted by the Peel Cabinet from 1841, but aroused complaints from the British interests involved in the campaign for settlement. In the end a not very satisfactory compromise was arranged; the government authorized its representatives on the spot to buy some land from native rulers and make it available for settlement by immigrants.

This process of the reluctant acquisition of colonies has been explained in various ways. One view, often dubbed the 'Imperialism of Free Trade', holds that, though there was little appetite for the acquisition of new territories, British governments were bent upon economic paramountcy in many parts of the world and, even if they much preferred economic influence and benefit to having to rule and protect, they were ineluctably driven by specific circumstances into taking over new colonies and responsibilities. Another argument is that economics was only one factor among many and that it was a host of differing circumstances and motives, such as military or naval considerations, pressures to protect colonists and traders, and the actions of 'men on the spot' and 'turbulent frontiers', that led to the unplanned acquisition of new colonies and the extension of others. Mid-nineteenth century British governments were by no means in thrall to economic pressure groups nor firmly committed to free trade.[47]

India

Further expansion and consolidation of imperial power took place in India. During the viceroyalty of Lord Auckland (1836–42), a forward policy in the northwest prevailed, although the first attempt to establish British influence in Afghanistan resulted in a British disaster there in 1842, only partially compensated by a later show of force on the frontier. The policy of expansion was more successful elsewhere. Lord Ellenborough, Governor General after Auckland, was not deterred by the Afghan setback. His military commander, General Sir Charles Napier, a radical in home politics, felt no compunction in overthrowing the

---

47. The idea of free trade as leading from informal to formal empire when obstacles were accounted was put forward a half century ago by J. A. Gallagher, and R. E. Robinson in 'The Imperialism of Free Trade', *Economic History Review*, vol. 6, 1953. J. S. Galbraith argued for the expansionist influence of protecting frontiers in 'The "Turbulent Frontier" as a Factor in British Expansion' in *Comparative Studies in Society and History*, II, 1960. More recently P. J. Cain and A. G. Hopkins have modified the theory of the link between economic interests and colonial expansion by suggesting that, rather than manufacturing interests, it was a 'gentlemanly capitalism' which linked the service sector, primarily finance and the city, and the aristocracy that promoted expansion. *British Imperialism: Innovation and Expansion 1688–1914* (1993).

Amirs of Sind and annexing their state to British India in 1843, in what he privately referred to as 'a very advantageous, humane piece of rascality'. The campaign in Sind had been aggressive, but Napier had no doubt that its success would bring to the native inhabitants a more beneficial rule than that of the displaced native princes.

At home opinion was much more mixed. Ellenborough made enemies by his flamboyant methods and displays of egotism. It was impossible for the home government to control the day-to-day decisions of their Indian proconsul when communications took a minimum of six weeks. Ellenborough eventually brought about his own downfall in April 1844 when his expensive wars and controversial behaviour finally brought the Court of Directors of the East India Company to exercise its surviving power to recall the Governor General, a relic of the company's earlier sovereignty. Ellenborough's behaviour had been sufficiently outrageous for the government to feel unable to resist his recall, but nothing could be done to reverse the practical results of his policy in India. Instead the forward movement continued.

In 1845 and again in 1848–9, there was war between British India and the military state of the Sikhs in the Punjab. This involved hard fighting, but in the end the result was the annexation of the entire Sikh territory. That Napier's robust faith in the superior advantages of British rule was not entirely unfounded may be gathered from the way in which the Sikhs proved loyal to their new overlords during the imperial crisis of the Indian Mutiny in 1857. British rule in India was further extended by annexations either imposed when native sovereigns died without direct heirs, or more simply when, as in the extensive territory of Oudh, the British government in India claimed a paramount right to intervene to protect a native population from chronic misgovernment.

Apart from these military campaigns and annexations, British dominance in India was marked by less obvious changes. As with the other parts of the Empire not extensively settled by British emigrants, we can discern a distinction between the desire for wealth and influence and a not always harmonious desire to impose British and particularly Christian mores. The latter impulse became more influential as evangelicalism increased its sway in Britain itself; missionary activity spread and evangelicals also began to demand that British rule should seek to civilize and Christianize the territories it controlled. The first printing press in the Punjab was established by missionaries as early as 1836, with 15,000 copies of the Sermon on the Mount as its first production. No longer was it permissible simply to rule India; India had to be improved.

Lieutenant Leech of the Bombay Engineers produced the first printed grammar of the Punjab's principal language in 1838, and by mid-century several books on both the language and the literature of that province had appeared.[48] India's

---

48. G. W. Shaw, 'The first printing press in the Punjab', *Library Chronicle*, 43 (1979), 159–79. I owe this reference to Vanessa Histon Roberts.

railway network expanded, accompanied by the telegraph system, which made British control easier. British engineering skill was applied to the building of irrigation canals and flood control schemes, to the benefit of the Indian economy. The use of English was deliberately fostered, and it became the established language of Indian administration, at least in its upper levels. During the early years of the East India Company, Indian culture, mores, and religions had been found interesting and often admirable by officials who sometimes had Indian wives or mistresses and made efforts to learn languages and absorb cultures. By the 1840s Indian languages and cultural traditions received only modest official recognition. A new law code reflected the introduction of further British influences. Although there were serious troubles ahead, by 1850 British paramountcy in India seemed ever more firmly established.

Other imperial concerns

In South Africa, the abolition of slavery in 1833 added to the restiveness of Boer settlers in Cape Colony under British rule. They believed that abolition had been enacted in ways which concentrated on the West Indian plantation islands and ignored the possible effects in South Africa; there was also dissatisfaction with the amount and the distribution of the compensation. Groups of Boer farmers moved out of British-controlled territory, especially during the Great Trek of 1837–44. Some of these migrants settled in Natal, where they came into conflict with the native military state of the Zulus. The Boer settlers succeeded in fighting off this threat and establishing a republic in Natal, but it soon began to feel growing British interference, in part motivated by missionaries in the interests of the local native peoples. The more determined of the Boer settlers moved on again, leaving Natal to be annexed to British South Africa in 1843.

Some Boers had founded a new community to the north of the Orange River, and in 1848 Britain formally annexed that territory also. Here, however, the advocates of the forward movement met a setback. The sequence of annexations, accompanied by wars with native states, was viewed with increasing alarm at home, both on financial and on humanitarian grounds. Accordingly, in the early 1850s the tide turned. Negotiations with the Boer settlers resulted in a British recognition of the autonomy of the two Boer republics of the Orange Free State and the more northerly Transvaal. This did not mean that Britain had given up claims to be the paramount power in South Africa. The existence on the frontiers of British South Africa of a pair of weak and chronically ill-governed pastoral republics could be accepted, but Britain remained wary of intervention in the region by any more weighty rivals.

The years after 1830 then brought a considerable increase in the British Empire, not because governments were bent upon a definite policy of continued imperial aggrandizement, but because they reluctantly shouldered additional commitments brought about by a variety of individual circumstances. Ministers repeatedly found themselves obliged to take on new commitments and unwelcome additional expenditure, in order to protect what were seen either as vital British interests or the legitimate activities of British citizens abroad. The quality of colonial administration reflected a mixture of progress and continuing weaknesses; it was not unlike what had been attained in both central and local government at home. By mid-century the resources of the State had shown considerable growth, a growth viewed with mixed feelings, especially by those who had to pay for it. There was still no general belief that the expansion of official activities, at the price of higher taxation, was likely to confer great benefits on the national community.

6

Economy and society

c.1830–1850

The pace of economic and social change accelerated in the years after 1830, but it is still necessary to be cautious in assessing the transformation which had occurred by mid-century. The concept of the 'Industrial Revolution' as a transforming agency in the late eighteenth and early nineteenth centuries has been immensely influential. Repeated demonstrations of its limitations have not succeeded in eradicating the widespread but erroneous belief that Britain was a predominantly industrial nation by 1850.

Nevertheless, in the 1830s and 1840s the physical impact of economic change was having a more obvious effect on parts of the landscape than in earlier years. The coming of the railway system was part of this, but so was the growth not only in the number but in the size and distinctiveness of such enterprises as factories and coal-mines. A royal commission in 1841 heard this account of change in a major mining area:

Within the last ten or twelve years an entirely new population has been produced. Where formerly there was not a single hut of a shepherd, the lofty steam engine chimneys of a colliery now send their columns of smoke into the sky, and in the vicinity a town is called, as if by enchantment, into immediate existence.[1]

Three years later, a visitor to the potteries of Staffordshire remarked that

A stranger might be tempted to believe that he saw a vast line of fortifications rising before him. The surrounding hills are all crowned with the lofty columns and the huge pyramids of the chimneys and with the great rounded furnaces, of which dozens are often seen close together, looking like colossal bomb mortars.

These changes were concentrated in limited areas, with the greater part of the environment affected either only slightly or not at all. Even areas of considerable industrial activity could offer little in the way of 'dark satanic mills'. Middleton was a silk-weaving centre seven miles from Manchester, and a visitor in 1849

---

1. N. McCord, *North East England: The Region's Development, 1760–1960* (1979), 41; B. Trinder, *The Making of the Industrial Landscape* (1982), 185, 191.

described the scene there:

I climbed a roughly paved lane, skirted by common-place mean houses, some of them little shops, and presently I heard on all sides the rattle of the shuttle. Still the aspect of the place was half rural. Trees here and there bowered the cottages and the noise of the flail mingled with that of the loom . . . I was met on the threshold by a decently dressed middle-aged woman who ushered me into the loom-shop where sat busy at his work her lord and master. The work-room boasted but an earthen floor, scratched and scraped by half a dozen cocks and hens which were jerking their heads about beneath the mechanism of the four looms which the chamber contained.

Scenes like this were still common in industrial Britain at mid-century.

One nation, one economy?

The catastrophic events that befell Ireland in the 1840s pointed to the massive differences between the British and much of the Irish economy and added to the political and religious animosities that made the Union of 1800–1 a failure in the long term. Within Britain, however, economic development and improved communications led to an increasingly integrated economy and society.

Historians have tended to become cautious when considering the transformation of the English economy, emphasizing continuity and the mixed nature of the economy even at mid-century rather than sudden revolution. By comparison, it was Scotland which experienced what one of its foremost economic historians has described as 'a social and economic transformation unparalleled in the Europe of the time in its speed scale and intensity'.[2] As in England, the manufacturing economy which sprang up in the late eighteenth and early nineteenth century did so in the context of an expanding agricultural and trading economy. The economic benefits of the Act of Union had not been immediately apparent but farming, particularly in the borders, quickly responded to new opportunities and changes to land ownership, landlord–tenant relations, and cultivation and breeding methods took place within a few decades, while by the late eighteenth century access to international markets had given an enormous boost to the tobacco trade and the manufacture of linen. Cotton manufacturing, coal mining, the chemical industry, pig iron production, and the jute industry followed, assisted by the building of canals and then railways. A comparison has been made with a latter-day Japan, as Scotland moved from imitation to innovation with a whole range of key inventions, not the least of which was Henry Bell's *Comet* of 1812, which pioneered steam propulsion for ships.[3]

The impact of the greater integration of the British economy upon senses of national identity was considerable. Towns or cities like Cardiff, Swansea,

2. T. M. Devine, 'Scotland' in R. Floud and P. Johnson (eds.), *The Cambridge Economic History of Modern Britain. Vol. 1: Industrialisation 1700–1860* (1994), 398.
3. Ibid. 411.

Glasgow, or Liverpool shared a common economic interest in the fortunes of Britain and its overseas possessions and trading partners. The objective similarities of this economic position made for societies and ways of life that had more and more in common: similar problems when it came to labour relations, the same network of working-class housing, nestling close to shipyards or factories, and a leisure culture which transcended national divides. Arguably, great seaports or industrial towns had more in common with each other than with their nearby rural counties. South Wales became more and more distinct from rural North Wales, a bastion of the Welsh language, because of industrial and social change and immigration from England. There were ostensibly contrary developments, such as the 'tartanization' of Scotland and its history and the invention of Eisteddfods and the reincarnation of Druids,[4] but the tide was with Britishness.

Population

Population growth continued at a rapid pace, and the evidence for it was increasingly firmly based as the census machinery became more sophisticated and more accurate.[5] There was still under-registration in some categories, but the scale of the demographic changes became clearer.

About 2 million were added to the population of Great Britain in each of the decades shown in Table 3. Within this increase a higher proportion was being added to the urban population than to the rural. By about 1850 the numbers living in communities above and below 5,000 people had evened out.[6] The

Table 3 Population of the United Kingdom, 1831–1851

	Number (millions)	Increase since previous census (%)
1831	24.1	14.8
1841	26.8	11.1
1851	27.4	2.2

The last percentage figure here is seriously depressed by the catastrophic effects of the Irish famine in the mid-1840s. For Great Britain only, the relevant figures would be

1841	18.5	
1851	20.8	12.4

4. H. Trevor-Roper, 'The Invention of tradition: The Highland Tradition of Scotland' and P. Morgan, 'From a Death to a View: The Hunt for the Welsh Past in the Romantic Period', in E. Hobsbawm and T. Ranger (eds.), *The Invention of Tradition* (1983), 15–101.

5. N. L. Tranter, *Population and Society, 1750–1940* (1985), 9–20, describes improvements in census procedures.

6. P. Mathias, *The First Industrial Nation*, 2nd edn. (1983), 226.

Table 4 Average annual birth- and death-rate, England
and Wales, 1841–1855 (per 1,000 population)

	Birth-rate	Death-rate
1841–45	35.2	21.4
1846–50	34.8	23.3
1851–55	35.5	22.7

Source: E. H. Hunt, *British Labour History, 1815–1914* (1981), 35.

growth of the larger urban communities continued at an impressive rate;
Sheffield, for example, had a population of 91,362 in 1831, 110,891 in 1841, and
135,310 in 1851.[7]

The overall increase in population derived from the relationship between
death- and birth-rates. Reliable information on these matters only became
available in the early-Victorian period, and even then there were awkward gaps
in the statistics; for instance, official registration of births in Scotland did not
begin until 1855. There is no reason to doubt, though, that the general picture is
reasonably well represented by figures like those given in Table 4.

By the early 1840s the annual death-rate had dropped below an earlier level of
well over 25 per 1,000 (in the mid-eighteenth century London's death-rate had
been something like 48 per 1,000), and with the annual birth-rate continuing at
about 35 per 1,000 this ensured a considerable growth. Within the overall figures
there were some striking variations. The Irish famine was responsible for the
higher United Kingdom death-rates from 1846. In the early 1840s the death-rates
for Liverpool and Manchester were twice as high as those for Anglesey and the
Isle of Wight. In the first years of Queen Victoria's reign the average life
expectancy for men was 39.9 years, for women 41.9 years; for the poorest groups
in Liverpool the figure may have been as low as 15.[8] Similarly, there were also
variations in the prevailing causes and circumstances. In 1847, the deaths of 3,200
mothers in childbirth were registered. Infant deaths were common; an average of
about 3 in every 20 died before the age of 1 year in the 1840s. In extreme examples,
such as some poor groups in Liverpool, half the children died before reaching the
age of 5. In the single year 1847, 75,507 infant deaths were registered. The British
figures were healthier, though, than those prevailing in the rest of Europe. In
Bavaria, well over one-third of all infants died before the age of 1 year at mid-
century.[9] Within the United Kingdom there were wide variations in infant
mortality. Although the rate varied between social classes and occupations, it is

7. S. Pollard and C. Holmes (eds.), *Essays in the Economic and Social History of South Yorkshire*
(1976), 276.
8. S. G. Checkland, *The Rise of Industrial Society in England, 1815–1885* (1964), 31; E. H. Hunt, *British
Labour History, 1815–1914* (1981), 42.
9. F. B. Smith, *The People's Health, 1830–1910* (1979), 13.

apparent that the main difference was between town and country. In Scotland and Ireland, both less urbanized than England, the rates were respectively 20 per cent and 40 per cent below that of England, where Dorset and Wiltshire, rural counties with low agricultural wages, had the lowest infant mortality rates in the country. The urban environment was clearly bad for the health of children.[10]

The reasons for the fall in the death-rate in these years are still not clear. We can be sure that it was not due to any significant improvements in medicine, though the case of smallpox is an exception. In the mid-eighteenth century it had been responsible for something like one-sixth of all deaths; the spread of vaccination must have been largely responsible for the drop to only 1–2 per cent of all deaths by 1850.[11] As far as most infectious diseases were concerned, doctors had little in the way of effective treatments to offer. Nor is there convincing evidence of higher standards of cleanliness, especially among the groups most at risk.

Apart from births and deaths, the size and distribution of the population were affected by migration. Much of this was short-distance. At mid-century, half of the adult population of Sheffield had been born outside that town, but usually in villages not far away. Most of the Highlanders living in Greenock had come only from the nearby county of Argyll; Perth and Dundee drew most of their immigrants from Perthshire.[12] As far as long-distance migration was concerned, with the great exception of the mass Irish migration of the famine years of the 1840s, emigration and immigration were pretty much in balance. Nearly 60,000 people left Britain in 1830, 100,000 in 1832, 130,000 in 1842, rising to over 250,000 each year in the later 1840s. Before the famine years from 1845, the Irish usually provided a narrow majority of the United Kingdom emigrants, about three-fifths Irish to two-fifths British, but the great famine altered this drastically. The absolute drop in the population of Ireland after 1846 was unique in contemporary European experience; between the 1841 and 1851 censuses there was a drop in population of 1,659,000, of which approximately 700,000 represented deaths and the remainder emigrants.[13]

Irish immigration into Britain and particularly into Scotland was on a considerable scale. The percentage of the Irish-born in England and Wales rose from 1.8 in 1841 to 2.9 in 1851 and for Scotland the rise was from 4.8 to 7.2. Outside Glasgow, the greatest proportions of the Irish-born were to be found in the textile towns of the western Lowlands.

The growing towns were the principal destinations of internal migration. This was not because country folk were driven from the land by the enclosure

10. F. M. L. Thompson, *The Rise of Respectable Society* (1988), 115–16.

11. Smith, *The People's Health*, 77.

12. For Sheffield, Pollard and Holmes, *Essays in the Economic and Social History of South Yorkshire*, 280; for the Scottish towns, C. W. J. Withers, 'The long arm of the law: migration of Highland-born policemen to Glasgow, 1826–1891', *The Local Historian*, 18 (3) (Aug. 1988) 127–35.

13. Hunt, *British Labour History*, ch. 5; Checkland, *The Rise of Industrial Society*, 34; J. H. Clapham, *An Economic History of Modern Britain: The Early Railway Age* (1930), 489.

movement or anything of that kind, but because of the attractive power of the urban scene, even with all the social ills which beset early-Victorian towns. There was no simple link between population increase, industrial development, and urban growth. Towns without a major industrial base, such as Edinburgh or Dublin, saw population increase and the growth of slums. Many country dwellers, suffering from over-population and underemployment, saw the towns as places where wages tended to be higher and employment opportunities greater, and perhaps where there was more individual freedom than in close-knit rural communities. As one modern writer has put it,

For every worker who sought refuge abroad or among O'Connor's toiling peasantry there were many more who could hardly wait to shake the mud of the fields from their boots. And while reactions to the new environment must have varied enormously, it seems reasonable to suppose that migrants were heavily weighted with those who were resentful of the monotony and repressions of rural life and who put the highest premium on the higher wages, excitement, and greater independence of town life. Factory work required no more exertion than much other work . . . Rather than a slave to the machine the worker was its overseer. His task was boring and he had to walk about a great deal, but the water-wheel or steam engine did the exhausting physical labour.[14]

In the countryside, of course, the exhausting physical labour was done by the workers themselves.

Nor was it the case that there was any necessary association between industry and squalor. In 1850 Henry Mayhew noted that in London 'Professional vagrants come to town as regularly as noblemen every winter.'[15] Towns without industrial development possessed some of the country's worst slums. Rising population without industrial expansion could have dreadful consequences. In Ireland population growth in the early nineteenth century was faster in the backward west and south, and the famine years of 1816–17, 1821–2, and 1845–6 showed only too clearly the dangers of population growth without economic development.

Occupations

In 1851 agriculture was still the biggest single source of direct employment and the absolute figure for those so employed had not declined, but the balance was changing drastically. Compared with other contemporary societies the percentage employed in British agriculture was not high; in France, Germany, and the United States about half of all workers were directly employed in farming.

As late as 1851, though, more than a quarter of all men over 20 were directly employed in agriculture.[16] About 1.75 million workers were employed either in farming itself or in closely related industries. Domestic service was the next largest employer, with well over a million. Compared with this, the cotton industry

---

14. Hunt, *British Labour History*, 67.   15. Ibid. 362 n. 7.
16. Mathias, *The First Industrial Nation*, 239–44.

Table 5 Approximate percentage distribution of labour force, Great Britain, 1821–1851

	Agriculture, forestry, fishing	Industry, mining, construction	Trade, transport	Services, public, professions all others
1821	28	38	12	21
1841	22	41	14	23
1851	22	43	16	20

Source: P. Deane and W. A. Cole, *British Economic Growth, 1688–1959* (1967), 142.

employed no more than half a million, about the same figure as the building industry; because of the overwhelmingly male employment in building, and the substantial female workforce in cotton, the numbers of families dependent on these two sectors were quite different. In textiles generally, women workers outnumbered male workers by 963,000 to 706,000, an exceptional situation. At mid-century the railways employed about 65,000 workers, but there were 145,000 washerwomen recorded in the 1851 census, certainly an underestimate. For long after 1850 most workers would continue to be employed in small productive units, and this included a large number of skilled workers. Printing, shops, hairdressing, jewellery, tailoring, furniture-making, shoe-repairing, and some shoemaking are examples of enterprises which cumulatively employed large numbers in sectors not usually thought of as industrial in nature. Much specifically industrial activity also took place outside the factory system in small workshops and similar conditions.[17]

The employment of children was in decline by 1851, although a greater fall was to come later in the century. For example, despite the big increase in the number of houses, there were fewer climbing boys employed in sweeping chimneys.[18] There is little evidence to suggest that the employment of children in factories exposed them to greater suffering than had existed previously but much to show a wide variety of conditions, some of them harsh by any standards. A leading modern authority on the history of children concludes that factory employment 'could not have surpassed the evils of apprenticeship to scattered masters and mistresses'.[19] Nor was it the case that factory employment necessarily brought a greater degree of separation between children and parents, for it remained common for children to be directly employed by male factory workers, who often employed their own children or other family connections in this kind of

17. Clapham, *Economic History of Modern Britain*, ch.5. The same view is expressed by J. Breuilly, 'Artisan economy, artisan politics, artisan ideology: the artisan contribution to the nineteenth century labour movement', in C. Emsley and J. Walvin (eds), *Artisans, Peasants &Proletariats, 1760–1860: Essays Presented to Gwyn A. Williams* (1985).
18. G. L. Philips, *England's Climbing Boys* (1949), 3.
19. I. Pinchbeck and M. Hewitt, *Children in English Society*, vol. i (1969), 257.

arrangement. In the 1830s such a system may have accounted for as many as half of all children employed in cotton factories.[20]

Industrialization

To contemporaries, and to subsequent writers, the continuing growth of industry was one of the most remarkable developments of the 1830–50 period. The relative novelty and the scale of the shift have been among the principal reasons for this. From another viewpoint, however, what was happening demonstrated a high level of continuity, as individuals in a position to do so sought to exploit opportunities open to them to secure advantages for themselves and their families. The opportunities changed, but not the willingness to exploit them. The cumulative effects of all of these individual decisions were, however, tremendous. By the middle of the century 93 per cent of British exports consisted of manufactured goods; only 7 per cent of British imports consisted of manufactured goods from elsewhere. About one-quarter of all international trade passed through British ports, most of it carried in British ships. This was a unique historical achievement.[21]

Even the prodigious achievement of British industry was not enough to give the United Kingdom a favourable balance between imports and exports. While exports increased in quantity, their prices fell to such an extent that accurate modern computations have demonstrated a deficit in the visible balance of trade. This was more than matched by other sources of national income, especially in the contribution made by the expanding carrying trade of British shipping. As early as 1830, the British merchant navy supplied two-thirds of the tonnage employed between Britain and the rest of Europe. Even if the prices of British exports fell, the uniquely dominant position achieved by Britain in world trading patterns led to a marked increase in the income generated by such items as shipping charges and financial services; this was more than sufficient to offset the adverse balance in visible trade.[22]

Within the general pattern of industrial growth, textiles changed most. In the early-Victorian years textiles contributed two-thirds of all British exports, and cotton alone almost half of the total. It was in the cotton industry, in the production of both yarn and finished cloth, that the factory system made the greatest progress. Weaving lagged behind spinning in the process of mechanization, and there were probably still about 50,000 hand looms at work in 1851, though the number was already in steep decline. Even in the cotton industry the introduction of bigger units of production had its limits. There were some large firms which had already developed into complex organizations, combining both spinning and weaving in one enterprise. Such firms might employ workforces of the order of 500, but they were still unusual.

---

20. S. Pollard, *The Genesis of Modern Management* (1968), 58.
21. Mathias, *The First Industrial Nation*, 242–5.   22. Ibid. 277.

Other textile sectors followed cotton in technical progress, at some distance in timing. In the worsted industry, the number of its power looms jumped from 2,768 in 1836 to 29,539 by 1850, while their individual productive power was also substantially improved. Worsted handloom weavers were increasingly forced out by machine competition; in 1836 John Foster of the Black Dyke Mills employed about 700 handloom weavers, but by mid-century only about 50.[23] In another process, combing, hand-work survived for a little longer. There were about 22,000 hand combers employed before Cunliffe Lister's invention of a practical combing machine in 1845 inaugurated an end to their livelihood. Overall, the textile industries experienced improvements in efficiency and productivity, introduced with such success that the total amount of employment increased considerably, even while the hand-workers were being forced out.

Textiles were exceptional in their level of growth and sophistication. In other industries, some firms could provide parallels to the textile giants, and in a few instances even more striking examples of growth. In the iron industry, the great Dowlais works employed more than 6,000 workers in the 1840s. This scale of operation was exceptional, although there were a few other iron works with a payroll of more than 1,000. In this situation it was already difficult for a new enterprise to enter the field successfully. A capital of something like £50,000 would be needed around 1850 to found an important new iron works; Dowlais was believed to represent an investment of £1 million. As in textiles, the giants were not particularly representative of their industry. If expensive technical requirements necessitated large capital investments for the mass production of iron competitively, there was a wide range of other metalworking activities with less demanding requirements. A workman who had contrived to accumulate savings of £60–100 could reasonably hope to set himself up in his own business in the secondary metalworking trades.[24]

The interlocking nature of much of the economic growth is illustrated by the way in which the iron industry was stimulated as a result of British predominance in sectors in which iron was increasingly employed. The railways provided one clear instance of this. Apart from locomotives and rolling stock, the growing demand for cheap mass-produced iron rails provided a major fillip to increasing iron production. In 1843 Lady Charlotte Guest, wife of the millionaire owner of the Dowlais Iron Works, noted proudly while on holiday at Mainz that her husband's firm had provided all of the iron used by the railways in that region. In a boom year like 1848 more than a quarter of the total British iron production was absorbed by railways.[25] The interlocking spiral of growth linked different sectors together in more complicated ways. The growing demand from iron works was one of the factors which encouraged the development of coal-mining,

23. E. M. Sigsworth, *Black Dyke Mills* (1958) provides much detailed information about the worsted industry in general, as well as the Black Dyke Mills themselves.

24. Mathias, *The First Industrial Nation*, 242–5.   25. Ibid. 259–60, 299.

which increased demand for coal-carrying railways, ships, mining equipment, and other elements requiring more iron.

Between the early 1830s and the early 1850s total coal production more than doubled. This growth was uneven in time and in place. The Great Northern Coalfield of Northumberland and Durham came to produce one-third of the total tonnage mined, while in the short period between 1836 and 1843 total national tonnage increased by around two-thirds.[26] Despite this prodigious growth, increases in technical understanding, including the adoption of the miner's safety lamp, meant that the human cost of winning coal was reduced. In the early years of the century, something like 8 out of every 1,000 miners died each year; by 1851 that figure had been halved.[27]

Some important industries were little affected by technical change and mechanization. Building was one, and it provided a major occupational category which (like the cotton and iron industries) possessed examples of large enterprises. In the 1840s Thomas Brassey's workforce often topped 8,000, while Morton Peto's even larger firm was at times employing as many as 14,000 in the highly labour-intensive construction business. Again the spurt in railway building provided opportunities for such giants; in 1840 railway projects alone employed about 100,000 workers, a figure which in boom conditions later in the decade soared temporarily to 300,000. However, these large-scale operations only accounted for a minority of those employed in building; most building workers worked for much smaller concerns. A modern assessment of the building industry concludes that

the technology of the industry was still basically medieval (for building the structure of most houses it still is in the 1980s) and the small man was dominant in the industry. Standards of efficiency, the amount of capital behind production, the size of the firm, remained as old-fashioned as the technology, apart from those very few working for specialized contracts.[28]

Despite this continuity, the growth in building operations of all kinds, from piecemeal house building to major construction contracts, gave a substantial boost to related industries. Again the railways provide a good example of this kind of economic catalyst. In the boom year 1848 about one-third of all British brick production was absorbed by the railways. The transport of bricks was itself an important item in internal communications, the making of bricks consumed a great deal of coal, and by 1850 railway locomotives themselves were using something like 1 million tons of coal each year.

Railways

In a famous phrase, Samuel Smiles remarked that the coming of the railways had 'virtually reduced England to a sixth of its size'. Much of the network was built in

---

26. Checkland, *The Rise of Industrial Society*, 18; Mathias, *The First Industrial Nation*, 244.
27. Hunt, *British Labour History*, 45.   28. Mathias, *The First Industrial Nation*, 241, 258.

these years, but the story is complicated because of the time lag between the formulation and approval of railway schemes and their construction. In 1836 nearly 1,000 miles of track were planned, but 227 of these miles were actually built in 1839, 528 in 1840, and 277 in 1841 (the lagging construction did have a beneficial effect in mitigating the impact of the depression of the years after 1837). In 1846, 4,540 miles were approved, and 1,253 miles of this were actually constructed in 1848. By 1851 the total mileage completed had reached 6,802 miles, representing an enormous expenditure on wages and materials, especially since British railways were relatively expensive to build, at something like £40,000 per mile. The profitability of the numerous lines varied. In the mid-1830s the Stockton and Darlington Railway was paying dividends of about 6–8 per cent, and in the early 1840s this had risen to 15 per cent. Such gratifying returns were rare, and in the early-Victorian period the average railway dividend did not exceed 8 per cent, a return which nevertheless compared favourably with other forms of investment.[29]

A problem with railways was that the initial expenditure was large and profits were delayed. By the early 1840s most of the early railways had become profitable and this led to a euphoric expansion. By November 1845, 620 schemes with a capitalization of £563 million were before Parliament. By the end of the year, the boom had burst and 'by 1848, even the best companies had lost 50 percent of their net worth.'

It has been argued that the 'railway boom' rescued a lagging British economy and came at a timely moment when investment opportunities seemed exhausted.[30] A more extreme view is that, by broadening the basis of an economy which 'rested precariously on textiles', it resolved 'the crisis of capitalism'.[31] The frenzied rush of investors into railway shares in two bursts of speculative activity, 1838–40 and 1845–7, had several effects, a boost to the economy, the building of the main lines of the British railway system, and losses for many investors. It also illustrates one of the cycles that mark modern economies: a new invention, far-sighted pioneers, over-optimistic speculators, devious entrepreneurs like George Hudson, whose railway companies were based on very creative accounting, a crash and, in the long term, tangible gains.

The impact of railway construction varied between different areas. The most glaring anomaly here was Ireland, where only about 400 miles had been completed by mid-century. On the other hand, the boost given by railway construction was not simply a domestic matter, for skills in railway design, technology, and construction were profitable exports. British navvies helped to build the Paris–Rouen line in 1843, after £600,000 of the necessary capital had been raised in London. For

29. Clapham, *Economic History of Modern Britain*, 385.
30. Checkland, *The Rise of Industrial Society* (1964), 24–5.
31. E. Hobsbawm, *Industry and Empire* (1968), 109–19.

the St Petersburg–Moscow line in 1851, £5.5 million was similarly raised in London. Apart from money, British railway experts were frequently employed in foreign projects, and it was understandable in these circumstances that much of the material required was bought in Britain and carried by British ships. Investment in railways overseas could be precarious, but there were some safer items available. A safe and profitable investment could be found in the Indian railway system; railway building there was backed by the authorities, and the debts incurred were serviced by taxes collected by the British authorities in India.[32]

Risks were present in the construction of lines in Britain, but in 1846–8 as much as 5–7 per cent of total national income was being invested in railways. By mid-century the railway system was itself a substantial employer of labour. After the early spurts of construction, there were signs of rationalization. There were about 200 separate railway companies in 1843, but a series of amalgamations brought the figure down to a more manageable 22 by 1850. Some order had been brought into the system by the establishment in 1842 of the Railway Clearing House, on the lines of the mutual clearing facilities already operated by the banks. The volume of railway traffic by mid-century was already justifying the building of most of the lines, and on the main lines average speeds of 30–40 m.p.h. were normal, a significant quickening in internal transport.

This new element in the country's communications inevitably affected existing interests. Some canals could contrive to continue in business as carriers of bulky cargoes where speed mattered little, but few could return attractive profits by 1850. The road system continued to improve, but the turnpike trusts had seen their most profitable days. This shift was indicated by the greatest manager of turnpike trusts, Lewis Levy; in 1839 he told a select committee that he still managed turnpikes with business totalling about £100,000 per annum, but that at one time the turnover of his road interests had amounted to five times that figure.[33]

What the economic effects of railways were has been much debated. For long it seemed axiomatic to historians that railways not only stimulated the wider economy but had profound effects in lowering the costs of transport. In fact, the early railways seem to have had more effect on the transport of people than goods and it was not until after mid-century that passenger train receipts were exceeded by those of freight transport. There were other means to transport freight and the efficiency of the pre-rail transport system has been underestimated but for passenger journeys over a dozen miles or so the superiority of rail was quickly demonstrated. It was only in the late 1850s, when freight overtook passengers as the slightly larger earner, that railways became profitable. Attempts to quantify the economic contribution of railways have been confounded[34] but it

32. Mathias, *The First Industrial Nation*, 294.
33. Clapham, *Economic History of Modern Britain*, 403–4.
34. In the early 1970s the counterfactual cliometric historians, R. Fogel and G. R. Hawke attempted to estimate the cost benefits of railways on the transport of goods in both Britain and the USA. They were cliometric because they used quantitative methods in historical study and counterfactual because

is in any case impossible to separate economic from social or psychological effects. Improvements in passenger transport were themselves an economic stimulant, while railways made the country effectively smaller, more centralized, and more uniform; symbolically clocks and watches became set to the same Greenwich Mean Time throughout the land.

Mechanization

The railways offered one striking example of increased use of powered machinery, but the extent of such changes was still limited. Within the secondary metal-working industries, in such sectors as chain-making, lock-making, and the manufacture of metal harness pieces, hand-work remained predominant, and small-scale production normal. Machinery was, however, making progress in other sectors. Steam-driven machinery was increasingly common in textiles and iron-making. In other areas unpowered machinery made significant changes in productivity and organization. From the later 1840s, sewing machines entered large-scale use. As technical developments improved the capacities of these machines, their applications multiplied; from about 1847 there was an increased use of sewing machines in footwear manufacture. Such new machines were relatively expensive, and their acquisition and profitable application involved capital, the organization of raw materials, and marketing on a different scale from earlier methods of production.[35] Similarly, machinery began to make some headway, if not on building sites themselves, then at least in the preparation of some building materials. In 1836, for example, John McDowall invented the first practicable planing machine for the production of tongue-and-groove floor-boards.[36] Overall, the increasing use of machinery was then and later seen as one of the most striking changes during these years.

One of the less obvious results of the economic depression experienced in the years after 1837 was an accelerated decline of older forms of production which had seen little technical innovation. The victory of the West Riding over such older centres of woollen production as East Anglia and the West Country was hastened. This was not simply a matter of one area succeeding another as the main centre of an industry, for the decline of a principal industry involved serious implications for the whole economy of the affected district. Local craftsmen and suppliers of all kinds of services could see their livelihood diminish or disappear with the defeat of their region's industrial base. This included the food, clothing, and building industries, as well as other suppliers of services.[37]

they used the hypothesis that railways had not been invented as the basis for their extrapolations. Useful as their work was in posing the question of the importance of railways, it has generally been considered that there were just too many variables for firm conclusions to be drawn. See R. W. Fogel and S. L. Engerman (eds), *The Reinterpretation of American Economic History* (1971) and particularly G. R. Hawke, *Railways and Economic Growth in England and Wales* (1970).

35. Checkland, *The Rise of Industrial Society*, 26.
36. *Newcomen Bulletin*, 133 (Dec. 1985).   37. Hunt, *British Labour History*, 27.

Mechanization made itself felt in other sectors of the economy too. The rural disturbances of the early 1830s were in part sparked off by the spread of the horse-driven threshing machines already commonly used in the north. This was not the only example of technological innovation in farming. The introduction of steam pumping engines, already common in mining, for drainage in the fenland areas was another, as was the application of improved machinery for the cheap mass production of earthenware drainage pipes and tiles.[38] It was soon possible for one reliable steam engine to drain as much as 6,000–7,000 acres, while drainage schemes on farms expanded rapidly with the fall in the price of pipes and tiles.

The factory system

Factories, if not the dominant form of industrial organization, were increasingly common in these years, and in them the hours of work could initially be long, even if the burden of physical labour might be less than in other forms of production. Long hours of work were not to be found only in factories. From about 1830 there was a trend towards shorter working periods in such areas as cotton factories; excessively long hours of work were increasingly subjected to criticism, both on humanitarian grounds and also on those of efficiency and productivity. Factory hours in the early 1830s were still long by later standards, but appreciably lower than levels obtaining abroad. In 1833 an inquiry into factory conditions estimated average weekly working hours in British factories as 69, with comparable figures including France and Switzerland 72–84, Prussia 72–90. This relationship persisted throughout the period covered by this book; reductions in working hours took place generally, without disturbing the relative placings of different European countries.[39]

It is apposite, nevertheless, that Britain was seen as the 'workshop of the world' at mid-century and not as the 'factory of the world'. Major industrial towns like Birmingham and Sheffield remained largely untouched by the factory system and remained worlds of small workshops.

Rural conditions

In 1831 more than one-third of all families in Britain were employed in agriculture. Farm work was still a matter of hard physical labour and there was only a very modest increase in the application of machinery. The replacement of the sickle by the scythe was the most general development of the nineteenth century. The standard of living which this toil gave the farm worker and his family varied. The poorest conditions existing over large areas were to be found in Ireland, especially in the undeveloped south and west. Famine brought the dangers of

38. Mathias, *The First Industrial Nation*, 310.   39. Hunt, *British Labour History*, 80.

this situation into stark prominence, but even in normal times the diet of the Irish farm labourer was poor.

Scotland is the most difficult country to generalize about when it comes to rural conditions for they varied enormously. Even in the Highlands there were differences between the eastern and southern districts on the one hand and the northern and western on the other with the former being better off, but the Highlands as a whole had a lower per capita income than any other part of Scotland. The basic diet of parts of the Highlands consisted of the herring and the potato so that when the potato crop was destroyed by blight in 1846 mass starvation was only prevented because charitable organizations reacted swiftly and the government '(in contrast to its inefficiency in Ireland) organised the distribution of food and seed corn from depot ships stationed in the principal firths'.[40] The northern lowlands were similar to the Highlands in that their economy was characterized by fishing and farming though kail was more important than the potato in the diet of the poor and this area that runs from Kincardineshire to Caithness had more in the way of medium-sized family farms as well as crofts. In contrast the southern Scottish countryside was much more prosperous and the Border counties of the south-east were large and in the avant-garde of farming methods. The farms of Lothian and Berwickshire could epitomize almost a factory mode of cultivation. As an English visitor to a famous farm, Fentonbards outside Dunbar, wrote: 'The great farm almost reached the sublime. It went like clockwork. Its fields, of from 20 to 30 acres, were all rectangular. There were no odd corners, no thickets, no hedgerow trees, no ragged, any shaped pastures.'[41] Such a farm employed large numbers of farm-workers or 'hinds' who lived in rows of cottages attached to the farm.

Even in relatively prosperous England, there was little improvement in the standard of rural diets in many regions until after the 1830s except for the lucky ones who enjoyed continuous employment. In some regions growing population without additional work opportunities brought a considerable measure of unemployment or underemployment. Before the middle of the nineteenth century three-quarters of all local taxation was raised to meet Poor Law expenses. In areas where industrial expansion provided rival employment possibilities, agricultural wage rates were usually higher than in areas without such alterna-tives. An expert observer of the rural scene, James Caird, noted in 1850 that farm labourers in Dorset were paid only about half what their opposite numbers received in Lancashire. William Sturge, a land agent who knew both the Bristol slums and the rural south-west, considered that many rural villages were in a worse state than the towns at mid-century.[42]

Variations in rural conditions often depended on social relationships. In England there was usually, though not invariably, some sense of a common

40. T. C. Smout, *A Century of the Scottish People, 1830–1950* (1986), 12.
41. Quoted by T. C. Smout, ibid., 15.
42. Ibid. 101, for Caird; for Sturge, J. H. Bettey, *Wessex from A.D. 1000* (1986), 272.

interest between a landlord and his tenant farmers. In many parts of Ireland, sectarian and national differences could produce alienation. A competent farmer was scarcely likely to show indifference to the condition of the workers he employed, but not all farmers were competent. Rural areas also varied in the use of child labour in farming. Some agricultural regions were among the sectors in which child labour was most common. Lancashire farms used child labour as much as, if not more than, Lancashire mills. Child labour was commonest in the poorer areas, where the wages of adult workers needed any supplements which could be found. In those northern counties of England where farm wages were relatively high, including Cumberland, Durham, and Northumberland, children usually received an above average period at school, and very young children were not formally employed in farm labour. Overt employment of young children on farms was less common overall in Scotland than in England. On both sides of the English-Scottish border an agricultural labourer was obliged to supply for his annual employment the labour of a female worker, a 'bondswoman'.

Poor conditions in rural areas gave rise to outbursts of discontent and protest. Earlier studies tended to emphasize the political implications of the rick-burning and other violence in the early-Victorian countryside. More recently it has been appreciated that the disturbances tended to be sporadic and localized. Recent studies have also indicated that personal spite and the activity of professional criminals formed part of the story.[43]

Standard of living

As in earlier years, generalizations about wages are difficult to substantiate; moreover, there is no doubt of the continued existence of variations in real wages over time, place, and type of employment. We can be sure that the statement made in the *Communist Manifesto* in 1848 that 'Machinery obliterates all distinctions of labour and nearly everywhere reduces wages to the same low level' was as erroneous at the time it was written as it has proved to be in subsequent periods. The modern historian, unable to indulge in such bland misrepresentation, is faced with problems in identifying meaningful wage trends in these years. In any event the place of wages in the overall standard of living is limited. Apart from problems arising from price levels, other ingredients in social conditions must also be considered. Poor housing and sanitary conditions could do much to counterbalance relatively good wages and better employment opportunities in early-Victorian industrial towns.

---

43. A good example of earlier more polemical interpretations is D. Jones, 'Thomas Campbell Foster and the rural labourer: incendiarism in East Anglia in the 1840s', *Social History* 1(1976). In that paper the tabulation of rural disturbances offered scarcely warrants the estimate of their extent and importance given in the text. For a more recent study, P. Muskett, 'The Suffolk incendiaries, 1843–45', *Journal of Regional and Local History*, 7 (2) (1987), 31–44.

At the same time, there is now substantial agreement among historians that broadly—but with many variations involved—wages improved by 1850, despite the considerable population increase. At mid-century there were complaints that in the industrial districts the higher wages and better conditions to be found in factories were causing an increasing disinclination among young women to take up domestic service. This is not to say that factory workers were receiving the lion's share of the increased wealth generated by increases in productivity. In 1842 a cotton manufacturer noted that the greater part of the increased profit was retained by the entrepreneurs 'by whose enterprise and industry the interests of our manufacturing towns have been directed'. The same witness supported this conclusion with the remark that 'On every hand the sides of the hills are adorned with the commodious dwellings of the master manufacturers, manifesting wealth and comfort.'[44]

Lower down the social scale the increase in 'wealth and comfort' was less obtrusive but none the less real. It is also reasonably clear when the improvement took place. A comparison of the purchasing power of wages in 1750 and in 1850 suggests that over the 100 years there was roughly a doubling in value, but that most of this substantial advance came in the last thirty years of the period, with little sustained change in real wages before about 1820.[45] The sizeable overall increase after about 1820 had important and pervasive results. In a situation in which medical science was able to make only modest contributions to a reduction in the death-rate, and when in some areas living conditions were deteriorating, higher wages, with their implications for improved diets, might have an important part to play in keeping the death-rate below the birth-rate and contributing to population growth. Again an international comparison is instructive. It is probable that wages in labour-hungry America were higher than in Britain, but British wages were higher than in other European States, probably on average by something between a third and a half.[46] Nor were the increases in British money wages eroded by concurrent price rises, for the general level of prices was falling in the years up to 1853.[47]

The overall figures conceal much diversity. A good example of this is the impact of the economic depression, which deepened in the years after 1837 and caused widespread unemployment and suffering well into the next decade. The impact of this setback was heightened because it interrupted a period of sustained improvement in the 1820s and early 1830s. One cause of the depression was a series of bad harvests between 1836 and 1842; food prices rose and capital had to be exported to buy food abroad. Setbacks in key overseas markets also made a damaging contribution. Exports to the United States amounted to £12.5 million in 1836, less than £5 million in the following year. Railway construction at

44. A. J. Taylor (ed.), *The Standard of Living in Britain in the Industrial Revolution* (1975), p. xxxvi.
45. Tranter, *Population and Society*, 86.   45. Hunt, *British Labour History*, 107.
47. Checkland, *The Rise of Industrial Society*, 12.

home slumped by 1842–3. Average real wages were lower in 1840 than they had been in 1830, and the figures for the consumption of such taxable items as tea, sugar, tobacco, beer, wines, and spirits all showed reductions in the early years of Queen Victoria's reign.

For some areas, the troubles of these years were compounded by the presence of specifically local problems caused by economic readjustments. In Montgomeryshire, for example, 1836 was a boom year in the local flannel industry, centred on the towns of Welshpool and Llanidloes. Money was spent on expensive new equipment, which could only be justified by the maintenance of high levels of sales; the first power loom was introduced into the area in 1835. This transitional stage was hit, not only by the widespread depression after 1837, but also by the development of damaging competition from the Rochdale area.[48]

Social categories

The 'common people' or the 'lower orders' continued to make up the great bulk of the population, the 'middle orders' about a fifth, and the aristocracy and gentry a small but immensely influential fraction. The nomenclature changed as terms like 'the lower orders' or 'the middling sort' gave way to class terminology. Yet, as in earlier years, it is difficult to see in the Britain of 1830–50 clearly defined social groups on a scale and coherence which could justify placing reliance on the vocabulary of class however widely contemporaries used it. Asa Briggs tells us, for instance, that 'The difference in experience and outlook of different sections of the labouring population makes it difficult to employ the term "working classes" with any degree of precision.'[49] Studies of both Birmingham and Sheffield in the early-Victorian period have stressed the absence of any firm class divisions, and the absence of homogeneity within what might be superficially construed as 'the working class'.[50] Mayhew, in the course of his inquiries into the condition of the poorer people of London, noted that 'In passing from the skilled operative of the West End to the unskilled workman of the eastern quarter of London, the moral and intellectual change is so great that it seems as if we were in a new land and among another race.'[51]

Part of these distinctions was represented by the disparities in wage rates. In the South Wales iron industry at mid-century, while an ordinary general labourer's weekly wage might be about 10s. 6d., a labourer directly working with a skilled puddler would be paid slightly more, perhaps 11s., the puddler

48. We owe this information to Dr Barrie Trinder.

49. A. Briggs, *The Age of Improvement, 1783–1867*, 2nd edn. (1979), 287. It should be noted though that Lord Briggs is of the opinion that the rivalry between the Chartists and the Anti-Corn Law League was 'essentially class antagonism'.

50. T. R. Tholfson, 'The artisan and the culture of early Victorian Birmingham', *University of Birmingham Historical Journal*, 4 (1953–4), 146; Pollard and Holmes, *Essays in the Economic and Social History of South Yorkshire*, 278.

51. *Morning Chronicle*, 21 Dec. 1849, quoted by Hunt, *British Labour History*, 99.

himself 21s., while in the same works exceptionally skilled workmen might be receiving £2 or more.[52] Wage differentials of this kind were often associated with differences in housing, representing the variations in the rents which could be afforded. Especially in areas dominated by small-scale production, it was common for supervisory grades and even small owners and managers to live in close proximity to workers. There was an overlap in earning potential between the better-paid groups of workmen in industry and a range of relatively poorly paid white-collar occupations. Clerks, teachers, trainee doctors, and some clergymen, for instance, might be less well paid than skilled industrial workmen, though such an overlap did not usually lead to any strong feelings of identity of interests between the social groups involved.

As well as such economic divisions, we have to take account of the many vertical divisions which divided society and in particular the gaps between the respectable and those who were not and those who were religious and those who never went to church or chapel. The Earl of Derby and a groom could enjoy a conversation about horse racing but many of those in intermediate stations couldn't have joined in.

There were other causes of disunity. In some contexts, racial distinctions could be effective. By 1850 about half of Britain's Jews were living in London, not always much liked by their native neighbours.[53] Irish immigration to Great Britain was not always accompanied by harmony between different groups of workers. By 1841 the Irish contributed about 10 per cent of the railway construction workers, and conflict between racial groups in that context has brought one modern investigator to conclude that in 1845 'there was near civil war among the railway navvies'.[54] Anti-Irish prejudice could appear in a variety of contexts; Engels once expressed the opinion that Irish emigrants provided Britain and America with 'pimps, thieves, swindlers, beggars and other rabble'.[55] The development of such social linkages as marriages between British and Irish working families in Great Britain was a slow process. Even among the Irish immigrants themselves there was no conspicuous uniformity, for Orange traditions appeared as well as nationalist elements.[56] Irish immigration was a major reason why Orange lodges multiplied to such an extent among resentful Englishmen that the government felt obliged to legislate against the Orange Order in 1825 and 1836. Another divisive factor was introduced by the patchy success of religious evangelism in these years. A study of Methodist miners in the Great Northern Coalfield, for instance, noted that Methodist pitmen did not share in leisure pursuits with their unregenerate brethren.[57]

52. Hunt, *British Labour History*, 99.   53. Ibid 177.
54. T. Coleman, *The Railway Navvies* (1968), 94, quoted by Hunt, *British Labour History*, 127.
55. W. O. Henderson (ed.), *Engels: Selected Writings* (1967), 95.
56. D. Macraild, *Faith, Fraternity and Fighting: the Orange Order and Irish Migrants in Northern England c.1850–1920* (2005).
57. R. Moore, *Pitmen, Preachers and Politics* (1974), 176.

Women

A vertical division in society was that between the sexes, though it is questionable whether an aristocratic lady felt she had much in common with a factory girl. It has become fashionable to distinguish between sex and gender. The two, once used as synonyms, are now thought of as different by many historians: the former as physiological and given, the latter a social construct. What is certain is that gender roles adapted and were modified but not in their essentials, in the first half of the nineteenth century.

The compelling image of womanhood at mid-century is that of the 'Angel of the Hearth', most lovingly described in Coventry Patmore's sequence of poems, 'The Angel in the House' (1854–63). Many historians have seen a change in the position of women in the first half of the nineteenth century as their role was defined as domestic, within the private, as opposed to the public sphere, and supportive and passive. The ideal woman was ultra-feminine, domestic, pious and, above all, pure and without sexual passion. This has been contrasted with earlier periods in which women were supposedly more involved with the world of work and were less subordinate to men. This alleged change has been seen as bound-up with and even caused by the increased numbers and influence of the more prosperous commercial and professional groups in society.[58]

Whether there was really such a change has been challenged: 'At a very general level, eighteenth and early nineteenth century women were associated with home and children, while men controlled public institutions, but then this rough division could be applied to any century or any culture.'[59]

The dominance of the view of woman's place and role put forward by Patmore and by Ruskin[60] among many can, indeed, be questioned on several grounds: that it was an ideal, which many a husband ruled by his wife might not have found reflected in reality; that it was largely confined to certain social strata; and that it was just a new, prescriptive, if rather sentimental, way of describing an age old reality. We cannot, however, dismiss too easily the increased emphasis upon home, family, and the almost saintly role assigned to women. The insistence upon it by writers, artists, and polemicists gives it significance, however far it diverged from reality. The dress, language, and deportment of women did change in the period 1815–50 towards greater modesty, more overt subservience to husbands, and an apparent sweet domesticity.

The emphasis upon propriety as the basis of respectability owed much to evangelicalism and the search for a new moral order. Several evangelicals came from aristocratic or gentry backgrounds and many more of the upper orders

58. A nuanced restatement of the separate spheres interpretation of women's history in the nineteenth century is contained in L. Davidoff and C. Hall, *Family Fortunes: Men and Women of the English Middle Class, 1780–1850* (1987).

59. A. Vickery, 'Golden Age to Separate Spheres? A Review of the Categories and Chronology of English Women's History', *Historical Journal*, 36, 2 (1993), 413.

60. John Ruskin, *Sesame and Lilies* (1865).

were receptive to the evangelical message but its roots lay in the merchant and commercial layers of society and its ethos was almost overtly a reaction against the values of aristocratic society. Another factor, which may have contributed to both the seriousness and earnestness that were a major element in early-Victorian thought and behaviour, was the uncertainty and apprehension with which many in the rapidly expanded middle orders of society regarded their position: how to behave, how to demarcate themselves firmly from the lower orders, how to define themselves as opposed to the aristocracy, and how to make themselves secure in their new positions. The home for some became a citadel against a dangerous world and the wife its guardian angel.

The ideal was imperfectly followed by all social groups but was given most credence by sections of the middle classes. A number of studies have demonstrated that aristocratic women could be the real administrators of estates whether they possessed them themselves or looked after their husbands' interests, while society hostesses often exercised real if concealed power in politics.[61] Nor did the sexual promiscuity of a number of aristocrats, both male and female, end in the 1830s, even if it was less overt and had for women, as previously, to be delayed until after the birth of legitimate heirs. For those towards the bottom of the social ladder, it is unlikely that the much trumpeted social and sexual codes for women had any influence, but respectable members of the working classes, who had independent aspirations to respectability, paralleled aspects of the separate spheres vision, the division between work and home and the importance of a wife not going out to work. 'Separate spheres' was therefore common to much of society but the Patmore–Ruskin ideal was most influential among its middle. Yet, Ruskin's argument, that a woman's duty was centred in the home and 'a public duty which is also the expansion of that', handed the wives and daughters of merchants, lawyers, and industrialists a pathway to public life via charity and good causes.[62]

There were more males than females during this period, around 5 per cent more in England and Wales and 10 per cent more in Scotland, but most formally employed workers were male. In 1851, for example, there were nearly twice as many boys as girls employed in the under-15 age group.[63] Marriage did not normally take place at an early age, and in 1851 more than two-thirds of all women aged 20–4 were unmarried.[64] Only a small minority of married women worked outside the home though many working-class women took paid work, such as washing or sewing, into the home. Even in the textile industry, where there were more female than male workers, married women made up only between a fifth and a quarter of cotton workers. That some of these workers might have a man staying at home and looking after the children was, nevertheless, a shocking thought. Friedrich Engels was aghast: 'One can imagine' he

61. K. D. Reynolds, *Aristocratic Women and Political Society in Victorian Britain* (1988).
62. Vickery, 'Golden Age to Separate Spheres', 400.
63. Hunt, *British Labour History*, 13.   64. Ibid. 33.

wrote, 'what righteous indignation this virtual castration calls forth and what reversal of family relations result from it.'[65] For most working-class men, it was important for their self-respect that their wives did not go out to work and separate spheres was as much an aspect of working-class as of middle-class life.

The subordinate position of women in the employment structure was well established and little challenged in these years. In 1840 Witham National School advertised for a new teacher, offering £55 to a male teacher, £35 for a woman.[66] Nurses might be paid as little as 7s. per week, though those who showed competence and reliability might earn appreciably higher wages as attendants on wealthy private patients. Less fortunate female nurses would find themselves in a downtrodden position, with poor food and low status. Not surprisingly in these circumstances, hospital records presented a dismal tale of nurses dismissed for drunkenness, theft, ill-treatment of patients, and similar offences.[67] The attitude of most male workers towards women's working conditions seems to have ranged between indifference and hostility.[68]

Children

There is considerable disagreement among historians of marriage and the family as to the extent of change in the late-modern period. Some have seen the nuclear family of parents and children emerging in the eighteenth and early nineteenth century and replacing the extended family, which included a wider network of relations.[69] It has been suggested that upper- and middle-class marriages became affective during the same period[70] and that attitudes towards children and childhood were transformed. It now seems clearly established that much of this, like the general notion of a great gulf between a pre-industrial and industrial society, is mythical; the nuclear family was a long-established norm[71] and affection within marriage and love of children was no modern invention. Sentiment did increasingly come to colour family relationships and to reinterpret them amongst all sections of society and particularly amongst the more prosperous. There was a growing interest in the education of children, an emphasis upon their charm, vulnerability, and supposed innocence but also on the need for discipline.[72] Since the middle of the eighteenth century, a literature designed for them had developed. If much of this was of the didactically improving variety, there were chapbooks of alphabets and rhymes and tales. The classic fairy tales of the brothers Grimm and Hans Christian Andersen were translated in 1822 and

---

65. Quoted in Thompson, *The Rise of Respectable Society*, 75.
66. Davidoff and Hall, *Family and Fortunes*, 295.
67. Smith, *The People's Health*, 260.   68. Hunt, *British Labour History*, 258.
69. See for instance E. Shorter, *The Making of the Modern Family* (1976).
70. L. Stone, *The Family Sex and Marriage in England 1500–1800* (1977).
71. P. Laslett, *Household and Family in Past Time* (1972); A. Macfarlane, *Marriage and Love in England 1300–1840* (1986).
72. J. Walvin, *A Child's World: A Social History of English Childhood, 1800–1914* (1982).

1846 respectively. J. D. Wyss had pioneered the novel for children with *Swiss Family Robinson* (1814) and Captain Frederick Marryat had begun with *Masterman Ready* (1841) the genre of ripping yarns for boys.

For the great majority of children, these developments made little difference. Childhood was short but there was some improvement in their position in these years, apart from the drop in the number of those in work. Very roughly, while a quarter of all British children obtained some kind of schooling in 1815, by 1850 about a half did so, despite the increase in population. Much of this expansion was concentrated in the years 1830–50.[73]

The 'middle class'

Contemporaries made much of the importance of a middle class in this period and in this they have been followed by many historians. The boundaries of such a class are not clear and, in practice, its exemplifications are generally drawn from what Marx called the *bourgeoisie*, well-to-do merchants and industrialists rather than Dickens's Bob Cratchit, while farmers are rarely included. One common denominator of the great majority of those described as middle class was the aspiration towards gentility and respectability. The former was more likely to be found amongst the richer sections for, although the notion of being a gentleman was beguiling, it took a degree of wealth to carry it off. Respectability could more easily be achieved and was also an ambition of most working-class people for, if the concept was embroidered by conformity in matters of religion, dress, and manners, at its core was economic independence.

Housing provides a striking illustration of the astonishingly wide range of people that the term 'middle class' was applied to in both contemporary and later discussions.[74] On the outskirts of Sheffield, for instance, George Wostenholm, a wealthy cutlery manufacturer, began from 1835 to buy up the landholdings on which the Kenwood Park Estate was to be developed. William Flockton, who had established his architect's practice in Sheffield in 1830, designed some of the bigger houses in this development, including one for Wostenholm himself. Even on this single estate the houses varied so much in size as to rule out any social homogeneity.[75]

The professions

One group of occupations, which can be distinguished by some commonality of ethos and function but yet displayed almost as many variations in status as the middle class or classes to which they are usually assigned, were the professions.

73. Hunt, 344 n. 12.
74. See e.g. M. A. Simpson and T. H. Lloyd (eds.), *Middle Class Housing in Britain* (1979), where the illustrations alone will indicate the extraordinary range of housing conceived of as 'middle class'.
75. Pollard and Holmes, *Essays in the Economic and Social History of South Yorkshire*, 178, 183.

The premier professions were undoubtedly the church and the law, followed by the senior ranks of the Civil Service, but the members of their different echelons had widely varied social status. It was not just that a bishop was superior to a curate but that it was more than likely that a bishop came from an aristocratic family. There was an enormous difference in the lifestyle and status of a rector or a vicar with a well endowed living to that of a vicar on a poor stipend or the curate who might never get a living of his own. Senior judges received peerages and barristers enjoyed much more prestige than solicitors in part because they did not receive money direct from clients. Largely because of the prestige of church and law, new occupations and members of previously unregulated old ones queued up to be recognized as professions. The professional ideal, as a study of the rise of the professions has argued, is based on the idea of trained expertise, a form of human capital.[76] In this professionals resembled craftsmen.

Many extensions of government activity in these years aimed at improving social conditions, especially among the poorer elements in society. These extended functions also involved an increase in the number of official positions, some of them well paid. Clerks to the new boards of Poor Law guardians were usually well-connected local lawyers. At Greenwich in the 1840s the Clerk was paid £350 p.a. for this part-time work, with additional sums soon added for the extra work as Superintendent Registrar for the district. A further role as parish Vestry Clerk brought in another £300 p.a. His local connections brought him this lucrative array of offices, and to this were added his earnings as an election agent. In practice his responsibilities as Clerk to the Poor Law Union were carried out by two deputies, to whom he paid £150 and £80 p.a. respectively.[77]

At national level, the new office of the Poor Law Commission brought new jobs for thirty-three clerks, as well as a variety of other staff. The salaries of the Poor Law Commission's ordinary clerks were not high—a few hundred pounds a year at most—but at least the security of this income in both good and bad years was assured. Royal commissions and other official inquiries, inspectorates of various kinds, some growth in the services of central and local government generally, all provided new and often lucrative opportunities for professional groups.

The development of recognized professions was a continuing process. This involved both the further definition and organization of groups with a longer history, and the evolution of previously unknown professional categories. The medical profession provides one of the most obvious examples. There had been doctors for a long time, but by the middle of the nineteenth century it was increasingly possible to identify a definite medical profession. Even then there was no simple uniformity of status within it. The members of the prestigious Royal Colleges of Physicians and Surgeons occupied a different social niche from

76. H. Perkin, *The Rise of Professional Society: England Since 1880* (1989), 5–6.
77. Smith, *The People's Health*, 360.

that of lowly practitioners in the provinces. In the early-Victorian years the Royal College of Physicians excluded from its principal offices any members who stooped to the menial role of regularly attending at childbirths.[78] There was, however, an unmistakable tendency among doctors to seek professional defin-ition. The Provincial Medical and Surgical Association was founded in 1836, as a coalition of a number of small regional associations of doctors. In 1838 and 1839 additional regional groups joined, and in 1856 the association became the national British Medical Association.[79] The generalized use of the title 'doctor' to denote most medical practitioners also dates from around this time. The strug-gle for professional respectability was not an easy one. In early-Victorian novels doctors do not always appear in a flattering light, and in the early-Victorian years the prestigious English Club at Rome maintained its exclusive character by, among other restrictions, specifically banning doctors from membership.[80]

The campaign for a formalized medical profession was impeded by a number of factors. On the one hand, in harsh reality there was little that an early-Victorian doctor could do to help the seriously ill. In addition, loosely attached to medicine was a broad range of quacks of various kinds, many of whom adopted a pretentious parade of superior knowledge which could in prevailing circumstances appear convincing. A study of medical practice in Lancashire reveals how despite the increase in doctors with recognized qualifications, they still had to compete with patients' own medical lore, herbalists, 'wise women', and quacks.[81] Patients who preferred quack remedies to normal medical care included many distinguished people. Purveyors of patent medicines (some of which were poisonous) could acquire substantial fortunes. James Morison, a retired merchant turned patent-medicine maker, was by 1843 paying the govern-ment £7,000 per annum in duty on his pills. Thomas Holloway and Thomas Beecham were other examples of men who acquired fortunes from patent medicines skilfully marketed. Faced with this kind of competition, and a wider range of charlatans, doctors tried to preserve their own position by professional definition and organization, while governments began the supportive moves which were eventually to lead to decisive legislation in 1858.

The determined attempt to institute professional restrictive practices in favour of the established medical men met opposition from those who doubted both the capacity and the motivation of contemporary doctors. Early attempts by back-bench MPs (instigated by doctors) to obtain regulatory legislation failed. In 1844 and again in 1845 the Home Secretary, Sir James Graham, tried his hand but he too had to withdraw his proposals, partly because the doctors had not yet contrived to establish a united front. A select committee inquiry into the medical profession led to further abortive bills in 1847 and 1849. It was not until 1858, with

78. Ibid. 23.   79. Ibid. 365; W. L. Burn, *The Age of Equipoise* (1964), 202–11.
80. Smith, *The People's Health*, 376.
81. S. King, *A Fylde Country Practice: Medicine and Society in Lancashire, circa 1760–1840* (2000).

the statutory registration of medical practitioners and the creation of the General Medical Council, that the medical profession secured their regulated professional monopoly.

Other groups found less difficulty in establishing a coherent professional status. The Institution of Civil Engineers secured a royal charter in 1828, the Institution of Mechanical Engineers dates from 1847, the Royal Institute of British Architects from 1834. The prestige acquired by such men as Robert Stephenson helped to determine and consolidate the professional status of their successors. Even within the increasingly formalized professions, however, there was always a hierarchy of achievement and status, rather than any uniformity. Many of their members never earned more than a merely local reputation, while a few might be figures of international renown and considerable wealth.

The aristocracy

The total number of wealthy people in early-Victorian Britain, even with recent recruits from such areas as the top echelons of the professions, remained small. In 1851 only about 10,000 men and women were assessed for tax at income figures of more than £300.[82] Among this fortunate minority the landed aristocracy still retained much of its earlier dominance. Some aristocrats also retained their close involvement with economic development in areas other than agriculture. The collieries owned by Earl Fitzwilliam expanded their workforce by about 300 in the ten years after 1845. In this case noble paternalism plainly extended into the mining sector of the estate. The houses built for the earl's pitmen were of above average quality, and there were pension arrangements for retired miners and miners' widows. The safety record in the Fitzwilliam collieries was also above average. St Thomas's Day was an annual estate holiday, when presents in cash and food were given to all employees. Lord Fitzwilliam sent many of his miners on trips to the Great Exhibition in 1851 at his own expense. In return for all this consideration, a loyal gratitude was expected. When some of his pitmen joined the miners' trade union in 1844, Lord Fitzwilliam closed all his pits and kept them closed until the miners made it plain that they preferred His Lordship's bounty to trade union membership.[83] The third Marquis of Londonderry was a fair man: when his Irish tenants paid their rent and did not vote for his candidates, they remained secure; when they failed to pay their rent but voted his way, they were not evicted; but when they were both in rent arrears and failed to vote for his candidates, they were evicted. In a different economic context, by 1833 the first Duke of Sutherland had spent something like £60,000 derived from his English possessions in developing the estates of his wife, Countess of Sutherland in her own right.[84] Accompanied by the deliberate clearance of 'surplus' population

82. Hunt, *British Labour History*, 358 n. 126.
83. Pollard and Holmes, *Essays in the Economic and Social History of South Yorkshire*, 47–56.
84. J. D. Mackie, *A History of Scotland* (1969), 317.

from economically backward areas, this investment was made in property which produced no significant income, the main objective being the creation of better conditions in the area concerned.

Recent recruits to the aristocracy shared the mixed interests of their longer-established brethren. In 1831 E. J. Littleton, who was to become the first Lord Hatherton four years later, owned eight brickfields, two quarries, two lime works, and three collieries, in addition to an extensive estate with profitable urban properties. He was responsible for the first reasonably effective legislation against the truck system in the early 1830s.[85] Arrival in the ranks of major landowners did not dampen the commercial propensities of wealthy entrepreneurs. It was noted that when brewing families like the Barclays, Hanburys, and Whitbreads were buying land, their new estates included some of the best barley-growing properties in England.[86] Similarly, old-established aristocrats often showed themselves capable of coping with the problems of newer areas of British society with considerable skill. During the troubles of the Chartist period in Shropshire, for example, the Earl of Powys coped competently with the problems caused by the industrial grievances of the local miners.[87]

Some aristocrats displayed a high degree of social responsibility. This was not always as easy as might appear at first sight. In one of the most famous cases, that of the seventh Earl of Shaftesbury, this preoccupation coexisted with difficult problems in his private affairs.[88] Others were uninterested in matters of politics, government, or society. During the crisis of 1846 Sir Robert Peel had bitter things to say on this score:

How can those who spend their time in hunting and shooting and eating and drinking know what were the motives of those who are responsible for the public security, who have access to the best information, and have no other object under Heaven but to provide against danger, and consult the general interests of all classes?[89]

A more charitable opinion might indicate that for the aristocracy, as for other groups, there were many interests other than politics which might attract attention in these years. A complex pattern of recreation, including field sports, was beguiling for many. For others the management of their estates was a matter of continuous personal attention. Similarly varied patterns of interest existed at all points on the social spectrum. There was no easy homogeneity at any social level. Instead society was complex and diverse; in the months which saw the drafting of the People's Charter, the elder Johann Strauss was making his first very successful British tour, performing at dozens of concerts and balls in many parts of

---

85. We are grateful to Mr Jack Tucker for this information.
86. Mathias, *The First Industrial Nation*, 244.
87. We owe this information to Dr Barrie Trinder.
88. For Shaftesbury's financial problems, for instance, see G. F. A. Best, *Shaftesbury* (1964), 36–9. The most recent full-scale biography, G. B. A. M. Finlayson's *The Seventh Earl of Shaftesbury* (1981) offers a full discussion of its subject's complex personality.
89. G. Peel, *Private Letters of Sir Robert Peel* (1920), 273.

the country. There were no clear demarcations between major social groups. Contemporaries often employed broad categories such as 'the middle class' or 'the working class' to try to cope with society's increasing complexity, but these intellectual inventions made a poor match with reality.

Trade unions

The trade union movement remained small between 1830 and 1850. In Sheffield, for example, the trade unions themselves claimed a total of only some 8,000 members in the late 1830s, when the population was about 111,000, and that claim may be inflated.[90] It is unlikely that there were more than 100,000 committed trade-unionists in the whole country at that time.[91] Apart from the understandable hostility of many employers, and the suspicions with which their operations were regarded by governments, the unions had powerful enemies. The Roman Catholic Church saw them as possible nests of subversion and anticlerical activity; from 1833 for at least a decade there was a deliberate anti-union campaign by that Church.[92]

Some grandiose and impractical schemes for national mass unions apart, trade unions remained small and localized, with little sense of unity among them. During the Chartist years, London had four separate shoemakers' unions, two for those making men's shoes and two for women's. A strict demarcation was maintained between those who did the finest work and those who made cheaper footwear. The reputation of trade unions suffered not only from the failure of such grandiose schemes as Robert Owen's Grand National Consolidated Trades Union in the 1830s, but also from the sporadic occurrence of brutal violence in the course of industrial disputes. On Whit Monday, 1832, a magistrate in his seventies was brutally beaten to death by two striking pitmen on Tyneside, in the course of a dispute which also saw a blackleg kicked and beaten to death by a group of strikers and their wives. In 1844 a man was killed when strikers blew up the boiler of the steam engine at the Deep Pit near Sheffield.[93]

The contemporary occupational structure, with its heavy emphasis on such groups as farm labourers and domestic servants, was not an auspicious field for union organization. Where attempts were made to spread unionism among the larger work categories, the results could be disastrous, as one notorious case demonstrated. In October 1833, some farm workers in the small Dorset village of Tolpuddle joined the Friendly Society of Agricultural Labourers. The declared aim of that society was to secure for its members, by fair means, a just reward for their labour. Like other early trade unions, the rules of the society prescribed

90. Pollard and Holmes, *Essays in the Economic and Social History of South Yorkshire*, 139.
91. Clapham, *Economic History of Modern Britain*, 594.
92. Hunt, *British Labour History*, 168.
93. McCord, *North East England*, 86; J. Stevenson, *Popular Disturbances in England, 1700–1870* (1979), 283.

rituals and oaths which could bring the infant organization within the ambit of the laws aimed at political subversion; secret oath-taking could be seen as a serious offence under this legislation. Six members of the union were prosecuted on these grounds and received sentences of transportation. It is clear the Home Secretary, Melbourne, used the law on illegal oath-taking to secure the prosecution of these agricultural trades unionists. The fact that the case of the 'Tolpuddle Martyrs' received an unusual degree of notoriety and that it damaged the reformist image of the government suggests that, like Peterloo, it was an exceptional rather than a typical incident and an example of hasty over-reaction. If trade-unionists had commonly been treated in this way in the 1830s, it is unlikely that we would have heard so much of this particular incident. The fact that there was an outcry against the sentences, with much respectable support, and that the convicts were pardoned and returned to England at public expense, is less often remembered. The normal course of trade union activity in these years was much less dramatic. The small unions of skilled workers generally pursued a restrictive and exclusive attitude in their membership qualifications. They often continued to operate within the registration provisions of the legislation covering friendly societies. Those who took this course could be found taking effective action in the courts in their own interests even in early-Victorian times.[94]

The period 1830–50 saw attempts to create a quite different kind of trade union, the mass association covering a variety of workers. While the unions which survived concentrated upon immediate issues affecting a limited membership, some trade-unionists and sympathizers sought to use trade-unionism as an agency of social and economic change. These attempts have been criticized as utopian system-building rather than effective working-class labour organization at this epoch. The great schemes were effective mainly on paper, in the enthusiasm of their authors and travelling orators or in the uncritical fears of employers and the Home Secretary. All proved ephemeral. They collapsed at the touch of a trade depression, or with the arrest of some leaders, with other leaders defaulting with the funds or even by a strike which made the funds run out.[95]

The most famous of all of these attempts to use mass trade unionism for purposes of national regeneration, Robert Owen's Grand National Consolidated Trades Union, was a resounding failure even in the boom conditions prevailing in 1834–6. The growth of trade unions was to depend more on hard-headed practical men concerned with the interests of specific groups of workers than on utopian idealists out of touch with existing realities, yet this must not lead us to underestimate Owen, one of the most remarkable figures of the period. Like his plans for a single trade union many of his ideas were not so much ahead of his time but at variance with reality at any time. A capable businessman and manufacturer in his early career and the founder of the model mill community

94. Mathias, *The First Industrial Nation*, 336.   95. Ibid. 337.

at New Lanark, he went on to establish utopian communities and to influence the cooperative movement. Owen and his followers were influenced by and influenced almost every radical and romantic development of the day. A secular millenarian, radical in his view of the position of women and sexual relations and a communitarian who wanted to control and make the rules for his communities, his main legacy was the increased acceptance by later periods of the emphasis he placed upon environment and upbringing as the formative influences upon character.[96] Many of his ideas would still be considered in the early twentieth-first century as 'New Age'.

The cooperative movement which actually developed like the trades unions and became firmly established was far removed from Owenite utopianism. Early efforts at organizing cooperatives saw catastrophic failure for romantic visionaries, and modest successes for practical people with limited but realizable aims. Grandiose schemes of national social engineering through cooperative ventures, sometimes based on concepts of communal living, led to repeated disappointment. On the other hand, the foundations of modest growth were laid by the development of retail cooperative trading through the work of such pioneers as Dr William King in London, and the more famous example of the Rochdale Pioneers of 1844. Instead of utopian visions, the retail stores practised competent trading, with a regular dividend based on amount of purchases being returned to members.[97] We can be confident that many of the pioneers in both trade unions and the cooperative societies entertained broadly radical views; indeed there could be a good deal of individual movement between support for such movements as Chartism and trade-unionism or cooperative societies. In general, however, progress in both unions and societies depended on concentration on limited but realistic aims.

Attempts to create organizations of employers were no more successful than schemes for mass trade unions. Most employers' groupings were ephemeral and ineffective. The most common form was a local or regional association in a given branch of industry, formed when that trade was facing problems. Attempts at concerted price-fixing took place in many sectors of the economy, but they rarely displayed any lasting coherence or effectiveness.[98] Such organizations, whether of workers or of employers, were not a major force in the day-to-day working of the British economy in these years.

Friendly societies and savings banks

Savings banks and friendly societies commanded a wider range of support than either trade unions or cooperative societies, and continued to be regarded benignly by those in power as valuable agents of self-improvement. Largely

96. Ian Donnachie, *Robert Owen: Owen of New Lanark and New Harmony* (2000), 262.
97. Briggs, *The Age of Improvement*, 288.
98. Mathias, *The First Industrial Nation*, 354–5.

building on the example of Scotland where the first savings bank had been established in 1810, savings banks expanded rapidly throughout Britain and by 1844 had more than a million depositors, and looked after a total sum of £27 million. The usual method of establishing such a bank was for a group of local 'principal inhabitants' to come together to back such a project and lay down rules which ensured that deposited funds were safe, and offered a rate of interest which would attract customers. Local savings banks often stipulated a modest maximum deposit, to ensure that the financial advantages of the institution were confined to the poorer groups for whom they were designed.

Savings banks and friendly societies had much in common, and generally appealed to the same social groups. The number and variety of friendly societies, providing welfare benefits on the basis of regular subscriptions, continued to grow in these years, in both rural and urban contexts. Legislative approval of their activities was consolidated in 1842, when the Conservative government strengthened provisions for registration. There was now to be a salaried Registrar of Friendly Societies to maintain an official register of the approved societies which were entitled to legal recognition and statutory protection. Many small local societies continued without such formalities, but a feature of these years was the expansion of the bigger societies. These large societies, sometimes organized on a national basis, and including quasi-masonic rituals and ceremonies in their activities, proved a considerable attraction. They included the Hearts of Oak society (1841), the older Order of Foresters (reorganized in 1834), and various branches of the Oddfellows, which ceased to be merely local bodies during the 1830s and 1840s. By mid-century total membership of friendly societies must have been well over 1.5 million, with some areas, notably Lancashire, notching up a particularly high level of membership. While many friendly society members were respectable church- or chapel-going folk, the social pattern was varied; many local societies had their headquarters and regular meetings in a public house. The very poor, and those dependent on intermittent employment, were largely excluded from the friendly societies with their continuous regular subscriptions. On the other hand, friendly society membership and savings banks could provide a measure of security against hard times, and played a significant part in the lifestyles of many respectable working families. These societies testified not just to working-class self-help but to the appetite for clubs that all strata of male nineteenth-century society shared.

Temperance

Another development with similar implications was the temperance movement, already exhibiting considerable growth in the early-Victorian period. By 1837, for example, the Leeds Temperance Society had 14 branches, 29 specified centres for regular meetings, and a roll of 118 speakers. A national temperance society, founded in 1842, developed by 1856 into a much larger National Temperance

League after an amalgamation with the London Temperance Society. By mid-century the various manifestations of the temperance movement possessed a larger committed following than any of the specifically political activities of the day. Despite all the efforts made, and the considerable degree of success attained, the cause of temperance never came close to total victory. In 1850 the annual consumption of beer was still running at about twenty gallons per head of the whole population. A select committee inquiry in the early 1850s reported that since 1830 the number of outlets for drink had risen from 88,930 to 123,396.[99]

Alcohol and its abuse was the subject of great attention. The problem of drug-taking was largely ignored. Opium and opium derivatives were freely available and, in addition to those who consciously took drugs for pleasure or to blot out life's worries, there were many unconscious or passive drug addicts whose numbers would increase as more and more proprietary medicines and sleeping draughts came to include laudanum and morphine; even babies were dosed and silenced with Godfrey's Cordial whose efficacious qualities relied upon the amount of laudanum it contained.

Education

One widely canvassed method of effecting social improvement and combating drunkenness, brutality, and other social evils was the expansion of education. The belief that schooling could lead to moral regeneration was one reason why the Churches played an important part in the education question, though of course the specifically religious element in education had ensured their earlier interest. In addition to the national school-building societies, many Churches were active at a local level. In Sheffield the Anglicans founded a local Church of England Instruction Society in 1839, and soon Methodists and Quakers responded to this initiative by founding their own educational associations in the town.[100] A belief in the importance of increased literacy in improving character was also a principal motive behind the State's first hesitant intervention in this field. The first meagre State grant of £20,000 in 1833 was raised to £30,000 in 1839, but as yet represented only a modest subsidy given to the two principal voluntary school-building societies—the British and Foreign School Society of 1807, which included both Anglicans and Nonconformists, and the exclusively Anglican National Society of 1811. Until 1869 all of the inspectors employed to check the use of the State grants to schools were clergymen. The substantial number of schools provided by the societies, with their religious base, was

---

99. Burn, *The Age of Equipoise*, 282; B. Harrison, *Drink and the Victorians: The Temperance Question in England, 1815–1872* (1971), is the best general discussion. An extensive bibliography is given in B. Harrison, 'Drink and sobriety in England, 1815–1872', *International Review of Social History*, 12 (1967), 204–76.

100. Pollard and Holmes, *Essays in the Economic and Social History of South Yorkshire*, 286.

complemented by the growing number of privately founded and operated schools; at mid-century, for example, Sheffield had about 180 private schools.

Although these schools extended literacy, despite the rapidly growing population, they rarely managed to cater for the needs of the children of the very poor. As this deficiency became obvious, attempts were made to meet it by such devices as the spread of Ragged Schools, institutions which offered basic elementary education, some food and clothing, and instruction in public and religious duties. At mid-century moves were also under way for the creation of a network of reform schools aimed at the rehabilitation of juvenile criminals. Other agencies such as mechanics' institutes and the extensive Sunday School movement supplemented the work of the ordinary elementary schools.

In country areas the contribution of aristocracy and gentry to the provision of education was considerable. Such philanthropy is often seen as more common in the southern counties of England but a study of Northumberland reveals the widespread provision of schooling and close supervision of schools by landowners. As with most charitable work, women were prominent.[101]

The educational attainment of the first half of the nineteenth century was impressive, and much of it was concentrated into the 1830–50 period. However, the highest hopes of the social reformers who prompted this expansion were never fully realized. Alike in town and country, crime, brutality, violence, and drunkenness continued, though probably not so commonly as in earlier periods. A modern study of popular disturbances in Britain has concluded that 'Victorians were not indulging in self-deception when they claimed to be living in a more stable and orderly society.'[102] The achievement was real, even if it was relative rather than absolute. The expansion in education was often cited as a principal reason for the relative social tranquillity attained by mid-century, despite population growth, the expansion of towns, and the pace of economic and social change.

Scholarship and learning

In addition to the increased provision of schooling, the second quarter of the nineteenth century saw advances in different fields of scholarship, though as yet this progress mainly took place outside the formal structures of universities and schools. The increase in the number of learned societies, both national and local, was one indication of growing interest, and also of the prevailing preference for voluntary action. Examples of such bodies were the Geographical Society (1830), the Statistical Society (1834), the Botanical Society (1836), the Ornithological Society (1837), and the Royal Archaeological Institute (1844). An example of the

101. A. E. Hattersley, 'Philanthropy of Landed Estates in Northumberland during the Nineteenth Century', Ph.D. thesis, University of Teesside (2004).
102. Stevenson, *Popular Disturbances in England*, 300.

local or regional parallels to these national societies was the Warwickshire Natural History and Archaeological Society, founded in 1846. The outstanding success of the Great Exhibition of 1851 contributed to a considerable public interest in art and science.

A lively intellectual and cultural life continued. Technical improvements in paper-making and printing facilitated the spread of cheap magazines and books. Religious works continued to provide a high proportion of this output, but there was a growing variety of both educational and recreational reading. By mid-century publishers like John Cassell were producing many cheap non-fiction works which found ready buyers. Serial publication in magazines influenced both the length and the structure of the early-Victorian novel, a literary form which reached high levels in these years. Some of its exponents have retained an honoured place in English literature. If Dickens and Thackeray were the giants here, they were followed by many others, including the Bronte sisters, Trollope, and Disraeli. Apart from such luminaries, the increasing volume of published novels incorporated a much larger number of once-popular writers now relegated to obscurity. In other literary spheres, writers such as Tennyson, Carlyle, Macaulay, and Ruskin were achieving distinction, and they too had many competitors of lesser later reputation.

For an age which has been seen as one of 'progress' or 'improvement', it is odd that a concern for the problems and challenges of its present figured so little in the popular reading of the day. Nostalgia for either the recent past or an idealized mediaeval past was the dominant theme of so much of its literature. For the most part the attitude of novelists and of poets and painters towards science, industry, and the town was negative. The popularity of Sir Walter Scott's works outlived his death in 1832, while the influence of Kenelm Digby's *The Broadstone of Honour* (1822) was influential long after its publication. Tennyson also contributed to the cult of the mediaeval, the 'return to Camelot' as it has been called, with his *Morte d'Arthur* (1842).[103] Another theme was that of upper-class life, the so-called 'silver fork' novels, exemplars of which were Disraeli and Edward Bulwer-Lytton. Dickens's great best-seller of the 1830s was *Pickwick Papers*, published in twenty instalments, beginning in 1836 and set in the recent past. For the most part novelists ignored the problems of industrialization and urbanization until the years immediately before mid-century.

The first influential work on what he called 'the Condition-of-England question' came from the historian and philosopher, Thomas Carlyle, with *Chartism* (1839) and *Past and Present* (1843). There followed what have been termed the 'Condition of England' novels. Disraeli's *Coningsby* (1844) and *Sybil* (1845); very different from his earlier novels in their concentrations upon the social problems of the period, they followed Carlyle in contrasting the dismal present with a

---

103. For the cultural and social influence of the mediaeval concept of chivalry see, Mark Girouard, *The Return to Camelot: Chivalry and the English Gentleman* (1981).

more kindly, chivalrous, and paternal past. There was, in general, a significant pause between the hardships endured by much of the population in the 1830s and early forties and the appearance of the novels which dealt with them. Mrs Gaskell's *North and South* was not published until 1855 and Dickens's *Hard Times* was published in 1854. *Oliver Twist* (1837–8) did, of course, deal with workhouse conditions, but with those of workhouses before the controversial 1834 Poor Law Amendment Act.

The age was also one of notable progress in science. The exact nature of the connection between scientific progress and industrial development has been the subject of historical controversy in recent decades, but there is now substantial agreement that the relationship was important. Certainly the significance of the connection was appreciated at the time by expert observers. Charles Babbage noted in 1835 that 'it is impossible not to perceive that the arts and manufactures of the country are intimately connected with the progress of the severer sciences; and that, as we advance in the career of improvement, every step requires, for its success, that this connexion should be rendered more intimate.'[104] Nowhere else in Europe at that time was there such a close link between technology applied in industry and the work of research scientists. Although France possessed scientists at least as able as those of Britain in these years, their impact on productive processes was slight.

As yet the British lead in the application of science had little to do with the universities. It was not until 1852 that Oxford introduced an honours school in natural science, following Cambridge's lead in 1848. In technical education such bodies as the engineering institutions and the national scientific societies played a more important role, as they had done earlier in the century. The British Association for the Advancement of Science was founded in 1831, and its regular meetings thereafter provided a platform for the discussion and dissemination of scientific ideas. In 1833 professorships of chemistry and physiology were created at the Royal Institution. The College of Chemistry was founded in 1845, primarily to encourage the application of chemical techniques in farming. Compared with these specialized agencies, the scientific contribution of schools and universities was limited. A national survey of provision in 1851 found only thirty-eight formal classes in science with a total of about 1,300 pupils.[105]

Religion

If science continued to progress and exert influence in these years, this did not mean that religion was taking a back seat. Instead these decades saw the continuation of the spread of religious zeal. The continuing evangelical revival was

---

104. P. Mathias, *The Transformation of England: Essays in the Economic and Social History of England in the Eighteenth Century* (1979), 46–60. The Babbage quotation is at p. 50.

105. R. L. Archer, *Secondary Education in the Nineteenth Century* (1928), 138.

important in both the Anglican and the Nonconformist traditions, but there was also a counter-current which included the Oxford Movement within the Established Church. In part this was a theological reaction to the fervour and the 'Low-Church' implications of the evangelical approach to religion; in part also it resulted from resentment at the increasing willingness of the secular State to interfere in the affairs of the Established Churches.

The protagonists of this movement emphasized the importance of the Church as a divinely ordained institution, and stressed the importance of the sacraments and the clergy possessed of the apostolic succession from the days of primitive Christianity. The concept of a society in which Church and State were complementary authorities was endangered by such actions as the setting up of a royal commission in 1832 to investigate the revenues of the Church of England. The fact that this intervention was encouraged by such leading clerics as the Bishop of London, C. J. Blomfield, did nothing to reassure the champions of the Established Church's independent authority.

The willingness of Parliament to interfere in religious matters increased as the years went by. The Tithe Commutation Act, the introduction of civil registration of births, deaths, and marriages, and the Act which gave permanent status to the Ecclesiastical Commission, thereby giving a body with a majority of laymen control over the Church's property, all encroached upon ecclesiastical authority. In 1837 the Whig government even tried to abolish the parochial church rates altogether, though this was frustrated by the House of Lords.

Oxford University, where theological discussion and argument was a major interest, became the principal centre of the 'High-Church' response. A series of 'Tracts for the Times', which expressed this reaction against both lay interference and evangelical tendencies, began in 1833. As the Oxford Movement continued to stress the unique importance of the Established Church, a fillip was given to anti-State Church agitation among dissenters. The Religious Freedom Society of 1838 and the more militant and vociferous Anti-State Church Association of 1844 added to the increasing volume of religious dissension. It was widely believed that views such as those pressed by the Oxford Movement involved a danger to Protestantism in general. Some of the leading members of the Oxford Movement, such as Dr Pusey, always remained within the Anglican communion, but the conversion of the prominent clergyman and scholar John Henry Newman to Roman Catholicism in 1845 fed the suspicion that the High-Church party represented romanizing tendencies. These fears were heightened when in the Maynooth affair of 1845 the British State showed itself willing to subsidize a Roman Catholic institution (see pp. 180–1 above).[106] Evangelicals both Anglican and Nonconformist came together to form the Evangelical Alliance in 1846, to defend the Protestant tradition against these dangers.

---

106. W. O. Chadwick, *The Victorian Church*, vol. i (1966); A. D. Gilbert, *Religion and Society in Industrial England: Church, Chapel and Social Change, 1740–1914* (1976), ch. 7.

These dissensions were not confined to theological dispute. In January 1845 a curate of High-Church persuasion insisted on wearing a surplice when preaching at Exeter; in a strongly evangelical area this provoked the hostile reaction of a crowd of about 2,000, and the clergyman concerned had to be given police protection. A serious anti-Catholic riot at Stockport in 1851 saw 1 death and 100 serious injuries. Roman Catholic chapels were sacked; 62 arrests were made, and a ringleader in the violent affray received a sentence of 15 years' transportation.[107] The establishment at mid-century of a new Roman Catholic episcopate in Britain provoked a major outbreak of anti-Catholic feeling, in which government and Parliament participated (see pp. 187–8 above).

Religious controversies created a great deal of noise, and engaged the energies of the most fervent partisans involved. Most early-Victorian religious life was less controversial. Within the Church of England, reform by the use of the political power of the State was welcomed by many clergymen as a necessary purification. Bishop Blomfield was one of the key figures here, and in his London diocese he encountered problems in his relations with adherents of the Oxford Movement. He also played a part in linking the Church with schemes for social amelioration. In a sermon preached before the royal family in 1832, he emphasized that it was a religious duty for those in authority to act to 'increase the comforts and improve the moral character of the masses'. In another sermon he told his congregation that they should appreciate that it was 'certain that persons immersed in hopeless misery and filth were for the most part inaccessible ... to the gospel'.[108]

Evangelicals were often found in the forefront of social reform movements because of this belief that those steeped in misery and disease were unable to devote time and energy to discovering God. Lord Shaftesbury's reforming zeal sprang directly from his determination to 'stand by that which alone was the pillar and the ground of the truth—the Bible, the whole Bible and nothing but the Bible'. Reforming governments were well aware that the religious implications of their proposals might arouse energies which could produce dangerous upsets. Sir James Graham as Home Secretary took great pains in trying to forestall such trouble in the preparation of the 1842 Factory Bill. Advance copies were sent to the Archbishop of Canterbury and other bishops known to be concerned with such questions. This attempt to conciliate the Established Church, and the privileged position accorded to Anglican authority in the management of the proposed factory schools, instead aroused a level of Nonconformist opposition which wrecked Graham's intentions.[109]

One of the most important ecclesiastical events of the 1840s took place in Scotland. A prolonged internal dispute within the Established Presbyterian Church about the presentation of ministers by lay patrons culminated in 1843 in

107. Stevenson, *Popular Disturbances in England*, 279.
108. Smith, *The People's Health*, 218, 230.
109. N. Gash, *Sir Robert Peel* (1972), 376–7; T. L. Crosby, *Sir Robert Peel's Administration, 1841–1846* (1976), 66.

a massive 'Disruption'. Out of a total of about 1,200 ministers of the Church of Scotland, 450 withdrew from it, and by 1847 the new Free Church of Scotland had contrived to establish about 700 churches of its own. In Scotland this event outweighed any other development of the decade and produced far-reaching results, including an increased need for reform of the provision for the poor, something which had been very much left to the Established Church in earlier years.

Religious affairs were important and occupied much public attention in the society of those years. Much historical discussion has been directed to such questions as the nature and extent of the evangelical revival among the poorer elements in society. In addition, however, some studies have drawn attention to the ways in which the religious revivals of these years affected many within the dominant minorities in Britain, with significant consequences on the ways in which they chose to use their power.[110] In these years genuine religious fervour exercised a major influence upon the lives of millions of men, women, and children drawn from all levels of society, without establishing complete dominance at any level.

The solitary official religious census of 1851 provides us with the best clue to the actual extent of religious observance, even though its evidence is flawed. Attendance at church or chapel cannot give a satisfactory measurement of religious feeling. It was shocking to many people to discover that more than 40 per cent of the whole population did not attend any place of worship, though it is of greater interest to us that the majority did. The proportion of church attendances varied. For the devout it was worrying that the level of attendance was low, and often very low, in some of the growing centres of population like Manchester, Liverpool, and Birmingham. The opponents of the Church of England could take comfort in that the 1851 census showed that the Anglican claim to be the national Church was vulnerable; if the Established Church produced 3.8 million attendances on census Sunday, other sects collectively saw 3.5 million, while in most of the large industrial centres Anglicans were in a minority. If in the rural south-east the Church of England enjoyed a 2 to 1 majority, its score fell to 1 in 5 for Wales, where evangelical Nonconformity was strong. In Yorkshire, the dissenters recorded twice as many attendances as the Anglicans. It was also clear that religious observance was much weaker among the poorer elements in society than among more respectable folk, and this too was worrying to the champions of religion. However disappointing the 1851 figures were for the devout, they leave no doubt that religion was still among the most pervasive influences within that society, and that the building and operation of churches and chapels was one of the most important activities of the day. No secular political movement could match the extent of Christianity's appeal.

110. I. Bradley, *The Call to Seriousness* (1976). The 1851 religious census results appear in *Report on the 1851 Census of Religious Worship*, Parliamentary Papers (1852–3), 89, and a commentary on them is K. S. Inglis, 'Patterns of religious worship in 1851', *Journal of Ecclesiastical History*, 11 (1960), 74–86.

Philanthropy

The continuing importance of religion remained a force behind the proliferation of charitable institutions. Medical charities continued to multiply, even if the prevailing level of medical science meant that their effectiveness was limited. The regulations governing such institutions continued to reflect contemporary social attitudes. It was normal for voluntary dispensaries to exclude domestic servants (whose masters were properly responsible for their care), paupers (for whom the Poor Law was the correct agency for medical treatment), individuals entitled to obtain medical care at the expense of their friendly societies, or families in receipt of what were considered incomes adequate to pay for medical facilities. Many hospitals excluded people suffering from diseases known to be seriously contagious, an understandable precaution in the light of contemporary inability to limit infection within a crowded institution.[111] The number of voluntary hospitals continued to grow. By 1843 London had more than twenty maternity hospitals, even if the level of facilities they provided would not have been regarded as anything like satisfactory by later generations. Probably about 4,000 women a year were treated in these institutions in the early-Victorian period.[112]

It was still exceptional for the State to take any decisive action in matters of health, except on occasions of national peril such as the visitations of cholera. The action of the new Poor Law Commission in establishing more systematic medical treatment for paupers after 1834 was that body's administrative decision (see p. 211 above). The Vaccination Act of 1840 was an exception to Parliament's general inaction in such matters; there the recently revamped administrative machinery of the Poor Law provided a convenient and inexpensive way of encouraging vaccination against smallpox. It took thirteen years, however, before the legislature could be persuaded to make vaccination compulsory. Even then the measure was attacked by libertarians, and often evaded in practice.

The expanding philanthropic activity of the 1830–50 period, following on the advances of earlier years, was varied in time and place. It was not able to prevent a great deal of suffering in a period of limited medical understanding, rapid population growth, and drastic economic and social change. It did, however, demonstrate that this was not a society in which callousness reigned unchallenged.

The ameliorative measures attempted were not always implemented competently; that leading philanthropist Lord Shaftesbury was once described by Disraeli as 'a kind of amiable bull in a china-shop of good intentions'. Much misery and hardship was left untouched, but if the record is compared either with that of earlier generations in Britain or with contemporary societies elsewhere it is far from discreditable. The history of philanthropy has been defined as the 'history of kindness'[113] and recent work has emphasized help given

---

111. Smith, *The People's Health*, 73, 252.   112. Ibid. 34–5.
113. F. K. Prochaska, *The Voluntary Impulse: Philanthropy in Modern Britain* (1988), 7.

within communities, the role of those women released from domestic tasks by their employment of servants, and the reinterpretation of aristocratic paternalism in these years.[114] If the Dickensian Christmas, which developed in the 1840s,[115] celebrated one major theme in Victorian society, the family, it also addressed the new emphasis on the need for charity and fellowship. Despite the strains placed on British society in these years, its inner cohesion, while occasionally showing signs of stress, never came within measurable distance of breaking.

Popular leisure

Too great an emphasis upon seriousness, sobriety, the work ethic, and improvement can give a false impression of developments in British society in the 1830s and 1840s. People were attracted to towns by higher wages but also by the prospect of more varied leisure pursuits. There was a buzz to the life of towns and, instead of fields, muddy lanes, the village inn, and the occasional fair or visit by itinerant entertainers, there were gas-lit pubs, street entertainers, hippodromes, and singing and dancing. The entrepreneurs of popular leisure catered for all classes, sometimes at the same place and time, though there were usually separate sections at differential prices. A hedonistic pursuit of pleasure, marketed with commercial skill, was the other side of life. Historians, like early Victorians, have found it difficult to come to terms with the extremes and contrasts of British society as mid-century was approached.

Popular culture demonstrated considerable continuity and resilience in the face of attempts to improve the mores and pastimes of the people. Moralists, improvers, and rational recreationalists did their best and had their victories, the abolition of many fairs and annual events such as bull-runnings and violent and rule-less 'football matches', while cock-fighting and bare-fisted boxing were driven underground. Such victories were marginal as the business of leisure was adaptable.[116] The more sensible reformers realized that positive alternatives had to be found and the result was the Mechanics Institutes and the entertainments provided by Temperance Societies. Thomas Cook organized the first of his railway excursions in 1841 to take 3,000 children from Leicester to Derby so that they would escape the evil temptations of Leicester on race-day. It must also be noted that railway excursions to view public executions were also popular. A start was made in the provision of public parks with the government purchase of Primrose Hill in 1842 and Battersea Park in 1846 while, outside London, Birkenhead and Manchester Parks were opened in the same decade. Both the Museums Act of

114. D. Roberts, *Paternalism in Early Victorian England* (1979).
115. J. M. Golby and A. W. Purdue, *The Making of the Modern Christmas* (2000), ch. 3.
116. H. Cunningham, *Leisure in the Industrial Revolution, c.1780–1880* (1980); P. Bailey, *Leisure and Class in Victorian England: Rational Recreation and the Contest for Control 1830–1885* (1978).

1845 and the Public Libraries Act of 1850 gave local authorities permission to build museums and libraries out of the local rates. When some were built they were not always well-patronized, though parks were popular when not over-regulated. When well-meaning reformers in Birmingham sponsored a three-penny concert at the People's Hall and it was badly attended, their conclusion was that 'the working classes did not appreciate even such a cheap and rational amusement as that'.[117]

Rural sports and pastimes transferred and were adapted to the urban environment. The public house remained the main focus for entertainment. Skittle alleys were usually appendages to public houses as were rat pits while betting on horse, rowing, or pedestrian races took place there. The music halls were emerging from the entertainment rooms of drinking establishments and maintained both the link with drink and the rowdy and bawdy atmosphere of their origins.

The life of the streets of major towns and especially London was characterized by vendors of food, street entertainers, and innumerable prostitutes, at once a colourful canvas and challenge to the novelist whose books would circulate in respectable homes but who, like Dickens, would have to disguise salient features. There was a hierarchy amongst prostitutes as among other professions and a rising and falling. Rising is illustrated by the famous 'Skittles' Walters, one of those Cyprian horsewomen, who attracted clients and protectors as they rode through Hyde Park; her nickname was supposedly due to her father's proprietorship of a skittle alley but she was kept in luxury by a succession of aristocratic protectors, including the future Duke of Devonshire. At the other end of the scale was the archetypal fallen woman, diseased, drab, and doomed to an early death. Such was the lot of some, though a not dissimilar fate awaited many poor women who were not prostitutes. The oldest profession shared with newer professions the concept of human capital but the capital diminished with age and ill-health.

The term the 'other Victorians' has sometimes been used to describe those sections of society who did not subscribe to or disobeyed that image and code which has become synonymous with 'Victorian'. In fact there was no single set of Victorian attitudes or values although certain moral precepts were rarely publicly questioned, however often they were ignored. British society at mid-century was a mass of contradictions; most societies have been the same and have encompassed great contrasts between the rich and poor and between their formal ethos and the real way of their world but few found such difficulty in reconciling them.

117. D. A. Reid, 'The Decline of St Monday', *Past and Present*, No. 71, 1976, 79.

Part III

7

Political developments

1852–1880

The Aberdeen coalition ministry

The general election of 1852 produced a House of Commons without a clear majority. The minority Conservative government which had been cobbled together after the collapse of Russell's ministry made some gains, but the allegiance of other newly elected members remained unclear. Optimistic calculations of Conservative strength put them at over 300. There were about 120 Whigs and 150 radicals on the opposition benches, although these terms were not very precise. A crucial balancing position was held by the Irish nationalists and the Peelites, both numbering 40 or slightly fewer.[1]

The fate of Derby's first ministry was sealed in the Budget debates in December 1852, when the other parties combined to reject Disraeli's proposals. The attacks made on the Conservative Budget by Peelites, and especially by Gladstone, made it clear that there could be no Conservative reunion in the near future. The Conservatives had, however, brought 286 MPs to the crucial division, which indicated that a coalition of opposition groups would be needed to create a viable administration.

Lord John Russell believed that he ought to be chosen to head the new ministry, but he had made too many enemies. Instead a coalition was formed under the Peelite Earl of Aberdeen; his Cabinet of thirteen was made up of six Peelites, six Whigs, and one radical. Sir William Molesworth was given the lowly Cabinet position of First Commissioner of Works, the first deliberate recognition of radical participation in government. Earlier radical ministers, such as Lord Durham in the 1830s, had been appointed because of their own personal importance. The relative insignificance of Molesworth's post indicated the continued predominance of the older governing groups.

The problems associated with the prickly relations between the two senior Whig politicians were apparently solved by making Russell Foreign Secretary and

---

1. R. Blake, *Disraeli* (1966), 322; J. B. Conacher, *The Aberdeen Coalition, 1852–5* (1968) gives a full discussion of political events in these years as does Muriel Chamberlain, *Lord Aberdeen: A Political Biography* (1983).

Palmerston Home Secretary. The latter accepted his new position with reasonably good grace, although he would have preferred to return to the Foreign Office. Palmerston proved at least as competent at the Home Office as most mid-Victorian Home Secretaries. He remained no great admirer of either Russell or Aberdeen. Russell, nursing his own ambitions, was to prove a troublesome and disloyal colleague for Aberdeen, whose primacy he resented, while the developments which culminated in the Crimean War showed his limited ability in foreign affairs. Yet despite these problems, at its inception the Aberdeen coalition looked as if it contained the germ of a stable governing arrangement. Its parliamentary support included a clear majority in the existing House of Commons and at least a substantial minority in the Upper House. In its early months, too, the new ministry scored some significant successes, notably the widely admired Budget of 1853, which Gladstone, as Chancellor of the Exchequer, devised and piloted through in masterly style. A number of useful if unspectacular domestic reforms were also enacted before events abroad brought the ministry to an ignominious collapse.

The Crimean War

From summer 1853 onwards, Britain was drifting into war with Russia. Misunderstandings of discussions in 1844 about the future of Turkey lay behind the Tsar's belief that the Ottoman Empire was moving towards inevitable collapse and that he could bring pressure to bear there without arousing British hostility. In 1853 religious quarrels within the Turkish Empire induced Russia to demand recognition as protector of Turkey's Christian subjects. To the Tsar's surprise and disappointment, opposition was at once aroused in Britain and France. Both of these governments were unwilling to see any increase in Russian influence in the Near East. In so far as the British Cabinet had any formed policies in the early months of the crisis, they lay in hopes that the situation could be resolved without war. Perhaps Austria's interests in south-east Europe might induce that power to suggest some compromise solution which would have a restraining effect on Russia. Before these schemes could materialize Russia acted, by invading and occupying the Turkish provinces of Moldavia and Walachia (areas eventually incorporated in the later State of Romania). Western opinion hardened against Russia. After diplomatic attempts at compromise failed, the majority of the British Cabinet supported a proposal for a naval demonstration in support of Turkey. In September 1853, the British Mediterranean fleet, backed by French units, moved to a covering position in the straits below Constantinople.

Although the Tsar also favoured a peaceful solution if an acceptable compromise could be found, this proved elusive. In October 1853 the Turkish government, emboldened by the presence of the Anglo-French fleets and their assurance of Western support, presented Russia with an ultimatum demanding the immediate evacuation of occupied Turkish territory. Russia refused such an obvious surrender, and war was declared. On 30 November 1853 a Turkish squadron was annihilated in a Russian naval attack on the port of Sinope; this aroused an anti-Russian reaction in British public opinion, where the battle was stigmatized as a massacre.

During these transactions the British government had failed to give any clear indication to other powers of British intentions in the area of dispute. Ministers were divided; Aberdeen was anxious to push negotiations with Russia for a peaceful solution, while most of his colleagues were more bellicose. The Queen and Prince Albert repeatedly but unavailingly pointed out to ministers the dangers of allowing Turkey to take the bit between her teeth in the belief that Britain and France would have to back her up. In January 1854 the British and French fleets entered the Black Sea and Anglo-French pressure for Russian concessions to Turkey increased. The prolonged dispute, continuously ventilated in the newspapers of both Western powers, aroused patriotic fervour. Pushed by public opinion, in February 1854 Britain and France abandoned attempts to find a peaceful solution of the crisis and in March declared war on Russia.

The British armed forces were hopelessly unready for such a contest. Neither army nor navy had a body of vigorous and able senior commanders, and in both services the operational organization was seriously defective. The army had neither the numbers nor the experience for the mobilization of an effective expeditionary force, and was especially deficient in its transport, supply, and medical services. Derby's brief minority government had succeeded in 1852 in some reform of the militia system, but there was no effective way of mobilizing adequate reserve forces as a backup to the small professional army.

A few months after the war began, the Russians withdrew from the occupied Turkish provinces on the Danube after some military setbacks. To Russian anger, this was followed by a peaceful occupation of those areas by Austrian troops, which prevented any significant fighting between Russia and the Anglo-French expeditionary force which had been dispatched there. It was now difficult to find any worthwhile military objective for the allied forces, but in the late summer the decision was taken to transfer the expeditionary force to the Crimea with a view to destroying the Russian base at Sebastopol; arguably this would be a blow to the enemy and an increase in security for Turkey. The aim was to launch a swift attack on Sebastopol; a long campaign was never envisaged. The first allied landings took place in September 1854, but instead of an immediate assault on the enemy base the allied commanders inaugurated a formal siege. After a couple of months it became obvious that a quick solution was not to be obtained by such tactics, and a Crimean winter for the troops became inevitable. Bloody battles marked by heavy casualties, failures in professional generalship on both sides, and by the doggedly determined fighting qualities of the troops engaged, punctuated the siege.

When, from mid-November, the winter weather set in, the shortcomings in British Army organization came home to roost. Even when ample supplies lay in ships offshore, the army commissariat was incapable of ensuring that they reached the front-line troops. It was not until the spring of 1855 that progress in such matters had reached anything like an adequate state. In the meantime many more British soldiers had died from disease and neglect than the Russians had killed. Medical services had proved disastrously deficient. It took months before the efforts of many different agencies, including the gallant women who came out from Britain as nurses under such leaders as Florence Nightingale and Mary Stanley, could bring order into this chaos.[2] Even if the hapless officials responsible for such matters during the winter did not display high levels of competence, they were not primarily responsible for the administrative collapse. It was the fruit of decades of neglect, fostered by an economy-minded legislature and electorate. However, the men in office at the time bore most of the brunt of criticism, at least in the first instance. A growing volume of reports of appalling conditions began to reach home, partly in letters from the army, partly in dispatches from the newspaper correspondents covering the war. Increasing literacy and wider reading of newspapers made these reports influential in shaping public opinion.

Ironically, this publicity reached its peak at a time when the worst deficiencies had actually been remedied. The Russians had suffered at least as badly, and in September 1855 Sebastopol was finally taken and its fortifications destroyed. Meanwhile, at home the revelations of conditions in the Crimea during the 1854–5 winter had produced a political explosion.

The fall of the Aberdeen ministry

Having blundered into a war, the Aberdeen ministry now had the responsibility for the situation presented by forty years of neglect of the armed forces. This necessarily involved trying to introduce useful reforms at a time when the temporary disruption they involved was particularly damaging. A modest improvement is all that could be claimed for these efforts (see pp. 317–21 below). The attempts of the Aberdeen government to compress into a few months a mass of long overdue reforms in the armed forces (most of which had been suggested years earlier) did not succeed in pacifying public opinion. It was obvious that the government was merely reacting to the pressure of events. Some of the most outspoken critics came from among the ministry's original supporters. The old leaders of the Anti-Corn Law League, headed by Cobden and Bright, openly opposed the war and blamed the ministry for drifting into it. A war of this kind starkly offended their vision of a peaceful world in which free exchange gave rise to an economic interdependence which made armed conflict impossible. For them, the bloodshed in the Crimea could have been avoided by any reasonably

---

2. The work of the West Indian, Mary Seacole, who patriotically came out to the Crimea and using her own money set up a combined nursing, home, club, and restaurant for officers and men was recognized at the time but then forgotten until recently. See E. Anionwu, *A Short History of Mary Seacole: A Resource for Nurses and Students* (2005).

competent government. Yet Cobden and Bright in these matters spoke only for a small and unrepresentative faction. Even among British radicals, there were other and stronger voices. Since 1846, two lines in radical thinking had become evident. Besides that of the group headed by Cobden and Bright, which advocated the pacific conduct of international relationships and the substantial reduction of armaments, there was that of other radicals, less interested in such matters, who preferred to pursue their sympathies with the oppressed nationalities of Europe, such as the Poles, the Italians, and the Hungarians. The linchpin of the reactionary system of the Continent, set up after the failure of the 1848 revolutions, was provided by the Tsar and his armies. A war against Russia could be seen by someone like the radical MP J. A. Roebuck as a noble crusade; if Russia could be crushed then perhaps national freedom could rise again in Europe. Radicals who entertained these hopes were therefore appalled and infuriated by the growing volume of evidence of the ineptitude with which the Crimean campaign was conducted under an aristocratic government.

When Parliament met in January for the 1855 session, press reports of the state of the army had already produced a dangerous political situation. On 23 January Roebuck proposed that the House of Commons should appoint its own committee of inquiry into the conduct of the war; this was plainly equivalent to a motion of censure on the executive. Russell, the government's Leader of the House of Commons, promptly resigned, seriously damaging the ministry even before the debates on Roebuck's motion. Russell bore as much personal responsibility as anyone both for the inept drift into war and for the shortcomings of the armed forces. He was now widely regarded as an irresponsible deserter. At the end of January 1855, Roebuck's motion was carried against the government by 305 to 148 votes, one of the greatest humiliations ever experienced by a British administration. The resignation of the ministry immediately followed.

Palmerston's first government

The formation of a new government was not easy. The Queen sent for Derby, but he could not obtain the adherence of any significant politicians outside his own party and gave up the attempt, knowing that a Conservative ministry formed in these circumstances must be weak, which was not what the country needed in the midst of a war. An attempt by Russell to form a ministry merely showed the decline in his own reputation, for few men of standing were prepared to support his return to the premiership. Finally the Queen commissioned Palmerston to form an administration. Of all the senior ministers in the Aberdeen government, he had emerged with least damage to his reputation, though of course bearing his share of responsibility for recent events.

Palmerston succeeded in producing a revised version of the Aberdeen coalition, omitting a few ministers such as Aberdeen himself and his army minister, the Duke of Newcastle, who seemed most damaged by the attacks on the previous administration. At first, with some hesitation, the other Peelite ministers, including Gladstone and Graham, agreed to stay in office. Palmerston tried to persuade Roebuck and the House of Commons to drop the committee of inquiry into the conduct of the war, as a sign of confidence in the new ministry, but his pleas were rejected and he had to accept this decision. His Peelite ministers, however, saw the House of Commons' persistence as a deliberate censure of the previous Cabinet and insisted on resigning.

In the early months of 1856, after the death of Tsar Nicholas and the fall of Sebastopol, peace negotiations were set on foot, which by March succeeded in bringing the war to an end on terms reasonably satisfactory to Britain. Despite the criticisms which had been launched against the system of government dominated by the aristocracy, there was no major shift in the balance of power within British society. The revelations of official disorganization and ineptitude in 1854–5 produced a violent radical outcry against aristocratic misgovernment, but the fruits of the noisy campaign for 'administrative reform' were meagre (see pp. 315–17 below).

The Second China War

Although peace had returned to Europe, the first Palmerston government was soon embattled elsewhere. The outbreak of the Indian Mutiny in 1857 coincided with a crisis in the Far East, which meant that British forces were already on their way there when the Mutiny broke out. Relations between Britain and China had been deteriorating for some time, and fighting began in October 1856. Both parties believed that they had legitimate grievances; Chinese officials were reported to have encouraged the killing of Europeans, including Britons, while the business practices of European merchants were not always fair or honest. The Chinese Empire was manifestly weak, but tried to maintain pretensions of superiority to all other States. Ironically, the British agent on the spot, Sir John Bowring, who was responsible for the outbreak of hostilities, had been in earlier years a free trade radical associated with Cobden in the Anti-Corn Law League. He was now much more aggressive in his views. Bowring's relations with the Chinese authorities at Canton were rarely cordial; there were faults on both sides. In October 1856 Chinese officers boarded a small vessel named the *Arrow* and arrested some of her crew who were accused of being pirates. The ship had been registered in Hong Kong and was flying the British flag at the time, although her registration had in fact expired. Bowring chose to regard this as an affront; when the Canton authorities refused his demands for the return of the arrested men, an apology, and compensation, he brought in British warships which bombarded the city. Open war between the two powers resulted.

The *Arrow* affair was only the last of a series of incidents which had brought friction between Britain and China. These had included brutal murders of British subjects and other Europeans, including a French missionary, as well as the flouting of Chinese authority by British merchants seeking to exploit and extend the commercial opportunities wrung from China at the end of the previous war. Bowring's drastic action in October 1856 seemed, however, to rest on a flimsy foundation. Although privately well aware of this, ministers concluded that they had no real choice but to back up their distant representative in a difficult situation, and accepted responsibility for the outbreak of hostilities.

When the news of the outbreak of war in the East reached Britain, with details of Bowring's provocative behaviour, a political crisis ensued. In the House of Commons, Cobden moved a resolution censuring the government for its persistence in an unjust war. In early March 1857, after one of the finest parliamentary debates of the century, the censure motion was carried by a majority of sixteen, with many of the government's nominal supporters either in the hostile lobby or abstaining. The temper of the Commons majority on this issue was not in step with public opinion, much of which shared the doubts entertained by some parliamentarians. Chichester Fortescue, a well-connected and sensible Whig politician, had noted in his diary on the last day of February that

I was, and am still, very much provoked at Bowring's conduct, and at first had some inclination to vote with Cobden before I heard his speech, merely to condemn Bowring. But Cobden's speech, Bulwer's, and indeed all the speakers on that side of the question, made it more and more impossible for me to have anything to do with Cobden. They were so un-English, so ingeniously unfair against ourselves and in defence of the Chinese.[3]

Instead of resigning, Palmerston obtained a dissolution of Parliament. In the ensuing general election, although he did not sweep the field, Palmerston's position was effectively endorsed by the mid-Victorian electorate. The principal opponents of the China War, including Cobden at Huddersfield and Bright at Manchester, lost their seats, and the government's parliamentary position seemed to be strengthened.

The outbreak of the Indian Mutiny in the early summer of 1857 necessitated the diversion of troops sent to the East, but with the suppression of the Mutiny by early 1858, the war against China was energetically pursued. France had her own grievances against China which brought her into the war as a British ally. In June 1858 China was brought to sign a peace treaty embodying further commercial concessions to the allies, but these preliminaries were not fulfilled. There was renewed fighting, with some temporary setbacks for the allies, and the murder of four British envoys by the Chinese. In October 1860 the allied armies entered Peking in triumph, after looting and destroying the Emperor's summer palace near the capital. Later in that month the imperial Chinese government surrendered, agreeing to implement the earlier treaty, and to pay the allies an indemnity which more than covered the cost of the war to them. Further British intervention in the Far East came in 1862, with the dispatch to Japan of a British force to

---

3. N. McCord, 'Cobden and Bright in politics, 1846–1857', in R. Robson (ed.), *Ideas and Institutions of Victorian Britain: Essays Presented to G. Kitson Clark* (1967), 111.

ensure the payment of substantial compensation for the recent murder there of a British citizen; this expedition also secured the opening of Japanese ports to British trade.

Palmerston's electoral victory of 1857 proved unexpectedly short-lived. In January 1858 there was an attempt to assassinate Napoleon III in Paris. This failed in its main object but the explosion killed or maimed a number of innocent bystanders. Not surprisingly, the French government complained to London when it became clear that the bombing had been the work of Italian refugees living in Britain. It then transpired that a defect in British criminal law prevented prosecution for conspiring in Britain to commit a murder outside British juris-diction. The Palmerston government introduced a Conspiracy to Murder Bill to rectify this, and found itself denounced by a motley collection of opponents for undue subservience to Napoleonic France. The normally pacific John Bright, who had returned to Parliament in a recent by-election at Birmingham, affected to denounce Palmerston for 'truckling to France'. In a confused parliamentary situation, the second reading of the proposed bill was defeated; with Parliament less than a year old, a general election would be unwelcome if an alternative government could be formed, and the Palmerston administration resigned.

Derby's second ministry

Lord Derby now formed his second minority government, but this could not last long unless it could acquire more strength. The Conservative ministry hung on into 1859, with some achievements to its credit, such as the admission of Jews to Parliament, the abolition of the property qualification for MPs (the first of the six points of the People's Charter to be implemented), and the successful piloting through as a non-party measure of a reformed scheme for the government of India in the aftermath of the Mutiny.

For its main legislation of the 1859 session, the Conservative Cabinet decided to introduce a parliamentary reform measure. Although this was drafted with an eye to improving Conservative electoral chances, it demonstrated that the 1832 settlement was no longer seen as final. Russell had, despite his nickname of 'Finality Jack' and an absence of enthusiasm on Palmerston's part, already adopted the policy of moderate parliamentary reform and had introduced bills in 1852 and 1854 which aroused little interest. The Crimean War had then overtaken these efforts. The Conservative Reform Bill of 1859 signalled that both possible governing groups were no longer committed to defending the 1832 dispensation. There was no reason why the Conservatives should feel any great need to preserve electoral arrangements which had only once, in 1841, provided them with a parliamentary majority.

The Conservative attempt to increase support by embracing parliamentary reform failed. The bill was too obviously in the government's party interest, and the opposition groups managed to combine to defeat it in March 1859. A general election followed in May; the Conservatives made a number of gains, returning more than 300 MPs for the first time since 1841. The Peelites were now shrinking as a distinct group, and most of the twenty-two returned in 1859 were soon to be absorbed into the emerging Liberal Party. The Conservative gains were still short of a majority and in June 1859 the ministry was ejected when the opposition groups came to an agreement which led to Palmerston's return to the premiership.

Palmerston's second ministry

The Liberal government formed in 1859 represented a deliberate consolidation of the various liberal groups in British politics—Whigs, radicals of various shades, Peelites, and Irish nationalists. Palmerston tried hard to conciliate Liberal politicians who had opposed him in the past. He offered Cobden a seat in the Cabinet as President of the Board of Trade; although Cobden maintained that their past differences had been so intense that this offer could not be accepted, he was otherwise willing to accept Palmerston's leadership of a united Liberal front. Gladstone and some other leading Peelites agreed to join the new ministry. For the remainder of Palmerston's life the political alliance established in 1859 kept him in power.

During those years political life seemed tranquil. The Conservatives were unable to cause much trouble to the ministry, and Palmerston's personal prestige and popularity remained high. Internally, the new Liberal Cabinet was not without its problems. At the Exchequer, Gladstone advocated a continued reduction in taxation. This stance was broadly acceptable to his colleagues, but on two counts its implementation was less simple. Like most economizing Chancellors, Gladstone saw in the annual defence estimates, still a major element in government spending, one easy source for saving. Palmerston was not prepared to sacrifice national security to financial expediency, and insisted on maintaining higher levels of spending on defence than Gladstone wanted. The revolutionary changes in naval design seemed to have increased the danger that a hostile France might employ her growing fleet of steam warships in a surprise attack on British naval bases. Palmerston was determined that those bases should receive new fortifications. Some of the Conservative Opposition, including Disraeli, tried to exploit ministerial divisions by posing as opponents of excessive expenditure on armaments. In the event, Palmerston had his way, despite the reluctance of his Chancellor of the Exchequer.

In his financial proposals for 1860, which marked a substantial reduction in indirect taxation, Gladstone included a long-standing radical demand, the abolition of the duties on paper which increased the cost of publications of all kinds. This apparently innocuous proposal unexpectedly sparked off a constitutional crisis. At that time the annual Budget procedure involved a Commons debate on resolutions outlining the Chancellor's proposals; once these were approved, their technical implementation was carried out by framing a number of Finance Bills which were then passed into legislation, usually with little difficulty. Constitutional convention held that the House of Lords would not initiate or amend a financial bill, but retained the right to reject it. In 1860 the Conservative majority in the Upper House chose to reject the specific bill framed to abolish the paper duties. The ostensible reason given was reluctance to accept a reduction in revenue while British forces were still engaged in an expensive war with China; probably an absence of enthusiasm for cheap publications was a more important motive.

Gladstone was furious, and by threats of resignation forced the Cabinet to endorse his tough response. Despite Palmerston's barely concealed indifference, he induced the House of Commons to pass resolutions warning the Lords that such interference in financial business was unwise and resented. In 1861 Gladstone altered the Budget procedures, embodying all of the year's financial proposals, including the repeal of the paper duties, in one omnibus bill, more or less daring the House of Lords to reject the entire Budget. The peers, despite much grumbling at such coercive tactics, chose to swallow the affront. The encounter played a part in Gladstone's emergence as a popular Liberal politician, and also seemed to have vindicated the supremacy of the House of Commons in financial matters.

Apart from Gladstone's successes in the financial sphere, which included a substantial reduction in the remaining duties on imports, the Palmerston government in its latter years was responsible for a continuing flow of reforming legislation. In a rather torpid political climate, these rarely caused much in the way of conflict, and they have in consequence been undervalued in comparison with the more hectic period which followed. Some of the reforming statutes of these years took the humdrum but essential form of consolidating and codifying masses of earlier piecemeal legislation. This was true of the criminal law enactments of 1861 and the great Companies Act of 1862. The Poor Law was significantly if undramatically overhauled and reformed by such measures as the Union Chargeability Act of 1865 (see p. 332 below). Factory reform, local government reform, law reform, and public health reform continued in solid if unspectacular fashion.

The last years of Palmerstonian Britain were not, however, devoid of excitement. The relative tranquillity of an Ireland experiencing a slow but real recovery from the catastrophe of the Great Famine of the 1840s was broken by the recrudescence of nationalist violence by the militant Fenians both in Ireland and in Great Britain. Abroad the precarious peace of Europe was broken in 1864 by a conflict between Denmark and the German powers over the duchies of Schleswig and Holstein. This episode was one from which Palmerston and his colleagues emerged with little credit, for they gave verbal expressions of support for Denmark which proved worthless when Bismarck called their bluff. The Parliament elected in 1859 ended not because of any political crisis but because of the approaching expiry of its maximum legal term. At the general election held in July 1865 the government made a few gains at the expense of their Conservative opponents, but there was little excitement. In general the British public seemed satisfied with the benign rule of the octogenarian Palmerston. His death in October 1865 ushered in important changes in the political world. Gladstone's success as Chancellor had enhanced his status, and he had been during the past few years at pains to project a more popular image. But Palmerston's immediate successor was his senior colleague, the elderly Lord Russell, although it was plain that his tenure of the premiership could not be a long one.

The reform crisis of 1866–1867

Russell's determination to crown his career by enacting a second parliamentary reform ushered in a political crisis. The majority of the political nation no longer regarded the 1832 Reform Act as having any claim to permanence. By 1865 both Liberal and Conservative ministries had attempted a further instalment of reform, as yet without success.

When the parliamentary session of 1866 opened, the Russell government had thrashed out a set of moderate reform proposals. The property qualification for the borough vote, fixed in 1832 at £10, was to be lowered to £7, and the occupancy qualification in the counties from £50 to £14. A narrow voting category would enfranchise perhaps 60,000 men who were not householders but lived in expensive lodgings. A vote could also be earned by maintaining a £50 deposit in a savings bank. Overall the Cabinet surmised that their proposals would add a total of about 400,000 new voters. A modest measure of redistribution of seats was also proposed; 49 small boroughs would lose their separate representation, with 26 of the suppressed seats going to the counties and 22 to the boroughs. The growth of the University of London was to be recognized by the grant of a single seat for which its graduates would provide the electorate.

Modest though they were, these proposals provoked serious opposition. The House of Commons elected in 1865 had been returned to support Palmerston rather than to forward parliamentary reform. Some of the government's nominal supporters opposed the bill. Although the reformers of the 1850s and 1860s were happy to adopt an optimistic assessment of recent social progress, this roseate view was not universally shared, even on the government benches. During the discussion of the 1866 reform proposals, the Conservative Opposition left much of the running in debate to dissentient Liberals. The most active of these was Robert Lowe, who had seen the rough-and-ready practice of a political system with a wide franchise at work in Australia, and had not enjoyed the experience. On his return to Britain he had entered politics in 1852 as MP for Kidderminster; this was a rough borough, and in 1857 Lowe received a nasty injury there during a political meeting. In 1859 he thankfully changed constituencies to sit for what was still effectively Lord Lansdowne's pocket borough of Calne. Lowe's opposition to the reform proposals of 1866 was in part inspired by his appreciation that there remained much that was rough and barbaric in British society, as against the optimism displayed by such reformers as Gladstone, but there was more to his arguments than this negative aspect. Even the keener reformers of 1866 did not see the franchise as a natural right which ought to be enjoyed by every adult male; instead, they aimed at an extended but selective electorate. For Lowe, however, the concept of the vote, not as a right but as a valuable privilege to be earned or deserved, went further. In his view the 1832 franchises were broad enough, in that they were accessible to any man who worked hard and displayed responsibility and thrift. He also pointed to the fact that the number of voters was increasing in any case as more and more men qualified as £10 householders. The franchise could be socially useful if seen as an incentive, a status to be gained by the exercise of virtue; it was, as Lowe contended, 'a lever to raise men'.

In a series of skilful contributions to the 1866 reform debates, Lowe rallied a band of Liberal MPs to reject their leaders' proposals. Government majorities sank to critical levels as the debates proceeded, until in June a Conservative amendment, cleverly worded so as to bring in forty-eight dissentient Liberals, was carried during the committee stage of the bill. It was plain that the government's principal legislation could not be enacted, and after some hesitation the Russell Cabinet resigned.

The third Derby government

Derby now formed his third minority Conservative ministry, after some half-hearted negotiations with the dissident Liberals who had helped to bring about the previous government's defeat. Once again the Conservatives had only a precarious hold on office, since if the various opposition groups came together they would be defeated. Both Derby and Disraeli came to the conclusion that the only way to retain the political initiative was to take over the cause of parliamentary reform. A colourable basis for doing so could be found in the decision of the House of Commons to accept the principle of reform by giving a second reading to the previous government's bill. In addition the Conservatives could not be seen as enemies of reform in view of their own unsuccessful proposals of 1859.

There were, however, serious problems to surmount, since the new Cabinet was not united in its attitude to reform. A group of right-wing ministers was hostile to any extensive reform, and soon became suspicious of the intentions of Derby and Disraeli. Disraeli's first idea was to proceed by way of resolutions in the House of Commons rather than a government bill, but when it became clear that this would lead to defeat it was decided to propose a bill. The government's difficult parliamentary position and internal divisions resulted in tricky manoeuvring by the two Conservative leaders, until they decided that they could afford to incur some defections from the Cabinet and press on with definite proposals. Lord Cranborne (the future Conservative leader as Lord Salisbury),

Lord Carnarvon, and General Peel (a younger son of the Prime Minister Sir Robert Peel) resigned early in March 1867, and Disraeli embarked upon a remarkable parliamentary tour de force to keep the new Reform Bill alive and with it the Conservative ministry.[4] Once again Liberal disunity provided a key element. Gladstone could not believe that Derby and Disraeli were sincere in their reforming stance, and wanted to kill the Conservative proposals. He could not control all of his followers in the House of Commons, however, and Disraeli exploited Liberal disunity brilliantly. A group of radical MPs, including James Clay, who had been a close friend of Disraeli in their unregenerate youth, had thought the Liberal Reform Bill of 1866 much too moderate. They now entered into a tacit understanding with Disraeli, to prevent Gladstone from wrecking the new Reform Bill if the Conservatives would in return accept amendments which widened its scope.

The government's proposals passed through several versions before the last of a series of bills was introduced in March 1867. It was not very different from the abortive Liberal proposals of the previous year, embodying some general lowering of the 1832 borough and county franchises, together with some specific 'fancy franchises' to be earned by such publicly useful qualities as the payment of income tax or a thrifty deposit in a savings bank. These latter proposals were in line with the general belief that it was desirable to reward the thrifty and worthy and with the ideas of John Stuart Mill.[5]

In April, Gladstone made a determined attempt to kill the bill on its second reading, moving an amendment which was designed to bring the radicals back into line. The bill proposed that the new borough franchise should be limited to householders who paid their own rates. This would deprive poorer householders of the vote in many towns because of the practice of 'compound householding', whereby the landlord paid the rates in a lump sum, while the tenant met the cost more conveniently as a small regular addition to his rent. Gladstone's amendment would have given the vote to all borough householders, but Clay and his radical group rejected this proffered bait and kept to their informal alliance with the government. Gladstone's defeat, with forty-five Liberal MPs voting against him, was an unmistakable setback.

During the committee stage of the bill Disraeli allowed the radicals to obtain their reward. Amendments widened the bill until it became a more extensive reform than the Liberal bill of the previous year. Thinking on his feet, Disraeli opposed amendments he thought he could beat, accepted amendments which he could not defeat, and throughout prevented Gladstone from pulling the Opposition majority together. Among the successful amendments were the

4. Blake, *Disraeli*, ch. 21. The reform crisis of 1866–7 produced an important crop of centenary studies, including E. J. Feuchtwanger, *Disraeli, Democracy and the Tory Party* (1965); F. B. Smith, *The Making of the Second Reform Bill* (1966); M. J. Cowling, *1867: Disraeli, Gladstone and Revolution: The Passing of the Second Reform Bill* (1967).

5. J. S. Mill, *Considerations on Representative Government* (1861).

reduction of the period of residence necessary for the vote from two years to one, and the addition of a limited voting qualification for those occupying expensive lodgings. Amidst the confusion of the debates the Conservative leadership kept the support of the overwhelming majority of their own party; 'Their bemused followers scarcely knew to what they were committing themselves other than that it was a measure recommended by their own leaders rather than one introduced by the hated Gladstone.'[6]

The most important incident during the confused debates on the Reform Bill's committee stage took place on 17 May. The borough franchise was still complicated by the problem of the compound householders; this system of paying rates rested upon permissive legislation which had been adopted by some towns but not by others. Gladstone still hoped to use this difficulty to defeat the bill, but his scheming was forestalled by a proposal by a backbencher. Grosvenor Hodgkinson, MP for Newark, suggested that the problem be avoided by simply abolishing the system of compounding for rates. His proposal, making the personal payment of rates by householders compulsory, was accepted by Disraeli, who saw here a chance of avoiding another dangerous manoeuvre against the bill by Gladstone. The decision to accept the amendment was taken by Disraeli on his own responsibility; such a concession had seemed so unlikely that only about 100 MPs were present at this crucial stage of the debates. This decision effectively brought household suffrage to the boroughs, and in itself probably added about half a million new voters. It was, however, a thoroughly unworkable device; the abolition of compounding threatened chaos in the finances of many local authorities. Within two years an amending statute was carried, restoring the practice of compounding without affecting the right to vote granted in 1867.

With the passage of the Hodgkinson amendment the remaining 'fancy franchises' ceased to be of much use as agencies of enfranchisement, and most of them were deleted. The Conservative measure encountered no difficulties in completing its remaining stages, with its third reading carried without a division in July. Derby's influence kept the House of Lords loyal, and before the end of 1867 the Reform Act for England and Wales reached the statute book after one of the most extraordinary legislative episodes in modern British history. Parallel Reform Acts for Scotland and Ireland followed within a few months. In addition an Act providing for a modest redistribution of parliamentary seats was passed. Of the seats taken away from small boroughs, the lion's share (25 out of 45) was given to the counties.

A third seat was given to Manchester, Liverpool, Leeds, and Birmingham. The House of Lords inserted an ingenious provision here, whereby electors in these cities could cast only 2 votes, in an attempt to ensure that a substantial minority might obtain representation by winning 1 of the 3 seats. Eleven new borough constituencies were created, and the University of London was given a single seat

6. N. Gash, *Pillars of Government, and Other Essays on State and Society, c.1770–1880* (1986), 61.

(choosing to elect Robert Lowe as its first MP). Scotland received an additional 7 seats, bringing the total to 60, 8 fewer than a strictly arithmetical settlement based on population would have warranted. The Scottish electorate was greatly extended, almost tripling in number. In Wales the electorate was almost doubled. Neither Ireland nor Wales received any additional seats.

Proposals for parliamentary reform in the 1850s and 1860s faced a practical problem already encountered in 1831–2. Most politicians were prepared to consider a widening of the electorate, but it was difficult to devise tests which would recruit the deserving without also admitting groups who might be useless or even dangerous. Much of the confusion surrounding the reform debates of 1866–7 derived from this. The legislation which resulted, like the 1832 Act, was an imperfect instrument for realizing the intentions of the reformers.

In England the enfranchisement of 1867 was most marked in the larger towns. In Birmingham the number of voters increased threefold, in Leeds fourfold, in Blackburn more than fivefold, and in most large towns the electorate at least doubled. With most urban householders now entitled to the vote, workers now provided a clear majority of borough voters. In the counties the lowering of the occupation franchise from £50 to £12 brought less striking results than in the towns. The overall addition of about a million new voters had important effects on the working of the political system. In the smaller constituencies, and in rural areas, it was possible for older conventions to persist, but the management of the larger urban electorates required more sophisticated agencies. Local party associations became more important, for MPs depended increasingly on party support to ensure that voters were persuaded to the polls. A striking instance of political organization is provided by Birmingham where the Liberal caucus, under the leadership of Joseph Chamberlain, was efficient enough to organize the dominant Liberal vote so that all three seats could be won despite each voter having only two votes.

The 1867–8 reform settlement was the product of confused debates and Disraeli's political sleight of hand. The legislation contained deficiencies in drafting which made its prolonged acceptance unlikely, as the abolition and speedy restoration of the system of compound householding showed. Another weakness concerned miners living in colliery houses. Whether or not a miner received the vote after 1867 rested on nothing more substantial than where his house happened to be; if in a borough he was enfranchised, but not if his house happened to fall within a county division. The new provisions for Scottish county voters were different from those for English county voters. The 1867–8 dispensation contained sufficient anomalies to encourage demands for further reform and more rational electoral arrangements. Several important clauses were so poorly drafted that their effect was not clarified until the next decade.

After 1846 the fluidity of the party situation and the instability of governments had given individual MPs considerable independence. The House of Commons collectively, rather than the electorate, was the decisive influence in determining changes in government. After the Second Reform Act, many MPs were more dependent on party support, and increasingly party discipline became tighter. For twenty years there was a clearer two-party situation, and even after the Liberal split over Home Rule in 1886 there was to be no return to the instability of the governments of the 1846–68 period.

Two groups were particularly bitter in their reaction to the passage of the parliamentary reform legislation of 1867–8. The right-wing Liberals like Robert Lowe, who had defeated their own leaders over reform, now saw their Conservative opponents unscrupulously enact a more extensive measure which they were powerless to prevent. On the other hand a group of right-wing Conservatives were appalled at what they saw, with some justice, as a want of Conservative principle on the part of their leaders. The future Lord Salisbury used the words 'political perfidy'. Certainly the creators of the settlement had no real idea of what its consequences would be and had been uncertain about the results which any specific provision for altering the franchise might entail. Still more uncertain was the question of how the new electors might choose to employ their votes. Each of the main parties could hope to be the principal beneficiary. The Conservatives might expect that the new electors would demonstrate gratitude; the Liberals could anticipate that a less wealthy and privileged electorate would not support a right-wing party.

The role played by 'noises off' the central stage of high politics has been much debated. Demands for parliamentary reform by radical organizations had been muted in the 1850s but in April 1864 a National Reform Union, a substantially middle-class body, was founded to be followed in February 1865 by the Reform League which had a membership that mainly consisted of skilled workers although a number of manufacturers supported it financially. The League pressed for extension of the franchise to every registered and resident adult male of sound mind and not convicted of a crime. As the debate over reform went on in Parliament, there were peaceful demonstrations throughout the country and a riot in Hyde Park in July 1866, when the Reform League insisted upon holding a demonstration despite a ban by the Home Secretary, followed by a further peaceful, if illegal, demonstration in the park in May 1867. Despite the claims of some historians that these demonstrations of radical support for reform were critical in pressurising the passing of the Reform Act,[7] most writing on the subject has seen the Act of 1867 as mainly the result of parliamentary manoeuvres for advantage and power, of unexpected and opportunistic alliances, and deft amendments.[8]

Particularly in the last years of his life, and in the following period when his posthumous reputation remained good, it was common for Disraeli to be

7. M. Beer, *History of British Socialism* (1921); R. Harrison, 'The Tenth April of Spencer Walpole: the Problem of Revolution in relation to Reform', *Before the Socialists: Studies in Labour and Politics 1861–1881* (1965).

8. See Cowling, *1867: Disraeli, Gladstone and Revolution*; Smith, *The Making of the Second Reform Bill*; and Blake, *Disraeli*.

credited with far-seeing wisdom as far as the 1867–8 reforms were concerned, the man who had discerned the 'angel in the marble', the working-class Conservative voter. The editor of *The Times* described the extension of the electorate as 'an experimental mining operation', designed to reach below the limited 1832 voters to find a new vein of Conservative support. It worked out like that in ensuing years, but modern studies of the reform crisis of 1866–8 have confirmed that Derby and Disraeli were at the time actuated by political expediency rather than constructive vision. Derby, who played a crucial role in the early stages of the Conservative move to reform, was old and in failing health, but still relished the sense of being on the crest of a wave and responsible for major events. That Disraeli was actuated by a desire to preserve the Conservative hold on office above any other considerations has been amply demonstrated by modern researches.

The 1867 measures may well have more than doubled the borough electorate in England and Wales and tripled it in Scotland, but the distinction between the borough and county franchises and the revision of seats which firmly demarcated county divisions from the boroughs were of clear party advantage to the Conservatives. Historical mythology, once established is, however, difficult to destroy and the idea that the 1867 reforms were in the interests of an abiding belief by Disraeli in 'One Nation' survives against the evidence.

To some extent the hopes of both of the major parties were realized. Immediately, the Liberals seemed to have benefited from the Second Reform Act, in their clear victory in the general election of 1868. In the longer term, however, the Conservatives proved the gainers. Whereas in aggregate the voters under the 1832 dispensation had given the forebears of the Liberals a clear margin in seats won, in the period between the Second and Third Reform Acts the Conservatives enjoyed a narrow margin in total election victories. Moreover, after 1867–8 there were already signs of increased Conservative voting strength in the larger urban centres, with even greater improvements in the London area. The 1867 extension increased the number of Roman Catholic voters in constituencies which had seen considerable Irish immigration, and on most occasions this could help the Liberals. On the other hand, it also strengthened an anti-Irish and anti-Catholic backlash, which was a major cause of Lancashire becoming an important centre of Conservative strength in the later nineteenth century.

One thing about the behaviour of the new voters is clear; there was no uniformity in their political allegiance, no solid voting in terms of broad social classes. Moreover, although 1866–7 had seen a growth in popular demonstrations in favour of reform, this out-of-doors pressure had never reached the same level as that of 1832. The way in which parliamentary reform had returned to the political arena in the 1860s, and the parliamentary proceedings of 1867, demonstrated that the Second Reform Act was not something exacted by an embattled people from a reactionary aristocracy, but primarily the work of the established dominant groups in society.

Political changes

Russell retired from the leadership of the Liberals before the end of 1867 and was replaced by Gladstone; Lord Derby too withdrew from active political life, in February 1868. For the next twelve years the rivalry between Gladstone and Disraeli was a prominent feature of British politics. Gladstone combined a powerful religious conviction and a capacity for emotional commitment to causes with a certain blindness and lack of scruple about the means employed for what he thought worthy ends. His hostility towards Disraeli was not simply a matter of political differences, but embodied also a strong personal enmity, stemming in part from Disraeli's attacks on Peel in the mid-1840s. The new Conservative leader disliked his Liberal rival.

During the 1850s and early 1860s, Disraeli's position of heir presumptive to the Conservative Party leadership had been far from certain, but after the triumph in the 1867 reform debates there could be no doubt about his claim to the leadership and with it the succession to the premiership. For him to arrive 'at the top of the greasy pole' in British politics was one of the most remarkable personal success stories in British history. In part Disraeli's success had been derived from the dearth of alternative leaders in his party after the 1846 split. In part it owed something to his personal qualities. He relished the great game of politics, despite occasional periods of reduced enthusiasm. The political world of those years was a small one, and there was much truth in the comparison drawn between the House of Commons and a club. Disraeli could be a good hater on occasion, but he was also a good friend. Radical MPs sometimes reflected that as Leader of the House of Commons Disraeli could be more considerate towards them than their Whig leaders.[9] If his rhetoric was sometimes too high-flown for complete effectiveness, at his best he was a great House of Commons man. He also had a great sense of fun, which could be an asset in that narrow parliamentary world. An eyewitness recalled his reaction when an obsessively anti-Catholic MP asked if the Conservative government had any new information about the machinations of the Jesuits against the Established Church:

Disraeli arose … and began with a manner of portentous gravity and a countenance of almost funereal gloom to give his answer. 'Her Majesty's Ministers,' he said 'had not been informed of any absolutely new machinations of the Jesuits but they would continue to watch, as they had hitherto watched, for any indication of such insidious enterprises. One of the favourite machinations of the Jesuits', he went on to say with deepening solemnity, 'had always been understood to be a plan for sending into this country disguised emissaries of their own, who, by expressing extravagant and ridiculous alarm about Jesuit plots, might bring public derision on the efforts of the genuine supporters of the State church. He would not venture to say whether the honourable member had knowledge of any such plans as that—', but here a roar of laughter from the whole House rendered further explanation impossible, and Disraeli composedly resumed his seat.[10]

9. McCord, 'Cobden and Bright', 103.   10. J. McCarthy, *Portraits of the Sixties* (1903), 150–3.

In the years since 1846, Disraeli had experienced dislike, distrust, and suspicion from many members of the Conservative Party, some of it tinged with anti-Semitism. His remarkable performance during the reform debates of 1867 had stilled any doubts entertained by most Conservative politicians, and when Derby's ill health enforced his retirement Disraeli was the obvious successor.

However gratifying this promotion might be, the last few months of the Conservative ministry were not easy. There were some achievements to the minority government's credit. The obstreperous King Theodore of Abyssinia, responsible for the imprisonment of British citizens, including a British envoy and a British consul, was defeated and driven to suicide, and the prisoners rescued. The expeditionary force which achieved this was conveniently drawn mainly from forces maintained in India on Indian revenues. There was a respectable showing in domestic reforms, including the abolition of public exe-cutions (not a popular reform), and the nationalization of the telegraph system. Another Act transferred jurisdiction in cases of disputed parliamentary elections to the Court of Common Pleas; the judges were not eager to accept this difficult additional function, but the new system was an improvement on earlier sanc-tions against electoral malpractices. The appointment of a royal commission to inquire into the effectiveness of existing public health legislation was a step which led to important developments during the next few years. On the other hand, the minority status of the government placed ministers in a difficult situ-ation. When defeated in the House of Commons, they did not have the option of immediate dissolution, because of the need to implement the changes in the electoral system before the next general election. As it was, when the 1868 general election was held, many of the new voters had not yet found their way on to the electoral registers.

Meanwhile Gladstone succeeded in restoring his authority within the Opposition majority, and used this situation to inflict a number of defeats on the Conservatives. In particular Gladstone tied the Liberal Party to a policy of major reform in Ireland, with the disestablishment of the minority Anglican Church there as his first objective. He had become convinced that the privileged position of the minority Church of Ireland was morally indefensible and that disestab-lishment was a necessary reform which would improve Anglo-Irish relations more generally. Other factors were making the question of Ireland more acute. September and December 1867 had seen the most notorious of the Fenian acts of terrorism in Great Britain, with the murder of an unarmed police sergeant at Manchester and the Clerkenwell explosion in London, which had caused many casualties in nearby tenements. It was possible to draw different conclusions from these events. Gladstone assumed that the proper response was to make an earnest attempt to remedy legitimate Irish grievances; others preferred the suppression of terrorism. During the session which ended in July 1868, Gladstone passed a series of resolutions against the government, foreshadowing the disestablishment of the Church of Ireland. These votes represented a humiliation for the Conservative ministers, and the end of the session provided something of a relief from a difficult parliamentary situation for them.

The general election of 1868

The general election which followed was a Liberal victory. The new House of Commons had a larger Liberal majority than that elected in 1865—116 as against about 82—but otherwise the distribution of party strength showed a remarkable resilience despite the 1867–8 reforms. The Conservatives retained much of their core electoral strength, and received a few notable gains as some consolation for their general defeat. They remained stronger in England than in the other parts of the United Kingdom, holding three-quarters of the English counties and a respectable proportion of smaller boroughs. The Liberals took about three-quarters of the seats in Ireland, Scotland, and Wales and most of the seats for the larger English boroughs—125 out of a total of 159. The strength of the Liberal Party in Ireland was not to persist; a new nationalist party aiming at Home Rule for Ireland was to come into existence during the next few years.

There were some surprises in the results. Lancashire returned 21 Conservatives as against 13 Liberals; the Conservatives took Salford, Bolton, Preston, and Blackburn, while Gladstone himself was beaten in the South-West Lancashire county division. In Lancashire industrial boroughs like Blackburn and Preston, there were Conservative mill-owners whose influence over their workforce was strong, while anti-Irish and anti-Catholic feeling was also intense. The London area also produced two striking results. At Disraeli's request, Lord George Hamilton, a subaltern in the Coldstream Guards, stood as Conservative candidate for the increasingly suburban county of Middlesex and came top of the poll by a considerable margin; during the past century there had been only one Tory win in that constituency. A prominent Conservative businessman, W. H. Smith, defeated John Stuart Mill at Westminster, previously another Liberal stronghold. These urban gains were, to an extent unrealized at the time, important portents for the future.

Gladstone's first ministry

However, the immediate Conservative defeat was clear, and Gladstone formed his first ministry. It was a strong Cabinet, though scarcely representative of the grass roots of Liberal support; eight of its fifteen original members sat in the House of Lords, and the Cabinet included such blue-blooded figures as the Duke of Argyll and the Marquis of Hartington, heir to the Duke of Devonshire. Robert Lowe was Chancellor of the Exchequer. Radicalism was represented by the ageing John Bright at the Board of Trade, but the composition of the Cabinet had a marked Whiggish tinge.

Liberal reforms

In a strong parliamentary position, the ministry was able to effect a considerable programme of reforms. In 1869 the Church of Ireland was disestablished, with a substantial portion of its endowments alienated for social improvement in Ireland. Instead of occupying a privileged position, the Irish sister Church of the Church of England was now only one of Ireland's Churches, with less popular support than Roman Catholicism. In 1870 Gladstone unfolded the other main element in his Irish policy, an attempt to reform the landlord–tenant relationship which lay at the root of much though not all of Irish unrest. The 1870 Land Act approached this problem by extending throughout Ireland a customary practice existing in Ulster and patchily elsewhere, which gave a tenant a claim at the end of his tenancy to compensation for any improvements he had made to his holding. The Act was well meant, and aroused the opposition of many landlords both in Britain and in Ireland by its interference with established property rights, but it was not very effective. The legal problems involved were complicated. The Act's most radical provision, compensation for evicted tenants when the rent charged was excessive, was emasculated when the House of Lords replaced 'excessive' with 'exorbitant', a shift in emphasis which reduced the chances of a court decision favourable to the tenant. However, it took some time for the ineffectiveness of the statute to become apparent, and the passage of the Land Act could be seen as a considerable reform at the time.

In the same year, Forster's Elementary Education Act cut through the tangle of contemporary religious controversies by providing a means to remedy deficiencies within existing facilities for elementary education (see pp. 311–13). Not surprisingly, in face of bitter sectarian controversy, the 1870 Act won few friends for the Liberal government. In both Houses the number of Liberal opponents and abstainers was so large that only a measure of support from Conservatives allowed the bill to pass. Militant Nonconformists were outraged at the continued financial support given to the voluntary schools, most of them controlled by the Church of England. Enthusiastic supporters of the Established Church looked with disfavour on the creation of the new Board Schools, which were often outside the influence of the 'national' Church.

Also in 1870 Gladstone procured an Order in Council which aimed at opening the home Civil Service to open competition. The War Secretary, Cardwell, was well advanced in his army reforms, and Childers' naval reforms (see pp. 317–21 below) were in their early, apparently successful phase. In 1871 Cardwell introduced a bill which would have abolished the system of purchase of army commissions and provided compensation for their current holders. There was stiff opposition in the House of Commons, mainly based on arguments that the purchase system ensured that commissions would be held by gentlemen, who alone could secure effective obedience. Even greater difficulty was experienced in the House of Lords, an obstruction circumvented by Gladstone's action in arranging for the cancellation of the early-eighteenth-century royal Order in Council, which provided the purchase system with its legal basis. He could not see that in the Britain of 1871 there might be valid objections to using the royal prerogative to sidestep parliamentary procedures. The distinguished Liberal intellectual E. A. Freeman later expressed the opinion that 'The thing did not look well... This is one of those cases in which a strictly conscientious man like Mr. Gladstone does things from which a less conscientious man would shrink.'[11]

Also in 1871 the Liberal government enacted a Trade Union Act which sought to give the unions a secure legal basis, and a Criminal Law Amendment Act which tried to define the legal limits of persuasion or picketing in industrial disputes. The latter Act was couched in terms which did not please the unions; although only a minority of workers was in the unions, their members included many who would have received the vote in 1867–8. University reform, too, was taken a step forward by an Act of 1871 which abolished most of the religious limitations on university degrees and appointments. In 1872 an old radical demand—and another of the Six Points of the People's Charter—was met in the enactment of voting by secret ballot. This issue had been controversial for many years, and it was something which the government did not take up voluntarily. John Bright refused to join the Liberal Cabinet unless this reform was included in the government's programme, and Gladstone was determined to secure this demonstration of Liberal unity, despite his own previous lukewarmness on the ballot issue.[12]

In 1873 a consolidating statute completed the reorganization of the upper courts which had been under way in piecemeal fashion in previous years. This involved the fusion of the two traditional sources of British law, common law and equity, and the creation of a more rational High Court of Justice and Court of Appeal. Originally this Act extinguished the judicial role of the House of Lords, but an amending Act of 1876 subsequently restored this function; the House of Lords in its judicial capacity was a committee of peers who were also distinguished judges. Other peers, by long-established convention, took no part in this work.

In the next general election, the Liberal government was to be accused by Conservatives of neglecting the kind of social reform which would be of benefit to the mass of the people. This polemic was for long accepted by the received historical tradition. In fact, the record of Gladstone's first ministry in this area was a good one, certainly not inferior to that of its Conservative successor, despite the latter's claims. Legislation affecting the regulation of mines, merchant shipping, public health, and local government enacted in the early 1870s followed on lines laid down by earlier legislation, but took the protective role of the State a great deal further. Altogether Gladstone's first ministry was responsible for a

11. *Pall Mall Gazette*, 12 Feb. 1874, quoted by P. Magnus, *Gladstone: A Biography* (1954), 221.
12. B. Kinzer, *The Ballot Question in Nineteenth Century British Politics* (1983) gives a full discussion of the political manoeuvrings which preceded the 1872 Ballot Act.

major legislative programme, made possible by its initially strong parliamentary position and the competence of most ministers. By 1872, however, there were signs of a turn in the political tide. Many of the reforms enacted had made enemies; this was true of the education, trade union, Irish, army and navy, licensing, university, and social reform elements within the government's programme. The British electorate has never been in the habit of rewarding reforming administrations with enhanced support, has indeed evinced a remarkable consistency in rejecting them.

Conservative recovery

During the first years of the Liberal ministry the Opposition had made little headway; Disraeli himself was in poor health, while the defeat of 1868 had provoked a new round of criticisms of his leadership of the party. By 1872 he had recovered his fighting spirit, and his vigorous attacks on the ministry received some striking popular endorsements. At Manchester in April 1872, and at the Crystal Palace in the following June, the Conservative leader made slashing attacks on the Liberal record which were well received by large audiences and widely reported. It is still not entirely clear what precisely led to this Conservative reaction. By 1872 the Liberal government had run into difficulties on a number of issues. Robert Lowe had tried to impose an unpopular tax on matches in 1871, which had to be withdrawn after demonstrations by the pathetic street-sellers who sold them. Also in 1871, the Home Secretary, Bruce, introduced a Licensing Bill which would have imposed severe restrictions on the sale of drink; this was not popular with the country's many drinkers and was strenuously opposed by the influential brewing and distilling interests. The bill could not be passed, but a more moderate Act which struggled to the statute book in 1872 was enough to harm the government in broad reaches of British society.

In 1872 Gladstone himself came under severe criticism. In two cases of patronage, a sensitive subject, he resorted to sharp practice, exhibiting the same kind of blinkered vision as when he used the royal prerogative to circumvent parliamentary proceedings in the abolition of the purchase system for army commissions. By mid-Victorian years ministers were expected to possess more integrity than this, and a vigilant public opinion, fed by a watchful press, was not inclined to acquiesce in such manipulation in public affairs. The first occasion arose over the strengthening of the Judicial Committee of the Privy Council by four salaried members, two of whom, under legislation of 1871, had to be judges or ex-judges. There was some difficulty in filling these places, and Gladstone eventually selected Sir Robert Collier; to meet the restrictions imposed by his own statute, Gladstone arranged for Collier to be appointed a judge of the Court of Common Pleas, where he sat for two days before being promoted to the Judicial Committee. On behalf of the judges collectively, the senior judges protested to the Prime Minister that he had deliberately violated the spirit, though not the letter, of the legislation involved. The second incident arose over university reforms. Some Church livings had previously been attached to certain university posts. To fill one of them, the Oxfordshire living of Ewelme, Gladstone selected the Revd W. W. Harvey. The 1871 Act had separated the Ewelme rectory from a university professorship to which it had earlier been tied but still stipulated that only Oxford graduates were eligible for the living. Harvey was a Cambridge graduate. Gladstone, on learning of the difficulty, insisted on arranging for him to become a member of Oxford University too, in order to fit him for the appointment. Even a sympathetic biographer has felt bound to describe this obstinate behaviour as a 'wanton act of high-handed folly'.[13]

On both occasions Gladstone exposed himself to damaging parliamentary criticism. In debates of February 1872 over the Collier case, the government avoided formal censure in the Lords by only two votes, in the Commons by only twenty-seven. In the following month, the Ewelme rectory affair produced another damaging parliamentary debate. The impact on parliamentary and public opinion would have been less serious if the Liberal government's position had been more secure on other grounds. A series of naval disasters (see p. 321 below) reflected on the competence with which the ministry looked to national security. Compared with the reputation of Lord Palmerston, and even with the previous ministry's successful defence of British interests in Abyssinia, the Liberal government's handling of foreign affairs, too, seemed lacklustre. Gladstone accepted the principle of arbitration in a long-standing dispute with the United States over the depredations of the British-built Confederate commerce raider *Alabama* during the US Civil War. This decision, and the payment by Britain of more than £4 million as a result, may have been wise but it was not popular. The 1872 Ballot Act allowed disgruntled Liberal supporters of 1868 to switch their votes without publicity on the first opportunity.

It is possible that extraneous events also played a part. Since the death of her husband in 1861, the Queen's secluded widowhood, accompanied by repeated claims for the provision of incomes from public funds for her family, had increased criticisms of the monarchy. The noisy if unrepresentative republican agitation was centred in the radical wing of the Liberal Party. Ten years after his father's death from typhoid fever, the Prince of Wales was stricken by the same disease and for some time his life was in danger. His recovery in early 1872 was the occasion for a remarkable display of public interest and support, with huge crowds in London lining the approaches to St Paul's for the thanksgiving service held on 27 February. It is possible that a revival of monarchist sentiment may have played a part in the growth of Conservative feeling.

In his Crystal Palace speech of 1872 Disraeli had defined the basis of his Conservatism as 'the maintenance of the empire of England, the preservation of the national institutions, and the elevation of the condition of the people'. As

13. Magnus, *Gladstone*, 222.

one historian of the Conservative Party has put it: 'There was more than a little fuzziness about detail here, and Disraeli himself damagingly conceded in 1873 that his party was not ready for an election because it did not yet have a policy, but for most observers (and apparently for many electors too) that crucial gap had been filled in 1872.'[14]

The fall of the Liberals

In the parliamentary session of 1873 Gladstone ran into new troubles. One legislative proposal was a bill to reform higher education in Ireland, with the establishment of a new university there, primarily for Roman Catholics. Gladstone believed that he had obtained the consent of the Roman Catholic bishops of Ireland for his proposal, and had made important concessions to secure their approval. The bill included an explicit provision that teachers in the university who offended the religious beliefs of the students would be dismissed, and excluded the teaching of such potentially controversial subjects as moral philosophy, modern history, and theology. Such sweeping limitations exposed the scheme to criticism, and in the event failed to secure the approval of the Irish hierarchy. After Gladstone had committed himself to the proposal, it was denounced by the Roman Catholic Church, with the result that an alliance of Conservatives and Irish Catholic MPs defeated the second reading by three votes in March 1873.

Gladstone's Cabinet decided to resign and the Queen invited Disraeli to form a government. He refused, on the slender ground that the Liberal defeat had been inflicted by a temporary and unusual grouping remote from the normal working of the political system. Faced with this bland and persistent refusal, Gladstone and his colleagues resumed office, but their fortunes were clearly in decline. From the formation of the Liberal ministry, by-elections had reduced their majority, to a trivial extent at first, but from 1871 this adverse electoral trend accelerated.

Late in 1873 Gladstone tried to counter some of the ministry's unpopularity by Cabinet changes. Some of the ministers who seemed to have been unsuccessful, like Lowe at the Exchequer and Bruce at the Home Office, were moved to other posts; Gladstone himself replaced Lowe at the Exchequer. The new ministerial appointments involved additional by-elections; some of the ministers concerned were defeated, which added to the decline in the ministry's reputation. Early in 1874 Gladstone decided to hold a general election. He was aware of the decline in the standing of his government and his party, and believed that only by securing a new electoral mandate could the trend be reversed. However, Gladstone miscalculated in the ground on which he chose to fight, though perhaps this could not have been clear at the time. His main proposal was to return to the fiscal

14. John Ramsden, *An Appetite for Power: A History of the Conservative Party since 1830* (1998), 117. Richard Shannon, *The Age of Disraeli 1867–1881* (1992) provides a valuable analysis of Disraeli's political outlook and the policies pursued by the 1874–80 Conservative ministry.

objective of the 1850s and 1860s and abolish income tax altogether. Although this was no doubt attractive to many voters, the overwhelming majority of the new electors added in 1867–8 would not have a sufficient income to bring them into the income tax bracket, while presumably they would have no objections to other people paying the tax. Nevertheless, the pledge wrong-footed Disraeli and his party who were unsure whether to denounce it or claim that they would do the same thing.[15]

The general election of 1874

In other ways too the sudden dissolution was not propitious for the Liberals. Gladstone's decision gave no opportunity for a well-prepared election campaign, and the Conservatives were by now better organized to face a snap election. After the defeat of 1868 Disraeli had commissioned an able Conservative lawyer, John Gorst, to take in hand the inefficient party organization. During the next few years an immense amount of organizational work was put in, forming or reviving local Conservative associations, and ensuring that Conservative candidates were selected and ready. National party organs too were either created or invigorated; the Conservative Central Office and the National Union of Conservative and Constitutional Associations were energetic agencies of electoral activity. A similar shaking up of Liberal organization still lay some years in the future. Electoral calculations were still relatively primitive, and both parties were to be surprised at the extent of the electoral shift in 1874. For the first time since 1841 a substantial Conservative majority was returned. Some of the trends shown in the previous election were intensified. The overall Conservative majority was less than 50, but in England alone they had a majority of more than 100. Although they increased their Scottish seats from 7 to 19 they remained in a minority there. The Irish results were difficult to interpret.[16] Many of the successful candidates there had made some kind of declaration in favour of Home Rule, but the party allegiance of many of the 57 nominal Home Rulers was uncertain. The emergence of a distinct Home Rule Party was more damaging to the Liberals than the Conservatives in Ireland, but a revelation of the extent of this damage still lay in the future. Conservative strength in the larger towns continued to grow. At Newcastle an increasingly popular local Tory candidate, who had been heavily beaten in 1868, took the second seat by a safe margin. In Leeds the Liberal vote was disastrously split by a radical candidate advocating Irish Home Rule, and 2 Conservatives were returned. At Salford the 2 seats were again won, though by a narrow margin, by strident Conservative campaigning, including a strong anti-Catholic and anti-Irish tinge. The overall results were Conservatives 350, Liberals 245, Irish Home Rulers 57.

15. R. T. Shannon, *Gladstone: Heroic Prime Minister 1865–1898* (1999), 136.
16. D. Thornley, *Isaac Butt and Home Rule* (1964), ch. 5, gives a full discussion of the complexities of the 1874 Irish results.

Gladstone was bitterly disappointed and, having come second in his Greenwich constituency to a distiller, complained about being 'swept away literally by a torrent of beer and gin'. He withdrew from his party's leadership and Lord Hartington became the Liberal leader in the House of Commons; during the next few years Gladstone's appearances in Parliament were few and unpredictable. The Conservatives' working majority was in practice greater than the nominal figure. The Liberals had been badly hit by the election, and in addition some of the first substantial group of Irish Home Rulers were on other matters inclined to support the Conservative side. During the first years of the new Parliament, the Irish party gave the government little cause for alarm.

Disraeli's second ministry

In forming his government Disraeli was able to call on a wider pool of talent than for his previous administration.[17] With some difficulty, Lord Salisbury was persuaded to join the Cabinet as Secretary of State for India, which represented a notable reconciliation and a recruit of ability and influence. The Earl of Derby, son of Disraeli's old chief, became Foreign Secretary; he proved less of an asset. The appointment which caused most comment was that of R. A. Cross as Home Secretary. It is unlikely that this promotion of a man who had never previously held ministerial office represented the new Prime Minister's intuitive assessment of his ability, much more likely that the selection reflected Disraeli's appreciation of the importance of that Lancashire Conservatism of which Cross was a prominent and popular representative. The choice proved a successful one. Adderley, the President of the Board of Trade, on the other hand, was a failure. He quarrelled with his officials and his increasingly obvious ministerial limitations brought the government into a scrape in 1875, involving the loss of an important piece of merchant shipping legislation. The new First Lord of the Admiralty, G. W. Hunt, proved a poor choice from the point of view of both naval efficiency and official performance as a minister; his principal interest lay in agriculture and during his tenure of the Admiralty it remained so. The Chancellor of the Exchequer, Northcote, was determined to show that a Conservative administration could govern as cheaply as the Liberals. Hunt failed to defend the navy against additional cuts in its funding, which further impaired its operational efficiency, at the same time as the government was embarking upon a more spirited foreign and imperial policy which knowingly involved the risk of war.

Conservative reforms

These problems were still in the future when the government took office. However unfairly, Disraeli and other Conservative polemicists had made much

17. Blake, *Disraeli*, ch. 24. This major biography and Shannon, *The Age of Disraeli*, are the most important secondary sources for the history of this ministry.

of the previous government's supposed failure to make adequate progress in social reform. They had promised that a Conservative ministry would show a higher level of care for the condition of the people. During the first years of the new government's tenure there was a programme of social legislation which the Conservatives claimed to be a break with the previous government's actions. A more dispassionate assessment might find instead a considerable element of continuity, just as the Liberal reforms of 1868–73 had owed much to the reform legislation of the 1850s and earlier 1860s.

When the new Cabinet met for the first time, some of the ministers were surprised to discover that Disraeli had no concrete policies to offer, despite his earlier references in major speeches to the need for change. Cross later recalled how

From all his speeches I had quite expected that his mind was full of legislative schemes, but such did not prove to be the case; on the contrary he had to rely entirely on the suggestions of his colleagues, and, as they themselves had only just come into office, and that suddenly, there was some difficulty in framing the Queen's speech.[18]

Criticism of this dearth of prepared policies may be tempered by the reflection that there was nothing unusual about it. Many later administrations, including the Liberal government which took office at the end of 1905, were to be in the same boat. There was a Factory Bill on the stocks already, which the new government could take over and pass in 1874. A Licensing Act to modify the previous government's highly unpopular statute did not involve much planning or preparation. Any substantial body of reforming legislation had to wait until 1875, when the new departmental ministers had found their feet. It was in that session that most of the constructive legislation which forms the ministry's main claim to be seen as a great reforming agency was passed. Two Acts relating to trade unions capitalized on dissatisfaction with the Liberal legislation in that field. The Conservatives offered a less restrictive limitation on picketing and similar activities, and also the removal of the privileged position previously held by employers in comparison with workers in the law respecting breaches of contract. This latter Act was styled the Employers and Workmen Act, instead of the earlier terminology of 'Master and Servant'. The Public Health Act of 1875 was an important statute, but its most useful attributes were as a consolidation and clarification of the complex mass of sanitary legislation passed in earlier years, including that of the previous government. Similarly, a Sale of Food and Drugs Act provided a simplification and codification of another area of piecemeal earlier legislation. Another Factory Act was also passed in 1875, marking a further step along what was by now a well-established legislative road, as did Northcote's Friendly Societies Act, which offered additional legal safeguards for this admired form of saving and insurance. The 1875 Artisans' Dwellings Act gave local

---

18. Blake, *Disraeli*, 543.

authorities the power to provide houses at the expense of their ratepayers; only a tiny handful (six by 1880) made any effort to use it. In 1876 an Education Act increased the powers of local authorities to compel attendance at elementary education. This was done without materially increasing the powers of the School Boards, which the Church of England viewed with suspicion. A poorly drafted Merchant Shipping Act was passed, again not a novel field for additional regulation. A Rivers Pollution Act was more a well-meaning gesture than an effective control on that environmental problem. The pace of domestic reform then slowed, although there was another Factory Act of some importance in 1878.

It is difficult to see the Conservative record of reform as superior to that of the previous Liberal ministry. It can be more reasonably seen as another instalment in a sequence which was well established earlier in the century. The extent to which the government tried to compel recalcitrant local authorities to take effective measures for the improvement of social conditions was limited, the extent to which the government was prepared to spend from central taxation for such purposes even more so. A limited acquaintance with some of the investigations into the slums and poverty of later years will induce a modest evaluation of this phase of Conservative paternalism.

After 1876, too, the ministry's concentration moved from domestic matters, with foreign and imperial policies receiving more attention. Disraeli had a genuine but nebulous ambition to vindicate the greatness of the country and the empire.[19] In the autumn of 1875 he had already acquired for Britain a large block of shares in the Suez Canal Company, not far short of half the total, as a result of a personal initiative, the necessary £4 million being borrowed on his own responsibility. The actual impact of the deal, as far as control of this key link with the East was concerned, was less dramatic, because of the limited powers over the canal which the company itself actually enjoyed, but as a stroke of policy it made a considerable impression on public opinion, as well as providing Britain with a useful and profitable investment for many years. Another spectacular gesture, the Royal Titles Act of 1876, which gave the Queen the title of Empress of India, was not well managed. The move was partly inspired by the Queen herself, and the Act should have reached the statute book with little controversy. But Disraeli made no attempt to obtain the agreement of the opposition leaders in advance, with the result that the measure was strongly opposed in both Houses of Parliament and in the press. The step was in part inspired by one of the most significant international developments in the previous twenty years or so, the effective expansion of Russian control in Central Asia over the relics of the old Mongol khanates. Now Russian power seemed to be approaching the north-west frontier of India, and an imperial title might serve to emphasize and consolidate the British dominance of the subcontinent.

19. Ibid, 562–3, 581–7.

The crisis in the Near East

This was not the only place where Russian expansionism seemed to threaten British interests. The Crimean War had been fought to obstruct Russian attempts to extend her influence towards the Mediterranean, and seemed to have succeeded in doing so for the time being. Then, in the summer of 1875, events in the Balkans detonated another international crisis in the Near East. A series of conflicts between Turkey and her subject peoples culminated in a Bulgarian rising which was met by massacres and other atrocities at the hands of ill-disciplined elements in the Turkish Army. The danger, from the British point of view, was that Russia would be unable to resist the temptation to intervene to protect the Bulgarians, tied to Russia by shared religion, shared Slav origins, and by contemporary panslavic enthusiasm in Russia.

Unfortunately for the Cabinet, the British ambassador in Constantinople was both staunchly pro-Turkish and in poor health. His reports played down the atrocity reports (the Bulgarian rebels, too, were capable of nasty behaviour), and were at first accepted by Disraeli as reliable. In any event the Prime Minister was more concerned with British national interests than with the fate of the Bulgarians. But further information, including reports from British consuls in the affected areas, soon provided better evidence and led to a good deal of press coverage of the atrocities. By August 1877 it was all too clear that the Turkish forces had been guilty of massacres of men, women, and children. A British public opinion ready to absorb accounts of violence and bloodshed, as had already been demonstrated during the Indian Mutiny, with a press very willing to supply them, embraced the stories with enthusiasm. A chorus of denunciation of Turkish malpractices in the Balkans erupted, with the support of a wide range of the morally outraged.

Disraeli's problem was that the adverse publicity given to Turkey made it difficult for Britain to intervene if Russia decided to rescue her fellow Christians by armed intervention. Derby, his Foreign Secretary, was convinced by the evidence that British support of the oppressive and discredited Turkish rule in the Balkans was out of the question. Derby's reaction to the news from Bulgaria had something in common with Gladstone's. During the first years after the Liberal electoral disaster of 1874, and his subsequent resignation of the leadership, Gladstone had largely withdrawn from the ordinary political scene, concerning himself more with the current policy of the Vatican. He played no part in the inception of the anti-Turkish agitation which followed the revelations of the Bulgarian atrocities, but the publication of the horrific details involved produced in him a kind of personal explosion of moral revulsion. This led directly to his unexpected return to the centre of the political stage.[20] In September 1876 he published his pamphlet *The Bulgarian Horrors and the Question of the East*,

20. For a detailed discussion of this episode, R. T. Shannon, *Gladstone and the Bulgarian Atrocities, 1876* (1963).

written with passionate concentration; it proved a remarkably successful piece of propaganda.

Gladstone followed this up with a sustained campaign of speeches in which he condemned the Conservative ministry as wilfully blind to great moral questions for the sake of power politics. In the last months of 1876 and the early part of 1877, the Eastern Question provided a great divide within that portion of the nation which was interested in such matters. Passionate expression of opinion was aroused on both sides. The outbreak of war between Russia and Turkey in April 1877, though, seemed to revive British fears of Russian imperialist expansion, while unexpected early successes by the Turkish armies aroused some admiration. Early in 1878 there was a marked change in military fortunes. The main Turkish field armies were forced to sue for an armistice and peace negotiations were set on foot. Turkey's plight alarmed Disraeli and most of his colleagues, but as yet there was little that they could do to defend British interests in the area, given the divided state of British public opinion. Moreover, the level of preparedness of the British armed forces was such that armed intervention could not be easily contemplated. Added to these difficulties was the presence within the Conservative Cabinet of ministers, especially Derby, who were strongly opposed to British support of a discredited Turkish government. Derby was even prepared to leak to the Russian ambassador confidential information about Cabinet discussions in order to undermine Disraeli's Eastern policies.[21]

As Russia seemed more and more likely to be able to dictate draconian terms to a defeated Turkey, support for Disraeli's anti-Russian position grew. In February a British naval squadron was sent to Constantinople, with orders to oppose any Russian attempt to seize control of the Dardanelles. A vote of credit for possible emergency military expenditure was carried in the House of Commons. Preparations for an expeditionary force were set on foot and, in March, Indian troops were ordered to Malta, while at home orders were issued mobilizing the reserves of the British Army. These moves provoked Derby's resignation. Now secure in the support of a Cabinet majority, including Lord Salisbury, who had gradually come round to his point of view, Disraeli could afford the inevitable breach with the son of his old leader. During the next month the danger of a major war receded, as the Tsar, aware of increasingly threatening moves from Britain, recoiled from his original intention of occupying Constantinople.

Nevertheless, Russian peace negotiators imposed upon Turkey a peace (the Treaty of San Stefano) which included terms unacceptable to the British government on a Balkan settlement and because of the proposed Russian annexations on the east side of the Black Sea. After intensive negotiations, in which British diplomacy succeeded in largely isolating Russia, the Tsar was forced by international pressure to agree that this settlement would be subject to reconsideration

21. Blake, *Disraeli*, 621–7. Lord and, it was suggestively hinted, Lady Derby were certainly close to the Russian Ambassador, Count Schouvaloff. John Vincent (ed.), *The Derby Diaries 1869–78* (1994), 28–9 has mounted a qualified defence of the Derbys' role.

at a gathering of representatives of all the major European powers, to be convened at Berlin in June 1878. In the intervening months intensive negotiations took place to ensure that the Congress of Berlin would provide a satisfactory solution to the Eastern crisis. Salisbury, the new Foreign Secretary, had succeeded by June in obtaining the concessions which Britain wanted. The Russian aim of creating a large Bulgarian satellite State, stretching from the Black Sea to the Aegean, at Turkey's expense, was replaced by the agreed definition of a smaller, weaker, and divided Bulgaria, with part remaining under at least nominal Turkish rule. The Tsar retained most of his gains on the far side of the Black Sea, but this was counterbalanced by an agreement with Turkey which transferred Cyprus to Britain for use as a base in the eastern Mediterranean.

During the Congress of Berlin Disraeli experienced the culmination of his strange political career; he was now widely seen not only as a major British figure, but as one of the most influential figures on the international scene. The agreements ratified at Berlin duly gave Britain the safeguards which she required, and Disraeli and Salisbury returned home to a rapturous public reception. The Queen had agreed with her Prime Minister's view of the crisis from the beginning, and made her opinion clear by conferring the Order of the Garter on both British plenipotentiaries, although Disraeli declined the dukedom she offered him. The prestige of the Conservative ministry stood at a high level in the country.

Conservative decline

The 1874 Parliament still had some time to run, however, and during the next two years a variety of factors eroded this favourable standing. The Eastern Question had not been the only overseas question at issue in the 1870s. Anglo-Russian friction had also surfaced in Indian affairs. The Viceroy appointed by Disraeli in 1876, Lord Lytton, proved a poor choice. Over-confident and headstrong, Lytton was not content to be an agent of policies decided in London. During the 1870s there was mounting anxiety about the situation in Afghanistan, as the Russian drive across Central Asia drew nearer to that border State. The previous Liberal government had rejected Afghan overtures for a defensive alliance against Russian pressures, and Afghanistan had suffered from internal strife in recent years. In the summer of 1878, a Russian mission headed by a general arrived in Kabul. Lytton decided that this required a decisive intervention to reassert British influence there. Ignoring the government's instructions to respond with as little friction as possible, he dispatched his own mission to Afghanistan. When the Afghan regime refused entry to the British envoy, the situation deteriorated until war broke out in November. The Indian Army invaded Afghanistan and in May 1879 a treaty was signed which provided for the reception in Kabul of a British resident mission. A few months later, in September, a mutiny in the Afghan Army at Kabul led to the massacre of the entire British mission. The Indian Army once again invaded Afghanistan and fought a successful punitive campaign, but the massacre had been a serious setback to the ministry's Indian policies. Gladstone had recently been selected as Liberal candidate for Midlothian and subsequently entered upon a campaign of major speeches—the Midlothian campaign—in which he included denunciations of the arrangements under which four-fifths of the cost of the fighting in Afghanistan fell upon the Indian revenue (though when he took office he chose to do nothing about it).

Lytton was not the only example of an impetuous agent providing problems for the home government. A parallel crisis which erupted in South Africa owed something to the appointment as Colonial Secretary of Lord Carnarvon, another of the right-wing rebels of 1867 who had been won back to the fold by 1874. As Colonial Secretary in Derby's last minority administration, he had presided over the federation of the different components of British North America (except Newfoundland) into the Dominion of Canada in 1867. It was not surprising that this welding together of the two traditions of British and French Canada into one federal structure aroused ambitions to repeat the success in South Africa, where the white settlers represented the twin British and Boer traditions. In the mid-1870s the time seemed auspicious for such a change. The republics created by the Boer settlers who had left British territory after the abolition of slavery, the Transvaal and the Orange Free State, had never been strong or well organized. By 1876 they faced considerable danger from the growing strength and increasing expansionism of the native Zulu confederacy. Carnarvon determined to use the opportunity to fulfil his own scheme for the creation under British auspices of a federation of all the white-dominated areas of South Africa. In April 1877, therefore, Britain annexed the Transvaal, ostensibly to prevent the Zulus from slaughtering the Boer settlers. At the same time Sir Bartle Frere, a convinced supporter of Carnarvon's aims, arrived in South Africa as the senior British representative in the area. At first the Transvaal Boers, themselves well aware of their precarious situation, acquiesced in the annexation. During 1878 Frere moved towards his ulterior aims by taking provocative action against the Zulus, something which the government at home certainly did not want. Early in 1879 his actions brought about open war, marked on 22 January by the overrunning of an important British base, Isandhlwana, by a Zulu force, in a stinging defeat which did nothing for the government's prestige at home. Not until early July did the reinforced British Army in South Africa succeed in inflicting a crushing defeat on the Zulus at the battle of Ulundi. The annexation of the Transvaal had seen the installation there of a British colonial government of no great competence, which showed little understanding of the beliefs and attitudes of the Transvaal Boers. With the removal of the Zulu threat in the summer of 1879, Boer dissatisfaction with the British regime mounted until it culminated in open revolt during 1880. By that time, though, the Liberals were back in power.

These imperial adventures and their incidental setbacks had tarnished the laurels of the Conservative ministry. They also provided Gladstone and his allies with additional ammunition in the crusade against 'Beaconsfieldism', begun in the aftermath of the Bulgarian atrocities. (Disraeli had moved to the House of Lords as Earl of Beaconsfield in 1876.[22]) The forward moves in Afghanistan and South Africa were condemned as vicious examples of imperialist oppression, crushing the liberties of Boer farmers on the one hand and Afghan tribesmen on the other; the virtues of these victims were exaggerated in this campaign.

Such overseas problems might have been less harmful to the Conservative government had they not coincided with problems at home. The ministry was reluctantly forced to budget for increases in taxation, due in part to an adventurous policy overseas, at a time when to do so was particularly unwelcome. The years after 1876 saw an acute commercial and industrial depression, an uncomfortable experience for 'the workshop of the world', and an early warning that this privileged economic position might not be secure or permanent. By 1879 there had been a striking rise in the number of bankruptcies and in unemployment. These setbacks were to prove temporary, but they coincided with the onset of a more long-lived and severe depression affecting sectors of British farming. At first this situation could be associated with purely temporary factors, such as a series of long, wet summers which ruined crops, and epidemics among both cattle and sheep. But behind these there lay much more enduring problems for British agriculture. After 1846 the price advantage entailed by the cost of transport and limitations in available foreign food supplies had continued to give British farmers a kind of indirect protection in the home market, despite the removal of protective tariffs. In the later nineteenth century both of these factors dwindled away. Innovations in naval architecture and marine engineering produced the economical modern merchant ship which cut the cost of sea carriage. After the US Civil War, development of the prairies brought the production of immense quantities of cheap grain. To this came to be added cheap meat supplies from South America and Australasia, aided eventually by the development of refrigerated shipping. Not all British farming suffered to the same extent; for example, with continued urban growth, dairy farming was less hard hit than the major grain-producing areas.

In the later 1870s the prices of some food items began to drop drastically. This was not of course a purely British phenomenon; it affected all Europe. Most European States saw an obvious remedy in the imposition of tariffs on imported food. In Britain, however, even for a Conservative ministry, such action was politically impossible. The memories of the 1846 break-up of the party were still alive, and most of the ministry's younger members and supporters had grown up in a milieu in which the verdict of 1846 was scarcely questioned. Cheaper food might be disastrous to some landowners and farmers, but it was an undoubted asset in the industrial communities on which Britain increasingly relied for her

---

22. When asked how he felt after his introduction to Lords, he replied, 'I am dead; dead but in the Elysian fields.' Sarah Bradford, *Disraeli* (1982), 334. His wife who died in 1872 had been made Viscountess Beaconsfield at Disraeli's request in 1868.

livelihood. The result was that the Conservative government took no effective action to protect the landed interest against competition from imported food (an omission which did nothing to maintain its support in rural areas).

A deepening agricultural depression was an uncomfortable experience in Great Britain; in Ireland it was disastrous. The real if slow recovery of the previous quarter-century or so was dependent on the continuity of agricultural prosperity there. The adverse conditions and the falling prices of the late 1870s produced a sharp deterioration in the condition of Ireland. Depression brought a renewed cycle of evictions for non-payment of rent, leading to an increase in violence. In Parliament the Irish Home Rule Party exchanged its moderate leader, Isaac Butt, for the more stridently nationalist Charles Stewart Parnell in 1877. The deliberate obstruction of parliamentary business, embarked upon as an individual ploy in earlier months, now became a regular party tactic, in ways which impaired the orderly and dignified working of the legislature. The Conservative government appeared to have no constructive policy in response to the deteriorating situation in the Irish countryside.

In 1879 Gladstone was selected as Liberal candidate for Midlothian at the next election, and he embarked upon a major propaganda exercise, using his own candidacy as a platform from which to appeal to the electorate more generally. Wide publicity was arranged for a series of mass meetings and powerful speeches. These campaigns in 1879 and 1880 caused a considerable stir, though their actual electoral effect cannot be measured. Gladstone was not the nominal leader of the Liberal Party, but these exertions marked his effective return to that position.

Disraeli (like Gladstone in 1874) underestimated the extent of the ministry's loss of popularity; senior party officials calculated that a general election early in 1880 would involve a Conservative loss of only sixteen or eighteen seats, an estimate which was to demonstrate that the Conservative Party machine was not in as satisfactory a state as it had been in 1874. Two by-elections in Liverpool and London also seemed to offer grounds for Conservative optimism, and Parliament was dissolved in late March. The result was a disaster for the Conservatives even worse than the Liberal catastrophe of 1874.

The general election of 1880

The first results presaged a defeat for the government, with a net loss of 50 seats in the boroughs. The county results arrived later, and would usually have offered some compensation. In 1880, however, Conservative inaction in face of agriculture's problems, and the presence in some counties of farmers' own candidates in consequence, saw the loss of another 27 seats. The Conservatives did badly in Scotland, Wales, and Ireland. In Lancashire, Lord Derby's considerable influence was now given to the Liberals, and the Conservatives lost ground. The new House of Commons contained 353 Liberals, 238 Conservatives, and 61 Irish

Home Rulers; within this third party the 1880 election saw the disappearance of many of the more moderate Irish MPs, and their replacement by more militant representatives. The Liberal Party machine had been improved by the time of the general election, but this was less important in deciding the result than the decline in the popularity of the Conservative government. The overall defeat was so clear that Disraeli resigned before the new Parliament met.

The change of government in 1880 has often been seen as symptomatic of a watershed in the history of nineteenth-century Britain. The mid-Victorian consensus in Britain had involved the widespread acceptance of certain assumptions about the proper ordering of society. These included a considerable faith in the means which seemed to have brought increased prosperity, comfort, and tranquillity. If some theoretical economists had begun to doubt the overriding efficacy of private enterprise, these doubts were not widespread in 1880. Individual progress was still generally seen as the root of common prosperity. A process of gentlemanly debate in Parliament seemed to be the proper mode for coping with any difficulties, and for the creation of beneficial reform. There had not as yet been any very significant change in the exercise of power in Britain; Cabinets continued to be largely drawn from established governing groups, with the aristocracy still prominent. There was still, despite some actual shortcomings in matters of defence, a sense of national and imperial security. Britain had outgrown her fear of a now weakened France, and had not yet learned to fear Germany; Russia was the principal focus of dislike, a dislike bolstered by a comfortable assumption of superiority over a semi-barbaric rival. Although there were some dissenting voices, and some continuing problems, there was still room for considerable complacency as Britain entered the last decades of the nineteenth century.

8

Government and administration
c.1850–1880

During the years after 1850, both central and local government saw a continued growth in official intervention and regulation. There was also improvement in the quality of public administration, but it was limited and patchy. There remained widespread doubts about the efficiency and reliability of official agencies.

Parliament

The legislature itself was changing, if not very drastically. In 1858 the property qualification for MPs was abolished. This had been one of the demands of the Chartists, though they were not responsible for its enactment. The reform was more symbolic than influential. The House of Commons continued to be overwhelmingly drawn from the wealthier sections of society, who could afford to fulfil an unpaid legislative role. In 1872, after protracted debates covering several years, another Chartist demand, the secret ballot, was conceded. The 1872 Act provided for an eight-year trial of the new system; thereafter it was for many years prolonged annually. Gladstone's decision owed more to political expediency than to any care for the arguments which the Chartists had advanced (see p. 290 above). Again change was the work of the established political groups, rather than a response to outside radical pressures.[1]

The supremacy of the House of Commons within Parliament had been strengthened by its success in forcing an unwilling House of Lords to accept parliamentary reform in 1832 and its superiority was apparently confirmed during the conflict over the repeal of the paper duties in 1860–1 (see pp. 277–8 above). The parliamentary reforms of 1867–8 further enhanced the representative status of the House of Commons, and in so doing relatively weakened the hereditary chamber.

The 1850s were not, however, a period when political parties were strong and united nor one when it was obvious who the Queen should ask to form a

---

1. B. L. Kinzer, *The Ballot Question in Nineteenth-Century English Politics* (1983) gives a full discussion of this topic, demonstrating that Gladstone accepted the ballot as the price of Bright's entry into the 1868 Cabinet, despite his own record of hostile votes on this issue.

government. The Repeal of the Corn Laws had split the Conservative Party but had not resulted in a united Liberal Party while the Peelites lingered on for a decade as a group with some influence. Until at least 1859 when Palmerston was able to consolidate the various liberal groups and perhaps until Gladstone formed his first ministry in 1868, there was a domination of political life by Liberalism but not by a united Liberal Party. It was in this context that the monarchy in the person of the Prince Consort exerted considerable influence.

That the monarchy was a constitutional monarchy was certain but what exactly the powers of a constitutional monarch were was less so. As ever, the development of the monarchy was affected by chance, in this case the early death of Prince Albert in 1861. Albert's capacity for hard work led to him being assiduous in monitoring and advising on many of the activities of governments, while the Queen's many pregnancies had meant that many decisions were left to him. The Prince Consort saw the role of a constitutional monarch as maintaining neutrality between political parties while making interventions in government policy. The Crown should provide providential leadership, encourage progressive forces, and be a bulwark against democratic excesses. This Albertine idea of monarchy worked reasonably well in the 1840s and 1850s and the Prince's intervention is usually recognized as having helped avoid war with the USA in 1861 over the *Trent* affair.[2] Nevertheless the Prince's quarrels with Lord Palmerston and his great unpopularity when he sought to prevent war with Russia in 1854 showed its limitations and whether it would have thrived in the circumstances of mass democracy or even in the circumstances of the limited mid-nineteenth century electorate with stronger parties and an accepted Liberal leadership is questionable.

Queen Victoria's retirement into seclusion after her husband's death put an end to such a proactive role for the monarchy. She continued to see and often commented upon a wide range of official papers but, whatever she believed, she did not determine policies and her power in the State was limited. In a Europe still dominated by monarchies, Victoria's personal and family connections continued to play a minor role in State affairs. But whatever power the House of Lords retained, or whatever influence the Crown might exercise, the constitutional focus of the country was increasingly clearly the House of Commons.

Legislation

By 1850 the public was growing accustomed to the annual enactment of a mass of new law, more and more of it in the form of public general statutes rather than local or personal 'private' legislation. In a number of ways mid-Victorian lawmaking remained a hit-and-miss business, as the 1867–8 parliamentary reforms

---

2. Confederate envoys were removed by force from the British mail packet *Trent* by a US warship. Stanley Weintraub, *Albert: Uncrowned King* (1997) describes Albert's conception of constitutional monarchy and his interventions in policy.

demonstrated (see p. 283 above). In matters of legislation, as in other spheres, the House of Commons was not always amenable to government control. After a number of well-publicized crimes in 1862, the House of Commons insisted on the immediate enactment of legislation against violent robbery. The Home Secretary opposed this as panic legislation, but the House of Commons carried the second reading against him by 131 votes to 68.[3] Not that the government's own legislation was always well designed. Often, major Acts had to be quickly followed to the statute book by amending or clarifying measures. The long sequence of Acts regulating merchant shipping, notably those of 1854, 1862, 1867, 1871, and 1876, showed that legislative success did not come easily. The Local Government Act of 1862 gave to the local boards created under it immunity from levies for highway maintenance imposed under the Highways Act of the same year. When it was discovered that many small communities were acquiring local boards solely to avoid increased expenditure on roads, an amending Act was hurriedly devised. This effectively prevented such action by communities of less than 3,000 population, but that then ensured that many small communities were left without any form of effective local government for another ten years.

Legislation against pollution was usually ineffective, partly because of the negligible penalties for such offences as the uncontrolled emission of industrial smoke, partly because of resistance from influential local interests. The attempt to provide a public vaccination service against smallpox began in 1840, and an Act of 1853 tried to enforce compulsory vaccination, but this statute was ineptly drafted, and further legislation was needed in 1858, 1867, and 1871. The important Public Health Act of 1875 included an extension of the discretionary powers given to local authorities for the building of isolation hospitals. Past experience led to the inclusion of reserve powers to order the creation of such facilities in case of default. These clauses were so badly drafted that in practice they impeded rather than encouraged the provision of such hospitals. An Act of 1850 allowed the creation of public libraries, but even thirty years later many local authorities had made no attempt to take any action here.

Experience of the unwillingness of most local authorities to incur additional expenditure resulted in a gradual tightening by Parliament of the controls involved. The 1855 Nuisances Removal and Disease Prevention Act empowered local authorities dealing with obstructive individuals to obtain court orders for the removal of public health dangers, at the expense of the property owner involved. An Act of 1869 gave the central government new powers to appoint the necessary officials for this purpose if a Poor Law union failed to do so. The 1875 Public Health Act gave the Local Government Board power to obtain court orders compelling any recalcitrant local authority to fulfil its sanitary responsibilities. There was an unmistakable trend towards compulsion and less local discretion in carrying out socially useful legislation.

In 1851, after a number of notorious poisonings, statutory provision was made for the compulsory registration of purchases of arsenic, and for the compulsory colouring of arsenic before sale. In 1854 an important Merchant Shipping Act prescribed a meticulous code of regulation for merchant ships and their crews. In 1871 another Act provided for the compulsory muzzling of dogs when rabies was about. In 1872, following a national conference on safety in mines, a new Mines Act enforced a variety of detailed regulations, including stipulations about the formal qualifications of colliery managers, provision for compulsory daily inspection of working spaces, and arrangements for the weighing of coal to ensure proper wage payments. In 1876 Parliament established a compulsory licensing system for vivisection. These examples illustrate the expanding range of statutory regulation, also indicated by the increasing size and number of the published volumes of new Acts of Parliament.

Parliament still chose to walk warily in some matters. Despite campaigns by such bodies as the United Kingdom Alliance, and the undoubted harm caused by excessive drinking, legislation regulating the drink trade was limited, and usually left to local authorities to implement. In 1877 the prison system finally became a national service; since this meant a reduction in local financial responsibility, opposition was negligible. Legislation involving the police was more cautious. There were advocates of a centralized national police, but also strong opposition to this strengthening of the State's coercive power, and a sustained attempt was made to balance efficiency with local control. The 1856 Police Act made the establishment of 'Peelite' police forces compulsory in every county, but sweetened this intervention by providing for central grants to cover a quarter of the cost of pay and uniforms in borough and county forces, provided those forces satisfied inspectors appointed by the Home Office. The proportion of police expenditure met from national taxation was doubled in 1874, but Parliament still expected police forces to be largely controlled on a local basis.

The device of enabling Acts, already used before 1850, was further extended in the third quarter of the century. By 1880 the Local Government Board, created in 1871, had been given wide powers to take action by executive Order, reducing the need for specific local legislation. Acts involving this kind of provision included the Pier and Harbour Acts of 1861 and 1862, the Tramways Act, 1870, the Gas and Waterworks Acts of 1870 and 1871, and the Public Health Act of 1875. The increasing resort to this kind of delegated power represented a considerable extension of the powers of the ministers and departments concerned.

Governments (which were responsible for most of the increasing flow of legislation) were well aware of the frequent technical shortcomings of the drafting involved, something which often exposed ministers to damaging criticism in Parliament and public opinion. In 1869 action was taken to remedy this deficiency. Henry Thring, an able lawyer who had acted as an adviser to the Home Office since 1860, was appointed to the new post of Parliamentary Counsel to the Treasury. Thring had previously written the first textbook on legislative drafting.

He was now to head a small office, staffed by a handful of barristers, with the duty of overseeing the technical aspects of legislation proposed by government departments. Although this reduced the chance of ambiguous or imprecise drafting of legislation (and incidentally further extended Treasury influence), it did not eliminate it.

Official inquiries

The use of royal commissions and other forms of official inquiry to precede (or on occasion to delay) legislation continued. Such agencies could still be manipulated either by government or by other interested parties. A classic example is the 1867 royal commission on the trade unions, which preceded the trade union legislation of the 1870s. Agencies friendly to the unions, including some members of the royal commission itself, fed that inquiry with evidence favourable to the unions, much of it carefully prepared and pre-digested. The result was that, despite much evidence of trade union malpractice, the majority of the royal commission agreed to a report which recommended no impairment of the legal status of trade unions, while a minority offered an alternative report in even more favourable terms. The resulting Liberal legislation did not satisfy the unions, though. The succeeding Conservative ministry appointed another royal commission on taking office in 1874. When the second inquiry recommended no significant changes in the legal framework, Disraeli's Cabinet ignored its findings and enacted legislation giving further concessions to the unions.

A more typical example of the continuing use of royal commissions can be seen in education. Apart from inquiries of this kind into the universities, the years around 1860 saw three royal commissions investigating different types of school, each of them chaired by an aristocrat of high standing. The Newcastle commission of 1858, the Clarendon commission of 1861, and the Taunton commission of 1864 investigated respectively ordinary elementary schools, the great public schools, and the varied schools for 'those large classes of English society which are comprised between the humblest and the very highest'. The evidence gathered by these inquiries provided the necessary basis for further State intervention, including the Elementary Education Act of 1870.

Much mid-Victorian legislation represented further travel along well-established roads. Factory legislation is a good example, since much of the legislation of the years after 1850 either extended provisions already enacted, or built upon the experience accumulated from the implementation of earlier statutes. The Factory Acts of 1850 and 1853 effectively brought in a maximum sixty-hour working week in steam-powered factories, with the normal working week ending at latest by 2 p.m. on Saturdays.[4] Considerable piecemeal modification then led to further major factory legislation in 1867, which greatly extended the scope of

4. E. H. Hunt, *British Labour History, 1815–1914* (1981), 79.

the factory regulation system. Apart from bringing in some specific additional categories, such as iron works, engineering works, and glass works, there was a blanket inclusion of all workshops employing more than fifty workers. Children under 8 were not to be employed in any kind of workshop; between 8 and 13, employed children were not to work more than a thirty-hour week, and had to receive at least fifteen hours' schooling each week. In the 1860s and 1870s, further legislation imposed additional limits on the employment of boys in mines, as part of the building up of a code of mining legislation parallel with that for factories.

Although this legislation was well meant, and accompanied by some extension and tightening up of the provisions for inspection, it was not possible to make it completely effective, even in the range of employment specifically included. Factories and mines only covered a relatively small part of children's employment. More girls were employed in domestic service than anywhere else. It was common for children to be employed in family businesses of one kind or another, and in such small-scale activities abuse and exploitation could continue unchecked.

Ireland

The impression is sometimes given that Ireland was neglected in the years between the great famine of the 1840s and the inception in 1868 of Gladstone's first ministry and his 'mission to pacify Ireland'. This is misleading, for there was a great deal of Irish legislation during the years after 1846. It included the Encumbered Estates Acts already discussed (p. 200 above), as well as a major measure of consolidation and codification of the Irish land law in 1860, for which Richard Deasy, an active Attorney General for Ireland, was responsible. Much Irish legislation of these years was relatively or wholly non-controversial and passed in comparatively tranquil times; a low level of political noise left little mark on the historical record. But, as the years after 1880 were to show only too clearly, the mid-Victorian Irish legislation failed to get to the heart of the problems of the sister island. Some of it involved the application to Ireland of concepts of property rights which worked tolerably well in England. After the catastrophe of the famine years of the 1840s there was a slow recovery in Ireland, which governments and Parliaments were inclined to attribute, at least in part, to the wisdom of this policy. Yet much of Ireland was in a state which made these concepts inappropriate. There were deep-rooted differences in culture, religion, and thinking between many tenants and their landlords. For many Irishmen, British governments and Parliaments, and their land laws protecting landlords' rights, represented not legitimate authority, but alien impositions derived from past aggressions and confiscations. A tenacious sense of historical injustice meant that the comparative harmony of British society was not present in much of the Irish countryside. While relative prosperity continued, Irish hostility to

British domination might be muted; it never disappeared, and there was plenty of inflammable material available if the agriculture on which most of Ireland depended should come to face another crisis.

Education

Elementary education was another area of continuing State intervention. The system of grants inaugurated in 1833 evolved into a relatively sophisticated system of official subsidy, regulation, and inspection. Like the factory inspectors, the official schools inspectors developed into a kind of pressure group, frequently arguing for greater intervention and more public expenditure, arguments not always welcomed by ministers. Draft annual reports were sometimes referred back, with requests for the omission of items which could be seen as political or controversial. The attempts of the schools inspectorate to achieve consensus in regular joint meetings were also forbidden in the mid-1860s. Nevertheless, pressure for more government intervention in elementary education mounted, as evidence accumulated in various forms of existing gaps and inadequacies. From the early 1850s, a leading Conservative MP, Sir John Pakington, spearheaded a parliamentary campaign for more educational spending. The 1850s saw some extension in the scale of grant aid, more tied to school attendance figures. In the 1860s came the controversial Revised Code of regulations, the work of Robert Lowe. This sought to make grants to schools dependent on the attainments of pupils in a limited range of elementary education. The royal commission chaired by the Duke of Newcastle, which investigated the working of the system in 1858, produced a mass of detailed descriptive and statistical evidence, which strengthened the case for more intervention. The minority Conservative ministry of 1866–8, which included Pakington, gave serious consideration to education policy, but came to no firm decisions. The vexed question of religious education, inflaming sectarian rivalries, was a main reason why this nettle was not grasped earlier. There was also uncertainty on other grounds; not only a dislike of increased taxation and government spending, but also fears of entrusting to the State the potentially great influence which the control of education might entail.

For these reasons the Act finally passed in 1870 was 'a messy compromise'.[5] There was no question of the State stepping in to replace the existing agencies for elementary education. Instead, the State would, after an appropriate interval, intervene only where voluntary effort, aided by public subsidy, could not provide adequate schooling. When that regrettable situation occurred, after giving the voluntary agencies an opportunity to make up any deficiencies, a local School Board, elected by ratepayers, could be created, with power to levy a rate and with it build and maintain its own schools. In future years, this avowedly

5. G. Sutherland, *Elementary Education in the Nineteenth Century* (1971), 21. This booklet provides a convenient summary of issues in elementary education. For a fuller discussion, G. Sutherland, *Policy-Making in Elementary Education, 1870–1895* (1974).

supplementary public system of elementary education was to grow to an extent unforeseen and unintended by its creators. The extended access to public money provided resources greater than the voluntary educational agencies could match, especially as economic growth increased the rateable value of property, and therefore increased the revenue derived from a given level of rates. Gradually the Board Schools outstripped the voluntary system in scale and in resources.

In many rural areas, where voluntary schools had long been established, usually by landowners, a partnership between the State and private philanthropy endured. As before the 1870 Act, school buildings were provided by aristocracy and gentry while school finances came from a combination of State grants and private benefaction. Schools were inspected and children tested by officials but their management remained largely under the control of the country gentry.[6]

An enlarged teaching profession, with its own hierarchies, standards, and qualifications, came into existence, providing new employment opportunities for many talented men and women. Overall, the coming of the Board Schools marked an acceleration in educational expansion, even though the full results of the 1870 changes could not be gathered immediately. In the early years of this new dispensation, School Board elections were commonly fought on the basis of religious affiliation, and on support or opposition to public subsidies to voluntary schools. Since the majority of assisted schools had been created under Anglican auspices, militant Nonconformists and dogmatic advocates of non-sectarian education opposed the system of grants to voluntary schools. Supporters of the voluntary schools, including most Anglicans and Roman Catholics, sought to elect School Boards friendly to them. This led to considerable local variation in policy in time and in place. In seven large towns, including Lincoln, opposition to the 1870 Act was strong enough to prevent the establishment of a School Board for the remainder of the century.

The 1870 Act gave School Boards a discretionary power to pay school fees for poor children. Some militant School Boards refused to use this power for any children attending Church schools. In 1876 the Conservative government tried to sidestep this controversy, by transferring this power to Poor Law Boards of Guardians, a device which in contentious districts merely transferred the field of conflict. In the same year a step towards compulsory education was taken with the establishment of local school attendance committees, with a discretionary power to issue bylaws enforcing attendance. In 1880 a short Act supported by both major political parties made the adoption of such by-laws compulsory.

In Scotland an Act of 1872 set up a Scotch (later Scottish) Education Department and popularly elected School Boards replaced the ministers, hereditors, magistrates, and town councillors who had controlled most schools on behalf of the Presbyterian Churches and these became national or as they were

---

6. A study of philanthropy on landed estates in Northumberland demonstrates the workings of this partnership between State and private charity. A. E. Hattersley, 'Philanthropy on Landed Estates in Northumberland During the Nineteenth Century', University of Teesside Ph.D. thesis (2004).

known public (in the opposite of the English sense) schools. As in England continuing provision was made for some church schools, those run by the Episcopalian Church and the Roman Catholic Churches and these were eligible for government grants but the previous system whereby the education of the majority was in the hands of the Presbyterian Churches was no more.[7] There were significant differences between the reforms in Scotland and those in England. The Scottish Act set out to establish a public system of education while allowing separate religious schools to continue; the English Act of 1870 was intended to fill in the gaps of a voluntary system. Under the Scottish Act education was immediately made compulsory.

Administrative developments

Some of the administrative functions acquired earlier in the century were now being carried out with greater thoroughness and competence. This was true of both the decennial census and the system of registration of births, deaths, and marriages. The 1851 and 1861 census returns showed a higher level of competence among enumerators, as well as greater sophistication in ordering and interpreting the information collected. Later generations of demographers were to regret that successive censuses did not employ consistent inquiries or consistent categories, which made long-term correlations of census data difficult. Civil registration was only introduced into Scotland in 1855, and Ireland in 1864; in the former case certainly, the delay was largely caused by vociferous complaints about the cost of the system.[8] There were still limits to the accuracy of the registration returns. The published figures for infant deaths may have underestimated the total by as much as 10 per cent; nevertheless, they were sufficiently reliable to make it plain that, with the possible exception of Sweden, the infant mortality figures for mid-Victorian Britain were the lowest in Europe.[9] After 1874 the registration of births became effectively compulsory, with marked effect on the reliability of these statistics. By 1880 the official registration, for live births at least, was 'practically perfect'.[10] There was by now convincing evidence of the continuance of great disparities in health between different parts of the country. One disquieting element was the variations in the number of deaths of mothers in childbirth, some of them accompanied by evidence of shortcomings in the medical services of some Poor Law unions.[11]

The extension of 'Peelite' police forces to cover the whole country produced from 1857 onwards (though not until 1869 for Scotland) an improvement in national statistics of crime, which had existed in a highly imperfect state since earlier in the century. Even here, local oscillations in the returns could result

7. J. D. Mackie, *A History of Scotland* (1964), 338.
8. N. L. Tranter, *Population and Society, 1750–1940* (1985), 10, 13, 18.
9. F. B. Smith, *The People's Health, 1830–1910* (1979), 65–6.
10. Tranter, *Population and Society*, 20.   11. Smith, *The People's Health*, 54–5.

from changing police practices, often caused by sporadic campaigns against specific problems such as drunkenness or prostitution, rather than any real shift in the incidence of offences. Sometimes important statistical information could be gathered in a single rather than a continuing effort; good examples of this are the religious census of 1851 and the survey of landownership carried out between 1871 and 1876.

After the 1867–8 franchise reforms, Parliament enacted more legislation designed to improve the condition of the people. This was not a response to a sustained popular pressure for further intervention by the State, at the price of higher taxation, but something made necessary by the increasing volume of evidence of existing social evils. There was still a widespread disposition to view increases in government spending with dislike or dismay. Much of this pressure continued to come from the left wing of the political spectrum, suspicious of both the efficiency and the integrity of the government agencies of the day. In the years after the repeal of the Corn Laws, many radicals, including Richard Cobden, adopted as their first priority a campaign for the reduction of public spending. For the 1868 general election, the radical Reform League urged its supporters to give their votes to candidates who would benefit 'not only yourselves but the whole nation . . . [by] reducing the enormous expenditure and taxation'.[12]

Taxation

The House of Commons was often in sympathy with such views. In 1848 Russell tried to persuade the House to accept a five-year prolongation of the income tax at the relatively high rate of 1s. in the pound.[13] Many government supporters joined the Opposition on this issue, and the Prime Minister experienced a humiliating defeat. In 1851 the radical MP Joseph Hume, one of the most energetic of the parliamentary critics of public spending, carried against the government a resolution limiting the income tax to one further year. Two years later, Gladstone persuaded the House of Commons to accept a further seven years of the income tax, but only as part of a scheme to extinguish it by 1860.

The Crimean War torpedoed this plan; income tax stood at 1s. 2d. in 1854 and 1s. 4d. in 1855, more than double the level imposed by Peel in 1842. The increased income tax itself paid for about one-third of the whole cost of the war; current revenue actually paid for more than half of the Crimean War expenditure, with borrowing kept as low as possible. Sir Stafford Northcote, a future Conservative Chancellor of the Exchequer, expressed in 1862 an anxiety common in political circles that the war had 'not only rendered large expenditure necessary, but infected the whole nation . . . with ideas of extravagance'.[14] The level of direct taxation hardly justified such fears. Income tax was down to 6d. in the pound by

12. N. Gash, *Pillars of Government and Other Essays on State and Society, c.1770–1880* (1986), 52.
13. i.e. 12d. in the pre-decimal 240d. pound.
14. Gash, *Pillars of Government*, 43–54 explores this point more fully.

1869, and Disraeli's second government, at the cost of drastic cuts in expenditure, brought it down to only 2*d*. in 1875 and 1876. One reason for that government's growing unpopularity after 1878 was a rise in income tax to 5*d*. in 1879 and 1880.

In order to secure a grudging parliamentary consent to essential levels of expenditure, governments found it necessary to make concessions which included Civil Service reform and the creation of new checks on government spending. It would be too simple to see this development as entirely forced upon ministers by public and parliamentary opinion. Some ministers, including Gladstone and Northcote, were themselves keen advocates of low taxation and rigid economy in public spending. In 1853 the Conservative Northcote joined the Liberal Charles Trevelyan in an inquiry into the Civil Service. Their report recommended substantial changes, including the application of the principle of competition for appointments. However, by the time this report appeared in 1854, public attention was concentrated on the Crimean War and the practical effect of the report was limited. The changes introduced in 1855 were much watered down from the Northcote–Trevelyan proposals. Instead of open competition for Civil Service posts, most of the home civil departments acquired a system whereby ministers nominated to posts, and the new Civil Service Commission then examined the successful candidates to confirm that they were suitable. Departments laid down the scope and standard of the examination, which need not be demanding; one prescribed a test 'not much more than an ordinary boy of fourteen, with a poor education, ought to be able to answer'.[15]

This compromise lasted until 1870, when an improved form of genuinely competitive examination under Treasury control was instituted. Even the Foreign Office, exempted from the 1870 Order in Council, was induced to tighten up its examination system in 1871. In practice, there was little widening of the pool from which Civil Servants were chosen, and patronage retained a strong hold on the system. The atmosphere of government offices was not normally calculated to inspire an energetic performance of duties. Here is the Colonial Office as seen in the 1860s: 'A sleepy and humdrum office, where important work was no doubt done, but simply because it had to be done, where there seemed no enthusiasm, no *esprit de corps*, and no encouragement for individual exertion.'[16] A few years later, an increase in Colonial Office salaries was matched by a reduction in the number of senior officials from twenty-six to only eighteen. Open competition began in this department, after a prolonged rearguard action, in 1877: the first two successful candidates had been educated at Winchester and Oxford.

Yet despite the shortcomings which remained, the quality of the Civil Service improved. Some men of energy and ability were recruited to the slowly changing

15. V. Cromwell and Z. S. Steiner, 'The Foreign Office before 1914: a study in resistance', in G. Sutherland (ed.), *Studies in the Growth of Nineteenth-Century Government* (1972), 176–7.

16. R. C. Snelling and T. J. Barron, 'The Colonial Office: its permanent officials, 1801–1914', in Sutherland, *Studies in the Growth of Nineteenth-Century Government*, 153.

public service. Arrangements for entry, career opportunities, and superannuation became more systematic. The reforms of the 1850–80 period, while unable
to transform the situation, marked an important stage in the evolution of an
administrative profession of considerable if uneven merit. One modern writer
has praised 'The small self-confident organization of first-class men, the exclusive elite of the Victorian civil service . . . the deliberate creation of reforms which
reached completion between 1850 and 1870'.[17] No doubt many mid-Victorian
taxpayers would have thought this an over-optimistic verdict, nor is it entirely
clear that late-Victorian administrators included many men who were markedly
more effective than a Chadwick or a Simon, a Tremenheere or a Walsham, all of
them products of the earlier patronage system of selection.

Senior civil servants were still numbered in hundreds, though the total
number of State employees was rising at a rate which alarmed contemporaries.
Civil servants numbering 32,000 in 1861 had become 50,000 twenty years later.
This inexorable rise was accompanied by continuing pressure for rigid economy
in public expenditure. The relationship between the two developments was
not simple; pressure for economy could produce higher standards in public
administration, and help inspire a somewhat higher level of public confidence in
increased official activity.

Governments were compelled to accept new checks on the way they spent the
public money entrusted to them by Parliament. Some ministers, and Gladstone
in particular, were willing to cooperate in such innovations. In 1861, as
Chancellor of the Exchequer, Gladstone supported the creation of a Public
Accounts Committee of the House of Commons, a new watchdog on official
spending; in the following year he proposed the resolution which made that
committee a permanent part of parliamentary machinery. In 1866 the Exchequer
and Audit Department Act reorganized the procedures for the auditing of central
government spending. In future the Comptroller and Auditor General possessed
a tenure fully protected from government interference, and had a direct responsibility for drawing the attention of the House of Commons to any shortcomings
in the official accounts.

These changes made it all the more important that government accounts
should not be vulnerable to such intervention, and thus led to the extension and
consolidation of the Treasury's authority in government finances generally. In
1868 a formal Treasury Minute invited the Comptroller and Auditor General to
suggest items of departmental spending which ought to be subjected to specific
Treasury authorization. In the previous year, the first Permanent Secretary to the
Treasury had been appointed; George Harrison was a tough and able administrator who did much to establish an overall Treasury control over central
government spending. In the 1880s it could be confidently asserted that 'nothing
whatever can be done which in any way involves the expenditure of public

17. H. Roseveare, *The Treasury 1660–1870: The Foundations of Control* (1973), 75.

money without the consent of the Treasury.'[18] The imposition of this kind of tight control, especially if carried out in an inflexible and unimaginative fashion, might not always work towards better government, but it could help to promote public confidence that taxpayers' money was not being wasted. There still remained enough evidence of official shortcomings to justify public scepticism about the degree of efficiency attained by 1880.

Nevertheless, the expenditure of the State continued to rise, reaching £70 million by 1860, and £81 million by 1880. Many contemporaries were appalled by such extravagance, but economic growth meant that the State was taking a smaller share of the national income than it had done earlier in the century, though this was noticed less than the increase in the sums involved. Advocates of useful reform repeatedly emphasized that beneficial change necessarily involved a higher level of spending. In 1869 the head of the public registration system, Horace Mann, noting that the cost of the Civil Service had risen by more than half since 1848, warned:

If the public is inclined now to give up the various advantages... if we should be content with fewer public improvements, less police protection, fewer sanitary safeguards, a harsher poor law, fewer and dearer courts of justice, fewer postal facilities, and fewer and less useful schools for three-fourths of the community—then it will be easy enough to reduce the civil service estimates by abolishing several departments and attenuating others. But if the public really wants the things for which it, and not the departments, has been crying out, it can get them only by paying for them.[19]

Such warnings were unpalatable. In any event there was no sustained public demand or 'crying out' for more government. Instead the revelation of some serious problem or scandal might inspire a fitful public opinion to demand immediate legislative or administrative intervention, and then soon to lose interest. There was a more sustained public concern for economy and efficiency. It was a widespread belief among voters, although not confined to this enfranchised minority, that official administration was often extravagant, wasteful, and incompetent, and sometimes corrupt. Extensions of the franchise did nothing to dampen this belief, and may have enhanced it. As in earlier years, governments sought to pare expenditure, even to an extent they knew to be harmful. Popular outcries at revelations of inadequacy or mismanagement in public affairs rarely included any willingness to find additional revenues with which to remedy them.

National security

The defence of the realm was an undoubted responsibility of government. The manner in which this responsibility was discharged provides a fine test of

18. Ibid. 72–88. The quotation is from F. W. Maitland, *The Constitutional History of England* (1908), 409, and seems to have been written in 1887–8.

19. Quoted, from *Journal of the Royal Statistical Society*, 32 (1869), 38–60, by E. Evans, *The Forging of the Modern State: Early Industrial Britain, 1783–1870* (1983), 286.

government competence. Britain stumbled into war in 1853 with an inherently inefficient military administration. In order to save money, the War Office and the Colonial Office shared a single Cabinet minister; that much of the army was deployed in colonial garrisons provided some justification for this arrangement. The artillery possessed a separate administration under the Master-General of the Ordnance, while the militia was controlled by the Home Office. Army supply and transport were a Treasury responsibility, discharged inefficiently. The Aberdeen government tried to introduce a reformed system while the Crimean campaign was under way. By the summer of 1855 some progress had been made. Most army administration was centralized in a partially reformed War Office with its own Secretary of State. The potentially awkward relationship between this civilian minister and the military Commander-in-Chief of the Army was not satisfactorily resolved. Under the pressures of the war, and the public anger at the sufferings of the soldiers in the Crimea, the army experienced more beneficial change than in the forty years since Waterloo, but the progress made was limited. Little was done to improve the operational efficiency of the army, nothing to ensure that British industry could provide the necessary spurt of supplies in case of future conflicts (a defect which continued long after the period covered by this book). That the army and, indeed, the admiralty were both producers and purchasers of armaments was a continual problem. Whether armaments production should be in public or private hands or what the relationship between private firms and the Royal Ordnance Factory or the naval dockyards should be were questions that were the subject of a number of public enquiries but were never resolved.[20] What made matters worse was that, because of the administrative reforms after the Crimean War, the navy was not even in charge of the procurement of its own guns. The Royal Navy's Bureau of Ordnance was abolished in 1856 and thereafter the navy had to order guns through the War Office's Ordnance Department. This unsatisfactory arrangement led to much interdepartmental muddle and bickering. A senior naval officer noted in 1884 that, 'Nothing could be more unsatisfactory than the manner in which naval gun estimates were put forward year after year to be criticised, manipulated and reduced by the war Office.'[21] In the years after the return of peace in 1856, government spending on small arms and ammunition was drastically reduced. Even the tiny sums available were spent without any ingenuity; orders were distributed to a list of known producers in a fixed proportion which ensured 'that all market and technological initiative was lost'.[22] Public interest in army conditions during the war, though short-lived, produced some beneficial results.

20. Marshall J. Bastable, *Arms and the State: Sir William Armstrong and the Remaking of British Naval Power, 1854–1914* (2004) gives many examples of the difficulties arms manufacturers experienced in their dealings with the War Office and Admiralty.

21. J. Beller, *Birth of the Battleship: British Capital Ship Design, 1870–1881* (2001), 78–83.

22. R. B. Saul, 'The mechanical engineering industries in Britain, 1860–1914', in B. Supple (ed.), *Essays in British Business History* (1977), 41.

Barrack accommodation was improved and the more savage aspects of military discipline were toned down. Acts of 1859 and 1867 reduced the use of flogging for offences against military law; after 1867, flogging in peacetime was effectively limited to violent insubordination and a few sexual offences.

Gladstone's first government brought changes in both army and navy. Operational efficiency was not the first priority here, especially for Gladstone himself. The armed forces remained the most expensive item in the national Budget, and the Liberals saw further savings here as part of a general campaign of retrenchment which would be economically rewarding to the country and electorally rewarding to the Liberal Party. The army reforms were carried out by the ex-Peelite Edward Cardwell, and at first appeared a great success. The system of purchase of commissions in the cavalry and infantry was abolished, expensive overseas garrisons were reduced, the regimental structure reformed, and new terms of army enlistment introduced.

These reforms contained serious flaws. The new short-service engagements were long enough to disrupt a civilian career without providing a long-term army substitute. The abolition of purchase of commissions was more symbolic than effective. Officers' pay remained low, and in many regiments they needed substantial private incomes. There was little effective change in the sources from which army officers were drawn. The nominal subordination of the Commander-in-Chief to the Secretary of State for War made little effective difference to military administration. When, in the South African War of 1899–1902, the British Army again faced an even modestly efficient enemy, the results showed that the reforms had not eradicated Britain's military weaknesses in a dangerous world. The suppression of the Indian Mutiny ostensibly marked a triumph for British arms, but the performance of the army in the early months of the conflict had not been satisfactory. Similar defects were revealed by the Zulu War of 1879 and the first Boer War of 1880–1.

The outbreak of the Crimean War had faced the navy with problems, too. The government decided to attack Russia in both the Baltic and the Black Sea, but manning these fleets proved an administrative nightmare. When Britain had last sent the fleet to sea in force the impressment system had been available, but the idea of forcibly conscripting seagoing men was scarcely practicable in the more liberal Britain of the 1850s. The effective disuse of the old method of manning the fleet had not been accompanied by the provision of an effective alternative. Many of the warships during the Crimean years were not adequately manned and therefore much less than efficient fighting units, another legacy of the cheap government of earlier years.

With the end of the Crimean War in 1856, the Admiralty found itself grappling for the remainder of the century with technical revolutions in naval design and armaments. A distinguished naval historian of the early twentieth century wrote that 'The least ship existing in 1867 would have been more than a match for the entire British Fleet existing in 1857, and again the least ship existing in 1877 would have been almost if not equal to fighting and beating the entire fleet of only ten years earlier.'[23]

As late as 1859 the first-rate warship HMS *Victoria*, although she possessed a steam engine in addition to her full outfit of sails, was wooden-built and armed with 120 smooth-bore cast-iron guns. When completed, she was already obsolete in comparison with the new iron-built armoured battleships which were under construction. The first of these to join the Royal Navy, HMS *Warrior*, was a mixture of successful innovation and serious weakness. Although she was fast, combining a heavy armament and an armoured defensive belt, her steering gear was unprotected. In succeeding years, British naval preponderance was maintained by the building of a substantial 'Black Battlefleet' of ironclads, which saw continuing technical progress in design, armour, and armament. There was less attention to operational cohesion, and the British battle fleet remained a motley collection of individual or small-group designs.[24]

The record of the Liberal government of 1868–74 and the Conservative government of 1874–80 provided ample evidence of deficiencies in naval administration. In both cases, the received historical account has oddly neglected the revealing tale of ministers' handling of naval affairs. Disraeli's second government embarked upon a spirited foreign and imperial policy which ran the risk of major war. At the same time, a determination to show the country that a Conservative ministry could govern as cheaply as Gladstone led to a continued pressure on the defence estimates. As far as the navy was concerned, this meant that few warships were built and that these were designed with an eye to economy rather than fighting efficiency. Income tax was reduced, but HMS *Ajax* and *Agamemnon*, the two battleships of the 1876 programme, were 'two of the most unsatisfactory battleships ever built for the Royal Navy'.[25] When the ministry's forward policy did blow up into the international crisis of 1877–8, the government bought up a weird collection of warships under construction in British yards for foreign navies; none of these expensive acquisitions was of real fighting value.

These events may have marked the nadir of the Victorian navy, but the previous government's record had been much less than perfect. Hugh Childers had been appointed to the Admiralty in 1868 to parallel Cardwell's military reforms, with the twin objectives of saving money and reforming the navy. At first all went well, the excessively long list of naval officers was pruned, and some administrative reforms were achieved. However, personal relations in the upper reaches of the Admiralty soon deteriorated, as Childers pressed on his changes with energy

23. Sir William Clowes, quoted by D. H. P. Braid, 'The armament of naval ships in the nineteenth century', *Transactions of the Newcomen Society*, 56 (1984–5), 111–12.

24. G. S. Ballard, *The Black Battlefleet* (1980) provides a wealth of information about the mid-Victorian navy, including such incidents as the loss of HMS *Captain*.

25. O. Parkes, *British Battleships* (1957), ch. 36; assesses the naval policy of Disraeli's second government.

and tactlessness. There were embittered resignations of senior admirals and officials, followed by a series of naval disasters which exposed both Admiralty and government to serious criticisms.

HMS *Captain* was a battleship of unorthodox design and defective construction, which had been unwillingly accepted by the Admiralty, after a publicity campaign by her designer and his supporters. Childers had accepted these arguments, and showed his confidence in the ship by placing one of his sons in her crew. In September 1870, shortly after joining the fleet, the ship capsized and sank with the loss of almost all of her complement. In July 1871 HMS *Agincourt*, an ironclad battleship, was almost lost when in perfect weather conditions she ran on to a well-known navigational hazard near Gibraltar; two admirals were relieved of their commands in disgrace as a result. A third disaster was already in train.[26] In the summer of 1871 an obsolete and unseaworthy naval transport, HMS *Megaera*, had to be run aground on a tiny volcanic island in the Indian Ocean because her corroded iron hull developed uncontrollable leaks. Dockyard reports of her unsuitability for the long trooping voyage on which she had been dispatched because she was cheap had been lost in the Admiralty files. The whole episode revealed a long story of incompetence and mismanagement in naval administration. The government staved off immediate attacks by appointing a royal commission. When the commission reported in 1872, it presented well-documented and scathing criticisms of the government's handling of naval affairs, as well as the inefficiency of Admiralty administration. The appearance of the report was followed by damaging debates in both Houses of Parliament, and a great deal of adverse public comment.

Before this conclusion, Childers had been driven into a nervous breakdown and enforced resignation by his cumulative problems. Gladstone transferred the able G. J. Goschen from the Poor Law Board to the Admiralty. The new First Lord tried to persuade the Prime Minister that if the navy was to be run on a financial shoestring its commitments would have to be reduced. The Prime Minister's response was to renew his demands for further cuts in the next naval estimates, without evincing any interest in matters of operational efficiency. It is a remarkable instance of historical selectivity that Cardwell's army reforms usually appear prominently in accounts of Gladstone's first ministry, while the naval record has been largely ignored.

A dispassionate evaluation of the record of mid-Victorian governments in relation to their crucial responsibility for national security will suggest that contemporaries were often right to doubt the competence and efficiency—and sometimes perhaps the integrity—of those in office. At the same time, this unimpressive record marked an improvement in comparison with some earlier periods.

---

26. N. McCord, 'A naval scandal of 1871: the loss of HMS *Megaera*', *Mariner's Mirror*, 57 (1971), 115–34. This paper discusses naval administration in these years, its defects, and the impact of these on contemporary opinion.

Colonial administration

The administration of the Empire was another government responsibility in which the record was mixed. As we have seen, the Colonial Office was not noted for initiative and energy. Imperial administration was complicated by another factor, because, in the years after 1846, colonial affairs attracted the attention of a vociferous band of radicals, who entertained powerful suspicions of the activities of the British government abroad. Cobden and Bright were among the better-known politicians adopting this stance, believing that imperial expansion often included subservience to unsavoury vested interests and unprincipled oppression of native peoples.[27] They knew that the Colonial Office was not a paragon of administrative competence, and did not even credit it with integrity. Men of this stamp were always ready to believe the worst of British activities abroad, whether in the Burmese War of 1853, Rajah Brooke's adventures in Sarawak, or the settlement in New Zealand. Even if they were not powerful in the politics of these years, they were capable of making a great deal of noise, and inspiring doubts about the competence and honesty with which Britain's imperial possessions were governed. In addition, the continuing obsession with cheap government meant that colonial administration, like other areas of government, had to be economically conducted. In Natal, for instance, a hut tax levied on the native population produced in 1875 a yield equivalent to the whole of that colony's administrative costs.[28]

Cost-cutting was one strong motive for the grant of increased autonomy to the more settled colonial possessions. From about 1859, British governments were increasingly willing to give the self-governing colonies more leeway in conducting their economic affairs, even if this might involve some breaches in the canon of free trade. In 1867 the British North America Act created the Dominion of Canada, with extensive self-governing powers. This development was in part a step to forestall any dangers of US expansionism in the aftermath of the Civil War there, but it owed something also to the wish to reduce the cost of colonial administration. Cardwell's army reforms after 1868 included a substantial reduction in the costly garrisons maintained in the self-governing colonies.

India

The most important, valuable, and remarkable of Britain's overseas dependencies was the Indian subcontinent. India was always a special case, to be governed separately from the mass of colonial possessions. At mid-century, the imperial hold there seemed permanent and secure, with little official awareness of possible

27. N. McCord, 'Cobden and Bright in politics, 1846–1857', in R. Robson (ed.), *Ideas and Institutions of Victorian Britain: Essays Presented to G. Kitson Clark* (1967), 87–114.

28. R. J. Hind, 'We have no colonies: similarities within the British imperial experience', *Comparative Studies in Sociology and History*, 26 (1984), 14–18.

threats to British control of the subcontinent. The Indian Mutiny of 1857 came as a tremendous shock to Britain, though not to such sceptics as Cobden and Bright. Queen Victoria reflected a widespread feeling when she lamented that the Mutiny was the work of 'our own people whom we had trusted'.

In previous years the British authorities in India had continued an expansionist policy, as well as providing reforms in such spheres as communications, education, law, and financial administration. Many of these reforms assisted the growth of the Indian economy but the degree to which they ignored Indian cultural sensitivities and went hand in hand with missionary endeavours affronted sections of Indian opinion. The 'doctrine of lapse' enunciated during the viceroyalty of Lord Dalhousie (1848–56) allowed the annexation of a native state if the direct line of its rulers died out. In 1856 Dalhousie had gone further, annexing the considerable state of Oudh simply on the basis of the corruption and oppression experienced there under a native ruler incapable of exercising effective authority. This expansionism was one of the factors behind the 1857 Mutiny, although the immediate causes were grievances connected with both the Hindu and the Muslim religions. The area involved in the rebellion, and the numbers taking part, were limited, and most of India remained loyal. However, a substantial part of the native army on which the East India Company depended joined in the rising. Some of these rebels perpetrated atrocities, including the massacre of 200 British women and children at Cawnpore. These atrocities were widely publicized, and sometimes exaggerated, both in India and in Britain; the suppression of the Mutiny by British regiments and loyal native units was marked by retaliatory atrocities. The repressive measures adopted during the suppression of the Mutiny were generally welcomed by a British public fully informed of the conduct of the more savage mutineers.

The catastrophe of the Mutiny, with its unavoidable implications of shortcomings in the system of government there, meant that the old pattern of administration in India could not remain unchanged. At home the rival political parties agreed on setting up a new system of government for India. In 1858 the minority Conservative ministry carried an Act which finally ended the political role of the East India Company. Indian affairs were now entrusted to a new department, headed by a Secretary of State; in India the Viceroy was to be a Governor General and the sovereign's representative. The events of 1857–8 marked a shift in Anglo-Indian relations and were to exercise an influence which subsisted until the end of British rule nearly a century later.

The quality of imperial administration remained uneven. During Disraeli's 1874–80 ministry, the course of events in India and South Africa exhibited deficiencies both in the framing of policies and in their execution on the spot. In these two cases, the result was an unwanted involvement in wars which did not reflect much credit on Britain (see pp. 300–1 above). It was rare in these years for British overseas policies to be determined by men who were well informed on matters of foreign and colonial policy. Certainly neither Gladstone nor Disraeli was.

Local government

In local government at home too, there were grounds for dissatisfaction with official performance. Parliament enacted more regulatory legislation, but rarely provided central grants for its local implementation. Much reforming legislation in areas like public health depended on the willingness of local authorities to take action financed by their own ratepayers. There is ample evidence of reluctance or obstruction in this area, understandably perhaps in a context in which comprehension of the nature of disease remained defective, and in which official agencies were widely distrusted. Local hostility towards national legislation which imposed additional local costs also ensured the failure of one of the most ambitious initiatives in the field of public health, the General Board of Health established in 1848. The Board, modelled on the Poor Law Board created in 1847, was empowered to create local boards of health on the request of 10 per cent of the local ratepayers. In addition, in areas where the annual death-rate exceeded 23 per 1,000 the General Board could simply order the creation of such a local board. Local boards, elected and financed by the ratepayers, were given powers over a range of public health concerns such as sewers, water supply, and street cleaning. The General Board had little control over them and was often unable to enforce effective sanitary improvements, although it did its best with the small staff of inspectors and medical officers it was given. One of its most useful agents was Dr John Simon, who joined the new department's staff after a short period of similar work in London. He was an able social reformer, who was to do much in future years to spread the sanitary gospel of improved public health engineering and medical services. In the short term, the work of the General Board of Health involved sufficient interference with local vested interests to make it unpopular. The ministries in office during the 1850s were not willing to give the Board the political backing it needed to succeed. It was weakened by a redefinition of its duties and powers in 1854 and abolished in 1858.

Events in Croydon exemplify the conflict and fury that could accompany attempts to improve public health. Croydon's water and sewage scheme was one of the first to be completed under the aegis of the General Board so that it was a considerable blow to the Board when a typhoid epidemic hit the town in the winter of 1852–3, only a year after the opening of the town's water works. A decade later mortality rates were to suggest the efficacy of the actions of the Croydon Board of Health but throughout the 1850s the case of Croydon exhibited the sort of dissension that such improvements could bring to a town, ratepayer opposition, litigation, and quarrels with riparian landowners. Croydon, it has been said, 'contributed materially to the termination of the public career of Sir Edwin Chadwick and to the remodelling of the General Board of Health in 1854'.[29]

29. Brian Lancaster, 'The "Croydon Case": Chadwick's model town under siege', *The Local Historian*, February 2004, 17–27.

By now, however, the principle of intervention was so well established in government that the Opposition won only a symbolic victory in this matter. The functions of the General Board of Health survived its abolition, in the hands of other government agencies, the Home Office, the Poor Law Board, and the Privy Council. Simon moved to become Medical Officer to the Privy Council, a position he exploited in subsequent years in a continuing crusade for sanitary improvement, with modest success.

The brief existence of the General Board of Health formed part of a good deal of tinkering with the relationships between central and local government during the mid-Victorian period. In 1872 G. J. Goschen, a successful banker and merchant who had become a Liberal minister, summed up recent developments here: 'We have a chaos as regards authorities, a chaos as regards rates, and a worse chaos than all as regards areas.'[30] By that time, the country had acquired, as a result of haphazard legislation, a variety of overlapping local authorities of different kinds—borough councils, poor law unions, school boards, rural sanitary authorities, urban sanitary authorities, highway districts, port authorities, and others. In 1858 there was an attempt to make new local health authorities coincide with the boundaries of existing Poor Law unions, but this provision disappeared during the parliamentary debates on the measure.[31] Legislation in 1872 and 1875 completed a nationwide system of local sanitary authorities, after patchy provision in earlier years, but in no very orderly fashion. Within the area of a Poor Law union, for instance, urban sanitary authorities would be separately elected bodies, while the remaining districts would, for sanitary purposes, be administered by their own elected Poor Law guardians operating as rural sanitary authorities. Until late in the century, individual rate assessments were made for a variety of local government functions, such as Poor Law, town improvement, lighting, sewering, education, highway maintenance, and police. In 1862 ratepayers in Newcastle upon Tyne were liable to seven separate rates for different purposes, and the number was to grow in ensuing years.

London continued to present huge problems of its own. Before the Metropolitan Management Act of 1855, the capital possessed a chaotic array of about 300 local authorities levying an assortment of rates and performing different functions. In the 1840s, legislation had begun to clear this mess by creating two overall metropolitan authorities for sewerage and building controls. The 1845 Act set up the Metropolitan Board of Works, with members representing the main existing local authorities. At first this Board was given only limited functions, but it gradually extended its duties by a piecemeal acquisition of additional roles—a fire brigade for the capital in 1865, parks in 1866, tramways in 1870, for example.[32]

Parliament made several attempts to improve the road system by imposing new responsibilities on local authorities. The 1862 Highways Act provided for the

30. H. Finer, *English Local Government* (1933), 21.   31. Ibid. 88.
32. Ibid. 469–70.

grouping of parishes into highway districts for road maintenance. A further Act in 1878 introduced a distinction between local roads, which remained the responsibility of these districts, and more important roads, for which county funds would repay to the districts half of the costs incurred. These stipulations were not accompanied by any effective supervision, with the result that there remained great variations in the extent to which districts and counties troubled to fulfil these responsibilities.

The hotchpotch of local authorities which had emerged by 1880 could not provide efficient and economical management. At the same time, there was a continual growth in the duties entrusted to such bodies. If the boroughs normally showed the sharpest growth in local government activity and expenditure, there was also expansion of the role of county government. In 1856 the police role of the counties was finalized; the 1875 Food and Drug legislation, the Highways Act of 1878, and the statutory regulation of weights and measures, also in 1878, were other examples of legislation which increased county responsibilities.

Although popular suspicion of the efficiency and integrity with which local authorities would use the revenues entrusted to them continued, there were some developments which helped to improve the public image of local administration. One of the most important of these was the continuing evolution of the post of District Auditor, originally a Peelite creation of the 1840s. The Poor Law Act of 1868 and the District Auditors Act of 1879 established this officer as a qualified auditor, appointed and paid by central government, charged with the duty of checking the finances of local authorities. Although the boroughs were partially excepted from this supervision, by 1880 most local government expenditure was checked by this agency; the auditors could disallow improper expenditure of public money and surcharge the responsible individuals with the cost to the public.

In 1871 Gladstone's first government tried to improve local government by creating a department which would bring together the varied links between central government and the complex network of local authorities. The new Local Government Board took over the work of the Poor Law Board, and most of the local government functions of the Home Office and Privy Council Office. Other legislation, such as the Local Taxation Returns Acts of 1860 and 1877, and the Municipal Corporations Act of 1882, provided other supervisory roles; these Acts required local authorities to provide the LGB with regular accounts of income and expenditure.[33] G. J. Goschen, as President of the Poor Law Board, had envisaged this new ministry as a fresh start in social reform, but Gladstone found such potentially expensive zeal unwelcome. Goschen was transferred to the Admiralty before the Local Government Board came into formal existence. James Stansfield, the first President of the Local Government Board, did not possess the personal or political weight needed to impose drastic changes in policies on

33. Finer, *English Local Government*, 303.

either his ministerial colleagues or his senior officials. With a Prime Minister determined to reduce expenditure, and senior officials conditioned by previous experience, there was no likelihood of vigorous and innovative policies. The different elements which came together under the umbrella of the LGB were not effectively amalgamated, but continued to exist as separate sections with a good deal of effective autonomy. The staff of the old Poor Law Board, the largest component in the new department, exercised a dominant influence. The LGB inspectorate was largely drawn from the old Poor Law inspectorate, which had rarely exhibited much originality or energy in recent years.

One early casualty of the new LGB system was the medical department which had grown up under the aegis of the Privy Council since 1855.[34] Under the leadership of John Simon, this unit had actively campaigned for more vigorous official action in matters affecting public health. After the incorporation of his department within the new LGB structure, Simon pressed on with attempts to make the new ministry an active reforming agency, especially through his published reports for 1874–6. Such zeal was increasingly unwelcome, both to ministers and to senior LGB officials. Simon played into the hands of his opponents with an injudicious ultimatum in 1876. When his demands were refused he had no choice but to resign. The medical department he had headed was now firmly placed under the control of the LGB's general secretariat, where it could be effectively muzzled.

Neither Liberal nor Conservative governments sought to make the LGB an effective instrument for accelerated social reform. The Conservatives did not include its President in a Cabinet until 1895 and, though the Liberals were more accommodating in that respect, Gladstone had no intention of sacrificing his general policy of retrenchment to expensive policies of social improvement. The LGB soon acquired a poor reputation for initiative and even for ordinary efficiency, and its relations with local authorities were often difficult. Before looking at some examples of this, it should be noted that the years after 1871 did see limited improvements in local government for which the LGB deserved some of the credit. After the local government and public health legislation of Gladstone's first government, the country was covered by a network of local authorities concerned with public health. One of the provisions of the legislation was the compulsory appointment by these authorities of a doctor as Medical Officer of Health. This was usually a part-time salaried post, but might be a full-time occupation in a large community. These officials were obliged to provide reports on the sanitary state of the district for which they were responsible, monthly to their own local authority and annually to the LGB. This meant an increasing regular flow of detailed information about local conditions. It took some time before this system was reduced to proper order, but the LGB headquarters staff

34. Ibid. 340. R. Lambert, *Sir John Simon, 1816–1904, and English Social Administration* (1963), 360, 573. The latter source is particularly useful both for Simon's career and for the administration of the Local Government Board.

soon acquired the habit of chasing up MOHs who failed to submit adequate reports on time, or whose successive reports seemed to present discrepancies requiring explanation.

This improvement in information gathering and digestion was real but incomplete. The headquarters of the LGB, often active in chivvying defaulters among local officers, itself acquired a reputation for mislaying documents. Some examples of exchanges between the LGB and local authorities will illustrate the presence of friction. In September 1876 Hexham Urban Sanitary Authority was in trouble with the LGB, which complained that despite repeated requests it had received no response to specific questions about the sanitary state of that country town (which was not good). The central department threatened to take action by Provisional Order dissolving the local authority unless there was an immediate improvement. In February 1879 the nearby Hexham Rural Sanitary Authority complained to the LGB of a negligent delay in sanctioning by-laws, and it transpired that the relevant documents had been mislaid in the LGB office.[35] In 1879 different sections of the LGB headquarters received requests for approval of plans for extensions to the Houghton-le-Spring Poor Law Workhouse and for the building of a new wing for a local school; both were approved in isolation, with the result that the new workhouse infectious wards were built next to the new school building.[36] In July 1871 the Sunderland Board of Guardians decided to appoint a new office boy. In accordance with regulations, the nomination was submitted to the new LGB office, which replied with a refusal to sanction the appointment until furnished with a list of the duties to be performed by the new officer. Understandably irritated, the guardians solemnly resolved at their next meeting 'That the . . . Board be informed that the duties of the office boy will be such duties as are normally performed by boys in offices'.[37] Such incidents, which were numerous and varied, were not simply trivial matters. When the LGB was inept in its dealings with local authorities, this displayed the failings of central government to influential local groups in many parts of the country. The local authorities themselves displayed a mixed record in these years, with some progress accompanied by areas of uneven attainment.

Police

After the 1856 police legislation, the country possessed a complete coverage of county and borough police forces. Over the years the standard of recruitment, conduct, and effectiveness of these forces showed an overall improvement.

---

35. G. Cadman, 'The administration of the Poor Law Amendment Act, 1834, in the Hexham Poor Law Union', M.Litt. thesis, Newcastle University, 1976, 70, 405.

36. R. G. Barker, 'The Houghton-le-Spring Poor Law Union', M.Litt. thesis, Newcastle University, 1974, 163.

37. P. A. Wood, 'The activities of the Sunderland Poor Law Union, 1834–1930', M.Litt. thesis, Newcastle University, 1975, 134.

This was accompanied by a continuing rash of examples of inadequacy, which often received wide publicity. During 1863 the Metropolitan Police dismissed 3 sergeants and 212 constables for drunkenness.[38] The Metropolitan Police also came out badly over the Fenian explosion at Clerkenwell Prison in 1867; a constable who was on the scene while the explosives were placed against the prison wall made no attempt to interfere. The Prime Minister told the Queen that the London police were 'especially deficient as a detective force'. In consequence a special 'detective branch' of the Metropolitan Police was established; in 1877, three of its four inspectors were convicted of corruption in a spectacular police trial.

Provincial forces had their problems too. The West Riding county force sacked more than a quarter of its recruits during 1856–9. During the major engineering strike of 1871, which involved many minor disorders locally, the Newcastle police force was in a turmoil, with mass resignations provoked by poor pay and conditions, together with the harshness of an overbearing chief constable.[39] The neighbouring Northumberland county force also had its troubles, some trivial, some undoubtedly damaging.[40] In 1859 a constable was required to resign; he was in the habit of taking a friend along for company on his beat, and had been seen in the streets playing an accordion while in uniform. In 1879 there was an ugly burglary at a country rectory, with shots fired when the burglars were disturbed. Soon afterwards two men, Brannagan and Murphy, both notorious poachers, were arrested and charged with the crime; at their trial police evidence secured their conviction, and they were sentenced to long terms of penal servitude. Ten years later, the real culprits confessed, and it became clear that the police evidence had been fabricated. Brannagan and Murphy received free pardons and £100 for every year they had spent behind bars. One incident of this kind could have a greater effect on public opinion than a much greater amount of unobtrusive good service.

The view of the development of British policing that has stressed the unarmed character of nineteenth-century police forces and their moral authority has been questioned by a number of studies. As one historian has pointed out the truncheon itself could be a formidable weapon while it was not unusual for cutlasses to be issued or for inspectors to be armed with revolvers.[41] Yet when the small numbers of police responsible for policing a swollen town like Merthyr Tydfil[42]

38. D. Ascoli, *The Queen's Peace: The Origins and Development of the Metropolitan Police, 1829–1979* (1979), 131–4; T. A. Critchley, *A History of Police in England and Wales, 900–1966* (1967), 161.

39. E. Allen, J. F. Clarke, N. McCord, and D. J. Rowe, *The North-East Engineers' Strikes of 1871* (1971), 137.

40. Anon., *Northumberland County Constabulary, 1857–1957* (n.d.), 16–17, 51, 57–9, 64–5; J. J. M. Perry, *The Edlingham Burglary; or, Circumstantial Evidence* (1879); E. Grierson, *Confessions of a County Magistrate* (1972), 119–20.

41. Clive Emsley, '"The Thump of Wood on a Swede Turnip": Police Violence in Nineteenth-Century England', *Criminal Justice History*, 6, 1985, 125–49.

42. D. J. V. Jones, *Crime in Nineteenth Century Wales*, 1992.

or a rapidly expanding new town like Middlesbrough, 'Britain's Ballarat', are taken into account, the achievements of nineteenth-century police forces in assisting the creation of a more orderly society appear astonishing. It was only on the insistence of central government in the shape of Her Majesty's Inspectorate of Police and inducement of financial support under the County and Borough Police Act that in the 1850s Middlesbrough could be persuaded to increase the size of its force to thirteen, not a large number to police a town of more than 13,000 inhabitants.[43]

Rates

In other respects too the system of local government exhibited only modest improvements in these years, although its cost continued to mount. The overwhelming bulk of local official expenditure continued to be met from local taxation; this revenue was collected and spent by local authorities elected by those who paid the rates. The total levy of rates rose from less than £10 million in the early 1850s to about £25 million thirty years later.[44] The local impact could be equally striking. At Leeds the town council was responsible for collecting the rate imposed by the new School Board after 1870; the amount rose from £13,000 in 1875 to £49,000 in 1880.[45]

Apart from the complexities of the rates themselves, valuation for rating purposes was still a source of trouble. This was one area where legislation did make improvements, but not with a completely reassuring effect on public opinion. The County Rates Act of 1852 and the Union Assessment Committee Act of 1862 tightened up the assessment system; under the latter Act the parishes ceased to be responsible for valuation and were replaced by one assessment committee for each Poor Law union. This reduced the approximately 15,000 separate assessment agencies to a more manageable 640, and also introduced a standardized appeals procedure. After these changes the Poor Law valuation system was so much improved that its assessments were usually accepted as the basis for the rates levied by borough councils. Suspicions that backstairs machinations could still influence rate assessments were often voiced. In mining areas it was inevitable that Poor Law boards of guardians and their rate assessment committees would include dependants of mineowners. In 1876 the District Auditor for County Durham complained that 'No change in Valuation Lists of the Large Proprietors such as Collieries have been made since 1870—and some good times for the latter have been allowed to go by.'[46] Powerful interests could play the

---

43. David Taylor, *Policing the Victorian Town: The Development of the Police in Middlesbrough c.1840–1914* (2002).

44. Finer, *English Local Government*, 434.

45. B. Barber, 'Municipal government in Leeds, 1835–1914', in D. Fraser (ed.), *Municipal Reform and the Industrial City* (1982), 103.

46. Barker, 'The Houghton-le-Spring Poor Law Union', 81–2.

system in other ways too. In 1871 the Hartlepool Malleable Iron Company, and in 1876 the North Eastern Railway, refused to accept valuations imposed by the Hartlepool Poor Law Union. In both cases the Union won the court cases which followed; the legal costs were so high that the Union had to impose a special levy on its ratepayers to meet them, something unlikely to encourage such challenges in future.[47]

Attempts to persuade ratepayers that immediate expenditure might produce larger long-term savings continued to be received with scepticism. After an inquiry into a major cholera outbreak in 1853, a government inspector concluded that

in the actual exercise of those powers, the local Board does not appear ever to have lagged behind, but on the contrary to have been generally in advance of public opinion in the borough and of the views and the wishes of the ratepayers at large... the main obstruction... appears to have consisted in the impatience of sanitary rates on the part of the ratepayers at large, who have hitherto been more alive to the direct pressure of those rates than to the indirect effect of unremedied sanitary evils upon life and death, and ultimately upon the poor rates.[48]

Such attitudes were widespread; a recent study comments that 'In many respects Leeds, with its privies, its dilatory record of sewage disposal, and its epidemic victims lying under canvas was not unique, but simply represents an exaggeration of the worst features to be found in many other towns.'[49] Local ratepayers often distrusted their local authorities, an attitude picturesquely instanced in an editorial comment from one provincial newspaper in 1861: 'There may be some truth also in the somewhat tart definition that Boards of Health are bodies more prone to poke their noses into the privies of other people than to sit in judgement upon their own.'[50]

If such attitudes towards local authorities were common, there was at least as much suspicion of central interference in local affairs. Two comments on the Poor Law Board from local newspapers in industrial districts will make this clear:

The busybodies of the Poor Law Board have shown their official insolence this week by sending a letter to the Sheffield Guardians telling them to get on with their work and send it up for examination... The Guardians know that no workhouse is necessary and 8000 ratepayers have voted them into office on that knowledge. The Poor Law Board know all this and the more they are told to mind their own business and be idle, the better for those who have to pay their wages. We can manage our business in Sheffield without their insolent dictation and we mean to do so.

47. K. Gregson, 'The operation of the Poor Laws in the Hartlepool Poor Law Union', M.Litt. thesis, Newcastle University, 1976, 130–1.

48. *Report of Commissioners Appointed to Inquire into the... Outbreak of Cholera in the Towns of Newcastle, Gateshead and Tynemouth* (1854), p. xxxix.

49. Barber, 'Municipal government in Leeds', 78.

50. *Darlington Telegraph and Gisbro' Mercury*, 22 June 1861; we owe this reference to Dr Brian Barber.

and

Gentlemen of business who had been accustomed throughout their whole life to manage their own business in a proper manner did not like to be called over the coals from time to time as they had been upon the most trivial matters even down to the thickening of the people's porridge in the workhouse.[51]

The Poor Law

The Poor Law system continued to take the largest share in local government activity and expenditure. The rating reforms mentioned above, together with the Union Chargeability Act of 1865, which prescribed a uniform rate throughout each Poor Law union, remedied some of the worst defects in the Poor Law's structure. For the first time, wealthier parishes within a union were obliged to contribute to the maintenance of the poor from less fortunate districts. Modifications were also made to the law of settlement. From 1846 five years' residence gave a legal claim to poor relief; this was reduced to three years in 1861 and one year in 1865. The performance of local Poor Law authorities continued to be uneven. There was still a great deal of talk about the Poor Law as a device which could produce independence and effort among the poor, especially by providing relatively harsh treatment for the undeserving. Religion, which in other ways was one of the major forces for social amelioration, could sometimes present a stern aspect, exemplified in this statement by a leading Yorkshire radical:

It is no derogation from the bounty of God, but the reverse, that to a great extent He makes men the authors of their own happiness or misery...such is the order of things established by Infinite Wisdom and Goodness; and if in particular cases the rule may seem to be attended with hardship its general operation is productive of the highest good as stimulating men's virtues.[52]

In practice, though, 'the principles of 1834' were already much diluted, largely because of the obstinate refusal of many local Poor Law authorities to implement them. One of the main targets of the Poor Law Commission in the years after 1834 had been the ending of the practice of using the rates to subsidize inadequate wages; a report of 1853 showed that while 8,041 unemployed workers were receiving relief, 18,182 individuals were receiving out-relief in addition to inadequate wages. In 1874 a Poor Law inspector in north-east England noted in passing that 'cases of relief given in aid of wages are of course common enough.'[53]

The obstinacy with which local Poor Law unions obstructed policies which they disliked did not always help the poor. A recurring theme was the inadequacy

51. *Sheffield Free Press*, 19 July 1856; *Blackburn Standard*, 18 Jan. 1860; We owe these references to Dr Derek Fraser.

52. We also owe to Dr Derek Fraser this quotation from E. Baines, jun., *Life of Edward Baines* (1851).

53. M. E. Rose, 'The allowance system under the Poor Law', *Economic History Review*, 19 (1966), 608. This paper also gives a valuable discussion of the problem of inadequate outdoor relief, referred to in the next paragraph of the main text here.

of many out-relief payments, including many of the pensions paid to the aged poor. Successive central Poor Law authorities tried to induce cheese-paring local unions to award adequate out-relief, instead of doling out small sums which involved hardship but which could just keep the recipients out of the workhouse. As in other aspects of Poor Law administration, local authorities who were themselves financing their work from local resources were in a strong position to resist central pressures.

In Scotland the reform of the Poor Law in 1847 and 1854 embodied principles which in some respects differed from the 1834 dispensation in England and Wales. The Scottish Poor Law in theory still did not accept that the able-bodied destitute person had any claim on public funds. In practice, as the reformed system settled down, this harsh principle was not implemented, as a result of a series of evasions which became widely established; this included the assumption that destitution necessarily led to disablement and therefore to a valid claim for relief.[54]

A principal reason for the Poor Law reforms of the 1860s was a series of revelations of appallingly bad conditions within some union workhouses, especially in relation to medical care.[55] In 1865 the Poor Law Board ordered all unions to see to it that medical facilities in the workhouses were adequate; in the following year a doctor was added to the Poor Law inspectorate, with the specific responsibility of checking workhouse medical wards. Some of the worst Poor Law scandals had been in London; the 1867 Metropolitan Poor Law Act provided for the creation there of large modern Poor Law hospitals and asylums. From 1874, the central government made a grant of 4s. per week towards the maintenance of each pauper lunatic housed in appropriate accommodation. In Leeds, the Poor Law guardians were spending about £2,000 per annum on medical relief in the late 1860s, and by 1874 they could nerve themselves to build a new Poor Law infirmary for 456 patients at a cost of £18,000.[56]

The mid-Victorian Poor Law modifications brought about improvement, but not a transformation. Poor Law expenditure was still dependent on the rates, and controlled by boards of guardians elected by the ratepayers. Some of those in need exhibited traits which were disliked by those who provided the money for poor relief. It was still a locally intimate system, with recipients often personally known to many ratepayers. This could be a recipe for generosity where applicants inspired sympathy; public attitudes towards 'the undeserving poor' could be less indulgent.

Some Poor Law unions developed an able management, marked by long service by interested guardians. At South Shields, Richard Shortridge, the first chairman of the board of guardians, served from 1836 to 1854. When he died in 1884 he bequeathed £13,500 to various charities, and allotted £60,000 in legacies

54. R. Mitchison, *A History of Scotland*, 2nd edn. (1982), 388–9.
55. Smith, *The People's Health*, 388.   56. Barber, 'Municipal government in Leeds', 76.

to men and women whom he considered deserving but in need of money. He was succeeded by William Anderson, who had been an active guardian since 1836, and served until 1876. From the 1870s, the workhouse programme there came to include treats like Hamilton's Panorama, visits to the theatre, Punch and Judy shows, pantomime visits, magic lantern shows, and band concerts.[57] Such extra treats became increasingly common during the last third of the century. The money for them normally came from unofficial donations, sometimes taking the form of a private collection among guardians to pay for items which no District Auditor would pass as proper public expenditure.

In a number of ways Poor Law administration became more sophisticated. Regional and national groupings and conferences for staff and union authorities developed. The Northern Counties Poor Law Conference was one regional forum which was held annually from 1872; the 1883 Poor Law Conference Act legitimized payment from the rates of expenses incurred in such meetings. Poor Law staffing developed professional standards and qualifications, and hierarchies of promotion became established. An officer might begin his career in a subordinate workhouse position, then become master of a small workhouse and perhaps graduate to a more senior and better-rewarded position in a bigger institution. By 1880 the proportion of clearly unsuitable officials was smaller than it had been in earlier years, but there were still sufficient to affect public confidence in the whole system. In 1851 John Scott, Poor Law official and local tax collector, left his Tyneside home ostensibly on a visit to the Great Exhibition, but in reality fleeing abroad after embezzling some £3,000 of public money; in 1880 another local official in a neighbouring area fled to the USA with his employers' petty cash.[58] All parts of the country experienced similar failures in public office.

Despite the continued shortcomings, there was a continuing growth in local official activity. Both in scope and in quality, this was a patchy business. The buoyancy of local rate income was an important variable. The total assessed rateable value increased from less than £70 million at mid-century to well over £120 million by 1880.[59] In areas of economic growth, increases in rateable value could bring in higher local revenues without raising the level of the rates beyond what a critical local electorate would tolerate. Increased rate income also enabled prosperous authorities to borrow more easily; by 1880 local authorities had a total debt of nearly £140 million, most of it representing recent borrowing to finance local improvement schemes. Other areas might face considerable problems with little growth in resources. Joseph Chamberlain's work as a reforming Mayor of Birmingham in 1873–6 depended upon local rate income, as had earlier if less publicized efforts on similar lines at Liverpool and Glasgow. The pace of local improvement often depended upon the presence or absence of energetic local

57. P. Mawson, 'Poor Law administration in South Shields, 1830–1930', MA thesis, Newcastle University, 1971, 36, 49, 116, 150.
58. N. McCord, *North East England: The Region's Development, 1760–1960* (1979), 167.
59. Finer, *English Local Government*, 379.

reformers. If Joseph Chamberlain did much for Birmingham, Newcastle upon Tyne never produced an equivalent campaigner for improvement during Victoria's reign.[60]

This local variation is part of the general impression conveyed by the performance of public administration in the years before 1880—some significant progress, coupled with continued weaknesses, often well publicized in the expanding press, and feeding a continued public distrust. In 1876 a local cooperative society in a mining district met to celebrate the opening of a new shop. The main speech was delivered by a prominent local radical, who was warmly applauded when he asked his audience of coal-miners and their wives,

When, in a country like this, they raise for the government yearly the sum of £70,000,000, and they had the confounded impudence to tell them it is not enough, was it not time the people stood upon their independence, and told the government that, if they could not conduct the business of the nation in a better manner than to be compelled to spend £75,000,000 a year, it was time they went away, and that someone else took their place?[61]

60. This is amply demonstrated in M. Callcott, 'The Municipal Administration of Newcastle upon Tyne 1835–1900', Ph.D. thesis, Newcastle University, 1988.

61. E. Lloyd, *History of the Crook…Co-operative Society, Ltd.* (1916), 141. In 1875 this society cancelled its annual tea party in favour of a trip to a neighbouring port to visit naval ships.

9

Economy and society

c.1850–1880

Historians, almost inevitably and probably necessarily, divide the past into periods. One example is the 'mid-Victorian' period, extending according to different authors from the mid-1840s to as late as 1886 or more narrowly from 1852 to 1867 or 1851 to 1875.[1] More controversial is the allocation to them of inherent characteristics[2] though it is difficult to see how one identifies a period without making certain characteristics the basis of the division.

Few periods are as indelibly stamped by contemporary proclamation and historical interpretation as the mid-Victorian period, especially when it is defined within the narrower timescale. The concept of an age of stability, of confidence, or of equipoise is inescapable whether we question, modify, or attempt to dismiss it. The view that relative to the turbulence and problems of the 1830s and early 1840s, times when economic change was experienced by many as dislocation, and to the later pressures of mass democracy and renewed economic difficulties, the mid-Victorian period was, unusually, a time of felicity for many is enduring. Recent problems seemed surmounted or at least soluble, the present was better than the past, and the future could be looked forward to with hope.

That this concept and interpretation has lasted far better than most such depictions of a society or period is not because it is necessarily true but is in part because many influential contemporaries believed it be true and expressed themselves volubly and confidently to that effect, while many later in the century looked back upon the mid-Victorian years as a stable time. We can, notwithstanding this, find plenty of mid-Victorians who were angry, pessimistic, or even nostalgic and discerned some instability or lack of balance. It is also because for many, 'most people above the poverty line', the prospects of a more comfortable

---

1. K. Theodore Hoppen, *The Mid-Victorian Generation 1846–86* (1998); W. L. Burn, *The Age of Equipoise* uses the dates 1851–67; Geoffrey Best, *Mid-Victorian Britain 1851–75* (1979).

2. Hoppen ibid. argues that 'periods' may well 'be a mischievous conception' but are 'a methodological necessity' though he eschews the characterization of a period with a designation of a word or a term considering this 'historical brigandage', 1–2.

life beckoned; the downside is, of course, that for most people below the poverty line there was little real improvement.[3]

Perhaps the contented and the optimistic were the majority of the articulate. As one eminent historian has written: 'Mid-Victorian confidence was based not only on economic strength but on social balance. Taking the years from the Great Exhibition to the Second Reform Bill of 1867 as a whole—and they have a remarkable unity—almost all sections of the articulate community were able to show substantial gains.'[4]

Such felicity was not to last. Agricultural depression was to hit many farmers and landowners in the 1870s, early fears about foreign competition to British manufacturing were evident by then, and if many welcomed the 1867 Reform Act there were others who shared Thomas Carlyle's foreboding about the consequences of 'Shooting Niagara'.[5]

No period is, of course, one of pause and at mid-century Britain was changing rapidly. The 1851 census provides a snapshot of one momentous development, the move from a mainly rural society to one which was predominantly urban and industrial. The census showed a small majority of town-dwellers for the first time, but part of this slim margin came from the market towns of the countryside. Towns continued to grow, and the number of large industrial enterprises increased, but the scale of these changes in the years after 1850 should not be exaggerated. In 1861, with one exception, no provincial town occupied more than about nine square miles.[6] This limited urban expansion, nevertheless, was associated with a more striking change, the continuing leap forward in population.

Population

The population of Great Britain in 1851 was about 21 millions, having grown by well over 2 millions during the previous ten years. Ireland was still suffering from the famine years, and continued to record a decline in population until the First World War, when the total was not much more than half that of the early 1840s. Population growth in Great Britain continued at a high level. In 1861 the total reached well over 23 millions, over the next ten years 26 millions, and then there was another leap forward to nearly 30 millions by 1881.[7] As in earlier years, this growth was unequally distributed. If the 1851 census offered an equivocal indication of urban dominance, by 1861 the margin was more convincing, for

3. Best, *Mid-Victorian Britain*, 309–10.
4. Asa Briggs, *The Age of Improvement* (1959), 402.
5. Carlyle penned a furious pamphlet, *Shooting Niagara: and After* portraying the Act as a dangerous leap into the rapids of democracy.
6. D. Cannadine, 'Victorian cities: how different?', *Social History*, 4 (Jan. 1977), 462. Newcastle upon Tyne was the exception. The complexities of municipal boundaries, and their varying relationships to built-up areas, affected the picture. Newcastle's area, for instance, included the extensive Town Moor, still surviving as open space.
7. S. G. Checkland, *The Rise of Industrial Society in England, 1815–1885* (1964), 27.

the proportion of urban to rural population was by then 5 to 4. By 1881 the shift was clear; more than two-thirds of the country's inhabitants lived in cities and towns.

Although the annual death-rate was still high by later standards, around 22 per 1,000, with little fluctuation in the overall annual figures, it did not prevent growth because in crude general figures the annual birth-rate was around 35 per 1,000 in these years. There were many local variations. In 1874, Bristol, Edinburgh, and Portsmouth returned death-rates of only 17 per 1,000; London and Norwich 18; Oldham 22; Glasgow 25; Nottingham 26; Manchester and Hull 27; Birmingham 28; Leeds, Bradford, Leicester, and Sheffield 29; Liverpool, Newcastle, and Wolverhampton 32. Individual districts within these towns could also exhibit discrepancies. Average life expectancy at birth, too, varied greatly from place to place; nationally a newborn baby had a poorer chance of surviving for another ten years than a man of 65.[8] There were also differences in the toll of accidents and work-related diseases; seafaring and coal-mining, tin-mining and file-making, were among trades where risks were high. Yet, although the death-rates in the most unhealthy communities were alarming, 'the towns never were allowed to devour people as they had done before 1750 and as several French cities were still doing in the 1870s. British cities were the healthiest in Europe and among the healthiest in the world'[9] though the overall expectation of life at birth in France, a much more rural country, had almost caught up with Britain's by mid-century.[10]

The overall birth-rate remained steady until the 1880s, although limited by such factors as age at marriage. In 1851 about 70 per cent of British women aged 20–24 were not yet married.[11] The birth-rate reached a peak in about 1876 at more than 36 per 1,000, but as with the death-rate the national average concealed many local variations. Individual communities reached their high point in birth-rates at different times: Blackburn 1851, Glasgow 1857, Liverpool 1864, Preston 1866, Huddersfield 1872.[12]

Occupations

If overall birth- and death-rates were relatively steady, patterns of occupation within this growing population were still changing (see Table 6).[13] Agriculture's share had already declined relatively before mid-century, and after 1850 it fell absolutely. Employment in mining and heavy industry increased, as these sectors took a more central role in economic growth. (At mid-century agriculture still

8. E. H. Hunt, *British Labour History, 1815–1914* (1981), 47.   9. Ibid. 49.

10. E. A. Wrigley, *People, Cities and Wealth: The Transformation of Traditional Society* (1987), 274.

11. Hunt, *British Labour History*, 33. The author offers a contrast with mid-20th-cent. India, where 82% of the 15–24 age group of women were married.

12. Checkland, *The Rise of Industrial Society*, 60. In some cases it is not possible to be precise in relation to these intercensal years, but these dates will be accurate to within a year or two.

13. P. Deane and W. A. Cole, *British Economic Growth, 1688–1959* (1967), 142–3.

Table 6 Approximate percentage distribution of labour force, Great Britain, 1851–1881

	Agriculture, forestry, fishing	Manufacture, mining, industry	Trade, transport	Domestic, personal	Public, professional, all others
1851	21.7	42.9	15.8	13.0	6.7
1861	18.7	43.6	16.6	14.3	6.9
1871	15.1	43.1	19.6	15.3	6.8
1881	12.6	43.5	21.3	15.4	7.3

Source: P. Deane and W. A. Cole, *British Economic Growth, 1688–1959,* 2nd edn. (1967), 142.

provided about half the total employment in France, Germany, and the USA.) The expanding industries continued to attract migrants into the towns, but this did not necessarily involve a straight transfer of agricultural workers into urban industry. The industrial concentrations developed a hinterland of mixed occupational patterns, and the new recruits to industry often came from these adjacent districts, rather than a purely rural environment.[14]

Apart from the increase in industrial employment, there were more subtle changes in occupation. Even where there was little industry, the second half of the century brought a decline in local handicraft work, and an increase in services of many kinds supplied by towns, both varying from trade to trade and from place to place in their timing. In Pinner, Middlesex, for example, farm work and local handicrafts declined in the 1851–81 period, although the wage-earning population increased from 507 to 883. Domestic service, general labouring, transport, and professional work were the expanding sectors in that community's employment pattern.[15]

Growth was not necessarily accompanied by drastic change in techniques or organization. London remained the biggest concentration of industry, but most of it was small scale. The expansion of the great industrial complexes might attract most contemporary notice, and the number of enterprises employing thousands of workers might continue to grow, but most workers still worked in small units.[16] Most building operations, most farming, much clothing and footwear production, printing, the jewellery trade, shops, hairdressing, furniture-making, and many other forms of work were still small-group operations, with little or no mechanization involved.

14. B. Lancaster and T. Mason (eds.), *Life and Labour in a 20th Century City* (1986), 61.
15. K. Kirkman, 'Mid-nineteenth century rural change: the case of Pinner', *The Local Historian*, 17 (4) (1986), 199. For another area, R. W. Ambler, 'Social change and religious experience: aspects of rural society in south Lincolnshire, etc.', Ph.D. thesis, University of Hull, 1985, 14.
16. The point was made over half a century ago by Sir John Clapham, and has more recently received powerful endorsement in J. Breuilly, 'Artisan economy, artisan politics, artisan ideology: the artisan contribution to the nineteenth-century European labour movement', in C. Emsley and J. Walvin (eds.), *Artisans, Peasants & Proletarians, 1760–1860: Essays Presented to Gwyn A. Williams* (1985).

Mining

In mining, underground work was little affected by mechanization; coal-hewing remained a hard, dangerous, and unpleasant physical labour. Nevertheless, mining provided an increasing number of relatively well-paid jobs. Within this general pattern of growth, the industry experienced mixed fortunes during the third quarter of the century. Lead-mining had expanded earlier, but by 1880 faced such unbeatable competition from cheaper foreign producers that a calamitous decline was under way. The 1850s brought an increase in the exploitation of the iron ore deposits of the Cleveland area of North Yorkshire, which helped the growth of the Teesside iron industry. Coal-mining remained one of the country's most important assets and large-scale expansion continued, though increases in production were jerky rather than regular. Between 1857 and 1859, production increased by about 15 million tons per annum, a quantity just about equal to the total mined in 1816. The years 1871–3 brought another boost in output of about 14 million tons per annum. During the 1860s total annual coal production passed the 100 million tons mark and continued to grow. An increasing population required more domestic fuel, more steam engines needed more boiler fuel, and coal-using industries like gas and chemicals continued to expand. Moreover, these developments were not confined to Britain, and a growing export trade absorbed much of the increased output of some of the biggest coalfields, including those of north-east England and south Wales.

Some danger signals accompanied the increased output, though the major impact of these lay in the future. Mining wages went up, but there was a drop in individual productivity. In the ten years from 1865 output per man-day fell from 21 cwt. to 17.5 cwt.[17] In part, this was because greater production involved the sinking of deeper pits as more accessible seams ran out. There were reductions in working hours, too; in 1872 the pitmen of the Great Northern Coalfield effectively won a five-day week. (From early in the century the north-east coal hewers had worked only an eight-hour day.) In 1872 the Mines Regulation Act limited the working week of boys under 16 to a maximum of 54 hours, which in practice meant a reduction for other miners too. However, during the mid-Victorian period such adverse factors seemed of little significance, as British coal consolidated its position as a vital element in the energy supplies not only of Britain herself but also of a Europe experiencing urbanization and industrialization.

Other industries

The iron and steel industry provided one growing appetite for coal. Although technical innovations reduced the amount of coal it needed to produce a given quantity of these metals, output rose at a high rate, if unevenly. In 1875–9 Britain

17. Checkland, *The Rise of Industrial Society*, 59.

still produced 46 per cent of the world's pig-iron and 36 per cent of its steel.[18] Between 1862 and 1865 iron production rose by one quarter to 5 million tons; between 1873 and 1883 there was another increase from 6.5 to 8.5 million tons, accompanied by loud complaints from producers about inadequate prices.[19] In 1852–6 the value of exported iron and steel rose from £6.6 million to £12.9 million; much of the increased output of the 1860s and 1870s represented additional exports.[20] Again there were worrying features within a general expansion. Though foreign competition was growing, the application of scientific and technological insights within the industry was limited. In 1854 hand-pointers destroyed a new needle-pointing machine at Redditch. In the early 1880s a witness told an official inquiry that 'the finest steels in the world were made in Sheffield . . . but we do not know why it is. We do it but it is really by rule of thumb.'[21]

Industrial growth in the later nineteenth century was interlocking and interdependent. Apart from the obvious links of mutual dependence such as iron- and steel-making's need for coal, and that of many different branches of engineering for iron and steel, the connections were often closer. A leading entrepreneur might be a director of several companies which possessed some kind of association—coal-mining, railway, iron and steel, engineering, for instance. As manufacturing firms increased in size and complexity, some developed their own engineering facilities. At the Black Dyke Mills, the mechanics and smiths moved from mere maintenance to the acquisition of workshops capable of meeting most of the company's requirements for new machinery.[22]

Engineering

The engineering industry continued to grow in size and complexity, both in specialized engineering sectors—such as marine engineering or the making of textile machinery—and in firms which spread their interests widely.[23]

One successful specialist enterprise was the Singer sewing machine company. Its first British venture was the establishment on Clydeside in 1867 of an assembly plant for machines made in America. This was followed three years later by manufacture at Clydebank; after fifteen years the British factory was producing more than the American parent.[24]

British machine tool manufacture faced increasing competition, mainly from America. Some firms showed that they could succeed against this opposition;

18. W. H. Chaloner, 'Was there a decline of the industrial spirit in Britain, 1850–1939?', Sixteenth Dickinson Memorial Lecture, *Transactions of the Newcomen Society*, 55 (1983–4), 212.

19. Checkland, *The Rise of Industrial Society*, 43, 56.   20. Ibid. 38, 46.

21. For Redditch, A. Briggs, *Victorian Things* (1988), 180. For Sheffield, *Second Report from the Royal Commission on Technical Education*, Parliamentary Papers (1884), 31, p. 752.

22. E. Sigsworth, *Black Dyke Mills* (1958), 184–5.

23. S. B. Saul, 'The mechanical engineering industries in Britain, 1860–1914', in B. Supple (ed.), *Essays in British Business History* (1977), 32.

24. Supple, ibid. 41.

Cravens, for instance, retained a dominant position in the manufacture of heavy machine tools.[25] But in some engineering sectors British producers were plainly unsuccessful. Although manufacturers of farm machinery continued to flourish in many markets, they were outmatched by American rivals in the production and sale of reapers and binders, where the transatlantic manufacturers established market dominance during the 1870s.[26] In many fields, though, the British engineering manufacturers competed effectively. They consolidated a prominent position within the infant electrical industry, for example. The laying of the transatlantic cable link in 1865 was not only a British technical triumph; such a success encouraged manufacturers of such items as electric cables, insulators, coils, and meters. By 1882 £7 million had already been invested in electric supply schemes in Britain.

There was also progress in technical standardization, something rarely seen in earlier years. Between 1858 and 1874 the railway workshops at Crewe built 857 almost identical locomotives for the London & North West Railway and another 86 for the Lancashire & Yorkshire Railway. This obviously facilitated economical maintenance and repair. From the late 1860s onwards James Tangye was producing a simple, standardized steam engine which could be used in many different contexts.[27]

Industrial successes were not won solely on quality or price, but also depended on successful selling techniques. In a highly competitive environment, there were some very successful salesmen. They were not always scrupulous in the techniques adopted to secure the orders essential for company profits and continued employment of the workforce. In particular, the armaments and shipbuilding industries took salesmanship very seriously.[28] On Tyneside the firm which W. G. Armstrong built up from mid-century relied heavily on the contributions of such salesmen as Stuart Rendel, who sought orders from the Confederacy during the American Civil War by cultivating its London banker, Gilliat. He also made a friend of the Italian naval attaché and recalled how 'I used my acquaintance with him for the furtherance of the first order for guns from the Italian government.' On another occasion the company was approached by 'a gentleman whose relations with Spain enabled him to obtain early information with regard to any future programme of armament and ship-building, and in some degree to influence orders'. We need not doubt that such contacts could be matters of mutual profit. If, in evaluating the causes of continued industrial growth, the role of the major industrialists receives pride of place, many companies owed their success to the ability of their owners to sell as well as to manufacture.

---

25. Supple, *Essays in British Business History*, 40.
26. Ibid. 38.   27. Ibid. 34–7.
28. D. Dougan, *The Great Gun Maker* (n.d. [1971]), 105–6. F. Manning, *The Life of Sir William White* (1923), 140. M. D. Noble, *A Long Life* (1925), 65–6. Marshall J. Bastable, *Arms and the State: Sir William Armstrong and the Remaking of British Naval Power, 1854–1914* (2004).

Textiles

Textiles were still a mainstay of the British economy. Their importance was appreciated, their interests anxiously watched by many people without immediate connection with the industry. A prolonged attempt to domesticate the Andean alpaca in Britain as a source of raw material was supported by Prince Albert and an impressive list of aristocratic patrons.[29] Many aristocratic ladies supported a 'Buy British' campaign in fashionable wear when foreign competition seemed threatening. Such efforts, though, can hardly account for the fact that in the short period 1852–6 British textile exports grew by a quarter, largely owing to continued improvements in manufacturing techniques. By 1872 there were 42 million spindles at work in cotton alone.[30] Before then the long-drawn-out tragedy of the hand-workers in textiles was effectively over.[31] Among the last major groups to go were the hand-combers in the worsted industry. By 1860 the application of Cunliffe Lister's combing machines had greatly reduced that employment; redundant hand-combers scattered into a variety of other occupations: farm labourers and servants or, for the more adventurous, dock work in Liverpool or the expanding iron industry of Teesside.[32]

The transformation in the textile industry was not simply the replacement of hand-work by machines, for the improvement in machinery was a continuing process.

Silently and gradually the machines increased in efficiency and in the range of tasks which they could accomplish—the result of modifications and improvements which, however small they might be individually, added together over the years to consign earlier versions of power driven machines to the same scrap heaps upon which, at lower levels, the old wooden hand operated machines were rotting away.[33]

Detailed improvement in textile machinery was rapid during the third quarter of the century. Another indicator of interest in improving technology was provided by the foundation of a technical college with a particular interest in textile manufacture at Bradford in 1879. The cost of equipping and operating textile mills steadily grew; by 1867, the capital invested in the Black Dyke Mills was approaching £1.5 million.[34]

Growth was irregular in scale and timing; overall expansion was compatible with setbacks and even crises. In 1879 Bradford saw 417 bankruptcies, compared with only 165 four years earlier.[35] Dependence upon the import of raw materials and the export of manufactured goods meant that external events provided both problems and opportunities. The cutting off of cotton supplies during the American Civil War is well known, although its actual results were not uniformly adverse. Markets had been showing signs of saturation in the earlier 1860s; stocks

29. Sigsworth, *Black Dyke Mills*, 136.
30. Checkland, *The Rise of Industrial Society*, 38, 56.
31. Sigsworth, *Black Dyke Mills*, 43, 72.   32. Ibid. 40.
33. Ibid. 189.   34. Ibid. 218.   35. Ibid. 77.

had grown, prices were threatened. The shortage of cotton during the war emptied warehouses at a profit. As overseas countries developed their own textile industry, weaving usually expanded first, and this produced increased demand for British yarn. The British textile industry had to adapt to changing market situations, and did so with considerable success. Yet the process of adaptation was accompanied by complaints about falling prices and reduced profits, which helped to feed the later notion of a serious depression in these years. Complaints of entrepreneurial failure among British manufacturers began to be heard. Critical comparisons were made with a supposedly more efficient textile industry in France; it was less often noted that French manufacturers were regularly exhorted to imitate the superior British producers. The British worsted industry was quick to exploit the opportunity offered by the disasters which France experienced in 1870–1.[36]

Entrepreneurial failure?

The textile industry provides a well-known case study for the argument that British industry lost momentum during the second half of the nineteenth century, losing the capacity for innovation, risk-taking, and effective management which had presumably characterized it at mid-century. Various factors have been advanced in support of this thesis: over-reliance on skilled labour rather than on new machinery, the lack of technical education, and the nature of the family firm which entrusted management to sons rather than expert managers. A leading proponent of the view that British entrepreneurship declined has written that late nineteenth-century Britain

basked complacently in the sunset of economic hegemony. In many firms, the grandfather who started the business and built it by unremitting application and by thrift bordering on miserliness had long died; the father who took over a sold enterprise and, starting with larger ambitions, raised it to undreamed of height, had passed on the reins; now it was the turn of the third generation, the children of affluence, tired of the tedium of trade and flushed with the bucolic aspirations of the country gentleman.[37]

A wider thesis on these lines sees English culture as opposed to industry and economic growth. No sooner had a British class of entrepreneurs arisen and put Britain temporarily in the vanguard of progress, then, instead of creating an entrepreneurial ethos and culture, they succumbed to the delights of a gentrified way of life and left science for the arts and the factory for the country house. This echoes the complaint of Richard Cobden who complained, 'Manufacturers and merchants as a rule seem only to desire riches that they may be enabled to prostitute themselves at the feet of feudalism.'[38]

36. Sigsworth, *Black Dyke Mills*, 75.

37. David Landes, *The Unbound Prometheus: Technological Change and Industrial Development in Western Europe from 1750 to the Present* (1969), 336.

38. M. J. Wiener, *English Culture and the Decline of the Industrial Spirit, 1850–1980* (1981). The quotation from Cobden is on p. 14.

Yet, when allowances are made for size of home markets and the fact that the British economy was relatively mature, the evidence for entrepreneurial failure is thin, especially when objective comparisons are made between British and foreign manufacturers.[39] The charge against the cotton industry is that it was unduly slow in adopting ring spindles and automatic looms but the abundant supply of skilled labour and the nature of British markets would have made any rush into new technologies uneconomic. The British textile industry remained generally successful. Studies of the iron industry and the chemical industry have similarly found the charges of entrepreneurial failure to have been much exaggerated.[40] One pointer to this is the way in which foreigners sought to enter British industry. By 1861 a substantial proportion of the successful merchant families in Bradford had come from abroad to settle there.[41] Moreover, British expertise was exported in the shape of subsidiary factories established in other countries, such as the German factories established by the Foster family, which depended upon key workers seconded from the parent company.[42]

Shipbuilding and shipping

The country's overseas trade, and the important coasting traffic, were largely carried in British-owned and British-built ships. There was a major shift in shipbuilding, from wooden sailing ships to iron, and then steel, steamships. In 1851 the tonnage of sailing ships on the British register was almost twenty times that of steamships, and even the latter were still mostly wooden. This sailing fleet reached its peak around 1865, when its tonnage was still five times that of the steamers. The balance was shifting quickly, however, and steam was predominant by the 1880s. By that time shipbuilding in wood had become of minor importance.[43]

This had transformed working practices for ships' crews and for shipyard workers. The shift in technology was not painless. Seafaring never is a safe occupation, and for most of the century merchant seamen were more at risk than coal-miners. As competition from steamships grew, owners and masters of sailing ships were tempted to cut corners on costs and take risks which might have been avoided in easier times. But at the same time, early steamships were subject to faults in design or construction which could be dangerous. Between 1856 and 1878, 17,564 lives were lost in shipwrecks around the coasts of Great Britain, though many masters of both sailing and steam ships with long seagoing careers never lost a single man, and the safety standards of shipping continued to improve.

39. L. G. Sandberg, 'The entrepreneur and Technological Change' in R. Floud and D. McCloskey (eds.), *The Economic History of Britain since 1700, Vol. 2: 1860–1939* (1981). L. G. Sandberg, *Lancashire in Decline* (1974).

40. P. H. Lindert and K. Trace, 'Yardsticks for Victorian Entrepreneurs' in D. N. McCloskey (ed.), *Essays on a Mature Economy: Britain after 1840* (1971). D. N. McCloskey, *Economic Maturity and Entrepreneurial Decline: British Iron and Steel, 1870–1913* (1973).

41. Sigsworth, *Black Dyke Mills*, 65.   42. Ibid. 284, 293.

43. P. Mathias, *The First Industrial Nation*, 2nd edn. (1983), 286.

Britain's industrial eminence in the age of iron, steam, and coal favoured the growth of shipbuilding in such places as Clydeside and the harbours of north-east England. By the mid-1870s, Clydeside had 40,000 shipyard workers, while on Tyneside it was a local joke that Palmer's yard built its iron colliers by the mile and then chopped them into convenient lengths. The second half of the century brought increases in the average size of ships and the extent of technological innovation. Britain not only built most of the ships of the British merchant navy, but could claim to be the shipyard of the world, since a majority of new ships came from British yards.

By the 1870s Britain's seagoing shipping was as great as that of the rest of the world combined. Even in 1860 the merchant navy's contribution (nearly £40 million) to national income was crucial in balancing the national accounts; it was to grow to over £75 million by the early twentieth century.[44] The importance of Britain as a producer of manufactured goods and of coal, and the key role of British shipping, worked together to mutual advantage. In the age of coal and iron, Britain had initial advantages, but the extent of dominance in commercial shipping also owed much to the entrepreneurial talents of British shipowners. Apart from shrewd management at home, shipping lines built up a network of agents throughout the world which provided commercial intelligence and facilitated orders.

Railways

After their early heroic phase, the railways settled down into an established system. The 6,000 miles of track built by mid-century more than doubled by 1871; the number of passenger journeys more than quadrupled, with third-class passengers providing most of the extra business. Experience, often painful, accumulated a body of railway lore, covering such matters as commercial operations, technical reliability, and safety regulations. British engineering knowledge and experience, and the availability of British capital, provided opportunities for lucrative contracts for building foreign railways. The first Norwegian trunk railway was built in the 1850s by British contractors under the supervision of British engineers, and the locomotives came from Robert Stephenson's Newcastle works. The line remained under British management during its early years.[45] Despite increased traffic, too, the safety record of British railways improved. Techniques of signalling and train braking became more sophisticated, but some aspects of railway work remained dangerous. Even late in the century, shunting produced high levels of accidental death and injury.[46]

---

44. Checkland, *The Rise of Industrial Society*, 146. Deane and Cole, *British Economic Growth*, 234.

45. P. Perkins, Report on lecture in *Newcomen Bulletin*, 133 (Dec. 1985), 5–6. In this case the locomotives were not an unmixed success.

46. Hunt, *British Labour History*, 349 n. 39.

Many of the later railways were never profitable, the traffic never justifying the initial investment and the running costs, from the time they were built until their closure in the mid-twentieth century,[47] but the developed railway network facilitated the delivery of farm produce to market and the evolution of postal services. Telegraph wires ran alongside the railway lines, carrying urgent commercial intelligence, swift personal and family communications, and a growing supply of national and international news to the expanding provincial press. The number of letters increased; by 1871 there was an annual average of 32 letters per head for the whole population and this almost doubled by the end of the century. A widely read magazine of 1862 observed that 'when we find that the town of Manchester equals in its number of letters the empire of all the Russias... we obtain a means of estimating the relative degrees of British and Russian civilisation.'[48] The postal services greatly extended communications within, as well as between, the growing urban areas. In 1863 nearly half of all the letters delivered in London originated there.[49]

Retail trade

Much commercial correspondence came from the expanding retail sector. During the third quarter of the century the number and variety of shops continued to grow. The North Staffordshire mining community of Silverdale was not in the forefront of sophisticated lifestyles; it had only 13 shops in 1851, but 95 thirty years later.[50] Although most shops were privately owned, the cooperative retail societies had a respectable minority share of them. There were at least 138 of these societies active in the early 1850s, and their numbers continued to grow, finding favourable conditions in northern mining villages and the textile manufacturing towns of the West Riding. Bradford's first cooperative society was founded in 1860; 201 members shared a first dividend for the first six months' trading of £33. 2*s*. 5*d*. By 1874 the same society had 3,184 members and a half-year's profits had reached more than £2,300.

A retail revolution was under way. A number of shops which had started with one line of business, usually either food or drapery, had like Bainbridges of Newcastle, Harrod's, Whiteley's, and Derry & Toms of London, and Kendal

47. In rural Northumberland for instance the Border Counties Railway from Hexham to Rickerton Junction was never a commercial success and nor was the railway from Alnwick to Cornhill. For the latter see N. D. Mackichan, *The Northumberland Central Railway* (1997).

48. D. Vincent, 'Communications, community and the State', in Emsley and Walvin (eds.), *Artisans, Peasants & Proletarians, 1760–1860: Essays Presented to Gwyn A. Williams* (1985), 167. Although the article quoted in the text appeared in *Fraser's Magazine* in 1862, the calculation was based on a Post Office report of 1855.

49. Ibid. 177.

50. E. Billingham, 'Silverdale: a demographic study of a North Staffordshire mining village, 1841 to 1881', MA thesis, Wolverhampton Polytechnic, 1985, 120. We owe the information on the Bradford co-operative society to Dr Barbara Thompson.

Milne of Manchester opened several different departments and soon most cities and large towns had department stores dealing in many different articles.[51] Department stores worked on the principle that customers liked to be able to purchase an array of goods from one shop and once in the shop to buy a table-cloth might be attracted by a display of hats in the next department. The chain stores which began to appear in the 1870s were based on the different principle that shoppers liked to find specialist shops with well-known names in every high street. Thomas Lipton started with one grocer's shop in Glasgow and expanded so as to have branches over most of Britain. The Maypole Dairy Company and the Home and Colonial Stores followed the same path.

For the most part chain stores were confined to the food trade until the 1880s but in 1877 Jesse Boot opened his first chemist's shop in Nottingham. The grand-son of a farm labourer and son of a vendor of herbal remedies, Boot was a self-taught pharmacist. Much of the business of a mid-Victorian retail chemist consisted of the sale of patent medicines. One of Jesse Boot's early activities was an agency for one of the followers of the well-named American quack Dr J. A. Coffin, whose 'medicines' were poisonous. In 1859 Thomas Beecham moved his head-quarters to St Helens, and from this new base the production of Beecham's Pills continued to grow. The 1875 Sale of Food and Drugs Act put out of business many lesser purveyors of patent medicines, by making it easier for larger concerns to establish proprietary brands containing the more popular ingredients. In 1880 over 17 million duty stamps for patent medicines were issued, the official stamp conveying to the ill-informed a misleading indication of official guarantee.[52]

Large-scale promotion was to be seen in the marketing of other goods, too. There were 145,000 licensed tobacco sellers in 1860, offering a market which became the target of the West Country Nonconformist Wills family. In 1849 that firm introduced, with their Bristol cigarettes, the idea of pushing popular brand names on a national basis. By the 1860s it was spending heavily on advertising skilfully packaged wares, and employed a national network of travellers.

Though the expansion of retail trade must be judged a social improvement, the results were not entirely unmixed. An extended milk supply system, with higher sales, contributed to the danger from tuberculosis, in a society which had no idea that there might be a connection between infected milk and that disease. The increased supply and consumption of meat also presented public health dangers. By 1868 Leeds had nearly 300 slaughter houses, without adequate means of dealing with the consequent pollution.[53]

---

51. There is considerable dispute as to which was the first department store. Bainbridges of Newcastle or Whiteley's or Galleries Lafayette in Paris are often quoted.

52. F. B. Smith, *The People's Health, 1830–1910* (1979), 343–5. This book gives much information about the patent medicine business, its extent, and its effects on health. Boot and Beecham have entries in *ODNB*.

53. B. Barber, 'Municipal government in Leeds, 1835–1914', in D. Fraser (ed.), *Municipal Reform and the Industrial City* (1982), 83.

The overall result of the coming of the mass market was beneficial: 'for most of the people, industry was able to offer an ever-widening range of choices for their food, their clothing, their domestic furnishings and for their entertainment.'[54]

Financial services

The growth and elaboration of the retail sector could not have taken place without widespread literacy among those who were far from rich.[55] The development of financial services also shows an increased sophistication in society, as banks, insurance, and stock exchanges multiplied and the third quarter of the century brought advances in accounting techniques. At the Black Dyke Mills, the primitive accounting which had sufficed earlier in the century was by 1867 replaced by the systematic keeping of financial records.[56] Not all industrial firms were capable of accurate estimates of costs or profit, but there were moves towards more professional office management and bookkeeping techniques. The Scottish Institute of Chartered Accountants was established in 1854, and smaller bodies in England and Wales came together in a similar organization in 1880.

Bitter experience helped to make banking practices more responsible during the second half of the century. The banking crisis of 1857 was largely caused by irresponsible or fraudulent practices by some provincial joint-stock banks and provided a useful lesson. It also marked a stage in the growing cohesion of the banking sector. The Bank of England had, by mid-century, stopped trying to discourage the growth of the joint-stock banks, adopting instead a policy of cooperation: from 1854 the Bank allowed the admission of joint-stock banks to the London Bankers' Clearing House. During the 1857 crisis the Bank did its best to help the provincial banks most at risk, although some of them were so unsound that their failure could not be averted. Governments, far from adopting any laissez-faire attitude towards banking, continued to try to enforce better standards. Acts of 1858 and 1862 gave a degree of limited liability to banks which observed specified conditions.

Scotland was badly affected by the 1857 crash as the Western Bank with its 100 branches closed leaving liabilities of £9,000,000. In 1878 another major Scottish bank, the City of Glasgow Bank, went down amidst charges of fraud and incompetence. In both cases Clydesiders blamed the reluctance of Edinburgh banks to come to the aid of their Glasgow counterparts. Nevertheless, Scottish banks were well placed to invade England but the opening of branches of Scottish banks over the border in 1874 produced such an outcry from English bankers that apart from their London offices, Scottish banks confined themselves to Scotland for a century and English banks agreed not to open in Scotland.[57]

54. W. H. Fraser, *The Coming of the Mass Market 1850–1914* (1981), 239.
55. Hunt, *British Labour History*, 111.   56. Sigsworth, *Black Dyke Mills*, 218.
57. John Keay and Julia Keay, eds., *Collins Encyclopaedia of Scotland* (1994), 62.

During the third quarter of the century, banks extended their role in the economy. Not only did companies and individuals at home make greater use of banking facilities, but the growth of overseas trade and the extended activity of British shipping offered increased opportunities for overseas banking business.

Over the same period, the London Stock Exchange established a commanding position, partly because of its openness in recruiting members and its ready acceptance of new enterprises for trading. The London practice of fixed periods for settlement, without payment being required before the end of the nineteen-to twenty-day period, encouraged an increase in share transactions. Compared, for instance, with the practices of the New York Stock Exchange, London was positively welcoming. This involved risks, for it was not only shares in sound, well-managed concerns which were traded there, yet its business doubled in the ten years before 1872.[58] The provincial exchanges also developed. Dealings in railway shares had been a major factor in their creation; in the third quarter of the century their interests widened, with a natural concentration upon enterprises within their own regions.

Insurance also grew. By the third quarter of the century, the habit of insuring persons and property was well established. In 1862 two-thirds of all property was covered in some measure, including the majority of properties for which fire insurance was practicable. As early as the 1860s the annual premiums for life insurance, mostly on a small scale, passed the £1.5 million mark, and were to go on increasing rapidly. Nor does this take account of the large numbers who enjoyed equivalent provision through friendly societies and similar bodies. As in other sectors of the economy, selling techniques improved; in 1850 the Royal Exchange Assurance Company employed 600 agents, and their number grew rapidly during the second half of the century.

Growth within the financial sector was punctuated by other crises in addition to that of 1857. The failure of a major banking house, Overend & Gurney, which behind a facade of high respectability had taken to unsound practices, provoked another financial panic in May 1866. This involved the collapse of some construction firms; even the greatest of them all, Thomas Brassey, had only a narrow escape. A boom was followed by another financial crisis in 1873, again accompanied by the failure of important enterprises where high reputation had concealed incompetence and even fraud.[59]

The overall expansion of financial services had important results. One was the appearance of a much expanded group of 'City men' who took an increasingly prominent part in national life.[60] There was more to the growth of financial services than this, however. Their activities were by no means confined to the domestic market. They became increasingly important overseas earners. In the

---

58. We owe this information to Dr Ranald Michie.
59. Checkland, *The Rise of Industrial Society*, 44–50.
60. P. J. Cain and A. B. Hopkins, 'Gentlemanly capitalism and British expansion overseas. 1: The old colonial system, 1688–1850', *Economic History Review*, 2nd ser., 39 (4) (1986), 507.

later nineteenth century, as some sectors of home insurance became saturated, British insurance companies expanded overseas; by 1900 two-fifths of their premiums for fire insurance came from overseas policies.[61] Income from financial services abroad, like the dues earned by British shipping, provided a crucial credit item in the national balance sheet. In the years around 1880, there was an annual deficit of about £100 million from the surplus of imported goods over exports. This imbalance was more than matched by other income, including a crucial contribution from financial services. Industrial and commercial strength gave Britain a central position within the expanding international economy, and within this 'London's financial hegemony was the reflection in a golden mirror of commercial and maritime strength.'[62] Between 1870 and 1913 industrial production rose by about 150 per cent; the income generated by financial services rose tenfold.[63]

Britain's credit balance in international economic activity provided the basis for a growing overseas investment which generated additional income. In 1850 Britain had a relatively modest £225 million invested abroad. This was already fast increasing. By 1857 British investors had sunk some £80 million in US railways alone. Not all overseas adventures proved safe, let alone profitable (some American railways were notorious), but the overall results were satisfactory enough to encourage imitation. By 1875 total overseas investment had jumped to £1,000 million and it reached £1,500 million ten years later.[64] With this expanding source of income, Britain's overall credit balance seemed secure. The extent to which the British economy depended on this factor, and on the income from various 'invisible earnings', was not generally appreciated. British prosperity was usually attributed to industrial growth and increased exports.

Agriculture

Despite its relative decline in importance as a source of employment and income, farming remained prosperous on the whole during most of the third quarter of the century. Although employment in agriculture declined, investment did not. In the years after 1850, Lancashire landowners were investing in improvements as a means of maintaining or increasing income.[65] The fall in cereal prices which was to occur after 1879 could not be foreseen in the 1850s and 1860s, when the practice of 'high farming' seemed to promise a satisfactory return on capital employed in improvements. (It would have taken remarkable prescience then to foresee that the cost of transporting food to Britain would be halved in

61. B. Supple, 'Corporate growth and structural change in a service industry, 1870–1914', in Supple (ed.), *Essays in British Business History*, 70.

62. Mathias, *The First Industrial Nation*, 329.

63. B. Supple, 'A framework for British business history', in Supple (ed.), *Essays in British Business History*, 15.

64. Checkland, *The Rise of Industrial Society*, 65.

65. G. Rogers, 'Lancashire landowners and the great agricultural depression', *Northern History*, 22 (1986), 250–68, for an illuminating regional study.

the 1870s.) The growth in urban markets, developments in fertilizers and cheap pipes for field drainage, and the availability of capital and credit for improvement schemes, all contributed to the trend. Even during the 1870s, there was a marked increase in such investment in Lancashire, Cheshire, Yorkshire, Gloucestershire, and Northumberland, to name only a few of the most active areas. Much of it was ultimately to prove unprofitable. Most of the capital required was borrowed, and in the last quarter of the century became a burden on many estates, as prices ceased to offer a reasonable return.[66]

In the 1850s, 1860s, and earlier 1870s, however, such dangers lay in the unknown future. British farming not only seemed to have rosy prospects but stimulated associated elements in the economy. In the 1850s about 100,000 tons of guano for fertilizer were shipped into Britain each year.[67] The willingness of landowners and farmers to invest in improved techniques encouraged agricultural machinery manufacturers.[68] Britain was, however, already importing food on an increasing scale.[69]

Free trade

The increasing reliance on foreign food imports reflected the continuing uncritical confidence in the concept of free trade which had finally triumphed in 1846. It was generally associated with increasing prosperity, though there were a few dissentient voices. For instance, by 1880 the textile manufacturer and inventor Cunliffe Lister was urging the use of tariffs, or the threat to use them, to force foreigners to give access to their markets.[70] As yet such pleas went unheeded, even within some of the trades exposed to foreign competition in the home market. Among the reasons for the faith in the existing economic orthodoxy was the belief that free trade had done much to improve the condition of the people. Free trade appeared to enable Britain to buy her imports in the cheapest market, while continuing industrial growth at home offered higher earnings.

The economy generally

Generally the decades after 1850 saw continuing expansion in the British economy. Annual increases in output ran at between 2 and 3 per cent.[71] Overall growth left room for failures both in individual enterprises and in less successful sectors of the economy, but the economy as a whole maintained an impressive standing in international terms.[72]

66. Rogers, 'Lancashire landowners', 260.
67. Checkland, *The Rise of Industrial Society*, 312.
68. Saul, 'The Mechanical Engineering Industries in Britain', 37.
69. Checkland, *The Rise of Industrial Society*, 313.
70. Sigsworth, *Black Dyke Mills*, 106.
71. Supple (ed.), *Essays in British Business History*, 9–10.
72. Chaloner, 'The Industrial Spirit in Britain'.

Despite this achievement, later economic historians accepted for many years that a 'Great Depression' occurred after about 1873. Modern reconsideration of the evidence suggests that this belief was exaggerated and mainly reflected the loud complaints of interests facing problems at that time. At most, there was some slowing down in the rate of growth.[73] Many of the complaints were about the falling prices obtainable for manufactured goods. This was not simply a British experience but rather a worldwide phenomenon caused by improved productivity and reduced transport costs. In many sectors, in fact, British industry did well, and maintained progress. For example, in the worsted industry there were striking increases in productivity in both spinning and weaving.[74] Such achievements were realized despite the fact that British wages were generally higher than those of her European competitors; French worsted workers probably received wages about one-third lower than their British equivalents, but this did not prevent British products from holding their own.[75]

Nor was the competitiveness of British industry yet much eroded by restrictive practices either of employers or of workers. Attempts to control markets and fix prices in the third quarter of the century were generally ephemeral and ineffective.[76] By the 1880s, trade unions had recruited fewer than 10 per cent of workers, and a modern study notes that

British workers... responded readily to cash incentives and were willing to take up new occupations, to adopt new work patterns, and to move about the country in response to changing work opportunities. There was an abundance of inherited skill in Britain and the shortcomings of working-class education appear to have had little effect on labour productivity. British labour was also conciliatory towards employers. Strikes, arson, machine breaking, and politically motivated violence have been highlighted in the literature, but they were not often serious impediments to industrial advance in the nineteenth century. The high quality of British labour was one of the chief causes of high wage levels in Britain.[77]

There were signs that this open situation, favourable to economic growth, might come under threat from more than one direction. In 1869, the rules of the Manchester Bricklayers' Association stipulated that 'any man found running or working beyond a regular speed should be fined 2s. 6d.'[78] Samuel Cunliffe Lister, who invented the first practicable wool combing machine in 1845, subsequently sought to prevent competition by buying up the patents for similar innovations.[79]

---

73. For argument in this sense see the works of B. Supple and W. H. Chaloner cited in nn. 71 and 72.
74. Sigsworth, *Black Dyke Mills*, 67.
75. We owe this information to Dr David Jenkins.
76. Mathias, *The First Industrial Nation*, 354–5.
77. Hunt, *British Labour History*, 340.   78. Ibid. 290.
79. Sigsworth, *Black Dyke Mills*, 40.

Wages

British wage levels were still generally higher than those in other European countries, often by as much as 50 per cent for comparable work.[80] The rewards offered for different classes of work did not reflect any equitable principle. For example, in 1876, many middle-ranking civil servants were paid more than twice the salaries offered to Post Office engineers, reflecting social status rather than levels of skill.[81]

Even historians who have little affection for the workings of a 'capitalist' economy accept that the later nineteenth century brought improvement in the real incomes of most people in Britain. This did not mean the elimination of poverty. By the end of the century perhaps 15 per cent of the population lived on incomes which were by any reasonable standard inadequate, even with frugal management. At mid-century the proportion must have been higher. In 1850, 5.7 per cent of the population were in receipt of poor relief; by 1880, this had dropped to 3.2 per cent (in 1834 the figure had been 8.8 per cent). Given the increase in population, to have reduced the proportion of the very poor was no slight achievement.

Moreover, although there was an overall price rise during the third quarter of the century, wages increased faster than prices, allowing for variations in both time and place.[82] The overall improvement became more substantial and more widespread from the 1860s onwards. While total national income was growing, so was the share in it taken by wages and salaries. Economic development reduced the proportion of the workforce employed in poorly paid jobs such as farm labour, and increased the number of jobs which required technical skills. Gains were often erratic; some key coal-miners increased their earnings by half during the short period 1873–5.[83] There were marked differences between the earning powers and the social status of different groups. The differences between wages paid to the skilled industrial worker and the unskilled labourer (the former perhaps three times as high as the latter) could mean different lifestyles. Even the smaller differentials between skilled and unskilled workers in the building industry could, at around 50 per cent, entail cultural differences. A trade union of skilled workers might enunciate the determination 'to get the labourers to keep their places ... the helper ought to be subservient and do as the mechanic tells him'.[84] Later in the century, rivalries between different groups of skilled workers in matters of demarcation, especially in the shipbuilding industry, could be as bitter as any disputes between the skilled and the unskilled.

Social mobility

There was increasing mobility within British society. The numbers of the rich continued to grow, although from no very high figure. The existence of many

80. Hunt, *British Labour History*, 107, together with information from Dr David Jenkins.
81. Hunt, ibid. 100.   82. Checkland, *The Rise of Industrial Society*, 229.
83. Ibid. 47, 230–2.
84. H. A. Clegg, A. Fox, and A. F. Thompson, *A History of British Trade Unions since 1889* (1964), 132.

small enterprises meant that it was still possible, with skill, hard work, and good fortune, for a working man to enter the ranks of employers. One of many individual success stories was that of Sir Josiah Mason. He was born into poverty, and began work at the age of 8, selling cakes as a street hawker. He later obtained an industrial job, and invented a method of making split key-rings by machine. In 1829 he set up his own pen-making business with a small workforce. By 1874 he employed 1,000 workers. Much of his fortune was devoted to philanthropy, including in 1880 the provision for Birmingham of a College of Science out of which the university there was to grow. Mason spent at least £150,000 on this single objective, and more than £250,000 on orphanages.[85] Success on a smaller scale was exemplified in the career of John Cooke of Lincoln, who began work as an apprentice wheelwright in Lincolnshire but progressed to become a manufacturer of agricultural machinery; he invented a new kind of plough in 1857, and at the time of his death in 1887 he employed seventy men in his Lincoln works. [86] Other industrial sectors provide many comparable successes.

Despite the many instances of successful and well-to-do manufacturers, industrialists as a group seem to have found entry to the very top echelons of society or to the ranks of the very rich difficult. Next to the fortunes of the great landowners and the considerable wealth accumulated by many in the commercial and financial communities the wealth of most industrialists appears modest. Finance had long been considered a gentlemanly occupation and seems not only to have been the path to the greater fortunes than most other occupations but to high social status.[87]

In addition, business organization was developing so as to increase the number of 'white-collar' workers—clerks, draughtsmen, salesmen, for example—whose ranks were filled from other groups of workers, either by the movement of individuals, or by the recruitment of the sons of other workers into 'white-collar' jobs.[88] As this development became more pervasive and complex, it introduced further diversity into the social structure.

Access to advancement was far from equal, it is true. A vast web of patronage, for instance, governed entry into apprenticeships in the skilled wage-earning trades. Opportunities to reach better-paid and more secure employment depended on personal links, family connections, shared membership of Church or chapel, or some such channel of influence. Walter Runciman, a major shipowner at the end of the century,[89] obtained his first command at the early age of 22 because of the owner's connection with his father, 'who, as a Wesleyan

85. *ODNB.*   86. Ambler, 'Social change and religious experience', 124.

87. W. D. Rubinstein, *Men of Property: The Very Wealthy in Britain since the Industrial Revolution*, 2nd edn., (2006), ch. 3. Among exceptions were William Crawshay, the Welsh iron master, who became a millionaire early in the nineteenth century, and a number of coal-owners including David A. Thomas, 1st Baron Rhondda, and James Joicey, 1st Baron Joicey.

88. Hunt, *British Labour History*, 279, 358 n. 126.

89. Shipowners exhibited a very high degree of social mobility and 'made great strides into the aristocracy and into titled and landed society'. W. D. Rubinstein, *Men of Property*, 124.

local preacher, was a comrade of his'; the ship concerned was a new clipper barque and Runciman's appointment involved passing over more experienced commanders.[90] Nevertheless, the increasing opportunities for individual improvement, though more limited than many contemporary observers were willing to allow, provided at least some foundation for the prevailing contemporary belief in social progress.[91]

Trade unions

The trade union movement cannot be credited with responsibility for overall social improvement, for it was not large enough to exert much leverage. Yet the absence of formal trade union organization did not necessarily prevent workers from effective action in pursuing such objectives as a shorter working week, and absenteeism for recreational purposes remained common.[92] Although there was some increase in trade union membership, the total in 1880 cannot have amounted to as much as 10 per cent of the adult male workforce, and probably numerically not much more than half a million people. Trade-unionism among women was almost negligible. At the same time there were factors which helped union growth. Improved communications made union organization easier, and facilitated the development of national rather than local or regional associations. Other factors were less obvious. Improved technology and larger enterprises made negotiations about wages and conditions more complex and difficult; this called for representatives who were literate, numerate, well-informed, adept in discussion, and aware of the increasingly complex code of regulation of working conditions.[93] The legal position of trade unions changed, too. The concessions granted by mid-Victorian governments are not altogether easy to understand. Unions were still small, and their reputation was not uniformly good. The 1860s saw a number of well-publicized 'trade union outrages'. In the Sheffield area attempts to force workmen into union membership culminated in October 1866 with the blowing up of the house of one non-unionist. Manchester brickworks provided further well-publicized examples of bullying and violence by unionists. Even Frederic Harrison, one of the movement's most useful friends in these years, felt bound to complain about such abuses.[94] Yet many trade unionists were respectable, often devout Christians, stalwarts of Church or (more commonly) Nonconformist chapel.

This helps to explain the countenance given to trade unionists by prominent churchmen. Leading Anglican clergymen such as Edward Girdlestone, a canon of

---

90. W. Runciman, *Before the Mast—and After* (1924), 165.

91. For a perceptive discussion of the contemporary concept of 'removable inequalities', W. L. Burn, *The Age of Equipoise* (1964), 103–7.

92. For an emphatic recent demonstration of this, M. Huggins, 'Stockton Race Week 1855–1900: the growth of an unofficial holiday', *Journal of Regional and Local Studies*, 6 (1) (1986), 49.

93. Hunt, *British Labour History*, 384 n. 8.   94. Ibid. 266–7, 385 n. 22.

Bristol, and James Prince Lee, the first Bishop of Manchester, were impressed by some of the unions' respectable leadership. During the first large-scale attempts to organize unions of agricultural labourers, help from both Church and chapel played a part.[95] The role of religion here was not uniform, though. The secular nature of the activities and objectives of the unions could be seen as a distraction from higher things; salvation should have mattered much more than working conditions.[96] Moreover, devoutness among workers was a variable; relations between the godly and the ungodly were not always good. Two popular cultures, that of drink, gambling, and sport, and that of the chapel and the temperance movement, contended in these years, a contest which did not make for social solidarity.[97]

The limited extent to which trade unions had learned how to work together may have been another reason for legislative indulgence. Although the Trades Union Congress is usually dated from the 1868 Manchester meeting, individual unions remained suspicious of attempts by any national body to limit their independence.[98] At local level, attempts to form trades councils as coordinating bodies achieved only partial success, with some important unions ignoring them.[99] A more coherent and united movement would have alarmed government and legislature more, and might have hindered the legal concessions which were forthcoming.

The stress laid by many trade union leaders on the limited objectives, the respectability, and the orderliness of their activities was tactically sensible in a society still profoundly unequal. Yet such assertions were often deceptive. The Amalgamated Society of Engineers' evidence to the 1867–9 royal commission on trade unions included a bland assurance that strikes were the last thing that unions would think of encouraging. One of the better-endowed unions, the ASE had subsidized strike action by other workers on 179 occasions during the previous thirteen years. In emphasizing the way in which its rules reserved to national headquarters the decision on whether a strike should take place or not, the union omitted to mention that this power was used to prevent unsuccessful strikes, not strikes generally.[100] As the great engineering strikes of 1871 demonstrated, the trade unions' skilful leaders could combine a moderate and law-abiding public image with effective intimidation in the background.[101]

The efforts to invest trade-unionism with an aura of moderation and respectability prevailed against the evidence of other characteristics. This, as much as any anticipated electoral advantages, explains the legislative concessions of the 1860s and 1870s. As unionism became increasingly formalized and in the

---

95. Ibid. 257.   96. Ambler, 'Social change and religious experience', 379–89.
97. R. Moore, *Pitman, Preachers and Politics* (1974), 176.
98. A. E. Musson, *Trade Union and Social History* (1974), ch. 3.
99. Hunt, *British Labour History*, 385 n. 26.   100. Ibid. 261, 384 n. 19.
101. E. Allen, J. F. Clarke, N. McCord, and D. J. Rowe, *The North-East Engineers' Strike of 1871: The Nine Hours League* (1971).

public eye, the shortcomings of its legal position became apparent. During the 1860s, court decisions had highlighted the vulnerability of the movement. Some trade unions had tried to take advantage of their welfare provisions to obtain a legal status by registering under the Friendly Societies Act of 1855. In 1867, the decision in the case of *Hornby v. Close* exposed the weakness of this device; the Bradford branch of the boilermakers' union took legal action against a dishonest treasurer, but the court rejected the union's claim to be a valid suitor. Another decision later that year, *Regina v. Druitt*, showed that the courts could take a broad view of what constituted intimidation during a strike.[102] The unequal legal position given to employer and employee under the Master and Servant Acts also caused dissatisfaction.

Even before the 1867 extension of the franchise, Parliament showed a willingness to make concessions; an Act earlier that year removed some of the worst inequalities of the Master and Servant laws. Although the evidence before the royal commission on trade unions appointed in the same year was far from uniformly favourable, the commission's report in 1869 was immediately followed by interim legislation specifically overturning the doctrine laid down in *Hornby v. Close*. The Trade Union Act of 1871 then sought to provide the unions with a clear status at law. It was more difficult, as later governments repeatedly found, to frame clear rules specifying the limits of permissible conduct during an industrial dispute. The 1871 Criminal Law Amendment Act tried to tidy up this situation, but disappointed trade unionists. In 1875 Disraeli's second government offered a revised and less restrictive form, which went some way to satisfy their objections. It is mistaken to suppose that the 1871 Act inhibited peaceful picketing, while the 1875 Act allowed it; this area of legislation is not amenable to such simplicities. The legislative changes were concessions rather than extorted privileges and the successes of the unions in these years provoked some response from the more anxious or more spirited employers. In 1873 a National Federation of Associated Employers of Labour was founded, though the extent to which most employers feared the unions is indicated by the fact that this defensive move fizzled out during the next ten years.[103]

Friendly societies and savings banks

The friendly societies continued to be larger than the unions, both in numbers and in resources. At mid-century their membership was at least three times as large.[104] Like the unions, the friendly societies moved towards organization on a national rather than a local basis, with many smaller societies joining larger bodies.[105] The benefits offered by the societies were improving, too; in 1872, the

102. Musson, *Trade Union and Social History*, 34–40.
103. Hunt, *British Labour History*, 388 n. 71.
104. W. H. Chaloner, *The Skilled artisans during the Industrial Revolution, 1750–1850* (1969), 13.
105. Ambler, 'Social change and religious experience', 378.

friendly societies in Bradford banded together to provide medical facilities for their members.[106] Parliament continued to view this movement with benevolence, improving legal safeguards for funds and consolidating the societies' legal status.

A similar benevolence extended to another major engine of respectable self-help for the labouring man, the savings banks, with helpful legislation in 1860, 1866, and 1880. Here, as elsewhere, the State imitated unofficial initiatives. The Post Office Savings Bank was founded in 1861 and attracted more than a million depositors in its first ten years; its deposits amounted to more than £8 million by 1866 and £31 million by 1878. Further imitation followed, as the Post Office extended its activities into the provision of small-scale insurance and annuity arrangements.

Social changes

The increasingly complex organization of society and the economy involved a growing need for specialists with distinctive qualifications. After 1850 there was a continuing crystallization of professions.[107] Engineers and architects had already acquired national organizations, and these continued to grow. Although often small—the Institution of Civil Engineers had fewer than 1,500 members by 1868—such bodies were important and influential in their own specialized areas. Within the professions there was a tendency for specialization to increase during the third quarter of the century, although this was not a universal development. Among architects J. H. Morton cultivated a market in the design of institutional buildings such as workhouses and hospitals; Thomas Hawksley supervised the design and construction of more than 150 waterworks. By the 1870s there were well over 5,000 professional architects. Even if some of these had only a dubious claim to professional qualifications, their numbers had increased by something like twelvefold over the previous half-century. Architects and engineers varied in social status, income, and specialized interests, but other factors, such as the development of professional journals or the institution of professional examin-ations, encouraged national professional identities. The best example of devel-oped professional status was that of the doctors. During the 1850s, efforts to produce a defined and disciplined profession finally bore fruit. An Act of 1858 created a legally limited medical profession, with its own register of qualified practitioners and its own disciplinary powers and procedures.[108] In 1852 Parliament had also begun a statutory regulation of pharmaceutical services, which encouraged professional identity among pharmacists. Changes in educa-tion, especially after the 1870 Elementary Education Act, brought greater defin-ition to the school-teaching profession. Apart from the consolidation of existing

106. Barber, 'Municipal Government in Leeds', 21.
107. Burn, *The Age of Equipoise*, 285.   108. Ibid. 202.

professions, new groups emerged. Repeated attempts to bring order into the work of valuation for purposes of national and local taxation saw a profession of valuer evolve, with the official position of District Valuer an important element in this process.

By 1880 the professions in Britain were more clearly demarcated and more firmly established than ever before. Not all of those who were accorded professional status were rich. Some teachers or doctors, or lesser officials in central and local government service, earned incomes no larger than those of many skilled wage-earners. They were, however, increasingly aware of belonging to groups possessed of their own identities, their own qualifications, and their own hierarchies of employment, though this did not mean that those groups were uniform in status or in social and political attitudes.

Social continuity

Traditional patterns of authority exhibited considerable tenacity. Landowners still enjoyed much of their earlier eminence in British society. To some extent this influence was bound up with the fortunes of the agricultural sector of the economy (see pp. 351–2 above). In the years after 1850 many landowners were still investing heavily on their estates, and some of them were still buying land. It was not until after 1880 that debt charges incurred for such purposes became embarrassing to many estates.[109] Until then landownership was thought to offer unqualified advantages—a secure investment, together with social prestige. For many landowners, agricultural rent-rolls were buttressed by additional sources of income and influence such as urban rents, mineral royalties, and lucrative company directorships. In some areas, where rival interests could aspire to prominence, the status of the landowner might be impaired before 1880. In 1868, one Lancashire aristocrat complained that 'We have the misfortune to belong to a county where merchants and wealth are far above, in their own opinion, the aristocracy and the old landed gentry,' though this opinion was not universally accepted.[110] The Earl of Derby continued to possess an influence in Lancashire far beyond that of any industrialist or merchant.[111]

In the third quarter of the century, successful businessmen were still acquiring landed estates. The Foster family of textile magnates spent more money in acquiring land than they did in accumulating stocks and shares, spending £709,700 in buying land between 1860 and 1873.[112] The purchase of landed estates had never, however, been a universal practice amongst wealthy businessmen and seems to

109. Rogers, 'Lancashire landowners and the great agricultural depression', 250–68, gives a good regional study.
110. Ibid. 268.
111. The extent of the involvement of the Earl of Derby in the affairs of Lancashire is revealed in John Vincent (ed.), *The Diaries of Edward Henry Stanley, 15th Earl of Derby (1826–93) Between 1878 and 1893* (2003).
112. Sigsworth, *Black Dyke Mills*, 225.

have declined from the 1840s though it remained a reasonable investment until the late 1870s and even subsequently a major asset to the socially ambitious. Where an aristocratic landlord cultivated an urban community in which he had property interests, the result could be a useful extension of influence. At Gateshead the James family inherited much of the property of the old Ellison lords of the manor, and during the century continued to take a paternalistic interest in the town's affairs, providing recreational facilities, contributing substantially to local charities, and so on. This cultivation paved the way for the election as the town's MP in 1874 of young Walter James, who held the seat without difficulty until he succeeded as the second Lord Northbourne in 1893.[113] On the other hand, although the Duke of Cleveland was the biggest landowner in Wolverhampton, the influence which this entailed was reduced because he was an absentee from the town.

In addition to the influence derived from its property, the aristocracy still exercised an enormous range of patronage. Apart from the staff needed by their estates and houses, and the tenancies at their disposal, aristocratic patronage was important in access to many careers. Moreover, flattering notice by magnates was an unmistakable indicator of local prominence; invitations to functions at aristocratic seats were eagerly sought and no doubt boasted about; societies of many kinds recruited aristocratic patrons to signify their status. Some aspects of the aristocracy's power were summed up in 1880: 'There is no other body of men in the country who administer so large a capital on their own account, or whose influence is so widely extended and universally present. From them the learned professions, the church, the army and the public services are largely recruited.'[114] The vast majority of really wealthy men were still the great landowners. Recent research into the fortunes left at death has shown that by far the greatest number of those leaving £500,000 or more were, until the 1880s, landowners and they still accounted for over two-fifths at the end of the century.[115] The complexion of governments and Parliaments remained predominantly aristocratic.

Women

The position of women in mid-Victorian society was marked by a number of paradoxes. A queen was on the throne and women formed the majority of the population yet women were treated as inferiors. The dominant rhetoric of the day insisted upon distinct and separate roles for the sexes, the exclusion of women from the political sphere, and male dominance with regard to divorce and property. Yet, this was the period in which the cluster of issues on which what became known as the 'Women's Movement' campaigned was first seriously raised.

113. N. McCord, 'Gateshead politics in the age of reform', *Northern History*, 4 (1969), 179–80.
114. James Caird, *The Landed Interest and the Supply of Food* (1880), 56–64.
115. W. D. Rubinstein, *Men of Property*, 78–9.

Whether the position of Victorian women was significantly different to that of women in previous periods and, in particular, to that of women earlier in the nineteenth century is a subject that has occasioned much debate (see Ch. 3 pp. 137–40). Certainly there was an insistent emphasis upon women's role as wife, mother, and pure guardian of moral values and the home. The ambitions and fears of many among the more prosperous sections of society were influential here: the world was marked by rapid change, even progress, but life could be insecure, while away from respectable districts, towns could be rough, insalubrious, and dangerous. The ideal of the comfortable home as a retreat and a pocket of stability was attractive as was the associated notion of womanhood separate from the working world and supposedly oblivious to the roughness, unpleasantness, and immorality of much of the life of Victorian towns. The image of the ideal woman presiding over the ideal home was one which only the comfortably off could approximate to but as an aspiration it affected the lower-middle classes and even respectable workers. It was powerfully reinforced by art and literature as was its obverse, the 'fallen woman'. One thing that the majority of married women had in common was that they did not go out to work, though in the cotton districts and in north Staffordshire potteries around 30 per cent were employed,[116] while many working-class wives supplemented family incomes by taking in work such as washing or sewing. For unmarried women and those married women who did go out to work employment opportunities were limited. In the textile-producing areas there was work in mills and elsewhere in factories and workshops producing such goods as pottery, ceramics, ornaments, or artificial flowers. In London, the 'slop trade' producing cheap clothing and uniforms employed over 11,000 females earning miserable wages at mid-century. The wages of dressmakers producing expensive garments were not a great deal better. For the majority of daughters of workers, domestic service was the obvious path to follow and until early in the twentieth century it employed the greatest number of women. The circumstances of servants varied widely but, in general, the larger the houses, the richer the family, and the more numerous fellow servants, the better were the conditions; to be in the service of a duke was more desirable than to be the 'tweeny' in a junior clerk's home.

Another form of employment constituted the great scandal of the age; the large number of prostitutes was a fact of life unmentionable in polite society though it must have been well-known. There are no firm statistics for the number of prostitutes in mid-Victorian Britain, nor indeed for any other period. Even the return of the Metropolitan Police for the number of brothels and prostitutes for May 1857, which compares the figures for that year with those for 1841 must be treated with caution. It estimated the number of brothels as 2,825 and the number of prostitutes as 8,600 as compared with 3,325 and 9,409

116. Joan Perkin, *Victorian Women*, (1993), 192.

respectively in 1841.[117] Other estimates were much higher but may have been exaggerated in the interests of sensationalism. At the least, it seems obvious that the number of prostitutes in London, ranging from those eking out a living in poorer areas, to those working in the West End, and the select band of high-class 'Cyprians' kept by men of wealth, was high.

Henry Mayhew's exposure of conditions in the clothing trades[118] shocked contemporaries as much because low wages forced many female workers to supplement them by part-time prostitution as because of the low wages themselves. The relative prosperity of prostitutes was a fact rarely mentioned. A study of prostitution in Southampton and Portsmouth has concluded that the standard of living of 'prostitutes was perceptibly higher than that of other poor working-class women'.[119]

Essentially work opportunities for women were limited. As the Society for Promoting the Employment of Women noted, 'the texture of English society is such that the number of reputable employments for females in the middle and humble ranks is very small.'[120] As there were more than a million women who remained unmarried in 1851 and the number rose thereafter to some million and a half in 1911, the lack of female employment opportunities was a major problem.

The problem was worst for those in 'the middle'. Upper and middle class women of independent means could live independent lives if they failed or chose not to marry but those from comfortable backgrounds fallen on hard times had few options other than posts as governesses or ladies' companions. The 1861 census attributed only 1 per cent of office employment to women; by 1881 this had grown to 3 per cent. This small minority might expect to see male colleagues paid twice as much for similar work. Generally women's wages were lower than for men in comparable employment. Of all workers employed by central government, including the Post Office, 8 per cent were women in 1861.[121] Shop work was still largely a male preserve as far as wage-earners were concerned.

Other factors would have made work for women of the middle orders difficult even had it been available: the difficulty of getting to work through muddy and jostling streets in the cumbersome crinolines and sweeping dresses of the day at a time when urban public transport was in its infancy; the lack of lavatories, for a respectable woman couldn't just use a back-alley; and the absence of tea shops or restaurants which women could visit without embarrassment. In time the need for female clerks and shop assistants would help produce and would

117. *Return of the number of Brothels and Prostitutes within the Metropolitan Police District, as nearly as can be Ascertained,* May 1857. Quoted in Liza Picard, *Victorian London: The Life of a City* (2005), 255.

118. Mayhew's series of 82 articles published in the *Morning Chronicle* in the late 1840s were published with some alterations as *London Labour and the London Poor* (1851).

119. Judith Walkowitz, *Prostitution and Victorian Society* (1980), 195.

120. Quoted in Liza Picard, *Victorian London,* 252.

121. Hunt, *British Labour History,* 18, 22, 103.

grow alongside an infrastructure which would facilitate their employment but its absence should not be underestimated as a barrier to such employment at mid-century.

Changes in the economy and in society that would bring more work for women were beginning to take place. There were some kinds of work in which women played a greater part. In 1871 the number of women teachers was approaching 100,000. There were already a number of places for female clerks, some limited opportunities in nursing and the beginnings of the massive increase in the retail industry that would require so many shop assistants. The number of jobs open to women increased by 33 per cent between 1851 and 1871.

The 'Women's Movement' found its main protagonists and supporters amongst the daughters of the upper-middle classes. Working-class women were on the whole too busy, either at work before they were married or at work in the home managing households afterwards and taking pride in their marital status, to be concerned that they did not have the vote or property rights. Aristocratic women continued to enjoy considerable influence and often heavy responsibilities, while their personal wealth and property rights were underpinned by the complex legal systems that the aristocracy had devised to protect a bride's dowry. There were, however a few aristocratic feminists such as Lady Amberley, whom Queen Victoria thought 'ought to get a good whipping'.[122] Some of the characteristics of the movement can be explained by the backgrounds of its leaders: a determined respectability, which often moved from a detestation of sexual immorality to a dislike of sex itself; and ambivalence as to whether women were equal to men or different and probably superior.

The franchise was only one of a number of goals of the movement. Langham Place in London was the meeting place for women of advanced views in the 1850s and 1860s. It was satirised by Anthony Trollope in *Is he Popenjoy?* (1868) as the 'Rights of Women Institute; instituted for the Relief of the Disabilities of Females'. The 'Ladies of Langham Place'

founded the Society for Promoting Women's Employment in 1859, tried to extend higher education for women, promoted female emigration to the colonies, and demanded entry into the medical profession; they established the Married Women's Property Committee and the Ladies National Association for the repeal of the Contagious Diseases Acts. Only in the aftermath of John Stuart Mill's election at Westminster in May 1965 did the parliamentary vote emerge as a significant goal.[123]

They were remarkably successful. In 1857 judicial divorce became possible (in 1861 in Scotland), but this was a limited measure which enabled men to divorce women more easily than women could divorce men. Grounds for judicial divorce were slightly widened in 1868. The 1870 Married Women's Property Act

122. Queen Victoria to Theodore Martin, March 1870. Quoted in Hywel Williams, *Cassell's Chronology of World History* (2005), 428.
123. M. Pugh, *The March of the Women* (2000), 7.

provided some financial independence for propertied women, and this legislation was later extended. Progress in gaining entry to the medical profession was slow but significant. The first woman to obtain any kind of recognized medical qualification was Elizabeth Garrett Anderson in 1865; a medical training centre for women opened in London in 1874, and two years later statutory access to the medical register was conceded. By 1881 there were twenty-five women doctors. The campaign led by Josephine Butler to repeal the Contagious Diseases Act, which provided for the compulsory medical examination of women suspected of being prostitutes in military and naval towns, was ultimately successful when the Liberal victory in the general election of 1880 led first to the suspension and then to the abolition of the Acts.

It would be unrealistic to suppose that the Women's Movement enjoyed much support among the majority of men or women. Most working men were insistent upon their position as master of their households even if the large share of the running of the households fell to their wives. Married working-class women invested great pride in their marital status. Working-class households had little in the way of property, so female property rights were a somewhat arcane issue for working-class wives. Even when their husbands had the vote, it is doubtful whether the desire to vote themselves was widespread among wives. Attempts to spread trade-unionism among women were met by indifference or enmity by most male unionists; what little progress was made before 1880 depended more on help from sympathetic outsiders than any support from the established union movement.[124] The relative success of the early women's movement had a narrow but an influential basis of support. Its leaders were articulate, were able to access a network of influential women and men, and on the issue of the Contagious Diseases Act they were at one with many clergymen.

On the franchise question, the movement was fractured. Mill's motion of 1867 that would have given women the vote on the same basis as men gained 73 votes against 194 but the cause of female enfranchisement had several disadvantages: most men did not want it; most women were opposed to it; and even many of the most prominent female social reformers were against it, including Octavia Hill and the young Beatrice Potter, later Beatrice Webb. Nevertheless, women who qualified as ratepayers were shortly to participate in local elections; after 1869 they could vote in municipal elections, after 1870 in School Board elections, and after 1875 in elections to Poor Law Boards.

Children

There was some change in attitudes towards children. Some historians have argued that the concept of childhood is a modern invention[125] and, though this

---

124. Hunt, *British Labour History*, 258.
125. Philippe Aries, *Centuries of Childhood* (1962); E. Shorter, *The Making of the Modern Family* (1976).

seems fanciful, a greater concern for children and the drawing of firmer lines between adults and children were gradual but persistent developments during the nineteenth century. Amongst the reasons for this was a general growth of sensibility which led to opposition to callousness in many forms, cruelty to animals, public executions, and a more enlightened attitude towards the deaf and the blind. The ill-treatment of children and child labour came to be seen something society and government should provide against. Another influence was romanticism, which encouraged the view of children as innocent and childhood as a special and formative period in life. The idealization of the home went hand in hand with an idealization of children. If only the prosperous classes could afford to indulge children and protect them from the harsher aspects of life, it was difficult to ignore the conditions of the children of poorer families. Gradual improvements in the standard of living for many led to such sentiments moving down the social scale.

The circumstances of children varied considerably. The children of rich families might well still be being educated ten years after a working-class contemporary had begun work. Childhood was thus shorter for the working-class boy or girl. Poor families needed their children to make a contribution to family incomes as soon as possible and legislation preventing children working was far from popular.

The view that children needed legal protection became influential nevertheless and was notably acted upon in the area of children at work. Parliament had begun legislating in the area of child employment in 1802 (see pp. 203–4) and it continued to limit and regulate children's employment. State intervention in the provision of education tuned in with employment legislation. The formal employment of children (and especially young children) continued to decline after 1871; this was one effect of increased schooling. The level of children in the 10–15 age group engaged in formal employment probably peaked at about 28 per cent in the years around 1871, thereafter dropping rapidly. Parliament continued to limit and regulate children's employment. An Act of 1867 regulated agricultural employment; the 1873 Agricultural Children's Act forbade the employment of children under 8 in farming, and provided for their education. Nor was employment the only area in which Parliament intervened to protect children. The Infant Life Protection Act of 1872 sought to regulate the fostering of children. Women fostering more than a single child had to register with the local authority, which was given power to inspect the premises concerned whenever it wished. The law relating to registration of infant deaths and establishing their causes was also strengthened. In the same year the law relating to illegitimate children was altered so as to make it easier for a mother to obtain maintenance payments from the father. Poor Law officials could now initiate the appropriate legal proceedings, something which had been expressly forbidden in 1844. In such extensions of provision for the care of children, as in many other spheres, government adopted, rather than created, changing attitudes, already visible in the increasing provision of charitable foundations for children, such as Dr Barnardo's Homes, founded in 1866. Often such institutions, begun on a small and local scale, grew very large. The Revd Thomas Stephenson opened a small refuge for destitute children off London's Waterloo Road in 1869; over the next century this initiative grew into a major charitable enterprise, the National Children's Home, operating more than 150 establishments. An increasing number of local charities specifically for children also appeared, such as the Newcastle Children's Hospital established in 1863.

Children could of course be seen as a problem as well as be the objects of compassion:

Throughout the nineteenth century children—growing in numbers as the century advanced—presented society with some of its most taxing and seemingly intractable problems. Knots of children crowded the Victorian landscape; gangs dominated the streets and alleys of towns and cities. They can be seen crowded together in contemporary illustrations and, from the mid-century onwards, in the revealing early photographs of Victorian life. The noise and play of children was a constant feature of life, forever disturbing the peace of their elders. Children at work were similarly ubiquitous, and although the worst excesses had been brought under control by mid-century, child labour was a feature of British life well into the [twentieth] century. To feed or house these children, to employ or educate them, to control and regulate their daily lives, to care for their physical and spiritual well-being, all these were major preoccupations of caring men and women and the encroaching Victorian state.[126]

Housing

Many children continued to be born into the squalor and danger of slums and poor housing. At mid-century Sheffield, Birmingham, and Leicester enjoyed reasonably good reputations for accommodation; Bradford would have been in the same group had it not been for the appalling conditions in which many Irish immigrants lived. Nottingham, Leeds, and Manchester, on the other hand, had much poor housing, as had London and Liverpool, neither of which was a centre of factory development. The expanding towns of north-east England had notorious black spots, while both Edinburgh and Glasgow possessed slums as bad as anything further south.[127] The inclusion of Edinburgh again indicates that there is no automatic correlation between industrial growth and bad housing. The evidence collected in 1869 for the Royal Commission on the Employment of Children, Young Persons and Women in Agriculture provided a formidable dossier on the poor living conditions in much of rural Britain.

In considering housing problems, the limited understanding of infectious diseases must be borne in mind; throughout the century it was possible to argue credibly in favour of back-to-back houses. This is one reason why there was little

126. James Walvin, *A Child's World: A Social History of English Childhood 1800–1914* (1982), 17.
127. Hunt, *British Labour History*, 92–3.

pressure for effective official action in housing matters from within the groups most affected.[128] Pressure for improved conditions came overwhelmingly from concerned minorities within influential sectors of society, who possessed the education, the information, the means, the time, and the interest in general welfare to provide it. This pressure was responsible for the growth of legislative intervention and the slowly developing compulsion imposed on recalcitrant local authorities in sanitary matters.

One way of improving conditions was to build 'model' housing. Schemes of this kind appeared in many places during the mid-Victorian years. Prince Albert's model houses erected in connection with the Great Exhibition of 1851, or the model estate villages built for the ninth Duke of Bedford, Lord Hatherton, and the Lucy family, exemplified an aristocratic involvement. The model industrial community of Saltaire, begun in 1851, and the housing erected for railway workers at Swindon and Crewe provide other examples. At Saltaire the houses had at least three bedrooms, kitchen, scullery, pantry, cellar, with piped water and gas supply laid on.[129]

Overall there was a tendency for new housing to be better than that which had gone before. Earlier in the century prosperous workers in London had begun to expect houses with at least four principal rooms, usually two up and two down in two-storey terrace housing. From mid-century, housing like this became increasingly the norm in new building, with local variations in design, and diversity in the quality of materials and construction. From 1875 it was illegal to build houses without lavatories. By 1876 four-fifths of the houses in Manchester had their own water taps. The development of suburban transport made it easier for new houses to be sited away from expensive central areas, so that a better house could be acquired for the same investment.

Especially in high-wage areas, more workers came to own their own homes, often as a result of the work of the building society movement. Cooperative societies also entered the housing market, providing new houses for their members on a kind of hire-purchase basis. In the growing industrial community of Wallsend, the local society built a little estate from the 1870s, with street names like Mutual Street, Equitable Street, and Provident Terrace. Even if such small property-owners represented only a minority of wage-earners, they included men of influence in their own communities and their own trades. At Woolwich Arsenal in 1873, workers demonstrated against the level of poor rates imposed on house owners. During the Local Board election for Heslington in Yorkshire in 1875, society members were given the following advice: 'Co-operators, remember the unfair attempt that has been made to force your Directors to increase the privy accommodation of your cottages... vote straight.'[130]

The comfort of new houses was improving in other ways, too. A satisfactory process for machine-printing of wallpaper was developed in 1851, and ten years

128. Hunt, *British Labour History*, 358 n. 115.   129. Ibid. 91.
130. For Woolwich, ibid. 97. We owe the Heslington example to Dr Derek Fraser.

later the wallpaper tax was abolished. The mass production of a cheap, decorative, and durable floor covering, linoleum, began in the mid-1870s. In general, workers' housing in Britain was already better than in any other European country.

Public health

Despite this improvement, many families continued to live in older, poorer housing. In some places sewers were either non-existent or defective. Elsewhere sewers were constructed which merely collected human excrement and other noxious matter and dumped them into some nearby river, moving a pollution problem without solving it. By the late 1850s, Birmingham's sewage had transformed the river Tame into a horrible black and filthy stream. In the 1860s Lord Dudley complained that 'Kidderminster stank from end to end'.[131] Public health engineering was developing from a relatively primitive base. It was not until the 1880s that any effective method was found of coping with the stench emitted by sewers without a continuous water flow; the provision of WCs did not lead to improvement in health unless water supply and drainage arrangements were effective and reliable.

London provides the great example of the inadequacy of water closets without good sewers to take sewage away from heavily inhabited areas. It took the 'Great Stink' of 1858 to bring home to the London authorities that the Thames had become a noxious sewer. It was Joseph Bazalgette, who became head of the Metropolitan Commission of Sewers, whose 'sweeping vision, executive drive and engineering genius' provided London with a modern sewage system. By the mid-sixties, after miles of tunnels had been dug and numerous pumping stations erected, the Thames at Westminster no longer stank or at least not so much. Bazalgette's ingenious notion of incorporating in his scheme an embankment along the riverside provided London with a new highway between Westminster and the City, tree-lined and with 'dolphin wreathed lampposts and seats adorned with sphinxes'.[132] While by the late 1860s these pioneering large-scale sewerage projects for London were nearing completion, Bradford Corporation was still building sewers so defective as to be health hazards to those who lived near them.[133] Yet the direction of change was towards higher standards and improved provision, even if progress was patchy.

The refinement of steam technology meant that in the third quarter of the century reliable steam engines became available, which could deliver the power for pumping stations and so improve water supplies. In many areas, economic growth provided both the capital and organizational skills needed to create new water supply companies; their timing and their success were other variables. This

---

131. For Birmingham, Smith, *The People's Health*, 219. For Kidderminster, D. J. Martin, 'The Kidderminster Paving Commission, 1813–1856', MA thesis, Wolverhampton Polytechnic, 1985, 51.

132. Picard, *Victorian London*, 5, 26.

133. Hunt, *British Labour History*, 51; Barber, 'Municipal government in Leeds', 14.

was part of the process by which water, gas, and eventually electricity became generally available public utilities. The implications of this development went much further than immediate questions of supply. This was part of a pervasive change in patterns of interdependence within society. A community relying on local streams, springs, or wells for its water exhibited a different pattern of dependence from one in which thousands of people depended for a vital supply on a handful of specialized workers employed by water companies. Instead of an intimate communal dependence, the customers of a more sophisticated water supply became dependent on the continuing work of a group with whom they were unlikely to have even the slightest personal acquaintance. This was part of a broad shift in interdependence which was to accelerate in later years and become even more pervasive in the society of the following century.

Some progress was made in reducing food adulteration. Already at mid-century there were complaints of the dilution of food by useless, sometimes even poisonous, ingredients. Although a range of ineffective statutes in such matters stretched back to medieval times, the first effective legislation was the Adulteration of Food, Drink and Drugs Act of 1872, extended by the Sale of Food and Drugs Act of 1875. There was some improvement in standards of personal cleanliness. The consumption of soap per head doubled in the twenty years from 1841, and more than kept pace with the growing population. This was part of a developing sense of respectable behaviour, in which dirtiness was seen as a reprehensible habit over wider reaches of society. But the extent to which personal cleanliness and official public health provision before 1880 contributed to improved social conditions must not be exaggerated.[134]

Medicine

Medical facilities were slowly, though patchily, improving, and so making an increased contribution to health. There was certainly room for this, as a recollection of conditions in Newcastle upon Tyne's principal hospital in 1870 suggests:

There were no trained nurses in the Infirmary, some could neither read nor write; no specific uniform was worn, the few nurses were underpaid and their accommodation was such that it was impossible to obtain a better class of woman. There was a dirty, ignorant but kind old woman who had charge of Wards 7 and 8. I can see her now with her dress tucked up, petticoats exposed and stockings wrinkled, waddling from bed to bed with a huge linseed meal poultice to be applied gently and kindly to a suppurating stump.[135]

This situation was transformed with the appointment in the same year of a new Resident Medical Officer, who secured the creation of an efficient school of nursing and the appointment of a professional nursing superintendent. In 1874

134. Smith, *The People's Health*, 217–18; N. L. Tranter, *Population and Society: Contrasts in Population Growth, 1750–1940* (1985), 81.

135. F. J. W. Miller, 'The Infirmary on the Forth, 1753–1906', *Archaeologia Aeliana*, 5th ser., 14 (1986), 160.

the appointment of a surgeon who had worked with Lister at Edinburgh brought antiseptic techniques to this hospital; over the next few years the number of operations quadrupled. By 1861 there were at least 130 voluntary general hospitals in England and Wales, and 23 hospitals with medical schools for training doctors.

New specialist hospitals were set up at a rate appreciably faster than the growth in population. So were extended facilities for such categories as the blind, sick children, and expectant mothers; for example, the Leeds United Institution for the Indigent and Industrious Blind opened its doors in 1877. In the 1870s unofficial exertions produced for Bradford a Fever Hospital, something which the local authorities of the town had discussed ineffectually as long ago as 1848. Hospital provision for rural areas, previously lacking, was improved by the cottage hospital movement; there were 16 of these small rural hospitals in 1865, 180 by 1880.[136]

In addition to the growth of voluntary hospitals, there was expansion in the hospital facilities provided by official agencies such as the Poor Law. As early as 1861, the Poor Law system provided more hospital beds than the voluntary sector, though the quality of many of them remained poor. From 1870, Poor Law policy favoured the provision of hospital wards, and in addition embarked upon a programme, again borrowing the idea from unofficial philanthropy, of establishing dispensaries for the supply of medicines to the poor. Voluntary organizations continued to be the pacemakers in improving medical services. In 1873 there were not far short of 1,000 provident dispensaries in the London area, run by friendly societies for their members. The Home Medical Mission campaign, which began in 1859, spread to most urban centres, providing medical teams, free medicines, and usually convalescence facilities also. An indication of the scale on which these voluntary services operated is given by the voluntary dispensary at Stockton, a town of about 13,000 inhabitants; between 1851 and 1868, the doctors serving that institution made a total of 102,426 visits to 10,347 patients.[137] Even with the facilities and techniques which many hospitals could offer by 1880, social conditions could limit their efficacy. A report from the Leeds Charity Organization Society in 1879 noted that 'a great many of the cases of sickness and suffering visited by the Dispensary Officers were so destitute of food and clothing that any medicine and medical attention could do no good.'[138]

Progress in tackling diseases was mixed. The sources of typhus and typhoid were identified in 1861. Tuberculosis, common in both urban and rural society, remained a mystery, although a major killer.[139] TB deaths were often ascribed to physical weakness in the individual victims, but such deaths were in decline by the 1870s, when deaths from smallpox and typhus were also falling. Typhoid and

---

136. Barber, 'Municipal government in Leeds', 19; Tranter, *Population and Society*, 69–70; Smith, *The People's Health*, 277–8. For a regional example, J. V. Beckett, *The East Midlands from A.D. 1000* (1988), 235.

137. Tranter, *Population and Society*, 69–71.

138. D. Mirick, 'Misery and illusion: the local welfare services in Leeds, England, and Philadelphia, U.S.A.', *Journal of Regional and Local Studies*, 6(2) (1985), 17.

139. Hunt, *British Labour History*, 350 n. 66.

some of the common infectious diseases of childhood—measles, whooping cough, scarlet fever, and diphtheria—remained common. The death of Prince Albert from typhoid in 1861 was an indication of continuing dangers which threatened not only the poor. Alcoholism and venereal disease remained serious causes of ill health and death.[140]

Vaccination was important in the decline of smallpox. The first Vaccination Act in 1840 established the principle of State intervention here, but was badly drafted and not wholly successful. The 1853 Act made infant vaccination compulsory, there were further Acts in 1858 and 1867, and the 1871 Act prescribed a simple summary process of fine or imprisonment for parents who failed to see that their offspring received vaccination.[141] Even though this repeated intervention was never wholly effective, it was enough to reduce the smallpox danger.

Improvement in diet, some improvement in housing standards and techniques of building, some improvement in water supplies and medical facilities, all of them varying in their impact from place to place, had together brought about a general improvement in health by 1880, despite the increased population and the persistence of appallingly adverse conditions in some places. From the mid-1870s in particular, death-rates showed a significant decline, despite the large numbers of the population in the vulnerable infant age group. Health standards in Britain remained better than those prevailing in other European countries and indeed in the rest of the world.

There was no ground for complacency, though. The 1848 Public Health Act stipulated an annual death-rate of 23 per 1,000 as an unacceptably high level, in that this figure could lead to the compulsory rather than the permissive implementation of the Act's provisions. In one major industrial region, admittedly perhaps the worst for such conditions, Newcastle upon Tyne returned a death-rate of 24.8 as late as 1874–9, with Middlesbrough at 23.96 in 1871–3, and Gateshead close at 22.9 in 1881–3. It was not until the next century that Newcastle's death rate fell permanently below 20 per 1,000. Apart from death-rates, other indices of health revealed distressing conditions. An individual who reached the age of 45 might seem to be already aged, and at that age susceptibility to disease rose sharply, to double among those between the ages of 50 and 60.[142]

Philanthropy

Charitable activities continued to play an important role, not only in providing medical facilities and housing but in philanthropic activity in many forms. Some individual contributions were on a grand scale; between 1853 and 1887 the Duke of Sutherland invested £1.65 million on improving his Scottish estates in ways unlikely ever to return a profit but which contributed to the welfare of the local

140. F. Cartwright, A *Social History of Medicine* (1977), 114.
141. Smith, *The People's Health*, 161.   142. Ibid. 320–1.

population.[143] Some industrial companies, though by no means all, adopted a paternalistic stance towards their dependants.[144] Philanthropic schemes often displayed ingenuity. At Leominster a Quaker philanthropist who founded a new orphanage in 1869 paid a visit to Germany in 1872, in which he was impressed by a printing works in Hamburg attached to one of that city's orphanages. On returning home, he created the Leominster Orphans' Press to provide the orphans with training and experience in what was one of the town's busiest trades, while at the same time it specialized in the printing of religious tracts and other works of an edifying nature; profits from the press subsidized the orphanage. Orphans' presses followed soon elsewhere in Britain, and the idea was exported by missionaries to India, with similar institutions established at Poona, Agra, Mirzapore, and Calcutta.[145]

As the scale and the variety of charitable enterprises continued to grow, animals as well as humans were among the beneficiaries. During the third quarter of the century, interest in pets, especially dogs, was growing. This led not only to the establishment of national organizations (the Kennel Club was founded in 1873) but also to the creation of a network of charities for animals. For example, the Battersea Dogs' Home was founded in 1868.[146]

The total charitable activity in Britain was probably double that of France, a country which possessed no public service on the scale of the British Poor Law.[147] British philanthropic activity in the third quarter of the century was greater than that of any other contemporary society. It was also sufficient to arouse fears that it might not have wholly good effects. The voluntary nature of most activity meant some overlapping provision and many gaps. Some feared that excessive kindness might sap the invaluable impulse to self-reliance and self-improvement. Such fears, together with a desire to introduce a more businesslike administration to philanthropy, resulted in the Charity Organization Society in 1869.[148] It sought to bring order to philanthropy, by eliminating duplication of effort and bringing about a rational approach to giving. The deserving among those in need were to be given help tailored to their needs, while those who had brought troubles upon themselves by fecklessness, vice, or extravagance might be left to the Poor Law. A network of local bodies developed under the national umbrella of the COS. This work was often carried on in cooperation with official

143. E. Richards, *The Leviathan of Wealth: The Sutherland Fortune in the Industrial Revolution* (1973), 68–70.

144. For a good local example, N. Greatrex, 'The Robinson enterprises at Papplewick, Nottinghamshire. I', *Industrial Archaeology Review*, 9 (1) (1986), 49–51. The reward for this paternalism included the deliberate creation for political purposes of a myth of harsh treatment, late in the 19th cent.

145. V. Histon, 'The Leominster orphans' press', *Nineteenth Century Short Title Catalogue Newsletter*, 4 (1987).

146. J. K. Walton, 'Mad dogs and Englishmen: the conflict over rabies in late Victorian England', *Journal of Social History*, 13 (2), (1979–80), 219–39.

147. Smith, *The People's Health*, 422.

148. C. L. Mowat, *The Charity Organization Society, 1869–1913* (1961).

agencies; Poor Law unions and local charitable organizations often shared a common leadership drawn from the 'principal inhabitants' of the district. The COS also operated as a kind of national focus for the philanthropic movement, issuing appeal literature and advice, and operating as a pressure group with some success in influencing government and Parliament.

Education

Philanthropy experienced a relative decline in one important sphere. In education, public intervention expanded, especially in elementary education after 1870. In the 1850s most school places were provided either by privately owned schools or by the schools founded by religious sects. In 1851, for instance, Sheffield possessed at least 180 schools which were the livelihood of their proprietors.[149] The quality of education provided in such schools varied. Even where 'writing' was described as a regular part of the curriculum, in poorer schools this could amount to no more than the routine copying of set passages.

Time at school varied. In some regions, such as Northumberland, Cumberland, and Westmorland, it was normal for children to have a continuous span of several years in school, up to the age of 12 or even 13.[150] In other areas, especially where child labour was common, attendance might be shorter and intermittent. Factory legislation of the mid-Victorian period, such as the Factory Acts Extension Act and the Workshop Regulation Act of 1867, tried to ensure regular schooling for factory children, with limited results. Many parents and employers could see little need for it; it has been suggested that in the Black Country local industries only

required bodily strength and endurance, a modicum of skill, and virtually no intellectual abilities. Even small employers who had risen from the lower ranks of the working-class never acquired the rudiments of learning. An innate shrewdness and hard work, not an education, was required for success . . . The need for education was not apparent to parents who could see relative prosperity achieved without it. The people who could read and write could not command greater wages than those who could not.[151]

Despite such restraints, educational provision continued to grow. Here as elsewhere official action followed philanthropic initiatives. As evidence accumulated that poor children engaged in criminal activity, a campaign for reformatory institutions developed, under the inspiration of a group of social reformers of whom Miss Mary Carpenter, a skilful and well-connected campaigner, was the key figure.[152] She set up her first reformatory school in 1852, and within the next four years another forty were established; an interest in conditions in India led to

149. S. Pollard and C. Holmes (eds.), *Essays in the Economic and Social History of South Yorkshire* (1976), 265.
150. Hunt, *British Labour History*, 16.
151. J. Pegler, 'A comparative study of popular education in Dudley before 1870', MA thesis, Wolverhampton Polytechnic, 1985, 65.
152. Miss Carpenter and her father have entries in ODNB.

the extension of Miss Carpenter's work there. It was only towards the end of her long and busy life that she overcame her reluctance, as a woman, to take part in public campaigning for her philanthropic causes.[153] Parliament proved willing to listen to arguments about the state of poor children. An Act of 1855 allowed Poor Law guardians to pay school fees for poor children out of the rates. The Industrial Schools Act of 1857 allowed magistrates to send convicted children to reform schools and provided grant aid for them. A parallel movement to provide a mixture of feeding, clothing, trade training, and basic schooling for very poor children, the voluntary Ragged Schools movement, received similar encouragement; an Act of 1869 excluded Ragged Schools from local taxation.

The biggest change came with the passing of the controversial Elementary Education Act of 1870. Although avowedly a supplementary measure, it provided in certain circumstances for the building and operation of schools at public expense. The new School Boards were established in areas where the voluntary provision of schools was inadequate. As some of the Act's critics had foreseen, the result was an increase in the extent of public control over schooling. In Leeds, although the School Board spent only £13,000 in 1875, the education rate rose to £49,000 in 1880 and £81,500 by 1896.[154] The coming of the Board Schools was accompanied by improvement in the quality of elementary education generally. Training in writing became more systematic, with English composition established in the curriculum for older classes, although in practice the number of children who reached that standard was limited. The official schools inspectorate, 59 strong in 1859, rose to 98 by 1869, followed by a leap forward to 244 by 1880. School inspectors penetrated even rural areas but in many counties State intervention did not mean a sharp break with the pre-1870 order. The philanthropy of the aristocracy and gentry was not replaced by the State and a partnership emerged in which State money and State inspection blended in with the financial and paternalistic input of landed families, while the needs of the agricultural year and of the household economies of rural families demanded that schools were thinly attended in certain seasons.[155]

The Scottish Education Act of 1872 gave the State a larger role. Scottish education was made universal and compulsory and, whereas the English Act sought to fill the gaps in the voluntary system, the intention in Scotland was to establish a standard public system of education. The Scottish Act also made some provision for secondary education.

Progress in education in these years was not confined to official intervention. Technical education was seen as an important requirement in many areas. The City and Guilds Institute was established in 1876 to provide examinations and qualifications in a range of technical crafts. Increasingly, industrial centres

153. Burn, *The Age of Equipoise*, 151–2. Ibid. 44, for the source of Miss Carpenter's zeal.
154. Barber, 'Municipal government in Leeds', 103.
155. A. E. Hattersley, 'Philanthropy and Landed Estates in Northumberland during the Nineteenth Century', Ph.D. thesis, University of Teesside (2004).

acquired technical colleges associated with local industry, Bradford in 1879, Birmingham in 1880.

In higher education Manchester led the provincial cities in the creation of new educational institutions.[156] Owens College came into existence there in 1851 when nearly £100,000 was made available under the will of a wealthy merchant and industrialist, John Owens. Among the few stipulations he made were the exclusion of women and the absence of religious tests for entry. The college received a more satisfactory legal status when it was incorporated by Act of Parliament in 1871; the Manchester Medical School joined with the college in the following year, and in 1880 a royal charter as the Victoria University signalled the attainment of full university status in association with a sister institution at Leeds founded in 1874. University College, Liverpool, joined as the third element in the federal Victoria University in 1881. Other foundations from which modern universities were to develop came into existence in Southampton (1861), Newcastle (1871), Sheffield (1875), Bristol (1876), Birmingham (1880), Nottingham (1881), Dundee (1883), and Reading (1892). The inspiration for these new institutions of higher education came from local enthusiasts rather than official intervention.

The authority of Parliament was employed to reform the established universities, often settling questions which had been fought over between reformers and conservatives within those institutions. A royal commission into Oxford University appointed in August 1850 provided the basis for two Acts of 1852 and 1856 which, among other things, opened Oxford degrees to non-Anglicans. Another royal commission on Cambridge University in 1856 paved the way for a new set of university statutes there in 1858. London University received a new charter in 1858, its own MP in 1867, and from 1878 women could take London degrees. Similarly, inquiries into the Scottish universities resulted in a reforming Act in 1858 which was followed by the institution of a new range of honours degrees there. In 1850 the university colleges founded in 1845–9 at Belfast, Cork, and Galway were united into the Queen's University. In 1879 there was another reorganization. Queen's University was dissolved: the constituent colleges received more autonomy, and a Royal University of Ireland was created, operating essentially as an examining body for the separate colleges. In Wales the first university college was founded at Aberystwyth in 1872; Cardiff followed eleven years later.

Scientific development

There was scientific progress in the universities, too.[157] Though Durham had taught mining engineering since 1838, Cambridge only acquired a department of

---

156. M. Sanderson (ed.), *The Universities in the Nineteenth Century* (1975) gives a selection of relevant documents, together with a commentary. W. H. G. Armytage, *The Civic Universities* (1955).

157. C. Singer, *A Short History of Science in the Nineteenth Century* (1949). M. Argles, *South Kensington to Robbins: An Account of English Technical and Scientific Education since 1851* (1964).

engineering in 1875, though it established a chair of political economy in 1863 and another in experimental physics in 1871. The contributions to scientific know-ledge of university-based scholars increased. William Thomson, the future Lord Kelvin, had become a professor at Glasgow in 1846. James Clerk-Maxwell, the first Cambridge professor of experimental physics, published a major work on *Electricity and Magnetism* in 1873. He was succeeded at Cambridge by Lord Rayleigh, a scientist born into the aristocracy, who managed to reconcile such varied activities as the lord lieutenancy of Essex and the discovery of the gas argon. At the same time much scientific research and discovery still took place outside the formal academic structure of education. James Joule, a pioneer in thermodynamics, was the son of a wealthy brewer and financed his own research. Sidney Gilchrist Thomas, inventor in 1875 of a process which enabled phosphoric iron ore to be used in steel-making, had previously been a schoolteacher and a police court clerk. Joseph Wilson Swan, the British discoverer of the incandescent electric light bulb and a number of other important inventions, left school at the age of 12 and was essentially self-taught. Achievement in science and technology could lead to wealth and social advancement. Patents taken out by men like Gilchrist Thomas and Swan to protect their discoveries produced substantial incomes. Others, like William Thomson and James Joule, won distinguished public recognition and the conferment of honours of various kinds for their work. There continued to be a close connection between scientific research and practical application. Thomson was consulted in connection with the laying of the transatlantic cable, while Joule's discoveries in thermodynamics between 1843 and 1878 were to have an important influence on the design of various kinds of engine in later years.

Historical research and writing

Another area of scholarship which developed significantly in these years was history. Again progress occurred both within the universities and outside the formal structure of education. The Royal Historical Society was established in 1868, and Earl Russell became its first president. A standing royal commission, the national Historical Manuscripts Commission, was set up in 1869, and embarked upon a systematic programme of publication of important sources.

William Stubbs was a Church of England inspector of schools before becoming Regius Professor of Modern History at Oxford in 1866 and later a bishop (first of Chester and then of Oxford). In 1870 he published his *Select Charters*, a collection of medieval documents which was to run through many editions and be a familiar source book to generations of history students. A three-volume *Constitutional History of England* followed in 1874, 1875, and 1878. His greatest service to historical scholarship lay in his editing and publication of a varied sequence of medieval documents. This provided an important stimulus to medieval studies generally, as did E. A. Freeman's widely read *History of the*

Norman Conquest, published in 1879. The spread of literacy provided a market for more popular historical writing, such as J. R. Green's *Short History of the English People* of 1875 and his *The Making of England* of 1881. Publishers such as Collins, Cassells, and John Murray found a ready market for cheap history books. This wider public interest in history had been foreshadowed by such earlier pointers as Thackeray's popular and profitable lectures on 'The Four Georges' in the 1850s. Another powerful influence was Macaulay's *The History of England*, the first volumes of which had appeared in 1848, and the later volumes in 1855. By 1880 an interest in history was more widespread and more sophisticated than at any earlier period.

Literature

In literature, Dickens, Trollope, Thackeray, and George Eliot continued to appeal to a wide readership in the years after 1850. The first collected edition of Thackeray's novels was published in twenty-two volumes only a few years after his death in 1863. Younger novelists, such as Thomas Hardy, George Meredith, and the American Henry James, proved more limited in their appeal. A reflection of more widespread literacy, coupled perhaps with unsophisticated tastes, was the appearance of another kind of popular fiction.[158] The early-Victorian years had seen a wide range of cheap and crudely printed imitations of the fashionable novelists of the day, but there now emerged a substantial volume of widely popular fiction which made no great intellectual demands on the reader but which appeared in a more respectable publishing format. Perhaps the only one of these once popular writers whose reputation has survived into modern times is Mrs Henry Wood. From the appearance of her melodramatic *East Lynne* in 1861, her numerous novels sold very widely. Ouida (Louise de la Ramee) achieved a similar popular success with such works as *Under Two Flags* (1867) and *Moths* (1880).

The most sensational novel of the period was Mrs Mary Braddon's *Lady Audley's Secret* (1862). The central character, a bigamous blonde, deserts her child, murders her husband, and contemplates poisoning her second husband. Amongst all this wickedness what may have fascinated or horrified many readers was the idea of poisoning a husband. Divorce was difficult and its consequences undesirable in mid-Victorian Britain but widowhood was an honourable estate and poison was easily available at the chemists.

By 1880 there was a clearer distinction between the novels which received critical literary praise and those which were widely read, a distinction which has survived into modern times. There were always some works which nevertheless contrived to combine enduring appeal with literary distinction. The mathematician Charles Lutwidge Dodgson, writing as Lewis Carroll, produced two

158. R. D. Altick, *The English Common Reader: A Social History of the Mass Reading Public* (1957). V. Neuberg, *Popular Literature: A History and Guide* (1977).

masterpieces, *Alice in Wonderland* (1865) and *Through the Looking Glass* (1871), in which endearing fantasy blended with gentle satire of human foibles:

'I can't believe that!' said Alice, '. . . one can't believe impossible things.'

'I daresay you haven't had much practice,' said the Queen. 'When I was your age I always did it for half-an-hour a day. Why, sometimes I've believed as many as six impossible things before breakfast.'

In addition to a growing variety of respectable reading material, a substantial volume of semi-pornographic and pornographic writing remained in circulation.

With Wordsworth's death in 1850 a great era in English poetry seemed to have ended, and his best work had been written much earlier. Of the mid-Victorian poets, only Tennyson achieved a major reputation in his own day; contemporaries such as Browning and Swinburne were less well known. Even in Tennyson's case, his popular reputation largely rested on works such as *The Charge of the Light Brigade* and *The Idylls of the King*, which literary critics did not think his finest work.

Art and architecture

Much of the growing volume of published writing required illustration. This affected the styles of artists in other areas and encouraged the production of pictures which told a story.[159] Frederic Leighton and John Millais were among the prominent artists who worked in this style. By the third quarter of the century such leading painters, with others like Sir Edwin Landseer, could command prices running into thousands of pounds for their works. As always, artistic taste among the dominant social groups was influential. The preferences of the Queen and Prince Albert were known and imitated. While awaiting the birth of one of her sons, the Queen had a Millais painting sent to Windsor for her inspection. Many of Landseer's most famous pictures had appeared in the years before 1850, but in the 1850s and 1860s he painted some of his best-known royal portraits.

Distinguished patronage was available for some new departures in art. One significant development was the emergence from about 1848 of 'the Pre-Raphaelite Brotherhood', a talented group which included William Morris, Dante Gabriel Rossetti, Ford Madox Brown, and Holman Hunt, and which received the enthusiastic encouragement of the influential critic and writer John Ruskin. Allied to their aesthetic determination to reintroduce a purer and more natural expression to art was an ambition to spread their message to sectors of society previously ignored by

159. R. C. K. Ensor, *England, 1870–1914* (1936), 152–61, has some perceptive comments on art, architecture, literature, and recreation in these years. His severe criticism of some aspects, including much architecture and the degree of cultivation attained by businessmen, reflect the widespread dislike of 'Victorian' attributes in the 1930s, and would not be so readily accepted today. A. P. Oppe, 'Art', and A. E. Richardson, 'Architecture', in G. M. Young (ed.), *Early Victorian England*, vol. ii (1934), chs. 10 and 11, contain much useful material. The former exaggerates the decline in aristocratic patronage, but is useful for the Pre-Raphaelites and for the position of eminent artists in society.

the world of high art. These endeavours ranged from Morris's romantic socialism and support of excellent craftsmanship to the patronage of individual working men. The connection between the Sunderland cork-cutter Thomas Dixon and Ruskin, Rossetti, and other eminent figures in artistic circles provides a good example of these well-meant liberal endeavours, and also of their very limited success.[160] Ruskin published his own letters to Dixon, but made no attempt to publish the other side of the correspondence. Other prominent artists and writers found Dixon's continued attentions something of an embarrassment. In practice, the Pre-Raphaelites, like previous generations of artists, still depended heavily on the support of influential supporters and patrons who represented both old and new wealth. In the north of England enthusiastic support for the Pre-Raphaelites came from the ninth Earl of Carlisle and his wife (the Earl was himself an artist of considerable talent), Sir Walter Trevelyan, Bt., and Lady Pauline Trevelyan.[161] In their interest and patronage, these aristocrats were joined by a substantial number of northern industrialists, including the ironmasters Henry Bolckow and Sir Isaac Lowthian Bell, the shipbuilders Charles Mitchell and T. E. Smith, and the chemical manufacturers R. S. Newall and W. W. Pattinson. Such patrons built up substantial private collections and often donated works of art to the growing number of local art galleries (which usually owed their existence to similar endowments). In practice, this encouragement was much more effective than any response to the artists' romantic and liberal sympathies from workers.

Opinions of Victorian architecture have oscillated markedly. Frequently condemned, as with other 'Victorian' attributes, during the second quarter of the twentieth century, a more sympathetic appraisal is now common. Economic, social, and demographic changes involved an enormous mass of new construction, facilitated by such developments as the mass production of cheap bricks and slates and the lower cost of transporting them. Decorative fashions in building saw a filtering down the social scale, with Gothic ornament first introduced for stately homes and public buildings increasingly used to embellish houses in such places as suburbs and mining villages. Although A. W. Pugin died in 1852, and Sir Charles Barry in 1860, both men left sons who continued to be influential in the next generation's architectural standards. In the year of Barry's death, the completion of the new Houses of Parliament provided a model which found imitators both in general design and in detailed decoration for many years to come. Civic pride provided one avenue for architectural distinction; St George's Hall, Liverpool (opened 1854) and the new Town Hall at Manchester (opened 1877) were among many manifestations of provincial architectural distinction.

---

160. G. Milburn, 'Thomas Dixon of Sunderland', *Sunderland's History*, 29, (1984), 5–45.

161. Lady Trevelyan was a great admirer of the Pre-Raphaelites and combining her beliefs in progress, art, and Christianity commissioned William Bell Scott to paint a series of paintings depicting the history of Northumberland to adorn the central hall in the Trevelyans' mansion, Wallington (see front cover). A recent work on Lady Trevelyan is: John Batchelor, *Lady Trevelyan and the Pre-Raphaelite Brotherhood* (2006).

Newspapers

Changes in society were also reflected in the periodical press, where growth was facilitated by improvements in printing technology and wider literacy. Fiscal changes also helped. A tax on advertisements was repealed in 1853, the newspaper tax was abolished in 1855, and the duty on paper was removed in 1861. These changes were part of the general move to free trade policies, but they also embodied the intention to encourage literacy and the dissemination of information. The most eminent journal *The Times*, with a circulation of about 63,000 in 1870, was believed to exercise a considerable influence in national affairs. Other national newspapers such as the Liberal *Daily Telegraph* and *Daily News* and the Conservative *Standard* were similar in character. Far from sprightly in their layout and contents, they provided a solid diet of home and foreign news. In 1870 the *Telegraph* was selling about 190,000 copies, the *News* 90,000, and the *Standard* 140,000. Improvements in communications, including the transmission of news by telegraph, enabled leading provincial newspapers such as the *Manchester Guardian* and the *Newcastle Chronicle* to provide regional journals of high quality. Increasingly, however, newspapers of a different character also spread among the less cultivated but basically literate. By the 1860s the *News of the World* and *Lloyds Weekly News* claimed weekly circulations of about half a million each. They offered reading material of a very different kind from the more staid daily papers. An advertisement for *Lloyds* in 1868 promised the following fare in its next number:

The Emperor Napoleon on Assassination
Fearful stabbing case through jealousy
Terrible scene at an execution
Cannibalism at Liverpool
The Great Seizure of Indecent Prints
A man roasted to death
A cruel husband and an adulterous wife.[162]

The expanding range of newspapers was complemented by a rapidly increasing volume of periodical publications of other kinds. Specialized magazines appeared such as the *Field* (1853, largely for country gentlemen), *Building News* (1854), the *Engineer* (1856), the *Solicitors' Journal* (1857), the *Queen* (1861, for ladies), the *Garden* (1871), *Iron* (1873), the *Illustrated Sporting and Dramatic News* (1874), the *Accountant* (1874), the *Electrician* (1878).

Religion

Religion remained a major influence in British society during the decades after 1850. This is not to say that the majority of the population was sincerely devout,

162. J. M. Milne, *Newspapers of Northumberland and Durham* (1971), 30. This book provides more generally a good example of the developing provincial press.

or punctilious in attendance at church and chapel. Rather, the basic concepts of Christianity found wide acceptance in various degrees at all levels of society. Overt opposition to organized religion, expressed in the work of activists like G. J. Holyoake and Charles Bradlaugh, possessed little influence outside relatively small groups of enthusiasts.

The Established Church of England continued to be by far the biggest Christian communion in England, with an entrenched position in national life. Many who were not regular Anglican worshippers resorted to the parish church for the major rituals of family life—marriage, baptism, funerals; in 1851, the Church of England conducted 84.9 per cent of all English marriages, a figure far above the ratio of its regular attenders.[163] Within the Established Church, there were continuing squabbles between different sections. Anglican evangelicals opposed the High-Church men inspired by the Oxford Movement of early-Victorian years. In Salford, when a High-Church vicar was appointed to St Stephen's in 1864 evangelical outrage at his practices led to his being forced to resign two years later.[164] Such concern in an industrial centre, and the wide support which evangelical Anglicanism enjoyed in industrial Lancashire, demonstrate that the Established Church was still lively in these years.

Other forms of evangelical religion also continued to be active after 1850. Primitive Methodism retained much of its original crusading fervour. In a PM mission in rural Lincolnshire in 1857, the ungodly were left in no doubt about their fate:

Your employment, instead of singing salvation with the white-robed multitude in heaven, will be to gaze on terrific forms, to listen to frightful sounds, to breathe sulphurous air, and to roll in liquid fire, where the prospect of eternal woe fills the mind with constant horror. Would you escape this agony? Repent of sin, pray for pardon, believe in Christ, 'wash and be clean'.[165]

The importance of salvation made many evangelicals fear the dangers of too great an involvement in such worldly affairs as politics and trade-unionism, though this was not a uniform reaction. In December 1875 one rural Primitive Methodist circuit condemned the use of chapels for 'political or other agitating meetings'.[166]

The force and nature of Evangelicalism was, nevertheless, abating and changing. Perhaps the major development affecting most Christian churches was the diminishing place of Hell. Much of the influence of the ideas of salvation and atonement came from the belief that the fate of the vast majority was an eternity in Hell from which only the elect in Calvinist terms or the worthy and repentant in evangelical terms would be saved. Heaven rather than Hell became prominent in most Christian teaching as God was increasingly portrayed as a

163. D. I. Coleman, *The Church of England in the Mid-Nineteenth Century* (1980), 7.
164. R. N. Greenall, 'Popular Conservatism in Salford', *Northern History*, 9 (1974), 123–38.
165. Ambler, 'Social change and religious experience', 154.   166. Ibid. 382–4.

God of love. Hell was increasingly portrayed in terms of the withdrawal of God's approval or a state of nothingness, rather than a place where positive punishment was meted out, while the possibility of the eventual entry into Heaven even of the hardened sinner began to be muted. 'In 1853 [F. D.] Maurice was dismissed from his professorial post at King's College London for arguing in effect that Hell did not exist in any literal sense, yet within ten years of that date his "more indulgent Gospel" was on the way to becoming a commonplace.'[167] Probably the state of heightened emotion demanded by early nineteenth-century Evangelicalism was too demanding and made it impossible for most people to maintain it over a lifetime. A more consolatory form of religion became dominant in the Anglican Church and spread slowly to many of the non-conformist churches after mid-century.

Even in Calvinistic Scotland, there was some decline in the religious certainties as regards Heaven and Hell. John McLeod Campbell's, *The Nature of the Atonement* (1856) expressed the view that salvation was available to all who genuinely repented, while William Logan edited a book of essays, *Words of Comfort for Parents Bereaved of Little Children* (1872), which argued that most of those who died in childhood, being less corrupt than adults, got to Heaven.[168]

Although for many men and women religion, including sectarian controversies, remained of crucial importance, there were signs of growing religious toleration. Nonconformists were admitted to degrees of the older universities; Jews were admitted to the House of Commons (1858) and the House of Lords (1866). Yet anti-Semitism and anti-Catholicism continued to be common, the latter often combined with anti-Irish sentiments. In 1853 *The Times* declared that 'We very much doubt whether in England, or indeed in any free Protestant country, a true Papist can be a good subject.' In 1857, it was thought advisable to ask candidates for entry to the East Riding county police force if they belonged to any Orange Lodge.[169] Popular anti-Catholicism was strong and often virulent. During the 1868 election campaign, Salford electors, including many workers enfranchised the previous year, were asked 'whether you will have the Pope or the Queen?'.[170] In 1851 an anti-Catholic riot at Stockport involved one death and many injuries, as well as the sacking of Catholic churches. Late in 1858 there was another riot when radicals advocating Italian national independence clashed violently in Hyde Park with Irish supporters of the papacy. One of the worst sequences of riots was associated with the stormy career of the Irish anti-Catholic lecturer William Murphy. This agitator, himself an ex-Catholic, was backed by the Protestant Evangelical Mission in his tours attacking the Catholic

167. Boyd Hilton, *A Mad, Bad & Dangerous People: England 1783–1846* (2006), 632.
168. T. C. Smout, *A Century of the Scottish People, 1830–1950* (1986), 192–3.
169. D. Foster, *The Rural Constabulary Act, 1839* (1982), frontispiece. For a wider discussion of anti-Catholicism, G. F. A. Best, 'Popular Protestantism in Victorian Britain', in R. Robson (ed.), *Ideas and Institutions of Victorian Britain: Essays Presented to G. Kitson Clark* (1967), 115–42, and E. R. Norman, *Anti-Catholicism in Victorian England* (1968).
170. Greenall, 'Popular Conservatism in Salford', 132.

Church and publication of scurrilous anti-Catholic propaganda. Visits by Murphy in 1867–8 provoked serious rioting, in which Irish Catholics took a prominent part, in many places, including Wolverhampton, Birmingham, Aston, and Stalybridge. Murphy's career came to a violent end; he died in 1872, never having recovered from being savagely beaten and kicked by Irish miners at Whitehaven.[171] The disappearance of Murphy brought to an end some of the most serious clashes of anti-Catholic agitators and their Irish enemies. But violence could still be provoked by religion. Later in the century it more often took the form of attacks, sometimes brutal, on such groups as the Salvation Army in their attempts to bring evangelical Christianity to some districts which had remained essentially pagan communities.[172]

There was another dimension to religion in Victorian Britain reflected in the number of fringe religious groups or cults of millenarians, followers of messiahs, Swedenborgians and spiritualists. Mary Anne Girling was in a long tradition going back to the seventeenth century of charismatic religious leaders and prophets. Her followers, the New Forest Shakers, spoke in tongues and danced in ecstatic frenzies as they awaited the apocalypse. The great sage of mid-Victorian Britain, John Ruskin, attended his first seance in 1864 and was progressively drawn into the spiritualism that was to fascinate so many eminent Victorians. Henry Prince, an ex-curate, founded a sect with a rather more fleshly character; as he considered himself incapable of sin, he was able to indulge in sexual union with his female followers in his 'Abode of Love' in Spaxton, Somerset, during the 1850s.[173]

Evolution

Charles Darwin's theory of biological evolution aroused consternation and angry debate in Victorian society. It caused some to lose their faith in Christianity and others to attack it as a vile heresy which lowered man to the status of animals or insects. What is just as obvious is that many were able to adapt it to their religious beliefs or to adapt their religious beliefs to it.

That it occasioned such a wide public debate reflected the range of contemporary publishing. Religious works still provided the biggest single volume of publications and such works were widely read and printed in great quantity. During the earlier nineteenth century, geology had been developing in ways which cast doubt on the biblical story of the Creation. In 1830–3 Charles Lyell had published his *Principles of Geology*, which argued for a long and varied development of the earth. Other writers, such as Robert Chambers, Erasmus Darwin, Jean-Baptiste Lamarck, and Herbert Spencer, had speculated on the possible emergence of

---

171. Stevenson, *Popular Disturbances in England, 1700–1870* (1979), 277–80.
172. Ibid. 282.
173. For Prince see, Aubrey Menon, *The Abode of Love* (1957). For a more general survey of the religious cults of the period see, Philip Hoare, *The Lost Eden: Adventures in a Victorian Utopia* (2005).

animal species by a process of gradual evolution rather than an act of creation. The potential conflict between such studies and the Genesis account came into the open after the publication in 1859 of Charles Darwin's account of *The Origin of Species by Natural Selection*. This crystallized ideas which different scholars had been approaching at much the same time, and awoke a reaction among those holding a dogmatic faith in the literal truth of the biblical account of the Creation.

The Darwinian controversy coincided with other disputes arising from developments in biblical scholarship, involving revisions of long-accepted texts and interpretations. German scholars, in particular, had been subjecting the Bible to historical criticism and their findings had influenced British theologians. In 1860 a group of liberal churchmen published a collection of *Essays and Reviews*, which included arguments against a literal and uncritical interpretation of the Bible, and other revisionist themes. The book was condemned by the Anglican Church's Convocation and two of its authors were tried for heresy before an ecclesiastical court, being acquitted only on appeal to the Judicial Committee of the Privy Council. These conflicts made a great deal of noise, especially during the 1860s, but became more muted in later years. Many leading scientists continued to be practising and sincere Christians, while more sophisticated arguments were put forward to accommodate geological realities, a belief in a natural process of evolution, and critical biblical scholarship within the Christian fold. To a great extent Darwinism was interpreted in ways that made it more friendly to Christian belief and the gospel of progress. Darwin postulated the survival of the fittest, whether the fittest were nasty or good didn't come into it, but many adapted the theory to give credence to a progressive view of human development.

The temperance movement

The relationship between the Churches and the temperance movement was close. Religious motivation was at least as strong as any other in the campaigns to reduce drinking. In 1881, the strength of Nonconformist Wales was reflected in an Act to close public houses in the principality on Sundays. Already an Act of 1854 had forbidden the opening of public houses (except for bona fide travellers) between 2.30 and 6 p.m. on Sundays. This was followed in 1864 by an Act which closed London public houses daily between 1 and 4 p.m.; this Act could be adopted by other local authorities and often was.[174] The Forbes-McKenzie Act of 1853 was a major victory for the temperance cause in Scotland and resulted in the pubs being shut altogether on Sundays (though genuine and bogus travellers could get a drink at a hotel) and an 11 p.m. closing time on weekdays. Such legislation was, of course, open to the charge that it was class legislation, preventing

174. Burn, *The Age of Equipoise*, 283 n.

the poor enjoying their Sunday off while the rich were free to drink at home, in restaurants, or in their clubs.

The earlier advocates of temperance had been few and subject to ridicule, but by 1870 temperance organizations were an accepted and respectable element in local society. In 1858, for example, 1,000 Wolverhampton teetotallers took a day trip to Hagley, marching to the railway station with their brass band playing and their colours flying. The ramifications of the movement could be curious. In 1861, the 'Temperance Lifeboat' movement began in Staffordshire, aiming to rescue individuals threatened with the wrecking of their lives through drink. In its first three years, forty lifeboat 'crews' were established, with a hierarchy of naval ranks and quasi-masonic rituals of their own. Some of the crews combined temperance missionary work with expressions of devotion to the popular hero Garibaldi.[175]

Some temperance organizations were local or regional, some national or even international in scope. The Sons of Temperance was an Anglo-American friendly society for teetotallers, which numbered Abraham Lincoln among its members and recruited widely in Britain. A very moderate calculation would count at least 100,000 fervent and active temperance workers in mid-Victorian years, with much larger numbers attached more tenuously to the movement. Religion and the associated temperance movement recruited support from different social groups, ranging from the aristocracy to the poor. Among the poor there was often a crucial difference between a popular culture associated with respectability, perhaps with attachment to Church or chapel, temperance movement or mechanics' institute, and another popular culture of a less edifying kind, whose roots lay in gambling and drinking, and no great respectability. Even this distinction is an over-simplification, for there were groups who might not be devout, might indulge in moderate drinking, and might take a deep interest in recreation of various kinds, and yet be accepted as respectable. There was nevertheless a distinction to be drawn, and which often was drawn at the time, between the respectable and disreputable elements in society. This distinction was not confined to the poorer sectors of society, but it was frequently observed there. In Sheffield 'The cultural division of the city was ... not so much between middle class and working class, but between "rough" and "respectable" ... the working man who was respectable was traditionally a church or chapel goer, active in the running of his congregation, who sent his children to Sunday school.'[176] A study of Durham miners concludes that 'The Methodists did not share leisure-time activities with their non-Methodist workmates ... they were divided from the bosses as workers, but united with them as "respectable" men.'[177]

175. R. J. Gohlich, 'The temperance cause in Wolverhampton and Walsall, 1850–1870', MA thesis, Wolverhampton Polytechnic, 1985, 33–45.

176. C. Reid, 'Middle class values and working class culture', in Pollard and Holmes, *Essays in the Economic and Social History of South Yorkshire*, 278.

177. R. Moore, *Pitmen, Preachers and Politics* (1974), 386–7 n. 51.

Popular tastes

As such comments suggest, tastes in leisure activities varied widely. Despite statutory prohibitions, blood sports such as cock-fighting flourished with varying degrees of secrecy in many parts of the country, including the industrial Midlands and north. Ratting, dog-fighting, and badger drawing still had considerable followings.[178] Other activities shunned by the respectable worker included the pervasive gambling: in some areas large pitch-and-toss schools were common, usually on Sundays, with children often employed as lookouts to forestall police interference. Gambling went on over dog-fighting, rabbit-coursing, cock-fighting, football, athletics, and whippet racing, as well as horse racing. Even in industrialized areas of Lancashire traditional wakes and the customs and recreations associated with them continued with remarkable consistency.[179] In towns like Birmingham with many small workshops the old tradition of St Monday by which workers, often hung-over from heavy drinking on Saturday and Sunday extended the weekend off until Tuesday morning, was still observed.[180]

If many traditional leisure activities reflected an older popular culture, rooted in the countryside yet demonstrating a capacity to adapt to and endure in urban environments, innovations were discernible after mid-century. Sport became more organized with standard rules while the improved transport system enabled teams and spectators to travel greater distances. Entertainment was promoted on a larger scale as the music hall developed from the sing-songs and stand-up comedy of the public house. The public house remained central to the leisure of the majority but its all-embracing importance declined as sports became organized separately and the music hall developed. Popular leisure pursuits had always had their commercial promoters but the new entrepreneurs of the leisure industry did things on a far wider scale.

Popular leisure and working-class leisure have often been seen as synonymous and, as the vast majority of the population could be defined as working-class, the great proportion of the consumers of popular leisure were working-class or rather, so far its public manifestations were concerned, working men. It is not only the many layers and divisions within the working classes but the multitude of taste cultures and the great distinction between rural and urban Britain that make 'popular' a more apposite word than working-class together with the fact that in all sections of society there were those who participated in popular leisure pursuits and others who regarded them with abhorrence. Queen Victoria delighted in her visits to the circus, while the aristocracy organized and patronized horse racing and boxing.

178. L. Faultless, 'The leisure pursuits of the working class in late Victorian and Edwardian Wednesbury, 1879–1914', MA thesis, Wolverhampton Polytechnic, 1985, 27–35.

179. Robert Poole, 'Oldham Wakes' in John K. Walton and James Walvin (eds.), *Leisure in Britain, 1780–1939* (1983).

180. Douglas Reid, 'The decline of St Monday, 1766–1876', *Past and Present*, 71 (1976).

Then there is the question of cultural transmission. Handel's *Messiah* may be regarded as part of high culture but, through Methodism and the choral movement, it became widely popular, while it has been argued that the brass bands which became associated with coal mines and factories originated with the middle classes.[181] Music halls varied considerably both regionally and in the social composition of audiences. They have fascinated historians who have pondered such questions as the degree of control exercised by working-class audiences over the entertainment they were offered, whether music halls constituted an arena for cultural negotiation or appropriation, whether they provided culturally conservative or radical fare, and to what degree different sections of the audience, depending on social status or gender, took away different meanings from the same programmes.

There was an increasingly varied and rich leisure culture available to mid-Victorians. Working people may have had limited leisure time and wages allowed for only a modest expenditure on leisure but small sums added up to big totals as the business of leisure was well aware. The burgeoning seaside holiday trade is an example of this. Seaside holiday resorts like Brighton and Scarborough began as resorts for the upper classes and by mid-century there were several seaside towns catering for the middle orders of society. After mid-century, though few working people could afford a week's holiday, cheap railway excursions made a day trip to the seaside a possibility. During Whit week in 1850 some 2,000 trippers left Manchester by train and Blackpool regularly received up to 12,000 excursionists during the 1850s. Gradually more workers were able to afford a few days' holiday and then a week's. The appearance of the 'day tripper' was not welcomed at first but soon, not just publicans and shopkeepers but some town councils would be striving to attract them, even as they tried to segregate them from more respectable visitors.

An important development expressive of the ideals and contradictions of the period was refurbishment of the festival of Christmas. Much of what the early twenty-first century still regards as the traditional Christmas dates from the mid-nineteenth century: the Christmas tree, the Christmas card, and Father Christmas. Literary influences were important here and, in particular, that of Charles Dickens. Central to the changes in the way Christmas was observed were, however, the Victorian idealization of the family and the indulgence of children.[182]

Popular politics were part of popular culture and expressions of political partisanship especially during elections were not confined to those who had the vote. As a study of popular political activity in the textile districts of Lancashire and Yorkshire has revealed the workplace was a centre of cultural influence and employees often took the workplace into politics by supporting the political

181. Dave Russell, *Popular Music in England, 1840–1914* (1987); Trevor Herbert, 'Nineteenth-century brass bands; the making of a movement', idem, (ed.), *Bands: The Brass Band Movement in the Nineteenth and Twentieth Centuries* (1991), 7–56.

182. J. M. Golby and A. W. Purdue, *The Making of the Modern Christmas* (1986).

party favoured by the factory owner.[183] Undoubtedly workers enjoyed volatile political meetings and the public disruption that came with elections. Indeed elections were times when normal rules of behaviour and the usual formal relations between different levels of the social hierarchy were suspended amidst the provision by candidates of much food and drink.[184] Especially after 1867, the electorate contained many wage-earners, but there was no uniformity in their voting behaviour. There was as yet no strong move to create a workers' party; instead,

working-class voters attached more significance to the differences between Liberals and Conservatives than to those between themselves and other classes. Few of them were disposed to support a working-class candidate who was neither Liberal nor Conservative, or necessarily to support a working-class Liberal or Conservative over candidates of the accustomed kind.[185]

Sympathies often stretched across social differences. On the royal commission on trade unions in 1867–9, the Earl of Lichfield was in the minority which was most favourable to the unions. Many of the effective social reformers of these years, such as the seventh Earl of Shaftesbury, were drawn from the ranks of the aristocracy or other wealthy groups. Within industrial Britain, similar sympathies could also be found, as in the Hornby textile-manufacturing family of Blackburn. W. H. Hornby represented the town in Parliament for twenty-four years but seems never to have spoken in the House. In local affairs he was a philanthropic employer, prominent in local charities and sporting activities.

Blackburn in the 1880s was a bastion of 'clog Toryism', where ideals of self-help and evening class wilted before the appeal of the corner pub and the Rovers. Blackburn became known as a place of pubs, clog fights, pigeons and greyhounds, and a population made up of ebullient horse-riding, fox-hunting cotton bosses and stout-hearted weavers who ejected disloyal voters from the mill and threw dead cats at socialist orators in the Market Square.[186]

No doubt this is largely true, but Blackburn also had its churches, its chapels, and its temperance movement.

In addition to their other political, economic, and social attributes, aristocrats continued to hold prominent positions in sport and recreation. This included participation in sports, playing a role in the administration of sporting regulations, and often large-scale gambling. As with religion, sport and recreation provided examples of activities which stretched over many different sectors of society. If W. H. Hornby was a fanatical supporter of cricket in his home town,

---

183. Patrick Joyce, *Work, Society and Politics: The Culture of the Factory in Later Victorian England* (1980).

184. James Vernon, *Politics and the People: A Study of English Political Culture, c.1815–1857* (1993).

185. Hunt, *British Labour History*, 270.

186. R. L. Walton, 'The Labour Movement in Blackburn, 1880–1914', MA thesis, Huddersfield Polytechnic, 1981, 13–15. Although the quotation includes a specific reference to the 1880s, the context makes it clear that the judgement can be broadened to cover both mid- and late-Victorian Blackburn.

other men of influence were devoted followers of horse racing. Lord George Bentinck and Admiral J. H. Rous achieved national reputations in trying to stamp out corruption on the racecourse. At the Stockton races local peers, including the Earl of Durham, the Earl of Zetland, and the Marquis of Londonderry, regularly attended with large parties, and often ran their own horses. This interest was widely shared, and employers protested vainly about the high level of absenteeism during race meetings.[187] Boxing was another popular sport which enjoyed support from varied social groups. In 1860 the great Sayers–Heenan fight was watched by 12,000 people; seven years later the eighth Marquis of Queensberry devised a famous set of rules to govern the sport. The field sports of the countryside continued to be popular, and hunts were often supported by groups of followers of varied social status from adjacent urban or industrial areas. In north-east England, miners often cheered on fox-hunters in nearby country areas.

There were, however, important areas of leisure activity in which the aristocracy did not retain a dominant position. Association football, which became the most popular of sports, had its origin in the wealthier social groups.[188] Stoke City FC was set up by ex-public schoolboys working as premium apprentices in the local railway workshops. The first important soccer rules were the Cambridge (University) Rules of 1863, the year in which the Football Association was founded. The sport was later the scene of a popular takeover, but this point must not be pushed too far. If most soccer spectators were wage-earners, many clubs depended to a varying degree on help from wealthier supporters. Like other sports, association football was infused with a spirit of contest and rivalry. National, regional, and local leagues and competitions developed and for such rituals as the presentation of trophies eminent individuals were much in demand. Although no northern team won the FA Cup until 1883, football was well established in the northern industrial and mining areas before then. At Wednesbury the football team was founded in 1873, two years before the equivalent cricket team. Cricket remained less popular, although it did have a large following and received more early newspaper reporting than other sports. *Wisden* first appeared in 1864 and the first Test match took place in 1880, after a number of earlier international matches had taken place less formally. Lawn tennis, developed in the 1870s, was for many years dominated by wealthier groups in society; a widespread popular interest did not develop until much later. The first major golf tournament was held in 1857, but for many years the game was primarily a Scottish activity.[189]

187. Huggins, 'Stockton Race Week' provides an excellent example of such occasions.
188. For a general study of leisure and recreation in these years, J. Walvin, *Leisure and Society, 1830–1950* (1978). For soccer, J. Walvin, *The People's Game: A Social History of British Football* (1975). Emma Griffin, 'Popular Culture in industrializing England', *The Historical Journal*, vol. 5, 3 September 2002, is a useful historiographical essay.
189. For an account of the development of sport see: R. Holt, *Sport and the British: A Modern History* (1989).

The increasingly urban society developed an enormous variety of leisure activities. For those of a more scholarly disposition, many local societies were set up in such fields as natural history, archaeology, and geology. It was normal for such societies to seek the patronage of local magnates. Gardening was another expanding activity. By 1871 Nottingham had acquired more than 10,000 allotment gardens.[190] As with sport, much gardening enthusiasm was channelled into competitions, often for trophies and prizes given by local employers or other leading figures. Societies devoted to the cultivation of specific plants began to be formed, with national associations and national competitions, their governing bodies frequently graced by aristocratic patrons.[191] Music also widened its appeal. The Triennial Handel Festivals at the Crystal Palace, established in 1862, attracted attendances of around 70,000–80,000, drawn from a wide social spectrum. Choral societies, brass bands, and a variety of other musical enterprises multiplied.

Generally, an increase in leisure time during the third quarter of the century gave enhanced recreational opportunities to more people. The 1871 Bank Holiday Act was an example of statutory provision for holidays; the Factory Acts of 1850 and 1853 had already brought about early closing on Saturdays to many textile factories, and from about 1874 a full Saturday half-holiday was normal in the textile districts.[192] These developments facilitated both participation in leisure activities and the emergence of a mass audience of spectators for sporting events, such as football matches or the great rowing matches on the Thames, Tyne, and Mersey in the 1860s and 1870s. The greater recreational opportunities derived from increased leisure and increased earnings were one part of the improved conditions enjoyed by the majority of British society by 1880.

Violence and crime

The increases in comfort during these years were real and important, but there were limits to what was achieved. It was not a uniformly tranquil or orderly world. There were parts of society in which violence could readily erupt. Industrial disputes could generate ugly incidents. In June 1869, a serious riot took place in the little town of Mold in Flintshire when a crowd tried to prevent the police taking to gaol two local miners who had been sentenced to one month's confinement with hard labour for their part in a dispute at a local colliery. When the situation looked dangerous a local magistrate ordered troops to fire on the rioters; four of them were killed and many wounded.[193] During a weavers' strike in north-east Lancashire in 1878, the house of the principal employer involved

190. We owe this information to Dr Martin Gaskell.
191. Anne Wilkinson, *The Victorian Gardener: The Growth of Gardening and the Floral World* (2006).
192. Hunt, *British Labour History*, 79–81.
193. P. F. Nolan, 'The Flintshire magistracy, 1830–1879', MA thesis, Wolverhampton Polytechnic, 1985, 50.

was sacked.[194] Wife-beating was sufficiently notorious to induce Parliament to pass the Criminal Law Procedure Act in 1853, which was not very effective. In 1878 the Matrimonial Clauses Act introduced a judicially protected separation with maintenance awards granted against an erring husband.[195]

Parliamentary elections provided another volatile arena. During the general election of 1865, there was violence at Nuneaton, Leamington, Atherstone, Warwick, Nottingham, Bristol. At Blackburn rival mobs sacked the campaign headquarters of their opponents and fought pitched battles with the police in the streets: 'All along the pavement streams of blood were flowing, and the sickening sight of men with blood flowing from their heads and faces met one at every turn.'[196] In the North Durham constituency during the general election of 1874, the candidates included rival local employers, whose workmen indulged in violence which included the sacking of a police station; the election was subsequently disallowed because of intimidation.

It was also a society with much crime. Most of this was less terrible than the serious outrages which were well publicized in the press. In the Black Country, 75–80 per cent of the prosecutions for indictable crimes in the 1835–60 period were for theft, mostly of a minor kind.[197] The Criminal Justice Act of 1855, which extended the range of minor offences which could be tried locally in Petty Sessions by two magistrates, brought about an increase in prosecutions for minor thefts and the like, but presumably no great increase in the actual incidence of such crimes. Similarly, the improvement in the maintenance of criminal statistics, from the 1850s onwards, could give a misleading impression of increasing criminality. The poorer sectors of society were the most common sufferers from crime, including the thousands of minor thefts, and understandably they usually showed no reluctance to see the law invoked against wrongdoers. Foreign visitors were struck by the absence of popular opposition to the working of the criminal law system.[198]

Some social groups were believed to be more likely to turn to crime than others. One modern writer has noted the 'cheerful, predatory attitude' of the Irish towards the Poor Law, and statistical evidence suggests that there was more to it than that; in the thirty years after 1860, when the Irish formed less than 8 per cent of Bradford's population, they were responsible for 14–24 per cent of appearances in the magistrates' courts of the town.[199] The Welsh provided evidence of another kind. In 1857 the level of crime in Wales was 20 per cent above that of England, but by 1881, perhaps because of the increased grip of Nonconformist religion in the principality, there was no significant difference.[200]

194. Stevenson, *Popular Disturbances in England*, 283–6.
195. Burn, *The Age of Equipoise*, 155.
196. Stevenson, *Popular Disturbances in England*, 287.
197. D. Philips, *Crime and Authority in Victorian England: The Black Country, 1835–1860* (1977), 283.
198. Ibid. 285.
199. Hunt, *British Labour History*, 162. The modern writer quoted by Hunt here is E. P. Thompson.
200. D. J. V. Jones, 'The Welsh and crime, 1801–1891', in Emsley and Walvin (eds.), *Artisans, Peasants & Proletarians*, 86.

A sensible evaluation of these attributes of mid-Victorian society is offered in a modern study:

There is much evidence that it was a rough society, but little to show that people feared for their lives, or felt themselves unable to use the roads at night. There was roughness, much fighting, much casual violence, but little lethal violence and serious injury ... the forces of law enforcement were never very strong ... and were certainly never strong enough to coerce the population into obedience. The system of law enforcement and the administration of the criminal law could only have worked with the active co-operation or the passive acquiescence of the mass of the population—and the evidence suggests that the authorities received at least this passive acquiescence. The relatively peaceful, orderly and law-abiding Englishman seems to have been a reality by the 1850s already.[201]

On balance, the 1850–80 period had brought an acceleration of economic and social progress, and continued improvement in the condition of the people, despite the huge increase in population and the difficulties it entailed. Serious social problems remained, but knowledge and recognition of them was improving. Economic growth continued to provide the resources with which they could be tackled more effectively. This was not a simple or uniform society, but one in which economic and social conditions were varied, volatile, and rapidly changing. Despite the stresses of a growing population and economic transformation, there was little sign that the internal coherence of British society was seriously at risk.

201. Philips, *Crime and Authority in Victorian England*, 284–6. This source offers a more extensive argument on the point than that given in the quotation included here.

Part IV

10

Political developments

1880–1914

The general election in the spring of 1880 replaced an overall Conservative major-ity of about 50 seats with a slightly larger Liberal majority. The Conservative defeat was comprehensive (see pp. 303–4 above).[1] Altogether the Conservatives lost, and the Liberals gained, more than 100 seats. The Scottish, Irish, and Welsh results were especially striking. In Scotland the Conservative victories fell from 19 to only 7; in Wales the Conservatives held only 2 seats. In Ireland the Home Rule Party consolidated its position, winning 61 seats, 10 more than in 1874. Yet in some respects the Conservative defeat was less crushing than appears at first sight. It had been a hard-fought contest, marked by a sharp drop in the number of uncontested returns from 188 in 1874 to 109 and the Conservatives took nearly 44 per cent of the overall popular vote (only some 2,000 votes behind the Liberal total). There was, though, no gainsaying the result in terms of seats in the House of Commons.

On 2 April Disraeli informed the Queen of his defeat; on 21 April the Cabinet agreed to resign before the meeting of the new Parliament. The Queen, who had learned to admire Disraeli and dislike Gladstone, sent first for Lord Hartington, Liberal leader in the House of Commons since Gladstone's withdrawal from the Liberal leadership in 1875. Yet it was clear that the return of Gladstone to the premiership was inevitable. The Queen's hostility was to be one of the many difficulties which he had to face during the next few years.

The new Liberal majority was mixed, ranging from aristocratic Whigs like Hartington to strident provincial radicals like Joseph Chamberlain. Disunity was shown by a problem which arose before the work of the new session was fully under way. The electors of Northampton had returned, as one of their two MPs, Charles Bradlaugh, who was not only a convinced radical but an open opponent of orthodox religion and an advocate of birth control.[2] These beliefs were

1. R. Blake, *Disraeli* (1966), 707–8, discusses the general election and its aftermath. M. D. Pugh, *The Making of Modern British Politics, 1867–1939* (1982) provides additional insights into this election, especially at pp. 1, 65, as well as a perceptive general discussion of the workings of the political system in these years.

2. W. L. Arnstein, *The Bradlaugh Case: A Study in Late Victorian Opinion and Politics* (1965).

anathema to many Liberals. When the 1880 Parliament assembled, the government front bench in the House of Commons was vacant, as ministers were absent facing the by-elections legally entailed by their acceptance of office. During this interval, a combination of outraged Liberals and militant Conservatives prevented Bradlaugh from taking his seat, asserting that an atheist could not be bound by the statutory oath of allegiance couched in religious terms. When Gladstone returned, he tried to solve the problem by introducing a measure which would have allowed someone without religious belief to affirm allegiance, rather than offer the prescribed religious oath. A hostile cross-party majority held together to reject this. The course of the 1880 Parliament was subsequently punctuated by attempts by Bradlaugh to take his seat; these repeatedly provoked divisions within the Liberal majority.

The fourth party

The Bradlaugh case had proved so troublesome largely because of the contribution of a group of Conservative backbenchers bent upon exploiting anything which seemed likely to embarrass the new government.[3] Their leader was Lord Randolph Churchill, a younger son of the Duke of Marlborough. The other principal members of what was called the 'Fourth Party' were Lord Salisbury's nephew A. J. Balfour, the experienced diplomat Sir Henry Drummond Wolff, and Sir John Gorst. Gorst had taken a leading role in the reorganization of the Conservative Party machinery after the 1868 defeat, but had for some years felt that his services were inadequately recognized. The Leader of the Conservative Opposition in the Commons, Sir Stafford Northcote, was unable to control these activists; he was not a brilliant leader and, moreover, he had a considerable respect for Gladstone (Northcote had served as Gladstone's private secretary in the early 1840s). Disraeli was capable of controlling this situation, but, after his death in April 1881, the Conservative leadership was shared between Salisbury in the Lords and Northcote in the Commons.

At first Northcote seemed the more likely man to succeed to the full leadership, for Salisbury was widely regarded as too uncompromisingly conservative in his views. In the next few years the situation moved to the latter's advantage, partly because of Northcote's failure to control his disobedient followers, who seized every opportunity to attack the Liberal ministers and exploit differences within the Liberal ranks. The other leading figures on the Opposition front bench in the House of Commons, R. A. Cross and W. H. Smith, had been competent departmental ministers, but neither of them exhibited much sparkle in debate, which again gave the sprightly 'Fourth Party' a better chance to show their mettle.

---

3. For the origins of the 'Fourth Party', and Churchill's career more generally, R. R. James, *Lord Randolph Churchill* (1959).

Their attacks on the new government, and especially its leader, joined with Irish obstructive tactics to use up parliamentary time. Together with the Prime Minister's preoccupation with Irish affairs, and problems overseas, this led to an undistinguished legislative record. The situation was infuriating to men like Joseph Chamberlain, who had expected the new Liberal administration to enact a programme of important domestic reforms. In his early months at the Board of Trade, his sole achievement had been a Merchant Shipping Act, and he had not found it easy to secure even that.

Liberal disunity

Disunity was present in the Cabinet as elsewhere in the Liberal Party. Gladstone himself preferred Whig aristocratic colleagues to radicals who might want to spend money on reform. He was determined to impose rigid economy and to reduce taxation.[4] He had only reluctantly accepted the need to give his radical followers recognition in constructing his government. An old-established radical like John Bright, now elderly and less active, was more acceptable than the new breed of militant provincial radical like Joseph Chamberlain. In previous years Chamberlain had emerged as an important political figure, partly because of his well-publicized work as a reforming Mayor of Birmingham, partly because of his association with a significant overhaul of Liberal Party organization in the West Midlands, which had contributed to Liberal victories there in 1880. In Birmingham itself, skilful electoral organization by the 'caucus' which controlled the Liberal organization succeeded in electing Chamberlain, Bright, and another prominent radical, P. H. Muntz, by an impressive majority. Gladstone could not ignore these developments, and room had to be found in the Cabinet for some representation of this vigorous radicalism which had made an important contribution to the Liberal electoral victory. Chamberlain became President of the Board of Trade, while Sir Charles Dilke, another prominent radical, was given a junior ministerial post as under-secretary at the Foreign Office. Bright became Chancellor of the Duchy of Lancaster, a post which provided little opportunity for radical initiatives. Most of the important ministries were held by Whig aristocrats, who contributed a duke, a marquess, and five earls to a Cabinet of twelve. Chamberlain and Bright were the only radicals in it. When the composition of the new Cabinet was announced, the Speaker remarked presciently that it would prove a difficult team to drive.

The incipient disunity within party and government was exacerbated by some of the government's policies. One of Gladstone's objectives was the pacification of an Ireland hard-hit by agricultural depression.[5] His first attempt, intended as

4. P. Magnus, *Gladstone: A Biography* (1954), 274–6.
5. For a general survey of Irish history in these years, F. S. L. Lyons, *Ireland since the Famine* (1971). For Parnell's career, and the story of the Home Rule Party, F. S. L. Lyons, *Parnell* (1977); C. C. O'Brien, *Parnell and his Party, 1880–90* (1957); F. S. L. Lyons, *The Fall of Parnell* (1960).

a stopgap measure pending more substantial proposals, was the Compensation for Disturbance (Ireland) Bill, which sought to ensure that Irish tenants evicted for non-payment of rent received compensation for any improvements they had made to their holdings (see p. 402 below). An obvious interference in the management of private property, this proposal was opposed by many Liberals in both Houses and defeated in the House of Lords.

Abroad, Gladstone enjoyed some success at first in getting rid of that 'Beaconsfieldism' which had been one of the targets of Liberal attacks. The Boers in the Transvaal had risen against a not very competent colonial administration after the British Army had destroyed the Zulu threat, and inflicted some irritating reverses on British troops. The new ministers had to decide whether to embark upon an expensive campaign to reverse these defeats or accept the repudiation of British rule. Given earlier Liberal opposition to the annexation of the Transvaal, withdrawal seemed the best policy. Gladstone succeeded in arranging a settlement which restored internal self-government to the Transvaal, while Britain retained control of its foreign relations and a vague 'suzerainty'; a lack of clarity within the agreement, and within a supplementary convention signed three years later, were to cause trouble at the end of the century. But this repudiation of a Conservative imperialist adventure pleased many Liberals. The settlement in the Transvaal was followed by a Liberal imperialist adventure which to many of Gladstone's followers seemed at least as bad as anything the Conservatives had perpetrated.

Egypt

Since the building of the Suez Canal, the strategic importance of Egypt had increased. Although technically part of the Turkish Empire, Egypt was largely autonomous. Among the fruits of this quasi-independence had been the running up of a considerable foreign debt, mainly borrowed in London and Paris. Egyptian debt repayments fell into arrears, and there were complaints from those who had lent the money. During the later 1870s, the governments of Britain and France had compelled the Egyptian regime to accept a joint Anglo-French supervision of Egyptian finances. Nationalist resentment at this sparked off a rising late in 1881, and many foreigners were murdered. The rebels forced the Egyptian ruler to repudiate European domination and accept a nationalist government.

The Mediterranean fleets of Britain and France were concentrated at Alexandria, but a political crisis in France resulted in a French withdrawal, leaving the British Liberal government to face difficult decisions alone. Egyptian forces began to strengthen the fortifications overlooking the roadstead in which the British warships lay. Gladstone succeeded in persuading himself that, whatever he may previously have thought about the rights of Afghan tribesmen and Boer farmers, the Egyptian nationalists were barbaric and disloyal rebels against their legitimate ruler; he claimed a sacred duty to 'convert the present interior state of Egypt from anarchy and conflict to peace and order'. The British admiral on the spot was authorized to take drastic action against the fortifications threatening his fleet. In August 1882 a British army was landed and by the end of the year British control of Egypt had been established. It was difficult for many Liberals to follow Gladstone's view of the Egyptian involvement. Bright resigned from the Cabinet, regarding the government's Egyptian policy as worse than anything Disraeli had done. Gladstone himself seemed to have no qualms about the correctness of his decisions. On one occasion he told the House of Commons that 'We have carried out this war from a love of peace, and, I may say, on the principle of peace.'

The British conquest of Egypt coincided with a rebellion against Egyptian rule in the southern Sudanese provinces. Gladstone distinguished this situation from that in Egypt itself; he considered the Sudanese rebels as a nation 'struggling rightly to be free'. In reality fanatical followers of a religious leader, the Mahdi, they were to be regarded, he thought, as patriots. After they had destroyed an Egyptian army commanded by a British officer in November 1883, Gladstone determined to leave the Sudan to the Mahdi. The government sent out General Gordon, a British officer who had served as governor of the Sudan during the period of Anglo-French control, to supervise the withdrawal of the remaining Egyptian garrisons in the Sudan. Instead, he disregarded his instructions and sought to overthrow the Mahdi. Gordon had miscalculated the situation, and by March 1884 he was besieged in Khartoum by the Mahdi's forces.

Belatedly and reluctantly, the British government dispatched a relief expedition, which narrowly failed to arrive in time; in January 1885 the Mahdi's followers forced their way into Khartoum and Gordon was killed. The progress of the relief force, and Gordon's predicament, had become a major focus of national attention. The military disaster at Khartoum became a political disaster for the government, and especially for the Prime Minister, who had been the main obstacle to a speedy dispatch of the expensive rescue mission.

Ireland

Meanwhile, the government was in trouble elsewhere. Ireland posed urgent problems.[6] The Irish Nationalist Party in the House of Commons was a constant irritant. Its leader, the Protestant landlord Charles Stewart Parnell, had entered Parliament in 1875. By the early 1880s he had emerged as the leader of both the Irish parliamentary party and the agitation of the Land League in Ireland. He was a shrewd, cool, and tenacious politician, unhampered by sympathy for British parliamentary traditions. He faced difficult problems. His movement depended on financial support from Irish-American sympathizers, and to secure that he had to appear militant and even revolutionary in his stance. At the same time he had to persuade the Roman Catholic Church that his policies did not

6. See sources cited in n. 5.

tend towards a godless, communist Ireland. He was also aware that the best mode of actually attaining his objectives lay through parliamentary action, and cooperation with at least one of the major British parties.

When the Liberals took office, a crescendo of violence in the Irish countryside was reaching a climax. Agricultural depression sharply increased the number of tenants evicted for non-payment of rent, and that sparked off a powerful reaction. In 1877 there had been 273 'outrages', which ranged from crimes like cattle-maiming to murder; in 1880 there were 2,590. Gladstone's first attempt to deal with the crisis was the Compensation for Disturbance (Ireland) Bill, introduced in August 1880. This proposed that an Irish county court judge could order compensation to a tenant evicted for non-payment of rent if that default was due to circumstances beyond the tenant's control. This compensation was to be paid by the landlord, and the bill's opponents argued that this was an unfair burden; if the State wished for compensation in such cases then the State should pay for it. Moreover, the interference with private property worried those who foresaw that such devices might not be confined to Ireland. In the Commons, 50 Liberals abstained and 20 voted against the bill. Liberal defections in the Lords ensured its rejection there by the crushing majority of 282 to 51. Nothing had been achieved to alter the critical situation in Ireland. In the winter of 1880–1, the Land League, with its declared aim of enforcing security of tenure at fair rents, was effectively controlling much of the Irish countryside. The Irish police force was not a particularly efficient organization. It was over-centralized and over-regulated, and its detective branch was poor. During the 1840s Peel had tried to combine Irish reforms with a determination to maintain law and order there, and his disciple Gladstone now followed the same course. The Chief Secretary for Ireland, W. E. Forster, believed that he possessed the support of Prime Minister and Cabinet in a policy of firm government. It was still widely believed in Britain that the disorder in Ireland was fomented by only a small number of militant nationalists; if they could be neutralized, moderation and good sense would prevail. Such views lay behind the Coercion Act of 1881, which gave the Irish authorities power to detain persons suspected of treasonable practices.

The other side of the coin was represented by the 1881 Land Act. This sought to implement the principle of fair rents assessed by a quasi-judicial procedure, a much bigger interference with private property in Ireland than had been attempted before. It began a process whereby 10 million acres in Ireland were by the end of the century held by rents assessed in this way. Yet the Land Act of 1881 did not bring immediate peace. Many tenants could not take advantage of its provisions because they were already compromised by arrears of rent. Instead of a few test cases establishing principles of rent-fixing, an enormous volume of litigation ensued, with delays before many cases could be heard, even though the staff of the tribunals was increased. The quality of some of the valuation work involved was also defective. The Land League meanwhile campaigned against the implementation of the Act; a solution of the agrarian problem would be bad news for nationalist agitation.

The government responded with more coercive legislation. In 1882 the special powers were extended to cope with the problem of Irish juries who refused to convict, by prescribing a list of offences to be tried without juries. Power was also given to prohibit the publication of seditious newspapers. Forster countered the opposition of the nationalist politicians by using these emergency powers. After they had made fierce public attacks on the government's Irish policies, Parnell and two other Irish MPs were arrested for breaches of the coercion legislation and imprisoned in Kilmainham Gaol. Forster still had no doubt that he was implementing policies which had been endorsed by Prime Minister and Cabinet; he felt sure that given time these policies would work.

Many Liberals, including Gladstone himself, were troubled. It was surely wrong for Liberals to imprison political rivals without trial, or to suppress the freedom of the press. Parnell had made no attempt to avoid imprisonment in the first instance; safely in gaol, he could not be held responsible for anything done by his followers, while preserving a martyr's fame. By late April 1882 his views had changed. He was anxious to be released, partly for private family reasons, partly because he feared that the nationalist movement might slip from his control into extreme courses if he were not able to exercise his authority. A secret negotiation produced a kind of gentlemen's agreement between Gladstone and Parnell. The Irish leader and his companion MPs would be released, and Parnell would do his best to ensure the success of the Land Act, sweetened by the concession of an acceptable Arrears Act, to enable tenants already owing arrears of rent to take advantage of the Land Act's provisions.

Gladstone had carried out this intrigue without informing his Irish ministers. They had been carrying out and publicly defending government policy, while that policy was undermined by the Prime Minister. The Viceroy, Lord Cowper, and the Chief Secretary, W. E. Forster, submitted embittered resignations; in the ensuing Commons debate Forster made a damaging attack on Gladstone's policy, suggesting that one reason behind the pact was Parnell's agreement to give a general political support to the Liberal government.

Lord Spencer and Lord Frederick Cavendish were appointed to the vacant posts. On 6 May, Cavendish was walking in Phoenix Park, Dublin, with Burke, the permanent Irish under-secretary. They were attacked by members of an Irish extremist group, who slashed their victims with long surgical knives and then cut their throats. Both in Britain and in Ireland the result of these atrocious murders was immediate and catastrophic. Parnell and Gladstone tried to save the situation, but little could be done. The revulsion in Britain was such that the government could not have survived if it had not introduced further coercive legislation, which the nationalists were bound to oppose. An Arrears Act was duly passed, but this proved a limited concession which did not help many tenants. Parnell could not or would not openly condemn the Irish resort to violent crime in pursuit of Irish grievances. The next few months brought a continuing tale of Irish savagery, well publicized in the British press. In August came news of the Maamtrasna massacre, when a murder gang stabbed and battered to death father, mother, and three children of a family; one small boy, though badly injured, survived. The Irish police and army were not always restrained in their own methods of law enforcement. The Viceroy, Lord Spencer, and the new Chief Secretary, Trevelyan, managed to keep some kind of control of the situation, and in 1883 there was some improvement, aided by the settling down of the Land Act arrangements.

Among those in British politics who resented the disruption brought about by the Irish crisis was Joseph Chamberlain, whose hopes for radical social reform were repeatedly frustrated. He had a high opinion of his own ability to solve the Irish crisis and he now chose to work through the same intermediary as Gladstone had used to negotiate his agreement with Parnell in 1882—Captain O'Shea, the unsavoury husband of Parnell's mistress. If Parnell would do his best to keep Ireland quiet, Chamberlain would offer a minimum of coercive powers, together with a substantial measure of devolution in Irish administration. There would be county councils (not as yet established in Britain) together with a Central Board for Ireland which would control most administration there. There was no suggestion of a full Irish legislature. Parnell was willing to accept these proposals, but made it clear to O'Shea that for him they could only be steps on the road to Home Rule. O'Shea, who enjoyed his role as contact man, knew that this would not be acceptable to Chamberlain, and concealed Parnell's crucial reservation from the radical minister. Chamberlain therefore believed that his scheme had been accepted by the Irish leader, and determined to press it upon the Cabinet. The right-wing majority there refused to accept the plan, and Chamberlain prepared to resign.

Domestic reforms

While Irish affairs were taking up a great deal of government time, the government's record in domestic reform seemed modest. Reforming legislation was finding its way to the statute book, but much of it was not very controversial. In 1881, after curtailment in earlier decades, peacetime flogging as a punishment was finally abolished in the armed forces. The 1882 Married Women's Property Act gave married women more control of their own property. In the same year cooperation between the two major parties secured the enactment of a major reform of the English land law. Chamberlain was responsible for reforms of the bankruptcy law and patent law in 1882, but these were matters which caused little political excitement.

The main controversy over domestic matters resulted from parliamentary reform legislation introduced by the Liberal government. This development began with a Corrupt and Illegal Practices Act passed in 1883; based on limiting allowable electoral expenditure, this marked an important stage in the suppression of electoral corruption. Some members of the Liberal Cabinet had reservations over the type of suffrage extension which should be implemented. Pressure of other events and the absence of sustained popular demand resulted in a postponement of reform proposals until 1884. Their introduction then sparked off a crisis. The government's proposals passed through the House of Commons without much difficulty. The Conservative majority in the House of Lords viewed them with a marked absence of enthusiasm, but were disinclined to court the popular odium of outright rejection. Tactically, therefore, the Conservative leaders in the Upper House preferred to hold up the Reform Bill, claiming that it ought to be accompanied by a bill for the redistribution of parliamentary seats.

The Third Reform Act

The settlement of this crisis contrasted with the events of 1831–2 and 1866–7.[7] In the earlier cases, the House of Commons itself had played a major role in the reform process. In 1884–5 only three men played any significant part in the discussions which hammered out a compromise. Lord Salisbury, spokesman for the recalcitrant majority of peers, acted as the principal negotiator for the Opposition, thereby incidentally confirming his leading position in the Conservative Party. Gladstone and the radical politician Sir Charles Dilke, who was regarded as an expert in electoral matters, acted for the Liberals.

Gladstone himself had no precise objectives in relation to the details of the legislation, though he claimed to favour 'the enfranchisement of capable citizens'. Salisbury knew that outright opposition to electoral reform was unlikely to prove successful, and was prepared to accept a solution which included a redistribution of seats which might work to Conservative advantage. In these circumstances the crisis was settled by an agreement on reform and redistribution between the two party leaders; their followers in both Houses of Parliament were left to accept a fait accompli. The Reform Act was allowed through by the House of Lords later in 1884, and the agreed Redistribution Act was passed the following year. The redistribution was a sweeping measure. The old county divisions were now cut up into single-member constituencies. Lancashire received fifteen more MPs, the West Riding thirteen. Large urban constituencies were also divided, Liverpool was split into nine single-member constituencies, the old London borough of Tower Hamlets into seven. After 1885 constituencies were much more even in terms of population than they had ever been before.

The 1884 Reform Act was not a skilful example of legislative drafting, and its enfranchising effect, though considerable, fell far short of democracy. There was still no acceptance that the vote was a natural right. Instead new selective categories of franchises were added to the existing complicated pattern. The principal effects were in the counties, where the old franchises continued, but additional categories were added, including the household and lodger qualifications

7. N. Gash, *Pillars of Government, and Other Essays on State and Society, c.1770–1880* (1986), 59–61.

introduced into the boroughs in 1867. Otherwise the measure was distinctly moderate. After 1884 it was still possible for a voter to amass plural votes by acquiring several property qualifications such as forty-shilling freeholds in different county constituencies. One aspect of particular interest to Gladstone was the effect of the reform in Ireland. The Irish franchise was now to be assimilated to that of mainland Britain, with householders in the Irish countryside now enfranchised. The number of Irish seats remained unaltered (though a strict demographic test would have involved a reduction in Irish representation). The next general election would demonstrate just how powerful the nationalist hold over Irish opinion was.

Political crisis, 1885

Before then, however, the political scene shifted. Parnell concluded that, with nothing emerging from Chamberlain's scheme for Ireland, he had nothing more to hope for from the Liberals. On the other hand, the Conservatives were making encouraging noises. Lord Randolph Churchill had in the previous few years moved from his mosquito function with his 'Fourth Party' to become an important figure within the Conservative Party. His skills as a platform orator developed, and he exploited the party organization to take advantage of his growing grassroots popularity. By the beginning of 1885 he had acquired a national reputation. He scented opportunities for party advantage in the Irish situation, and publicly declared that a Conservative administration could govern Ireland without the coercion for which the Liberals were responsible. At the same time confidential contacts led Parnell to believe that he might gain more from the Conservatives, who could control the House of Lords, than he could from the Liberals. In early June 1885, the Conservatives moved an amendment to the Liberal Budget; ordinarily the balance of the parliamentary forces was such that the amendment could easily be beaten off, and seventy-six Liberals were absent from the division. Without warning, Parnell led a cohort of Irish Nationalist MPs into the opposition lobby, and Gladstone's government was beaten. Immediate dissolution was not practicable, because the recent parliamentary reforms were not yet fully implemented. Lord Salisbury therefore formed a minority government to hold office until a general election could be held.

Salisbury's first government contained many ministers who had gained experience under Disraeli, and one notable newcomer. Churchill's recent rise to political eminence had to be recognized, whatever doubts the new Prime Minister might have about the populist methods employed to reach that position. Although he had never held office before, Churchill entered the Cabinet as Secretary of State for India; his old enemy, Northcote, was induced to leave the leadership in the House of Commons and retire to the Lords. The new government held office for only seven months, a term which was very much a prolonged election campaign.

On the Liberal side, the campaigning for the ensuing general election brought into the open some of the divisions within the party. A radical wing, with Joseph

Chamberlain as its standard-bearer, openly advocated an 'unauthorized programme' of reforms which had not been accepted by the leaders of the party. These included public elementary education freed from remaining fees, elected local government for the counties, administrative devolution to the major elements in the United Kingdom, higher taxation on the wealthy, disestablishment of the remaining Established Churches of England, Scotland, and Wales, making smallholdings available for would-be small-scale farmers, payment of MPs, and full manhood suffrage. Chamberlain did not envisage any proposals for the government of Ireland which went beyond the concessions he had already advocated.

The radicals achieved notoriety not only because of the slate of reforms which they proposed, but also for the nature of the campaign with which they were advanced. Chamberlain himself asked 'What ransom shall property pay for the security it enjoys?', and such strident campaigning produced protests from right-wing Liberals. Gladstone himself went abroad before the election, and did little to bring order into the party.

Meanwhile the Conservatives continued their flirtation with the Irish Nationalists. Some coercive powers were allowed to lapse, Churchill continued to make encouraging noises about possible concessions, and the new Conservative Viceroy, Lord Carnarvon, sincerely believed in a measure of legislative devolution. Carnarvon embarked upon confidential discussions with Irish leaders, including Parnell, and made his own personal sympathies clear enough; he was careful not to commit the Conservatives to any specific proposals. The minority Conservative government succeeded in passing Lord Ashbourne's Act, which inaugurated the first substantial use of public funds (£5 million) to enable Irish tenants to buy their holdings. With no competing offer from the Liberal side, Parnell urged Irish voters in Britain to vote Conservative in the impending election. (It is not clear how effective this instruction was; it was not universally obeyed.)

Gladstone himself had already concluded that some form of Irish Home Rule was needed, but failed to make his conversion clear to his colleagues. Instead he confused the issue by leaving various leading Liberals with different impressions of his intentions. Chamberlain still had no inkling that his leader had moved beyond the administrative devolution discussed in Cabinet earlier in 1885. Lord Derby, who had moved from his old Conservative allegiance into the Liberal camp by 1885, concluded that Gladstone was prepared to accept some degree of Home Rule.

The 1885 general election

Late in November there was an excited general election. As was normal, the borough results came in first, and here the Conservatives established a narrow lead, but this was then swept away by their defeat in the county divisions. Out of the 377 seats in the counties the Conservatives held only 119; even in their old heartland of the English counties they could hold only 105 of the 239 seats. In Norfolk, for instance, the Liberals took 4 of the 6 county seats. There were two main reasons for this. Part of the newly extended county electorate seems to have been attracted by the land reform and some of the other features of the 'unauthorized programme'. More important were changes in the character of many county constituencies revealed by the 1885 Redistribution Act. The old county constituencies were now broken up into single-member divisions; in many of these, economic and social change had accelerated in recent decades. On the major coalfields, for instance, some of the new county constituencies and the new electorate were dominated by miners. Many nominally county constituencies were by now in reality industrial or suburban in character. For the next few years the Liberals were to enjoy an unusual degree of success in the counties. In Ireland, where Gladstone was particularly interested to see the results, Parnell's Nationalists won a clear-cut victory, with 86 MPs in the new House of Commons. As there were 335 Liberals and 249 Conservatives, this left Parnell in a position of considerable influence.

In December there were discussions behind the scenes. In the absence of any clear majority in the new House of Commons, Salisbury remained in office until the new Parliament met in January. Both Conservatives and Liberals were still in touch with Parnell, and Gladstone seems to have hoped that some kind of solution to the problem of Irish government might be found in a Conservative measure of devolution for which Gladstone would bring his own backing. Any chance of this taking place vanished when in mid-December Gladstone's son Herbert disclosed that his father was a convert to the principle of Home Rule. This indiscretion at least cleared the air. Parnell dropped any idea of alliance with the Conservatives, Salisbury's ministry shed its more pro-Irish members, including Carnarvon, and openly adopted an anti-Nationalist stance.

Irish home rule, 1886

When the new Parliament assembled, the new allies, Liberals and Parnellites, were in a clear majority, and the minority Conservative government was defeated. Gladstone took office again, but the prospects for Liberal unity were poor. Some important figures in the party refused to join a ministry committed to Irish Home Rule. Lord Hartington, the elder brother of Lord Frederick Cavendish, would not accept Gladstone's new concessions to Irish nationalism. Hartington led a group of right-wing Liberals, including a number of ex-ministers, in a serious defection from Gladstone's leadership. Another Liberal voice of some importance, John Bright, also refused to accept Gladstone's new prescription, largely on the moral ground that it represented a surrender to the wicked men responsible for violence in Ireland.

There were other dangers. Joseph Chamberlain had accepted office as President of the Local Government Board, after Gladstone had undertaken that there would be an inquiry into Irish affairs before definite decisions were taken, a pledge which was not fulfilled. Chamberlain's position was difficult. It was dangerous for a radical leader to come out openly against Gladstone's Home Rule aspirations. Chamberlain's own political standing owed much to his special influence within his 'Duchy', an important group of West Midlands constituencies centred on Birmingham. It was important for him to preserve this power base. Though determined to do all that he could to defeat Home Rule, he found it expedient to temporize at first.

Gladstone now prepared two interdependent proposals for Ireland; one of these was a considerable expansion of the land purchase scheme instituted by the previous ministry, the other a measure for the creation of an Irish legislature. His introduction of these proposals into the Cabinet in March provoked the resignation of Chamberlain and Trevelyan, both leading radicals. After a considerable struggle, Chamberlain succeeded in retaining the core of his West Midlands influence, though elsewhere the Liberal Party organization was predominantly loyal to Gladstone.

The Home Rule proposals were open to attack on a number of points. Irish MPs would no longer sit at Westminster, but the Irish contribution to national expenditure would be a fixed proportion of a total determined there. In addition a number of key functions, such as defence, foreign policy, trade regulation, currency, and the Post Office, were to be excluded from the purview of the new Irish assembly. There was no provision for separate treatment for the Protestant-dominated north-east of Ireland; Ulstermen could be seen as being handed over to the political control of their arch-enemies. The proposed new legislature in Dublin was a cumbrous mixture of one-chamber and two-chamber working.

Gladstone introduced his scheme in the House of Commons on 8 April 1886; the debate which followed was one of the greatest parliamentary occasions of the century, with a high standard of argument and oratory sustained over sixteen days. It soon became clear that the proposals were in jeopardy, despite Gladstone's belated willingness to compromise on some issues. The dissentient Liberals were largely responsible for the outcome. Both Hartington and Chamberlain made effective attacks on the detailed weaknesses of Gladstone's scheme as well as its general import. Bright did not join in these parliamentary attacks, but made his hostility to the proposals clear to other Liberals, which may well have affected some waverers. In the early morning of 8 June, the second reading of the first Home Rule Bill was defeated by 343 votes to 313, with 93 Liberals, including Hartington, Chamberlain, and Bright, in the hostile majority.

Gladstone could only hope to reverse this defeat by victory at the polls. The general election of 1886 was fought on the issue of Irish Home Rule, and the verdict of the electorate settled that matter for the time being. The election had been sprung on the country, and there was no opportunity for prolonged campaigning. Not surprisingly in these circumstances, there was a significant number of unopposed returns—42 Liberals, 86 Conservatives, 66 Irish Home

Rulers, and 24 Liberals opposing Home Rule. In most cases a Liberal who had voted against Home Rule was not opposed by a Conservative candidate.

In terms of seats the results were a rejection of Home Rule. Gladstone's Liberals shrank to only 191 MPs; Parnell led his Irish phalanx of 85. Against this the Conservatives returned 316 strong, and the anti-Home Rule Liberals, or Liberal Unionists as we may now call them, held 78 seats. In July, when the result was known, Gladstone promptly resigned, and Lord Salisbury formed his second ministry. This was a Conservative rather than a coalition government, although if the Liberal Unionists had gone into opposition on any crucial issue the ministry would have been defeated. Early in 1887 there were some discussions between the various Liberal groups but it soon appeared that reunion was unattainable; a trickle of Liberal Unionists back to Gladstone during this Parliament was not substantial enough to be decisive.

Rather more than the Third Reform Act, it was the Irish Question that destroyed the continuity of British politics. The Reform Act weakened the hold of the aristocracy in politics but the divisions over Home Rule made aristocratic influence almost completely one-sided. The largely peaceful and evolutionary path of political change in nineteenth-century Britain had depended much on the fact that there were not one but two aristocratic parties or, at least, a formidable aristocratic component in each. The massed ranks of the middle orders had never, as in many continental states, been faced with the closed ranks of an *ancien regime*. The decline in the number of Whig supporters of Liberal administrations removed brakes upon rash reformist measures. All was well while the electorate had its attention focused upon Irish Home Rule, which was highly unpopular, but, when other questions were highlighted, the paucity of Whigs would prove to be a great disadvantage to the Upper House.

The fall of Churchill

During the Home Rule debates and the general election Lord Randolph Churchill had continued to play a key role in Conservative campaigning, consolidating his position as a popular figure. In his campaigning, the 'Ulster card'— the claim that Gladstone was sacrificing loyal Protestants in Ireland to their Catholic foes—had played a prominent part. His importance was recognized by his advancement to Chancellor of the Exchequer in the new Conservative administration. There followed one of the most dramatic personal catastrophes in modern British political history. Churchill had a high and largely justified opinion of his services to his party, and was not willing to accept Salisbury's authority readily. His rapid rise meant that he had not worked with his ministerial colleagues for long periods; instead he was a relatively isolated figure in the Cabinet. Believing himself to be indispensable, he tried to use threats of resignation to impose his views on Salisbury, in both domestic and foreign affairs. Churchill was determined to use his popularity and his Chancellorship to establish his own and his party's position more firmly. In particular, he intended to show that the Conservatives could govern as economically as any Gladstonian administration, while bringing forward reforms at the same time. In his first Budget, he wanted to offer reductions in expenditure. His colleagues were willing to make concessions, and did so, but Churchill was not satisfied. He pressed upon the army and navy demands for further spending cuts which the service ministers believed to be dangerous to national security. Though he did not have a strong following in the Cabinet, a display of flexibility and patience by Churchill would have secured the adoption of most of his proposals. But such qualities were not among his strong points. When he could not have his own way, without taking advice or time to consider, Churchill sent a letter of resignation to Salisbury. The Prime Minister, who was well aware of the challenge to his authority which Churchill represented, and the weak ground which the Chancellor had taken, simply accepted the resignation. Churchill's apparent position of strength evaporated, for his impetuous resignation naturally gave rise to hostility within the party; only a few months after the Home Rule crisis, Churchill had in personal pique endangered the security of the ministry. Salisbury was also able to find an impressive replacement for Churchill at the Exchequer in G. J. Goschen, an able debater and acknowledged expert in financial matters, who joined the government from the ranks of the Liberal Unionists. Churchill's meteoric political career was over.

Conservative Irish policies

Ireland was bound to provide the new ministry with its most pressing problems. Salisbury was fortunate in finding two successive Chief Secretaries for Ireland who were capable of facing the difficulties of that office. His first choice, Sir Michael Hicks Beach, was forced to resign on health grounds in early March 1887. He was replaced by the Prime Minister's nephew A. J. Balfour. Balfour had been perhaps the least active of Churchill's 'Fourth Party' in the early 1880s, and had contrived to project an image of a somewhat languorous man of fashion. In his new role he revealed another side of his character, as a tough-minded minister well able to cope with Irish opposition and invective. The Conservative ministry reverted to an older Irish policy. On the one hand Coercion Acts equipped the Irish executive with special police powers, which Balfour showed no reluctance to employ; his Irish administration enjoyed some success in reducing the level of crime. The other side of this policy was a continued expansion in land purchase schemes and other aspects of agrarian reform in Ireland. In 1887 rents fixed by quasi-judicial process were extended to leasehold property, and provision was made for lowering earlier rent determinations where this seemed justified. Further Land Acts in 1888 and 1891 extended official encouragement and subsidizing of land purchase by Irish tenants. A Congested Districts Board was set up in 1890 to help the most backward regions of Ireland (see p. 482 below).

The Conservatives nevertheless suffered one important reverse, largely of their own making. In 1887 *The Times* published a series of letters which purported to show that Parnell and other leading Irish politicians secretly encouraged Irish political violence, including the Phoenix Park Murders. The government tried to exploit this opportunity by setting up a special judicial tribunal to examine these charges. However, in February 1889 this dubious expedient backfired, in a demonstration before the tribunal that some of the key documents concerned were forgeries. The final report of the special commission did link some Irish leaders, though not Parnell, with the encouragement of violence. This result was scarcely noticed in relation to the revelation that the attacks by *The Times* had been in great measure founded upon forgeries, with little real effort having been made to establish the letters' authenticity. Parnell's vindication brought him a temporary popularity in Britain and seemed to bring new hope to the cause of Home Rule. Another development now intervened and transformed the Irish situation yet again. In November 1890, Captain O'Shea succeeded in a divorce case in which Parnell was branded as an adulterer. This was a catastrophe for the Home Rule party. Parnell's leadership had been riveted upon it during the 1880s, and his personal tragedy entailed serious harm to the party he led. Neither the Roman Catholic Church in Ireland, on which so much depended for the nationalists, nor the Liberals within the British Churches, could continue cooperation with someone so discredited in terms of personal morality.[8] Gladstone made it clear that if the Irish wished to keep that Liberal alliance which was their main practical hope for Home Rule, then the Irish leader must go.

Parnell refused to relinquish his party leadership, and the Home Rule Party split, with the majority of the Irish MPs repudiating their leader. He declined to accept his rejection, and fought back vigorously. His campaigning in Ireland was strenuous and at the same time discouraging in its results. Parnell's health collapsed and he died in October 1891. His devoted followers continued to fight against those who had rejected their champion and driven him to his death. For the remainder of the century, two Irish nationalist parties were locked in bitter hostility.

This disaster for the Irish cause came at a time when the horizon otherwise looked favourable. The 1886 Parliament enjoyed the unusual experience of lasting out almost its maximum legal existence, but in its last years the Conservative government seemed to be losing ground. Since the heady days of the original Home Rule crisis in 1886, the government's by-election record had been poor. Indeed Goschen had been beaten at the by-election on taking office, and a vacancy had been hurriedly made for him in a safe Conservative seat. The ministry was responsible for a continuing flow of reforming legislation, much of it

8. Parnell was not the only politician whose career foundered after a sensational divorce case. Sir Charles Dilke, a rising Liberal politician, was discredited by a divorce case in 1886 in which he was cited as a co-respondent.

relatively uncontroversial and unable to generate any partisan support among the electorate. Examples included the major local government reforms of 1888 (see pp. 471–2 below), an 1889 Act for the expansion of technical education, an Act of 1890 enlarging the powers of local authorities in housing, free elementary education in 1891, and an extension of factory regulations in the same year. Conservative reform was embarked upon with one eye on the need to conciliate the Liberal Unionists, but much of the legislation involved was merely an extension of earlier measures, based upon accumulating experience and information. Some of the Conservative reforms probably contributed to the party's decline in popularity. However admirable in principle the creation of elected county councils might be, for many voters what they meant in practice was an increase in expenditure and higher rates.

One factor which offset Conservative decline was the creation of an increasingly effective popular organization, the Primrose League.[9] This was launched in 1883, with Churchill's 'Fourth Party' much to the fore, and established itself over the next few years as an important accompaniment to the normal party organs. It developed a novel structure, with its own hierarchy of ranks, titles, functions, and awards for members of both sexes, and indeed for children too. A wide round of social activities accompanied its political work. Reasonably reliable membership figures suggest totals of nearly 100,000 by the end of 1885, more than 650,000 by 1912. Ostensibly a separate organization, the League could carry out electoral activities on behalf of the Conservatives without falling foul of legislation fixing limits on candidates' election expenditure. The Primrose League was much larger than any of the small socialist groups of these years, enjoyed more popularity among both sexes, and was more effective politically. In the early 1890s the Primrose League had not yet reached its peak in size and effectiveness, but it helped to limit Conservative losses in the general election of 1892.

In 1891 the Liberal Party's annual conference, meeting at Newcastle, drew up a programme on which to fight the approaching general election. Irish Home Rule appeared in the forefront, accompanied by a miscellaneous and not particularly coherent list of other proposals. These included disestablishment of the Established Churches in Scotland and Wales, local polls to decide whether or not alcoholic drinks could be sold, abolition of all plural votes, shorter (three years maximum) Parliaments, land reform, and the creation of elected district councils within the counties. To supporters, the Newcastle Programme could be defended as a policy of liberal decentralization of authority. To opponents, it seemed to be designed to attract a heterogeneous array of cranky groups at the risk of undermining legitimate authority. Gladstone was little concerned with matters other than Home Rule, and the programme was not well designed to arouse popular enthusiasm or indeed Liberal unity.

9. For a cogent study of the Primrose League see M. D. Pugh, *The Tories and the People* (1985).

Gladstone's fourth ministry

The general election in July 1892 was a defeat for Salisbury's second administration, but the Liberal gains were far fewer than Gladstone had counted on, fewer than he needed to force Home Rule through against the hostile majority in the House of Lords. The results saw Liberals and Conservatives not far apart, 272 Liberals, 268 Conservatives, with the overall result resting upon their respective allies, 81 Irish Home Rulers and 46 Liberal Unionists. In England Gladstone remained in a clear minority, while the other elements in the United Kingdom gave him most of their seats.

Salisbury declined to accept the result of the election as a clear-cut verdict, but in the new Parliament his ministry was soon defeated. Gladstone formed his last government in August 1892. He was now nearly 83 years old, increasingly deaf, and cantankerous. Most of his colleagues now belonged to a different political generation, and did not share all of his basic views. A second Home Rule Bill was framed, and accepted by the Cabinet. Like its predecessor, it was vulnerable in detail. The problem of loyal, Protestant Ulster was again ignored, something which the Opposition could easily exploit. Ireland was to have its own legislative assembly, but was also to send eighty representatives to Westminster; defence, foreign relations, and trade regulation were to be reserved to the United Kingdom Parliament. A cumbrous and probably unworkable provision to prevent Irish MPs from voting on matters concerned only with Great Britain was dropped during the Commons debates.

Gladstone introduced his proposals in February 1893, and another major series of debates ensued. Chamberlain opposed the bill fiercely and skilfully, but could not prevent its final passing in the Commons by 43 votes on 1 September. No one could have had much doubt about its ultimate fate, but the margin by which the peers killed the bill was a striking one; the second reading in the House of Lords was rejected on 8 September by 419 votes to 41.

Gladstone urged an immediate dissolution of Parliament, and an appeal to the electorate against the action of the hereditary House. His Cabinet colleagues, who had a better idea of what the electorate would have decided, refused his advice. Relationships within the Cabinet, especially between the aged Prime Minister and some of his younger colleagues, were not cordial, and in March 1894 Gladstone finally resigned. Ill health was the ostensible reason for this step, but the reality was different. The majority of the Liberal Cabinet was convinced that its responsibilities included the maintenance of Britain's maritime strength. The continuing proposals for the expansion of the navies of Russia and France meant that to do this necessitated a considerable programme of warship construction. Gladstone refused to sanction the increased naval expenditure involved, but found himself virtually isolated in the Cabinet and chose to go.

During the long-drawn-out struggle over the Home Rule Bill, the government had managed to make only modest progress with other reforms. The Local

Government Act of 1894 created a range of new elected local councils. Married women could now vote in local elections if otherwise qualified, and women could be elected to local councils. The legislative fruits of the government's first years were not very great. There was no effective temperance legislation, no disestablishment.

Lord Rosebery's administration

Finding a new Prime Minister was not easy. The obvious candidate, Harcourt, Chancellor of the Exchequer, had served in Liberal governments since 1873 and came from an impeccable social background, but his overbearing personal manner had alienated so many of his colleagues that he lost the prize.[10] The other possible candidate was the Foreign Secretary, Lord Rosebery. The Queen made no attempt to take advice from Gladstone, and commissioned Rosebery to head the ministry. Rosebery was not an ideal leader for the Gladstonian Liberal Party.[11] He had great gifts (including considerable skill as a historian). He was a rich aristocrat, who had married a Rothschild heiress, and enjoyed good food, good drink, good tobacco, witty conversation. His horses won the Derby twice during his short ministry. Rosebery was not well attuned to some Liberal interests, including the temperance workers and earnest Nonconformists; he supported working men's clubs, including their right to supply alcoholic drinks to their members. He was prepared to accept Irish Home Rule, but was scarcely enthusiastic about it; elsewhere he believed sincerely in the grandeur and the goodness of the British Empire. Some of the other younger members of the government, including the rising lawyers Asquith and Haldane, were inclined to share such views.

Rosebery's premiership was short and inglorious. Its successes were few. In the 1894 Budget Harcourt extended the principle of death duties, including the imposition of graduated levies varying with the total size of estate on death; on estates of more than £1 million, the State confiscated 8 per cent of the total. This increased revenue was needed for naval expansion, but it was not enough, even with an extra penny added to income tax. Additional taxation was levied on drink, including beer, which may have given moderate pleasure to temperance workers, but was not a popular line with the extended electorate. Governments responsible for increased taxation were still courting electoral dangers.

Some of the individual members of the government contrived to improve their reputations; they included a future premier, Sir Henry Campbell-Bannerman, at the War Office. At the top, however, the tenure of the Rosebery Cabinet was marked by factious infighting. Harcourt was embittered by being passed over for

10. For a recent biography of Harcourt see, P. Jackson, *Harcourt and Son: A Political Biography of Sir William Harcourt 1827–1904* (2004).

11. For Rosebery's career, R. R. James, *Rosebery: A Biography of Archibald Philip Primrose, Fifth Earl of Rosebery* (1963) and L. McKinstry, *Rosebery: Statesman in Turmoil* (2005).

the premiership, and did nothing to help his new chief. By 1895 Prime Minister and Chancellor were scarcely on speaking terms. The government's problems were exacerbated by the House of Lords which, emboldened by the apparent impunity with which Home Rule had been dispatched, mutilated the Liberal government's legislative programme.

Meanwhile, the growing weakness of the ministry was accompanied by a growing confidence among its enemies. Relationships between Conservatives and Liberal Unionists became closer, including cooperation at by-elections. On 21 June 1895 the government suffered a snap defeat in the House of Commons on an Opposition resolution criticizing the War Office for inadequate supplies of the explosive cordite. Such a defeat was scarcely a matter of major importance, especially since the censure was not based on any reliable evidence. Instead of making a fight on the issue, however, Rosebery determined to resign and escape from an increasingly uncongenial situation.

The 1895 general election

On 26 June, two days after the Liberal Cabinet's resignation, Salisbury again took office. He led a coalition government; the two principal Liberal Unionist leaders, Joseph Chamberlain and the Duke of Devonshire (the former Lord Hartington), joined the Cabinet. The Unionist coalition was now poised for an election victory, and Parliament was dissolved in July. Rosebery had tried to persuade his colleagues in the Liberal leadership to agree upon a united campaign, but his arguments fell on deaf ears. He had wanted the Liberal campaign to concentrate on an attack on the partisan actions of the House of Lords, but Morley (Irish Secretary in Rosebery's Cabinet) made Irish Home Rule his main platform, while Harcourt gave more prominence to the cause of temperance. Morley was defeated at Newcastle, Harcourt at Derby, and both had to take refuge in areas outside urban England, in Montrose and Monmouth. The 1895 election also demonstrated the electoral impotence of independent labour candidates, even in constituencies dominated by voters who were workers. In 1892 Keir Hardie had won West Ham, largely because the Liberal candidate there died just before the election was held. The Independent Labour Party was founded at a meeting held in Bradford in January 1893, but it remained small and insignificant in electoral terms. In 1895, faced with a new Liberal candidate, Keir Hardie lost his seat; he was defeated again at a by-election at Bradford in 1896. All twenty-eight parliamentary candidates backed by the Independent Labour Party in 1895 were defeated.[12]

There was little Liberal fighting spirit in the 1895 general election; 124 seats were left without Liberal candidates. The Unionists gained seats almost everywhere, including a further expansion of their strength in urban England. The

---

12. For the ILP see: D. James, T. Jowitt, and K. Laybourn (eds.), *The Centennial History of the Independent Labour Party* (1992).

London area returned 53 Unionists and only 8 Liberals, including Unionists elected for constituencies like Poplar and Shoreditch which were far from being haunts of the rich and privileged. There had been 25 Liberals from the metropolitan area in 1892. Many provincial cities also evinced increased Conservative strength. Even in Scotland the Liberal lead was cut to a handful of seats. In England the county seats returned to the Conservatives for the most part, after about ten years of flirtation with the Liberals. The overall result gave Conservatives 340, Liberals 177, Irish Home Rulers 82, Liberal Unionists 71. The new coalition had a convincing majority of seats, though a less decisive lead in total votes cast, for this was one of those elections in which a relatively modest shift in voting behaviour produced a massive reversal in electoral fortunes. Even so, with more than 49 per cent of the total votes cast, the Conservatives were clearly ahead of any other party.

Unionist predominance

The scene was now set for ten years of Unionist coalition predominance, accompanied for much of the period by Liberal disunity and weakness. For most of this period, Lord Salisbury's pre-eminence in the State was not seriously challenged. The presence of the Prime Minister in the House of Lords did not involve any serious problems, and Salisbury had become a statesman of ability and prestige at home and abroad. He was not imbued with any strong sense of optimism for the future, and saw in the contemporary world many reasons for anxiety. His preoccupation with foreign affairs stemmed in part from his apprehension that the gravest dangers lay there. What concerned him most was a world in which masses of people grouped in national states, largely literate but in his view essentially uneducated and uncultured, could be worked up so as to collide in major conflict over national interests. He saw the statesman's main duty as a need to take precautions against outbursts of popular national feeling. He was too acute to suppose that this could be done by trying to repress national feelings; he preferred a policy which gave national feeling adequate expression and backing in ways which would give reassurance about the greatness of the country. He was unable to believe in the political reliability of the mass of the people, either in Britain or elsewhere. Perhaps the expanding popular press would come to occupy a position of real influence in moulding opinion, and the day of the statesman at the helm of a country's destinies would be over. Probably European statesmen could not indefinitely succeed in avoiding major international conflict. Salisbury believed that it was becoming harder for leaders to preserve freedom of manoeuvre; instead they seemed in danger of becoming merely ineffective figureheads. The best that he could hope to do was to prevent matters from getting worse, there being little chance of substantial improvement in international relations. It was this kind of fundamentally pessimistic thinking which had been one reason for Salisbury's distrust of Churchill's populist activities in the 1880s, which seemed to him devoid of principle and devoted entirely to immediate political expediency.[13]

Nevertheless, the flow of reforming legislation to the statute book continued unabated during the 1895–1905 period, and the activity and the resources of both central and local government continued to grow. A predominantly urban and industrial society required more sophisticated provision for sanitary and educational purposes, while intervention in such matters as health, welfare, and industrial relations was already at a level which would have astonished earlier generations. Yet the government's domestic legislation, although substantial, did not inspire popular enthusiasm. The only measure to arouse much attention was the Workmen's Compensation Act of 1897. This provided for the payment by employers of compensation for accidents over a wide range of work. Some groups at risk, including seamen, farm workers, and domestic servants, were still excluded, but these exceptions all came to be included by simple supplementary legislation in ensuing years.

There was much talk about old-age pensions during these years, and a number of official inquiries into various pension schemes. Nothing effective was done, partly because the concept was opposed by the influential friendly societies. This attitude was widely supported by their numerous members, who were already prudently paying for their own benefits from their own limited resources. The friendly societies were understandably unhappy at the prospect of either non-contributory pensions for the aged poor provided out of taxpayers' money, or of the State taking the field as a competitor in some sort of contributory scheme. By 1900 the membership of friendly societies amounted to some 5.5 million, a high proportion of whom would be on the electoral registers. The existence of friendly society and insurance alternatives did not help the advocates of State pensions at the taxpayers' expense.

In 1887 Queen Victoria celebrated her Golden Jubilee, with festivities held throughout Britain and the empire. These loyal ceremonies were transcended in 1897, when the Diamond Jubilee was an occasion for immense national and imperial rejoicing. The occasion was also marked by a meeting of principal ministers from eleven self-governing colonies, and the acceptance of the principle of holding such meetings regularly. That was as far in the direction of imperial cooperation as the self-governing colonies were prepared to go. A few of them were willing to contribute to the cost of imperial defence, or even to make limited concessions in matters of trade, but there was a resolute opposition to any kind of constitutional federation. Some were already engaged in different projects. Plans were on foot for the federation of the Australian colonies, to be finalized in the Commonwealth of Australia Act of 1900. The increased interest in imperial affairs in these years was reflected by one significant political move.

---

13. For Salisbury see: Andrew Roberts, *Salisbury: Victorian Titan* (1999); David Steele, *Lord Salisbury: A Political Biography* (1999), and Michael Bentley, *Lord Salisbury's World: Conservative Environments in Late-Victorian Britain* (2001).

When Salisbury formed his third ministry in 1895 he had given Joseph Chamberlain a wide choice of office. The Liberal Unionist leader had chosen the Colonial Office, not normally seen as one of the more important Cabinet posts. His own interests had moved increasingly towards the empire, and the possibility of his being responsible for a programme of major domestic reform had evaporated.

South Africa

The empire provided the most dramatic events of these years of Unionist government, in the South African War of 1899–1902.[14] In previous years there had been an increasing confrontation between the Boer republics of the Transvaal and the Orange Free State, and the British colonies of Cape Colony and Natal. Their relations were complicated by the presence of a considerable Boer population within the British colonies, and a growing immigrant population, much of it British, within the developing mining areas of the Transvaal. The discovery of gold there in 1886 had transformed that republic. A poor, chronically ill-governed, pastoral state had become wealthy, capable of arming itself against foreign intervention, and sensitive to the dangers facing it. The Transvaal apprehension of danger was enhanced by the work of the British South Africa Company, inspired by Cecil Rhodes, which had taken British influence to the north of the Boer states, in the area which was later to be Rhodesia and then Zimbabwe. British power in various forms seemed to be hemming in the Boer enclaves and depriving them of opportunities for expansion.

Rhodes was strongly placed as Prime Minister of Cape Colony, where he drew support both from British settlers and from many of the Cape Dutch or Boer elements. He was determined to secure British paramountcy in Southern Africa, but to do this he needed to curb the independence of the Transvaal, where the dominant Boers, headed by Paul Kruger, were resolute in resisting British encroachments. Rhodes hoped to use as his lever the grievances of the British immigrants in the Transvaal mining areas, who were denied equal political rights by the Transvaal establishment. He secured from the Unionist government in its early months the implementation of a promise made by the previous Liberal ministry; the British South Africa Company was granted control of a narrow strip of British territory running alongside the Transvaal's western frontier in order to complete a railway link with the Cape. At the same time British residents in the Transvaal were encouraged to complain about their treatment by the government there. Both the Rosebery and the Salisbury governments were prepared to exploit these complaints to bring pressure on the Kruger regime.

14. J. Van der Poel, *The Jameson Raid* (1951); B. Porter, *The Lion's Share: A Short History of British Imperialism, 1850–1970* (1975), 167–82; G. H. L. Le May, *British Supremacy in South Africa, 1899–1907* (1965).

Rhodes was also preparing a more sinister adventure. He concentrated a force of company armed police in the newly acquired frontier strip, with the intention of launching them into the Transvaal to support an anticipated rising on the Rand goldfield. The planned rising fizzled out, but at the end of 1895 the police commander, Dr L. S. Jameson, launched his little force into the Transvaal, only to be rounded up with little difficulty by government forces. This ill-starred adventure both morally and politically damaged the British position and prestige in South Africa. Rhodes had to resign as premier of the Cape, since his support among the Cape Dutch collapsed. The Orange Free State joined in closer alliance with the Transvaal. Kruger was encouraged by expressions of overseas sympathy, including a telegram of congratulation from the German Emperor. Abroad, British government complicity in the adventure was widely assumed, though it will probably never be certain how far British ministers and officials were involved in the affair. The most likely position is that some of them, including Chamberlain, knew that something of the kind was in the wind, but prudently protected themselves from inconvenient knowledge.[15]

Chamberlain formally condemned the Jameson Raid as soon as he had definite news of its occurrence, but he was for some time exposed to political danger. A select committee of the House of Commons was appointed to investigate the affair. The committee had a Unionist majority, including Chamberlain himself, but it also possessed a strong Liberal element, including Harcourt, Campbell-Bannerman, and the radical Labouchere. The select committee may not have been too searching in its inquiries, but the final report was adopted by all except two of its members, Labouchere and an Irish Home Ruler. That report exonerated Chamberlain and his department from any charges of complicity in the Raid, while blaming Rhodes for his share in the affair. In the subsequent parliamentary discussion, Chamberlain went out of his way to claim that Rhodes had done nothing dishonourable. It now remained to pick up the pieces of the British position in South Africa. In 1897 Chamberlain sent a man of great ability and a convinced imperialist, Sir Alfred Milner, to represent Britain there as High Commissioner and Governor of the Cape. His brief included the repairing of relations between the British and Boer elements in Cape Colony, and the resumption of pressure on the Transvaal government to confer political rights on its immigrants. The Transvaal, in ways which the Jameson Raid apparently justified, was spending an increasing proportion of its revenue on the purchase of arms.

In March 1899, a petition to the Queen was sent by 21,684 British subjects living on the Rand goldfield in the Transvaal, complaining of the refusal of the Transvaal State to give them full political rights, and of tyrannical conduct by the Transvaal police. Milner backed the petition, and urged the home government to take it up, in a dispatch which spoke of 'thousands of British subjects kept

---

15. See Peter T. Marsh, *Joseph Chamberlain: Entrepreneur in Politics* (1994), 372–86.

permanently in the position of helots, constantly chafing under undoubted grievances and calling vainly to Her Majesty's Government for redress'.

There followed months of tortuous negotiations between Milner and Kruger. Milner was convinced that Kruger's Transvaal embodied an imperialism of its own, bent on destroying the British position in southern Africa. By September Kruger had concluded that he could only conciliate the British by offering concessions to the 'Uitlander' elements in the Transvaal mining areas which would fatally dilute Boer control over the republic. Both sides embarked upon preliminary military preparations, and in October, with preparations for an invasion of British territory completed, the Transvaal delivered an ultimatum couched in terms which were plainly unacceptable.

Once again, and not for the last time, British servicemen in the field paid the price exacted for past neglect of the armed forces. The number of British troops involved eventually reached 450,000, more than half of whom were drawn from the expanded British Regular Army. Of these, nearly 6,000 were killed, more than 16,000 died of disease, and nearly 23,000 were wounded. The Boer forces were much smaller, and their casualties both from military action and from disease were proportionally much fewer than those of the British.

At first the Boer armies were superior in numbers and equipment to the British units opposing them; even when substantial British reinforcements were in the field, inadequate intelligence and incompetent generalship resulted in a series of humiliating military reverses culminating in 'Black Week' in December 1899. Within a few days, three British armies were decisively beaten. January and February 1900 saw further defeats for the main British field force in its attempts to relieve the besieged town of Ladysmith. Britain had already taken steps to mobilize more of her undoubtedly superior resources. The appointment of Lord Roberts as Commander-in-Chief, with Kitchener as his Chief of Staff, brought a higher level of military skills to bear, while a flow of reinforcements established and consolidated British numerical superiority. The Boers failed to take advantage of the early British weakness to strengthen their position in the Cape. The besieged British outposts, Ladysmith, Kimberley, and Mafeking, held out against Boer forces unskilled at siege warfare.

By mid-February the military tide had turned. Roberts devised a strategic plan appropriate to the situation, which his predecessors had signally failed to do. At the end of February one of the principal Boer field armies was surrounded at Paardeberg and forced to surrender. British forces in great strength swept into the two Boer republics. The capital of the Orange Free State, Bloemfontein, fell on 13 March and by the end of May that republic had been annexed to the British Crown. On the last day of May British forces entered Johannesburg. On 11 September President Kruger left the Transvaal for exile, and in the following month the Transvaal too became formally a British colony.

Victory seemed achieved, and Roberts relinquished his command and returned home. But Kitchener, as his successor, soon learned that the war was far from over. The remaining Boer forces resorted to guerrilla warfare with considerable success. In December substantial British reinforcements were still arriving to cope with this unexpected prolongation of hostilities. In response to the Boer tactics, Kitchener embarked upon new and expensive expedients. The guerrillas depended heavily on the support they could obtain from the countryside within the occupied republics. Kitchener responded by clearing large areas of their inhabitants, who were rounded up and placed in 'concentration camps'. Guerrilla mobility was restricted by creating fortified lines running for many miles across country.

British servicemen were not the only victims of the limited efficiency of the British military organization. Boer farming families usually had little or no experience of living in concentrated communities. The organization of the internment camps in their early months was defective. The death-toll from disease, much of it due to insanitary conditions, reached more than one-sixth of the internees. When these circumstances became known at home, the British government, and Chamberlain especially, reacted sharply to enforce improvements, but by then many Boer women and children had died in the camps.

Gradually, the British military pressure wore down the remaining Boer forces, and in March 1902 their leaders embarked upon negotiations for surrender. At the end of May the Peace of Vereeniging was concluded. The terms were in the circumstances generous. The remaining Boer armies were to surrender; with only a few exceptions, everyone who accepted the British annexation could return home freely. British military control of the conquered areas would be kept as brief as possible. The cost of the war to the victors would be paid by the British taxpayers; a substantial grant would in addition be made by Britain to rehabilitate the Boer farming areas. Rhodes did not live to see the end of the war, but died on 26 March 1902. He left a substantial part of his great personal fortune to found scholarships at Oxford, to be held by students from South Africa, elsewhere in the empire, the USA, and Germany.

The 1900 general election

The South African War had important political results at home. In the years after 1895 the Unionist government had been losing ground; a series of by-election defeats was linked with economic problems. The war aroused public enthusiasm, and in its early years opponents of the war became extremely unpopular. Chamberlain persuaded Salisbury to take advantage of the opportunity to hold a general election in October 1900. The justification offered for the premature dissolution was that it must be made clear to the Boers that the British government enjoyed public backing in its war policy, and that the Unionists would be empowered to fight the war to a victorious conclusion. In what was known as the 'khaki' election, the ministry offered itself for re-election as a united and patriotic party.

In contrast the Liberal Opposition was disunited and in disarray. A substantial section of the party, including Rosebery and Asquith, themselves imbued with imperialist ideals, were prepared to give the war effort a wholehearted support. A smaller group of 'pro-Boers' included the vocal Welsh radical MP, David Lloyd George; in the early years of hostilities, his forthright opposition to the war brought him risks of serious injury at excited public meetings. Some Liberals saw the war as just and necessary, others saw it as an immoral imperialist adventure, embarked upon in the interests of the capitalist mine-owners of the Rand. Sir Henry Campbell-Bannerman, who was consolidating a position of personal leadership within the party, tried to occupy a balancing position. He did not openly condemn the war, but attacked the ministry for some of its war policies. When the concentration camp scandal broke publicly, he accused the government of fighting the war by 'methods of barbarism'.

Against the background of the war, older questions like Irish Home Rule scarcely surfaced in the constituencies. There was some criticism of the government's limited achievements in social matters, including pensions, but what Salisbury called 'a layer of pure combativeness' against the Boers was more effective. As a result the Conservative urban vote rose again, seats won narrowly in provincial cities in 1895 being now held by a larger margin. By a narrow margin, the government won an absolute majority of the votes cast. In Scotland the Unionists secured a narrow majority of the seats. Overall the Salisbury government was backed by 334 Conservatives and 68 Liberal Unionists in the new House of Commons. The Liberals again did badly, with only 184 seats; the still-squabbling Irish Home Rulers returned 82 strong. The infant movement for independent labour representation, headed now by the newly formed Labour Representation Committee (see pp. 426–8 below), had two victories. The veteran Keir Hardie was narrowly elected for Merthyr, where one of the two Liberal candidates had become personally unpopular; the other Liberal was way ahead of Hardie at the head of the poll for this two-member constituency. The other new 'Labour' MP, Richard Bell, returned for Derby where his railway union was strong, was essentially a Liberal trade union official of the old Liberal–Labour school represented by men like the northern miners' leader Thomas Burt. Such men found the radical wing of the Liberal Party more congenial than any more militant labour alignment, and Bell himself was to defect to the Liberals in 1904.

Tariff reform

The war which consolidated the electoral position of the Unionist coalition also sowed the seeds of its eventual collapse. Joseph Chamberlain's imperialist fervour had been strengthened by the war. The official British position had been that the mother country had sought to protect British subjects exposed to oppression in the Transvaal. This aroused considerable sympathy elsewhere in the empire. All of the self-governing colonies were eventually represented in the imperial armies fighting in South Africa. Colonial contingents from Canada, Australia, New Zealand, and the British South African colonies provided more than 60,000 men; others came from the Indian Army and other overseas territories.

These demonstrations of imperial cooperation impressed men like Chamberlain, who saw in them an opportunity to exploit for schemes of imperial consolidation. Soon after the war, in July 1902, the fourth colonial conference was held, when the colonial ministers came to London for the coronation of King Edward VII. But Chamberlain's hopes of persuading the self-governing colonies to accept some kind of imperial council or other institutional link proved a complete failure. On the other hand there were some encouraging noises as far as imperial economic cooperation was concerned. But this would require the imposition by Britain of tariffs on non-imperial imports, if any meaningful system of mutual imperial preferences in trade were to be implemented. This would entail a challenge to the doctrine of free trade, which had since early-Victorian times become deeply entrenched, both among economists and among the public at large. Earlier challenges such as the Fair Trade movement of the 1880s had proved ineffective. The Liberal Party was wedded to the concept of free trade, and the late-Victorian Conservative Party, conscious of its alliance with the Liberal Unionists, had walked warily in such matters. The electoral dangers involved in embracing 'protection', which might include such items as the taxation of imported food, were appreciated, and were soon to be made clear.

Chamberlain made a lengthy visit to South Africa which ended in March 1903. This served to confirm his ideas on the need to foster imperial unity and to use economic policy for that purpose. Moreover, before he left Britain he had thought of a way to introduce the principle of imperial preference in a painless fashion. As part of the extra taxation imposed to meet the cost of the war, a small duty had been imposed on imported cereals. This was expressly a revenue-producing expedient, not a tariff imposed to protect British producers, and was not seen as an infringement of the general free trade principle. Chamberlain urged the Cabinet to include in the 1903 Budget a remission of this duty for colonial produce only. When he returned, however, it was to discover that the Chancellor of the Exchequer, Ritchie, had instead persuaded the Cabinet to drop the corn duty entirely. The financial implications were minor, for the 'registration' duty on corn brought in only £2 million, but the affair was an important test case for Chamberlain and his supporters.

After some weeks of internal debate within the government, Chamberlain determined to speak out. On 15 May 1903 he made his first public speech advocating a reconsideration of the country's free trade policies. His arguments were not confined to the question of imperial unity, although that was a key element. If Britain were to embark upon further social reforms, including old-age pensions, then additional revenue must be found. The imposition of tariffs within an imperial preference system could tap a new source of government income. In addition, by abandoning a one-sided free trade stance, Britain should be able to enforce the reduction of foreign tariffs which were an impediment to British exports. In September 1903 Chamberlain resigned his ministerial position in order to have a free hand to pursue his tariff reform crusade. This had already produced a critical political response, which was to bring to an end the long period of Unionist dominance.

Salisbury had remained Prime Minister until July 1902, when Balfour succeeded him without difficulty. Balfour shared many of his uncle's views but could not inherit his full authority, in part because Chamberlain was himself an increasingly influential figure in these years. That leading ex-radical was by now a convinced believer in the importance, the merit, and the civilizing mission of the British Empire. This belief owed something to wider ideas of a kind of neo-Darwinian principle of natural selection. Put crudely, the different racial blocs differed widely in their characteristics, with the 'Anglo-Saxon' group embodying the peak of present human development. This racial bloc, represented most obviously by Britain, Germany, Scandinavia, and the United States, ought to have a natural affinity. At the same time these peoples were the best-fitted to carry out a civilizing mission to the more backward regions of the earth. Chamberlain wanted to see not only the development of the British Empire, but also the growth of a closer cooperation between the kindred communities of Britain, Germany, and the United States.

When he raised the banner of tariff reform in 1903, Chamberlain was unwittingly laying the ground for one of the greatest electoral reversals in modern British history. The immediate effects of his campaign were twofold; on the one hand the Unionist coalition was plunged into irremediable confusion, while on the other the defence of free trade enabled the various segments of the Liberal Party to come together in a coherent campaign with popular appeal.

The end of Unionist rule

By the end of 1903, the Unionists had split three ways on the question of tariff reform. Most of the senior figures in the ministry had been reared in a British society committed to free trade as the foundation of British prosperity. Lancashire had been one of the great bastions of late-Victorian Conservatism, and Lancashire feared anything which might impede the free import of the raw materials, especially cotton, on which its industries depended. Other Unionists feared the electoral reaction if they openly jettisoned free trade. Chamberlain succeeded in getting support from industries particularly worried by foreign competition, and in recruiting a number of keen young Unionists, but his views were repudiated by many others.

Balfour had demonstrated that he could be tough and determined while Secretary of State for Ireland but he was not to be a successful prime minister or leader of the Conservative Party. A philosopher, he was perhaps somewhat detached from the political fray and found it difficult to be enthusiastic about political causes.[16] On tariff reform he had 'unsettled convictions' but struggled hard to keep the Unionist coalition together. Accepting the resignation from the government of the principal Unionist free traders and of Chamberlain himself, he tried to reconstruct his administration in a way which would keep links with both wings. He himself proffered a compromise policy, which would promise not to tax food imports, but would allow the use of other tariffs as a fiscal weapon; the imposition of tariffs, or the threat to impose them, would be used to oblige other countries to accept British exports if they wanted access to the British market for their own goods. All of these expedients proved unavailing. The Liberal Opposition repeatedly brought about debates on the tariff question in the House of Commons, increasingly revealing the disarray within the government majority on this issue. Balfour was by 1905 reduced to the humiliating expedient of advising his followers not to take part in such divisions, in order to avoid displays of disunity. At the end of 1905 the crisis within the Unionist coalition had reached a point at which resignation became inevitable.

By that time a number of other issues were contributing to Unionist unpopularity. The Education Act of 1902 had marked an important extension of public intervention in that sphere, but had also aroused hostility from Nonconformist militants incensed at the additional help given to church schools, mostly operated by the Established Church. It also meant more public spending on education, something unpopular with many taxpayers and ratepayers. The ministry had, after considerable hesitation, allowed Milner to implement a scheme to import indentured Chinese workers into South Africa for a limited period, to help to get the Rand mines into production again and provide the revenue needed for reconstruction in the areas affected by the recent war. This was denounced by the Liberals and their allies as 'Chinese Slavery' and played a part in their campaigning.

The opposition was also strengthened by an alliance between the Liberal Party and the Labour Representation Committee.[17] This latter body's foundation

16. For Balfour see Kenneth Young, *Arthur James Balfour* (1963) and Ruddock Mackay, *Balfour Intellectual Statesman* (1983). For a discussion of his attempts to deal with party disunity see ch. 8 of John Ramsden, *An Appetite for Power: A History of the Conservative Party since 1830* (1998).

17. The relationship between the Liberal and Labour Parties in the years around 1900 has given rise to a substantial volume of historical research. Examples include F. Bealey and H. Pelling, *Labour and Politics, 1900–1906* (1958); D. Howell, *British Workers and the Independent Labour Party, 1883–1906* (1983). For the distribution of electoral strength in these years, a key reference work is H. Pelling, *Social Geography of British Elections, 1885–1910* (1967). The Liberal–Labour relationship has also been studied in a variety of regional settings. These include P. F. Clarke, *Lancashire and the New Liberalism* (1971); P. Thompson, *Socialists, Liberals and Labour: The Struggle for London, 1885–1914* (1967); K. O. Morgan, 'The new liberalism and the challenge of Labour: the Welsh experience, 1885–1929', *The Welsh History Review*, 5 (1972). A. W. Purdue has contributed studies on this theme in relation to north-east England: 'George Lansbury and the Middlesbrough election of 1906', *International Review of Social History*, 18 (1973), 333–52; 'Arthur Henderson and Liberal, Liberal–Labour and Labour politics in the north-east of England', *Northern History*, 11 (1976 for 1975), 195–217; 'The Liberal and Labour Parties in north-east politics, 1900–1914', *International Review of Social History*, 26 (1981), 1–24.

resulted from a resolution in favour of independent labour representation in Parliament, carried in the Trades Union Congress in 1899 by 546,000 votes to 434,000. One motive was apprehension that legal interpretation of the statutes relating to trade unions was undermining the position believed to have been won by 1875. The *Lyons v. Wilkins* case of 1899, which laid down tight limits for acceptable picketing activities, was an important event in this respect. In February 1900, the creation of the LRC had aroused little public attention, as Lord Roberts's victorious troops swept through the defeated Boer republics. A federation of affiliated organizations, some trades unions, a number of trades councils, the ILP (the Social Democratic Federation joined but soon dropped out), and the Fabians, it had scarcely come into existence by the time of the 1900 general election, and made little impression on either of the major parties. At first many trade unions were cool towards the new initiative too; many of their leaders were Liberal–Labour and antipathetic to the ILP which they feared would have too much influence over the LRC. This changed in 1901 with the Taff Vale decision, which served to confirm trade union fears of developing legal interpretations and made many consider that the labour movement needed a party of its own.

The Taff Vale case

This celebrated case arose from a strike on the Taff Vale Railway. The railway company sued the union for damages arising from the action of union agents in persuading employees to break their contracts of employment. The High Court gave judgment in favour of the employer, and awarded costs and substantial damages against the Amalgamated Society of Railway Servants. The Court of Appeal subsequently reversed this verdict and found for the union. The employers then appealed to the House of Lords, who reinstated the decision of the High Court judge.[18] The division of opinion among the learned judges demonstrated that a difficult point of law was involved. This aspect was of little interest to the trade union movement, which now wanted the law to be changed and clarified in order to safeguard their capacity for effective industrial action. The Unionist ministry would only offer a royal commission to look into the question. These developments led to a rise in union affiliations to the Labour Representation Committee, which more than doubled in 1902–3.

Labour gains

Meanwhile, the LRC won a few more seats in by-elections. The Liberals did not put up a candidate in what was for them a hopeless contest in the Clitheroe division in 1902, but the seat was won from the Unionists by David Shackleton,

---

18. Of course the House of Lords in its judicial capacity was different from its legislative form and consisted of a court of appeal staffed by senior judges.

leader of a textile workers' union, standing as an LRC candidate but enjoying support from local Liberals. In 1903 Will Crooks won another seat from the Unionists at Woolwich, again with significant Liberal backing in the constituency, and Arthur Henderson won Barnard Castle against both Liberal and Conservative opponents. A close scrutiny of these victories demonstrates that they represented only a modest degree of support for independent labour candidates. During the Barnard Castle by-election of 1903, for instance, the Labour candidate, Arthur Henderson, who had acted as the paid agent of the previous Liberal MP, was forced against his will to accept the name of Labour instead of Liberal, and said nothing during his campaign which a radical Liberal candidate would have objected to. Moreover, his Liberal rival was a very unorthodox candidate disliked by most of the local supporters of that party, who preferred Henderson. Henderson's majority over the Unionist candidate was only forty-seven. In any event these by-election successes, however fragile, did provide some evidence that the LRC might be worth cultivating.

The Liberal Chief Whip, Herbert Gladstone, concluded that Labour might be able to beat Unionists in some constituencies which the Liberals could not win. In 1903 he had confidential negotiations with Ramsay MacDonald, the secretary of the LRC. The outcome was a secret electoral pact, whereby the Liberal leaders agreed to do their best to see to it that in the next general election LRC candidates should not face a Liberal opponent in about fifty constituencies, in return for general LRC support for Liberals where there was no Labour candidate. Two years later, a similar understanding between the LRC and the Trades Union Congress ruled out contests between LRC-sponsored and trade union 'Lib–Lab' candidates at the approaching general election. Without these agreements, the infant Labour Party would have been unable to make significant gains. The LRC's organization in the constituencies was weak; there were affiliated groups in only seventy-three constituencies by 1906.[19]

The 1906 general election

In timing his resignation at the end of 1905, Balfour entertained hopes that the Opposition would face problems in forming a ministry. It was known that within the Liberal leadership there were competing claims, and that the party had seen bitter divisions in the recent past. Balfour's hopes had some foundation. As the Unionist decline accelerated, a group of ambitious Liberal politicians, Asquith, Haldane, and Grey, agreed among themselves that they would not take office under Campbell-Bannerman unless the new premier agreed to lead the ministry from the House of Lords, leaving them a free run in the Commons, the essential forum of power. This attempted coup by the trio of Liberal imperialists evaporated when put to the test. Once Campbell-Bannerman was commissioned to form a

---

19. Pugh, *The Making of Modern British Politics*, 146.

government, and had the distribution of offices in his grasp, the plotters accepted the major posts they were offered. Asquith went to the Exchequer, Grey to the Foreign Office, and Haldane to the War Office. Campbell-Bannerman stayed in the House of Commons. Moreover, Campbell-Bannerman's new Cabinet proved to represent a wide spectrum of Liberal opinion. Lloyd George at the Board of Trade represented the radical wing of the party, while the presence of John Morley at the India Office and James Bryce at the Irish Office gave places to an older school of Liberalism. John Burns, whose working-class background made him appear to many as a radical but who was by now a Gladstonian, was President of the Local Government Board. Winston Churchill, whose views, with the exception of free trade convictions, were little known, was Colonial Under-Secretary. Every significant section of the party was brought together in support of the new administration. With this established, the Liberal government was well placed to face its crumbling opponents at a general election held early in the new year.

The 1906 general election proved an even greater disaster for the Unionists than had been anticipated. They returned only 157 MPs, less than a quarter of the seats in the new House of Commons. The Liberals gained a clear overall majority over the other parties, with 400 seats, including 23 Liberal–Labour MPs, who held aloof from the new Labour Party, preferring to stay within the radical wing of the Liberals. Moreover, they could usually count on the support of the 83 Irish Home Rulers, finally reunited under John Redmond, and the 29 members who accepted the whip of the new Labour Party,[20] as the Labour Representative Committee's MPs now chose to call themselves. Again the result in terms of total votes cast was much less dramatic than the shift in seats. The Liberals had just under 2.7 million votes, Labour fewer than 0.3 million; the Unionists polled under 2.5 million. The total Unionist vote actually held up relatively well, and the turn of the tide was most evident in the larger number of electors who chose to turn out in support of the new ministry.

One view of the 1906 election is that it marked a widespread desire for social reform and was the result of a transformation of Liberalism as a New Liberalism embraced a social reformist agenda and found a temporary alliance with that proportion of the labour movement which, via the Labour Representation Committee, was demanding its own political voice. It was, in short, a triumph for 'Progressivism'.[21] Despite the fact that radicals and 'new Liberals' were undoubtedly well-represented amongst those who gained seats in 1906, it must, nevertheless, have been far from clear to the electorate what the agenda of a Liberal government would be. Indeed, the Liberal Party had no clear-cut programme of social reform, while retrenchment had figured prominently in most Liberals' electoral addresses. Campbell-Bannerman in his election manifesto stressed the

20. It was not possible for an individual to join this new party. As with the LRC, it continued to be made up of affiliated organizations.
21. See P. F. Clarke, 'The Progressive Movement in England', *Transactions of the Royal Historical Society*, 24, 1974.

'time-honoured principles of Liberalism—the principles of peace, economy, self-government and civil and religious liberty'.

An alternative explanation is that the election result was due to a temporary mix of contingent factors which turned a Unionist defeat into a major loss of seats. If it had been the Liberals who had been divided in 1900, it was the Unionists who went into the 1906 election with major divisions. The three-way split which followed Joseph Chamberlain's conversion to tariff reform was deeply unsettling to Unionist supporters, even in seats where rival Unionist candidacies were avoided. Tariff reform aroused the fervent opposition of the most half-hearted Liberal and this, together with the irritation of the Education Act, created a final crusade for the old Liberal causes of support for free trade and nonconformity. Balfour did not handle the crisis within his party well and the Unionist cause was not helped by Home Rule for Ireland, usually an electoral handicap for the Liberals with British voters, not being an issue at the election. The tactic of resigning in order to expose Liberal divisions backfired, when the prospect of office was attractive enough to bring about Liberal unity.[22]

The impact of the Labour Representation Committee, which reformed itself as the Labour Party after the election, made little difference to the result. Balfour's philosophic detachment may have deserted him when he thought he detected ripples from socialist revolutionary activity on the continent in the election of some 29 LRC MPs: 'what is going on here is a faint echo of the same movement which has produced massacres in St Petersburg, riots in Vienna, and Socialist processions in Berlin' but he showed foresight when he felt that the development would lead to 'the break-up of the Liberal Party'.[23] That we know that the coming of a formally independent group of Labour MPs was to be of great importance in the long run should not obscure the fact that such MPs were thought of by most contemporaries as just a pressure group within the Liberal tent.[24] The Gladstone–MacDonald entente obscured for the time being the potential threat that Labour posed to the Liberals, though some more traditional Liberals were worried. As it turned out, the Liberals had no real need of the secret pact with Labour, which had largely been a consequence of their lack of confidence in their chances of gaining a clear victory over the Unionists. Out of the 29 LRC candidates elected in 1906, 24 won by virtue of Liberal withdrawals. The Liberals had given the new political party a place in Parliament.

The impact of the 1906 election was greater even than its numerical result indicated. In the previous twenty years there had been an increasing move of the right wing of the old Gladstonian Liberal Party into the Unionist fold. This had been well illustrated by the 419–41 majority in the House of Lords against the

22. The most detailed study of the 1906 election is A. K. Russell, *Liberal Landslide: The General Election of 1906* (1973).

23. Young, *Arthur James Balfour* (1963), 255.

24. An authoritative account of the Labour Party's development and influence is Duncan Tanner's *Political Change and the Labour Party 1900–1918* (1990).

second Home Rule Bill in 1893. The Unionists had come to embrace not only the old Conservative governing groups but also much of what had earlier been Whig. The rejection of the Unionists not only involved the fall from power of forces which had dominated the political situation in recent years, but the setting aside of groups long accustomed to holding power in Britain.

True, it was a relative rather than an absolute shift. The Liberal Cabinet formed in December 1905 still included a substantial minority of aristocratic elements, including six peers; the new Prime Minister was himself possessed of a substantial inherited fortune. Nevertheless, the Liberal majority contained more than 200 new MPs, many of them concerned-to break the mould into which they conceived British politics had set since the Home Rule crisis in 1886. Two characteristics of the 377 Liberal MPs were the number of nonconformists, 157, and of those who could be loosely termed 'professional' (85 lawyers, 25 writers and journalists, 9 teachers, and 5 doctors). Property and wealth continued to be well represented for the parliamentary party 'included amongst its ranks 57 landowners, 97 manufacturers, 47 large merchants and financiers and 12 newspaper proprietors. Bankers, colliery owners, shipping magnates and men famous in every sphere of commerce were well to the fore'.[25] One effect of the election result and the subsequent policies of the Liberal governments was that political life became more impassioned and bitter.

The new government

The government, immensely strengthened by its election victory, fulfilled two of the requirements for a powerful ministry: a large majority in the Commons and a Cabinet reflecting most shades of opinion in that majority. Whether it fulfilled another requirement, a consensus as to policy, had yet to be seen and was not to be discerned immediately. At first, retrenchment and the rewarding of interest groups, such as nonconformity and the trades unions, were the main domestic policies. Foreign affairs were the concern of only a minority of ministers. Important foreign and defence decisions were hidden from the majority of the Cabinet.

In the immediate aftermath of its sweeping electoral victory the Liberal government led by Sir Henry Campbell-Bannerman seems to have had little conception of what use it should make of its triumph. It was not yet clear whether the Liberal Party was to adhere to Gladstonian principles of limited state intervention and cheap government or emerge as a party committed to the extension of collectivism at the price of higher taxation. The Cabinet reflected the different strands of opinion within the Liberal Party but what its members could agree about save for free trade was uncertain.

In its early months of office some of the measures of the new government represented proposals which were being prepared in government departments

---

25. Peter Rowland, *The Last Liberal Governments* (1968), 33.

before the resignation of Balfour's government. Where the government differed from the policies of the previous ministry, it was not always conspicuously wise or successful. The concession in February 1906 of self-government in the conquered Boer territories paved the way for a Boer takeover of the Union of South Africa after the latter's creation in 1909, and for unintended consequences. The acceptance of a Labour proposal which conferred an exceptionally privileged legal position upon trade unions, in place of ministers' more modest preferences in relation to Taff Vale and kindred matters, was another ill-considered decision. It is still not easy to understand the magnitude of the concessions to the unions embodied in the 1906 Trade Disputes Act, except on the assumption that the Liberal ministers did not understand the implications of their action.[26]

As is usual after 'great political earthquakes', the immediate results seemed inadequate to the most committed of the government's supporters and mildly reassuring to those who opposed the government. Campbell-Bannerman's administration, secure in its enormous majority in the Commons, easily established its authority but had by 1907 little to show by way of legislative achievement. A downturn in the economy during 1907–8 increased unemployment and this made the argument that tariff reform could protect jobs more attractive. Public opinion was increasingly exercised by the threat from Germany and there were demands for a more rapid naval rearmament programme. By-elections demonstrated that the government could be defeated at the polls, with two seats being lost to Labour candidates at Jarrow and Sheffield, while Colne Valley was won by a socialist. The Labour victory in Jarrow was not because of an increased Labour vote but was due to the disintegration of the previous personal vote for Sir Charles Mark Palmer, whose death caused the by-election. His shipyard was the basis of the town and in the election the Unionists contested the seat for the first time, coming second to the Labour candidate, Pete Curran, while there was also an Irish Nationalist candidate.[27] The Colne Valley election produced by far the most left-wing member of the House of Commons in Victor Grayson, who refused to join the Labour Party.[28] In 1908 the Unionists won seven seats including that of Winston Churchill who lost his Manchester constituency in the by-election that followed his promotion to President of the Board of Trade. The Unionists' allies also won control of London County Council.

The Unionists

In 1906 the Unionists were temporarily dazed by their defeat and there were inevitably recriminations. Tariff reformers claimed that full-blooded supporters of their cause had done well and that, if only the party had been united behind

---

26. N. McCord, 'Taff Vale Revisited', *History*, vol. 78, no. 253, June 1993.

27. A. W. Purdue, 'Jarrow politics, 1889–1914: the challenge to Liberal hegemony', *Northern History*, 18 (1982).

28. For Grayson see, D. Clark, *Victor Grayson, Labour's Lost Leader* (1985).

their standard, it could have won. There was little real evidence for this claim. The constituencies where tariff reformers had won tended on the whole to be metal manufacturing towns feeling the effects of European competition,[29] but the British economy as a whole was fairly buoyant and the threat to cheap food proved more of a scare than fear of unemployment. Nevertheless, amongst the depleted number of Unionist MPs, the percentage of tariff reformers had increased and they were in a position to press for a firm party commitment to fiscal reform. The 'Valentine Compact', an exchange of letters on 13 February 1906, found both Balfour and Chamberlain agreeing that fiscal reform 'is, and must remain, the first constructive work of the Unionist Party'. Had Chamberlain not been incapacitated by a stroke some months after the election, it is likely that he would have been able to hold Balfour to this agreement but, as it was, Balfour not only continued as leader but was able to put his own interpretation on the 'compact'. Dissensions were muted but they were still there. Chamberlain had streaked across the British political scene like a meteor bringing division and electoral disaster first to the Liberals and then to the Unionists; now his voice was silenced but his followers and his sons still pressed his final cause and tariff reformers continued to consolidate their position in the party organization.

The Unionists, vastly outnumbered in the Commons, possessed a potent weapon in the Lords, though it was one that was dangerous to use against any popular piece of legislation. Balfour had declared in January 1906 that 'the great Unionist Party, should still control, whether in power or in opposition, the destinies of this great Empire'. The Unionists proceeded to use their majority in the Upper House, but cautiously. By confining the Lords' rejection of government bills to those which excited Liberal partisans but left the country as a whole cold, they robbed the Liberals of the chance of asking for a dissolution and then fighting an election over the blocking power of the Upper House. They allowed the Trades Disputes Bill to go through unimpeded so as not to offend the labour movement but threw out or mutilated by amendments bills relating to education, licensing, and land.

Political divisions

Edwardian politics were characterized by conflicting ideological currents which divided all political parties. Liberal Imperialists shared with most Conservatives and Liberal Unionists beliefs on the Empire, foreign affairs, and defence, and for the need for empire and nation to become more efficient if they were to face the challenges of the twentieth century. They included Asquith at the Treasury, Sir Edward Grey at the Foreign Office, and Haldane at the War Office. This ensured some continuity with the foreign and defence policies of the previous government. The old Liberal retrenchment financial beliefs were weakened not

---

29. Marsh, *Joseph Chamberlain*, 627.

434 Political developments, 1880–1914

only by greater support for social reform within Liberal ranks, and within other parties too, but also by demands for increased defence spending. In a dangerous world, pressure for a bigger and more efficient army and for the maintenance of British sea power in the face of German rivalry was impossible to resist. There was broad agreement that the State could and should do more to nurture a healthier and better-educated population even if this meant greater public expenditure, but no such agreement as to whether this should be financed by tariff reform or increased direct taxation.

Within parties tensions continued. Unionist divisions over tariff reform were obvious enough, including strong opposition in Lancashire, an important Unionist stronghold for many years, but a county which had many factories dependent on raw cotton imports. Some Unionists were hostile to State interference and some disliked the social implications of aspects of the Liberal government's army and navy reforms. Others were keen supporters of improved defence and measures to improve social conditions. The divisions within the Liberal Party during the Boer War were not completely healed. Many Liberal businessmen feared the consequences of increased taxation and greater trade union influence. Where Liberal nonconformists supported some social reforms, their motives were different from those of Liberal Imperialists. The Labour Party, as the LRC became in 1906, was divided between those who pressed for socialism and those who saw themselves as the political voice of the trades unions.

The Asquith ministry

In the first period of Liberal government the Unionists appeared to be regaining ground and the new government's achievements were limited and reactive. For instance, it was a Labour initiative, which the Liberals accepted, which allowed local authorities to provide school meals for undernourished children. The resignation of the terminally ill Sir Henry Campbell-Bannerman in April 1908 and the succession of Asquith saw the government seize back the initiative. That a change of Prime Minister from the moderately radical Campbell-Bannerman to the Liberal Imperialist Asquith[30] led to a dramatic shift in government policy towards social reform and higher taxation reveals the difficulty of dividing Edwardian politics into a simplistic divide between right and left. The social reform legislation was devised for a mixture of motives. There was an element of humanitarianism and a degree of political calculation in the hope of electoral profit. There was also the belief that social reform would make for a more efficient society and one able to provide leadership for the Empire. Asquith had argued earlier that domestic reform was 'a question of social and Imperial efficiency'. The government profited from its success in focusing public attention on the question of taxation.

30. Two biographies of Asquith are: Roy Jenkins, *Asquith* (1964) and Stephen Koss, *Asquith* (1976).

Asquith's succession to the premiership saw ministerial changes which strengthened the government, notably the move of Lloyd George to the Exchequer and Winston Churchill to the Board of Trade. Asquith had advocated old-age pensions in earlier years and made some provision for it in his last Budget as Chancellor. The concept had been under discussion for at least a decade, but the time had not seemed right in view of such temporary factors as the high cost of the South African War. The principle of pensions for the aged poor, a social group unable to help itself adequately, was relatively uncontroversial and the Unionists did not oppose it. Despite the reputation for sound finance he had gained as Chancellor, Asquith's estimates of the possible costs proved to have been over-optimistic and pensions were much more expensive that he had envisaged.

Otherwise the Prime Minister took little part in the drafting of the social reforms which were to be one of the main claims to fame of his ministry. Lloyd George and Churchill were responsible for proposals which were novel in the early twentieth-century context, including a major scheme of National Insurance against illness and unemployment and the establishment of publicly funded Labour Exchanges to facilitate labour mobility.[31] In addition a Children's Act (1908) codified much earlier piecemeal legislation and extended the powers of the State to protect children against parental neglect and ill-treatment. The trio of Old Age Pensions (1908), Labour Exchanges (1909), and the National Insurance Act (1911) were significant moves in the direction of greater State intervention in the lives of the mass of the working population, although their immediate impact was limited by various restrictions and limitations in their coverage. Churchill, in his new Liberal incarnation, having left the Unionists over tariff reform, was now a full-blooded advocate of social reforms financed by increased taxation. Lloyd George, a more pragmatic individual, saw and grasped the way in which such reforms provided a great opportunity for a popular political initiative.[32]

It may seem natural to assume that these innovations would have the enthusiastic backing of the trades unions and the mass of working-class voters. In practice the Labour Party, heavily influenced by the trades unions, was never easy with the Liberal social reform agenda, which offered workers social improvement via other agencies. Labour leaders backed old-age pensions but were suspicious of labour exchanges and national insurance provisions. Most trade unionists were already paying for some kind of insurance, often through friendly societies or trade union benefit schemes. Many workers were unconvinced that State involvement would produce significant advances in social welfare.[33]

31. Derek Fraser, *The Evolution of the British Welfare State* (1973), ch. 7, 'Liberal Social Policy, 1905–14', 135–57, provides a clear account of these reforms.

32. For two useful though contrasting accounts of Lloyd George as a social reformer see: John Grigg, *Lloyd George, the People's Champion 1902–11* (1978) and Martin Pugh, *Lloyd George* (1988). Paul Addison, *Churchill on the Home Front 1900–55* (1992) considers Churchill as a social reformer.

33. For a discussion of the hostility to the State of many working-class people, see H. Pelling 'The Working Class and the origins of the Welfare State' in *Popular Politics and Society in Late Victorian England* (1968).

Lloyd George introduced into the Commons the legislation for pensions which had been devised by Asquith. Its passage was not very contentious and Unionists were not disposed to obstruct the measure. Chamberlain had for long favoured pensions and it was difficult for the Unionists to oppose Lloyd George's proposals especially as a non-contributory scheme had obvious popular appeal even if the initial benefits were distinctly limited in the amounts paid and the groups covered. Those over 70 whose annual income was less than £31.10.0 would receive five shillings weekly, but various limitations on eligibility, such as being in receipt of poor relief or being characterized as criminals or drunkards, reduced the number who qualified initially. Even so, Asquith's estimates of probable numbers were soon greatly exceeded, revealing, according to Lloyd George, 'a mass of poverty and destitution which is too proud to wear the badge of pauperism'. In practice the pensions were not enough to live on comfortably but the possession of this independent income did something to enhance the dignity of the aged poor and may often have made their position in family life more acceptable. Asquith had originally budgeted for an expenditure of £1,200,000 but by 1912 pensions were costing £12 million and the cost continued to rise. Such increase was significant at a time when the government was having to finance other serious expenditure, notably on naval construction. Unionists saw in this increased need for revenue an additional argument for tariff reform but the Liberals, committed to free trade, could only look to increased direct taxation.

Further expenditure was involved in other social measures signalled by the government. The National Insurance Act which reached the statute book in 1911 was divided into two parts. Part I was cleverly devised to conciliate the important vested interests of the friendly societies, the medical profession, and the insurance societies, all of whom were given a role in the statutory system of insurance against ill-health. Under this, wage-earners would contribute 4d. weekly, employers 3d., and the State 2d. to an accumulating fund which would finance medical treatment when needed. 'Approved' societies, including the friendly societies, were to provide the benefits which included a 10 shillings weekly payment and free medical treatment for an insured worker incapacitated by ill-health. Doctors were paid fees depending on the number of 'panel' patients on their lists. No provision for a worker's dependents was included. In this way the State did not act as an exclusive provider of the medical insurance but rather became a contributor and exercised a general supervisory role over the system. Lloyd George, in introducing these proposals, made it clear that he anticipated that the scheme would be extended as soon as possible.

Part II of the 1911 National Insurance Act embodied a selective scheme for insurance against unemployment, for which Churchill deserved much of the credit, although he left the Board of Trade for the Home Office before its final enactment. Again an accumulating insurance fund was established, to which the insured worker and his employer each paid 2½d. and the State added a third to this dual payment. When unemployed, an insured worker could receive

7 shillings a week for a maximum of fifteen weeks. Workers sacked for misconduct would not be eligible for these benefits. Initially the scheme covered workers in trades that were particularly susceptible to fluctuation in employment.
About 2¼ million workers were covered but, once established, the scheme could
easily be extended by simple amending legislation. Although the Unionists
opposed Part I of the Act, Part II proved uncontroversial.

There were other social reforms. In 1909 Churchill established Trade Boards to
enforce minimum wages in the 'sweated industries' where workers were notoriously exploited. Though this measure was undoubtedly well-meant, its effects
were not always those intended. Employers might find it more advantageous to
replace poorly paid workers by machinery rather than pay higher wages with
the result that the attempt to enforce minimum wages might mean that some
workers would receive nothing instead of a pittance. The Shops Act of 1911 gave
shop workers a statutory half-day holiday by compelling shops to close for a half-
day each week.

This series of social legislation paralleled and, in part, caused years of bitter
political crisis. The Unionists were prepared to accept much of the legislation but
not the means the government used to pay for it. To meet the cost of pensions,
national insurance, and labour exchanges together with new warships and
supplements to local government the government was prepared to increase
considerably direct taxation.

It has been suggested that Lloyd George was deliberately baiting a trap for the
opposition when he drew up his 1909 Budget. Certainly his rhetoric advocating
his proposals was deliberately provocative, emphasizing the way he intended to
tax the rich for the general benefit. A sliding scale for income tax made the
wealthy pay more and those with an income of more than £3,000 had to pay a
special additional income tax or super tax. For many years it had been a constitutional convention that the House of Commons held the power of the purse
and that the House of Lords would not amend purely financial measures,
although in theory the right of the Upper House to reject any legislation
remained intact. It seems unlikely that Lloyd George believed initially that the
Unionists in the Lords would take the risk of rejecting a Liberal Budget, even
though the fiscal measures he proposed were in some cases specifically aimed at
certain groups such as major landowners. For many Unionists, the Budget of
1909 was obnoxious on two counts: it suggested that the Liberals could raise the
additional revenue they needed without introducing tariffs; and it targeted the
rich by such devices as taxing the 'unearned increment' brought by development
to landed property (a measure which eventually proved unworkable), which
could be seen as social engineering rather than being strictly financial in scope.
This was only one of a group of proposed new taxes which were unmistakeably
aimed at the landed interest.

It is probable that the government was surprised when it became clear that the
Unionist majority in the Lords might take the extreme step of rejecting the

Budget. One historian has argued that 'The explanation of this extraordinary and quite unexpected result lies not in the budget provisions themselves but in the way the budget became inadvertently the focus of several distinct strands of political passion in 1909.'[34] The Unionists had been doing well in by-elections and were confident that a general election might bring down the government. On 30 November 1909 the Lords rejected the Budget.

This decision led to a hotly contested election early in 1910 and to a constitutional crisis which involved not just the powers of the Lords but also the prerogatives of the monarchy. It also brought the question of Home Rule for Ireland back to centre stage after a period in which the huge Liberal majority obtained in 1906 had enabled the government to delay action on the matter.

The 1910 elections and the Parliament Act

The Liberals and their allies fought the general election of January 1910 on the issue of 'The Peers against the People' with the result that the Unionists gained 116 seats, winning a majority of English constituencies, and the Liberals lost their independent control of the House of Commons. The election results demonstrated a return to normality after the Liberal landslide of 1906. Although the Unionists won more votes than the Liberals, they won back only about half the seats they had lost in 1906. What was also demonstrated was the divide between the south of England where the Unionists won the great majority of votes and seats[35] and the north of England, Scotland, and Wales where the Liberals largely maintained their position. Thereafter, the government depended for its existence on Labour votes and, even more crucially, on the votes of the Irish Home Rulers.

The paradox of this election[36] was that it weakened the position of both main parties for, despite the opposition gains, the government could still win a majority in the new House of Commons and was now determined to reduce the powers of the Lords. One historian has summed up the disastrous outcome of the election for the party which had gained so many seats as follows:

In its actual outcome, the result of the January 1910 general election made the tactical situation as bad as it could be for the Unionists, for the Liberals lost their overall majority and could now continue to govern only on Irish MPs' votes, which ensured that battle would be rejoined with the Lords as the prelude to achieving Home Rule as well as the budget.[37]

34. R. Shannon, *The Crisis of Imperialism, 1865–1915* (1974), 397.
35. In the traditionally Tory county of Sussex, the Liberals had won four of the nine seats in 1906 but did not win a single seat in either of the 1910 elections. We are grateful to Ian Ivatt who is writing a Ph.D. thesis on the politics of Sussex 1900–14 for this information.
36. For a detailed account of the election campaigns of 1910 and an analysis of results see: Neil Blewett, *The Peers, the Parties and the People* (1972).
37. John Ramsden, *An Appetite for power: A History of the Conservative Party since 1830* (1998), 208–9.

The Budget was reintroduced and in April the Lords allowed it to pass, but matters could not be allowed to rest there. The aggrieved Liberals were determined to use the crisis to limit the powers of the Lords to reject legislation. If this was done, the Upper House would no longer be able totally to reject a Home Rule Bill approved by the Commons.

A bill was prepared which would remove the ability of the Lords to impede a financial measure (the Speaker of the Commons was to decide whether a measure was financial or not) for more than a very brief period and reduce their veto on other legislation to a temporary delaying power. In an attempt to offset the overwhelming power thus conferred on the House of Commons, the maximum duration of a parliament was reduced from seven to five years (with the Lords retaining the right to reject any bill which sought to prolong a parliament beyond this term). The preamble to the measure spoke of an intention to replace the hereditary chamber with 'a Second Chamber constituted on a popular basis', an ambition as yet unrealized.

This Parliament Act had still to be passed by the chamber whose powers it would sharply reduce. Most Liberals seem to have assumed that Asquith had already secured from King Edward VII an agreement that, if necessary, he would secure the passage of the bill by the creation of enough Liberal peers to produce the required majority if the Unionists were determined to reject it. In fact the King had given no such promise and the crisis had brought the royal prerogative into the political arena. The King's own advisors were divided in their evaluation of the situation, while Edward was unwilling to place the royal creation of peers at Asquith's disposal unless a further general election confirmed the Liberal government in power.[38]

King Edward died in May and his death gave leading politicians on both sides an opportunity for reflection on the dangers of the charged political atmosphere. It was not just the Parliament Act which concerned them but its almost inevitable consequence, the passage of a Home Rule Bill. The immediate reason for the Constitutional Conference, held between June and late July 1910, was that Unionist miscalculations and Liberal reactions had led to a crisis that no one had wanted. A variety of possible expedients were discussed, including the institution of some kind of federal structure for the United Kingdom generally. The conference was marked by a great deal of backstairs intrigue affecting prominent members of both major parties, but in the end no compromise was possible. The Unionists would not accept Home Rule for Ireland at the cost of sacrificing Ulster Protestants to their hereditary enemies, the largely Catholic Nationalists. If the Liberal ministers abandoned Home Rule, their tenure of office could

---

38. If the concept of the creation of new peers to enable legislation to pass through the Lords recalled the demands on William IV at the time of the Great Reform Act, the possibility of the King dismissing a government with a majority in the Commons and asking the leader of the opposition to form a government recalled King William's decision to call on Peel in 1834. It was, nevertheless, the case that Asquith's request, in reality a demand, was of dubious constitutional propriety.

be speedily terminated by the Irish Nationalist MPs. In the end, Asquith saw that he had no alternative to soldiering on with the Parliament Bill. Though the Constitutional Conference failed, it has been seen as demonstrating that, behind the scenes, the political situation was more fluid than it appeared to be and that a number of senior political figures had a hankering for a coalition (see p. 442).

After much heart-searching and consultation, the new king, George V, now agreed to give a 'contingent guarantee' that, if another general election confirmed the government in power, he would, if necessary, create sufficient Liberal peers to ensure the passage of the Parliament Bill. Another general election in December brought little change in the composition of the House of Commons, although Liberals and Unionists were now equal there, with the Home Rulers still holding the balance of power. When Asquith revealed the understanding the King had given him, the Unionist leadership advised Unionist peers to allow the Parliament Bill to pass in order to avoid the creation of a Liberal majority in the Upper House. At least the peers' remaining powers were worth preserving for the Unionist majority. Unionist peers were advised to leave the House before the crucial vote, and most of them did, but a recalcitrant minority fought to the last and the eventual majority for the Parliament Bill on 10 August 1911 was only 131 to 114. Discredited by recent mistakes and setbacks, Balfour resigned the Unionist leadership in November 1911.

Home Rule to the fore

With the passage of the Parliament Act, the question of Home Rule for Ireland was at centre stage, even though Home Rule had not played a major role in the 1910 general elections. The House of Lords could now only delay for three years the implementation of a Liberal Home Rule measure, while the Liberal dependence on Irish votes made action by the government unavoidable. The Irish Nationalists had maintained the Liberal ministers in office, even though some Liberal policies, including proposals on education and licensing, were unpalatable in Ireland. Now the price had to be paid and a new bill for Home Rule was introduced in 1912. Some old problems reared their heads again in relation to this measure. It provided for an Irish legislature covering all of Ireland, and a reduced Irish contingent to the Westminster Parliament (which could still amend or repeal legislation passed by the Irish Parliament). Control of foreign policy and defence were still reserved to Westminster. Few British politicians supported the Bill enthusiastically.

In Ireland both the Nationalist majority and the northern Protestant minority adopted uncompromising attitudes. Andrew Bonar Law, a Scottish Presbyterian with Ulster connections, who had unexpectedly succeeded to the Unionist leadership after Balfour's resignation, had no hesitation in allying the Unionist Party in Britain with the Ulster resistance to the imposition of all-Ireland Home Rule with its built-in Catholic and Nationalist majority.[39] It could be, and was, argued that the government had no clear electoral mandate for its Home Rule proposals. In 1912 and 1913 the Home Rule Bill proceeded along its parliamentary path in accordance with the provisions of the 1911 Parliament Act. In Ireland both principal groups set up paramilitary organizations which succeeded with gun-running ventures, which produced two opposing armed militias as the bill approached its third parliamentary passage in 1914. Various last-minute schemes for compromise on the position of northern Ireland came to nothing, and the Liberal cabinet had little choice but to continue with the policy of implementing its Home Rule programme after the final parliamentary stages had been completed, whatever the consequences.

At this stage, ministers were responsible for a major misjudgement which gravely affected the situation. If Home Rule was to be enforced, against die-hard opponents in Ulster who were prepared to use force, then the role of the army would be crucial. The War Office raised the question of the position of the numerous army officers from Ulster in the event of any necessary military action to impose an all-Ireland Home Rule solution. It was decided that in such circumstances officers from Ulster would be allowed to disappear from their units during any such enforcement measures and would subsequently be reinstated without penalty. Officers from elsewhere who opposed Home Rule should be invited to say so and would at once be dismissed from the army. In March 1914 steps were taken in accordance with this decision. Among the first units affected was the 3rd Cavalry Brigade in camp at the Curragh, near Dublin. Faced with the government's terms, the brigadier commanding, his three colonels, and the great majority of other officers opted to be dismissed from their commissions rather than be party to the military coercion of Ulster. The army might well have reluctantly obeyed direct orders, but, having been offered these terms, the response at the Curragh was disastrous for the government's Irish policy. Further proceedings of this kind were immediately halted and it seemed that the government's willingness to use the army to enforce Home Rule against armed resistance was no longer viable. A situation of stalemate seemed to have been reached, which was only broken in August by the outbreak of the First World War.

National unity and national efficiency

The years 1901–1914, conventionally the 'Edwardian period' even though King Edward died in 1910, are sometimes seen as a time of relative tranquillity which was brought to a catastrophic close by the outbreak of war. Some have seen these years as a time of tensions. The problem of Ireland, culminating in the

39. R. Blake, *The Unknown Prime Minister: Life and Times of Andrew Bonar Law, 1858–1923* (1955) chs. 7, 9–13.

apparently insoluble crisis of 1914, is only one of the difficulties and political uncertainties that troubled the period.

The nature of the State posed a central question of Edwardian politics. Was the State an institution principally concerned to provide a perimeter within which individuals should enjoy the maximum freedom to exert their own abilities for their own advancement, thereby contributing to the improvement of society as a whole, or should the State play a more active role in providing a complete infrastructure within which individuals should operate? Should such bodies as trades unions and employers' federations be seen as entirely voluntary elements in civil society or should they develop into integral parts of a corporate State? Could Britain and her Empire flourish in the new century without a strong central State serviced by the most skilful, intelligent, and devoted of her citizens? Could the upbringing of children, even their conception, be left to the whims of the individual? Such concerns flew in the face of Victorian political attitudes whether those of Conservatives, conceiving of an organic society, or of Liberals, wishing for a loosely governed association of individuals.[40]

Among modern historians, there are essentially two views of Edwardian politics. One, perhaps a little old-fashioned now, sees a transition to a more democratic and welfare-orientated society in which a 'New Liberalism' paved the way, sometimes supported by the Labour Party which was destined to succeed it. A reactionary Conservative or Unionist Party provided the principal opposition. Another view holds that this is a somewhat superficial analysis, and instead stresses a general groundswell of opinion within a broad spread of elite groups who felt that Britain could not survive without a new harnessing of national energy and ability. In this view the old divisions, old parties, and hostility between classes could and should be overcome by cooperation between classes, and between expert and talented groups working together.

Despite their differences, tariff reformers, Liberal Leaguers, Fabians, and eugenicists[41] had a great deal in common. Above all, they concurred on the need for an efficient State and society which would enable nation and empire to face the challenges of the new century. The Constitutional Conference of 1910 had hinted at such a consensus with some of those who were most zestful in the battle between parties, including Lloyd George, F. E. Smith, and Winston Churchill, most attracted to the idea of coalition, while the Lloyd George Coalition during the First World War saw it realized.[42]

40. See G. R. Searle, *The Quest for National Efficiency, 1902–11* (1971).

41. Eugenicists held that breeding was too important to national well-being to be left to chance. It was important to encourage the brightest and fittest to have children and to discourage the lower strata of society, who were such because less intelligent, from having large families. It was especially important to prevent the mentally or physically deficient, especially when there was evidence that their failings might be hereditary, from reproducing their deficiencies.

42. See Robert J. Scally, *The Origins of the Lloyd George Coalition: The Politics of Social Imperialism, 1900–1918* (1975).

Foreign policy

Since the eighteenth century, it had never been easy to distinguish between Britain's relations with the other European powers and her need to protect her worldwide interests. By the early twentieth century the need to align and reconcile foreign and imperial policy and to provide for apposite military and naval power to further both had become urgent. For many years British policy-makers were somewhat distanced, though concerned, as the major European powers arranged themselves in alliance systems from which Britain stood apart, but they were increasingly worried as European rivalries were exported to Africa, the Middle East, and Asia. There were those who considered that Britain's response should be forceful and dynamic, proof that in a Social Darwinist scenario this was a virile nation, and there were radicals, opposed to any great adventures, who favoured a pacific foreign policy.

The great moderating influence until 1902 was Salisbury, perhaps the most conservative of British leaders, who appreciated both the strength and limitations of British power, saw Britain as a power with few needs other than to maintain her position, eschewed excessive expenditure because of the effect high taxation would have on the social order, and refused to get excited about setbacks or minor humiliations, which others saw as crises. Above all, he saw no need to buttress Britain's position by seeking allies, considering that 'isolation' served Britain well enough and that the advantages of alliances were outweighed by the obligations that came with them.

The standard view of the development of British policy between 1900 and 1914 sees the dangers of isolation brought home to Britain's leaders by continental hostility during the Boer War and by Germany's naval programme, which seemed designed to make Germany a rival of Britain as a naval power. The Anglo-Japanese Alliance of 1902 and then the *Entente Cordiale* with France of 1904 and the *Entente* with Russia in 1907 were the result. By 1905 a permanent sub-committee of the Committee of Imperial Defence had the remit of considering the technical problems of combined operations with the French and Admiral Fisher was thinking up wild plans for operations in the Baltic and 'Copenhagening' the German fleet. Owing in part to the pro-French views of influential officials in the Foreign Office and to a continuum of policy between Balfour's government and its Liberal successor, Britain grew ever closer to France. By 1914, though there were no treaty obligations, the military and naval staff talks between the British and the French had, without the knowledge of many Cabinet members, virtually committed Britain to go to the aid of France in a war with Germany.

An alternative view is that Lord Lansdowne, Salisbury's successor as Foreign Secretary, never really departed from his predecessor's policies. The Anglo-Japanese Alliance was restricted to a particular Asian sphere and solved a number of British problems, while the *Entente* was a resolution of Franco-British colonial problems. It was the next Liberal Foreign Secretary, Sir Edward Grey, who turned the *Entente* into an anti-German and pro-French agreement, added regular Franco-British military staff-planning to the mix, and led Britain away from the flexible foreign policy of Salisbury and Lansdowne towards a firm commitment to France.[43] In this he was assisted and in part persuaded by Foreign Office officials and generals; the constitutional thesis that politicians make decisions and civil servants and army chiefs carry them out has not invariably been the case in practice. The frenetic and impulsive foreign policy initiatives of Imperial Germany, which considered that the best way to secure an understanding with Britain was to probe British weaknesses, were counterproductive. Instead, with astonishing rapidity, an influential core of British diplomats and senior army officers[44] became convinced of the need to support the latter-day enemy, France, and the power which had been seen as the greatest threat to the British Empire, Russia.

Germany's erratic foreign policy played its part in pushing Britain closer to France. The Moroccan crises of 1905 and 1911 were the result of the German government's belief that an aggressive attitude towards France's position in Morocco would weaken the *Entente* but this had the opposite effect and persuaded the British that they had to be seen publicly to support France. An important effect of the 1911 crisis caused by the despatch of the German cruiser, *Panther*, to the Moroccan port of Agadir was that Lloyd George and Winston Churchill, not hitherto associated with Grey's and the Foreign Office's support for France, came out strongly against German ambitions.

By 1914, the conviction that Germany aimed for a European hegemony and that Britain was bound to support France had become military and diplomatic common sense and, despite the fact that most Liberal MPs and the majority of ministers did not share it, was to prove decisive in Britain's decision to go to war. What is striking is that until the early days of August 1914 such matters were not discussed in Parliament.

Defence

Defence followed awkwardly in the wake of the diplomacy it was meant to support. We can distinguish the outlines of a division between 'Continentalists', who considered that Britain needed European allies and the ability to place an army in Europe in the event of war, and those who felt that Britain's fundamental interests lay outside Europe and that the Royal Navy provided sufficient protection. This divide had a long history. There was little consensus on strategy between the army and navy.

43. John Charmley, *Splendid Isolation? Britain and the Balance of Power 1874–1914* (1999).
44. Prominent amongst Foreign Office officials who took this view were Eyre Crow, Louis Mallet, Francis Bertie, and Arthur Nicolson, while General Sir Henry Wilson was a perennial supporter of close coordination with the French military.

It is difficult to escape the conclusion that it was German naval plans that cemented British support for France. British strategic thinking mirrored Germany's. Germany was a major military power and her naval programme was a challenge, which brought her onto a collision course with Britain, the major naval power, for whom plans for an expeditionary force in Europe were a departure forced on her by Germany. The logic of Germany's ambitions to become a great naval power should have led her to improve her relations with Russia and reduce the extent of her support for Austria–Hungary but this was a course German leaders could not accept. It was this attempt to be both the major military power in Europe and a naval power threatening British naval supremacy that led to war in 1914.

In fact the disposition of political forces in Germany made it impossible to decide on one rational course or another. The emperor and Tirpitz and the powerful Navy League would never concede defeat for their naval plans ... On the other hand the Germans would never accept the logical Bismarckian corollary of this: good relations with Russia and refusal to support Austria.[45]

It was much easier to persuade British opinion to accept the need for a large and powerful navy than it was to gain acceptance for increased expenditure upon the army. The navy was seen, even by radicals, as essential to defence and a guarantee of freedom and liberty, while the army, though lionized at times of national emergency, was in general less favourably regarded.

Admiral Fisher, the First Sea Lord between 1904 and 1910, reacted to the German threat by redistributing naval forces and creating a formidable 'Home Fleet'. The launching of HMS *Dreadnought* in 1906 marked a considerable development in naval design and technology but the Dreadnought class of battleships had the effect of making all other battleships virtually obsolete, thus wiping out much of Britain's existing supremacy. In 1908 there was considerable concern over the speed of German naval construction and after much argument and a spirited press campaign eight battleships were ordered.

The size of the British Army was limited, not just by confidence that Britain was protected by the navy but by overwhelming opposition to conscription. Haldane's reforms were probably the best that could be done in the circumstances. The army's command was reorganized under a general staff; an expeditionary force of six infantry divisions and one cavalry division was created; and a territorial reserve formed out of the yeomanry and volunteers. Even then, the pretence had to be maintained that the expeditionary force was not necessarily meant for intervention on the continent.

During the Agadir crisis of 1911, when the Germans, who had perfectly valid reasons for opposing a French takeover of Morocco, overplayed their hand by sending a cruiser, *Panther*, to Agadir, plans for war were firmed up. At a meeting

45. R. Shannon, *The Crisis of Imperialism 1865–1915* (1974), 427.

of the Committee for Imperial Defence on 23 August attended by an inner circle of ministers (Asquith, Grey, Haldane, Lloyd George, McKenna and Churchill) a plan to transport the expeditionary force to France was imposed upon a reluctant navy. These military preparations paralleled the tough diplomatic stance reflected in Lloyd George's Mansion House speech, which implicitly warned the Germans that France enjoyed the support of Britain.

Ministers opposed to a close understanding with France had not been told of the CID meeting but soon found out and managed to have a resolution passed by the Cabinet that, 'no communications should take place between the General Staff and the Staffs of other countries which can, directly or indirectly, commit this country to military or naval intervention'. Asquith, nevertheless, allowed military exchanges to continue.

In early July 1914, ministers were more worried about the Irish situation than about the emerging European crisis. Even when Grey informed the Cabinet on July 24 that Serbia, rather than capitulate to Austro-Hungarian demands, would fight, that Russia would come to her assistance, and that it was likely that Germany and France would be drawn into a general war, Asquith wrote that although Armageddon was close, 'Happily, there seems to be no reason why we should be anything more than spectators.' A major reason why Britain did not remain a spectator and declared war on Germany on 4 August was that the Cabinet found itself constrained by tacit agreements and military plans known only to some of its members. Foreign Office staff and army generals had been more influential in determining Britain's obligations than the Cabinet as a whole or the Liberal members of the Commons.

The historical consensus has for long been that, whatever the errors made by politicians on the road to war, Britain could not have stood apart from the First World War and that, whatever the cost, it was in the long-term interests of Britain to see that France was not defeated and that Germany did not dominate Europe. Some recent studies have challenged this consensus[46] but it remains dominant.

---

46. Niall Ferguson, *The Pity of War* (1998); John Charmley, *Splendid Isolation?* (1999).

11

Government and administration
c.1880–1914

The period 1880–1914 ends with a burst of spectacular and radical change in the late Edwardian period which saw a considerable expansion in the role of government. In comparison both with those years and with the pattern of change in public administration in the decades before 1880, the growth of government in the years 1880–1906 is often undervalued, being seen as largely the continuation of trends established during the struggle for the growth of government before 1880.

Many of the changes of the 1880s and 1890s were, indeed, piecemeal and incremental. An example of this is the Mines Acts of 1887 and 1900 which limited the employment underground first of boys under 12 and then of boys under 13. Cumulatively, however, the changes were so extensive that they amounted to much more than a simple development of earlier moves. As early as the 1880s an acute observer noted that 'We are becoming a much governed nation, governed by all manners of councils and boards and officers, central and local, high and low, exercising powers which have been entrusted to them by modern statutes'.[1]

The knowledge on which to base legislation and the ability to implement it successfully depended on previous advances in the machinery of government. These included the development of census techniques, the general growth of official statistics, and the increased use of such information-gathering methods as royal commissions and parliamentary select committees. Without such improvements, much social reform would have been impossible. The coming of old-age pensions in 1909 depended heavily on the existence of accurate certification of age and of a sophisticated post office organization which could act as a network for payment distribution.

The efficiency of government and its place in public esteem continued to improve, even if the level of success with which national and local government tackled the problems of late-Victorian and Edwardian Britain varied greatly. To assume that passing laws and expanding the apparatus of government meant

---

1. F. W. Maitland, *The Constitutional History of England* (1911), 501. The lectures on which this book was based were first composed c.1887–8.

that problems were always successfully countered is an over-simplification which many perceptive contemporaries would not have shared.

The monarchy

Some developments would have been hard to foresee. One was the increased popularity of the monarchy. If the political influence of the Crown had now ebbed considerably, public interest and affection for the monarch and the royal family was increasing. The expanding popular press of the later nineteenth century regularly featured their activities. Princess Alexandra's genuine and active interest in hospitals and nursing was only one example of royal activities which received widespread public notice. Pictures of the Queen and of other members of the royal family adorned the walls of many homes, especially those of the less affluent sections of society. Queen Victoria's Jubilees in 1887 and 1897 gave rise to widespread popular celebrations, while her death in 1901 was seen as the end of an era. This was not simply a tribute to Victoria's longevity, for the interest continued into the next reign too; Edward VII's death in 1910 was to be marked by widespread popular mourning, which reflected that monarch's skill in the public performance of his role in society.

One of Edward VII's great strengths was his realization that the monarchy needed to present itself to its subjects, something which his mother never considered, and that ceremony and grand display were essential to this end.[2] The Jubilees honoured the Queen but she played little part in their organization; even so the contrast of the small dumpy figure of the widow in black, who was the head of the greatest empire in the world, set against the magnificent uniforms of her subordinates, was a compelling image.

There was a general tendency for governments to arrange public ceremonies and parades in order to project the image of nations. State capitals were turned into fitting stages for such theatre. London was no exception and its public buildings became monumental while the central stage for the celebration of the State and monarchy was created by 'the widening of the Mall, the building of Admiralty Arch, the re-fronting of Buckingham Palace and the construction of the Victoria Monument in front'.[3] Kings, robed or in uniform, made better centrepieces than frock-coated presidents or prime ministers and Edward cut an impressive figure.

The reign of Queen Victoria saw a marked decline in the political power of the monarchy, even if the Queen never admitted this, but the royal prerogatives remained important and royal action was still a legal requirement for a great variety of official business. In the late 1880s the constitutional historian

---

2. See David Cannadine, 'The Context, Performance and Meaning of Ritual: The British Monarchy and the "Invention of Tradition"', c.1820–1977', in E. Hobsbawm and T. Ranger (eds.), *The Invention of Tradition* (1983), 101–64; and D. Starkey, 'The modern monarchy: rituals of privacy and their subversion' in *The Monarchy: fifteen hundred years of British tradition* (1998), 248–68.

3. David Cannadine, 'The British Monarchy, c.1820–1977', *The Invention of Tradition*, 128.

F. W. Maitland pointed out that if the Queen were to lose the use of her hand for a month this would cause serious problems for the administration of official business. He also drew attention to the great mass of important public documents which the Queen regularly received and considered.[4]

King Edward, though accepting that his political powers were limited, was determined to maintain his prerogatives and felt that, especially in foreign policy and defence, he was entitled to exert influence. In 1910 he refused to give assurances to Asquith that he would create sufficient Liberal peers to allow the Parliament Bill to pass through the House of Lords. He insisted that a further general election would be needed before he would give his consent and even considered calling upon Balfour to form an administration. King Edward died before the Parliament Act crisis reached its culmination.

In foreign affairs Edward VII sometimes took independent initiatives, even if these paralleled his government's policies. His extended European tour in 1903, during which he visited Lisbon, Rome, and Paris, was a breach of the normal protocol in that it was arranged by his great friend the Portuguese Ambassador, the Marquis of Soveral, while neither the government, his private secretary, nor Queen Alexandra was informed in advance. The visit to France was the highlight of the tour and made Edward popular in Paris. It has been seen as important in preparing the way for the Anglo-French *Entente* agreed by politicians and diplomats in the following year.[5] Cambon, the French Ambassador to London, thought the King's role crucial: 'any clerk at the Foreign Office could draw up a treaty, but there was no-one else who could have succeeded in producing the right atmosphere for a *rapprochement* with France.'[6]

Edward's son and successor, George V, was the first monarch to confine himself largely to Walter Bagehot's view of the duties of a constitutional monarch, 'to be consulted, to encourage and to warn', though even he would play a more positive role when it came to the formation of governments later in the century. The new King inherited the crisis over the Parliament Bill and, like his father, took the line that he was not compelled to place the prerogative of creating peers at the prime minister's disposal without a general election mandate supporting the government's plan. His own advisers were not agreed on the correct course, and he may not have been aware that Balfour would have been prepared to try to form an alternative government if asked. It seems clear that the King's eventual agreement to accept Asquith's request was the wisest course to take. A second occasion in which the royal prerogative was brought into political immediacy came in 1912, as the Irish Home Rule Bill continued its parliamentary progress. The Unionist leader,

---

4. Maitland, *The Constitutional History of England*, 397, 408. Two other studies of the monarchy are J. A. Cannon and R. Griffiths, *The Oxford Illustrated History of the Monarchy* (1988); J. M. Golby and A. W. Purdue, *Kings and Queens of Empire* (2000).

5. See Gordon Brook-Shepherd, *Royal Sunset* (1987), 250–1.

6. Quoted in Simon Heffer, *Power and Place: The Political Consequences of King Edward VII* (1998), 163.

Bonar Law, bluntly told the King that the passing of the 1911 Parliament Act, which left the House of Lords with only a temporary veto over a Home Rule measure, had raised the question of the royal veto over legislation. He argued that it was ministers' duty to the sovereign to ensure that they had acquired such an electoral mandate for this purpose by fighting a general election on the issue. Well aware of the likely electoral verdict, Liberal ministers would never have accepted that course. In the absence of such a mandate, Bonar Law contended, the King would be justified in finding ministers who would support him and then vetoing the bill. The perils of such an action were obvious from Bonar Law's further comment that 'in either case, half your subjects will think you have acted against them'[7] and the worried monarch contented himself with urging Asquith to compromise.

Both Edward VII and George V considered that they had a special relationship with the armed forces and exhibited sympathies for both individual senior officers and for military and naval policies, though these never led to serious clashes with ministers. Uniquely in the annals of the dynasty, father and son were on friendly terms, but naval affairs produced one element of friction between King Edward and his heir. Edward warmly supported Admiral Fisher in his naval reforms, while George was a warm admirer of one of Fisher's most vociferous opponents, Admiral Lord Charles Beresford.

George's succession saw changes in the tone and style of monarchy. Edward was very much a European, conscious of his links with the intermarried royal families of Europe and happy to spend much of his time in continental resorts and spas. George V identified himself much more exclusively with Britain and with the Empire. The Indian Durbar of 1911 at which the new King-Emperor was acclaimed by his Indian satraps and subjects was symbolic of the change of direction. George's exemplary, if rigid, domestic life contrasted with that of his father and marked a return to the propriety of Albert and Victoria and the notion of a family monarchy. This was another phase in the long oscillation between determined respectability and colourful pleasure-seeking which has marked the British monarchy for many generations. Edward's robust appetite for pleasure and comfortable self-confidence appealed to a population, most of which continued to accept the social and moral proprieties of the nineteenth century, while wanting to have more fun. Those sections of the working classes who were fond of the variety theatre and the racecourse may have regretted that the new King was less fond of these pursuits than his father, while much of high society found George V and his consort a bit dull, even if few went as far as Max Beerbohm:

> Last evening
> I found him with a rural dean
> Talking of District Visiting...
> The King is duller than the Queen.[8]

---

7. H. Nicolson, *George V: His Life and Times* (1952), 200–1.
8. Max Beerbohm, *Ballade Tragique a Double Refrain.*

George's dull worthiness had its appeal to important sections of pre-war society and would come into its own as a positive asset after the Great War.

As the political power of the monarchy declined, its social influence grew. The 'Court' had only ever been for the aristocracy and gentry but the determination of royalty to make its mark on wider circles by visits to provincial towns and by taking on honorific positions at the head of charities and other worthy causes gave the monarchy a leadership of civil society that was to endure into the twenty-first century.[9]

Prime Minister and Cabinet

The predominance of the Prime Minister in the British political system was now firmly established. The wider electorate and greater literacy brought the principal political figures into a prominence unknown in the days of Lord Liverpool. The leaders of the main political parties, the actual or potential premiers, received unprecedented publicity. Party conferences, national political organizations, and local political parties were conducted in ways which fostered the personal importance of the leaders of government and opposition. A belated recognition of these developments came at the end of 1905, when for the first time the office of Prime Minister was accorded a settled official precedence. Previously the formal precedence accorded to a Prime Minister had depended either upon his own rank in society or upon some other ministerial post held in addition to the premiership. Yet the Prime Minister's pre-eminence in government still depended upon collective Cabinet acceptance of that leadership and the choice of ministers had to be made with some recognition of the strength of factions within the parliamentary party. Gladstone's last premiership and the experiences of Rosebery and Balfour showed that there were practical limits to a Prime Minister's authority.

In some ways the collective authority of the Cabinet increased in these years. The government's control of proceedings in Parliament was extended. Governments were increasingly expected to pilot through programmes of beneficial legislation, and this required the allocation of requisite amounts of time in both Houses. Obstructive tactics by Irish Nationalists and other refractory political groups led to the adoption of emergency procedural devices to allow Parliament to function effectively. This process began in the last months of Disraeli's second government in 1880, when a new Commons Standing Order gave committee chairmen power to suspend individual MPs. A more dramatic step came in the following year, when Irish obstruction prolonged debate on a Coercion Bill from 3.45 p.m. on 31 January until 9.30 p.m. on 2 February. Then

---

9. F. Prochaska, *Royal Bounty: The Making of a Welfare Monarchy* (1995) describes the way the monarchy since the late eighteenth century has put itself at the head of charitable causes and established a leadership in civil society.

Government and administration, c.1880–1914

the Speaker, on his own responsibility, ended the debate and enforced a vote. The Liberal majority subsequently amended Standing Orders to approve this initiative and provide for similar actions in future. In 1887 the ending of formal debate by a 'guillotine' resolution was introduced. With the Speaker's consent, a resolution ending discussion on a proposal could be moved; if it passed, a vote would be taken without further debate. In 1902, obstructive tactics during debate on the government's Education Bill produced a further device, a timetable resolution limiting the amount of time allowed for debate on various parts of a bill.[10] These innovations were initially responses to the deliberate obstruction of parliamentary procedures by opposition groups. Without such urgency, they would have aroused more hostility from MPs. Once adopted as emergency expedients, these measures furnished governments with procedural machinery which could be used to ensure the enactment of other legislation. By 1906, the government had gone far in consolidating its control of parliamentary business. Some compensation for individual MPs was derived from an increasing use of questions to ministers. This practice was not new, but had not been much used. By 1900 it had become a regular technique for backbenchers, with several thousand questions put to ministers in the House of Commons each year.

Campbell-Bannerman and Asquith were both competent prime ministers when it came to holding together cabinets composed of disparate elements together. In Edwardian terms the former, a radical of a traditional kind, was a middle-of-the-road Liberal who was a capable and shrewd chairman. His successor, who had been a successful Chancellor of the Exchequer, also proved adept at smoothing divisions while presiding over a Cabinet which included highly charged personalities of considerable ability. The success of both was facilitated by two factors. The Liberal governments were highly compartmentalized, with secretaries of state looking after their own departments without too much interference from other ministers (this disguised major differences especially when it came to foreign policy and defence). The Gladstonians, Loreburn, Morley, Bryce, and Harcourt, whose views probably represented those of most backbenchers, were amongst the Cabinet's weakest members; had they been more forceful, they might well have been able to persuade a majority of ministers to favour a more Gladstonian foreign and defence policy.

Asquith was wise in making skilful use of the two mercurial members of the cabinet who couldn't easily be categorized. Lloyd George and Winston Churchill have been described as not belonging to 'any easily definable species of Liberal. They were statesmen of genius in search of great roles to play in politics'.[11] The Asquith–Lloyd George alliance was a major reason for the strength of the Asquith government. The collapse of this alliance during the First World War was a major cause of Asquith's fall in 1916.

10. D. Read, *England, 1868–1914* (1979), 314–16.
11. R. Shannon, *The Crisis of Imperialism, 1865–1915* (1974), 403.

Politicians and parties

If in 1815 parties could hardly be discerned, by the early twentieth century they were the basis of political life. It was all but impossible to embark upon a political career without joining a party.

The independence of individual MPs was reduced, partly by greater government control over parliamentary proceedings, but also by extensions to the franchise and restrictions on electoral expenditure which made candidates more dependent on organized support than in earlier years. The 1883 Corrupt and Illegal Practices Act imposed tight restrictions on candidates' spending on parliamentary elections, increasing dependence on party organizations and such associated bodies as the Primrose League (see p. 413 above). In mid-Victorian years the control of the party leadership over individual MPs had been limited; in late-Victorian and Edwardian years, solid party voting became more frequent, although rebellions by individuals or groups on specific issues were not uncommon. At mid-century, governments had often lost divisions in the Commons a dozen times in a single year, but by the early twentieth century a government defeat was a rare event.

Gladstone's Midlothian campaigns in 1879 and 1880 have been seen as inaugurating a new kind of politics, mass politics. General elections became national with party leaders moving around the country and addressing great audiences. It has been argued that, far from leading to more participation in elections, the Gladstonian mass platform inaugurated a more passive form of politics as compared with the previous more rumbustious politics of the hustings; huge audiences and readerships listened to or read the speeches of leading politicians but there was less real participation.[12] Politics did become more orchestrated but Lloyd George besieged in Birmingham town hall in 1900 by an angry crowds because of his 'Pro-Boer' views would not have complained of lack of participation and, 'down to 1914 volatile meetings and public disruption remained widely accepted as an inevitable, even legitimate feature of a healthy polity.'[13]

More voters meant more political organizing and campaigning. Gladstone's Midlothian campaign had broken the taboo against national electioneering by party leaders but it was the Conservatives who had first accepted that the logic of a mass electorate meant nationwide organization and perpetual electioneering, though they were closely followed by the Liberals. The problem was that having invented nationwide, regional, and constituency organizations, in order to garner votes, the political elites were faced with the claims of these new organizations for influence. The National Union of Conservative Associations was formed in 1869 and the National Liberal Federation in 1879. Who was supposed to be in charge: party leaders, the parliamentary parties, or the party at large?

12. James Vernon, *Politics and the People: A Study in English Popular Politics, c.1815–1867* (1993).

13. Jon Lawrence, 'The Transformation of British Public Politics after the First World War', *Past and Present* 190 (2006), 187.

Factions devoted to particular causes and special interest groups complicated the picture. On the whole the political centre held, though it had to be increasingly alert to the need for some accommodation of the views of its supporters and activists.

There was, more or less, a two party system. The Liberal split over Home Rule in 1885 could, like the Conservative split over the Repeal of the Corn Laws in 1846, have led to a period of political flux but, although the Conservatives and Liberal Unionists remained ostensibly distinct parties for a quarter of a century, they worked together relatively amiably, utilized the common name of Unionists, and eventually fused in 1911. The Liberal Imperialists had never aspired to be more than a Liberal pressure group but the Labour Party did provide the potential for three-party politics, though before 1914 that was all it did provide.

Outside Parliament, the operation of the emerging mass political parties was increasingly expensive. The regular subscriptions of loyal party members were not sufficient to finance all of a party's work. Both Conservatives and Liberals depended on their ability to obtain substantial sums from their wealthier supporters. The temptation to involve the honours system in such relationships was inevitable. It was possible to argue that there was a difference in principle between the acceptance of a gift as an indication of gratitude from someone ennobled on a party's recommendation and the selling of honours in return for subsidies. In practice this was not an easy distinction to maintain. During his last administration, for example, Gladstone was less than scrupulous in his willingness to confer peerages in return for financial support to the Liberal Party.[14] In an age which produced many self-made plutocrats anxious for public recognition, such donors were not difficult to find.[15] On the whole this practice was relatively harmless with benefactors being rewarded with titles and honours but having no influence on party policies, though it did give an advantage to the party in power which controlled the honours list. Perhaps more worrying was the fact that more politicians served as directors of companies which might benefit from political decisions. Lord Selborne was, for a time, Under Secretary at the Colonial Office and a director of the P&O, a shipping company which did business with his department.[16] Widespread unease about ministers' business interests came to a head with the Marconi scandal of 1912–13 when Lloyd George and two other ministers were found to have dealt in shares in the American Marconi Company while the government was negotiating a major empire-wide contract with that company's parent company, the British Marconi Company.[17]

14. Read, *England, 1868–1914*, 319.
15. Wealthy supporters were not confined to the major parties and socialist parties also found millionaire backers. Joseph Fels, a soap manufacturer, consistently gave money to socialist groups. A. W. Purdue, 'George Lansbury and the Middlesbrough Election of 1906', *International Review of Social History*, XVIII (1973), 3.
16. G. R. Searle, *Corruption in British Politics, 1895–1930* (1987), 47.
17. Frances Donaldson's *Marconi Scandal* (1962) provides an authoritative account of the scandal, while G. R. Searle, ibid. 172–200, places it in the wider setting of other contemporary scandals.

The electorate

Electoral arrangements continued until 1914 to be those laid down by the reforms of 1884–5 with the exception that the Parliament Act of 1911 required that no Parliament could last more than five instead of seven years. Although the provisions of the 1884 Reform Act theoretically provided for something just short of universal male suffrage, only about 60 per cent of the adult male population was registered to vote at elections.[18] Only about 10–12 per cent of British adult males were not qualified to vote, but about 30 per cent were excluded in practice by complicated registration procedures and the fact that many had recently changed their addresses.

It has been suggested that the fact that only around 60 per cent of males were on the register as compared with some 95 per cent after the next major reform in 1918 accounts for the failure of the Labour Party to make rapid progress before 1918 and its greater success thereafter.[19] This depends upon the assumptions that those who were not on the register differed markedly from those who were and would have been more likely to vote Labour. It is probable that, instead of a mass of men who were continuously unable to vote, many people dropped off and came back to the registers from time to time because of the registration procedures. There is little to support the assumption that the poorer you were the more likely you were to vote Labour. Among groups formally disqualified by the suffrage rules, soldiers in barracks and living-in domestic servants were widely assumed at the time to be inclined to support Conservatism. Others were disenfranchised because they were living with parents or by the complexities of the lodgers' franchise, but many of these individuals belonged to groups which were neither poor nor underprivileged. The discrimination in the system reflected age and marital status rather than social position.[20] The pre-1918 electorate, with skilled workers in practice forming a high proportion of voters, probably worked to the advantage of a Labour Party closely tied to the trade union movement.[21]

The House of Lords

There were important shifts in the composition of the House of Lords. As the Liberal Party adopted more radical policies, especially in relation to Ireland, the balance of parties within the Upper House changed. For many years there had been a Conservative majority among the peers, but until the late nineteenth century there was also a large body of Whig–Liberal peers, who enjoyed considerable influence in the House of Lords and in the country more generally. The Irish

18. N. Blewett, 'The Franchise in the United Kingdom, 1885–1918', *Past and Present*, Dec. 1965.

19. H. G. C. Mathew, R. I. McKibbin, and J. A. Kay, 'The Franchise Factor in the rise of the Labour Party', *English Historical Review*, xci (1976), 736; and R. I. McKibbin, *The Evolution of the Labour Party, 1910–24* (1975), p. xv.

20. D. Tanner, 'The Parliamentary Electoral System, the Fourth Reform Act and the Rise of Labour in England and Wales', *Bulletin of the Institute of Historical Research*, vol. lvi, no. 134, Nov. 1983.

21. M. Pugh, *The Making of Modern British Politics, 1867–1939* (1982), 142–4.

Home Rule crisis of the mid-1880s brought a marked decrease in their number. Defeating a Home Rule Bill as the Lords did in 1886 because Home Rule for Ireland was not popular with the British electorate, the Lords had to be careful with bills backed by more popular support. By the end of the century, the House of Lords possessed an overwhelming majority of peers from the Conservative and Liberal Unionist Parties, while the Gladstonian Liberal Party in the Upper House numbered fewer than 100. In 1888 both Rosebery and Salisbury had advocated some remodelling of the Upper House to allow for the introduction of a substantial number of life peers, but these initiatives attracted so little support that they were speedily dropped. The inflated right-wing majority among the peers used its powers in a partisan fashion. The House of Lords rarely embarrassed a Conservative administration; the experiences of the weak Liberal governments of 1892–5 demonstrated the peers' willingness to exploit their powers to frustrate much of the legislative programme of a Liberal ministry. At the same time, the representative status of the House of Commons was increasing, especially after the parliamentary reforms of 1884–5. The full consequences of these developments were not to become fully obvious until the political crisis of 1910–11, which led to the clipping of the powers of the Upper House.

After the electoral landslide of 1906, the defeated Unionists deliberately resorted to using the Lords as a brake on the new Liberal ministry. Until 1909 the peers followed this policy with some caution, allowing through such measures as the 1906 Trades Disputes Act and rejecting or mutilating bills which seemed to be without strong support save among Liberal activists. This caution seemed to be working, as the Unionist recovery appeared firm in the first years of Liberal government and there seemed to be little popular resentment at the Lords' actions. This changed with the fateful Unionist decision to use the House of Lords to reject the Finance Bill implementing Lloyd George's 1909 Budget (see pp. 437–8). After the passage of the 1911 Parliament Act the powers of the Upper House were much reduced, though it retained significant functions in scrutinizing legislation and retained a suspensory veto over general legislation. Since 1911 no prime minister has sat in the House of Lords.

The preamble to the Parliament Act envisaged future legislation for a more accountable second chamber. Schemes for implementing this ambition were considered by both Conservatives and Liberals, and later by Labour, but they all foundered. On the one hand, the House of Lords as modified in 1911 worked reasonably well, while the House of Commons was always reluctant to contemplate another elected chamber with possible rival aspirations. It was one thing to reject the hereditary principle but far from easy to find an acceptable replacement.

The women question

Probably because no party perceived a great and certain advantage in it, the subject of enfranchising more male voters was not a vital issue in Edwardian politics, though there was a general acceptance that it should eventually come about. It became entwined in a more contentious matter, the question of votes for women. In 1867 John Stuart Mill had attempted to have women included on the same basis as men with his amendment to the Reform Act; it received a substantial minority vote but it was not until 1918 that women over the age of 30 received the vote in parliamentary elections. In the Edwardian period the women's movement revived and was divided into suffragists, who campaigned peacefully for the vote, and suffragettes who employed militant and illegal methods.

There is little evidence that the majority of women were in favour of their enfranchisement but there was a substantial lobby of middle- and upper-class women who were, while many influential males also supported the cause. The cause of votes for women tended to be most unpopular within the working-classes and was certainly no vote winner with working-class voters, who were, of course, men.[22] The problem for the Liberal government was that a mere amendment to the present electoral system that gave women the vote on the same basis as men might, by enfranchising female householders, bring into being a predominantly Conservative female electorate.

The militant suffragettes, members of Mrs Pankhurst's Women's Social and Political Union, have received rather more attention than the more numerous members of the National Union of Women's Suffrage Societies led by Mrs Millicent Fawcett. The latter organization has been described as 'constitutional, responsible, respectable—and dull'[23] but may have been more effective in promoting the cause than the suffragettes, whose increasingly violent tactics increased opposition to female enfranchisement.

Arguments against female suffrage ranged from the view that women were biologically incapable of consistent rational judgement in political matters to the separate-spheres concept by which women had different talents, interests, and abilities and these were best expressed in the domestic sphere. Many of the women who opposed the suffrage[24] took the latter view but widened the sphere of women from the home to a whole range of social and welfare matters. They could thus argue that as well as charities, local government was an area in which women could and should participate. Some women had already the right to vote in local government elections and to be Poor Law Guardians and in 1907 women became eligible to sit on County Councils. As social and welfare issues were increasingly on the agenda of national politics, however, it became increasingly difficult to support the argument for a confinement to local politics. The real

22. George Lansbury, a prominent socialist supporter of votes for women, found his views an impediment when he stood for predominantly working-class constituencies. He resigned his seat at Bow and Bromley and fought a by-election there in 1912 specifically upon the suffrage issue; he was easily beaten by a Unionist anti-suffragist.

23. M. Pugh, *Electoral Reform in War and Peace* (1978), 17.

24. The list of prominent women who opposed female suffrage includes several of the most individual and independent women of the day: Beatrice Webb; Mrs Humphrey Ward (a leading novelist and her family's main breadwinner); and Gertrude Bell, a much-travelled expert on the Middle East.

victory for the suffragists lay not in gaining popular support, which indeed they probably never succeeded in doing, but in securing the support of much of the elite, the well-educated and the influential.

By 1914 it was clear that what was holding up votes for women was not opposition to the reform itself but qualms over exactly what form enfranchisement should take and how it would affect the balance between political parties. Asquith remained ill-disposed to the whole idea but realized that the majority of the parliamentary Liberal Party was in favour, that the Liberals risked losing female activists, and that he might be 'outflanked by both the Labour and Conservative parties. As a result, the likelihood was that all three parties would have entered the election [which would have had, in normal circumstances, to have taken place before December 1915] with a commitment to votes for women'.[25]

Public expenditure and taxation

The growth of government during these years was reflected in the mounting official expenditure. During the late-Victorian and Edwardian periods, government spending was rising faster than population. In 1881 central government spent about £81 million; in the early twentieth century the figure was approaching £200 million. Local government spending increased in even greater proportion, rising from £36 million in 1880 to nearly £108 million by 1905.[26] By 1890 central taxation and expenditure had, after generations of economy, again reached the level attained in the last wartime years before 1815.[27]

The structure of public income also changed. Direct income and property taxation produced over £9 million in 1880 and then doubled over the next twenty years. Death duties trebled over the same period, to provide more than £18 million by 1900. The rate of increase in indirect taxation was less striking, although most revenue still came from customs, excise, and stamp duties all of which increased between 1880 and 1914. Customs and excise payments provided nearly £45 million in 1880, well over £60 million in 1900. Stamp duties doubled their contribution, to £8.5 million, over the same period. The older system of assessed taxes on land and similar items now made only a small contribution to revenue, well under £3 million annually and effectively static.

Although only a small minority paid income tax, they had some grounds for grumbling at the incidence of this, as yet ungraduated, tax by the early twentieth century. Peel's revival of it, avowedly as a temporary measure, in 1842, had been at the rate of 7d. in the pound. In 1874 the level came down to only 2d. in the pound. Increases in the scale of government spending took it back up to 8d. before the end of the century. The South African War brought a sharp rise to

25. M. Pugh, *The March of the Women* (2000), 283.
26. H. Finer, *English Local Government* (1933), 373–80.
27. N. Gash, *Pillars of Government, and Other Essays on State and Society, c.1770–1880* (1986), 52.

1s. 3d. and similar levels were retained until the First World War. In addition to increases in taxation, the total of the National Debt, somewhat reduced in the late nineteenth century, resumed its rise, to reach well over £700 million by 1906.

The two main items of increased public spending were the armed forces, and welfare provision in various forms. In 1890 defence at nearly £35 million was still in the lead, with welfare costs at over £27 million. In subsequent years both items rose, and welfare rose faster than defence. Expenditure grew against strenuous opposition in both major political parties and among the electorate. There was little public enthusiasm for more and more expensive government. Gladstone's commitment to rigid economy persisted throughout his years of eminence; in October 1886 the new Conservative Chancellor of the Exchequer, Lord Randolph Churchill, asserted that 'my own special object... is to endeavour to attain some genuine and considerable reduction of public expenditure and consequent reduction of taxation.'[28]

Continuing doubts about official competence were among the reasons for opposition to increased taxation. It was widely conceded that the quality of administration generally had improved from a previously low level, but there were still sufficient examples of official fumbling and mismanagement to buttress a widespread disbelief in the efficiency of the State. Many examples of official ineptitude in these years are readily available. In 1890 the Treasury finally agreed to a scheme for police pensions, after fifteen years of negotiation on the issue. The Metropolitan Police first urged the Home Office to buy Scotland Yard in 1878. It took the Home Office eight years to make up its mind to do so, and during that period the purchase price rose from £25,000 to £186,000.[29] The Local Government Board was the focus of much criticism on grounds of delays and inefficiency. Some of this criticism was justified as is demonstrated by the fact that it took the LGB some eight months to decide whether the Gateshead Poor Law Union could pay the licence fee for the workhouse dog without special permission from the Central Board itself.[30] The uses to which official patronage, too, was put could still arouse critical public comment. This extended even to senior judicial appointments, where damaging press comment followed several controversial elevations of political supporters to the bench.[31] It is understandable that the process of extending government activities at the cost of higher taxation did not command widespread enthusiasm. Nevertheless, the activities of government continued to expand.

28. Read, *England, 1868–1914*, 320.

29. T. Critchley, *A History of Police in England and Wales, 900–1966* (1967), 170; D. Ascoli, *The Queen's Peace: The Origins and Development of the Metropolitan Police, 1829–1979* (1979), 167.

30. Documents in PRO, MH 12/3107. Mr Frank Manders has drawn our attention to this example of a cumbersome bureaucracy.

31. For the controversial judicial appointments, J. R. Lewis, *The Victorian Bar* (1982), 129–32. Another example of limited efficiency was provided by the Quarries Act of 1895, under which a series of statistics for that industry was regularly published; the Act arbitrarily excluded all quarries less than 20 ft. deep. P. Ventom, 'The Freestone Quarries of Ackworth, Yorkshire, 1850–1914', MA dissertation, University of Leeds, 1989.

It was increasingly the income tax payers who had to shoulder the burden. Local government expenditure on social services increased by nearly £40 million between 1890 and 1910 but it was the 1 million taxpayers rather than the 8 million ratepayers who paid for most of this via the grants central government made to councils.

The burden on income tax payers became much greater because of the cost of the social measures of the Asquith government. The percentage of revenue gained by indirect taxation, customs and excise and stamp duties, fell rapidly and that which came from direct taxes, income tax and death duties, increased.

Old-age pensions turned out to cost far more than had been estimated. Lloyd George, Chancellor of the Exchequer in 1909, needed to find an extra £16 million in order to pay for pensions and armaments at a time of economic recession. With the Lloyd George Budget, income tax became graduated with three rates depending on the amount of income, while a distinction between earned and unearned income was introduced, with the latter being taxed more heavily. The amount of resentment this engendered amongst the well-to-do was considerable.

Government expansion

The expansion of government, both national and local, continued remorselessly. As well as the need for more regulation in an interdependent and increasingly complex society, there were factors built into the machinery of government itself. The appointment of specialist professionals, doctors, sanitary engineers, and surveyors, to local government posts was paralleled by an increasingly professional approach by other career administrators. Government departments increasingly contained expert civil servants. Despite continued opposition by many ratepayers, local councils, often reluctantly, expanded their responsibilities and staffing.

More information related to policy became available, though the methods used to gather it were rarely new. In discussions of the social problems of these years the social surveys carried out by Booth and Rowntree have been given a prominent place. Those surveys were only the tip of the iceberg. The Local Government Board, if not an administrative paragon, from its inception became the repository of an increasingly detailed mass of reports on local conditions. Although the indexing of this material was not perfect and documents were frequently mislaid, overall there accumulated a store of detailed information. Local Medical Officers of Health would find their annual reports cross-checked against what they had said in previous years; links were made between parallel circumstances in different places.

The collection and publication of official statistics continued to grow. In the early years of the twentieth century preparations were made for the first National Census of Production (actually carried out in 1907). The Board of Trade improved its monitoring of industrial relations, and published a mass of evidence on wages and prices, including international comparisons. Governments continued to appoint royal commissions to investigate many issues. A good example is the Royal Commission on Distress from Want of Employment, which in 1895 published a wide range of information on how unemployment was or was not being tackled in various localities. A similar inquiry in 1893 provided evidence of poor living conditions in many rural communities. Royal commissions could, it is true, also be employed to postpone unwelcome problems; this may have been one reason why the Unionist government appointed a royal commission to inquire into trade union law after the celebrated Taff Vale decision of 1901.

Parliaments were now faced with an increasing volume of legislation to be enacted every year, much of it bristling with detail and complexity. Sometimes the effects of particular legislation could have implications not fully appreciated by their creators. Although Local Acts frequently gave local authorities power to regulate housing and tackle slums, such legislation rarely led to constructive results in practice. One reason for this was that the old Land Clauses Consolidation Act of 1845 laid down rules which made compulsory acquisition of property expensive for local ratepayers. A change in these rules, little noticed at the time or later, embodied in the Housing of the Working Classes Act of 1890, went some way to reduce this burden. This was a principal reason why Leeds moved in the 1890s to deal with the notoriously unhealthy slum area of Quarry Hill after years of hesitation and prevarication.[32]

The expansion of government continued under the Unionist administrations between 1895 and 1905 and, after 1907, when Asquith became prime minister, it increased rapidly. Local government played some part in this process of its own accord, but what was more important was the way that central government thrust new responsibilities upon councils. The 1902 Education Act had not only made local authorities responsible for education but had made necessary an increase in central government grants to help pay for this new responsibility. This was a significant addition to growing government supplements to local government for a whole host of purposes which, if they protected ratepayers at the expense of taxpayers, had the effect of limiting the autonomy of local government and its becoming increasingly an instrument of central government.

The expansion of government in the first years of Liberal government was modest. School meals for needy children were subsidized and medical inspection of pupils introduced. Plans for old-age pensions were discussed and by 1907 the Cabinet had agreed to bring in legislation to provide for pensions but it was only when Asquith became prime minister in April 1908 that the Old Age Pensions Bill was introduced and then carried. This together with the setting up of Labour Exchanges and the National Insurance Act which followed represented a major expansion of the State (see pp. 435–7). The number of State employees grew as

32. B. Barber, 'Municipal government in Leeds, 1835–1914', in D. Fraser (ed.), *Municipal Reform and the Industrial City* (1982), 100–1.

a consequence. Between 1891 and 1911 there was an increase from 83,000 to 130,000 of those employed by central and local government in England and Wales.[33]

Administration in Scotland

In many ways administrative progress in Scotland shadowed that of England and Wales with the Poor Law gradually becoming similar in its responsibilities (see pp. 333 above and 466 below) and police forces being made obligatory for burghs and counties and subject to inspection by Her Majesty's Inspector of Constabulary. In important areas the general direction of change was similar but was in accordance with Scottish tradition and terminology. Local government was distinctive: from 1833–92 it was possible for a burgh to be governed either by a provost bailies and councillors or by 'Commissioners of Police' (an elective authority which had responsibility for public order, sanitation, and amenities) and magistrates.[34] The combined result of the 1892 Burgh Police (Scotland) Act and 1900 Town Councils (Scotland) Act was to establish a uniform system of burgh Councils under a provost, bailie, and councillors. The development of the counties was much more like that in England and Wales with a system of government by justices of the peace being succeeded as in England by county councils in the same year, 1899, though by a separate Act.

Along with the Law, which remained distinct in most areas from that of England and Wales, and the Church of Scotland, the educational system had been preserved by the Act of Union. The provision of education had for long been superior in Scotland both in its extent and the academic calibre of the staff in burgh and parish schools, though the ease by which the youth of ability could make his way from farmyard to university has been exaggerated. As in England, much of it was provided by the Established Church, in this case the Presbyterian Church of Scotland. In 1872 a new central authority, the Scotch Education Department, was created and popularly elected School Boards on the English model gradually replaced the schools provided by the Presbyterian Church, though Episcopalian and Catholic schools continued as voluntary schools in receipt of government grants.

The establishment of the Education Board followed on the creation of a number of boards with responsibility for such matters as prisons, poor relief, public health, and fisheries in Scotland. The need for a coordinating authority led in 1885 to the important step of the revival of the post of Secretary of State for Scotland, which had not been filled since the eighteenth century, and setting up of a Scottish Office in Whitehall.

33. Between 1891 and 1911 there was an increase from 83,000 to 130,000 of those employed by general and local government in England and Wales. Donald Read, *England, 1868–1914* (1979), 386. In 1902 there were 107, 802 civil servants (excluding industrial grades).

34. Mackie, *A History of Scotland* (1964), 326. The term 'Commissioners of Police' is somewhat confusing and they are not to be confused with Chief Constables, the commanders of police forces, which, after 1857, were obligatory in all burghs and counties.

Compared with those in later periods in the twentieth century the numbers of those directly employed by government prior to 1914 seems modest (the newly formed Scottish Office had only 22 staff in 1900), though in comparison with the mid-Victorian period it represented a considerable expansion. The delivery of services added to the cost of government subsidies to the aged, the sick, and the unemployed, while at the same time defence expenditure increased. To pay for all this, the Liberal government's answer was income tax, progressively graded according to income and to different kinds of income. The answer horrified many traditional Liberals as much as it did Conservatives.

Legislation

By the late-Victorian period the work of Thring and his associates (see pp. 308–9 above) had done much to refine the technical task of drafting legislation. There were still Acts of Parliament which proved defective, and amending Acts to deal with them continued to appear frequently. Even major legislative measures, such as the Third Reform Act of 1884, could be imperfectly drafted.

Most of the work of government and legislature in these years dealt with themes which were far from new. The list of statutes dealing with public health continued to lengthen and provided an increasingly comprehensive and complex code of regulation. The 1872 Adulteration of Food, Drink and Drugs Act had been the first modestly effective legislation in that field. It was strengthened by the Sale of Food and Drugs Act of 1875; the 1899 Sale of Food and Drugs Act was a much more thorough and efficient measure. Similarly, although earlier statutes had enforced the appointment of local public health officials, it was not until 1891 that an Act defined their qualifications. It prescribed, for example, that sanitary inspectors in London should either have had previous relevant experience with another local authority or should hold a certificate of professional competence issued by the Local Government Board. This was one of many examples of the development of professional hierarchies and qualifications within public service.

The effectiveness of much reforming legislation still depended on local willingness and capacity to implement it. An Act of 1897 allowed local authorities to provide allotments and five years later these powers were extended to include smallholdings. In the absence of compulsion the overwhelming majority of local authorities took little or no action. The 1890 Housing of the Working Classes Act codified earlier permissive legislation allowing local authorities to provide housing, and offered modest additional encouragement. These provisions were generally ignored; in most places there were always empty houses at any given time, while most ratepayers were opposed to the cost of such schemes, for which they would have to pay.

There were still many examples of reformers struggling hard to persuade taxpayers and ratepayers that a modest capital investment in improvements would prevent years of higher poor rates and other charges imposed by avoidable illness. This kind of social arithmetic, in both national and local terms, was rarely swallowed easily by those who would have to pay for extended intervention. In 1898 the reluctant decision of Bradford Town Council to employ direct labour to remove the contents of the town's dry lavatories was taken because the previous contract system had proved unnecessarily costly rather than merely inefficient.[35]

Parliament was still reluctant to compel local authorities to take on additional tasks. A respect for local knowledge and local responsibility, as well as distrust of central authorities and their intervention in local affairs, led to a preference for permissive legislation or local Acts inspired by local initiatives. When clear evidence of the need for more State intervention was available, however, governments and Parliaments were becoming less inhibited in the compulsory imposition of greater responsibilities upon local authorities.

Factory reform

Legislation on working conditions had begun in the early nineteenth century, and continued to be extended in scope and effectiveness. Some provisions in this legislation were often repeated, as, for example, the stipulation that the relevant regulations must be displayed in all of the places to which they referred. The powers of the factory inspectors were frequently increased. The Mines Act of 1872 marked a much extended regulation of mining practices; further major Acts of 1881, 1887, and 1900 produced a comprehensive code of intervention and regulation of mining which would have amazed and perhaps shocked an earlier generation. Merchant shipping also saw increasingly meticulous provisions. The strident public campaigns associated with men like Samuel Plimsoll concealed the reality of a continuous and expanding legislative control of conditions at sea, embodied in many Merchant Shipping Acts. As with factory and mines legislation, these measures were not the work of any single party, but represented the response to a steadily growing volume of experience and information.

Part of this information on employment conditions related to working hours. By the later nineteenth century governments possessed more specific information relating to the hours actually worked in various trades; this evidence led, for instance, to the Acts of 1886 and 1893 which limited the working hours for railwaymen and young shop assistants.[36] The 1905 Unemployed Workmen Act established a new administrative agency to coordinate measures for unemployment relief in London. Elsewhere the Act gave statutory recognition to the local voluntary Distress Committees which had already been established in many places, enforced their creation in all places with a population of more than 50,000, and empowered them to employ out-of-work men, establish labour

---

35. T. G. R. Wright, 'Poor Law administration in the city of Bradford, 1900–1914', MA thesis, Huddersfield Polytechnic, 1981, 39 n. 149.

36. E. H. Hunt, *British Labour History, 1815–1914* (1981), 46, 79.

exchanges, assist emigration, and embark upon schemes for settling unemployed workers in farming enterprises.[37]

Education

Education was another sphere of growing national intervention, following earlier precedents. By the early twentieth century the new Board of Education sought to exercise a national supervisory function over more than 3,000 local education authorities of one kind or another, most of them school boards created under the 1870 Elementary Education Act. In 1880 there were 244 HM Inspectors of Schools; another 124 were added in less than twenty years.[38] Successive statutes tightened the requirement for compulsory elementary education; the 1870 upper age limit of 10 years was raised to 11 in 1893 and 12 in 1899 (1901 in Scotland). At the same time, it should be noted that in 1892 there were 86,149 prosecutions of parents for failing to send children to school.[39]

The 1891 Education Act finally ensured that all public elementary education should be, as one cynical contemporary observed, 'what is called free'. The Conservative government which enacted this, after earlier and more tentative legislation on the subject, felt obliged to find the money from central funds to reimburse local authorities for their loss of fees. The relevant regulations were poorly drafted, but by 1900 these grants had become a major element in public expenditure on education, which was by then the biggest single item in domestic public expenditure.[40] The Education (Defective and Epileptic Children) Act, 1899, allowed local authorities to provide special schools for such children; in 1901, for example, the Wolverhampton School Board opened a special school with forty places for mentally defective children.[41]

The 1902 Education Act, which abolished the separate school boards, was one of the most significant and controversial measures in the history of the public education system.[42] The new municipal grammar schools established under this Act were modelled on the public schools. For example, the regulations for them issued by the Board of Education in 1902 stipulated that 'Where two languages other than English are taken, and Latin is not one of them, the Board will require to be satisfied that the omission of Latin is for the advantage of the school.'[43]

---

37. For a full discussion of these matters, J. Harris, *Unemployment and Politics* (1972).
38. Finer, *English Local Government*, 349.
39. Hunt, *British Labour History*, 12; E. Royle, *Modern Britain: A Social History 1750–1985* (1987), 214.
40. G. Sutherland, *Elementary Education in the Nineteenth Century* (1971), 37–9.
41. M. Forster, 'Secondary and technical education in Wolverhampton in the post 1902 era', MA thesis, Wolverhampton Polytechnic, 1985, 8.
42. There were also deficiencies in the Act. The structure of local government was not in step with population growth. After 1902 a town like Canterbury, small in population but high in municipal status, possessed much more extensive powers in education than urban districts like Willesden, Tottenham, and Rhondda, which had more than four times the population. Finer, *English Local Government*, 132.
43. Forster, 'Secondary and technical education in Wolverhampton', 31.

Overall the educational intervention of earlier years was greatly extended. In 1870 the total spending from central funds for education was just over £750,000; by 1895 the total was approaching £7 million.[44] What had begun in 1833 as a modest subsidy to voluntary efforts, and developed by 1870 into a limited provision of schooling where other agencies failed, was by the end of the century an important department of State. Before 1906 senior officials at the Board of Education, including the Permanent Secretary, Sir Robert Morant, were already planning further extensions of State intervention, such as the creation of a schools medical service. In 1907 school medical inspection came about under the Education (Miscellaneous Provisions) Act and a school medical service followed. A number of local authorities were already organizing school meals in 1905 but central government moved cautiously and it was only in 1914 that such provision was made compulsory.

The Poor Law

The Poor Law was another area of shared central and local government responsibility. The proportion of the population experiencing pauperism was dropping. There were 10 per cent fewer paupers in 1900 than in 1850. As a proportion of the growing population the drop was more striking—from 5.7 per cent to 2.5 per cent—an eloquent testimony to the success story of Victorian Britain.[45] The Poor Law remained, however, the aspect of official activity most familiar to the bulk of the population, either as ratepayers or as paupers. By the end of the century the Scottish Poor Law system, which in early- and mid-Victorian times was less effective than that for England and Wales, had developed into an essentially similar system.

Within the umbrella ministry of the Local Government Board, the Poor Law central department retained much effective autonomy, but its ability to exercise effective control over local boards of guardians remained limited. The LGB repeatedly urged the local Poor Law authorities to treat paupers, especially respectable paupers, more generously. In 1895 a general order urged that aid to outdoor paupers should be set at adequate levels. In the following year a further order stipulated that adequate outdoor relief should be the normal treatment of the respectable aged poor. In 1900 a further general order told local boards that the granting of adequate relief to all deserving aged persons was to be seen as standard and confirmed Poor Law policy. The frequency with which such orders were issued may induce doubts about their effectiveness.

A principal reason for the continuance of local control in Poor Law matters was that the money still came overwhelmingly from the local rates. At local level, the Poor Law was still administered by boards of guardians elected by a ratepaying electorate; many recipients of relief were personally known to many

44. Read, *England, 1868–1914*, 283.   45. Royle, *Modern Britain* (1987), 179.

ratepayers. The Poor Law system was peculiarly dependent upon the state of the local economy. Any serious slump exercised a double influence, increasing the number of applicants for relief while diminishing the capacity of ratepayers to meet additional charges. During a sharp recession in the mid-1880s, it was claimed that 'a considerable proportion of the rates are drawn from a class very little removed from pauperism, who had a hard struggle to pay the demands made upon them by the Overseers, and . . . any considerable increase in their burdens would have the effect of causing them to become paupers.'[46]

The local government reforms of 1894, which widened the electorate to include many poorer householders, and removed the ex officio magistrate members of the boards of guardians, did not usually inaugurate a more generous regime. Poor people considered deserving by local opinion might receive sympathetic treatment; from 1905, for example, the Bradford Poor Law Union, normally far from extravagant in its use of ratepayers' money, built new homes specifically for the deserving among the aged poor.[47] There was much less sympathy for those seen as undeserving. The Bradford guardians sent idle, drunken, or immoral applicants for relief to a special Test Workhouse, where monotonous work was regularly exacted and the diet was notably unappetizing. There was a considerable fund of sympathy for poor children. The Bradford Union provided more than 100,000 meals for poor schoolchildren in the six months from September 1905, taking advantage of a recent general order from the Local Government Board authorizing such expenditure.

There were always some, even if probably only a small minority, who tried to cheat the system. One northern union claimed in 1886 that 'Outdoor relief has for many years been, for good reason, kept down to the lowest point. Relieving officers have found imposture so rife among the applicants that they have wisely done all in their power to put an end to a system so fruitful of evil.'[48]

There were other forms of behaviour which alienated the rate-paying Poor Law electorate. A widow might spend extravagantly upon her husband's funeral, then claim to be destitute and apply for relief for herself and her children. There were always some among the poor who were violent, drunken, or obstreperous; their activities were likely to be noted by the increasingly popular local newspapers. One northern workhouse provides a reasonably typical range of such cases.[49] In 1890 a female inmate received fourteen days' imprisonment for riotous conduct; later in the same year two of her fellow inmates were in court, 'one for tearing and destroying the bed-clothes, and the other for disorderly and refractory conduct'. Next year another inmate was prosecuted for 'very cruel

---

46. Newspaper cutting in collection catalogued as 'Newcastle Relief Fund, 1885–6', Newcastle Central Library.

47. Wright, 'Poor Law Administration in the City of Bradford', 46, 52–4.

48. N. McCord, *North East England: The Region's Development, 1760–1960* (1979), 169.

49. R. G. Barker, 'The Houghton-le-Spring Poor Law Union', M.Litt. thesis, Newcastle University, 1974, 170–1, 227.

treatment' of a pauper infant. In 1893 a male inmate was in trouble for returning to the workhouse drunk; in 1894 two others returned drunk, bringing with them a bottle of laudanum. In 1902 another man received seven days' imprisonment for drunkenness; when released, 'on presenting himself for admission to the workhouse in a drunken condition, [he] had owing to his violent conduct been taken before a Justice and committed to prison for a further period of 14 days.' In 1905 a tramp kicked in the door of the relieving officer's office after being refused a ticket for a second night in the workhouse. The elderly did not always grow old gracefully, and the poor and the sick were not always pleasantly pathetic. It is understandable that ratepayers' enthusiasm for generous relief policies was often limited.

Nevertheless, in the Poor Law as in other areas of government, there was an unmistakable move towards better service. This was facilitated by an improvement in the quality of officials. By the end of the nineteenth century a more professional and reliable corps of public officials had been created. Local, regional, and national associations of Poor Law officials developed and there was a slow but definite improvement in qualifications and conditions of service. Wolverhampton workhouse held up to 500 inmates. Its long-serving (perhaps too long-serving) master received a salary of £70 plus double workhouse rations when he was appointed in 1839; when he retired in 1891 he was being paid £253 and his wife £172.[50]

Late-Victorian workhouses were usually much more sophisticated structures than their predecessors, larger, more complex, and endowed with separate infirmary premises. By 1891 there were 22,452 beds in Poor Law hospitals, and this number tripled over the next twenty years. Increasingly, workhouse design was entrusted to architects specializing in institutional buildings. Generally, Poor Law medical services improved, an advance facilitated by the clearer establishment of the medical and nursing professions as well as by the progress of medical science. All was not plain sailing here, however; the General Medical Council steadfastly refused to allow workhouse infirmaries to be used in medical education, despite the fact that they could provide experience of problems frequently encountered in medical practice.[51] It remained common for doctors holding Poor Law appointments to be excluded from the prestigious honorary appointments in voluntary hospitals.

The Local Government Board initiated a number of policy changes in the late-Victorian and Edwardian years. In 1885 the receipt of Poor Law medical treatment ceased to involve the electoral disqualification which pauperism normally entailed; since few of those involved were likely to be registered voters this may have been more important symbolically than practically. In the years around 1900, pauper children were removed from the workhouses and placed

50. M. B. Rowlands, *The West Midlands from A.D. 1000* (1987), 291.
51. F. B. Smith, *The People's Health, 1830–1910* (1979), 366, 387–94.

instead in quasi-family units with foster-parents. The workhouses themselves became 'Poor Law Institutions', and each union was instructed to devise a fictitious address to be used on the birth certificates of children born in the institution, a well-meaning attempt to avoid future stigma. Recourse to outdoor relief to the able-bodied in times of high unemployment was normal in many areas.

Other changes allowed the election of women to boards of guardians, though their numbers were small and their election by a predominantly male electorate precarious. The most radical electoral change was enacted in 1894. The property qualification for guardians was abolished, magistrates ceased to be ex officio guardians, plural voting in Poor Law elections ended, and elected guardians were to serve for three years. Boards of guardians were now allowed to co-opt a limited number of outside members. By 1905 the Blackburn Board of Guardians had eight 'labour' members, representing a variety of trade union and political groups.[52]

A cool recent assessment of the late-Victorian and Edwardian Poor Law has this to say:

> The reformed workhouses provided accommodation that was rather cleaner and certainly no more over-crowded than the worst urban housing, and workhouse food—monotonous, none too plentiful, and badly cooked as it often was—compared not unfavourably with what the poorest classes were accustomed to at home... It remained true also that English and Welsh paupers were still, on the whole, better fed, better housed, and less harshly treated than the majority of paupers elsewhere.

This modest commendation is contrasted with 'the harrowing, hopeless degradation of the French sick poor' in the later nineteenth century.[53]

The Poor Law Commission which reported in 1909 found itself unable to agree and there were Majority and Minority reports. The government did not take much notice of either but left the existing system substantially intact though separate and parallel to the National Insurance scheme it introduced in 1911. There were both ideological and pragmatic reasons for this. The Majority report favoured not just a retention but an expanded if reformed version of the existing system which would become the basis of all social welfare, while the Minority wished to destroy it completely and replace it by a grand scheme for social welfare with distinct departments devoted to the able-bodied unemployed, education, health, and pensions. Neither view appealed to Lloyd George or Churchill who were busy with a social insurance scheme which instituted eligibility based on contributions, a compulsory prudence organized by the State. To have done away with the Poor Law would in any case have involved a vast programme of change for the existing system had become increasingly diverse and adaptable. It would have been unpopular with a host of interests including the Local Government Board and Boards of Guardians, while it would have offended

52. R. L. Walton, 'The Labour Movement in Blackburn, 1880–1914', MA thesis, Huddersfield Polytechnic, 1981, 38.

53. Hunt, *British Labour History*, 138; Smith, *The People's Health*, 423; Read, *England, 1868–1914*, 409.

the many who considered that poverty if it needed to be ameliorated was often self-inflicted.

The government, while leaving the Poor Law as something more than a safety net, especially with regard to health, pursued a different agenda. Old-age pensions, which were initially non-contributory, enabled the majority of the elderly who were in reasonable health to escape the workhouse but convinced Lloyd George that non-contributory schemes were prohibitively expensive and could not be extended to the sick, the unemployed, or other needy groups. Insurance could call upon the contributions of workers and employers as well as those made by government. It also went with the grain of self-help and while it involved the State assisted the individual and was thus not socialist. Both Lloyd George and Winston Churchill consciously followed the Bismarckian State insurance principle.

The National Insurance Act of 1911 was far from the sweeping and clear-cut scheme originally envisaged, for a host of compromises had to be made to assuage the many vested interests of insurance companies, friendly societies, trades unions, and doctors. There were two parts to it, the first dealing with health and the second with unemployment benefit (see pp. 435–7).

Taken together with measures such as labour exchanges, pensions, and school meals as well as increased taxation for the well-to-do, the National Insurance Act has often been seen as part of a major move towards a 'welfare state'. This may be a misreading of the intentions of the Asquith government and various aspects of the measures contradicted each other as with the non-contributory and universal nature of old-age pensions and the contributory and specific principle of unemployment benefit. The state expanded its role but involved private agencies. Humanitarianism vied with national efficiency and paternalism with self-help. That the legislation changed the relationship of the State with the mass of the population is, however, incontrovertible.

The combination of the continuation of the Poor Law and introduction of new means of fulfilling some of its functions meant that the old system of providing State aid and an embryonic new system carried on side by side, the one 'all-embracing but socially unacceptable' and the other more acceptable but selective in much of its coverage. In time, 'When all its functions were appropriated by other social institutions the Poor Law would fall apart.'[54]

Other areas of administration

Some other areas of administration scarcely justified even such a modestly favourable verdict. The developing economy was not helped by the level of competence shown in maintaining the road system. An Act of 1882 provided for modest subsidies from central funds to help with the upkeep of major roads, but

54. D. Fraser, *The Evolution of the British Welfare State* (1973), 162–3.

the legislation was not well thought out. In practice there was no uniformity in the national road system's upkeep. Individual counties decided for themselves what they would do—or often not do—in designating main roads and maintaining them in a satisfactory state.[55]

Overall the structure of local government remained confused. During the mid-Victorian years agencies multiplied so that, for instance, town councils, Poor Law guardians, and school boards administered their own affairs within overlapping areas and disparate rating systems. At the end of the century town councils collected their own rates and also acted as collecting agents for the school boards' rates; the Poor Law authorities levied their own rates and paid their own collectors. In 1893 a Leeds Local Act brought some rationalization of the city's confused rating system; previously the council had levied separate rates under sixteen different assessments.[56]

For much of the century the Poor Law was the most important agency of local government, but it was ultimately overtaken by the borough councils and then also the county councils as the recipients of most additional functions. The 1888 local government legislation inaugurated the abandonment of specialist separate authorities in favour of unitary organs of local government. The abolition of the separate school boards in 1902 took this trend further. In 1888 the counties received elected councils for the first time, and major towns (mainly those with populations of more than 50,000) were designated as county boroughs outside county jurisdiction.[57] Other changes came in 1894, with the creation within the counties of urban district councils, rural district councils, and parish councils.

London received separate treatment. In 1888 the London County Council was set up, and in 1899 some of its functions were devolved on to twenty-eight new metropolitan boroughs. This reform was not due simply to disinterested zeal, though there was a strong case for some decentralization of the metropolis. The Conservative-dominated government disliked the radicals' hold on the LCC, a hold which they, nevertheless, broke when they won control in 1907. In addition many ratepayers in the wealthier London districts, such as Kensington and Westminster, resented the way in which legislation of 1894 had established an overall London valuation which obliged them to subsidize poorer districts like Poplar or Deptford. Numerously signed petitions from wealthier districts, asking for separate borough status, provided one of the initiatives behind the changes introduced in 1899.

It could not be said that rationalization and efficiency carried all before it. A recent study has commented that 'rationality and efficiency took second place to a determination to check centralising tendencies by stimulating civic pride and local self-reliance.'[58] The local government reforms of 1888 and 1894 left

55. Finer, *English Local Government*, 135.
56. Barber, 'Municipal government in Leeds', 103.
57. Finer, *English Local Government*, 22, 33, 40, 113; for London, ibid. 471–88.
58. G. R. Searle, *A New England? Peace and War 1886–1918*, (2004), 126.

the structure of local government extremely complex with much overlapping of authority. There were County Councils, County Boroughs, City Councils, Municipal Councils, Urban District Councils, Rural District Councils, and Parish Councils. There were also 640 Boards of Guardians and 2,500 School Boards,[59] while a number of other functions were exercised by independent bodies such as river authorities and docks and harbour and port authorities. Some towns went in for what became known as 'municipal socialism' and administered their own gas, water, and electricity services while others left such matters to the private sector. Local government boundaries often inaccurately reflected the realities of economic and urban development with large conurbations having no political or administrative existence.

By the end of the century, the local government franchise was wider than the parliamentary franchise; about three-quarters of all adult males could vote in local elections, although many of them did not bother to do so. A small minority of women had also acquired the local franchise and in 1907 were given the right to be borough or county councillors. Changes in the structure of local government did not necessarily herald any major shift in the patterns of local influence. In twenty-two of the new county councils, the first chairman was the chairman of the county's quarter sessions; in six counties the Lord Lieutenant became the first chairman. The 1888 Act reserved control of the county police forces to the local magistrates.

Despite some hesitations, Parliament was increasingly willing to add to the powers of local government. This owed something to the growing volume of evidence showing the need for more official intervention, but something also to the relative increase in efficiency and reliability of local administration. This increased confidence was shown in such measures as the Public Authorities Protection Act of 1893, which conferred a privileged legal status on local authorities, whereby law cases alleging unfair or illegal treatment by a local authority had generally to be instituted within six months of the cause of complaint.[60]

Between 1880 and 1905 local government expenditure nearly tripled, from £36.3 million to £107.7 million, or from 1.46 pounds per head of the population to 3.17 pounds. In 1906 the local rates were still meeting more than half of the total.[61] An increased share of costs was now being borne by grants from central government funds. In 1880 these had only amounted to £2.7 million, but by 1905 this had jumped to nearly £20 million, still a minority of local government spending but a much more important one, amounting to nearly 20 per cent.

There were two other significant contributions to local revenues. The increased rateable value of property resulting from economic growth meant higher income even when there was no proportionate increase in the level of rates imposed. The second source was a marked increase in local government borrowing; the total borrowed amounted to £136.9 million in 1880, but by 1903

59. Searle, *A New England*, 126.   60. Finer, *English Local Government*, 199.   61. Ibid. 373–80.

this had risen to £447.8 million. In both cases, the resources available to a local authority depended on the resilience of the local economy, and there were great discrepancies between the financial positions of different local authorities.

The experience of the growing Tyneside town of Wallsend illustrates some of the implications of increased prosperity. During the third quarter of the century local government expenditure there was derisively small; in 1868 a proposal to light the short stretch of road between railway station and high street was easily defeated, the local board's chairman remarking 'that such as were compelled to be in the place after dark must provide themselves, as their fathers had to do, with lanterns'. By the early 1880s the local board had gradually moved to appoint more salaried officials, usually under the compulsion of national legislation. By 1891 the board could nerve itself to build a hospital costing £6,500. The rateable value of the town had been less than £30,000 when the local board was set up in 1866; by 1891 it was almost £80,000. In these circumstances the board and the successor town council could face increases in spending with an equanimity denied to their mid-Victorian predecessors.[62]

Local government personnel

Similar increases in expenditure were reflected in many forms. In 1882 Newcastle's Medical Officer of Health had a total staff of 9; by 1906 this had risen to 38, in addition to additional staff employed in the city's own hospitals. It was not simply a matter of numbers, for the changes embodied developments in professional qualifications and techniques of organization. In the early twentieth century, Newcastle's cleansing department employed well over 500 men, organized in four districts and eight sub-districts, with a hierarchy of supervisory personnel. The experienced professional manager who headed this body was a regular attender at the annual National Conference of Cleansing Superintendents of Great Britain and Ireland. This level of sophistication would have astonished the handful of scavengers who a generation earlier had sporadically tidied up a few of the town's principal streets.

Hereditary local government officials were by no means unusual. At the first election for a Town Clerk in Gateshead in 1836, Thomas Swinburne lost on the mayor's casting vote. His son Joseph became Town Clerk in 1856 and died in office in 1893. He was succeeded by his son William, who had served as his deputy since 1891; William held the post until 1929. When in 1903 Thomas Crowther retired as Clerk to the Bradford Poor Law Guardians, a post he had held for twelve years, he had accumulated a total of fifty-four years' service in various Poor Law posts; he was succeeded by his son, who had been his father's assistant since 1894. In 1906 the union appointed its first shorthand-typist, to supplement

---

62. McCord, *North East England*, 165, 175.

the work of the office's five clerks; the union's total staff almost doubled in the early years of the twentieth century.[63]

Not all local government employees belonged to any impressive professional hierarchy. In the early twentieth century, the cleaning staff of the same union, known as the 'scrubbers', were taken from the pauper lists, usually from 'the least satisfactory of the outdoor relief cases', and paid 10s. 6d. weekly. By the end of the nineteenth century the Poor Law employed many nurses, but they were generally poorly rewarded, with wages much lower than those given to other staff such as relieving officers.[64]

However, the more professional aspect of local government was expanding. It was reflected in the growth of specialist organizations, whether trade unions, professional associations, or merely local societies. In 1901 the printed annual report of the Newcastle Municipal Officers' Association noted that

Subjects of extreme importance to the members have been under consideration, and action has been taken which it is hoped will be for the benefit of the members generally...It is hoped that the small proportion of the staff still remaining outside the Association will see that it is in their own interests and also in the interests of their colleagues as a whole that they should join the Association without delay.

These local associations usually reflected the hierarchical nature of local government employment, with senior officials dominating their management. National publications such as the *Local Government Chronicle* gave opportunities for the exchange of information and opinions among officials, and facilitated their emergence as a pressure group in matters relating to the work and the development of local government.

The improvement in the quality of local government staff, though real, was also incomplete. There remained a substantial number of scandalous breaches of duty by officials, often well publicized to a rate-paying electorate by an interested local press. The creation of the London County Council in 1888 was preceded by serious and well-founded charges of corruption involving some of the staff of the Metropolitan Board of Works.[65] During a serious trade depression in 1885–6, ratepayers in the hard-hit South Shields Poor Law Union enforced spending cuts which included a reduction in the Clerk's salary; when he retired a few years later an audit showed that he had informally evened things up by appropriating union funds.[66] In 1880 the Inspector of Nuisances employed by the Brandon Urban Sanitary Authority fled to America with that authority's petty cash. In 1899, in the same district, a rate collector received twelve month's imprisonment for embezzling public funds.

63. Wright, 'Poor Law administration in the city of Bradford', 31.
64. Smith, *The People's Health*, 360; Wright, 'Poor Law administration in the city of Bradford', 107.
65 Finer, *English Local Government*, 471.
66. P. Mawson, 'The South Shields Poor Law Union', MA thesis, Newcastle University, 1971, 128; McCord, *North East England*, 167.

The police

The police changed considerably during these years.[67] By the early twentieth century the extent of professionalism here, as in other areas of government service, had grown. This was not a uniform development, and there were still variations in quality between local forces. From 1835 onwards the borough councils had been given a major share in the control of the local police, forming joint watch committees with local magistrates for that purpose. Even in 1888, however, control of county forces was left to the county JPs.

In 1914 the overwhelming majority (over 90 per cent) of borough chief constables were career policemen who had worked their way up through the lower ranks. In contrast, only a minority of heads of county forces had taken that route. In the counties the police were less subject to supervision by local authorities than in the boroughs. County chief constables tended to be long-serving patriarchal figures who in practice enjoyed more independence than their brethren in the boroughs. The first Chief Constable of Surrey retired in 1899 at the age of 86. Monmouthshire's first Chief Constable, appointed in 1857 at the age of 33, retired in 1893; his successor served for forty-two years before retiring at the age of 73. The first Chief Constable of Kent, Captain Ruxton, served from 1857 to 1894; one of his officers described him as 'a typical English gentleman in cap and tweeds, building a police force in an English tradition of fair-play and no nonsense'. Most counties employed chief constables drawn from the aristocracy or gentry, with a number of ex-officers from the armed forces among them.[68] There were some exceptions; in 1902 County Durham received its first professional Chief Constable, who had previously served as Chief Constable of smaller forces, first at Reigate and then at South Shields.

The general level of police recruits improved, and their reputation increased. In 1896 only fifty-nine officers were dismissed from the Metropolitan Police for all causes. At mid-century fewer than one-third of all police recruits had lasted for as long as five years. There was still an unsatisfactory minority. In 1887 a constable was dismissed from the Northumberland force; while conveying two prisoners to Morpeth, he had adjourned with them to a convenient public house, all three subsequently arriving at the prison drunk. Such derelictions from duty, though they continued, were now infrequent. There were some setbacks in police standards within the general picture of improvement. In 1888 the terrifying murders committed by Jack the Ripper remained unsolved; it was scarcely surprising that when the Sherlock Holmes stories began to appear three years later the police detectives were not given flattering portraits. Some police forces were still

67. The main sources for this discussion of the police are Critchley, *A History of Police*, 124–70, and Ascoli, *The Queen's Peace*, 140–75.
68. In Northumberland a manor house was retained as the official residence of the Chief Constable until the 1940s. Joan M. Taylor, *England's Border County: A History of Northumberland County Council 1889–1989* (1989), 119.

capable of astonishing escapades. In 1897, for instance, the Head Constable of Reading ordered some of his officers to carry out a pretended break-in at the house of the Chief Constable of Berkshire in order 'to frighten the old man', in the course of a private quarrel.

As in other areas of public service there were dynasties of serving policemen. In 1906 there were policemen who were the grandsons of men who had served as watchmen under local Improvement Acts before 1835. Other aspects of professionalism also appeared. The possibility of using fingerprints for individual identification was demonstrated as early as 1858. Britain's Central Fingerprint Bureau was not created until 1901; by 1903 it had accumulated 60,000 fingerprints of known criminals.

The Post Office

Another area of government with both central and local elements, the Post Office, grew substantially. By 1900 nearly 2,000 million letters were dealt with annually, the largest flow of correspondence in the world. Greater literacy and spending power led the average number of letters sent per head almost to double between 1871 and 1900.[69] In 1884 the first public telephones arrived; picture postcards joined the postal flow in 1894. By late-Victorian years the Post Office was a major factor in communications and an important employer. Post Office work provided new opportunities for women's employment. If the wages for most Post Office work were not high, they were regular and reliable, factors which contributed to the respectability of this calling.

The Post Office fulfilled many functions. It provided a form of banking for the majority of the population who did not have bank accounts, with the Postal Order becoming the means of sending money to relatives. Telegram boys brought congratulatory messages at times of celebration though their arrival at working-class households was at other times likely to be as harbingers of the news of a death. It was also an arm of the State and it is difficult to see how old-age pensions could have been paid without it.

The Civil Service

The overall size of the Civil Service increased significantly. From about 50,000 in 1881, it grew to 116,000 by 1901 and then growth accelerated, partly as a result of changes introduced by the Liberals after 1906. Most of the increase in numbers came in the lower-paid echelons of the public service and the cost of the Civil Service remained relatively low.

69. D. Vincent, 'Communication, community and the State', in C. Emsley and J. Walvin (eds.), *Artisans, Peasants & Proletarians, 1760–1860: Essays Presented to Gwyn A. Williams* (1985), 166–85. Further information on postal growth is in A. Briggs, *Victorian Things* (1988), 336–46.

The number of senior posts in some important government offices remained small. The most prestigious and rewarding positions in both the home and foreign Civil Service remained perquisites of men drawn from the dominant minorities; they alone possessed the resources, the connections, and the education to win them. Even with the institution of entrance examinations, competition was confined to a minority who had the educational and social qualifications which enabled them to compete. It was rare for important posts to be filled by men of lowly origins, though there were a few exceptions. By the 1880s the various inspectorates had developed their own career structures; in 1882 the first man to rise from a shop-floor job to become one of HM Inspectors of Factories reached that level—this, though, was not common before 1906, or indeed for many years thereafter. In 1892 Edward Fairfield became an assistant undersecretary at the Colonial Office, after an official career which began as a junior clerk; this too was not a frequent achievement.[70] All of the twenty-eight clerks appointed to the Foreign Office between 1898 and 1907 had attended major public schools, twelve of them at Eton; nearly half of them had gone on to university, invariably Oxford or Cambridge.[71] Such privileged access to State appointments was normal in the great majority of contemporary societies.

The atmosphere in some of the major ministries was not conducive to enterprise or efficiency. The reputation of the Local Government Board has already been mentioned. Webb and Olivier, bright recruits to the Colonial Office, found the work there 'deadening to initiative'. In the early twentieth century, Foreign Office clerks 'lived a pleasant routine existence which stultified their education, dulled their wits and deprived them of every kind of initiative'. A modern study of that department is aptly entitled 'A Study in Resistance'.[72]

The Empire

The departments which earned these criticisms were responsible for Britain's external interests, including the administration of the world's greatest empire. When the twentieth century opened, the Queen-Empress Victoria reigned over about 400 million people, inhabiting more than one-fifth of the globe. The massive areas coloured red on contemporary maps exhibited an enormous range of differing conditions. Three-quarters of the empire's population lived in India, while the self-governing 'white' colonies held only a small proportion of the total; Canada's enormous area held only 5.4 million people, Australia 3.8 million, New Zealand 0.8 million. Economically, the empire was of less than overwhelming importance, with two-thirds of Britain's exports going elsewhere. Politically,

70. R. C. Snelling and T. J. Barron, 'The Colonial Office: its permanent officials, 1801–1914', in G. Sutherland (ed.), *Studies in the Growth of Nineteenth-Century Government* (1972), 164.
71. V. Cromwell and T. S. Steiner, 'The Foreign Office before 1914: a study in resistance', in Sutherland (ed.), *Studies in the Growth of Nineteenth-Century Government*, 179–86.
72. Ibid.

strategically, symbolically, and psychologically, the empire counted for much. This was demonstrated by the writings of authors like Kipling and the popularity achieved by such bodies as the Primrose League, which stressed the imperial connection. From 1884 the Imperial Federation League worked to promote empire unity and identity, recruiting many influential figures to this crusade; W. E. Forster, for example, was its first president.

The continued expansion of British overseas possessions involved an increase in business for a Colonial Office which was not particularly efficient. No doubt the authority of ministers there remained theoretically intact, but in practice faulty organization and procedures could mean that junior officials were left without much supervision. At one period a bright young graduate was effectively in charge of the Australian business of the Colonial Office after only six years' service.[73] The peak of activity in colonial administration in these years came during Joseph Chamberlain's term as Secretary of State for the Colonies between 1895 and 1903. His political importance and enthusiasm for the empire saw an injection of energy into the department. Modest subsidies helped the West Indian colonies to survive a crisis in the sugar trade—here Chamberlain even persuaded the Cabinet to threaten the imposition of retaliatory import duties on foreign sugar if unfair competition was not ended. Cyprus received railways and an irrigation scheme; the first railways were also built in Sierra Leone, Nigeria, the Gold Coast, and Uganda. A limited amount of public money, and much official encouragement in other ways, fostered the development of research institutes devoted to colonial agriculture and tropical medicine. Many of Chamberlain's ambitious schemes foundered on the unwillingness of Cabinet and Treasury to sanction spending which might produce political attacks on grounds of extravagance and excessive taxation. The cry for cheap government was far from dead. However, there was a distinct increase in the level of attention devoted to colonial matters in these years. This was not only felt in such a crisis area as South Africa, but also showed in improvements over a much wider sphere.[74]

There were also attempts to improve links between the mother country and the colonies, as in the development of occasional meetings between the home government and ministers from the self-governing colonies. Overall, there was little doubt in these years about the validity of Britain's imperial mission. The Conservative Lord Curzon thought that the British Empire was 'under Providence, the greatest instrument of good that the world has seen'; the Liberal Lord Rosebery agreed, claiming that the empire was 'the greatest secular agency for good that the world has seen'. In 1898, after an Anglo-Egyptian army in the Sudan had routed a Dervish army twice its size at the battle of Omdurman,

73. Snelling and Barron, 'The Colonial Office', 160.
74. Read, *England, 1868–1914*, 340–74; B. Porter, *The Lion's Share: A Short History of British Imperialism 1850–1970* (1975), 135.

revenging Gordon's catastrophe at Khartoum, Lord Salisbury claimed that 'All the wide territories which the Mahdi ruled with barbarous and atrocious cruelty have now been brought under the civilizing influence of the British Government.'[75] A. V. Dicey, an influential writer on political affairs, asserted in 1905 that 'The maintenance of the British Empire makes it possible, at a cost which is relatively small, compared with the whole number of British subjects, to secure peace, good order, and personal freedom throughout a large part of the world.' Dicey also noted that the empire performed a vital security function, helping to protect from foreign rivals 'one of the two greatest free commonwealths in existence'. From 1904 onwards, Empire Day was added to the list of annual national celebrations. It was natural that the way in which this small group of islands off the north-west corner of Europe had raised itself to such a position of worldwide power should arouse pride and satisfaction. There were voices which questioned the value and the glory of the empire, but they were little regarded. The 1897 Diamond Jubilee celebrations were a celebration of imperial grandeur, even if they took place in a world of diminishing security.

The empire was still growing in the early twentieth century, though most of the recent acquisitions represented Britain's share in 'the scramble for Africa' by European powers. British governments were not anxious to acquire additional colonies; one recent writer suggests that 'the mere existence of a "national interest" was not sufficient on its own to warrant British intervention. It also had to be shown that that interest was under threat from outside and would likely be lost if something were not done to secure it.'[76]

A dominant Conservative Party remembered the disastrous defeat of 1880, which could be attributed to colonial adventures, and was chary of alienating a tax-paying electorate by embarking on aggressive and expensive annexations. Where intervention seemed necessary and inevitable, overt annexation was avoided whenever possible; 'protectorates' or the activities of chartered but ostensibly independent companies were preferred. It was not possible to allow other European powers to extend their colonial empires while Britain merely stood on the sidelines. In the face of France's annexations in equatorial Africa, Britain acquired Nigeria. In the face of German penetrations in East Africa, Lord Salisbury negotiated agreements which secured British control of Kenya, Uganda, and Zanzibar. In 1898 British and Egyptian forces reconquered the Sudan, blocking any French expansion into the upper Nile valley; in the following year an Anglo-French agreement recognized the two powers' respective spheres of influence in that area. In all these cases, the British policy was a modest assertion of British power and British interests without provoking major conflicts with rival powers.

The South African War was a psychological setback to imperial enthusiasm. The cost of victory was high and the radical charges of 'methods of barbarism'

75. Porter, *The Lion's Share*, 189–91.   76. Ibid. 112–18.

and the intrigues of unscrupulous business interests were effective. The reversal of Milner's policies, designed to produce a British dominated South Africa, resulted in the South Africa Act of 1909, which instituted a Union of South Africa consisting of Cape Colony, Natal, and the two former Afikaner republics of the Transvaal and the Orange Free State. White manhood suffrage vastly increased Afrikaner influence and, although the Union seemed a successful solution in the immediate future, it was to have baleful results in the long term.

The empire which had grown so extensive by 1914 was a far from uniform entity. We can distinguish between the white dominions, where the British inhabitants had come to outnumber indigenous peoples; settler colonies, where Europeans, although dominant, were in the minority; and those colonies where Britain by means of a handful of administrators exercised suzerainty over societies where the social and political structures remained otherwise substantially unchanged. On the whole British governments displayed little enthusiasm for direct rule, preferring, as with the dominions, to hand over home affairs to representative assemblies or, as with much of Africa or the semi-independent princely states of India, to rule indirectly.

India

India remained a special case among Britain's imperial possessions. The Indian contribution to Britain's trade was more important than that of the rest of the empire. Britain's supremacy in the Indian subcontinent was her most remarkable imperial achievement, symbolized by the imperial title and the existence since 1858 of a special British department of state for Indian affairs. At the same time there was an inescapable weakness in the British position in India. As education, literacy, and knowledge spread among growing numbers of Indians, it became increasingly obvious that the imperial power denied her Indian subjects the kind of political rights which her own citizens increasingly took for granted.

Meanwhile, India was being tied together, under British auspices, by an improved network of communications, including a railway system of almost 25,000 miles. One result was easier contact and cooperation between nationalist elements in various parts of India. The first overt signs of such activity arose from an innovation by the Indian government in 1885. The Viceroy summoned a congress of leading Indians as a forum for discussion. This body, however, went on to establish itself as a continuing Indian National Congress, a vocal platform for the enunciation of grievances and claims in political, economic, and administrative matters. The nature of Indian society meant that its initial unity could not be maintained. In 1906, after years of communal conflicts, the Muslim section of the Congress abandoned it and formed their own Muslim League, a development which was to have important consequences for the history of twentieth-century India.

The dilemmas facing the British in India were illustrated by the experiences of a distinguished Viceroy, Lord Curzon, who took up this appointment in 1898.[77] In his early years in India, Curzon's hard work, administrative skill, and personal gifts secured apparent successes both in India and in Whitehall. He had positive achievements to his credit, including improved arrangements for famine relief, a major extension of irrigation, reforms in universities and police, and increased security on the north-west frontier. The tide of success was not maintained. A serious dispute over control of the Indian Army with the ambitious and unscrupulous Commander-in-Chief, Kitchener, formed part of the story, but there was more to it than that. Curzon's well-meant efforts to increase the efficiency of Indian government, as in the partition of the ancient province of Bengal or his interference with the Calcutta municipality, served to alienate Indian opinion without recruiting any alternative body of support anywhere. When he left India in 1905 his sojourn there had done little to enhance his political standing at home. By 1906 it was increasingly obvious to the well-informed that the pattern of British rule in India must change if control of the subcontinent was to be maintained. Such misgivings, however, were not widespread among British people.

There were broadly two approaches to governing India and indeed to the non-white empire as a whole. One was to preside over the country as it was and the other to reform, change, and modernize it by the export of British institutions. John Morley, who became Indian secretary in 1905, seemed just the man to implement the latter approach which dated back to Macaulay and which was motivated by the desire to produce a liberal and constitutional India. He had to work with a Viceroy, Lord Minto, appointed by the Unionists, but succeeded in persuading him to associate himself with the 'Morley–Minto' reforms of 1909 which extended Indian representation in the layers of Indian government. At the same time, however, the partition of Bengal was upheld and this resulted in considerable opposition from Congress leaders and led to civil disobedience. It was difficult to appease both Hindus and Muslims. When Morley and Minto were replaced by Lord Crewe and Lord Hardinge their abandonment of the Bengal partition was popular with Congress but their transfer of the capital from Calcutta to Delhi outraged Hindu nationalists and did little to satisfy Muslims. The Indian Under-Secretary, Edwin Montagu, promoted in 1912 the idea of provincial self-government but this was rejected by Lord Crewe. There was no easy solution to the problems of governing India. In the short term the Raj retained widespread support amongst the Princes and the masses, but such support was weakening. Bold moves towards greater democracy and limited self-rule did not have the backing of British opinion and were likely to exacerbate tensions between Hindu and Muslim.

77. D. Dilks, *Curzon in India*, vol. i, *Achievement* (1969), vol. ii, *Frustration* (1970); P. King, *The Viceroy's Fall: How Kitchener Destroyed Curzon* (1986).

Ireland

In Ireland British rule was severely tested.[78] The crisis of the early- and mid-1880s culminated in the rejection in 1886 of Gladstone's first Home Rule Bill. During the following twenty years the most important development in Anglo-Irish relations affected the land question, the root cause of much discontent. Conservative administrations, by the Land Acts of 1888, 1891, and 1903, provided for a massive shift in Irish land ownership by using the financial power and credit of the British State to encourage tenants to buy, landlords to sell. A Liberal Land Act in 1893 formed part of the same sequence. Under the 1903 Act, the British State provided the landlord with a bonus amounting to 12 per cent of the sale price, while tenants were enabled to borrow purchase money on exceptionally favourable terms. By the early twentieth century, this substantial settlement of the land question in its traditional form was no longer enough to ensure Anglo-Irish cordiality, but what had been done amounted to a significant success. Land reforms had much to do with the comparative peace in the early years of the twentieth century.

Apart from land reforms, governments and Parliaments resorted to other expedients to ameliorate the Irish situation. One administrative experiment was the creation in 1890 of the Congested Districts Board. This new Irish agency received an annual Treasury grant which it spent on its own authority. Its activities included subsidies for railway development, the improvement of farming techniques by grants for animal breeding projects, support for the fishing industry, encouragement to tourism, and assistance in emigration. This innovation was to be imitated in later years for a variety of purposes; the Arts Council and the University Grants Committee are among later descendants.

An independent Ireland or southern Ireland was far from inevitable in the early twentieth century. Irish Nationalist MPs were eager for an Irish Parliament but content that this should be combined with Irish representation at Westminster. Essentially, they demanded a limited independence for a state they did not conceive of as culturally or economically distinct from Britain. The importance of Sinn Fein and the Irish Republican Brotherhood has been much exaggerated in the light of subsequent history. Sinn Fein's solitary candidate in a by-election was unsuccessful and the party didn't even contest the general elections of 1910. The IRB, as the Fenian movement of the mid-nineteenth century was now called, was a secret organization dedicated to revolution but lacked the popular support to initiate one. A succession of events transformed the situation.

The results of the 1910 elections meant that the government was now dependent on Irish Nationalist votes and brought Home Rule back on the agenda. The refusal of Ulster unionists and the Conservative and Unionist Party to accept the passage of the Home Rule Bill led to the growth of extremism amongst both

---

78. F. S. Lyons, *Ireland since the Famine* (1971, rev. edn. 1973) provides a full discussion.

unionists and nationalists. The drilling of volunteers, gun-running, and outrages committed by both sides led to constitutional crisis in Britain as well as Ireland. Nevertheless, the outlines of a settlement by which a northern Ireland would remain within the Union were already discernible by August 1914 and with Nationalist MPs pledging their support for the war effort, the Home Rule Bill was passed, though its operation was suspended. The exigencies of war were to lead to the growth of a much more extreme form of Irish nationalism.

Security and the armed forces

The relative tranquillity in Ireland until 1911 was a boon to British governments increasingly aware that the security of Britain and her empire entailed new problems. The later nineteenth century saw the development of rival alliances between heavily armed European powers, from which Britain stood aloof. Relative isolation posed dangers, and enforced consideration of Britain's defences, one of the key responsibilities of the State. Compared with the great continental conscript armies, and the recent record of the German Army in particular, the British Army appeared puny. Its performance in combat during these years, especially in South Africa, displayed serious shortcomings, despite such earlier attempts at reform as those of Cardwell (see p. 319 above). During the 1899–1902 Boer War, the British Army assembled a force not far short of half a million men to crush an opponent who never had more than about 60,000. British losses from disease were twice those inflicted by the enemy; British casualties generally were far higher than those of the Boers. The circumstances of victory in South Africa suggested an urgent need to modernize the British Army.

Some steps were taken but public opinion remained firmly set against the European model of conscript armies. Top direction was improved by the creation of the Committee of Imperial Defence in 1903 but in general Unionist plans for army reform made little progress. The Liberal governments continued the process of army reform with the Haldane reforms. These included the amalgamation of the Yeomanry and the Volunteers by the Territorial and Reserve Forces Act of 1907, though it remained unclear whether the new force could be used outside the United Kingdom. An army general staff was set up in 1909, something which had been advocated after thorough inquiries years earlier, but shelved. Haldane's main achievement was the establishment of a well-equipped Expeditionary Force which could be sent to France at the outbreak of a war (its probable destination could not be named so it was officially there to be sent to 'any part of the world'). Central military administration was helped by the building of a new War Office between 1896 and 1906. There were still serious gaps in the assimilation of the lessons of the Boer War, while the recommendations of Lord Esher's Enquiry, which stressed the importance of maintaining an armaments industry which would be capable of supplying the armed forces in time of any future war, were ignored.

The navy continued to receive more attention than the army. The Royal Navy was seen as the main defence of the British Isles, the overseas empire, and the vital sea routes. By the 1880s it was in urgent need of reform. A good illustration of this occurred during a crisis in Anglo-Russian relations in 1885. At the height of the crisis, when Gladstone threatened Russia with war, the British Mediterranean Fleet possessed two battleships ready for action, one at Malta and the other at Port Said; even if the battle squadron had been concentrated, it would have presented a motley collection of individual designs rather than a coherent fighting force. In the previous year there had already been a public campaign, spearheaded by W. T. Stead's *Pall Mall Gazette*, complaining that the navy was not in a fit state to fulfil its operational role.

There were some face-saving government responses to public expressions of anxiety, but nothing effective was done until 1889. By that time two potential enemies, France and Russia, had drawn closely together and announced naval building programmes. In response the Salisbury government, backed by another temporary wave of public anxiety, passed the Naval Defence Act, which provided for the spending of £21.5 million over the next few years. This aimed at out-building the Franco-Russian combination, and also at equipping the fleet with squadrons of major warships designed to fight together; a total of 10 battleships, 9 large and 29 smaller cruisers, and 22 smaller warships were to be built under this Act.

Before this programme was completed, the Royal Navy experienced the most humiliating of all Victorian naval disasters. Designed before the Naval Defence Act, the battleships *Victoria* and *Sanspareil* represented 'a retrograde design' rather than 'a sound tactical conception'. A pair of very large guns provided their main armament; this weapon was 'a slow firer, never made good shooting, and proved costly to repair and reline'.[79] At the beginning of 1892, *Victoria* became the fleet flagship in the Mediterranean, then the main focus of British naval power; she ran aground on the way to her station in January. On 22 June the fleet was approaching its planned anchorage in the Syrian port of Tripoli, under the command of Vice-Admiral Sir George Tryon, one of the most distinguished of contemporary admirals. In giving the necessary order to move from two columns into one, Tryon made an elementary error which was not corrected in time to prevent catastrophe. The flagship of his second-in-command rammed and sank the fleet flagship, with the loss of the Commander-in-Chief and 358 others.

The general level of naval administration was, nevertheless, improving by that time. When the Naval Defence Act battleships entered service they were 'the finest group of fighting ships afloat'.[80] Maintaining the margin of maritime security which they represented was not easy, in political terms. The international scene did not become more tranquil, and in 1893 the Liberal Cabinet was

79. O. Parkes, *British Battleships: A History of Design, Construction and Armament* (1970), 330–6.
80. Ibid. 356.

faced with the need for a further large-scale naval building programme. The First Lord, Earl Spencer, encountered opposition in Cabinet on the issue, an opposition which culminated in Gladstone's final resignation as premier. Before this, the naval members of the Board of Admiralty had threatened a collective resignation if the Liberal Cabinet refused to adopt the new building programme.[81]

The Spencer programme involved an expenditure of a further £31 million on naval shipbuilding and costs continued to grow in ensuing years. Between 1894 and the laying down in 1905 of the *Dreadnought* (the first of the even more expensive 'all big gun' battleships), sixty battleships, in six main classes, were ordered. From 1904 Admiral Sir John Fisher, as First Sea Lord, did much to speed up the modernization of the Royal Navy; he scrapped older ships of insignificant fighting value and tried to ensure that key posts were filled by hand-picked officers of high quality. In doing so, he became embroiled in bitter disputes with other senior admirals, which sometimes erupted into public controversy. Fisher, who was adept in exploiting political and royal support, won most of his battles, but the early twentieth-century navy was riven by disputes involving both policies and personalities.

In the later stages of the international naval rivalry, Germany replaced the Franco-Russian combination as Britain's principal naval competitor, with important results in international relations. German economic rivalry was already arousing concern; Britain could not ignore the Kaiser's plan to equip Germany with a battle fleet capable of challenging the world's most powerful navy. By 1905 when the *Dreadnought* was launched Britain had realigned her foreign relations. In 1902 she signed her first modern peacetime alliance, an Anglo-Japanese Treaty which provided Japanese backing for the defence of major British interests in the Far East. British foreign policy also worked to eliminate any possible source of friction with the United States. In 1904 Britain and France succeeded in settling the principal disputes between themselves; at the beginning of 1906 the Liberal Foreign Secretary authorized the armed services to begin confidential staff talks with their French opposite numbers. It was thus principally against the German threat that the great shipbuilding programme took place under the aegis of the Liberal governments prodded by the agitations of the popular press. By 1914, it was clear that, although Germany had a powerful fleet, Britain had maintained her naval supremacy.

Events in 1914–18 were to show that the governments concerned had discharged this crucial responsibility for defence with moderate rather than complete efficiency.[82] In the political climate of late-Victorian and Edwardian years governments repeatedly faced hard decisions on matters of national and imperial security. A volatile public opinion, and a wider electorate, did not show

81. Ibid. 380.
82. Examples include the shell supply crisis of 1915, and on the naval side events such as the battle of Coronel and the sinking of HMS *Hogue*, *Cressy*, and *Aboukir*, both in late 1914.

any sustained high level of attention to foreign affairs, imperial policy, or matters of defence, but was perfectly capable of supporting occasional explosions of popular wrath. The death of the 'Christian hero' Gordon in Khartoum early in 1885, and successive naval scares and fears of invasion fanned by popular novels, were examples of issues which aroused a fickle public interest. For most of the time domestic and even local affairs proved more absorbing to most people.

Both the informed views of government and of generals and admirals and the spasmodic worries of the press and popular opinion did have an effect. The army and, especially, the navy were seen as important. Defence expenditure increased markedly in the Edwardian period and was both in absolute terms and as a percentage of government expenditure far higher than that in either the late nineteenth century or subsequently in the 1920s and early 1930s. The total services budget increased from £63 million in 1905 to over £80 million in 1914 though, even in a period when there was anxiety about defence, these figures represented a percentage drop from 44 per cent to 39 per cent of a swollen total budget. When it came to war in 1914 it was, inevitably, found to have been insufficient.

Summing up

In domestic history these years had brought development of the official machinery of central and local government to higher levels of activity and sophistication than at any earlier time. The celebrated reforms introduced by the Liberals after 1906 would have been impossible without the transformation of official resources which had occurred earlier. This crucial change was relative rather than absolute. The transformation in quality as well as quantity was not complete. The increased range of activity by both central and local government did, however, contribute to a shift in the nature of interdependence within British society, a shift which will be discussed further in the next chapter. By 1914 the nation depended upon the formal services of government to an extent which would have astonished and perhaps dismayed earlier generations, though this dependence still had far to go.

12

Economy and society

c.1880–1914

Whether monarch's reigns and the associations we attribute to them are helpful means of dividing the past into periods is debateable but there can be little doubt that 'Victorian' remains a term redolent in its expression of a cultural unity. The Queen died in 1901 but it can be argued that Victorian attitudes long outlived her and a recent study has conceived of the last Victorians and many of their attitudes dominating British society until after the Second World War;[1] this rather sidelines 'Edwardian' or 'Edwardianism'. Clearly the period 1880–1901 is objectively late-Victorian or even high-Victorian but the question of a discernible break with a new century and a new monarch in 1901 is a matter of interpretation while, save in the narrow literary sense of a school of poetry, few use the term Georgian to describe the last years before 1914.

The coming of mass politics and what has been seen as a 'mass society', preponderantly urban with efficient transport systems, well-organized spectator sports, the telephone, and newspapers and magazines with large circulations, do seem to give the late-Victorian period a new and modern character. Whether we should see the years between 1901 and 1914 as further development on the same lines or as a distinct period with different values that had more to do with the later twentieth century than with late Victorianism is a question that this chapter poses rather than answers.

A number of overarching characteristics do bind the years 1880–1914 together: Britain was ever more an urban society; religion remained important but was less central to the lives of the majority; there were cultural and moral challenges to the dominant ethics of the mid-Victorian period; a dynamic commercialism and consumerism transformed the lifestyles of all classes; more words and pictures were printed and were read and seen by more people; the views and the appetites of the majority of the population became more important, socially, politically, and commercially; government intruded more and more; and, although Britain remained powerful and confident, there were worries about economic competitiveness and military ability in a dangerous world.

1. John Gardiner, *The Victorians: An Age in Retrospect* (2002).

Table 7 Population of the United Kingdom, 1881–1911

	Number (millions)	Increase since previous census (%)
1881	35.0	10.8
1891	37.9	8.3
1901	41.6	9.8
1911	45.4	9.1

Population

Late nineteenth-century population figures showed further massive increases, but, as Table 7 shows, the relative rate of growth was slowing down.[2] Britain exhibited what was to be a general feature of advanced industrial societies, a declining birth-rate. The population continued to rise, albeit more slowly, and the result was a society in which the average age was higher. This led, as yet, not to an ageing, but to a middle-aged population.

As in earlier decades growth was not evenly spread. Some areas which had seen spectacular increases in earlier years now contributed to the slowing down in the rate of growth. The industrial town of Wednesbury had experienced a 100 per cent increase in the thirty years before 1871, but only 14 per cent in the thirty years after 1881.[3] Yet Coventry more than doubled its population during the latter period.[4] The local rate of growth was affected by a variety of factors. The railway centre of Swindon grew from 19,904 in 1881 to 45,006 in 1901; the seaside resort of Bournemouth grew from 16,859 to 78,674 between 1881 and 1911. Military developments saw the army centre of Aldershot, a mere hamlet before the Crimean War, reach 30,974 by the beginning of the new century. London continued its prodigious growth, almost doubling its numbers during the second half of the century, as it had done in the first; in 1901 the capital contained 6.5 million people, about 20 per cent of the total population of England and Wales.

Birth- and death-rates

Whatever the effects of local circumstances, the overall slowing of the rate of increase reflected a decline in fertility in the years after 1881.[5] Even among general labourers, where families remained relatively large, the average number of

2. Mitchell and Deane, *Abstract of British Historical Statistics* (1962), 6.
3. L. Faultless, 'The leisure pursuits of the working class in late Victorian and Edwardian Wednesbury, 1879–1914', MA thesis, Wolverhampton Polytechnic, 1985, 17.
4. B. Lancaster and T. Mason (eds.), *Life and Labour in a 20th Century City* (1986), 20. Boundary changes accounted for a small part of this increase.
5. P. Mathias, *The First Industrial Nation: An Economic History of Britain, 1700–1914*, 2nd edn. (1983), 363.

children per family dropped from 7.85 at mid-century to 5.32 for those who married in the last decade of the century. The national birth-rate peaked at 36 per 1,000 round about 1876, and by 1900 was down to 28.5. Such global figures again conceal considerable local variations in the scale and the timing of this development. The causes of the fall are not entirely clear, but it seems unlikely that it can be attributed in any simple way to an increased resort to artificial means of contraception. In the 1890s condoms were not cheap, costing at least 2s. a dozen, and other contraceptive devices were just as expensive.[6]

The death-rate fell too, but not as sharply, and again with local variations. The overall death-rate for England and Wales was 20.8 per 1,000 in the early 1880s, 17.7 in the years after 1900. In some northern industrial towns, and other black spots, the local death-rate was still as high as 20.4 in the late 1890s. Newcastle upon Tyne's remained effectively above 20 per 1,000 until after 1900; Birmingham's had fallen below that point nearly twenty years earlier. There were variations in time, too. The worst rate of infant mortality came as late as 1899, with 163 infant deaths per 1,000, though even this was still the lowest in Europe. Death-rates increased sharply after the age of 45 (which was quite old in nineteenth-century terms). A hard winter produced a significant increase in deaths, especially among the elderly. The falling death-rate meant an increased average life expectancy. Average age at death for men was 41.9 in the early 1880s, 44 by 1891, and for women the figures were 45.3 and 47, though it must be noted that the figures are much influenced by high infant mortality and that for those who survived infancy life expectancy was higher.

Some of the old killer diseases were losing their potency. Cholera was no longer a serious danger in Britain, although polluted water supplies could still allow disastrous epidemics elsewhere, as in Paris in 1884 and Hamburg in 1892. Deaths from consumption, the most common form of tuberculosis, fell from 380 per 100,000 in 1838 to 183 per 100,000 in 1894. This alone meant an annual saving of about 75,000 lives. Deaths from typhoid and typhus averaged 1.24 per 1,000 in 1847–50, but only 0.07 by 1906–10. In the case of typhoid, the association between the drop in mortality and better water supply and drains was increasingly appreciated. A typhoid outbreak in Lincoln in 1905 was attributed to the city council's unwillingness to spend money on public health improvements.[7] Scarlet fever exhibited another striking drop in mortality, from 106.2 per 100,000 in 1874 to only 17 per 100,000 in 1886.[8]

It is unlikely that the fall in death-rates owed much to improvements in medical science. The adoption of anaesthesia from the 1840s and then antiseptic and aseptic methods during the later nineteenth century must have had some impact in saving lives, but overall the principal cause of the falling death-rate seems to

6. E. Royle, *Modern Britain: A Social History, 1750–1985* (1987), 45–6.

7. J. V. Beckett, *The East Midlands from A.D. 1000* (1988), 246.

8. F. B. Smith, *The People's Health, 1830–1910* (1979), 65, 316, 320. This source further discusses TB, pp. 288–9, typhoid, p. 245, scarlet fever, p. 137.

have been economic growth. This brought improvement in nutrition and housing conditions. Other factors, such as the increasing mass production and cheapening of soap and disinfectants from the 1880s, and the building of more public baths, also made some contribution. Meanwhile, some groups remained more at risk than others. At the end of the century, tin-miners, potters, and file-makers, exposed to dangers involved in working practices, died at twice the rate of farm workers. Poorly paid unskilled labourers also had high death-rates, much higher, for example, than the relatively highly paid coal-miners. At the beginning of the nineteenth century, 8 miners in every 1,000 were annually killed in mining accidents; by the end of the century the figure was down to 1.33. Mining disasters still occurred; 164 miners were killed at Seaham in 1880, 168 at West Stanley in 1909.[9]

Migration

Considerable population movements continued, both within the United Kingdom and overseas. Nearly half of those reaching maturity in Ireland in the 1880s and 1890s left in search of better opportunities elsewhere. Almost half of the natural increase in Scotland's population was lost by migration during the forty years after 1880. Towns like Glasgow, Dundee, and Perth drew on nearby Highland areas in earlier years; by the late nineteenth century more remote areas like Ross and Cromarty, and Sutherland, also provided immigrants to southern Scottish towns.[10] Irish migration to Scotland, especially to the industrial areas of the west coast and to Glasgow in particular, was considerable.

A movement of another kind helped to swell the greatest cities. Persecution abroad, and opportunities in Britain, led to a considerable immigration of Jews. By 1900 there were probably as many Jewish as Irish immigrant workers in London (about 140,000 of each). Manchester and Leeds acquired Jewish communities of about 25,000 and 15,000 respectively, with other centres receiving smaller contingents. The Jews were not universally welcome, and anti-Semitism was common. In 1890, the *Cotton Factory Times*, a newspaper written primarily for textile workers, reported that 'The Leeds murderer Samuel Harrison has been respited on grounds of insanity. Harrison is a Jew, and Lord Rothschild has had the matter under hand.'[11] Resolutions against immigrant workers were passed at annual Trades Union Congress meetings in 1888, 1892, 1894, and 1895. Thereafter a more tolerant attitude seems to have prevailed in that body, though popular anti-Semitism was far from dead.

9. E. H. Hunt, *British Labour History, 1815–1914* (1981), 43–5.

10. N. L. Tranter, *Population and Society, 1750–1940* (1985), 39. C. W. J. Withers, ' "The long arm of the law": migration of Highland-born policemen to Glasgow, 1826–1891', *The Local Historian*, 18 (3) (1988), 127–8.

11. 22 Aug. 1890, quoted by M. A. Savage, 'Unions and Workers in the cotton industry of Preston, c.1890–1895', MA thesis, Lancaster University, 1981, 73 n. 3.

Irish immigrants were not assimilated easily into a British 'melting pot' and divisions between English, Scottish, and Welsh on the one hand and the considerable numbers of Irish who came to live among them produced many tensions. Such divisions were aligned with but not confined to the antipathy between Catholics and Protestants. They were particularly pronounced in Lancashire and Clydeside, producing a strong Protestant Unionist cultural and political reaction (see pp. 261, 288, 357 above).

The economy

The bigger population was supported by Britain's developing economy. Its fortunes have aroused much debate in recent years. This debate owes much to the contrast between the actual evidence of performance and the polemical claims in the late nineteenth century that, after a period of remarkable growth, Britain had become trapped in a 'Great Depression' during the last quarter of the century. It is now broadly accepted that although there was a slowing in the rate of economic growth, and faster expansion in some foreign competitors, the British economy continued to advance. Some of the relevant figures are impressive. Between 1870 and 1907 British industry increased its power consumption tenfold. In 1900 the London Stock Exchange handled well over twice the volume of business of its New York equivalent.[12] There was, however, a slowing down, especially from the 1890s. This applied both to the increase in the gross domestic product and to the overall level of productivity. This was a slowing of the rate of growth, not an absolute decline.[13]

There was also a continuing shift in the relative importance of different economic sectors. By 1901 the share in employment of agriculture, forestry, and fishing was down to only 6 per cent, while manufacture, mining, and building was 40 per cent. Within manufacturing, textile employment (with its high female component) grew slowly in the later nineteenth century, to reach 1,509,000 in 1901; employment in metal trades and engineering (almost all male) surpassed textiles by 1871 and reached nearly 2 million by 1901.[14] Additional employment growth also appeared in some non-industrial sectors. Building employment, after little growth in the 1880s, spurted from 833,736 to 1,130,425 between 1891 and 1901. There were still 1,285,075 indoor domestic servants in 1901. The service sector continued to expand.[15] Some of the most spectacular successes of the

12. We are indebted to Dr Ranald Mitchie for the Stock Exchange comparison. For power consumption (and for the question of depression more generally) W. H. Chaloner, 'Was there a decline of the industrial spirit in Britain, 1850–1939?', Sixteenth Dickinson Memorial Lecture, *Transactions of the Newcomen Society*, 55 (1983–4), 212.

13. B. Supple, 'A framework for British business history', in B. Supple (ed.), *Essays in British Business History* (1977), 9.

14. Royle, *Modern Britain*, 36.

15. Supple, 'A framework for British business history', 10–11.

British economy took place in such fields as insurance and financial services. In the forty years before the First World War, the total national product grew by about 150 per cent; banking, insurance, and financial services generally grew elevenfold, making a crucial contribution to national resources.[16]

The least satisfactory aspect of economic performance in these years was that competing industrial economies, especially the USA and Germany, grew faster. Britain was peculiarly dependent upon her foreign trade, and a failure to retain her relative standing there caused concern. In the early 1880s Britain produced more than a quarter of the world's manufacturing output; by 1900 this had dropped to less than one-fifth. The annual value of British exports was approximately £231 million in the 1880s, £237 million in the 1890s. At the same time imports rose from about £394 million to £436 million. The gap was bridged by the vital receipts from 'invisible' earnings such as shipping, insurance, banking, and earnings on foreign investment of British capital. These rose from approximately £161 million per annum. in the 1880s to nearly £200 million per annum by 1900. Overall Britain still enjoyed a favourable balance sheet, but the margin of safety was dropping.[17]

Historians have, like contemporaries, placed great emphasis upon Britain's relative decline as a manufacturing power and less upon Britain's success as a financial and trading centre and the provider of the greater part of the world's shipping. One example of this approach has argued: 'This sudden transformation of the leading and most dynamic industrial economy into the most sluggish and conservative, in the short space of thirty and forty years is the crucial question of economic history.'[18] It could alternatively be argued that the crucial question is to explain the extraordinary success of the City of London and the British trading and service economy. Modern economists take the view that there is no need to privilege the manufacture of goods over transport, services, and finance. What matters are the profitability and the spin-off in terms of stimulation and the provision of employment of any economic activity. It was as a result of its success as an agricultural and a trading, perhaps a buccaneering, economy that Britain became 'the first industrial nation' but the temporary lead in manufacturing can be seen as only an episode in its economic history. Analysis of the Edwardian economy suggests that manufacturing was only in relative decline, while other aspects point to the economy being, before its time, a prototype for a post-industrial economy. Britain's positive balance of payments in terms of the import and export of manufactured goods lasted less than twenty years and was long gone by 1900. Her domination of the world's financial and trading markets increased in the late nineteenth century as did her predominance in shipping. The number of wealthy men whose fortunes were made in the City of London testifies to the buoyancy of the financial, trading, and shipping world as does the

16. Supple, 'A framework for British business history', 10–11, 15.
17. D. Read, *England, 1868–1914* (1979), 221.
18. E. J. Hobsbawm, *Industry and Empire* (1968), 149.

fact that Liverpool produced so many millionaires and half millionaires in the period 1880–1919.[19]

Industry

Within British industry there were significant shifts in relative importance. The cotton industry, a prodigious contributor to the economy earlier in the century, no longer held pride of place for growth, although the Lancashire operatives were still accounted the most skilful in the world.[20] In the more mature industrial economy of the later nineteenth century, other sectors, such as engineering and shipbuilding, were now the key areas of innovation and expansion. In the last twenty years of the century the annual value of textile exports dropped from £105 million to £97 million. Coal-mining, on the other hand, produced massive increases in total output, reaching nearly 300 million tons per annum before the First World War. Coal exports soared, almost tripling to 100 million tons per annum by 1913. Mining employment rose rapidly, but this growth was accompanied by a continuing fall in productivity. The nature of British coal seams and the exhaustion of some accessible deposits were partly responsible, but it remained true that by 1914 American miners were twice as productive as their British opposite numbers. In coal there was not just a slowing down of improvement in productivity, but an absolute drop in the tonnage produced per worker.

In the early 1880s Britain still produced one-third of the world's steel; owing to American and German competition, this dropped to one-fifth by 1900. In some important steel-using industries the picture was more favourable. American primacy in machine tools grew, but never became complete. British firms remained prominent in some categories, with firms like Cravens and Alfred Herbert among world leaders. In the manufacture of farm machinery, firms like Richard Hornsby of Grantham held their own, achieving record exports to Russia and South America in the 1890s. Some firms in this sector successfully diversified into tea-processing machines, electric lighting, and mining equipment, including gold-dredging equipment.[21] With the exception of the USA (and even for some specialized elements there), the world's textile industries still obtained much of their plant from British engineering works.

In the growing manufacture of bicycles Britain succeeded in keeping the lion's share of export orders, despite strong German competition. By 1906 the single firm of Rudge employed 2,700 workers and produced 75,000 bicycles annually.[22] By 1905 Coventry had 29 firms making motor cars, and there were

---

19. W. D. Rubinstein, *Men of Property: The Very Wealthy in Britain since the Industrial Revolution*, 2nd edn. (2006), 128–38.

20. Hunt, *British Labour History*, 110.   21. Beckett, *The East Midlands*, 292.

22. S. B. Saul, 'The mechanical engineering industries in Britain, 1860–1914', in Supple (ed.), *Essays in British Business History*, 31–47.

more than 8,000 cars registered in Britain.[23] Many of them were not, however, British but American or French and by 1914 Britain was a net importer of cars. The record of the chemical industry was mixed. An often-quoted weakness was the dependence on foreign, chiefly German, supplies of chemical dyestuffs. On the other hand, Britain was strong in soap manufacture, in paint, in fertilizers, in heavy chemicals.[24] In engineering generally the British record was one of mixed achievement and disappointment; there is no convincing evidence of general failure.

Shipbuilding

Shipbuilding's record of continued success was even clearer. Like the Lancashire cotton operatives, the shipyard workers of north-east England were considered the best in the world.[25] In the 1890s British yards built more than 80 per cent of the world's new shipping, and would still in 1913 build more than 60 per cent.[26] Changes in ship design were readily assimilated by British firms; between 1870 and 1900 the average size of merchant ships jumped from 270 to 1,300 tons. The tenfold expansion of international trade during the 1850–1914 period was one of the most important of all historical developments. British shipyards made a vital contribution to the supply of the shipping involved, to both the direct and indirect benefit of the British economy.

The merchant navy

By 1880 Britain had almost 4 million tons of steam shipping registered. In the early twentieth century the British merchant navy included about a third of registered world tonnage. It carried about half of all international trade, earning millions of pounds which made a vital contribution to national income. British shipping companies developed a complex system of 'conferences' covering most regular long-distance hauls; these arrangements linked customers to exclusive use of the companies concerned, in return for discounts on the cost of carriage, thus consolidating British pre-eminence in international shipping.[27]

This success was associated with relative efficiency in British financial services; the use of British ships encouraged the use of British banking and insurance facilities in commerce, while these financial services could equally encourage the employment of British ships. British ports continued to expand to cope with the increased flow of traffic. The building of new docks, warehouses, and similar installations was a marked feature of these years. The Manchester Ship Canal, opened in 1894, allowed that city to develop into a major inland port.

---

23. Royle, *Modern Britain*, 17.   24. Read, *England, 1868–1914*, 226.
25. Hunt, *British Labour History*, 110.   26. Chaloner, 'The industrial spirit in Britain', 213.
27. Mathias, *The First Industrial Nation*, 357.

Railways

The British railway system was now substantially complete. The last major trunk line to be built, the Great Central, reached Marylebone from Sheffield in 1899. In London, the Inner Circle Underground line was completed in 1884.[28]

London had no rivals as the exemplar of urban growth because the Underground, tramways, and buses turned what had recently been countryside or village into parts of greater London, but suburban railway systems and tramways facilitated the physical expansion of many towns. On Tyneside, electrification of the suburban lines began early in the new century. Glasgow was the only city apart from London to acquire its own underground railway; opened in 1896, it was rather small-scale with a narrow gauge and was originally powered by cable. The expansion of tramway systems, first horse-drawn and then electric, also made commuting to work from residential suburbs easier. Victorian towns had been concentrated and densely populated but Edwardian towns were harbingers of the suburbs and sprawling urban areas of the later twentieth century.

Railway developments could still affect specialized communities; the railway town of Swindon more than doubled in population between 1881 and 1901, and in the latter year four-fifths of all employment there was provided by the railway. The railway tunnel under the Mersey, lined with 38 million bricks from British brickworks, was opened in 1886.[29] The expansion of transport facilities was not, until the early twentieth century, confined to advanced technical achievements. An immense increase in the transport of goods was largely responsible for a quadrupling in the number of horses employed in Britain during the half-century before 1900.[30]

Agriculture

British farming was another area of mixed fortunes in these years. Readily available and cheap foreign food posed major problems for many landowners and farmers, but this was not a universal experience. In Lancashire, expanding urban markets for dairy produce enabled many farmers to maintain incomes and standard of living.[31] Farmers in the Midlands also escaped the worst setbacks, but landowners there were obliged to accept reductions in rents; by 1905 rents in much of the region were back to 1870 levels.[32] Other long-established agricultural regions fared worse. The Earl of Pembroke's Wiltshire estate had produced an income of £11,138 in 1874; there was a loss of £2,122 in 1896. In the 1890s, Lord Wantage had more than half of his Berkshire estate—the largest in

28. Royle, *Modern Britain*, 12, 14.   29. *Newcomen Bulletin*, 133 (1985).
30. Royle, *Modern Britain*, 11.
31. G. Rogers, 'Lancashire landowners and the great agricultural depression', *Northern History*, 22 (1986), 250–1.
32. M. B. Rowlands, *The West Midlands from A.D. 1000* (1987), 267.

the county—in his own hands because of the impossibility of recruiting tenant farmers.[33] Many rural communities saw an absolute drop in population, which could be extensive. In Dorset the population of Cerne Abbas was halved during the second half of the century; the Wiltshire village of Great Bedwyn shared this experience.[34]

Even in the less hard-hit regions like Lancashire, there were problems. Falling prices for some farm products enforced rent reductions on landlords; wheat, which had sold for 70*s.* per quarter in 1847 was down to 46*s.* in 1870 and only 24*s.* in 1894. There was a sharp fall in wool prices in the late nineteenth century, and sheep flocks were drastically cut in several regions, including Wiltshire, Dorset, Hampshire, and Berkshire.[35] Those landowners whose incomes were boosted by sources such as mineral royalties, urban rents, or company directorships did not suffer as much as those who essentially depended on their agricultural rent-rolls. In Lancashire nearly half of the important landowners, including many gentry families, were in the latter category while the more fortunate Earls of Derby found their fortunes buoyant. In the end income counted and distressed gentry found that their social and political standing declined with their incomes.

The drop in the cost of sea carriage, together with the exploitation of productive areas like the American prairies, hit British cereal producers hard. In 1870 it cost nearly 16*s.* to carry a quarter of wheat from Chicago to Liverpool, a useful indirect protection for the British wheat farmer; by 1904 the figure had dropped to less than 5*s.*[36] The total acreage of wheat reached 3.75 million acres in about 1870, but by 1904 two-thirds of this was used for other purposes. In a society committed to the concept of free trade in food, 80 per cent of wheat was by 1900 imported. A small consolation prize was that mechanized milling techniques favoured the continued use of some British wheat, but the increase in imports was a blow to the old wheat-farming areas of south and east England. Although it was still possible to farm profitably on the basis of fruit orchards, market gardens, and dairy produce, the loss of rent income in the old wheat-growing districts may have been as high as 40 per cent, again with effects on the social and political status of landowning groups. By the mid-1890s Britain imported one-third of her meat. Some of this was frozen meat from New Zealand or Australia. An additional source was the cattle-rearing areas of South America, where better transport facilities were provided by British overseas investment in railways and ports.

Differential growth and mergers

Within a continuing overall growth of the British economy, there were some significant shifts in emphasis.[37] The contribution of manufacturing industry

33. J. H. Bettey, *Wessex from A.D. 1000* (1986), 260.   34. Ibid. 231.
35. Ibid. 259.   36. Read, *England, 1868–1914*, 234.
37. Supple, 'A framework for British business history', 15.

grew more slowly than that of the increasingly sophisticated network of financial services such as banking and insurance. Insurance spread widely in Britain, and before the end of the century was rapidly expanding abroad. In 1900, 40 per cent of fire insurance income came from foreign customers.[38] The process was encouraged by the creation of larger insurance companies, as a result of mergers; between 1886 and 1900 an average of nine insurance companies a year were taken over in this way. Some of the giant firms which developed were numbered among the greatest of British companies. At mid-century the Royal Exchange Assurance Company had employed 600 agents; by 1900 the figure reached 5,000, and in the early twentieth century successive mergers and increasing business took this to well over 15,000.

In banking too there was a tendency for amalgamation into larger firms organized on a national scale. The local banks which had played an important role in earlier years succumbed at an increasing rate. In north-east England, for instance, the long-established firm of Woods and Company was taken over by Barclays in 1897, while Lloyds Bank absorbed the Newcastle bank of Hodgkin, Barnett, Pease, and Spence in 1893 and the venerable Lambton Bank in 1908.

Takeovers and other forms of commercial federation were not confined to these sectors. We have already seen how the principal overseas shipping routes came to be controlled by 'conference' arrangements between the major companies concerned. In chemicals the United Alkali Company of 1891 represented a similar defensive grouping; like a similar combination among Cheshire salt interests, its success in defending an industry threatened by foreign competition was limited. The Imperial Tobacco Company (created in 1901) was a largely successful attempt to provide defences against American penetration of that domestic market. The English Sewing Cotton Company of 1897 united in close trading agreements fourteen companies which had previously been competitors. The pervasive move towards larger groupings affected altogether more than 1,600 companies in the twenty years after 1880.

Though the effect of this trend towards consolidation in industry, finance, and commerce was important, it should not be exaggerated. There remained many smaller enterprises, and it was still possible for the self-made man to rise into the ranks of independent businessmen and employers. Many firms remained on a small scale, including building, woodworking, decorating, shops, and engineering of various kinds. In early twentieth-century Lancashire it was asserted that three-quarters of weaving manufacturers had risen from the ranks of the workforce.[39] Thomas Mitchell, who as manager of the Constructive Department at Portsmouth Naval Dockyard supervised the building in 1905 of HMS *Dreadnought*, had risen to that position from the shop floor. In many spheres it was possible for ambitious, able, and fortunate workers to achieve remarkable success. Thomas Burt, ex-miner and trade union leader, became a long-serving

38. Ibid. 70.   39. Hunt, *British Labour History*, 279.

MP and junior minister. John Burnett, another leading trade-unionist, who led a major engineering strike in 1871, spent his last working years as a distinguished and respected senior civil servant. Even if such examples of promotion were not common, they were often cited in contemporary discussion of society.

The growth of the financial and service sectors involved some social changes. It generated an increasing number of 'white-collar' jobs for clerks, agents, and managers of various kinds. The number of non-manual wage-earning jobs doubled, from 2 million to 4 million, between 1881 and 1914. There had been only 100,000 clerks in 1861; there were nearly 700,000 by 1911.[40] For the most part these jobs were seen as more prestigious than shop-floor employment in industry. The new opportunities were often taken up by 'blue-collar' workers or their sons.[41] There were changes in upper levels too. Although the hold of the aristocracy on the most prestigious positions showed remarkable resilience, by the end of the century top financiers, many of them of extra-British origin, had obtained positions of wealth, influence, and status of almost equal importance; meritocracy or the 'survival of the fittest' ruled beneath a facade of gentility in the City.

An overriding result of the importance of trade and finance was the supremacy of London and the relative decline of provincial cities. Glasgow, Newcastle, Cardiff, and Liverpool continued to grow and prosper but the view from the 1840s, which had seen other cities poised to be more innovative and self-sufficient, was no more. The capital dominated.

Trade unions

Although there was a considerable increase in the number of more highly paid workers, the trade unions enlisted only a minority of wage-earners. The growth in union membership accelerated, rising from about 750,000 in the later 1880s to over 2 million by 1906, but only about a quarter of all workers were union members by 1914. The 1891 census estimated that there were 250,000 carpenters and joiners, but not more than 40,000 of these had joined a trade union. In part this limited response reflected the availability of other sources of support like friendly societies and the expanding insurance facilities. In 1888, when the trade unions probably held no more than 10 per cent of all workers, friendly societies may have recruited as many as 80 per cent. In 1890 union membership was about equal to that of cooperative societies, at about 1 million each.[42]

There were some areas in which trade-unionism was unusually strong. In coal-mining, unions enjoyed an above average influence, partly because of the peculiarly cohesive nature of mining communities. A stipulation in the 1887 Coal Mines Regulation Act, requiring the presence of men with at least ten years' mining experience in all mining operations, incidentally—and surely

---

40. M. Pugh, *The Making of Modern British Politics, 1867–1939* (1982), 89.
41. For a good example of this, Hunt, *British Labour History*, 279.   42. Ibid. 287.

unintentionally—strengthened mining unions against strike-breakers.[43] This pattern of concentrated support allowed the miners' unions (still exhibiting strong regional loyalties) to return five of the eight trade union MPs to reach Parliament by 1889.

The functions of trade unions became more important in the later nineteenth century, as many firms became larger and the production processes more complex. Negotiations over piece rates often called for superior qualities of technical knowledge and powers of expression on the part of workers' representatives, and enhanced the status of experienced union officials. There was also some increase in cooperation between different unions, illustrated by the growth of local trades councils. The unions were not uniformly convinced of the desirability of such contacts. A separate Trades Union Congress for Scotland was established in 1889. In 1904 the original Trades Union Congress altered its rules, excluding trades councils from membership and instituting block voting by the constituent unions.

When unskilled workers acted to create their own trade unions, the skilled unions often displayed hostility.[44] Unionism among workers considered unskilled did, however, develop in the later nineteenth century. The National Union of Gasworkers and General Labourers was founded in 1889, and its much publicized success in winning the eight-hour day for London gasworkers provided a fillip for similar moves elsewhere. On the other hand, membership of the National Agricultural Labourers' Union, which peaked at about 86,000 in 1874, had dropped to only 10,000 by 1886.[45] In 1892, unions of unskilled workers still had only about 200,000 members.[46] Unionism was also very weak among women. At the 1888 TUC, Mrs Annie Besant irritated male union leaders by accusing them of leaving the defence of vulnerable groups of working women (especially in that year the match girls involved in a major dispute) to 'a woman of the middle class' like herself; the irritation reflected the fact that the accusation was well founded.[47]

Individual union autonomy was jealously guarded; in 1889, for instance, union pressure was responsible for the clause in the Technical Instruction Act which forbade technical schools to teach the practice of any specific trade.[48] After a sharp depression in the mid-1880s, demarcation disputes between different unions in the shipyards intensified and in the next century were to develop into a threat to British competitiveness in that important industry. A similar development had already been seen in 1880 when the footplate men broke away from the main railway union to pursue their own sectional interests in the new Associated Society of Locomotive Engineers and Firemen.

43. Ibid. 383 n. 4; 382 n. 67.
44. H. A. Clegg, A. Fox, and A. F. Thompson, *A History of British Trade Unionism since 1889*, vol. i: 1889–1910 (1964), 132.
45. Pugh, *The Making of Modern British Politics*, 71.
46. Royle, *Modern Britain*, 138–9.　　47. A. Briggs, *Victorian Things* (1988), 203.
48. Hunt, *British Labour History*, 398 n. 114.

Despite such events, these years also saw a tendency for union mergers into larger units, a process which was to continue in the next century. There was also a continuing growth of unionism among new groups. The National Union of Elementary Teachers (the germ of the later National Union of Teachers), founded in 1870, reached a membership of 14,000 by the 1880s, and was soon acting as a pressure group in the determination of national educational policies. Similar developments were seen in the Postmen's Federation in 1891, the Tax Clerks' Association in 1892, and the Musicians' Union in 1893.[49]

Although trade unions were an increasingly prominent and increasingly accepted element in British society, their limited membership by the early twentieth century meant that they exercised only a modest influence. They played some part in campaigns for legislative concessions to workers, but such reforms owed more to a continuing element of State paternalism, and a desire to conciliate electors among the workers, than to any fear of organized labour. In any event, there was no political unity among union members, or workers in general, during these years. A parliamentary by-election in a mining area at Barnsley in 1897 gave a coal-owner, selected by a Liberal association mainly composed of workers, an easy win against a Conservative and a worker nominated by the Independent Labour Party.[50] In the 1890s the Liverpool Conservative Working Men's Association, with about 6,000 subscribing members, was an important factor in consolidating Tory dominance in that city.[51] In Birmingham municipal elections, Conservative candidates in the 1880s included plumbers, fitters, and small-tradesmen.[52] In armaments centres like Newcastle, Woolwich, and Sheffield, or dockyard towns like Portsmouth, Chatham, and Southampton, popular Conservatism was strong. As one study notes, 'Many a working-class family felt a keen sympathy with the colonies whither they had so often dispatched their sons, and took an immense pride in the Royal Navy in which sons and brothers enlisted.'[53]

In the 1890s, with workers forming a clear majority of the electorate, the Conservative Party dominated Merseyside and West Lancashire, Birmingham and the West Midlands, the East End of London, Portsmouth, Woolwich, and Sheffield, and showed considerable urban strength elsewhere.[54] While the years 1890–1910 saw the appearance of hundreds of labour or socialist periodicals, most of them had brief lives and tiny circulations. One significant exception, Robert Blatchford's *Clarion*, combined its own brand of radicalism with a strident patriotism and nationalism; on these lines it was much more successful than, for example, Keir Hardie's *Labour Leader*.[55] In fact, there was no particular reason for workers' allegiance to be given to either of the major political parties.

49. Hunt, *British Labour History*, 302.
50. Pugh, *The Making of Modern British Politics*, 76.   51. Ibid. 86–7.
52. M. Pugh, 'Popular Conservatism in Britain: continuity and change, 1880–1987', *Journal of British Studies*, 27 (3) (1988), 278.
53. Pugh, *The Making of Modern British Politics*, 83.
54. Pugh, 'Popular Conservatism', 271.
55. Pugh, *The Making of Modern British Politics*, 77–8.

The late-Victorian Liberal Party was no more favourable to labour than its rival. It was a weakening Conservative ministry which saw the House of Commons pass in 1891 a resolution requiring the payment of 'fair wages' by firms holding public contracts, which in practice helped trade unions a great deal. Another Conservative ministry enacted the important Factory and Workshop Act of 1901 and the Unemployed Workmen's Act of 1905.[56]

By the 1890s the union movement was probably more influential than the friendly societies, but its influence remained limited. Nor was it wholly beneficial. There were already accusations that trade union restrictive practices were limiting the competitiveness of some sectors of production, to the detriment of society in general. Miners often objected to the introduction of coal-cutting machinery, at a time when productivity in the mines declined in comparison with foreign competitors. The penetration of the home market by cheap American footwear was also blamed on union restrictive practices. In 1906 the Liberal government conferred on trade unions an exceptionally privileged legal status, which greatly increased their ability to take effective action in the pursuit of their own sectional objectives. It has even been asserted that a disruption of supplies of milk and some other foods during a major strike in 1911 contributed to the exceptionally high infant mortality figures of that year. Some recent writing on labour history has argued that by the early twentieth century the trade unions exerted an influence inimical to the overall efficiency of the British economy within a competitive world.[57] Criticism of union tactics was often voiced in contemporary writings on industry; a good example comes from a standard work on quarrying: 'the adoption of machinery to common use in these degenerate days of strikes, high wages and short hours is, without doubt, increasingly necessary to promote commercial prosperity and progress of a nation.'[58]

Caution is necessary in evaluating such strictures. Wage-earners were not the only groups capable of enforcing restrictive practices in defence of their own sectional interests. During the reforms of the law courts in later-Victorian years, barristers evolved and enforced a tight code of practice designed to protect their own interests. These stipulations included the ruling that if a QC appeared in a case then a junior barrister must also be employed and be paid two-thirds or three-fifths of the sum received by his leader. In 1896 the *Daily Telegraph* described the Bar Council as 'the strongest trade union in the world'.[59]

In the early years of the twentieth century trades unions appeared to have established themselves as part of the economic system. The 1906 Trades Disputes Act and the Osborne Judgement of 1909 gave them a privileged status in law but

---

56. Hunt, *British Labour History*, 316, 335.   57. Ibid. 336–8.

58. M. Powis-Sale, *Stone-Working Machinery* (1884), 6, cited by P. Ventom, 'The Freestone Quarries of Ackworth, Yorkshire, 1850–1914', MA dissertation, Leeds University, 1989, 25. Mr Ventom notes also (p. 47) that it was rare in the early twentieth century for Yorkshire quarry workers to begin work before 10 a.m.

59. J. R. Lewis, *The Victorian Bar* (1982), 172–9.

the number of strikes was sufficiently low to be considered an irritant rather than a challenge to economic efficiency. The years 1910–1914 saw, however, a fivefold increase with around 10 million working days lost because of strikes. The 'Great Labour Unrest' largely involved major unions, transport unions and miners' unions conscious of their power to bring economic life to a standstill. Worrying characteristics of labour unrest in these years were the threat of alliances between powerful unions (the NUR, the MFGB, and the National Transport Workers Federation took steps towards a 'Triple Alliance' in 1913–14), the use of the sympathy strike, and the fact that the union leadership did not always appear firmly in control of its membership. This militancy had numerous causes, the combination of near full employment and shrinking real wages, employers' attempts to achieve greater efficiency in the light of foreign competition, expanding trades union membership, the influence of socialists and syndicalists,[60] and, above all, a realization of the power of industrial action in the context of an increasingly interdependent and complex economy. Labour unrest was handled uneasily by the Liberal government dedicated formally to a harmonious view of society. It oscillated between support for employers or unions, sending in troops or despatching ministers with olive branches, coercing employers or threatening strikers. The unrest posed problems for the Liberal–Labour alliance, though leading Labour MPs and trades unionists like J. H. Thomas and Arthur Henderson were strongly opposed to the new militancy when it seemed uncontrolled and in the grip of syndicalist influence.

Between 1910 and 1914 trade union membership rose from 2.5 million to 4.1 million. It did so against a background of the economic prosperity which marked the last years before the First World War. It remains difficult to ascertain how much credit was due to trade unions for the improvement in the condition of the great majority of the British people by the earlier twentieth century, despite the phenomenal increase in population. It seems most likely that unions were able to have a limited effect in protecting members from even worse experiences in times of economic turndown and exercised an influence in maximizing wage rises in times of industrial expansion. Their very existence did contribute to feelings of security among their members and few organizations were able to inspire such loyalty but there is little to suggest that they were among the most effective causes of the improvement in the conditions of the majority of the population.

Standard of living

Evidence about the standard of living is fuller in these years than for earlier periods. Great variations persisted, even among wage-earners. In the 1880s many dock workers received only intermittent employment at low rates of pay.

---

60. Syndicalism was opposed to the idea that the position of the working class could be improved by gaining control of Parliament and legislating in the interests of workers but believed in direct action by which industries could come under workers' control.

A Wiltshire farm worker might receive only 14s. a week; a Tyneside blast-furnaceman could expect a regular weekly wage of £2 to £3. In general, wages were higher in the north of England and in other heavy industrial areas than in the south but the improvement in conditions affected most of the population. In part it stemmed from scientific and technological advances. Increased life expectancy was now to some extent the product of deliberate human action, based upon a greater understanding of dangers to health and how they could be tackled. Of at least equal importance was the availability of the greater resources made available by economic expansion. There were few parts of the world, and none elsewhere in Europe, where living standards were better than in Britain by the early twentieth century. One American investigator calculated that a batch of necessary purchases which had cost a British working family £1.14s. in early-Victorian times would cost only £1.9s. in 1898, at a time when the general level of wages had doubled. In 1884–5 a similar study, after careful comparisons, concluded that British wages were the highest in Europe.[61] The opportunities for spending matched increased incomes. The growth of the distributive and retail sectors of the economy brought an unprecedentedly wide range of goods and services to market, above all, food imports from all parts of the world, and played a considerable part in lowering their prices.

The benign combination of an increase in wages for many and a decline in prices seems to have come to an end at the beginning of the twentieth century. Much of the anxiety and labour unrest of the Edwardian years seems to have arisen not from a declining standard of living but from fears that recently acquired expectations might not be fulfilled. The Edwardian economy experienced a switchback ride with a depressed period from 1902–5 followed by a boom from 1905–7 and, after a brief decline, a period of strong growth between 1911–13. For workers there was no great falling back but rather a struggle to maintain real incomes.

Diet

Food supplies were improving in quantity, variety, and nutritional quality. Higher consumption of white bread, margarine, skimmed milk, and cheap jam brought little or no dietary advantage, but this was only part of a more varied picture. In 1905 the average annual meat consumption per head in the United Kingdom had risen to 122 lb. (as against Germany's 99 lb. and France's 80 lb.). Where detailed patterns of expenditure survive, a significant improvement in food supply is usually evident, even for such poor groups as Wiltshire farm labourers.[62]

---

61. D. A. Wells, *Recent Economic Change* (1898), 354–8. Wells was also responsible for a series of articles in the *Contemporary Review* in 1887, in which he explained the real causes of the recent fall in prices which so worried some interests in Britain. The American consular reports are noted in Hunt, *British Labour History*, 108–9.

62. Hunt, *British Labour History*, 85–7, 109.

Apart from food, these years brought a wider availability of goods and services. In domestic terms the use of linoleum as a cheap and durable floor covering, and of mass-produced wallpaper, was by now common. Comfort, cleanliness, and health were also assisted by the introduction and wide use of such cleaning agents as Zebra grate polish (1890), Lifebuoy soap (1894), Vim (1904), Persil (1907). The mass production of soap, washing soda, and various disinfectants was well established by the 1880s.[63] Large mechanized laundry establishments became common after 1890; the national census computed that employment in laundry work reached 167,607 in 1891, 205,015 in 1901, both certainly underestimates.[64] Gas cookers might have a grill from 1886 and in the following year the pre-payment gas meter was introduced. In the 1890s the use of gas for cooking and lighting spread rapidly.

By the end of the century Cadbury, Lipton, Home & Colonial, Lever, Rank, Boots, Wills, W. H. Smith, Burton, Raleigh, and Rudge were among a host of well-known names associated with a new availability of consumer goods on an unprecedented scale. In the last year of Victoria's reign more than 100,000 Brownie cameras were sold in Britain; there were 14 amateur photographic societies in 1880, 256 in 1900. The number of pianos bought trebled between 1850 and 1914.[65] By 1900, tearooms and cafes, such as those of the Lyons chain, proliferated in towns, enjoying the patronage of social groups who had not been accustomed to eating out before.

Despite the increase in population, consumer spending per capita increased by about one-third during the half-century after 1870, a development reflected in a great expansion of the distributive and retail trades. By 1898 the Lipton chain of grocery shops numbered 242. In the north Staffordshire mining community of Silverdale, there were 95 shops in the early 1880s, 148 in the early 1890s.[66] The cooperative movement continued to grow in the retail sector, and even achieved a modest success in manufacturing; the main producer here, the Cooperative Wholesale Society, was no more indulgent towards its workers than many other employers.

The growth in cigarette consumption was another indicator of a more prosperous society. In 1888 Wills introduced their cheap 'Woodbine', at five for 1d.; in five months nearly 5 million of these cheap cigarettes were sold. Three years later, 41,500,000 cheap cigarettes and 84,500,000 of more expensive brands were sold in Britain. In the jubilee year of 1897, Wills introduced another selling technique,

---

63. Rowlands, *The West Midlands*, 257.

64. P. E. Malcolmson, *Laundresses and the Laundry Trade in Victorian England* (n.d.), 2.

65. For photography, Briggs, *Victorian Things*, 135–6. For pianos, C. Ehrlich, *The Piano: A History* (1976) gives a full discussion of both the musical and the social implications of this development. Briggs records the contemporary comment that 'the piano makes a girl sit upright and pay attention to details' (p. 248).

66. E. Billingham, 'Silverdale: a demographic study of a north Staffordshire mining village', MA thesis, Wolverhampton Polytechnic, 1985, 120. It is possible that vagaries in directory inclusion may to some extent be responsible for these figures, but the general trend is clear enough.

the first cigarette cards, 'Kings and Queens', fifty cards from Alfred to Victoria; these were small, decorative items which the customer was encouraged to collect into complete sets.[67] Improved communications made it easier to set up national supply networks for such goods. The volume of persuasive advertising continued to grow and displayed increasing variety and ingenuity. In the early twentieth century Angus Watson spent £40,000–50,000 annually on advertising his 'Skipper' tinned Norwegian sardines, 'Sailor' tinned salmon, and 'My Lady' tinned fruit. By 1900 the shopping centres of provincial cities exhibited a range of goods for sale which would have astonished earlier generations. Anyone who lived say from 1830 to 1900 would have witnessed a revolutionary transformation in what could be bought by the mass of the population.

Housing

Despite the growth in population, housing improved, too. The decennial censuses gave estimates of the population living in overcrowded conditions which dropped from 11.2 per cent in 1891 to 8.2 per cent in 1901 and 7.8 per cent in 1911. By 1911, 80 per cent of British families of three or more in number had at least four rooms to live in. The British census defined overcrowding as more than two people to a room; the Austrian equivalent was five to a room. The British social investigator Rowntree calculated that when one-roomed dwellings provided 18 per cent of housing in London, parallel figures included Berlin 44 per cent, Stockholm 49 per cent, and Oslo 37 per cent.[68]

Housing developments in these years included some striking examples of model communities built at the expense of paternalistic employers. Lever's Port Sunlight, perhaps the most impressive of them all, was begun in 1888, Cadbury's Bournville in 1893, and Rowntree's New Earswick in 1901. Although such enterprises were exceptional, they were not without influence on wider developments. The general level of housing showed improvement, within a diverse range of conditions. By 1900 most British urban houses had gas lighting; by 1911 about half of Britain's towns were largely equipped with water closets. The housing situation was eased by a building boom beginning in the mid-1890s. There were 831,344 building workers in 1881; 833,736 in 1891; 1,130,425 in 1901. The social implications of this boom in building were not simple or uniform. Some of the new suburbs showed social homogeneity, with large tracts of similar houses; others contained diverse house types within a limited area.

Regional variations remained. The characteristic mass housing in Yorkshire towns like Leeds was the true back-to-back, in which two terraces shared a common back wall. Even here, the quality of the Edwardian back-to-backs was

67. B. W. E. Alford, 'Penny cigarettes, oligopoly, and entrepreneurship in the U.K. tobacco industry in the late nineteenth century', in Supple (ed.), *Essays in British Business History*, 49–58. For cigarette cards, Briggs, *Victorian Things*, 147.
68. Hunt, *British Labour History*, 94–8.

markedly superior to their mid-Victorian predecessors, although many of the latter were still in use in the early twentieth century. On the Great Northern Coalfield, colliery houses built around 1900 were bigger and better than those of fifty years earlier, but many mining families still lived in the latter. Some regional differences are not easy to explain in purely economic terms. North-east England, a centre of economic growth, and generally a high-wage area, had poorer housing conditions than those of other developing regions. Moreover, the bad overcrowding figures from the north-east came from industrial towns, mining communities, and rural villages alike.[69] Scottish working-class housing was particularly poor with half the Scottish population living in one- or two-roomed accommodation and overcrowding in Glasgow at the turn of the century between four and five times as great as in corresponding English cities.[70]

Pressure for housing improvements in the late nineteenth century still came predominantly from social reformers within the dominant minorities. There is little evidence of pressure from workers themselves; better houses might mean higher rents.[71] Most municipal authorities made no significant contribution to housing. When Coventry Corporation built forty-eight houses and some two-roomed flats from the 1890s onwards, their weekly rents began at 4s. 3d. when poorer accommodation in the city was available at less than half this sum.[72] Other authorities were even less adventurous; a prominent alderman in one northern city responded to a 1891 proposal to build council houses as follows:

There was a residuum of the population incapable of helping themselves. The residuum was the result, to a large extent, of hereditary causes, but mainly the result of a life of debauchery, sin and often crime... If it was right and incumbent upon them to provide shelter for these people, it was equally incumbent upon them to provide food and raiment for them. Therefore the Corporation might begin and erect bakehouses and clothing establishments tomorrow. By that means they would get themselves upon an inclined plane, which would land them in the vortex of pure municipal socialism.[73]

Nor did the overall improvement in housing during these years owe much to initiatives from central government. Official bodies helped to establish higher standards of public health in various ways and in 1909 the Town Planning Act gave the Local Government Board the power to order local authorities to submit town-planning schemes and build new housing to replace slums, but in the actual provision of housing the contribution of government was negligible in relation to population growth and the problems inherited from earlier years.

69. The remarks about the Leeds back-to-backs are based on photographic evidence collected and made available by Professor Maurice Beresford. For the north-east, N. McCord and D. J. Rowe, 'Industrialisation and urban growth in north-east England', *International Review of Social History*, 22 (1977), 57–8.

70. T. C. Smout, *A Century of the Scottish People, 1830–1950* (1986), 50.

71. Hunt, *British Labour History*, 358 n. 115.   72. Rowlands, *The West Midlands*, 262.

73. Newcastle City Council Proceedings, 3 June 1891.

Prices and wages

Movements in both prices and wages contributed to social improvement. Prices fell generally during the 1875–95 period, and changed little in the following years. This would have meant improved real wages even if money rates of pay had remained unchanged. In fact the share of the growing national income going to wages and salaries probably increased from about 52 per cent in the early 1870s to about 62 per cent in the early 1890s. Moreover, economic development and technological improvements meant that a higher proportion of workers now occupied better-paid jobs. The proportion of workers in agriculture and similar sectors continued to fall, while industry, commerce, and professional employment continued to increase. British workers experienced shorter working hours than their opposite numbers in other European countries.[74] Many groups of workers won reductions in the length of their standard working week. By 1880 the majority of industrial workers enjoyed at least a Saturday half-holiday, and by the end of the century only a minority were tied to a full six-day working week. This does not necessarily imply a reduction in the hours worked; instead higher wages in the form of more overtime payments might be the preferred result. In 1905 the normal working week in the Portsmouth naval dockyard was down to 41.5 hours in winter, 50 hours in summer. During the urgent construction of HMS *Dreadnought* the men working on her averaged a 69-hour week.[75] This represents an extreme case, but overtime working was common.

Within the overall improvement there were occasional setbacks, sometimes severe. In the mid-1880s, British shipbuilding experienced a short but acute depression. As many as 20 per cent of shipyard workers were then unemployed for a while and special relief funds were established in the main shipbuilding centres. In 1886 the overall national unemployment rate rose to above 10 per cent; 1892–5 and 1904–5 were also bad years in some important industries. The 1904–5 depression, however, followed a boom in the first years of the century, and was followed by another boom in 1905–7.

Women

Working men were not the only gainers. Families benefited from increased male incomes, but there were also other beneficial changes in the position of women. There was a shift in female employment. At mid-century about a quarter of all adult women were in paid employment, but by the early twentieth century this

74. Hunt, *British Labour History*, 108–9. In the mid-1880s an American consular investigation confirmed these points (US Consular Reports, 1884–5, *Labor in Europe*, i. 177).

75. R. Baker and L. J. Rydill, 'The building of the two Dreadnoughts', in F. M. Walker and A. Slaven (eds.), *European Shipbuilding: One Hundred Years of Change* (1983), 14. When electric lighting was installed in the dockyard in 1907, the basic working week became 48 hours all the year round.

had dropped to only one-tenth.[76] Increased real wages for men had reduced the need for supplementary family earnings.

For the minority of women in employment, there were new patterns of opportunity. The growth of local and central government provided some. At mid-century, women were only a tiny minority of official employees, certainly well under a tenth; before the outbreak of the First World War they formed the majority. Teaching and the Post Office were notable employers of women. Although the great majority of office workers were men and boys, the proportion of women clerks increased from a negligible figure at mid-century to about 3 per cent by 1881 and 25 per cent in the early twentieth century. The growth in retailing provided jobs for many women. Department stores and chain stores were set up in all major towns and the latter were to be found in suburbs and small towns as well.

The new pattern of employment created work mainly for unmarried women and, as much of it was based in the centres of towns, it created a stimulus for other forms of female employment. In London in particular the spin-off from large numbers of female workers was a considerable expansion of tea rooms and cafes catering for female clerks and shop assistants who required modestly priced meals in reasonably genteel surroundings. The success of the Lyons restaurants is an example of this.

There were marked local variations in female employment. In some of the textile centres, like Blackburn, Bolton, Bury, and Preston, a majority of women were still in paid employment in the years after 1900. On the other hand, in some farming regions, including East Anglia, female employment in agriculture was fading long before the end of the nineteenth century, though in Northumberland and the Scottish border the employment of female field workers, the 'bondagers', continued into the next century.

Domestic service was still a main source of work for women, and had its own complicated hierarchy in wages and status. Yet by 1900, although there had been a slow growth in numbers, the increased availability of alternative work, and a reduced need for many women to earn, brought about a relative decline in this sector. In 1881 there were 218 female domestic servants per 1,000 families in England and Wales; by 1911 this figure had dropped to 170. Associated with this trend was an improvement from about 1870 in the wages of women servants. It nevertheless remained normal for women to be paid less than men for similar work. In the early twentieth century it was still common in many different trades for women to receive between one-third and two-thirds of the relevant rates for men.[77]

The later nineteenth century saw a small-scale and arduous entry of women into professions which had been male monopolies earlier. By the mid-1880s some centres, including London, Edinburgh, Bristol, Leeds, Birmingham, and Manchester, had a small scatter of professionally qualified woman doctors.[78]

76. Hunt, *British Labour History*, 18–23.   77. Ibid. 104; Read, *England, 1868–1914*, 244.
78. Smith, *The People's Health*, 381–2.

There were 8 women doctors in 1871, 25 in 1881, 212 in 1901, and 477 in 1911. In other ways British society was slowly adopting a more enlightened attitude towards women. The law relating to divorce and to women's ownership of property was liberalized. Late nineteenth-century legislation gave some women voting rights in local elections.[79] From 1869 unmarried female ratepayers could vote in borough elections; from 1870 they could be elected to School Boards; and after 1875 they could become Poor Law guardians (nearly 1,000 women did so in ensuing years). By 1900 about a million women in England and Wales possessed a local franchise. This advance was not universally approved and did not go unchecked. The Local Government Act of 1888 excluded women from the new county councils, and the 1899 London Government Act did the same for the new metropolitan boroughs. These exclusions were not reversed until an Act of 1907, which unambiguously confirmed the eligibility of otherwise qualified women to vote in local elections.

The struggle for the parliamentary vote had not succeeded by 1914, although a National Society for Women's Suffrage had been founded as early as 1869. The issue became more highly publicized after the amalgamation of earlier groups into a National Union of Women's Suffrage Societies in 1897. Agitation became more strident when the Women's Social and Political Union, founded by Mrs Emmeline Pankhurst in 1903, decided two years later to adopt militant tactics. Most of the suffragettes came from groups who possessed the means and the leisure to take up such activities; most of their male sympathizers were similarly drawn from relatively affluent sections of society. Elsewhere, traditional views of a woman's 'proper place' remained stronger. Women were beginning to develop a greater public role in other ways. Political roles opened up for women in the Women's Liberal Foundation, created in 1886, and in the Conservatives' larger Primrose League. Women were also prominent in the national Charity Organization Society, founded in 1869. The British Women's Temperance Society was created in 1876. The National Vigilance Association was founded in 1885 as a pressure group primarily interested in the fight against prostitution, and grew into the wider Women's Local Government Society from 1888. The National Union of Women Workers was primarily a charitable society run by well-wishers, rather than a trade union; until 1902 it actually opposed women's suffrage.

Society responded slowly, but in many different ways, to the emergence of women in new roles. The press continued to extend provision specifically for them. From 1901 the *Illustrated London News* ran a special women's feature: some of the major provincial newspapers had begun to provide women's sections in earlier years. Women were allowed to play full rounds of golf from 1885, and were given their first Wimbledon tennis championship competition in 1886.[80]

79. These developments are fully discussed in P. Hollis, *Ladies Elect: Women in English Local Government* (1987), on which this brief account is based.
80. Royle, *Modern Britain*, 258.

Universities admitted women to their courses and degrees. At London University, Westfield College for women was added as an Anglican counterpart to non-denominational Bedford College in 1882, and Royal Holloway College for women was founded by a patent medicine magnate in 1886. Although Cambridge did not admit women to its degrees until 1921, they could take examinations from 1880. Girton College (1869) had been founded as the first college for women at the older universities, and was followed within ten years by Lady Margaret Hall as the first at Oxford. The Victoria University, a federation of provincial colleges, allowed women graduates from 1880; the Scottish universities followed suit in 1892, the University of Wales in 1893, and Durham in 1895.

By 1914, substantial progress had been made in liberalizing the position of women in comparison with the earlier nineteenth century, but the changes involved were limited in scope and patchy in incidence. Their main effect was on a minority of women among the more affluent and sophisticated social groups. As a recent study has concluded 'many of the more positive changes in women's standing came about as the result of feminism' but, although the efforts of those who articulated and pressed for such changes were a factor, it was largely economic change which was producing an economy and society which facilitated and needed a new role for many women.[81]

Children

Attitudes towards children were changing. Instead of treating them essentially as immature adults, society came to see them rather as a special category of individuals which required separate consideration. There was increased awareness, fed by an accumulation of evidence, that many children were in need of protection. As with other social crusades, reforming initiatives here usually came from within the more educated and leisured groups. Though the number of children in paid employment dropped sharply in the later nineteenth century, it was still common to find working families complaining about the absence of opportunities for children to earn, rather than disapproving of such practices.[82] For much of the nineteenth century many children had been at risk at the hands of parents or unscrupulous exploiters. Child prostitution was a frequent evil. After a famous campaign against 'The Maiden Tribute of Modern Babylon' spearheaded by W. T. Stead in his *Pall Mall Gazette*, the Criminal Law Amendment Act of 1885 raised the legal age of consent to sexual intercourse from 13 to 16. Four years later, the Prevention of Cruelty to Children Act gave courts powers to punish cruelty by parents and to remove children at risk from parental control. The National Society for the Prevention of Cruelty to Children was founded in the same year.

81. Susie Steinbach, *Women in England 1760–1914. A Social History* (2004), 318.
82. Read, *England, 1868–1914*, 215.

The later nineteenth century saw the creation of several organizations specially for children. In north-east England, the *Newcastle Chronicle* began to publish a children's section in 1876. By 1886 this initiative had ripened into a children's society with 100,000 members. 'The Dicky Bird Society' numbered Ruskin and Tennyson among its honorary officers. Its regular messages from 'Uncle Toby' stressed kindness to animals as one of the society's aims.

The concept of youth as a period between childhood and adulthood became established and was seen as both a time of promise and a problem, a phase of freshness and idealism without the scepticism and disillusion which would come with experience of the ways of the world and a threat to society because of its insubordination and disregard for social conventions. The 'Boy Problem' that was caused by young men in work with some money in their pockets and a lack of reverence for respectable adults was extensively analysed. How could the adventurous spirit of youth, too often misdirected, be properly channelled so as to serve the needs of society and nation?

The Boys' Brigade was founded in Glasgow in 1883, and had 35,000 members by 1900. The Church Lads' Brigade was established in London as an Anglican imitation in 1891, and soon enrolled 70,000 boys. The establishment of local boys' clubs was well under way by the early twentieth century. By far the most successful youth organization was the Boy Scouts founded by General Baden-Powell, the hero of Mafeking, in 1908. By 1914 the Scouts had 150,000 members. Although the Scouts had some obvious military features and drew upon the widespread feeling that nations required a youth that was patriotic, disciplined, and prepared to respond to a potential call to arms, the movement also drew upon a desire to promote social cohesion and neighbourliness and contemporary ideas of the benefits of fresh air, the virtue of the countryside, and the need of youth for a combination of responsibility and fun. Other movements, which had been founded with the primary purpose of strengthening religious belief, found that they had to emphasize the social and sporting sides of their activities. The Young Men's Christian Association had been founded in 1844 but by the early twentieth century rather than promoting Christianity with fellowship and sport as ancillary aims, it had come to provide social and sporting facilities with a Christian ethos.

Youths to most Edwardians meant males but girls were not to be left out. Young women of the aristocracy and gentry had, despite the mid-Victorian model of the domesticated female, too delicate for exerting exercise, continued to hunt, and, by the beginning of the twentieth century, were playing tennis and golf. These latter sports were increasingly taken up by females of the prosperous sections of society while bicycling became popular well down the social ladder. Sport and exercise, in moderation and with decorum, were becoming acceptable pursuits for women. Girls were at first allowed to join the Scouts but soon the Girl Guides was formed as a parallel organization. The Young Women's Christian Association, formed in 1877, followed a similar path to the YMCA.

The literature available to young people had, if it was to be successful, to be less didactic in religious and moral terms and present adventure and cater for the preoccupations of the young. The *Boys' Own Paper*, founded by the Religious Tract Society in 1879, proved unexpectedly successful, with a weekly circulation of 200,000. Less serious in purpose were *Comic Cuts* (1890–1953) and *Chips* (1890–1953).

Novels and magazines for the young fell largely into two categories, those which depicted young men proving themselves to be the equals of adults by playing significant parts in wars and on the outposts of the empire and those which depicted a world of the young in which adults were only intermittent authority figures. G. A. Henty was the master of the former genre and his young heroes proved their worth in wars in India, Canada, and South Africa (*With Clive in India* (1884), *With Wolfe in Canada* (1886), and *With Roberts to Pretoria* (1902)). Just as popular was the public school story; here was a boys' world with its own codes and values and adults only came in the person of the schoolmaster, the 'beak'. Rudyard Kipling's *Stalky & Co* (1899) drew on his own experiences as a pupil at the United Services College and was a seminal influence on future writers of the public school novel. C. H. S. Hamilton wrote under a number of pen names, the best known of which is Frank Richards. His stories of public-school life, published in the *Gem* (1907–39) and the *Magnet* (1908–40) and in novel form, made the worlds of Tom Merry and his chums and Billy Bunter of Greyfriars School familiar to a wide readership most of which had never come near a public school. Similar stories for girls were initiated by Angela Brazil and proved equally popular.

It was true of children, as it was of women, that attitudes towards them were already changing by 1914, but the process was to be taken much further in subsequent years.

Philanthropy

Most initiatives for social improvement continued to come from unofficial sources. The Charity Organization Society remained influential and continued its policy of developing social work into a professional activity distinguishing between those deserving and benefiting from charity and the undeserving who should be looked after by the Poor Law authorities, but the view that greater action by government was required was gaining ground. In the mid-nineteenth century, it had been possible to believe that the swelling tide of prosperity and properly targeted charitable work would solve Britain's social problems. By the last quarter of the century, the proliferating evidence of the continued existence of a great mass of poverty and suffering made easy optimism less defensible. Many well-informed people placed their influence behind various campaigns for further public intervention to combat social problems. It was increasingly appreciated that the aged poor represented a category at risk, and the momentum for some State scheme of old-age pensions was increasing. A group of prominent industrialists was among keen advocates of such a reform; they included Sir William Lever (soap magnate) and Sir John Brunner (chemicals) as well as the philanthropic Cadbury and Rowntree families.[83]

The Golden and Diamond Jubilees of Queen Victoria were commonly marked by charitable projects as commemorative activities. In Newcastle upon Tyne, the long-established voluntary hospital became the Royal Victoria Infirmary after 1897, with new buildings on a new site; two leading local industrial families each provided £100,000 for this ambitious project. In the same city a leading citizen provided a new children's hospital in 1888 as a memorial to his wife. Orphanages, convalescent homes, old people's homes, asylums for the blind, the deaf, and dumb, specialized hospitals of various kinds, societies for providing poor children with holidays, and a great variety of other philanthropic agencies continued to multiply. From about 1870 onwards there was a significant change in the administration and finances of many of the leading philanthropic institutions. Instead of being almost entirely dependent on gifts, subscriptions, and legacies from wealthier patrons, voluntary hospitals and similar institutions began also to derive income from regular small subscriptions from workers employed in local enterprises. This development led to the abolition of the old system of admission to voluntary hospitals and kindred institutions (except for emergency cases) only on presentation of a letter of introduction from a regular subscriber. A parallel change was the arrival on the governing bodies of such institutions of elected worker governors representing the new multiple subscribers. At Newcastle's principal hospital small regular subscriptions collected at works produced £2,503 in 1898, and nine worker governors were included in the thirty-two strong house committee.[84]

There was an increasing connection between official and unofficial welfare agencies, which was to develop as a key factor in the process leading to the 'Welfare State' of the later twentieth century. As unofficial initiatives multiplied specialist agencies, Poor Law unions in particular extended the practice of sending appropriate categories of paupers to such institutions at public expense. In one year before the First World War one northern union sent deputations of guardians to check that its dependants were being well treated in the following institutions: Wigton Convent of Mercy, Carlisle; St Joseph's Home, Darlington; Lancaster Asylum; Border Counties Home, Carlisle; St Peter's Home, Gainford; St Mary's Home, Tudhoe; Hospital of St John, Scarton; Storthes Hall Asylum, Huddersfield; Edgeworth Children's Home, Bolton; Sunderland Boys Industrial School; *Wellesley* Training Ship; Green's Home for Boys; Shotley Bridge Training Home for Girls; Deaf and Dumb Institution, Newcastle; Blind Institution, Newcastle;

83. Pugh, *The Making of Modern British Politics*, 112, 117.
84. W. E. Hume, *The Infirmary, Newcastle upon Tyne, 1751–1951* (n.d., but probably 1951), 51–2. By 1947 the annual income from such small subscriptions had reached £126,788 (p. 52).

York City Asylum; Beverley Asylum, Doncaster; Balby House, Doncaster; Dr Barnardo's Home, Ilford; Field Heath House, Middlesex; Leatherhead School for the Blind; Stoke Park Colony, Bristol; Midland Counties Institution, Chesterfield; Middlesbrough Asylum; Sedgefield Asylum[85] This cooperation between official and unofficial institutions was a natural development in a society in which the same dominant minorities effectively controlled both.

Religion

Though philanthropic agencies reflected an important role for religion in the provision of charitable institutions, there was some evidence that the hold of religion on British society was weakening. The religious census of 1851 had shown that a disturbingly high proportion did not attend church or chapel. Later surveys emphasized this aspect. In her celebrated study of Middlesbrough, published in 1907, Lady Bell calculated that about three-quarters of that boom town's 90,000 population were non-attenders. A London study of 1904 showed that in suburban areas nearly half of the population was churchgoing, but in the centre of the capital the proportion dropped to not much more than one-third.[86]

Church- or chapel-going had been far from universal among the working-class population during the nineteenth century, though apathy rather than outright atheism or agnosticism was usually the cause. There were strong social pressures on the middle orders and the social elites to put in appearances at church or chapel but it was among a minority of the upper classes that a quiet scepticism could be discerned. A. J. Balfour was without religious belief and, though Asquith rather enjoyed the liturgy of the Church of England, his stance was decidedly sceptical.

Alternatives to Christianity also found some support: spiritualism continued to fascinate as did the influence of eastern religions represented by Theosophy, while the interest and admiration for pre-Christian religions investigated by the twelve volumes of Sir James Frazer's *The Golden Bough*, printed between 1890 and 1915, produced advocates for Pan and pantheism in the Order of the Golden Dawn. Such esoteric beliefs were not for the overwhelming majority and the general development was the retention of religious belief but with a moderation of certainty and enthusiasm punctuated by revivalism.

Until the mid-1880s, the numbers of new churches and chapels increased at much the same rate as population growth, though the gap between the total number of seats provided and the size of the population continued to grow. Moreover, the building and administration of churches and chapels continued to absorb the energies of many people. The churches included a high proportion of those who occupied influential positions within society. Leading civil servants

85. P. Mawson, 'The South Shields Poor Law Union', MA thesis, Newcastle University, 1971, 96–7.
86. Read, *England, 1868–1914*, 421.

and trade union officials had often been brought up in a family tradition of piety; from 1868 to 1885 the Lord Chancellorship was held by three men who were all regular Sunday School teachers.[87]

In all parts of the country, the later nineteenth century was a time of religious exertion. One day in 1897 a group of twenty-four men and women formed a circle, holding hands, and formally decided to create a new Bethany Baptist Church in the little Welsh community of Six Bells. A year later a piece of ground had been acquired and cleared for building by volunteers. The first pastor was appointed in May 1899, and the foundation stone of the chapel laid in March 1901. By 1905 the first chapel was too small, and a larger one was begun. The little community had been caught up in one of the great waves of religious enthusiasm which convulsed much, though far from all, of British society during the late nineteenth and early twentieth centuries. The revival of 1904–5 was particularly strong in Wales; 'Caught by the wave of religious fervour that swept throughout Wales, the Church witnessed a mighty outpouring of the Holy Spirit and many were added to their numbers. Remarkable scenes were witnessed at Baptismal Services in January and February 1906.'[88] The effects of such revivalist episodes could be temporary, but during their peaks these events were among society's most absorbing interests, far transcending any political events for many people.

The influence of religion was not confined to the formal activities of church or chapel. Many individuals in many different social contexts were guided in their conduct by personal religious faith. The Bainbridge family was by 1900 well established in northern commercial life, with important interests in both Newcastle upon Tyne and Leeds. T. H. Bainbridge wanted to extend Christian stewardship among the employees of his large Newcastle department store; in about 1900 he wrote,

We have a good many Christian salesmen in the house, and I should like some of them to take a personal interest in some one apprentice by gaining his confidence, becoming his friend and counsellor, and sometimes inviting him to tea on Sunday afternoon or supper on Sunday night, and having a talk with him after the Sunday evening service.

A few years later, facing a serious operation, Bainbridge wrote this note:

I am now face to face with the possibility of death. It is, therefore, a solemn moment. I have been a very unprofitable servant. I have no hope except in a penitent trust in Jesus Christ as my Saviour. The first verse of the hymn 'Just as I am' represents, I trust, my attitude to Jesus Christ, on whose promise, 'He that comes unto me, I will in no wise cast out', I now rely for salvation.[89]

There was still much genuine religious devotion at all levels of society, as well as a great deal of merely outward conformity. Anyone embarking upon an openly

87. Lords Hatherley, Cairns, and Selborne (Lewis, *The Victorian Bar*, 157).
88. T. J. Mathias, *Souvenir of Jubilee Celebrations of Bethany Baptist Church, Six Bells* (1947).
89. A. and J. Airey, *The Bainbridges of Newcastle: A Family History, 1679–1976* (1979), 108; G. France (ed.), *Reminiscences: Thomas Hudson Bainbridge* (1913), 210.

irreligious stance would certainly have found it difficult if not impossible to enjoy a position of eminence and influence either in public life or in respectable society.

One feature of Church and chapel life in these years was the proliferation of ancillary activities which might be only marginally connected with religion. Social and sporting activities, annual trips, and youth organizations were among the ways the Churches adjusted to growing incomes, increased leisure, and a proliferation of alternative social activities. Other bodies did the same. The Conservative Primrose League leavened its political activities with such diversions as excursions, brass bands, singing, conjurors, ventriloquists, jugglers, waxworks, marionettes, Pierrots, and magic lantern shows.[90]

Whether such ancillary church activities demonstrated religious decline and were a desperate attempt to come to terms with an increasingly secular society troubled some contemporary churchmen, who thought that those who came to church attracted by amusements were unlikely to become true Christians. A more complex question arose when it came to the absorption of many clergy in social problems. Charity and good works had always been Christian duties but an emphasis upon social morality rather than upon spirituality, upon the redemption of society rather than the salvation of souls, could also suggest a creeping secularization. The legacy of F. D. Maurice's Christian Socialism was greater than its immediate impact had been and the Christian Social Union's less radical social idealism which was influential in the 1880s and 1890s owed much to it and founded centres for social work or 'settlements' in the East End of London of which Toynbee Hall (1883) was the first and most famous. The ex-Methodist preacher, William Booth, used very different methods to bring religion to the urban poor from those of the Anglican intellectuals who promoted settlements like Toynbee Hall. The Salvation Army with its uniforms and brass bands set out to save souls with evangelistic fervour but came to be respected for its social work amongst the poorest and least respectable as well as its aim of spiritual salvation. The ranks of Salvation Army officers grew from only 127 in 1878 to 2,260 in 1886 and 4,170 in 1899.[91]

The Society of Friends also became increasingly active in social reformist work in the last decades of the nineteenth century building upon its traditional pacifism, joining nonconformist campaigns on issues such as temperance, and involving itself in education. This move from evangelical certainty to a more liberal outlook has been described as a 'Quaker Renaissance'.[92]

Religion rather than being a matter of private practice and belief continued to mould political and social attitudes. As well as Anglican socialists there were Anglican Liberals and there were Nonconformist Conservatives especially among Wesleyan Methodists, but a major predicator of political allegiance

---

90. Pugh, *The Making of Modern British Politics*, 52; Read, *England, 1868–1914*, chs. 16 and 26, gives a perceptive discussion of changes in recreation and culture, which has been drawn on for this section.
91. Read, ibid. 269.   92. See E. Isichei, *Victorian Quakers* (1970).

continued to be religion with the majority of Anglicans voting Conservative and most Nonconformists voting Liberal. Few went as far as the Dorset minister, Rev. F. Hirst, who said that, 'Jesus was present at every election ... and that in voting for the Liberal candidate the electors would be voting for Jesus Christ himself'.[93] Scotland and Wales were much the same as England in this respect with the difference that Nonconformity and therefore Liberalism was much stronger; in Scotland, members of the United Presbyterian Church and the Free Church tended to vote Liberal while Episcopalians tended to vote Conservative. The Irish Home Rule issue modified this alignment with a number of English Nonconformists following Chamberlain while, in Scotland, Liberal Unionism became a significant force.

The denominations were also divided over drink, entertainment, and Sunday (to Nonconformists the 'Sabbath'). The Roman Catholic Church, whose members, despite prominent Anglican converts, were overwhelmingly of Irish extraction, took a relaxed attitude to alcohol, dancing, and the pursuit of worldly pleasures after Mass on Sundays. The breadth of the Church of England contained a spectrum of attitudes to such matters but it was from Nonconformity that the major opposition to drinking and much of popular entertainment together with support for Sabbatarianism came. The Scottish Sabbath was particularly strict and dour and, since there was no biblical evidence for the date of the birth of Christ, the one day in the year which in England was both a religious and a popular festival, Christmas Day, was an ordinary working day. Though the influence of rational recreationalists had modified it in some towns, where public parks and even art galleries could be open on Sundays, the essence of the Victorian Sunday was to persist well into the twentieth century.

High culture

A characteristic of mid-Victorian high culture had been that the whole range of the arts and the sciences were, at least in theory, accessible to the educated person. By 1914 this was no longer true and increasing specialization meant that, even within disciplines, practitioners, whether historians or physicists, did not share a fund of common knowledge. The 'man of letters', who effortlessly embraced a myriad disciplines when he wrote in the *Edinburgh*, the *Quarterly*, or the *Westminster Reviews* was being displaced. There were also developments in art, literature, and music that took art forms beyond the bounds and conventions which had previously distinguished them, bemusing in the process many of the educated and providing new barriers to those who wished to ascend the cultural ladder.

The arguments and disagreements between mid-Victorian intellectuals had been considerable and hard-fought but there had been a consensus based on the

93. A. K. Russell, 'The General Election of 1906', D.Phil. thesis, Oxford University, 1962, 388.

'homogeneity of society and intellect, a synthesis of progressive politics and moral art'.[94] The decline in religious belief among artists and writers had threatened this but the hope of many was that humanism working in a rational world underpinned by scientific certainty would provide a substitute. Advances in science increasingly failed to provide evidence for such a context. Darwinism pointed to the survival of the fittest, not the morally superior. In the early twentieth century, the Newtonian universe was much eroded: 'Through the discoveries of Planck, Einstein and Freud, rational man undermined his own world.'[95]

That art served a social and moral purpose had largely been accepted by most practitioners and critics until the 1880s and the aesthetic movement with its emphasis upon art for art's sake provided a disturbing challenge. It claimed that the creation of the beautiful rather than the morally uplifting was the aim of art. Oscar Wilde, James McNeill Whistler, and Alergnon Swinburne were amongst those associated with this approach, which horrified many contemporaries, not just because it was amoral, but because it seemed to favour the immoral, and not just because it favoured the beautiful, but because its ideas of beauty were new and disturbing. Much of its inspiration came from Paris's bohemia which damned it further in the eyes of moralists. With the launch of the *Yellow Book* in 1894 for which the swirling and sinuous lines and erotic imagery of Aubrey Beardsley are the enduring legacy, aestheticism seemed to approach the 'decadence' of the *fin de siècle*.

Just as challenging as a disassociation of art from morality and social purpose was a move away from representationalism by some artists. Whistler, who titled many of his paintings nocturnes or symphonies, favoured forms and shades of colour rather than a conventional presentation of his subject matter. When Ruskin accused him of 'flinging a pot of paint in the face of the public', the combative and litigious artist responded by taking his critic to court. He received only a farthing in damages but had the opportunity to express his view that he interpreted rather than represented what he painted. Walter Sickert presented a challenge to the artistic establishment both in his choice of subject matter, which included the music halls, and in his style of painting which was closer to that of the French impressionists than that of any other late-nineteenth century British painter.

If moves towards less conventionally realistic art were viewed with suspicion, a new realism in literature, which concentrated upon the slum, the outcast, and the deviant, was equally distasteful to much of public opinion. The novels of the French writer Emile Zola were in particular seen as an unhealthy and baleful influence and works such as George Moore's *A Mummer's Wife* (1885) and George Gissing's *Demos* (1886) owed much to his example. Though not a realist in the Zola tradition, Thomas Hardy faced the opprobrium of moral zealots for

---

94. Shannon, *The Crisis of Imperialism, 1865–1915* (1976), 269.
95. Modris Eksteins, *Rites of Spring: The Great War and the Birth of the Modern Age* (1989), 31.

his sympathy for those who strayed from conventional morality in *Tess of the D'Urbervilles* (1891) and *Jude the Obscure* (1895). On the stage, Ibsen's *Ghosts* and *The Doll's House* explored themes previously considered unsuitable for public discussion and were accordingly vigorously attacked for encouraging immorality.

'The late Victorian period', a recent study has observed, was 'Mrs Grundy's finest hour'.[96] During the previous decades, artists and writers had generally exercised self-censorship. There had always been a lively underground pornographic industry but those who hoped to appeal to a wide audience had had to bear in mind the sensitivities of the public which was interpreted by the galleries, the circulating libraries, and the publishers of the three-decker novels. The burgeoning defiance of the mores of the devout and the self-consciously respectable by writers and artists in the 1880s led to a confrontation with the self-appointed guardian of the nation's moral welfare, the National Vigilance Association, established in 1886, which was convinced that the nation's morals and health were ebbing due to a somewhat contradictory nexus of masturbation, birth control, homosexuality, prostitution, and sotto voce the morals of the Prince of Wales and his set. The influence of the NVA upon the censorship of art was indirect but powerful. In the end, however, it was only one manifestation of Mrs Grundy in the moralists' long war with the arts that was to continue well into the twentieth century.

The impact of the challenges to the established conventions and mores of literature and art by either the avant-garde or social realists before the later Edwardian period can be exaggerated. The Royal Academy made little attempt to accommodate them. So far as most purchasers or even admirers of painting were concerned, Lord Leighton and the Holland Park circle[97] or the paintings of beauties of the harem by Alma Tadema provided an eroticism sufficiently distanced by time and place to be acceptable. The trial and conviction of Oscar Wilde for homosexuality led to a major 'moral panic' which made artists and writers more cautious and Britain's equivalent of French *fin de siècle* 'decadence' was relatively restrained, more a luscious and ripe continuation of Pre-Raphaelitism than a permeation of British culture by the ethos of the French poet Baudelaire.

One tradition, which had been central to British art for most of the century, continued to be influential; the reaction of the majority of artists and thinkers to urbanization and industry had been negative and was expressed in an idealization of the rural as the repository of sound values and organic community. William Morris followed Ruskin's lead in his view that the good society was necessary for noble art and the good society was a rural community which valued craftsmanship. Morris's rural utopia described in *News From Nowhere* (1890) was an England where industry and towns had been abandoned and a merry

96. G. R. Searle, *A New England? Peace and War 1886–1918* (2004), 70.
97. Caroline Dakers, *The Holland Park Circle, Artists and Victorian Society* (1999).

socialist England been established in which everyone could fulfil themselves via husbandry and crafts. It is often pointed out that Morris's beautiful wallpaper was actually rather expensive but the vein of rural nostalgia he tapped, the concept of a 'deep England' that was still there, beneath mass production, urban streets, and industrial capitalism, awaiting rebirth was vital. In the arts it would lead to the Arts and Crafts movement and to architectural revivals of the English vernacular, in town planning to Ebeneezer Howard's Garden Cities, in music to the collection of English folk songs by Cecil Sharpe, and in politics to Robert Blatchford's *Merrie England* (1895), Guild Socialism, and to revivals of Chartist land schemes, via Joseph Chamberlain's 'three acres and a cow', to Lloyd George's land reform proposals.

The developments in the arts had implications for culture as a whole and the early twentieth century saw with 'Modernism' a more substantial challenge to the traditions of high art with what contemporary slang saw as a division between the 'high-brow' and the 'middle-brow'.[98] Virginia Woolf asserted that 'On or about December 1910 human nature changed.'[99] This seems unlikely but, if we ignore the fantastically short timescale and concentrate upon developments in high culture in the early twentieth century, there can be no doubt that the Edwardian period saw developments in the arts linked to changes in science and morality, which, if confined to a sub-section of the elite, were profound and seminal. Almost every development that we associate with modernism, abstract art, atonal music, and poems that don't rhyme was present before 1914. The exhibition of Post-Impressionism, organized by Roger Fry, opened in 1910, Diaghilev brought his *Ballet Russe* to London in 1911, Schoenberg's *Five Orchestral Pieces* and Stravinsky's *Rite of Spring* bewildered London's music lovers in 1912 and 1913, and D. H. Lawrence's *The Rainbow* was written before 1914.

One result of Modernism was to make high culture less accessible to the many and preserve it for the few. One writer, John Casey, has gone so far as to see this as its aim:

The intellectuals could not, of course, actually prevent the masses from attaining literacy. But they could prevent them reading literature by making it too difficult for them to understand—and this is what they did. The early twentieth century saw a determined effort on the part of the European intelligentsia, to exclude the masses from culture.

The fate of the lower-class Leonard Bast in E. M. Forster's *Howard's End* (1910) is seen as a parable. Poor Bast's wish to obtain culture proves fatal for he dies crushed by a bookcase.[100]

If there was thus some fragmentation of high culture and in particular a divide between the avant-garde and more traditional art and literature, the former

98. George V, who, with his liking for a tune he could hum, a picture which told a story and a novel with a plot, was firmly a middle-brow but never quite understood the terminology, mishearing as he did 'high brows' as eye-brows. Kenneth Rose, *George V* (1983).

99. Virginia Woolf, *Mr Bennet and Mrs Brown* (1924).

100. John Carey, *The Intellectuals and the Masses* (1992), 19.

impinged little on the majority of the reading public and of those who frequented art galleries or went to concerts. They had heard, no doubt, of Post-Impressionism, Futurism, and Vorticism and may have been aware of the Bloomsbury Group but there was a wide and rich cultural world they found accessible.

These decades witnessed a revival in various aspects of musical life in Britain, which commanded a wide audience. Some of this took place on a self-consciously high plane. Elgar, Parry, Stainer, and Sullivan composed notable oratorios, such as *The Dream of Gerontius* (1900) and *The Golden Legend* (1886), which catered for the growing interest in amateur choral activity (often, in Wales and the north of England, based upon the choirs of churches or chapels). For those of a less serious disposition, the Savoy operas of Gilbert and Sullivan provided lighter diversions. Popular songs could enjoy a considerable vogue; Sullivan's 'The Lost Chord' sold half a million copies between 1877 and 1900. Piano production in Britain doubled during the second half of the century.[101]

The novels of Thomas Hardy, John Galsworthy, R. L. Stevenson, Joseph Conrad, and H. G. Wells reached a relatively wide readership, though not equalling the position achieved by Dickens in an earlier generation. Hardy stopped writing novels, fed up with the attacks upon him by moralists. Then, as now, books which were to be acclaimed as literary masterpieces were less widely read than genuinely popular novelists. Writers such as Marie Corelli (in 1900 her romantic novel *The Master Christian* sold more than a quarter of a million copies), G. A. Henty, Baroness Orczy, Edgar Wallace, and Conan Doyle (his fictional detective Sherlock Holmes first appeared in 1891) sold in much greater numbers, and were much better known, than writers who have subsequently enjoyed greater reputations. The books and short stories of Rudyard Kipling, such as *The Jungle Book* (1894) and *Captains Courageous* (1897), many of them with imperialist implications, may perhaps be seen as one group which combined popular appeal with literary merit. Kipling's poem 'Recessional', with its note of high imperial responsibility, was taken as a chosen text of the 1897 Diamond Jubilee celebrations. A parallel instance of enduring popularity was the cooperation between Elgar and A. C. Benson, which produced an early version of 'Land of Hope and Glory' for Edward VII's coronation in 1902.

Popular culture

The division between high and popular culture had always been a generalization into which a multiplicity of 'taste cultures' had only awkwardly fitted but, by the early twentieth century, it was at best a rough-and-ready categorization. If divides or the possible emergence of mid-culture threatened high culture, it is arguable that popular culture was equally fragmented.

Many contemporary upper- and middle-class observers saw popular culture as monolithic, a culture of the masses; the concept of a 'mass society' was increasingly

101. Royle, *Modern Britain*, 256.

a worry. The old folk culture, a culture of the people, admired retrospectively by conservatives and socialists alike, had, supposedly, given way to a culture born of a sensationalist popular appetite pandered to by commercialism. Spectator sports in particular aroused concern that Britain was going the way of late imperial Rome with bread and circuses for the masses.

The Liberal MP, G. F. Masterman, expressed such worries:

> You may see it [the culture of the masses] in the Saturday football crowds in all the manufacturing cities: see it in concentrated form when a selection of all the Saturday football crowds has poured into London for the 'final contest' for the 'cup', which is the goal of all earthly ambition. All the long night overcrowded trains have been hurrying southward along the great trunk lines, and discharging unlimited cargoes of Lancashire and Yorkshire artisans in the grey hours of early morning. They sweep through the streets of the metropolis boisterous, triumphant. They blink round historic monuments. They all wear grey cloth caps; they are all small men with good natured and undistinguished faces. To an oriental visitor they would probably all appear exactly alike, an endless reproduction of the same essential type.[102]

Many contemporaries saw mass society, mass politics and mass culture as threats but one historian of the period has seen the rich popular culture available to the British workers as less a threat to the status quo than a factor underpinning it and a reason why the British working classes failed to accept socialism.[103] In *The Ragged-Trousered Philanthropists* Robert Tressel painted a sympathetic portrait of a working-class socialist but had to admit that 'He was generally regarded as a bit of a crank: for it was felt that there must be something wrong about a man who took no interest in racing or football and was always talking a lot of rot about religion or politics.'[104] Far from a 'culture of consolation'[105] popular culture provided an active alternative to politics which:

> Bred dogs and pigeons, grew flowers, raised canaries, founded angling clubs and cycling societies, put the factory or the local team together (or seized it from the possession of middle-class patrons) preached in church/chapel, attended Pleasant Sunday Afternoons or forgot what it learned at fourth standard but amazed the middle classes by its knowledge of football, racing, or even cricket.[106]

Sport provided a major extension of recreational activities. In the 1890s East London could already be described as 'football mad', an attribute which it shared with much of the industrial Midlands and North. In 1895, 45,000 spectators turned up to the FA Cup Final, and the figure reached well over 100,000 in the early twentieth century.[107] When Preston North End's Cup-winning team

---

102. C. F. G. Masterman, *The Condition of England* (1909), 103–4.
103. Ross McKibbin, 'Why was there no Marxism in Great Britain?', *English Historical Review*, xcix, 1984, 297–332.
104. Robert Tressel, *The Ragged-Trousered Philanthropists* (1965 edn.), 18.
105. A term employed by Gareth Steadman Jones in 'Working-Class Culture and Working-Class Politics in London, 1870–1900', *Journal of Social History*, vol. 7, summer 1973–4.
106. McKibbin, 'Why was there no Marxism in Great Britain?', 308.
107. Royle, *Modern Britain*, 267.

returned home in 1889, a crowd of about 27,000 turned out to greet them. In 1898, 20,000 came to St James's Park to watch Newcastle United's first game in the First Division; accommodation there was increased to provide for 50,000 spectators a few years later. By the end of the Victorian period, spectator expectations at major matches had led to the widespread employment of professional players; transfer fees of up to £1,000 were already known. Despite its popularity, soccer was not a particularly egalitarian activity. Apart from the increasing hero-worship of prominent players, major clubs were normally administered on an oligarchical basis, with a group of a town's 'principal inhabitants' often taking the lead. When disappointed, football crowds could be unruly. In 1890, when Lofthouse scored in a key match between Blackburn and Sheffield Wednesday, police and troops had to clear angry spectators from the pitch. In another Blackburn match that year,

the referee was mobbed at the close . . . The official had to be protected by the Committee and so demonstrative were the spectators that the police could not clear the field. [He] had to take refuge under the grandstand, and, subsequently, in a neighbouring house. The police force was increased and eventually the referee was hurried into a cab and driven away followed by a howling, stone-throwing mob.[108]

Rugby too had its problems in these years. Another fast-growing sport, its internal divisions produced a long-term split in 1895. Older accounts of this event, which involved the withdrawal of twenty-two Northern clubs from the Rugby Union, endeavoured to place it within a framework of class antagonisms. A more recent assessment pinpoints northern resentment at southern dominance and neglect of northern interests as a more credible explanation.[109]

As the working week became shorter, the appetite for more sedate entertainments such as excursions grew. In 1901, the annual holiday by railway from Crewe sold 20,000 tickets.[110] A farmer's daughter from a village near Nottingham, visiting Skegness in the 1890s, enjoyed walking on the pier and the sands, watching a ventriloquist, and riding on the switchback and the spiral railway.[111] Bicycling increased in popularity, especially after the invention of the 'safety' machine in 1886 and its subsequent mass production. A new bicycle cost between £12 and £25 in the 1870s, but only £4.10s. by 1894; there was also a flourishing second-hand market.[112]

Theatre and music-hall flourished, making their own contribution to the expanding service sector within society. The popular stars of the music-hall were

108. E. Dunning, P. Murphy, and J. Williams, 'Football hooliganism in historical perspective', *ESRC Newsletter*, 51 (March 1984); C. B. Korr, 'West Ham Football Club and the beginnings of professional football in east London, 1895–1914', *Journal of Contemporary History*, 13 (1978), 211–32; B. W. Prowse, 'The control and accommodation of Lancashire football crowds, 1886–1914', MA thesis, Lancaster University, 1981, 1–4; Royle, *Modern Britain*, 267.

109. B. Davies, 'Bifurcation in sport: some preliminary thoughts on the subject of rugby football', *Journal of Local and Regional Studies*, 8 (1988), 23–8.

110. Royle, *Modern Britain*, 264.   111. Beckett, *The East Midlands*, 269–70.

112. Royle, *Modern Britain*, 17.

employed at substantial salaries on a professional national circuit. By 1900 the music-halls, now increasingly termed theatres of variety, had broken their links with their public house origins and had become major businesses as with the Stoll and Moss empires. A final seal of respectability came when King George V attended a 'Royal Command' performance of variety stars in 1912. Cinema started off as a music-hall turn but was in the long run to supersede its patron. By 1914 elaborate temples were being built specifically for the projection of films.

The public manifestations of popular culture caught the eye. 'Mass society' was there for all to see at the football match, the holiday resort, or the public house but there were private worlds that attracted little attention. Most contemporary descriptions of popular culture come from those who were outside the culture. From a distance it was easy to see the mass but there were in fact a myriad of distinctions and hosts of pleasures, hobbies, and sports which outsiders ignored. Higher wages, the retail revolution, and more leisure made homes more comfortable and enabled many to garden, to collect stamps, go fishing, or race pigeons.

A feature of the world of private leisure was the way that sports and interests with rural origins were popular amongst the urban as well as the rural working classes. Coarse fishing became enormously popular and so did whippet racing. The smallest garden could be made productive while there was a great demand for allotments. Gardening could of course be a useful part of the household economy but the competitive urge and the lure of prizes meant that working men were by the early twentieth century entering flower shows and competitions for the biggest leek or marrow.

By 1914 there were dozens of publications devoted to the followers of hobbies, the breeders of pets, and the collectors of all sorts of things. A study of popular leisure in Cumbria has concluded:

Evidence for the nineteenth century is hard to come by, but newspaper reports of shows, of which there were a great many, indicate that, by the 1870s, there was already a widespread interest in domestic animals and birds in Cumbria. What relationship the numbers of entries bore to the actual number of pets in the region can only be guessed, but it seems likely that, as with gardening, shows reveal only the tip of the iceberg.[113]

Popular culture was now a literate culture, for a continuing extension of basic literacy, often coupled with relatively unsophisticated tastes, together with increased spending power, more libraries, and a flood of cheaper publications of many kinds, led to an increase in recreational reading. During the 1880s, although there continued to be a huge output of religious publications, fiction for the first time took the lead in publishing volume. There was also a substantial demand and supply for cheap, popular non-fiction in many forms, including popular histories. The end of the century, and the death of the Queen, inspired works such as *The Life of a Century* and *Sixty Glorious Years*. Most of them

113. Lyn Murfin, *Popular Leisure in the Lake Counties* (1990), 13.

reflected a complacent pride in British achievements at home and abroad. The South African War of 1899–1902 provided another focus for popular publishing.

Cheap popular magazines and newspapers were also growing in number, an increase owing much to increased revenue from advertising. Typical examples were George Newnes's *Tit-Bits* (1880) and Alfred Harmsworth's *Answers to Correspondents* (1888). Sometimes offering glittering prizes in competitions, they provided entertainment for a wide readership. By the later 1890s, these magazines each claimed circulations of between 400,000 and 600,000 weekly; Newnes became a baronet in 1895, Harmsworth a peer as Lord Northcliffe in 1905. A parallel development was the increasing circulation of popular newspapers.

Harmsworth launched the *Daily Mail* at a price of a halfpenny in 1896, and claimed that this venture reached a circulation of 1 million during the South African War. Advertising revenue was crucial; the *Mail* would have run at a loss without this income. From 1903 the *Daily Mirror* (originally designed as a newspaper specifically for women) was added to the Harmsworth stable. Some leading provincial newspapers, such as the *Manchester Guardian* and the *Newcastle Chronicle*, moved with the times; they took advantage of improved communications and printing methods to maintain a hold on their own regional readerships, and offered an increased range of news and special features. Altogether, newspaper readership probably doubled during the twenty years before 1906. That newspapers didn't dictate popular taste but had to reflect it is demonstrated by the fact that even those papers owned by the Quaker Rowntree and Cadbury families had, reluctantly, to publish the racing news.[114]

Did such publications represent a watered-down high culture, the emergence of a mid-culture, or the proliferation of a literate popular culture? Many contemporaries worried that mass literacy, rather than resulting in an elevation of popular taste, catered for the lowest common denominator. Yet, an itemization of the contents of *Tit Bits*, a favourite butt of intellectuals, has found 40,000 words of solid print per issue , serialized novels and excerpts from authors such as Dickens, Thackeray, George Eliot, Washington Irving, and Ruskin, together with guides to walks in the Lake District.[115]

A newspaper could be read in a work-break or at the pub but it seems likely that the new popular newspapers were largely bought to be read at home, while this is certainly true of magazines and popular novels. Contemporaries and historians alike have almost certainly concentrated too much on the public and therefore easily observable manifestations of popular culture, important as these were. The private lives of the seemingly indistinguishable masses were less accessible to observers but higher real wages and better housing had resulted in a flowering of private and domestic cultures. This had a considerable importance for women. The degree to which women were excluded from Victorian popular

114. *The Letters of Arnold Stephenson Rowntree to Mary Katherine Rowntree 1910–15* edited by Ian Packer, Camden Fifth Series, vol. 20, 2002, 10.

115. Carey, *The Intellectuals and the Masses*, 108–9.

culture has probably been exaggerated; women did go to public houses, though they had their segregated places, they and their children went on seaside holidays and they were to be found at the music-hall and the racecourse as well. There is, nevertheless, no doubt that, so far as its public manifestations were concerned, this was a predominantly male popular culture. Much of culture was work-centred; within the workplace and its network of social relations and hierarchies of status was a culture which permeated the rest of male life. Men socialized with their equals in a particular industry, drinking and going to football matches with them, while they confidently expected their sons to follow in their footsteps, for the British artisan was as convinced of the rightness of the hereditary system as any aristocrat. The developments in domestic culture and the early beginnings of a more consumerist society did not displace but did modify this predominantly male culture.

The culture of women was markedly different, being based upon home and neighbourhood rather than upon employment. If men's preoccupation was with earning a wage, women's was with making it stretch to support home and family. This sexual–cultural division was not displaced but was softened in the late-nineteenth and early twentieth century as men spent more time in the home with a domestic leisure shared to a greater degree by both sexes. The leisure opportunities open to women were also beginning to expand. Many of the younger women who went out to work found that clothing manufacturers, shops, restaurants, and the entertainment industry were beginning to cater for them while, by the very end of our period, the cinema was establishing itself as a place which respectable women could visit by themselves.

Education

These developments would have been impossible but for wider literacy. By 1900 it was accepted that elementary education and basic literacy ought to be available freely and generally. By then the board schools had overtaken the Church of England as the principal supplier of elementary education, although the total of all sectarian schools still outnumbered those provided by the school boards. There was much local variety. Many rural villages were served by only one school, often an Anglican foundation. The situation in urban areas often gave the board schools a bigger role, but even there variations existed. Blackburn in 1895 possessed 23 Anglican schools with 15,400 school places; 16 Nonconformist schools with 6,892; 7 Roman Catholic schools with 5,200; and only two board schools with 1,147.[116]

For wealthier people a separate educational provision existed, leading from the fee-paying preparatory schools to the growing number of fee-paying public schools. In 1894, Campbell College, Belfast, was founded to provide that region

---

116. R. L. Walton, 'The labour movement in Blackburn, 1880–1914', MA dissertation, Huddersfield Polytechnic, 1981, 30.

with a public school of its own. Other new foundations included the Methodist schools Culford (1881) and Kent College (1885). The Quakers set up Leighton Park in 1890, the Roman Catholics St Benedict's School, Ealing, in 1892. There was also expansion in older schools; Shrewsbury School moved to new and larger premises in 1881. The 1870s had seen the establishment of a range of girls' public schools, and this trend continued, with thirty-four new foundations in the last two decades of the century.

Public elementary education, though, was free from 1891, and by 1900 annual State educational expenditure had passed the £7 million mark. The increased public importance of education was recognized by the creation of the ministerial Board of Education in 1900. For a board school pupil to reach higher education was still a rare achievement, usually dependent upon contact with uncommonly devoted and able teachers at a lower level of schooling. Only a handful were able to reach the universities by means of scholarships open to candidates from elementary schools, but this select band was increasing slowly. The 1902 Education Act provided for the creation of the local grammar schools which were to be the main route to higher education for children from poorer families until the great majority of them were replaced by comprehensives in the later twentieth century. In 1904 the Board of Education issued amended regulations which aimed at making it easier for able pupils at public elementary schools to proceed to higher levels of education. In these early years the numbers benefiting from such opportunities remained small.

The universities received little help from the State. In 1889 the Conservative government established an annual Exchequer grant of £15,000, distributed on the advice of a special committee, ancestor of the present University Funding Council. In 1890 came the first tiny official subsidy for scientific education. By 1901, although the principle of official encouragement of university education and research had been accepted, the annual total awarded had only reached the trivial figure of £25,000. Local and regional initiatives were much more fruitful. University colleges were founded at Nottingham in 1881, Dundee in 1883, Reading in 1892, and Sheffield in 1895. The independent University of Birmingham was established in 1900 and the London School of Economics in 1905. Manchester and Liverpool became separate universities in 1903 and 1904, Sheffield in 1905, and Bristol in 1909. Success in the tobacco trade enabled H. O. Wills to finance the attainment of independent status by the University of Bristol.

Compared with today, the number of students remained small, particularly those reading for degrees. By 1890 the provincial university institutions produced only about 100 graduates annually; twenty years later the figure had risen to 500–600.[117] Most students did not proceed to degree-level work, but took a variety of certificates or diplomas, including teaching qualifications. The new colleges and universities were chronically short of money, although there were

117. Read, *England, 1868–1914*, 286.

some subsidies from local authorities; in 1904 Liverpool Corporation gave £10,000, Sheffield £7,500, and Leeds £5,500 to their local university institutions. London County Council gave the LSE the site for its first residential accommodation. In provincial centres, local industrialists often played an important role in forwarding higher education, and academic posts were created with local interests in mind. Glasgow University instituted the first professorship in naval architecture in 1883; Newcastle founded professorships of engineering and naval architecture in 1891 and 1906.

The older universities retained their high prestige, and most of their students came from the public schools, where curricula were commonly designed for this progression. Although there was some expansion in the teaching of science and technology at Oxford and Cambridge, the number of students enrolled in those courses remained low, especially in comparison with the numbers of trained scientists now being produced by Britain's principal economic competitors. In 1900 the Oxford Class Lists saw the following proportions: Classics 34 per cent, History 33 per cent, Natural Sciences 8 per cent, Mathematics 6 per cent; at Cambridge Natural Sciences came top with 27 per cent, but Classics still provided 25 per cent, Mathematics 16 per cent, and History 10 per cent.[118]

Violence and crime

Although an improved standard of living and of opportunity, coinciding with rapidly growing population, was a remarkable achievement in late-Victorian and Edwardian Britain, the success was not unqualified. From time to time troops had still to be called upon to aid the civil power. During a fiercely contested miners' strike in 1893, soldiers guarding pithead installations in Yorkshire fired upon an attacking crowd, and two men were shot dead.[119] In the same year the 1st Royal Dragoons were sent to Hull to help maintain order during a dockworkers' strike. By the early twentieth century, governments were more wary about the employment of troops in such situations. During the autumn of 1910 when there were violent incidents during a coal strike in the Rhondda Valley, the Home Secretary, Winston Churchill, stood firmly against pressure to use troops and halted at Cardiff the cavalry which had been summoned at the behest of the Chief Constable of Glamorgan. Even when strikers moved into the village of Tonypandy and wrecked many shops, Churchill insisted that law and order should be left to the police; he stationed a cavalry squadron as a precautionary measure but these troops were not used. For his pains, he was criticized by *The Times* for withholding troops and by Labour mythologists for seeking confrontation.[120]

118. Royle, *Modern Britain*, 372.
119. R. G. Neville, 'The Yorkshire miners and the 1893 lockout: the Featherstone "massacre"', *International Review of Social History*, 21 (1976).
120. M. Gilbert, *Churchill: A Life* (1991), 219–21.

The 'Jack the Ripper' murders of 1888 were among a series of atrocious crimes which aroused widespread publicity and concern. Robberies, often accompanied by violence, were still common. There were many prostitutes, whose services were utilized at all levels of society. Police regulations often reflected a tacit acceptance of their activities. Yet there was overall a welcome drop in the level of serious crime. There were 100,000 indictable crimes in the police records of England and Wales in 1882, only 76,000 in 1899. There was an even greater drop in the figures for assaults on police officers. It is unlikely that these trends can be attributed to any remarkable improvement in police skills, more probable that they reflect other factors such as better education, more widespread respectability, higher incomes, and a toughening attitude expressed in long prison sentences for convicted criminals.[121] The early twentieth century saw, however, a new role for the police which would cause friction between them and the wealthier members of society, the use of the law to control motorists.[122]

Poverty

Poverty and slum conditions remained. Though the proportion of the population formally listed as paupers dropped to below 3 per cent by the end of the century, less than half the figure for the 1830s, an increasing number of surveys and descriptions, from both official and unofficial sources, demonstrated the continued existence of substantial and intractable areas of poverty. In 1886 Booth estimated that 30 per cent of London's population lived in conditions which he described as poverty. In 1899 Rowntree's first survey of York calculated that 18 per cent of its inhabitants had absolutely inadequate resources, while a further 18 per cent lived in poverty partly because of inadequate management of income. In 1894 Booth claimed that 30 per cent of those over 65 were paupers (though this seems on the high side). A recent calculation suggests that in 1900 perhaps 15 per cent of British people lived in conditions which reasonable contemporary opinion would have regarded as serious poverty.[123] A foreign visitor to London in 1896 described those who lived in Whitechapel and Tower Hill as 'in abject poverty, squalid, wan, and forbidding in appearance', living in 'narrow, dirty, reeking streets'.[124] All major cities had slums into which much of the poverty and other social problems of the day were concentrated. Many of these slums lasted for generations, and it was not until well into the twentieth century that some of them were tackled effectively. Country towns and rural villages could also display slum conditions.

---

121. Read, *England, 1868–1914*, 255–6.
122. Clive Emsley, 'Mother, what did policemen do when there weren't any motors? The law, the police and the regulation of motor traffic in England, 1900–1939', *The Historical Journal*, vol. 36, 2 (1993).
123. Hunt, *British Labour History*, 117–20.
124. P. de Rousiers, *The Labour Question in Britain* (1896), 100–2.

Whether or not poverty in Britain was worse or better than in those countries where comparisons are realistic, western European countries, the United States, or the British dominions, is almost impossible to resolve. All that can be said is that by contemporary standards poverty in Britain was no worse and probably less extreme than in comparable states. Relative to the British past, it was less dire, while relative to the early twenty-first century it was dire indeed.

Despite these continuing problems, and the increases in the activities of local and central government, many people, perhaps a majority, took little or no interest in politics. In 1900 the total active membership of the Independent Labour Party, the biggest left-wing political organization, was probably about 6,000, about equal to the number of those paying Primrose League subscriptions in Bolton.[125] The attraction of the Primrose League, with its attachment to the empire and the monarchy, might have been its varied social programme as much as any political stance, but pride in Britain's achievements at home and overseas, and attachment to the existing order, were more pervasive than any desire for an alternative political, social, or economic system.

The 'classes' and the 'masses'

Gladstone famously distinguished between the 'classes' and the 'masses'. By the 'classes' he seems to have meant something rather wider than the aristocracy, a social and political elite composed of those of wealth, education, and influence. The decline of the British aristocracy has been much debated but it still possessed enormous social prestige and a large proportion of the nation's wealth[126] even if a decline in its political influence, discernible since the 1880s, was evident by 1914.

At the same time there was an increasing number of rich people, often ostentatiously displaying their wealth. Personal fortunes accumulated in industry and commerce could rival those of rich aristocratic landowners. In 1899, for example, the iron-master W. O. Foster left an estate of £2.5 million and Sir Charles Tennant, the Glasgow chemical manufacturer and father of Margot Asquith left over £3 million. Yet it remained easier to acquire wealth than status. Although the ranks of the peerage were becoming more open to newer forms of wealth and distinction, most new peers still came from within the charmed circle of established aristocratic interests, even though their families may have been relatively recent arrivals there.

One way to enter the aristocracy was by marriage and, although the great majority of aristocrats and gentry married within their own social strata, the late

125. M. D. Pugh, *The Tories and the People* (1985), 2.

126. D. Cannadine, *The Decline and Fall of the British Aristocracy* (1990) provides a detailed analysis of the position of the aristocracy at mid-century. W. D. Rubinstein, *Men of Property: The Very Wealthy in Britain since the Industrial Revolution* (2006) demonstrates that aristocratic fortunes tended to remain greater than those of industrialists.

nineteenth and early twentieth century aristocracy was no more inclined to spurn new money in the shape of an heiress than had been its predecessors. Much attention was given to the number of marriages between British noblemen and American heiresses. Between 1870 and 1914 there were 104 marriages by peers and the sons of peers to American brides. Among these brides were Consuela Vanderbilt who married the Duke of Marlborough, Jennie Jerome, who married Lord Randolph Churchill, and Mary Leiter, who married Lord Curzon. It has been argued that such marriages were more a sign of the coming of a 'transatlantic-cosmopolitan upper class' than a narrowing of social divides.[127]

The upper circles of power and prestige had long faced the problem of how to refresh itself with new men and new money without losing control of the process. The social rounds of high society were the important filter. New men and their wives queued up but it was aristocratic ladies who, for the most part, guarded the gate and let some through. High society had become ever more complex as the social calendar became more set and more noticeable to those outside it owing to the photographing of events and of society beauties and the coverage of balls and receptions by illustrated magazines. The magazine *The Queen* had a regular column called 'The Upper 10,000 At Home and Abroad'.[128] The pace at which social advancement was possible, was, nevertheless, increasing and it is possible to conceive of a greater symbiosis between wealth and birth or recent and old money.

Below the 'classes' was not just the 'masses' but complex layers for a myriad of intermediate positions separated the very poor from the very rich. Income tax was still paid only by the affluent but the number of income tax payers went far beyond the few thousand families that made up 'society'. In the mid-1870s about half a million people paid income tax; by 1900 the number had risen to 900,000. Every town and county had its mini-society and pecking order, its dominant families and those who longed to join them, while there were often alternative hierarchies determined by religion.

In 1889 Engels described British society as possessing 'numerous gradations each recognised without question, each with its own pride' and (he added significantly) with 'its inborn respect for its "betters" and superiors'.[129] A distinguished modern study of labour history has emphasized 'The remarkable diversity in every aspect of working-class life and the keen consciousness of sectional interests'.[130] By the early years of the twentieth century, the Board of Trade's *Labour Gazette* regularly provided a mass of evidence on the enormous diversity of contemporary patterns of occupation, wages, and earnings. The use of the terminology of social class was by now well established, it is true, but expressions like 'the working class' and 'the middle class' were a convenient (and often misleading) social shorthand rather than a precise vocabulary delineating social realities.

127. F. M. L. Thompson, *The Rise of Respectable Society*, 107.
128. Leonore Davidoff, *The Best Circles. Society, Etiquette and the Season* (1973), 62.
129. Hunt, *British Labour History*, 276.   130. Ibid. 340.

For most people, then as now, life was primarily about local, personal, and family matters, rather than broader affairs with national or international implications. Until the coming of the motor bus after the First World War, many rural communities went on living in relative isolation. There were increasing tendencies, though, towards wider association within society. The diversifying professions crystallizing out of British society continued to grow, with their regular provision of national conferences and national professional publications. Major trade unions too developed their national frameworks and institutions. Within the still-important friendly society movement, the large national societies like the Hearts of Oak flourished and expanded, and many local societies were swallowed up. An increasingly urban society was less tied to purely local concerns than earlier communities had been.

Identities

The period 1815–1914 was one in which the concept of a British identity steadily strengthened and the early twentieth century saw it at its most cohesive. This was assisted by the success of the economy and by the increase of Britain's power and influence in the world. Great cities like Glasgow, Cardiff, Liverpool, or Newcastle represented the British rather than Scottish, Welsh, or English economies and its worldwide links and manifestations. The popular culture of a mature industrial society was largely inclusively British, though English music-hall turns might have a rough reception in Glasgow, while Marie Lloyd found even English provincial audiences difficult. Englishmen represented Scottish parliamentary constituencies with little comment as did Scots who represented English seats. The British Army was an important factor in the growth of Britishness with, in 1829, 5 per cent and 12 per cent of colonels, being, respectively, Welsh or Scottish, and Ireland supplying 21 per cent.[131] The English could comfort themselves with the unspoken assumption that Britain was a euphemism for a greater England. Scots and Welsh combined without much difficulty an interest in their own pasts and a sense of a distinct identity with a common Britishness.

Much of the success of Britishness derived from the way in which it offered a layer of identity compatible with potentially conflicting loyalties. Numerous Scots took advantage of a formula which left them national self-respect while participating in the commercial and professional possibilities of an empire whose metropolis was London, not Edinburgh. So too, did many Irish, including some Catholics. And for Welsh, the ancient Britons, it was even easier to think of English ways as British.[132]

Internal migration seems to have made little difference. Scots who migrated to England and stayed were within a generation only identifiable by names. The Welsh, probably because the development of the industries of south Wales

131. Searle, *A New England?*, 15.
132. P. Langford, *Englishness Identified: Manners and Character 1650–1850* (2000), 13.

provided employment opportunities, seem not to have emigrated in great numbers either to England or the Empire but there was massive English migration to south Wales which eventually produced, not English enclaves, but a new form of Welshness, without the language. Catholic Irish identity was more tenacious, persisting over several generations in British towns with religion and an enduring Irish problem as its cement.

Borders could be, despite Britishness, sharp. There was no gentle transition for the traveller crossing the Tweed, despite a common Saxon ancestry in Northumberland and Berwickshire, nor if he journeyed from Carlisle to Longtown. As a German visitor had discovered earlier in the nineteenth century, the inhabitants of Northumberland were more zealous in their Englishness than Englishmen further south.[133] An exception on the Welsh-English border was Monmouthshire, for if the Severn provided a natural boundary between England and south Wales as it neared its estuary, the border between Gloucestershire and Herefordshire on one side and Wales on the other involved this contested English county.

Both Scotland and Wales had embraced, at least superficially, forms of identity that had developed from romanticism in the early nineteenth century (see pp. 90–2 above), identities which came to be accepted by many English. The more important factors which made Scotland different were those which had been preserved in the Act of Union, a different law, education system, and established church. Of these, the most important was the latter and it was Presbyterianism, combined, somewhat uneasily, with the literary, scientific, and educational inheritance from the Scottish Enlightenment, which underpinned Scottish identity. As with the English, who found the essence of England in the countryside, the Scots when in search of the *real* Scotland found it in a sturdy peasantry acclaimed in the Kailyard school of novelists rather than in the world of town and industry.

In the late nineteenth century and early twentieth century both Scotland and Wales received additional national institutions. Scotland had its Scottish Office and Wales its National University and from 1905 its National Library at Aberystwyth. A problem for England was the lack of a folk tradition and costume, real or invented, and a convincing ethnic identity, but the English, despite revivals/inventions in the field of folk culture and a nostalgia for a 'deep' England of manor village and country town, didn't really need either; success in the present and recent past was enough, while did it really matter whether institutions like the British Museum were classed as British rather than English?

It has been suggested that wider associations rested upon literacy and the literary forms which catered to it, novels and newspapers, which made possible 'imagined communities'.[134] The physical bonds between industries and cities also played a part creating common national and economic interests and interest groups. Just as employers' federations were British so was the trades union movement. Although

133. J. G. Kohl, *Ireland, Scotland and England* (1844) quoted by Langford, *Englishness*, 16.
134. B. Anderson, *Imagined Communities. Reflections on the Origin and Spread of Nationalism* (1991).

a common sense of being British, though still being Scottish, Welsh, or English, marked Edwardian Britain, the failure to associate the majority of the Irish with Britain was apparent. That Union had failed, though the failure was made complex by the fact that it was confined to Catholic Ireland while Protestant Ireland and especially predominantly nonconformist parts of Ulster had grown ever more enthusiastically Unionist.

The export of Irish antipathies and rivalries to Britain via the considerable Irish immigration of the nineteenth century had far-reaching effects. Much of Scotland divided itself politically between a Unionism which was self-consciously protestant and a Liberalism which gained much support from its association with home rule for Ireland. The politics of Liverpool were marked by fierce religious and national antagonisms, while on Tyneside two adjacent shipbuilding towns, Hebburn and Jarrow, were divided on similar lines, the one with its Orange Lodge and Protestant and Unionist Association, while the other, normally supportive of Liberalism because of the Home Rule question, provided over 2,000 votes for an Irish Nationalist candidate at a by-election in 1907.

Within Britain and the United Kingdom the English population continued to outpace in its growth the smaller nations. By the beginning of the twentieth century 82.5 per cent of the British population and 73 per cent of the United Kingdom population lived in England. This was significant in determining that a degree of Anglicization prevailed throughout the Kingdom even as it resulted in reactions to it. The preponderance of the English also made any proposals for devolution difficult. The English were fond of their counties and cities and towns but regions meant little to them and even less as the population became more geographically mobile; 'devolution all round' would result in a very unequal partnership.

The British and the Empire

There can be little doubt that the acquisition of a great empire affected British identity. Patriotism had moved in the late eighteenth and earlier nineteenth centuries from the constituent realms of the United Kingdom towards Britain and the Union flag and the Empire over which the flag flew reinforced this process. The British located their identity less and less with continental Europe and saw themselves as a people with worldwide interests. The Empire was also a unifying force in British society; it generated a sense of purpose and straddled class and politics. This is not to state that the greater part of the British public gave the priority to the Empire that we find with Cecil Rhodes, Lord Milner, Joseph Chamberlain, or Rudyard Kipling, or that they had any sophisticated understanding of imperialism as a political philosophy. There was rather a 'generalized imperial vision' which permeated many forms of popular culture.[135]

---

135. J. M. McKenzie, *Imperialism and Popular Culture* (1986), 9.

British attitudes towards the different kinds of empire differed markedly. The white dominions were regarded by many as Britain overseas, familiar societies where family members had emigrated and one might consider moving to oneself. There were considerable differences in the percentages of emigrants from the different parts of Britain to the empire: Scots emigrated in far greater numbers making up half of the British-born in Canada, Australia, and New Zealand in 1901, while 'the Welsh were rarities everywhere'.[136] The other parts of the Empire were an exotic growth, a source of pride when school children were introduced to the world map, the context for popular adventure stories and a colourful ingredient at jubilees and coronations.

A recent study has argued that imperial consciousness has been much exaggerated so far as the bulk of society was concerned. Most people knew surprisingly little about the Empire.[137] Yet what ordinary people did know was that much of the world was ours. To less ordinary people, to many scions of aristocratic or gentry families in particular, it has been suggested that its more exotic regions offered an escape from a world dominated by towns, industry, business, and democracy into a world of emirs, maharajahs, and sultans, where martial valour was still more important than business deals or trades unions. Rather than consider the 'Orient' an inferior other, many imperialists considered India or Arabia superior to dull western societies and strove to maintain their social and political structures under the British flag.[138] The opposite tendency was the desire, whether from religious or secular motives, to 'improve' colonial societies, to make them Christian, liberal, and modern.

What Britain or the British people, or what sections of British society, gained in material terms from the Empire is imponderable. No sensible profit and loss account can ever be drawn up. The profit from a Hong Kong or the loss from some African colony will not provide the answer. The view that manufacturing interests sought markets via the acquisition of colonies is confounded by the greater success of British exports to countries outside the Empire. The notion that a 'gentlemanly capitalism' based on the City of London, a capitalism of bankers and stockbrokers rather than of industrialists, lay behind imperial expansion has gained ground,[139] yet returns on investments outside the Empire were almost certainly greater than those from within it. The great benefit was the way that worldwide possessions and military, and, above all, the naval, might which they facilitated, underpinned and secured the international trade which Britain dominated.

Equally contentious are the questions of the benefits and the disadvantages of the Empire for the majority of its subjects and the degree to which the pre-1914

136. Ged Martin and Benjamin E. Kline, 'British Emigration and New Identities', in P. J. Marshall (ed.), *Cambridge Illustrated History of the British Empire*, 265.
137. Bernard Porter, *The Absent-Minded Imperialists: Empire, Society and Culture in Britain* (2005).
138. See D. Cannadine, *Ornamentalism: How the British saw their Empire* (2002).
139. P. J. Cain and A. G. Hopkins, *British Imperialism: Innovation and Expansion 1688–1914* (1993).

world order of which Britain was the principal pillar was beneficent. What can be said is that the British Empire did much to stimulate a global economy and promote its growth, that its subjects were governed under laws and with the aid of surprisingly modest military force, and that the world in which Britain was the greatest power compares favourably with the worlds that preceded and followed it.

Surveys of Britain and British power in 1914 can result in contradictory pictures, hubris or intimations of decline, a successful and prosperous society beginning to tackle its inherited problems or one deeply divided by social and political divisions. There is evidence enough for contradictory analyses but since 1815 Britain had become an even greater power, been the first to confront the major problems of massive economic change and urbanization and emerged as a society which, although far from equal, proffered a standard of living and opportunities to the majority beyond the expectations of most Britons at the end of the Napoleonic Wars.

Conclusion

The period 1815–1914 was one in which Britain was involved in many small wars but no great war in which the nation's fate hung in the balance. The Great War 1914–18 has been seen with much justice as marking a watershed or great divide in British history, demarcating the pre-war society, its politics, and economy from a very different post-war world. The actual effects of the war on the long-term development of Britain are difficult to evaluate for long processes of change already under way were to continue and intensify to our own day. The most obvious effect of the war and that which shocked both contemporaries and posterity was the enormous death toll yet this had relatively little effect upon the growth of the population.

The war has been seen as the cause of major changes in the nature of British politics leading to such developments as the decline of the Liberal Party, the complementary rise of the Labour Party, and the enfranchisement of women. Whether or not such developments were already under way in the Edwardian period has been the subject of much controversy. It has been suggested that 'Liberal England' was already in crisis before the war: the Liberal Party challenged by Labour; the Irish Home Rule question leading to challenges to constitutional government; trades union militancy increasing; and with the suffragettes mounting a campaign of disorder.[140] The debates are effectively represented by a post-mortem on the Liberal Party:

The Liberal Party can be compared to an individual who, after a period of robust health and great exertion, experienced symptoms of illness (Ireland, Labour unrest, the suffragettes). Before a thorough diagnosis could be made, he was involved in an encounter

140. G. Dangerfield, *The Strange Death of Liberal England* (1935).

with a rampant omnibus (the First World War), which mounted the pavement and ran him over. After lingering painfully, he expired. A controversy has persisted ever since as to what killed him.[141]

The notion that Edwardian Britain was in crisis is probably as overdone as the obverse, a long serene Indian summer. There was plenty of industrial unrest but wage rates rather than syndicalism were its main cause. Votes for women would almost certainly have come and, in any case, it was only a minority of women who were desperately interested in the cause. Some sort of compromise solution to the Home Rule question was on the cards.

What is certain is that British society in 1914 was far more prosperous than was the society of 1815 with which this study began, and far more complicated. Every century is, no doubt, that cliché and truism, a century of change, but the years 1815 to 1914 had seen massive economic, social, and political change. The term a 'mature industrial society' has been coined for late nineteenth century and Edwardian Britain.[142] The early stages of massive economic change and the growth of towns and cities had created the 'Condition of England question'. There is much to be said for the term 'an age of equipoise' for the mid-Victorian decades which followed. Late Victorian Britain had confounded Marx's prophesies of the progressive immiseration of the 'working class', despite the continued misery for many, while the middle orders of society had not only grown but become more variegated. Classes, strata, sections, or sub-cultures squabbled and saw other sections as 'the other' but, however it may be argued that there were discrete class cultures, there was overriding these a sense of national unity and common values. Edwardian society bickered and had its internal enmities but overall saluted common cultural and political values.

This was essential, for interdependence is crucial to any advanced society. In 1815 British society, outside a few major urban centres, had been primarily a matter of small, localized communities. Within them, interdependence essentially rested on an intimate family or neighbourhood basis. By 1914 there had been a great change. Interdependence now existed in a more intricate and sophisticated pattern. For food, clothing, government, entertainment, fuel, light, water, and a variety of other services there were now links between millions of people who did not know each other. The consequences of this change were to be pervasive and much more marked as the process continued to diversify in the course of the new century. Although the process has been incremental rather than revolutionary, and the consequences are not yet fully realized, this transformation has profound implications for the economic, social, and political evolution of modern British society. Nor has it been merely a British phenomenon, for it has been shared by all technologically advanced and administratively sophisticated societies. There seems no reason to doubt that similar experiences will continue

141. T. Wilson, *The Downfall of the Liberal Party 1914–1935* (1966), 20.
142. H. Perkins, *The Origins of Modern English Society 1780–1880*, (1969).

to be more widely shared elsewhere. History presents us with a thread of continuity stretching from our own day back to the most primitive human societies. Recent shifts in patterns of interdependence have shown that the modern world can give the long story a decisive twist of its own.

Britain had changed enormously between 1815 and 1914 but had the British changed much? They were much more governed and the degree of public order had increased markedly. All classes of society enjoyed a higher standard of living though the conditions of the poorest were still lamentable and differences in living conditions between the social strata were vast. The British of the early nineteenth century had been famous or notorious for their hedonism, nationalism, volatility, and independence. Government had relied upon custom and the local authority of gentry and urban worthies to maintain order with the army and the suspension of normal civil liberties to cater for emergencies when things got out of hand. Popular culture had been vital but often brutal and usually bawdy. If John Bull is one archetype of the quintessential Briton, steady and resourceful but dangerous when angered, Punch is his cousin, not very cerebral, quick to anger and likely to take it out on his family. Ally Sloper, the 'hero' of *Ally Sloper's Half Holiday*, a penny weekly comic published between 1884 and 1923, has been seen as the late Victorian descendent of Punch. He is out for pleasure, vaguely working- or lower-middle-class but wishing to be a 'swell'; he is worldly, sly, and full of sexual innuendo, rather than straightforward bawdiness.[143] To set against him we have many an image of hard-working artisans or dutiful clerks seeking to provide their front parlours with pianos and care for their families. The real or average citizen or subject can never be induced to stand up. What is certain is that there had been a certain taming of British society, whether by increased prosperity, the growth of government, evangelicalism of a religious or secular nature, or recognition of the need for interdependence and the benefits of regulation and order. Despite industrial conflict and deep political fissures, Britain had a reputation for orderliness, self control, and respect for authority which would last until the late twentieth century.

What the effects of the First World War on Britain and British society were, whether they led to a decline in British power, transformed political life, led to the final decline of the aristocracy, or retarded or accelerated social and economic developments is beyond the remit of this book. The very scope of the questions points, however, to the significance attached to the nature of Edwardian Britain as well as to the war which followed. If the major debates amongst historians can usually be summed up as change versus continuity, then the opposed views of Edwardian Britain, a society with more in common with the Britain of the previous century than with post-war society, or a period already exhibiting the traits and dealing with the problems that would characterize the rest of the twentieth century, exemplify the problems of analysing change over time.

143. Peter Bailey, 'Ally Sloper's Half Holiday', *History Workshop*, 16, (1983), 5–31.

Biographical appendix

(Individuals are entered under the names by which they are best known, even if they acquired different titles at some point.)

Albert, Prince Consort (1819–61). Second son of Ernest, reigning Duke of Saxe-Coburg-Gotha. He was educated by private tutors, and at Brussels and Bonn. In 1840 he married Queen Victoria; they had nine children. He took a keen interest in public affairs, and became the Queen's principal adviser. He presided over commissions for rebuilding the Houses of Parliament and for organizing the Great Exhibition of 1851. In 1847 he became Chancellor of Cambridge University. His last intervention in public affairs consisted of advice which was largely responsible for preventing conflict between Britain and the USA over the *Trent* affair in November 1861. Prince Albert possessed a strong sense of public duty and interest in social conditions and eventually overcame much early prejudice against his foreign origin. Overwork was one of the causes of his inability to resist the typhoid attack which killed him in December 1861.

Asquith, Herbert, Henry, first Earl of Oxford and Asquith (1852–1928). An orphan whose relatives were minor employers in the woollen trade, he won a scholarship to Balliol and was subsequently called to the Bar. He entered Parliament as Liberal MP for East Fife in 1885. In 1892 he became Home Secretary in Gladstone's final government. He could probably have become leader of the Liberal Party when Harcourt retired in 1898 but didn't put himself forward for largely financial reasons. A Liberal Imperialist, he supported the Boer War thus distancing himself from Campbell-Bannerman and much of the Liberal Party. Despite having plotted to have Campbell-Bannerman relegated to the Lords he became a member of the Liberal government in December 1905 as Chancellor of the Exchequer and upon Campbell-Bannerman's death became Prime Minister (1908–16). His government was responsible for instituting Old-Age Pensions and National Insurance and for the Parliament Act of 1911. After the general elections of 1910, the Asquith government was dependent upon the support of the Labour Party and the Irish Nationalists. The government's Home Rule proposals led to the threat of civil war in Ireland while the government also experienced difficulties with major strikes and suffragette agitation. In August 1914, Asquith led the country into war but did not prove a successful wartime leader. Criticized for not being energetic in the direction of the war, he was forced in May 1915 to form a coalition government and in December 1916 he was replaced as Prime Minister after a coup led by Lloyd George, who succeeded him, and the Conservatives. Asquith's fall left the Liberals a divided party and the section which continued to support him was badly defeated in 1918 with Asquith losing his seat. Although Liberal factions were reunited in 1923–6 under his leadership, the Liberal Party was at the end of his life a much weakened force.

Balfour, Arthur James, first Earl (1848–1930). The son of a Scottish landowner who married Lord Salisbury's sister, he was educated at Eton and Cambridge. He became a Conservative MP in 1874, acting as Salisbury's private secretary during the Congress of Berlin in 1878. During the early 1880s he was a member of Lord Randolph Churchill's 'Fourth Party'. Balfour was appointed President of the Local Government Board, 1885, Secretary for Scotland, 1886–7, Chief Secretary for Ireland, 1887–92, and Leader of the House of Commons, 1891–2. He was First Lord of the Treasury and Leader of the House of Commons from 1895 to 1902, when he succeeded Salisbury as Prime Minister.

In December 1905 he resigned after the Unionist split over Tariff Reform. He lost the Unionist leadership in 1911, after the Unionist defeat over the Parliament Act. He was First Lord of the Admiralty, 1915–16, Foreign Secretary, 1916–19, and was created an earl in 1922.

Bentinck, Lord George Cavendish (1802–48). The fifth child of the fourth Duke of Portland. Educated privately, he joined the army in 1819. He became an MP in 1828 and Canning's private secretary in the 1820s. He was deeply interested in field sports and horse racing. Offered office by Peel in 1841, he preferred to concentrate on his sporting activities. He effected reform of horse racing practices, exposing fraud and misconduct there. Deeply affronted by Peel's decision to repeal the Corn Laws, he took the lead in Conservative opposition to it, cooperating with Disraeli. In 1846 he sold his racing stud to concentrate on political affairs. He died suddenly in 1848.

Bright, John (1811–89). The son of a Rochdale textile manufacturer, he entered his father's business on leaving school. He became acquainted with Cobden about 1835, and subsequently joined him in activities of the Anti-Corn Law League. He became MP for Durham City in 1843, after the local Conservative leader, Lord Londonderry, quarrelled with the party leadership. As MP for Manchester, 1847–57, he opposed the Game Laws and the death penalty. Suspicious of various colonial activities by Britain, he opposed the Crimean War and the second China War. Defeated in Manchester in 1857, he sat as MP for Birmingham from 1857 to 1885. Bright supported the North during the US Civil War. President of the Board of Trade from 1868 to 1870, he retired because of ill health. He was Chancellor of the Duchy of Lancaster, 1873–4 and 1880–2, when he resigned in opposition to the invasion of Egypt. He opposed Gladstone's Home Rule Bill in 1886.

Brougham, Henry Peter, first Baron Brougham and Vaux (1778–1868). Son of a Westmorland squire, he was educated at Edinburgh High School and Edinburgh University. He became a barrister in 1803 and an MP in 1810. He defended Queen Caroline in 1820, and advocated reforms in various spheres including the law and charities. Elected MP for Yorkshire without expense in 1830, he became Lord Chancellor and was raised to the peerage in 1830. He effected several law reforms, and played a major role in reform debates in the House of Lords. Found to be an untrustworthy colleague, he was dropped from the Whig ministry in 1834. He was active as a judge and continued to support reforms in law and in education.

Campbell-Bannerman, Sir Henry (1836–1908). The son of the wealthy owner of a large drapery firm, Campbell-Bannerman was educated in Glasgow and at Cambridge. He was elected in 1868 as Liberal MP for Stirling, a seat he represented for forty years. A loyal Gladstonian and a supporter of Home Rule, he was a respected figure in the Liberal Party and was Chief Secretary for Ireland during Gladstone's last administration and then became Secretary for War (1892–5). A vote of censure on him for not having provided the army with sufficient cordite was the immediate cause of the Rosebery government's resignation. He emerged as Liberal leader in 1898 as very much the compromise candidate in a party split into warring factions but was to prove a practical and capable leader. On the resignation of the Balfour government in 1905, he became Prime Minister and after the 1906 election formed a ministry which included most leading Liberals. He died in office.

Canning, George (1770–1827). The son of an undistinguished lawyer whose widow became an undistinguished actress, his education was supported by an uncle, a Whig banker, who sent him to Eton and Oxford. He was a Tory MP from 1794, Undersecretary for Foreign Affairs, 1796–9, Member of the India Board, 1799–1800, Paymaster General, 1800–1, Treasurer of the Navy, 1804–6, Foreign Secretary, 1807–9. After quarrelling and fighting a duel with Castlereagh in September 1809, he resigned office. President of the Board of Control, 1816–21, he resigned over the Queen Caroline affair in January 1821. Canning was nominated Governor General of India in 1822, but instead became Foreign Secretary on Castlereagh's death. He was Prime Minister for a few months in 1827 before his death.

Cardwell, Edward, first Viscount (1813–86). Son of a Liverpool merchant, he was educated at Winchester and Oxford. He became Conservative MP for Clitheroe in 1842, and was Secretary to the Treasury, 1845–6. He followed Peel in the split over the Corn Laws in 1846. Cardwell was President of the Board of Trade in the Aberdeen ministry, 1852–5, Chief Secretary for Ireland under Palmerston, 1859–61, Chancellor of the Duchy of Lancaster, 1861–4, Colonial Secretary, 1864–6, and Secretary for War, 1868–74, when he was responsible for army reforms. He was created a viscount in 1874.

Castlereagh, Robert Stewart, Viscount (1769–1822). Son of the first Marquess of Londonderry, he was educated at Armagh and Cambridge. He was elected to the Irish Parliament in 1790 and to the British Parliament in 1794. As Chief Secretary for Ireland, 1798–1801, he steered the Act of Union between Ireland and Britain through the Irish Parliament in 1800. When · George III refused further concessions to the Catholics in 1801, he resigned. He was Secretary of State for War and the Colonies, 1805–6 and 1807–9, but resigned after the failure of the Walcheren expedition in 1809. He fought a duel with Canning in 1809. As Foreign Secretary, and Leader of the House of Commons, 1812–22, Castlereagh played a major role in forging a coalition against Napoleon. He succeeded as second Marquess of Londonderry in 1821, but committed suicide in 1822 and was buried in Westminster Abbey.

Chadwick, Edwin (1800–90). Born near Manchester, after slight schooling he entered a solicitor's office. He read for the Bar but became a journalist; his articles on social problems attracted Jeremy Bentham's attention, and he became effectively Bentham's secretary. Appointed a paid investigator for the Royal Commission on the Poor Laws, 1832, he was so successful that he became a full commissioner. He was Secretary to the Poor Law Commission, 1834–46, was made a CB in 1848, and knighted, 1889. Chadwick was an influential writer on public health and other social problems, though his tendency to alienate others limited his influence in practice.

Chamberlain, Joseph (1836–1914). Son of a London footwear manufacturer, he became a screw manufacturer in Birmingham. He took a leading part in the National Education League, opposing grants from public funds to church schools. As Mayor of Birmingham in 1873, 1874, and 1875, he adopted vigorous reforming policies. Elected MP for Birmingham in 1876, he made a national reputation as a leading radical. Chamberlain helped to improve Liberal organization, especially in his West Midlands 'Duchy', and played an important role in the Liberal electoral victory of 1880. He was President of the Board of Trade, 1880–5. He was largely responsible for the Liberal 'Unauthorized Programme' during the 1886 general election. He became President of the Local Government Board, but broke with Gladstone over Irish Home Rule and resigned in the same year. As a Liberal Unionist, Chamberlain became Colonial Secretary in Salisbury's government in 1895. After the South African War, he embraced the policy of Tariff Reform, and resigned from Balfour's government in 1903. His political career was ended by a stroke in 1906.

Childers, Hugh (1827–96). The son of a clergyman, he was educated at Cambridge. He emigrated to Australia in 1851, becoming Inspector of Schools in Melbourne and later Secretary to the Melbourne Education Department, Auditor General, and a Member of the Legislative Council. He was the first Vice Chancellor of Melbourne University. Childers returned to Britain in 1857, and became a Liberal MP in 1860. He was Financial Secretary to the Treasury, 1865–6, and First Lord of the Admiralty, 1868, resigning after a breakdown in 1871. He served as Chancellor of the Duchy of Lancaster, 1872–3, Secretary for War, 1880–2, Chancellor of the Exchequer, 1882–5, and Home Secretary, 1886. Childers supported Gladstone over Home Rule.

Churchill, Lord Randolph (1849–94). Third son of the sixth Duke of Marlborough, he was educated at Eton and Oxford. He was Conservative MP for Woodstock, 1874–85, and South Paddington, 1885–94. In the 1880–5 Parliament, he was leader of a small but active group of MPs—'the Fourth Party'—in attacking the Liberal government. He gained considerable support in the country and in the Conservative Party organization, showing great skill in platform oratory. Churchill held the posts of Secretary of State for India, 1885–6, and Chancellor of the Exchequer and Leader of the House of Commons, 1886. He resigned rashly over defence estimates in December 1886 and never held office again.

Churchill, Sir Winston Spencer (1874–1965). Son of Lord Randolph Churchill, he was educated at Harrow and Sandhurst and then served with the 4th Hussars in the Sudan. Between 1899 and 1900 he was a war correspondent in South Africa and was captured by the Boers from whom he escaped. In 1900 he was elected to Parliament as a Conservative but defected to the Liberals four years later. Campbell-Bannerman appointed him Undersecretary for the Colonies and Asquith brought him into the Cabinet as President of the Board of Trade in 1908 and then made him Home Secretary in 1910. He played a major role in devising the National Insurance Act of 1911. Appointed First Lord of the Admiralty in 1911, he held this post until his resignation in 1915 after the failure of the Dardenelles Campaign. After a spell commanding a battalion in France, he became successively Minister for Munitions (1917–19), Secretary for Air and War (1919–21) and Colonial Secretary in the Lloyd George Coalition. Re-elected as a Conservative in 1924, he was Chancellor of the Exchequer (1924–9) in the Baldwin government. With the outbreak of the Second World War he returned to government, as First Lord of the Admiralty once again and then succeeded Neville Chamberlain as Prime Minister in 1940 remaining so until the Conservative defeat at the 1945 election. He was again Prime Minister from 1951 till 1955.

Cobden, Richard (1819–1901). The son of a Sussex farmer; after early jobs as a clerk and a salesman he set up in business, first as a partner in a London calico warehouse, then from 1831 as a calico-printer near Blackburn. He took part in the campaign for the incorporation of Manchester after the Municipal Reform Act of 1835. He joined the Anti-Corn Law League soon after its formation and became its most effective leader. He became MP for Stockport, 1841–7, and for the West Riding of Yorkshire, 1847–57. After the repeal of the Corn Laws, Cobden embarked on an extensive overseas tour, which received much publicity. In 1846 he received approximately £80,000 from public subscription; he used part of this to buy a small country estate which included his birthplace in 1847. Unpopular because of his opposition to the Crimean War and the second China War, Cobden was defeated for Huddersfield in the 1857 general election. Elected for Rochdale in 1858, he was offered the Presidency of the Board of Trade by Palmerston, but refused because of his open differences with Palmerston's foreign policies in the past. Generally he supported the government; he negotiated a commercial treaty with France in 1859–60. He refused a baronetcy in 1860. Having lost heavily in financial speculations, Cobden received about £40,000 from a second subscription in 1860. He died on 2 April 1865.

Cross, Richard Assheton, first Viscount (1823–1914). Born in Lancashire, he was educated at Rugby and Cambridge. An MP from 1857 to 1886, he became expert on local government and similar matters. He played an important part in strengthening the Conservatives in Lancashire. He was Home Secretary, 1874–80 and 1885–6, Secretary for India, 1886–92, and Lord Privy Seal, 1895–1900. He was created a viscount in 1886.

Derby, Edward Stanley, fourteenth Earl of (1799–1869). Educated at Eton and Oxford, he became a Whig MP in 1820. In 1827 he joined the Canning ministry as Undersecretary for the Colonies. He was Chief Secretary for Ireland, 1830–3. As Colonial Secretary, 1833, he carried the Act abolishing slavery, but resigned in 1834 in opposition to concessions to Irish nationalists. He moved into Conservative ranks and became Colonial Secretary under Peel, 1841–5. He was called to the House of Lords in 1844, and succeeded as Earl of Derby in 1851. He was Conservative Prime Minister (in minority governments) in 1852, 1858–9, and 1866–8. He was responsible for drafting the Second Reform Act. A classical scholar, he translated the *Iliad*.

Disraeli, Benjamin, first and only Earl of Beaconsfield (1801–81). His father, Isaac, was wealthy and a well-known writer; the family were descended from Jewish refugees from Spain and had become Anglicans in 1817. He abandoned early plans to become a lawyer and instead embarked upon a career as a writer; his first novel, *Vivian Grey*, was written in 1826–7. Disraeli became a dandy and acquired a dubious reputation during the 1820s and early 1830s; he married a rich widow in 1839. He contested elections in a variety of political stances, before being elected MP for Maidstone as a Conservative in 1837. In the early 1840s he was a member of the 'Young England' group, advocating right-wing Tory paternalism. His best-known novels, *Coningsby* and *Sybil, or The Two Nations* were published in 1844 and 1845. After supporting Peel for some years, Disraeli began to criticize him, and went into strenuous opposition over the repeal of the Corn Laws. He emerged, with Lord George Bentinck, as a prominent member of the protectionist Conservatives after 1846. He was MP for Buckinghamshire from 1847 to 1876, and acquired the Hughenden estate in that county. He served as Chancellor of the Exchequer in Derby's minority administrations, 1852, 1857–9, and 1866–8. He gradually overcame much Conservative opposition to his leadership, and fought through the Second Reform Act, 1867, in a great parliamentary performance. He was Prime Minister in 1868 and 1874–80. He became Earl of Beaconsfield in 1876, and a Knight of the Garter after success at the Congress of Berlin in 1878. His last novel, *Endymion*, was published in 1880. He died on 19 April 1881, and was buried at Hughenden with a memorial in Westminster Abbey.

Durham, John George Lambton, first Earl of (1792–1840). The son of a Durham landowner, he was educated at Eton; he was in the army from 1809 to 1811. He sat as a Whig county MP for Durham from 1813 to 1828 and was elevated to the peerage in 1828. He was Earl Grey's son-in-law. As Lord Privy Seal from 1830 he was a leading member of the committee which drafted the parliamentary Reform Bill. He served as Ambassador to Russia from 1835 to 1837, and Governor General of Canada in 1838. In the mid-1830s he advocated further parliamentary reform; he was probably the most important radical of the 1830s.

Edward, King (1841–1910). The second child of Queen Victoria and Prince Albert, he was educated by private tutors and then spent four terms at Oxford. He became Prince of Wales when he was one month old. Queen Victoria did not share with him or delegate to him important royal duties and he devoted his attention to social life and was cited in two divorce cases. He showed good judgement in urging the Queen to fulfil more public engagements after her withdrawal into seclusion after Prince Albert's death. After his accession to the throne in 1901, he contributed to the rapprochement with France that resulted in the *Entente Cordiale*. He accepted without enthusiasm that the political power of the monarch had diminished but understood that the ceremonial side of monarchy had great appeal.

Eldon, John Scott, first Earl of (1751–1838). The son of a Newcastle merchant, educated at the Royal Grammar School, Newcastle, and Oxford, he eloped with the daughter of a rich Newcastle merchant in 1772. He became a barrister in 1776 and an MP in 1783. He was Solicitor General from 1788 to 1893 and Attorney General from 1793 to 1799, Chief Justice in the Court of Common Pleas from 1799 to 1801 and Lord Chancellor in 1801–6 and 1807–27. His elder brother, William, also had a successful legal career, which culminated in a peerage as Lord Stowell.

Gladstone, William Ewart (1809–98). The son of a wealthy Liverpool merchant and landowner, he was educated at Eton and Oxford. He was Conservative MP for the pocket borough of Newark, 1832–46; Vice President of the Board of Trade, 1841–3, and President, 1843–5, coming under Peel's influence. He resigned over the Maynooth grant in 1845, but sided with Peel over the Corn Laws. He was Colonial Secretary during the 1846 crisis. He strenuously attacked Disraeli's 1852 Budget and served as Chancellor of the Exchequer in the Aberdeen ministry, 1853–5, in the second Palmerston ministry, 1859–65, and in the Russell ministry, 1865–6. From 1858–9 he was High Commissioner in the Ionian Islands. He became increasingly liberal in his expressed views. Gladstone was Liberal Prime Minister in 1868–74, 1880–5, 1886, and 1892–4. His Home Rule policy split the Liberal Party in 1886, and he finally resigned over naval estimates in 1894. He died on 19 May 1898 at his country estate of Hawarden, and was buried in Westminster Abbey.

Graham, Sir James, Bt. (1792–1861). The son of a Cumberland baronet and landowner, Graham was educated at Westminster and Oxford. In 1818 he became a Whig MP, and succeeded to a baronetcy in 1824. He was First Lord of the Admiralty in 1830–4, but resigned in opposition to concessions to Irish nationalists. He moved into Conservative ranks and became Home Secretary under Peel, 1841–6. He became a leading Peelite after the 1846 split in the party. He served again as First Lord of the Admiralty in the Aberdeen coalition ministry, 1852–5, then under Palmerston until the Peelites resigned as a group later in 1855.

Grey, Charles, second Earl (1764–1845). His father was a distinguished general and Northumberland landowner, who was raised to the peerage in 1801. Educated at Eton and Cambridge, he became a county MP for Northumberland in 1786, joined the opposition Whigs, and introduced a parliamentary Reform Bill in 1797. He served as First Lord of the Admiralty in 1806 and Foreign Secretary in 1806–7; he resigned over George III's opposition to Catholic Emancipation. He emerged as principal opposition leader during the 1820s. As Prime Minister in 1830–4, he was responsible for the 1832 Reform Act and other reforms; he resigned when some colleagues intrigued with Irish nationalists behind his back.

Hunt, Henry 'Orator' (1773–1835). The son of a prosperous Wiltshire farmer, he ran away from school and quarrelled with his father. He married an innkeeper's daughter in 1796, left her in 1802, and lived with a friend's wife. He was fined and imprisoned in 1800 for challenging a yeomanry colonel to a duel and in 1810 for assaulting a gamekeeper. He became a prominent radical politician, and was arrested at the 'Peterloo' meeting of 1819, when he was sentenced to two years' imprisonment; he wrote highly unreliable memoirs while in prison. As MP for Preston, 1830–3, he opposed the government's parliamentary reform proposals as inadequate and abandoned politics in 1833, becoming a blacking manufacturer.

Huskisson, William (1770–1830). Born near Wolverhampton, he was educated privately in Paris where he witnessed the capture of the Bastille in July 1789. He became a Tory MP in 1796, Undersecretary at War, 1795–1801, and Secretary to the Treasury, 1804–5, 1807–9. He was a supporter of Canning. He served as Minister for Woods and Forests, 1814–23, and President of the Board of Trade, 1823–7. He became a noted expert in financial and economic affairs. After serving in the short-lived Canning ministry, Huskisson joined the Wellington government as Colonial Secretary and Leader of the House of Commons but resigned in 1828 after a disagreement over disfranchised parliamentary seats. Other Canningite ministers supported him and the split weakened the Tory governing coalition. He supported Catholic Emancipation. He was accidentally killed at the opening of the Manchester and Liverpool Railway.

Liverpool, Robert Banks Jenkinson, second Earl of (1770–1828). His father, an administrator and Tory politician, was given a peerage in 1786. He was educated at Charterhouse School and Oxford. He saw the capture of Bastille in Paris in 1789. He became an MP in 1790. With one short break he held ministerial office from 1793 to 1827. He was Foreign Secretary from 1801 to 1804, was given a barony in 1803, and succeeded his father as Earl of Liverpool in 1808. He served as Home Secretary, 1804–6 and 1807–9, Secretary of State for War and the Colonies, 1809–12, and Prime Minister, 1812–27. He supported Wellington's Peninsular campaigns and Canning's foreign policy.

Lloyd George, David, first Earl Lloyd George (1863–1945). His father died when he was a baby and he was brought up by his mother and his uncle, a shoemaker and Baptist pastor. Despite this Nonconformist background, he attended the village 'National' or 'Anglican' school. He became a solicitor before being elected as Liberal MP for Caernarvon Boroughs in 1890. He was a prominent opponent of the Boer War. He was President of the Board of Trade (1905–8) and Chancellor of the Exchequer (1908–15). During 1908–11 he introduced the Old Age Pensions Act, the 'People's Budget' and the National Insurance Act 1911. As Minister for Munitions (1915–16) and Secretary for War (1916) he acquired a reputation as a zealous prosecutor of the war and after Asquith was deposed became Prime Minister (1916–22) of a coalition of 'Lloyd George Liberals' and Conservatives. The 1918 election confirmed the wartime Coalition in office and he remained Prime Minister until 1922 when the Conservative Party withdrew its support. He never held office again although he headed a reunited Liberal Party from 1926 to 1931.

Lowe, Robert, first Viscount Sherbrooke (1811–92). The son of a clergyman, educated at Winchester and Oxford, he became a barrister and emigrated to Australia in 1842. He practised law in Sydney and was active in political affairs there. He served on the legislative council for New South Wales, 1843–50. In 1850 he returned to England and became a leader-writer for *The Times*. He sat as MP for Kidderminster, 1852–9, and for Calne, 1859–67. He was Secretary to the Board of Control for India, 1852–5, Vice President of the Board of Trade, 1855–8, Vice President of the Committee of the Privy Council for Education, 1859–64. He attacked the reform proposals of the Russell government in 1866. He was Chancellor of the Exchequer in 1868–73 and Home Secretary in 1873–4.

Melbourne, William Lamb, second Viscount (1779–1848). Educated at Eton and Cambridge, he was great grandson of a lawyer. He became a Whig MP in 1806. He was Chief Secretary for Ireland, 1827–8, under Canning and Wellington, and resigned with Huskisson and other Canningites in 1828. He succeeded to a peerage in 1829. Melbourne served as Home Secretary in Grey's ministry, 1830–4, and Prime Minister, 1834 and 1835–41. He was principal adviser to Queen Victoria during the early years of her reign.

Newman, John Henry (1801–90). The son of a banker, he was educated at Ealing and Oxford. He took Anglican orders. He began to write Tracts for *The Times* in 1833, emphasizing the high role and catholic attributes of the Church of England, and became a leading figure in controversies between evangelicals and the 'Oxford Movement' within the Church. He joined the Roman Catholic Church in 1845, a conversion which caused a considerable stir. He was Rector of the Catholic University of Dublin, 1854–8, and became a cardinal in 1879.

Northcote, Sir Stafford, first Earl of Iddesleigh (1818–87). The son of a long-established landed family, educated at Eton and Oxford, he succeeded to the baronetcy in 1851. He was a Conservative MP from 1855 to 1885. He served as private secretary to Gladstone in 1842; President of the Board of Trade, 1866; Secretary for India, 1867, Chancellor of the Exchequer, 1874–80; and Leader of the House of Commons 1876–80. He was leader of the Opposition, 1880–5, but his authority was challenged by Lord Randolph Churchill and his

'Fourth Party'. He was created Earl of Iddesleigh in 1885. He was appointed Foreign Secretary in 1886, but induced to resign after six months; he never recovered from a heart attack in Lord Salisbury's house on the day of his resignation.

O'Connell, Daniel (1775–1847). He was educated in seminaries at St Omer and Douai, and became a barrister in 1798. As a champion of Irish nationalism, he was dubbed 'The Liberator'. He formed the Catholic Association in 1823, supported from 1824 by 'Catholic Rent' or regular small subscriptions from Irish Catholics. The final Catholic Emancipation crisis of 1828–9 was sparked off by his election as MP for County Clare in 1828. He supported the Whigs after 1830. He agitated for repeal of the Anglo-Irish Act of Union from 1840. Elected Lord Mayor of Dublin in 1841, he acquiesced in official prohibition of a mass meeting at Clontarf, 1843. In 1844 he was arrested and convicted for political offences, but the judgement was reversed on appeal to the House of Lords.

O'Connor, Feargus (1794–1855). Born into an Irish landowning family with links to nationalist movements, he was educated at Trinity College, Dublin, and became a barrister. He supported the parliamentary reform agitation in 1831–2; from 1832 to 1835 he was MP for Cork, as supporter of O'Connell, with whom he quarrelled. He became a leading champion of the Chartist Movement after 1837. O'Connor acquired the *Northern Star* newspaper in 1837, which became the principal Chartist periodical and vehicle for O'Connor's personal ambitions. He played a part in stirring up agitation which led to the Newport Rising of 1839, but was absent in Ireland when it took place. In 1840 he was sentenced to eighteen months' imprisonment for seditious libel. He quarrelled with several major Chartist leaders. In 1846 O'Connor founded the National Land Company to settle Chartists in land colonies. He became MP for Nottingham (with some Tory help) in 1847. He acquiesced in the official prohibition of a mass procession in connection with the great Chartist petition in 1848. He became insane and was admitted to an asylum in 1852; in 1855 his funeral attracted a large crowd of mourners.

Palmerston, Henry John Temple, third Viscount (1784–1865). He spent much of his childhood abroad, and was educated at Harrow, Edinburgh University, and Cambridge. In 1802 he succeeded to the Irish peerage, which was compatible with a seat in the House of Commons. He was elected a Tory MP in 1807, and became Secretary at War from 1809 to 1828. He supported Catholic Emancipation in the 1820s, and left office with other Canningites in 1828. He joined Lord Grey's ministry as Foreign Secretary in 1830, and continued in Melbourne's administration until 1841. He advocated a spirited foreign policy; in Opposition from 1841 to 1846, he attacked Conservative foreign policy as too weak. After he returned to the Foreign Office under Russell in 1846, he was strongly criticized by the Queen for taking unauthorized initiatives in foreign policy, and was finally dismissed by Russell on such grounds in 1851. He played a part in Russell's fall in 1852 by attacking the government's Militia Bill. Palmerston refused invitations to serve under Derby. He served as Home Secretary in Aberdeen's ministry from 1853 to 1855 and Prime Minister in 1855–8 and 1859–65. He died in office just before his 81st birthday and was buried in Westminster Abbey.

Parnell, Charles Stewart (1846–91). He was born into an Anglo-Irish Protestant landowning family; his mother was the daughter of an American naval officer. He was educated at Cambridge. Elected MP for an Irish constituency in an 1875 by-election, he became leader of the Home Rule Party in May 1880 and employed obstructive tactics in the Commons against Irish legislation. He became leader of the Land League as well as of the Home Rule Party. Imprisoned in Kilmainham Gaol, October 1881, he negotiated the 'Kilmainham Treaty' with Gladstone and was released in May 1882. He resumed opposition to government measures, and, after negotiations with the Conservatives, caused the government defeat which precipitated the general election of 1885; he urged the Irish in Britain to vote Conservative in that election. He became allied with Gladstone after the latter's adherence to Home Rule. He was a central figure in the 'Parnellism and Crime' affair in 1887–9, when he was vindicated. He was cited as co-respondent in the O'Shea divorce case in 1890, but refused to give up the leadership of the Home Rule Party, which split into bitterly feuding Parnellite and anti-Parnellite factions. He struggled to retain his position in 1890–1, while in failing health, but died in October 1891.

Peel, Sir Robert, second Baronet (1788–1850). The son of a rich Lancashire manufacturer, he was educated at Harrow and Oxford. He became a Tory MP in 1807, and served as Undersecretary for War and the Colonies, 1810–12, and Chief Secretary for Ireland, 1812–18. As Home Secretary, 1822–7 and 1828–30, he was responsible for many reforms in criminal law. He was a leading opponent of Catholic Emancipation in the 1820s, and created the Metropolitan Police in 1829. Despite his earlier opposition to the measure, he was persuaded by Wellington to stay in office and help to pass Catholic Emancipation in 1829. He was leader of the Opposition in the House of Commons, 1830–41, and briefly Prime Minister from 1834 to 1835, when his Tamworth Manifesto proclaimed a new moderate image for the Conservative Party. After winning the general election of 1841 he served as Prime Minister from 1841 to 1846, introducing many moves towards freer trade which culminated in the repeal of the Corn Laws in 1846. This broke the Conservative Party, which Peel had done so much to build up. Defeated on the Irish Coercion Bill, he resigned in June 1846. He remained influential, though out of office, until his death after a riding accident on 2 July 1850; his death was marked by an unprecedented range of memorial tributes, statues, and so on, including a memorial in Westminster Abbey.

Rhodes, Cecil, John (1853–1902). The younger son of a clergyman in the Home Counties, he was educated at Oxford, but his education suffered owing to frequent ill health in his youth. Before going to Oxford, he spent some time in South Africa, where he began to accumulate a large fortune, at first in diamond-mining concerns; he was one of the founders of the De Beers Company. Later he acquired large interests in gold-mining. A member of the Cape Colony legislature from 1880, he was Prime Minister of Cape Colony, 1890–6. He became a Privy Councillor in 1895, but was forced to resign as Cape premier by his connection with the Jameson Raid into the Transvaal. Earlier he had founded the British South Africa Company, which secured British control of a large part of the future Rhodesia (Zimbabwe). Rhodes left a fortune of more than £6 million on his death in 1902, much of it destined to found scholarships at Oxford for students from Britain, the empire, the USA, and Germany.

Rosebery, Archibald Philip Primrose, fifth Earl of (1847–1929). Educated at Eton and Oxford, he succeeded his grandfather in the peerage in 1868, and became a prominent Liberal in the House of Lords. He served as Undersecretary in the Home Office, 1881–3, First Commissioner of Works, 1884–5, and Foreign Secretary, 1886 and 1892–4. He became Prime Minister after Gladstone's resignation in March 1894; Rosebery's final resignation in 1895 reflected divisions within the Liberal Party and the growing strength of Conservative–Liberal Unionist opposition. He supported Gladstone over Home Rule in 1886, but later became lukewarm on the issue. As first Chairman of London County Council in 1888–90, he supported progressive reforms there. He resigned this position on the death of his wife in 1890, but returned to it briefly in 1892 before joining Gladstone's last ministry. As a keen historian, he wrote notable biographies of Pitt the Younger and Napoleon. He married a Rothschild heiress in 1878, and was a well-known racing owner, winning the Derby twice while premier. Rosebery supported the South African War, and attacked the 'People's Budget' of 1909 and the Parliament Act of 1911.

Russell, Lord John, first Earl Russell (1792–1878). The third son of the sixth Duke of Bedford, he was educated at Westminster and Edinburgh University. A Whig MP from 1813, he was an advocate of parliamentary reform. In 1828 he secured the repeal of the Test and Corporation Acts. Paymaster General in 1830, he entered the Cabinet in 1831 and played a leading role in the enactment of the 1832 Reform Act. He served as Home Secretary and Leader of the House of Commons, 1835–9, and Colonial Secretary and Leader of the House of Commons, 1839–41. He supported the repeal of the Corn Laws in 1845–6. Russell was Prime Minister, 1846–52, Foreign Secretary, 1853, and Lord President of the Council, 1854, but resigned after attacks on the Aberdeen ministry in Parliament. He tried unsuccessfully to form a ministry after Aberdeen's resignation in 1855. In 1859 he opposed the Conservative Reform Bill. He was Foreign Secretary from 1859 to 1865, and was created Earl Russell in 1861. He became Prime Minister on Palmerston's death in 1865 and served till 1866, when the government's Reform Bill was defeated. An unimpressive personality, he was small of stature and weak of voice.

Salisbury, Robert Cecil, third Marquess of (1830–1903). The second son of the second Marquess (his elder brother died in 1865), he succeeded to the peerage in 1868. He was educated at Eton and Oxford. He was elected a Conservative MP in 1853 and became Secretary of State for India in Derby's third minority ministry in 1866, but resigned in March 1867 because of his opposition to the Reform Bill. He was reconciled with Disraeli after a breach of some years, and served as Secretary of State for India, 1874–8; he supported Disraeli's foreign policy and became Foreign Secretary, 1878–80. He partnered Disraeli at the 1878 Congress of Berlin. Salisbury was Prime Minister and Foreign Secretary, 1885–6, 1886–92, and 1895–1900; his health declined and he resigned as Foreign Secretary in 1900, and as Prime Minister in 1902.

Shaftesbury, Anthony Ashley Cooper, seventh Earl of (1801–85). Educated at Harrow and Oxford, he was a Conservative MP from 1826 to 1851. He served as a Member of the Board of Control for India in 1828, and Lord of the Admiralty, 1834–5. A philanthropist; active in campaigns to reform the lunacy laws, factory legislation, conditions of working children, education, housing, and so on, he was a strong evangelical Christian. He succeeded his father in the peerage in 1851.

Sidmouth, Henry Addington, first Viscount (1757–1844). Son of a prominent London doctor, he was educated at Winchester and Oxford, and became a barrister. He was elected an MP in 1783, and was Speaker from 1789–1801. Prime Minister in 1801–4, he was created a viscount in 1805. He was Home Secretary from 1812 to 1821. After leaving office, he opposed Catholic Emancipation and the Reform Bill.

Victoria, Queen (1819–1901). The daughter of HRH Edward, Duke of Kent, the fourth son of George III, who died in 1820. She came of age on 24 May 1837 and succeeded to the throne on 20 June 1837, on the death of her uncle, William IV. Her accession dissolved the connection between the thrones of Britain and Hanover dating from 1714; her uncle, the Duke of Cumberland, became King of Hanover, as female succession was not possible there. In 1840 she married her first cousin, Prince Albert of Saxe-Coburg-Gotha, who became Prince Consort and established a strong influence over the Queen; they had nine children. The Prince Consort died of typhoid in December 1861. During the early and middle years of her reign, the Queen was sometimes unpopular among some sectors of society, but in her latter years she was a centre of popular respect. Her political interventions were often partisan: she preferred Melbourne to Peel in the early years of her reign, disliked Palmerston for some years at mid-century, and later liked Disraeli and disliked Gladstone. Her Jubilees of 1887 and 1897 were occasions of great national rejoicing, especially the latter. She died in January 1901 and was buried beside Prince Albert at Frogmore near Windsor.

Wellington, Arthur Wellesley, first Duke of (1769–1852). The fourth son of the first Earl of Mornington; his grandfather had been given an Irish peerage in 1747. Educated at Eton, Brussels, and Angers (France) Military Academy, he entered the army in 1787. He was an Irish MP from 1790 to 1795. He served as a colonel in the Netherlands campaign of 1794–5, and in India, 1796–1805, both as a general and as an administrator, with successes in both to his credit. He returned to Britain in 1806 and became an MP. He was Chief Secretary for Ireland, 1807–9. He served in Portugal in 1808, winning the Battle of Vimiero and surviving the controversy which surrounded the subsequent Convention of Cintra. He took command in Portugal again in 1809, remaining there or in Spain throughout the remainder of the Peninsular War. He made his great military reputation by successive victories over various French commanders. Wellington's military success was accompanied by public recognition: he was made a viscount in 1809, an earl in 1812, a marquess in 1812, Field Marshal in 1813, KG in 1813, and duke in 1814. He invaded southern France in 1814. He was a British delegate, with Castlereagh, at the Congress of Vienna. When Napoleon escaped from Elba, Wellington was appointed Commander-in-Chief of the allied forces in the Netherlands and won the Battle of Waterloo on 18 June 1815. He commanded the allied army of occupation in France, 1815–18. He was Master General of the Ordnance, with a seat in the Cabinet, from 1818 to 1827. He was the British representative at international Congresses of Aix-la-Chapelle (1818) and Verona (1822). Wellington refused office under Canning in 1827, and became Prime Minister after Canning's death. He conceded Catholic Emancipation in 1829, and his government fell in November 1830. He was in the Cabinet, without ministerial office, from 1841 to 1846.

Select bibliography

(Place of publication is London unless given otherwise.)

Bibliographies and works of reference

Published bibliographies include J. L. Altholz, *Victorian England, 1837–1901* (Cambridge, 1970), L. M. Brown and I. R. Christie, *Bibliography of British History, 1789–1851* (Oxford, 1977), W. H. Chaloner and R. C. Richardson, *Bibliography of British Economic and Social History* (rev. edn., Manchester, 1983), I. R. Christie, *British History since 1760: A Select Bibliography* (1970), and H. J. Hanham, *Bibliography of British History, 1851–1914* (Oxford, 1976). Two series of bibliographical aids are the *Annual Bulletin of Historical Literature* published by the Historical Association and the *Annual Bibliography of British and Irish History* published by the Royal Historical Society. C. Cook, *British Historical Facts 1830–1900* (1975), D. Butler and G. Butler, *British Political Facts 1900–1994* (1994) and B. R. Mitchell, *British Historical Statistics* (Cambridge, 1988) are invaluable sources for students and researchers.

General works

There are many modern studies which cover all or part of the 1815–1914 period. Some books include that period within a wider survey, such as G. Alderman, *Modern Britain 1700–1983: A Domestic History* (1986), E. Royle, *Modern Britain: A Social History, 1750–1985* (1987), and R. K. Webb, *Modern England: From the 18th Century to the Present* (2nd edn., 1980). The last-named book, written by a distinguished American scholar, provides a good starting-point for anyone without previous knowledge of the period. G. Williams and J. Ramsden, *Ruling Britannia: A Political History of Britain 1688–1988* (1990) provides lively analysis and, despite the long period covered, much detail. Some of the useful surveys covering part of the 1815–1906 period are G. F. A. Best, *Mid-Victorian Britain, 1851–75* (1979), A. Briggs, *The Age of Improvement, 1783–1867* (2nd edn., 1979), W. L. Burn, *The Age of Equipoise: A Study of the Mid-Victorian Generation* (1964), E. J. Evans, *The Forging of the Modern State: Early Industrial Britain, 1783–1870* (1983), K. Robbins, *The Eclipse of a Great Power: Modern Britain 1870–1975* (1983), N. Gash, *Aristocracy and People: Britain 1815–1865* (1979), J. F. C. Harrison, *Early Victorian Britain, 1832–1851* (1979), G. Kitson Clark, *The Making of Victorian England* (1962), H. Perkin, *The Origins of Modern English Society, 1780–1880* (1969), M. D. Pugh, *The Making of Modern British Politics, 1867–1939* (1982), D. Read, *England 1868–1914* (1979), J. Roebuck, *The Making of Modern English Society from 1850* (1973), R. Shannon, *The Crisis of Imperialism, 1865–1915* (1974), F. O'Gorman, *The Long Eighteenth Century: British Political and Social History 1688–1832* (1997), and M. Pugh, *State and Society: British Political and Social History 1870–1992* (1994). B. Harrison, *Peaceable Kingdom: Stability and Change in Modern Britain* (Oxford, 1982) explores the reasons for the relatively peaceful evolution of Britain during a period of change. The two relevant volumes in *The Oxford History of England*, R. C. K. Ensor, *England, 1870–1914* (1936) and E. L. Woodward, *The Age of Reform, 1815–1870* (1938; rev. edn. 1946) are now rather elderly; on the whole the Woodward book has now more to commend it, but parts of Ensor, including chapter 10 on 'Mental and Social Aspects, 1886–1900' can still be read with profit. The relevant volumes of the *New Oxford History of England* are: Boyd Hilton, *A Mad, Bad, and Dangerous People: England 1783–1846* (2006), K. Theodore Hoppen, *The Mid-Victorian Generation 1846–1886* (1998), and G. R. Searle, *A New England? Peace and War 1886–1918* (2004); all are valuable works and all, especially Hoppen's book, are essentially British histories. An earlier work, G. M. Young (ed.), *Early Victorian England, 1830–1865*, 2 vols. (1934) contains articles by specialists on many aspects of life in that period; although in some respects corrected by later scholarship, the collection still contains much sound material.

Modern accounts of Scottish history include S. O. Checkland, *Industry and Ethos: Scotland 1832–1914* (1984), W. Ferguson, *Scotland from 1689 to the Present* (1968), T. C. Smout, *A Century of the Scottish People, 1830–1950* (1986). J. D. Mackie, *A History of Scotland* (1964), manages to compress a great amount of information into the two chapters devoted to our period. I. Donnachie and C. Whatley (eds.), *The Manufacture of Scottish History* (Edinburgh 1992) consider interpretations and inventions of Scottish history while C. Harvie, *Scotland and Nationalism* (2nd edn., 1994), addresses Scottish nationalism. Welsh studies include D. G. Evans, *A History of Wales, 1815–1906* (1989), G. Elwyn Jones, *Modern Wales* (1984), D. Williams, *A History of Modern Wales* (2nd edn., 1977), and G. A. Williams, *When Was Wales? A History of the Welsh* (1986). For Ireland, J. C. Beckett, *The Making of Modern Ireland, 1603–1922* (2nd edn., 1981), F. S. L. Lyons, *Ireland since the Famine* (rev. edn., 1973), L. J. McCaffrey, *The Irish Question, 1800–1922* (Lexington, Ky., 1968), E. R. Norman, *A History of Modern Ireland* (1972). Among Longman's series of regional studies of England are: J. V. Beckett, *The East Midlands from A.D. 1000* (1988), J. H. Bettey, *Wessex from A.D. 1000* (1986), D. Hey, *Yorkshire from A.D. 1000* (1986), and M. B. Rowlands, *The West Midlands from A.D. 1000* (1987) and N. McCord and R. Thompson, *The Northern Counties from 1000* (1998). All of these regional books contain valuable illustrations of British history after 1815 as well as much of interest relating to earlier periods. Other regional studies include N. McCord, *North East England: The Region's Development, 1760–1960* (1979), and J. D. Marshall and J. K. Walton, *The Lake Counties from 1830 to the Mid-Twentieth Century* (Manchester, 1981).

Economic history

Works on economic history include S. G. Checkland, *The Rise of Industrial Society in England, 1815–1885* (1964), the elderly but perceptive J. H. Clapham, *An Economic History of Modern Britain*, 3 vols. (Cambridge, 1926 (2nd edn. 1930, repr. with corrections 1950); 1932 (repr. with corrections 1952); 1938), F. Crouzet, *The Victorian Economy* (1982), R. Floud and D. McCloskey (eds.), *The Economic History of Britain since 1700*, 2 vols. (1981), P. Mathias, *The First Industrial Nation: An Economic History of Britain, 1700–1914* (2nd edn., 1983), R. Floud and P. Johnson (eds.), *The Cambridge Economic History of Modern Britain*, 3 vols (Cambridge 2nd edn. 1994). M. J. Daunton, *Progress and Poverty: An Economic and Social History of Britain 1700–1850* (Oxford, 1995) brings together work on economic growth and social and political perspectives. D. H. Aldcroft and P. Fearon (eds.), *British Economic Fluctuations, 1790–1939* (1972) includes a discussion of some of the methodological problems in this area, as well as a group of important papers on various aspects of the British economy, including the building industry and the balance of payments. For agriculture, J. D. Chambers and G. E. Mingay, *The Agricultural Revolution, 1750–1880* (1966). D. Bythell, *The Sweated Trades: Outwork in Nineteenth Century Britain* (1978) is inter alia a useful reminder of the limited spread of the factory system. A useful guide to the physical results of economic change is B. Trinder, *The Making of the Industrial Landscape* (1982). J. Butt and I. Donnachie, *Industrial Archaeology in the British Isles* (1979) provides a good introduction to a similar context. English Heritage's new series of regional studies, *England's Landscape* (2006), contains detailed chapters on the effect of economic change on the landscape region by region.

Population

A good general introduction is N. L. Tranter, *Population and Society: Contrasts in Population Growth, 1750–1940* (Harlow, 1985). Other useful studies include T. Barker and M. Drake (eds.), *Population and Society in Britain, 1850–1980* (1982), a group of related essays, M. W. Flinn, *British Population Growth, 1700–1850* (1970), and R. Mitchison, *British Population since 1860* (1977). A. McLaren, *Birth Control in Nineteenth-Century England* (1978) brings together the evidence on this issue. For the capital, D. J. Olsen, *The Growth of Victorian London* (1976). E. A. Wrigley, *People, Cities and Wealth: The Transformation of Traditional Society* (Oxford, 1987), contains a number of essays on population growth.

Social groups

The best general account of British workers in the nineteenth century is E. H. Hunt, *British Labour History, 1815–1914* (1981); this offers an admirably balanced and sensible account of a theme often affected by polemic. Other useful studies include J. Benson, *The Working Class in Britain, 1850–1939* (1989), K. D. Brown (with L. A. Clarkson), *The English Labour Movement* (Dublin, 1982), and E. Hopkins, A *Social History of the English Working Classes* (1979). E. P. Thompson, *The Making of the English Working Class* (1963) has been one of the most influential of modern history books. It brings together a mass of material on radical workers, but its conclusions are by no means generally accepted. E. J. Hobsbawm, *Labouring Men: Studies in the History of Labour* (1964) provides perceptive insights into various aspects of labour history. A revisionist interpretation of the consciousness of workers is provided by P. Joyce, *Visions of the People: Industrial England and the Question of Class 1848–1914* (Cambridge, 1991), which sees language as determining rather than reflecting the behaviour of social groups. G. Crossick, *An Artisan Elite in Victorian Society* (1978) analyses that important social group the 'labour aristocracy' in a case study of Kentish London. The best introductory study of trade unions remains H. Pelling, A *History of British Trade Unionism* (1963). A. E. Musson, *Trade Union and Social History* (1974) brings together a group of perceptive studies of various aspects of trade union history. K. Burgess, *The Origins of British Industrial Relations* (1975) discusses engineering, building, coal-mining, and textiles in this context. C. More, *Skill and the English Working Class, 1870–1914* (1980) discusses modes of training and levels of skill. A selection of contemporary documents with commentary is given in J. T. Ward and W. H. Fraser, *Workers and Employers: Documents on Trade Unions and Industrial Relations in Britain since the Eighteenth Century* (1980).

Wealthier and more influential social groups are covered in J. V. Beckett, *The Aristocracy in England, 1660–1914* (Oxford, 1986), W. D. Rubinstein, *Men of Property: The Very Wealthy in Britain since the Industrial Revolution* (2nd edn., 2006), D. Spring, *The English Landed Estate in the Nineteenth Century* (Baltimore, Md., 1963), and F. M. L. Thompson, *English Landed Society in the Nineteenth Century* (1963). M. Girouard, *Life in the English Country House: A Social and Architectural History* (New Haven, Conn., and London, 1978) broke new ground in analysing the workings of great houses. The relationship between the aristocracy and industrial development is discussed in J. T. Ward and R. G. Wilson (eds.), *Land and Industry: The Landed Estate and the Industrial Revolution* (Newton Abbot, 1971);

the first two essays in this volume are particularly valuable. D. Cannadine (ed.), *Patricians, Power and Politics in Nineteenth-Century Towns* (Leicester, 1982) discusses inter alia the urban influence exercised by the aristocracy while Cannadine's *The Decline and Fall of the British Aristocracy* (New Haven, 1990) charts the fortunes of the aristocracy from the late nineteenth century.

L. Davidoff and C. Hall, *Family Fortunes: Men and Women of the English Middle Class, 1780–1850* (1987) brings together a great deal of detailed information, but suffers from the lack of any convincing definition of the middle class involved. The rise of the professions is considered in W. R. Reader, *Professional Men: The Rise of the Professional Classes in Nineteenth-Century England* (1966) and in an older standard work, A. M. Carr-Saunders and P. A. Wilson, *The Professions* (Oxford, 1937). J. R. Lewis, *The Victorian Bar* (1982) and F. N. L. Poynter (ed.), *The Evolution of Medical Practice in Great Britain* (1961) provide useful examples. H. Perkin, *The Rise of Professional Society: England since 1880* (1989) discerns an increasing divide between the values of professionals and those of businessmen. G. Anderson, *Victorian Clerks* (Manchester, 1976) deals with that increasingly numerous occupational group.

P. Horn, *The Rural World, 1780–1850: Social Change in the English Countryside* (1980) brings together evidence on the effect of changes in farming and other developments in rural communities. A. Howkins, *Reshaping Rural England: A Social History 1850–1925* (1991) does the same for a later period. More material on rural conditions is in G. E. Mingay (ed.), *The Victorian Countryside*, 2 vols. (1981). For Scotland, T. R. Slater, *The Making of the Scottish Countryside* (1980).

Women

Older but still important studies are M. Hewitt, *Wives and Mothers in Victorian Industry* (1958) and I. Pinchbeck, *Women Workers and the Industrial Revolution, 1750–1850* (1930; repr. 1969) but from the early 1970s the history of women or women's history has been a major growth point in historical writing: A. V. John (ed.), *Unequal Opportunities: Women's Employment in England, 1800–1918* (Oxford, 1986), J. Lewis, *Women in England, 1870–1950: Sexual Divisions and Social Change* (Brighton, 1984), M. Vicinus (ed.), *Suffer and Be Still* (1972), and M. Vicinus (ed.), *A Widening Sphere: Changing Roles of Victorian Women* (1977). An important debate has concerned the position of middle- and upper-class women; contrasting interpretations can be found in: L. Davidoff and C. Hall, *Family Fortunes: Men and Women of the English Middle Class 1780–1850* (1987), Amanda Vickery, *The Gentleman's Daughter: Women's Lives in Georgian England* (1998) and 'Golden Age to Separate Spheres? A Review of the Categories and Chronology of English Women's History', *Historical Journal*, 36, 2 (1993), K. Reynolds, *Aristocratic Women and Political Society in Victorian Britain* (1998), P. Jalland, *Women, Marriage and Politics 1860–1914* (Oxford, 1986). L. Davidoff, *The Best Circles: Society, Etiquette and the Season* (1973) considers the social world of upper-class women. S. Steinbach, *Women in England 1760–1914* (2004) provides a useful overview.

Children

For children the standard work is I. Pinchbeck and M. Hewitt, *Children in English Society*, 2 vols. (1969, 1973). Also useful are M. W. Thomas, *Young People in Industry* (1945) and J. Walvin, *A Child's World: A Social History of English Childhood 1800–1914* (1982).

Government

An older but still helpful introduction to this topic is K. B. Smellie, *A Hundred Years of English Government* (2nd edn., 1950). H. Parris, *Constitutional Bureaucracy: The Development of British Central Administration since the Eighteenth Century* (1969) is another useful study. In addition to works on the individual parliamentary Reform Acts, mentioned below, two papers touch upon all three nineteenth-century Reform Acts: N. McCord, 'Some difficulties of parliamentary reform', in *Historical Journal*, 10 (1967), and N. Gash, 'Parliament and democracy in Britain: the three nineteenth century Reform Acts', in N. Gash, *Pillars of Government, and Other Essays on State and Society, c.1770–1880* (1986). Studies of individual topics include E. Cohen, *The Growth of the British Civil Service, 1780–1939* (1941), R. Jones, *The Nineteenth Century Foreign Office* (1971), H. Roseveare, *The Treasury: Evolution of a British Institution* (1969), K. Bourne, *The Foreign Policy of Victorian England, 1830–1902* (1970), and P. M. Kennedy, *The Realities behind Diplomacy: Background Influences on British External Policy, 1865–1980* (1981). D. M. Young, *The Colonial Office in the Early Nineteenth Century* (1961) illustrates more about contemporary government than its rather narrow title suggests. G. Sutherland (ed.), *Studies in the Growth of Nineteenth-Century Government* (1972) consists of a collection of essays which explore specific aspects, including patronage and recruitment. A collection of essays on the making of foreign policy is K. M. Wilson (ed.), *British Foreign Secretaries and Foreign Policy: From Crimean War to First World War* (1987). For imperial administration, R. Hyam, *Britain's Imperial Century, 1815–1914* (1975), and B. Porter, *The Lion's Share: A Short History of British Imperialism, 1850–1970* (1975). For the army, E. M. Spiers, *The Army and Society, 1815–1914* (1980); two standard works on naval history are P. M. Kennedy, *The Rise and Fall of British Naval Mastery* (1976) and C. J. Bartlett, *Great Britain and Sea Power, 1815–1853* (Oxford, 1963). The two principal political parties have been the subject of numerous works. Two of the most useful on the Liberal Party are T. A. Jenkins, *The Liberal Ascendancy 1830–1886* (1994), and M. Bentley, *The Climax of Liberal Politics: British Liberalism in Theory and Practice 1868–1918* (1987), while the older work J. Vincent, *The Formation of the Liberal Party, 1857–1868* (1966) remains essential reading. The nature of the support for Liberalism is discussed in E. Biagini, *Liberty, Retrenchment and Reform: Popular Liberalism in the Age of Gladstone* (Cambridge, 1992). For the Conservative Party broader histories include, R. Blake, *The Conservative Party from Peel to Churchill* (1970), B. Coleman, *Conservatism and the Conservative Party in Nineteenth Century Britain* (1988), and J. Ramsden, *An Appetite for Power: A History of the Conservative Party since 1830* (1998). E. Royle and J. Walvin discuss *English Radicals and Reformers, 1760–1848* (Brighton, 1982), and D. G. Wright provides a short account of *Popular Radicalism: The Working-Class Experience, 1780–1880* (1988). K. Burgess, *The Challenge of Labour: Shaping British Society, 1850–1930* (1980) brings together material on later years. For the Labour Party, F. Bealey and H. Pelling, *Labour and Politics 1900–1906* (1958) is still invaluable as an account of the party's early years but D. Tanner, *Political Change and the Labour Party 1900–1918* (Cambridge, 1990) is the definitive history of the impact of Labour in the first quarter of the twentieth century. For local government the fullest general account is still H. Finer, *English Local Government* (1933). An important modern study is D. Fraser, *Urban Politics in Victorian England* (Leicester, 1976), which inter alia depicts the obstacles in the way of accepting town councils as trustworthy and efficient agencies of improvement. Another study of urban developments is E. P. Hennock, *Fit and Proper Persons: Ideals and Reality in Nineteenth Century Urban Government* (1973). H. J. Dyos and M. Wolff (eds.), *The Victorian City*, 2 vols. (1973), is a major collection of varied studies on urban affairs. A. Briggs, *Victorian Cities* (1968) contains essays on Birmingham, Leeds, London, Manchester, Melbourne, and Middlesbrough, together with a general discussion on urban growth.

Poverty, philanthropy, and the Poor Law

J. Burnett, *Plenty and Want: A Social History of Diet in England from 1815 to the Present Day* (1966) is a standard work on that topic. Among many modern studies of responses to poverty are A. Digby, *The Poor Law in Nineteenth-Century England and Wales* (1982), D. Fraser, *The Evolution of the British Welfare State* (1973), D. Fraser (ed.), *The New Poor Law in the Nineteenth Century* (1976), N. Gash (ed.), *The Long Debate on Poverty* (2nd edn., 1974), D. Owen, *English Philanthropy, 1660–1960* (Cambridge, Mass., 1965), D. Roberts, *The Victorian Origins of the British Welfare State* (New Haven, Conn., 1960), M. E. Rose, *The Relief of Poverty, 1834–1914* (1972), P. Thane, *The Foundations of the Welfare State* (Harlow, 1982). M. E. Rose, *The English Poor Law, 1780–1930* (Newton Abbot, 1971) is a good introduction to the Poor Law, combining excerpts from primary sources with a perceptive commentary. M. B. Simey, *Charitable Effort in Liverpool in the Nineteenth Century* (1951) is an important local study. F. B. Smith, *The People's Health, 1830–1910* (1979) is a valuable study of social problems and the limited resources of nineteenth-century medicine. R. G. Hodgkinson, *The Origins of the National Health Service: The Medical Services of the New Poor Law, 1834–71* (1967) is a major work on this topic. A similarly comprehensive study is G. M. Ayers, *England's First State Hospitals and the Metropolitan Asylums Board, 1867–1930* (1971). For the pre-1834 Poor Law, J. D. Marshall, *The Old Poor Law, 1795–1834* (1968) and G. W. Oxley, *Poor Relief in England and Wales, 1601–1834* (Newton Abbot, 1974) are the best sources.

Police and crime

Among many modern studies, the most useful include three books by C. Emsley, *Policing and its Context, 1750–1870* (1983), *Crime and Society in England, 1750–1900* (1987), and *The English Police: A Political and Social History* (1991). Other relevant books include V. Bailey (ed.), *Policing and Punishment in Nineteenth-Century Britain* (1981), K. Chesney, *The Victorian Underworld* (1972), P. McHugh, *Prostitution and Victorian Social Reform* (1980), D. Philips, *Crime and Authority in Victorian England: The Black Country, 1835–1860* (1977), J. J. Tobias, *Crime and Police in England, 1700–1900* (Dublin, 1979). A balanced account of political and popular demonstrations of discontent is J. Stevenson, *Popular Disturbances in England, 1700–1870* (1979).

Popular culture, leisure, and recreation

Recent years have brought a great mass of research and publications relating to leisure, recreation, and that hard to define area, popular culture. The most useful studies include H. Cunningham, *Leisure in the Industrial Revolution, c.1780–1880* (1980), P. Bailey, *Leisure and Class in Victorian England: Rational Recreation and the Contest for Control 1830–1885* (1978), J. Walvin, *Leisure and Society, 1830–1950* (1978), J. Walvin and J. D. Walton (eds.), *Leisure in Britain, 1780–1939* (Manchester, 1983). There is also J. M. Golby and A. W. Purdue, *The Civilisation of the Crowd: Popular Culture in England, 1750–1900* (1984). On sport, the best single account is R. Holt, *Sport and the British: A Modern History* (Oxford, 1989) and football is well covered by T. Mason, *Association Football and English Society, 1863–1915* (Brighton, 1980). Other works in this wide area include D. Vincent, *Literacy and Popular Culture: England 1750–1914* (Cambridge, 1989) and M. Clapson, *A Bit of a Flutter: Popular Gambling and English Society, c.1823–1961* (Manchester, 1992). E. Griffin, 'Popular Culture in Industrialising England', *Historical Journal*, vol. 5, 3, September 2002 provides a useful historiographical essay.

The monarchy

The monarchy is a subject which has attracted many historians in recent years, a recognition that not only did its political influence endure rather longer than had previously been thought but that its social influence and popularity had waxed in the nineteenth and twentieth centuries. V. Bogdanor, *The Monarchy and the Constitution* (Oxford, 1995), though a late twentieth century constitutional study, provides information on and insights into its historical development. Frank Prochaska, *Royal Bounty: The Making of a Welfare Monarchy* (New Haven, 1995), makes the case for the monarchy's role as leader of civil society and of charitable organizations. Linda Colley, 'The Apotheosis of George III: Loyalty, Royalty and the British Nation 1760–1820', *Past and Present*, 102 (1984) argues that the foundations of the association of monarchy and patriotism were already established at the beginning of the nineteenth century. D. Cannadine, 'The Context, Performance and Meaning of Ritual: The British Monarchy and the "Invention of Tradition", *c.*1820–1977', in E. Hobsbawm and T. Ranger (eds.), *The Invention of Tradition* (Cambridge, 1983) provides a radical reassessment of the place of ceremony and ritual in the projection of the monarchy. J. A. Cannon and R. Griffiths, *The Oxford Illustrated History of the Monarchy* (Oxford, 1988) and J. M. Golby and A. W. Purdue, *Kings and Queens of Empire* (Stroud, 2000) both argue for the continued importance of the monarchy. Kings and Queens and other royals have ever attracted biographies and among recent publications are E. A. Smith, *George IV* (New Haven, 1999), Stanley Weintraub, *Victoria: Biography of a Queen* (1987) and *Albert: Uncrowned King* (1997). Philip Magnus, *King Edward VII* (1964) remains probably the best biography of that monarch.

Religion

Valuable studies here include A. Armstrong, *The Church of England, the Methodists and Society* (1973), I. Bradley, *The Call to Seriousness: The Evangelical Impact on the Victorians* (1976), which gives an interesting discussion of the evangelical impact on influential minorities, W. O. Chadwick, *The Victorian Church*, 2 vols. (1966, 1970), the standard account of the Church of England, A. D. Gilbert, *Religion and Society in Industrial England: Church, Chapel and Social Change, 1740–1914* (1976), a valuable general survey, and E. R. Norman, *Church and Society in England, 1770–1970: A Historical Study* (Oxford, 1976). J. Briggs and I. Sellers, *Victorian Nonconformity* (1973) provides a selection of documents with comment. Boyd Hilton, *The Age of Atonement: The Influence of Evangelicalism on Social and Economic Thought 1785–1865* (Oxford, 1988) argues that social and economic ideas were infused by theology.

Education

Broad studies include A. Digby and P. Searby, *Children, School and Society in Nineteenth-Century England* (1981), a selection of relevant texts with a commentary, J. Lawson and H. Silver, *A Social History of Education in England* (1973), and A. Tropp, *The School Teachers* (1957). Scotland is well served with R. Anderson, *Education and Opportunity in Victorian Scotland* (1983). G. Sutherland, *Elementary Education in the Nineteenth Century* (1971) is a useful introduction with guidance to further reading in that sector, as is M. Argles, *South Kensington to Robbins: An Account of English Technical and Scientific Education since 1851* (1964). A standard account of the aftermath of the 1870 Elementary Education Act is G. Sutherland, *Policy-Making in Elementary Education, 1870–1895* (1974). V. E. Chancellor, *History for their Masters: Opinion in the English History Textbook, 1800–1914* (1970) offers an interesting account of the history taught in schools. Useful works on higher education include W. H. G. Armytage, *The Civic Universities* (1955), M. Sanderson (ed.), *The Universities in the Nineteenth Century* (1975), and M. Sanderson, *The Universities and British Industry* (1972). The earlier sections of H. Perkin, *Key Profession: The History of the Association of University Teachers* (1969) contain interesting material on university conditions in this period.

Science and technology

Two classic studies are D. Landes, *The Unbound Prometheus: Technological Change and Industrial Development in Western Europe from 1750 to the Present* (1969), and H. J. Habakkuk, *American and British Technology in the Nineteenth Century* (Cambridge, 1962). A. R. Musson and E. H. Robinson, *Science and Technology in the Industrial Revolution* (1969) deals with earlier developments. R. Kargon, *Science in Victorian Manchester: Enterprise and Expertise* (Manchester, 1977) is less narrow in its scope than the title suggests. A useful introductory text is L. T. C. Rolt, *Victorian Engineering: A Fascinating Story of Invention and Achievement* (1970), which also suggests additional reading in the general field of engineering and technology.

Biographies

The 1815–1914 period has attracted many biographers. Just about every figure of any significance has been the subject of a modern study. These works vary greatly in size and in quality. The following list includes a small selection of works of high quality which go beyond their immediate subject matter and set it against a broader description of the background involved. Lord (Robert) Blake has written two major works, *Disraeli* (1966) and *The Unknown Prime Minister: The Life and Times of Andrew Bonar Law, 1858–1923* (1955), both of which provide a perceptive account of developments during the lifetimes of the two subjects. The latter is now challenged if not displaced by R. J. Q. Adams, *Bonar Law* (1999). Professor Norman Gash has provided an equally magisterial treatment of Peel in his two volumes *Mr. Secretary Peel: The Life of Robert Peel to 1830* (1961) and *Sir Robert Peel: The Life of Sir Robert Peel after 1830* (1972). The same author has also written a somewhat briefer but still very useful account of *Lord Liverpool* (1984). Gladstone has attracted many biographers; leading studies are P. Magnus, *Gladstone: A Biography* (1954) and R. T. Shannon, *Gladstone: Heroic Prime Minister 1865–1898* (1999). Two recent biographies of Lord Salisbury are: Andrew Roberts, *Salisbury: Victorian Titan* (1999) and D. Steele: *Lord Salisbury: A Political Biography* (1999). Three biographies of A. J. Balfour are: K. Young, *Arthur James Balfour* (1963), S. H. Zebel, *Balfour: A Political Biography* (Cambridge, 1973), and M. Egremont, *Balfour* (1980) though the enigmatic politician still proves an elusive subject. Roy Jenkins, *Asquith* (1964) remains the best study of that prime minister. John Grigg, *Lloyd George: The People's Champion 1902–11* (1978) and *Lloyd George: From Peace to War 1912–16* (1985) are the fullest accounts of Lloyd George's career in the years covered by this book. Roy Jenkins, *Churchill* (2001), chs. 1–15, deals with Churchill's early career. Other biographies will be mentioned below in relation to specific chapters.

Chapter 1

Among the most useful general accounts of the post-1815 years are A. Briggs, *The Age of Improvement, 1783–1867* (rev. edn., 1979), N. Gash, *Aristocracy and People: Britain 1815–1865* (1979), Boyd Hilton, *A Mad, Bad, and Dangerous People* (2006), and F. O'Gorman, *The Long Eighteenth Century 1688–1832* (1997). Jonathan Clark's challenge to the orthodox interpretations of the nature of English society until the late 1820s is contained in *English Society 1688–1832: Ideology, Social Structure and Political Practice during the Ancien Regime* (1985).Two biographies of leading Tory politicians are particularly useful; both are by Professor Norman Gash, *Mr. Secretary Peel: The Life of Robert Peel to 1830* (1961) and *Lord Liverpool* (1984). The very full work on Peel contains a great deal of associated information about contemporary politics. The Liverpool study took further the convincing revaluation of that premier and his government in J. Cookson, *Lord Liverpool's Administration, 1815–1822* (Edinburgh, 1975). B. Hilton, *Corn, Cash and Commerce: The Economic Policies of the Tory Governments, 1815–1830* (1977) deals with some of the governments' most important policies. Castlereagh has two modern biographies, both useful: C. J. Bartlett, *Castlereagh* (1966) and J. W. Derry, *Castlereagh* (1976). Canning too has a pair of modern biographies: P. J. K. *Rolo, George Canning* (1965) and W. Hinde, *George Canning* (1973); the latter is the fuller account. Lord Sidmouth is given a fair hearing in P. Ziegler, *Addington* (1965). G. M. Trevelyan, *Lord Grey of the Reform Bill* (1920) may well be that historian's weakest book and cannot be seen as a satisfactory study; E. A. Smith, *Lord Grey 1764–1845* (Oxford, 1990), provides a perceptive study. R. Stewart, *Henry Brougham: His Public Career, 1778–1868* (1986) is an excellent portrayal of that wayward character. For the Whigs more generally, A. Mitchell, *The Whigs in Opposition, 1815–30* (Oxford, 1967). There have been many studies of radical agitation in these years, of which the most important is E. P. Thompson, *The Making of the English Working Class* (1963). This influential and readable work is widely believed to exaggerate the extent of working-class coherence and popular radicalism in the post-1815 years, but it brings together a great mass of material on such themes. J. Stevenson, *Popular Disturbances in England, 1700–1870* (1979) gives a more succinct account of such matters, together with references to other relevant writing. E. Royle and J. Walvin, *English Radicals and Reformers, 1760–1848* (Brighton, 1982) is a later study. C. T. Machin, *The Catholic Question in English Politics, 1820–30* (1964) is the best modern study of that topic; the Irish dimension is discussed in F. O'Ferrall, *Catholic Emancipation* (1985) and J. A. Reynolds, *The Catholic Emancipation Crisis in Ireland, 1823–9* (New Haven, Conn., 1954). Daniel O'Connell has a competent biography in A. Macintyre, *The Liberator* (1965). Foreign policy is dealt with in two standard works, C. K. Webster, *The Foreign Policy of Castlereagh, 1815–22: Britain and the European Alliance* (1925) and H. W. V. Temperley, *The Foreign Policy of Canning, 1822–27* (1925). The nature and effectiveness of the Combination Laws of 1799–1800 were dissected many years ago in D. George, 'The Combination Laws', *Economic History Review*, 1st ser., 6 (1935–6). For the creation of the Metropolitan Police, D. Ascoli, *The Queen's Peace: The Origins and Development of the Metropolitan Police, 1829–1979* (1979). M. W. Flinn, 'The Poor Employment Act of 1817', *Economic History Review*, 2nd ser., 14 (1961–2), offers an interesting sidelight on government attitudes and policies in the post-war years.

Chapter 2

For a valuable collection of documents with perceptive comments, H. J. Hanham, *The Nineteenth Century Constitution* (1969). The monarchy is discussed in B. Kemp, *King and Commons, 1660–1832* (1957). R. Pares, *King George III and the Politicians* (Oxford, 1953), despite its title, contains material up to 1830. In addition to the already mentioned biography of George IV by E. A. Smith, D. Saul, *Prince of Pleasure* (1998) provides a lively account of the Regent. J. Black, 'The House of Hanover' in W. M. Ormrod (ed.), *The Kings and Queens of England* (2001), describes the development of the monarchy during the reigns of George IV and William IV. J. P. Mackintosh, *The British Cabinet* (1962) includes a historical survey which discusses relations between monarch and government.

A formative study of the role of the Cabinet is A. Aspinall, 'The Cabinet Council, 1783–1835', *Proceedings of the British Academy*, 38 (1952). For the House of Lords, A. S. Turberville, *The House of Lords in the Age of Reform, 1784–1837* (1958). C. Seymour, *Electoral Reform in England and Wales* (1915) is an old standard work of reference which has been supplanted in many respects by later work, but it still gives much evidence about pre-1832 elections to the House of Commons. F. O'Gorman, *Voters, Patrons, and Parties, The Unreformed Electorate of Hanoverian England 1734–1832* (Oxford, 1989) provides a reassessment of the pre-1832 electoral system. E. and A. C. Porritt, *The Unreformed House of Commons*, 2 vols. (1903, 1909) is an old standard work which has never been effectively supplanted.

The question of national unity and identity has been the subject of many recent books. Linda Colley, *Britons* (1992) has been highly influential with an account of the forging of a sense of British identity from the mid-eighteenth century. Paul Langford, *Englishness Identified: Manners and Character 1650–1850* (2000), considers English identity.

The working of the national census is described in D. V. Glass, *Numbering the People* (Farnborough, 1973) and Interdepartmental Committee on Social and Economic Research, *Census of Great Britain, 1801–1931: Guide to Official Sources No. 2* (1951). R. Lawton (ed.), *The Census and Social Structure: An Interpretative Guide to the 19th Century Censuses for England and Wales* (1978) is a collection of essays on the census as a source. The best general work on central government remains H. Parris, *Constitutional Bureaucracy: The Development of British Central Administration since the Eighteenth Century* (1969). D. M. Young, *The Colonial Office in the Early Nineteenth Century* (1961) is a perceptive study of one department which goes beyond its immediate theme in its analysis of the working of government. The patronage system is discussed there and in A. P. Donajgrodski, 'New roles for old: the Northcote–Trevelyan Report and the Clerks of the Home Office, 1822–48', in G. Sutherland (ed.), *Studies in the Growth of Nineteenth-Century Government* (1972).

The quality of naval administration, and the impact of 'cheap government' ideas on defence, are discussed in C. J. Bartlett, *Great Britain and Sea Power, 1815–1853* (Oxford, 1963). A. Bruce, *The Purchase System in the British Army, 1660–1871* (1980) gives a full discussion of the working of that system. D. Duman, *The Judicial Bench in England, 1727–1875* (1982) provides an account of the central judiciary, its social origins and status. A good general account of problems of public order in these years is in J. Stevenson, *Popular Disturbances in England, 1700–1870* (1979), chs. 10 and 11. For the pre-1834 Poor Law, J. D. Marshall, *The Old Poor Law, 1795–1834* (1968) and G. W. Oxley, *Poor Relief in England and Wales, 1601–1834* (Newton Abbot, 1974) are the most convenient accounts. G. B. Hindle, *Provision for the Relief of the Poor in Manchester, 1754–1826* (Manchester, 1975) describes one of the most advanced examples of local government in these years. A succinct account of colonial affairs is given in D. K. Fieldhouse, *The Colonial Empires* (1966).

Chapter 3

E. J. Evans, *The Forging of the Modern State: Early Industrial Britain, 1783–1870* (1983) includes as an appendix a valuable range of statistical information, including population figures for a variety of communities. For population growth more generally, M. W. Flinn, *British Population Growth, 1700–1850* (1970). For Scotland, M. W. Flinn (ed.), *Scottish Population History* (Cambridge, 1977). For Ireland, K. H. Connell, *The Population of Ireland, 1750–1845* (Oxford, 1950). R. M. Reeve, *The Industrial Revolution, 1750–1850* (1971), provides a good general account of economic change in these years. A. E. Musson, 'Industrial motive power in the United Kingdom, 1800–1870', *Economic History Review*, 2nd ser., 29 (1976) is a perceptive corrective to earlier views of the pace of industrialization.

A similarly salutary work is the splendid tour de force by F. M. L. Thompson, 'Some nineteenth-century horse sense', in the same volume of *Economic History Review*. There are many accounts of the development of science and technology in these years. Among the most useful are A. F. Burstall, *A History of Mechanical Engineering* (2nd edn., 1965), D. L. S. Cardwell, *Technology, Science and History* (1972), P. W. Kingsford, *Engineers, Inventors and Workers* (1964), and L. T. C. Rolt, *Victorian Engineeering: A Fascinating Story of Invention and Achievement* (1970). The lengthy scholarly debate about the 'openness' of the British aristocracy can be followed in L. Stone and J. C. F. Stone, *An Open Elite? England 1540–1880* (Oxford, 1984) and D. and E. Spring, 'Social history and the English landed elite', *Canadian Journal of History*, 21(1986). A major study is J. V. Beckett, *The Aristocracy in England, 1660–1914* (Oxford, 1986). For religion, the best account is in A. D. Gilbert, *Religion and Society in Industrial England* (1976). I. Bradley, *The Call to Seriousness* (1976) provides a perceptive account of the evangelical revival. For popular radicalism E. P. Thompson, *The Making of the English Working Class* (1963) brings together a mass of material, but its conclusions can usefully be tempered by other works such as D. Read, *Peterloo: The 'Massacre' and its Background* (Manchester, 1958), M. I. Thomis, *The Luddites: Machine Breaking in Regency England* (Newton Abbot, 1970), and R. Walmsley, *Peterloo: The Case Reopened* (1969). The case keeps getting re-opened and a recent article is, R. Poole, ' "By the Law or the Sword": Peterloo Revisited', *History*, vol. 91, 302, April 2006. A relevant local study is N. McCord, 'Tyneside disturbances and Peterloo', *Northern History*, 2(1967). M. W. Flinn, 'Trends in real wages, 1750–1850', *Economic History Review*, 2nd ser., 27 (1974) summarizes a lengthy scholarly debate on the standard of living and offers a convincing digest of the available evidence. The significance of charitable work is discussed by D. Owen, *English Philanthropy, 1660–1960* (1965); a regional example is N. McCord, 'The Poor Law and philanthropy', in D. Fraser (ed.), *The New Poor Law in the Nineteenth Century* (1976).

Chapter 4

Among biographies of William IV are P. Ziegler, *King William IV* (1971) and T. Pocock, *Sailor King: The Life of King William IV* (1991). S. Weintraub, *Victoria: Biography of a Queen* (1987) and *Prince Albert: Uncrowned King* (1997) are among the latest of many biographies of the royal couple. N. Gash, *Reaction and Reconstruction in English Politics, 1832–1852* (Oxford, 1965) is a perceptive account of the political developments of these years. G. B. A. M. Finlayson, *England in the Eighteen Thirties: The Decade of Reform* (1969) is a brief but competent summary, with a bibliography. R. Stewart, *The Foundation of the Conservative Party, 1830–1867* (1978) is the best account of the 'Peelite' recovery. For the historical background to the reform crisis of 1831–2, the standard work is J. Cannon, *Parliamentary Reform, 1640–1832* (Cambridge, 1973). The best modern study of the struggle for the Reform Act in 1831–2 is M. Brock, *The Great Reform Act* (1973). For the working of the post-1832 electoral system, N. Gash, *Politics in the Age of Peel* (1953) remains a standard work; an additional note is offered in N. McCord, 'Some difficulties of parliamentary reform', *Historical Journal*, 10 (1967). An illustration of the effects of the Great Reform Act on party organization is given in N. Gash, 'The organization of the Conservative Party, 1832–1846', pt. 1: 'The parliamentary organisation', *Parliamentary History*, 1 (1982), and pt. 11: 'The electoral organisation', *Parliamentary History*, 2 (1983). Reading on the 1834 Poor Law Amendment Act is suggested in the next section. For the Municipal Reform Act of 1835, G. B. A. M. Finlayson, 'The Municipal Corporation commission and report', *Bulletin of the Institute of Historical Research*, 36 (1963), and the same author's 'The politics of municipal reform, 1835', *Economic History Review*, 81 (1966). For a good local example, W. L. Burn, 'Newcastle upon Tyne in the early nineteenth century', *Archaeologia Aeliana*,

4th ser., 34 (1956), and M. G. Cook, 'The last days of the unreformed Corporation of Newcastle upon Tyne', *Archaeologia Aeliana*, 4th ser., 39 (1961). Among biographies, the second volume of the standard life of Peel, N. Gash, *Sir Robert Peel: The Life of Sir Robert Peel after 1830* (1972), is an outstanding source for these years. There are many other useful biographies of leading political figures. P. Ziegler, *Melbourne* (1976) and L. G. Mitchell, *Lord Melbourne, 1779–1848* (Oxford, 1997) provide contrasting studies of that politician. J. Prest, *Lord John Russell* (1972) is a substantial biography, though not in the same magisterial class as Blake's *Disraeli* or Gash's *Peel*. For Palmerston, D. Southgate, *The Most English Minister* (1966), J. Ridley, *Lord Palmerston* (1970), and J. Chambers, *Palmerston, The People's Darling* (2004) are the principal modern studies. Disraeli's own account of his political ally *Lord George Bentinck: A Political Biography* (1852) is still worth reading, if only for such high points as the account of Peel's fall in 1846. Disraeli's early career is analysed in C. Richmond and P. Smith eds., *The Self-Fashioning of Disraeli 1818–51* (1998) and J. Ridley, *The Young Disraeli* (1995). Revaluations of the protectionists after 1846 are A. Macintyre, 'Lord George Bentinck and the Protectionists: a lost cause?', in *Transactions of the Royal Historical Society*, 5th ser., 39 (1989) and R. Stewart, *The Politics of Protectionism. Lord Derby and the Protectionist Party, 1841–52* (Cambridge, 1971) and Anna Gambles, *Protection and Politics: Conservative Economic Discourse, 1815–1852* (Woodbridge, 1999). A convenient short account of Peel's second government is T. L. Crosby, *Sir Robert Peel's Administration, 1841–46* (Newton Abbot, 1976). D. Read, *Peel and the Victorians* (1987) describes the admiration of mid-Victorians for this less than charismatic politician. For the Irish aspect of this ministry, a full discussion is given in D. A. Kerr, *Peel, Priests, and Politics: Sir Robert Peel's Administration and the Roman Catholic Church in Ireland* (Oxford, 1982). D. Southgate, *The Passing of the Whigs, 1832–1886* (1962) is still the best discussion of the political role of the Whigs in these years. The starting-point for the Chartist movement is the standard bibliography of the extensive relevant publications, D. Thompson and J. F. C. Harrison, *Bibliography of the Chartist Movement* (1978). Two contrasting studies are D. Thompson, *The Chartists* (1984) and J. T. Ward, *Chartism* (1973). James A. Epstein, *Radical Expression: Political Language, Ritual, and Symbol in England, 1790–1850* (Oxford, 1994) is one of a number of studies emphasizing the salience of language and ritual to Chartism. A. M. Hadfield's *The Chartist Land Company* (Newton Abbot, 1970) provides a full account of that aspect and Malcolm Chase, *'The People's Farm': English Radical Agrarianism 1775–1840* (Oxford, 1988) describes the wider context of the Land Company's appeal. For the Anti-Corn Law League, N. McCord, *The Anti-Corn Law League* (1958), P. A. Pickering and A. Tyrrell, *The People's Bread: A History of the Anti-Corn Law League* (Leicester, 2000), and D. Read, *Cobden and Bright: A Victorian Political Partnership* (1967). Two modern biographies are W. Hinde, *Richard Cobden: A Victorian Outsider* (1987) and K. Robbins, *John Bright* (1979). G. Kitson Clark, 'Hunger and politics in 1842', *Journal of Modern History*, 25 (1953) discusses a critical stage in the early-Victorian depression. F. Mather, *Public Order in the Age of the Chartists* (Manchester, 1959) and J. Stevenson, *Popular Disturbances in England, 1700–1870* (1979) discuss the policing problems caused by the agitations of these years.

Chapter 5

For more general comment on government and administration in these years, N. McCord, 'Some limitations of the Age of Reform', in H. Hearder and H. R. Loyn (eds.), *British Government and Administration: Studies Presented to S. B. Chrimes* (Cardiff, 1974). A succinct general account of taxation is J. F. Rees, *A Short Fiscal and Financial History of England, 1815–1918* (1921). For the income tax, B. E. V. Sabine, *A History of Income Tax* (1966). For the rates, E. Carman, *The History of Local Rates in England* (2nd edn., 1912). For the development of the Civil Service, E. W. Cohen, *The Growth of the British Civil Service, 1780–1939* (1941). A good illustration of Civil Service recruitment is given by R. C. Snelling and T. J. Barron, 'The Colonial Office: its permanent officials, 1801–1914', in G. Sutherland (ed.), *Studies in the Growth of Nineteenth-Century Government* (1972). For problems of public health, and the limited official response, F. B. Smith, *The People's Health, 1830–1910* (1979) and R. A. Lewis, *Edwin Chadwick and the Public Health Movement, 1832–54* (1952). For education, G. Sutherland, *Elementary Education in the Nineteenth Century* (1971) provides a brief account with suggestions for further reading. For the Post Office, the standard modern account is M. J. Daunton, *Royal Mail: The Post Office since 1840* (1985); another useful study is D. Vincent, 'Communications, community and the State', in C. Emsley and J. Walvin (eds.), *Artisans, Peasants & Proletarians, 1760–1860: Essays Presented to Gwyn A. Williams* (1985). For railway regulation, H. Parris, *Government and the Railways in Nineteenth-Century Britain* (1965) and G. Alderman, *The Railway Interest* (Leicester, 1973). J. T. Ward, *The Factory Movement* (1962) gives the fullest account of the agitation leading to early Factory Acts; U. Henriques, *The Early Factory Acts and their Enforcement* (1971), a Historical Association booklet, gives a short account with further references. R. K. Webb, 'A Whig inspector', *Journal of Modern History*, 27 (1955) and U. Henriques, 'An early factory inspector: James Stuart of Dunearn', *Scottish Historical Review*, 50 (1971) provide illuminating examples of early inspectors. S. G. and E. O. A. Checkland published the text of *The Poor Law Report of 1834* with an explanatory introduction (1974). The Poor Law Amendment Act of 1834 is cited and discussed in M. E. Rose, *The English Poor Law, 1780–1930* (Newton Abbot, 1971). D. Fraser (ed.), *The New Poor Law in the Nineteenth Century* (1976) is a volume of essays on various aspects of post-1834 Poor Law administration, with useful bibliographies. A. Digby, *Pauper Palaces* (1978) is a full account of Poor Law development in one region, East Anglia. For local government more generally, H. Finer, *English Local Government* (1933). An illuminating local example is E. C. Midwinter, *Social Administration in Lancashire, 1830–1860: Poor Law, Public Health and Police* (Manchester, 1969). For imperial affairs, W. P. Morrell, *British Colonial Policy in the Age of Peel and Russell* (Oxford, 1966). H. T. Manning has contributed several papers on imperial history in these years, 'The colonial policy of the Whig ministers, 1830–7', *Canadian Historical Review*, 33 (1957); 'Colonial crises before the Cabinet, 1829–35', *Bulletin of the Institute of Historical Research*, 30 (1957); 'Who ran the British Empire, 1830–1850?', in *Journal of British Studies*, 5 (1965–6).

Chapter 6

For population change, N. L. Tranter, *Population and Society, 1750–1940* (1985). The growth of London is discussed in H. A. Shannon, 'Migration and the growth of London, 1840–91', *Economic History Review*, 5 (1934). For changes in the landscape through economic development, B. Trinder, *The Making of the Industrial Landscape* (1982). For changes in industrial organization, B. C. Hunt, *The Development of the Business Corporation in England, 1800–1867* (Cambridge, Mass., 1936) and S. Pollard, *The Genesis of Modern Management* (1968). For an excellent example of an industrial enterprise, with much general discussion added, E. M. Sigsworth, *Black Dyke Mills* (Liverpool, 1958). For the history of banking, B. L. Anderson and P. L. Cottrell, *Money and Banking in England: The Development of the Banking System, 1694–1914* (1974). A parallel study is E. V. Morgan and W. A. Thomas, *The Stock Exchange: Its History and Functions* (1962). Rural life is described in P. Horn, *The Rural World, 1780–1850: Change in the English Countryside* (1980). For the rural disturbances of 1830–1, E. Hobsbawm and G. Rude, *Captain Swing* (1969); for later rural disturbances an illuminating example of conflicting interpretations is provided by D. Jones, 'Thomas Campbell Foster and the rural labourer: incendiarism in East Anglia in the 1840s', *Social History*, 1 (1976) and P. Muskett, 'The Suffolk incendiaries, 1843–5', *Journal of Regional and Local History*, 7 (1987). For religion in these years, the best general account is in A. D. Gilbert, *Religion and Society in Industrial England: Church, Chapel and Social Change, 1740–1914* (1976). More specific studies include G. Kitson Clark, *Churchmen and the Condition of England, 1832–1885* (1973), G. I. T. Machin, *Politics and the Churches in Great Britain, 1832 to 1868* (Oxford, 1977), W. R. Ward, *Religion and Society in England, 1790–1850* (1950) and N. Yates, *The Oxford Movement and Anglican Ritualism* (1983). For the significance of charities, B. Harrison, 'Philanthropy and the Victorians', *Victorian Studies*, 9 (1965–6). For another context, N. Gash, 'Lord George Bentinck and his sporting world', in *Pillars of Government and Other Essays on State and Society, c.1770–c.1880* (1986).

Chapter 7

J. B. Conacher, *The Aberdeen Coalition, 1852–5* (Cambridge, 1968) gives a full account of that administration's history. R. Blake, *Disraeli* (1966) provides a full account of the fortunes of the Conservative Party in these years. P. Magnus, *Gladstone: A Biography* (1954) is useful, though not as full, for the Liberals. D. Southgate, *The Passing of the Whigs, 1832–1886* (1962) and J. Vincent, *The Formation of the Liberal Party* (1966) provide additional insights into Liberal developments in these years. For the free trade radicals, N. McCord, 'Cobden and Bright in politics, 1846–57', in R. Robson (ed.), *Ideas and Institutions of Victorian Britain: Essays Presented to G. Kitson Clark* (1967). The reform crisis of 1866–7 inspired an important crop of centenary studies, including M. J. Cowling, *1867: Disraeli, Gladstone and Revolution: The Passing of the Second Reform Bill* (1967), E. J. Feuchtwanger, *Disraeli, Democracy and the Tory Party* (1965), and F. B. Smith, *The Making of the Second Reform Bill* (Cambridge, 1966); the last named book gives the best narrative account of the episode. For the enactment of the secret ballot, a full discussion is given in B. Kinzer, *The Ballot Question in Nineteenth-Century English Politics* (New York, 1983). P. Joyce, *Work, Society and Politics: The Culture of the Factory in Later Victorian England* (1980) breaks new ground in ways which help to explain Conservative urban strength. For the political developments of the later 1870s, R. T. Shannon, *Gladstone and the Bulgarian Atrocities, 1876* (1963).

Chapter 8

W. L. Burn, *The Age of Equipoise: A Study of the Mid-Victorian Generation* (1964) offers inter alia a subtle and perceptive analysis of relations between government and society, and comments on many of the legislative innovations of these years. A standard work on the electoral system is H. J. Hanham, *Elections and Party Management: Politics in the Time of Disraeli and Gladstone* (1959). For the concept and impact of 'cheap government', N. Gash, ' "Cheap government", 1815–1874', in N. Gash, *Pillars of Government and Other Essays on State and Society, c.1770–c.1880* (1986). For changes in central administration, one key sector is described in the latter part of H. Roseveare, *The Treasury 1660–1870: The Foundations of Control* (1973). For the army and navy reforms of Gladstone's first government, E. M. Spiers, *The Army and Society, 1815–1914*, ch. 7, A. V. Tucker, 'Army and society in England, 1870–1900', in *Journal of British Studies*, 2 (1963), and N. McCord, 'A naval scandal of 1871: the loss of H.M.S. *Megaera*', in *Mariner's Mirror*, 57 (1971). For a succinct account of imperial affairs in these years, R. Porter, *The Lion's Share: A Short History of British Imperialism, 1850–1970* (1975). A broader discussion is in C. C. Eldridge, *England's Mission: The Imperial Idea in the Age of Gladstone and Disraeli, 1868–80* (1973). The course and significance of the Indian Mutiny of 1857 are discussed in M. Edwardes, *Red Year: The Indian Rebellion of 1857* (1975) and C. Hibbert, *The Great Mutiny: India 1857* (1978). The consequences are examined in T. R. Metcalf, *Aftermath of Revolt: India, 1857–70* (Princeton, NJ, 1954). For the government and public health, R. Lambert, *Sir John Simon, 1816–1904, and English Social Administration* (1963). For local government, D. Fraser, *Urban Politics in Victorian England* (Leicester, 1976), E. P. Hennock, *Fit and Proper Persons: Ideal and Reality in Nineteenth-Century Urban Government* (1973), D. Fraser (ed.), *Municipal Reform and the Industrial City* (Manchester, 1982); in the last-named work, B. Barber's essay on Leeds is particularly illuminating. Another study of the government of the growing towns, written as 'a community power study', is J. Garrand, *Leadership and Power in Victorian Industrial Towns, 1830–80* (Manchester, 1983). A recent study confirming the weaknesses in much urban administration is M. Callcott, 'The Municipal Administration of Newcastle upon Tyne, 1835–1900', Ph.D. thesis, Newcastle University, 1988.

Chapter 9

For economic developments generally, R. A. Church, *The Great Victorian Boom, 1850–1873* (1975). A contribution to the scholarly debate on the quality of entrepreneurial initiative is W. H. Chaloner, 'Was there a decline of the industrial spirit in Britain, 1850–1939?', Sixteenth Dickinson Memorial Lecture, *Transactions of the Newcomen Society*, 55 (1983–4); this paper also lists the principal earlier contributions to the debate. The thesis that gentrification stifled the spirit of industrial enterprise put forward by M. Wiener, *English Culture and the Decline of the Industrial Spirit, 1850–1980* (Cambridge, 1981) is denied by F. M. L. Thompson, *Gentrification and the Enterprise Culture: Britain 1780–1980* (Oxford, 2001). B. Supple (ed.), *Essays in British Business History* (Oxford, 1977) brings together information on various elements in the economy, including mechanical engineering, tobacco, and insurance. For overseas investment, P. L. Cottrell, *British Overseas Investment in the Nineteenth Century* (1975).

For the economic fortunes of landowners, G. Rogers, 'Lancashire landowners and the great agricultural depression', *Northern History*, 22 (1986). For an example of the management of a great estate, E. Richards, *The Leviathan of Wealth: The Sutherland Fortune in the Industrial Revolution* (1973). A contemporary description of the role of the landed interest is J. Caird, *The Landed Interest and the Supply of Food* (1880). A. E. Musson, *Trade Union and Social History* (1974) brings together a group of important papers on such topics as trade-unionism 1825–75 and the creation of the TUC in a form which provides useful correctives to earlier misunderstandings. Similarly, P. Joyce, *Work, Society and Politics: The Culture of the Factory in Later Victorian England* (1980) provides insights into many aspects of industrial society. H. Mayhew's famous description of *London Labour and the London Poor* of 1861–2 has been republished in several modern forms, including a four-volume edition (New York, 1968) and three volumes of extensive excerpts edited by P. Quennell, *Mayhew's London* (1949), *London's Underworld* (1950), and *Mayhew's Characters* (1951). More recent editions include E. P. Thompson and E. Yeo (eds.), *The Unknown Mayhew: Selections from the Morning Chronicle, 1849–50* (1971) and V. Neuburg, *London Labour and the London Poor* (1985). For another study of poor urban conditions, H. J. Dyos, 'The slums of Victorian London', *Victorian Studies*, 11 (1967). M. J. Daunton, *House and Home in the Victorian City: Working-Class Housing, 1850–1914* (1983) discusses 'respectable' housing. An analysis of the nature of crime and the reaction to it is D. Philips, *Crime and Authority in Victorian England: The Black Country, 1835–1860* (1977). P. McHugh, *Prostitution and Victorian Social Reform* (1980) provides a full discussion of the Contagious Diseases Acts and the agitation against them.

Chapter 10

M. D. Pugh, *The Making of Modern British Politics, 1867–1939* (1982) gives a perceptive general discussion of political events during these years. Electoral patterns are thoroughly delineated in H. Pelling, *Social Geography of British Elections, 1885–1910* (1967). The background to the Third Reform Act is discussed in A. Jones, *The Politics of Reform: 1884* (Cambridge, 1972). Conservative urban strength is considered in R. McKenzie and A. Silver, *Angels in Marble: Working Class Conservatism in Urban England* (1968) and R. L. Greenall, 'Popular Conservatism in Salford, 1868–1886', *Northern History*, 11 (1974). Other important studies include R. Blake and H. Cecil (eds.), *Salisbury: The Man and his Policies* (1987) and P. Marsh, *The Discipline of Popular Government: Lord Salisbury's Domestic Statecraft, 1881–1902* (Hassocks, 1978). Modern biographies of Joseph Chamberlain include R. Jay, *Joseph Chamberlain: A Political Study* (1981) and P. T. Marsh, *Joseph Chamberlain: Entrepreneur in Politics* (1994). Two papers which exercised a widespread influence on subsequent scholarship are by J. P. Cornford: 'The transformation of Conservatism in the late nineteenth century', *Victorian Studies*, 7 (1963–4) and 'The parliamentary foundations of the Hotel Cecil', in R. Robson (ed.), *Ideas and Institutions of Victorian Britain: Essays Presented to G. Kitson Clark* (1967). An important study of Liberal policies in these years is M. Bentley, *The Climax of Liberal Politics: British Liberalism in Theory and Practice, 1868–1918* (1987). For Rosebery see R. R. James, *Rosebery: A Biography of Archibald Philip Primrose, Fifth Earl of Rosebery* (1963) and L. McKinstry, *Rosebery: Statesman in Turmoil* (2005). For events during the Parliament of 1880–5, W. L. Arnstein, *The Bradlaugh Case: A Study in Late Victorian Opinion and Politics* (Oxford, 1965) and R. R. James, *Lord Randolph Churchill* (1959), which gives good examples of Churchill's speeches. The Primrose League and related topics are discussed in M. D. Pugh, *The Tories and the People* (1985). For the Irish crisis of the 1880s, F. S. L. Lyons, *The Fall of Parnell* (1960), F. S. L. Lyons, *Ireland since the Famine* (1971; rev. edn. 1973), C. C. O'Brien, *Parnell and his Party, 1880–90* (1957), and L. P. Curtis, *Coercion and Conciliation in Ireland, 1880–1892* (Princeton, NJ, 1963). P. Buckland's Historical Association booklet, *Irish Unionism* (1973), is essentially a precis of his major study, *Irish Unionism, 1885–1922*, 2 vols. (1972 and 1973). J. Van der Poel, *The Jameson Raid* (Oxford, 1951) is the standard account of that episode; a more general account of South African affairs is G. H. L. Le May, *British Supremacy in South Africa, 1899–1907* (1965). A broad background is given in D. Denoon, *Southern Africa since 1800* (1972). For the South African War of 1899–1902, R. Kruger, *Goodbye Dolly Gray: The Story of the Boer War* (1959) and T. Pakenham, *The Boer War* (1979). For the early history of the Labour Party, and Liberal–Labour rivalry, F. Bealey and H. Pelling, *Labour and Politics, 1900–1906* (1958), D. Howell, *British Workers and the Independent Labour Party, 1883–1906* (1983). D. Tanner, *Political Change and the Labour Party 1900–1918* (1990) is an authoritative account of the Labour Party's development and is also the best study of political change in its period, a subject it approaches region by region. Regional studies have been important in modern scholarship here; examples include P. F. Clarke, *Lancashire and the New Liberalism* (1971) and P. Thompson, *Socialists, Liberals and Labour: The Struggle for London, 1885–1914* (1967). A. W. Purdue has contributed studies of the North East: 'Arthur Henderson and Liberal, Liberal–Labour and

Labour politics in the north-east of England', *Northern History*, 11 (1976 for 1975) and 'The Liberal and Labour Parties in north-east politics, 1900–1914', *International Review of Social History*, 26 (1981). K. O. Morgan has examined Labour and Liberal rivalry in Wales, 'The New Liberalism and the Challenge of Labour: The Welsh Experience, 1885–1929', *Essays in Anti-Labour History*, ed. K. D. Brown, while M. Pugh, 'Yorkshire and the New Liberalism?', *Journal of Modern History*, 1 (1978) and K. Laybourn and J. Reynolds, *Liberalism and the Rise of Labour 1890–1918* (1984) have produced contrasting studies of Yorkshire politics. B. Lancaster's 'The Rise of Labour', *Labour History Review*, lvii (1992) deals with Liberal and Labour politics in Leicester. Liberal fortunes in rural areas are considered in, P. Lynch, *The Liberal Party in Rural England 1885–1910* (Oxford, 2000).

The general election of 1906 is discussed in A. K. Russell, *Liberal Landslide: The General Election of 1906* (1973), and those of 1910 in N. Blewett, *The Peers, the Parties and the People: The British Elections of 1910* (1972). The Liberal governments of 1905–14 are chronicled by P. Rowland, *The Promised Land 1905–1910* (1968) and *The Last Liberal Governments: Unfinished Business 1911–14* (1971). For changes in foreign and imperial policy, three books by P. M. Kennedy provide a good foundation: *The Realities behind Diplomacy: Background Influences on British External Policy, 1865–1980* (1981), *The Rise of the Anglo-German Antagonism, 1860–1914* (1980), and *Strategy and Diplomacy, 1870–1945* (1983). S. Heffer, *Power and Place: The Political Consequences of Edward VII* (1998) provides a forceful argument for the importance of the King's role in the *Entente* with France. John Charmley, *Splendid Isolation? Britain and the Balance of Power 1874–1914* (1999) is revisionist in its analysis of British foreign policy and in its account of how Britain became involved in the First World War.

Chapter 11

An older source which is still of considerable interest for the nature of government in these years is F. W. Maitland, *The Constitutional History of England* (Cambridge, 1908), based on lectures first given *c*.1887–8. For changes in parliamentary procedure, V. Cromwell, 'The losing of the initiative by the House of Commons, 1780–1914', *Transactions of the Royal Historical Society*, 5th ser., 18 (1968), P. Fraser, 'The growth of ministerial control in the nineteenth-century House of Commons', *English History Review*, 75 (1960), H. J. Hanham, *The Nineteenth Century Constitution* (1969). Government responses to unemployment are discussed in J. Harris, *Unemployment and Politics* (1972). F. B. Smith, *The People's Health, 1830–1910* (1979) remains a major source for public health problems. B. B. Gilbert, *The Evolution of National Insurance in Great Britain: The Origins of the Welfare State* (1966) provides as account of the Liberal government's social reforms. For education, J. E. B. Munson, 'The Unionist coalition and education, 1895–1902', *Historical Journal*, 20 (1977). For the Civil Service, good examples are given in R. C. Snelling and T. J. Barron, 'The Colonial Office: its permanent officials, 1801–1914' and V. Cromwell and T. S. Stainer, 'The Foreign Office before 1914: a study in resistance', both in G. Sutherland (ed.), *Studies in the Growth of Nineteenth-Century Government* (1972). For welfare provision, the early chapters of P. Thane, *The Foundations of the Welfare State* (1982) give a good summary. H. Finer, *English Local Government* (1933) remains a major source for these years. For the army, B. Bond, *The Victorian Army and the Staff College, 1854–1914* (1972), W. S. Hamer, *The British Army: Civil Military Relations, 1885–1905* (Oxford, 1970), and E. M. Spiers, *The Army and Society, 1815–1914* (1980), especially chs. 8 and 9. For the navy, A. J. Marder, *The Anatomy of British Sea Power: A History of British Naval Policy in the Pre-Dreadnought Era, 1880–1905* (1941) is the principal authority.

Chapter 12

For the economy generally, S. B. Saul, *The Myth of the Great Depression* (1969). N. L. Tranter, *Population and Society, 1750–1940* (1985) remains a guide here. L. P. Gartner, *The Jewish Immigrant in England, 1870–1914* (1960) discusses that increasingly numerous group. For public health, F. B. Smith, *The People's Health, 1830–1910* (1979). For trade unions, H. A. Clegg, A. Fox, and A. F. Thompson, *A History of British Trade Unions since 1889*, vol. i: *1889–1910* (1964). P. Hollis, *Ladies Elect: Women in English Local Government* (Oxford, 1987) discusses the role of women in local government in the years before the attainment of the parliamentary franchise. H. Fraser, *The Coming of the Mass Market 1850–1914* (1981) and A. Briggs, *Victorian Things* (1988) bring together a mass of information about the increased range of articles of consumption. C. Ehrlich, *The Piano: A History* (1976) gives similar evidence on greater availability. F. Howes discusses *The English Musical Renaissance* (1966) and R. Pearsall considers both *Victorian Popular Music* (1973) and *Edwardian Popular Music* (1975). D. Russell, *Popular Music in England 1840–1914: A Social History* (2nd edn., Manchester, 1997) provides the best overview of the subject, while D. Scott, *The Singing Bourgeois* (1989) and T. Herbert (ed.), *Bands: The Brass Band Movement in the Nineteenth and Twentieth Centuries* (1991) consider, respectively, parlour music and the development of brass bands. W. Bellamy assesses *The Novels of Wells, Bennett and Galsworthy: 1890–1910* (1971). S. Hynes, *The Edwardian Turn of Mind* (1968) and S. Nowell Smith (ed.), *Edwardian England 1901–14* (Oxford, 1964) are stimulating accounts of the intellectual climate and the arts in the early twentieth century. John Carey, *The Intellectuals and the Masses* (1992), provides a controversial explanation for the increasing gulf between high- and middle-brow art and literature. For popular reading habits, C. Cockburn, *Bestseller: The Books Everyone Read, 1900–1939* (1972) is illuminating, even if much of its material relates to later years. For periodicals, A. J. Lee, *The Origins of the Popular Press, 1855–1914* (1976). Two books by M. R. Turner (ed.), *The Parlour Song Book: A Casquet of Vocal Gems* (1972) and *Parlour Poetry: 101 Improving Gems* (1969), give selections of popular songs and verse. M. Girouard, *Victorian Pubs* (1975), B. Harrison, *Drink and the Victorians* (1971), and B. Spiller, *Victorian Public Houses* (1972) discuss a major element in leisure activities. For sport, B. Davies, 'Bifurcation in sport: some preliminary thoughts on the subject of rugby football', *Journal of Local and Regional Studies*, 8 (1988), E. Dunning, P. Murphy, and J. Williams, 'Football hooliganism in historical perspective', *ESRC Newsletter*, 51 (March 1984), B. W. Prowse, 'The control and accommodation of Lancashire football crowds, 1886–1914', MA thesis, Lancaster University, 1981, C. B. Korr, 'West Ham Football Club and the beginnings of professional football in east London, 1895–1914', *Journal of Contemporary History*, 13 (1978).

Index

Entries marked by an asterisk (*) are enlarged in the Biographical Appendix.